LIBERTARIANISM DEFENDED

In Memory of Jim Rosse

Libertarianism Defended

TIBOR R. MACHAN
Chapman University, USA

ASHGATE

Published by
Ashgate Publishing Limited
Gower House
Croft Road
Aldershot
Hampshire GU13 3HR
England

Ashgate Publishing Company
Suite 420
101 Cherry Street
Burlington, VT 05401–4405
USA

Ashgate website: http://www.ashgate.com

British Library Cataloguing in Publication Data
Machan, Tibor R.
Libertarianism defended
1. Libertarianism
I. Title
320.5'12

Library of Congress Cataloging-in-Publication Data
Machan, Tibor R.
Libertarianism defended / by Tibor R. Machan.
p. cm.
Includes index.
ISBN 0-7546-5214-9 (alk. paper)—ISBN 0-7546-5216-5 (pbk. : alk) 1. Libertarianism. I. Title.

JC585.M4414 2006
320.51'2—dc22

2005010998

ISBN-13: 978-0-7546-5214-4 HBK
ISBN-10: 0-7546-5214-9 HBK
ISBN-13: 978-0-7546-5216-8 PBK
ISBN-10: 0-7546-5216-5 PBK

Typeset by Saxon Graphics Limited, Derby
Printed and bound in Great Britain by TJ International Ltd, Padstow, Cornwall

Contents

Preface vii

Introduction: Defending Libertarianism 1

INDIVIDUALISM AND LIBERTY

1 Is It Responsible to be Free? 13
2 The Principles of the Declaration: Here to Stay? 21
3 Justice, Self and Natural Rights 31
4 Individualism and the Vitality of Community Life 71
5 Economics and Human Values 83
6 Finding the Rational Man 97
7 A Positive Libertarian View of Government 121
8 Liberalism and Atomistic Individualism 125

LIBERTARIANISM *PER SE*

9 Anarchists and Minarchists: Allies After All? 147
10 Robert Nozick and the Libertarian Alternative 163
11 Will Technology Make Us Free? 185
12 How Critical is Critical Legal Studies? 191
13 Should You Apologize? 203
14 Between Parent and Child 215
15 Should Ads for Hazardous Goods be Banned? 223

HARD AND SOFT STATISM

16 The Ideology of Death that Will Not Die 233
17 Libertarianism and Conservatism 241
18 Socialism Redux on the Horizon 261
19 Two Philosophers Skeptical of Negative Liberty 269
20 Does Libertarianism Imply the Welfare State? 285
21 Democracy in Public Life and Corporate Management 303

CONCLUSION

22 The Dependence of Equality on Liberty 313
23 Why Agreement Is Not Enough 321
24 Against Fairness 335

Epilogue 341

Index 343

Preface

Ever since the late Robert Nozick penned *Anarchy, State, and Utopia* in the mid-1970s, libertarianism has been treated with some measure of respect within political philosophy, science, and economics circles. But libertarianism and Nozick's version of it have been regarded as nearly identical, resulting in little attention to ideas and arguments other than his – despite the fact that Nozick himself acknowledged that there are impressive libertarian thinkers other than himself.

Yet while Nozick's version of libertarianism has occupied stage front, he has not formally responded to the many critical discussions of his work. Meanwhile, though, other libertarians have continued to talk. Jan Narveson, Loren Lomasky, Eric Mack, Douglas B. Rasmussen and Douglas J. Den Uyl, and many others have marshaled impressive arguments in support of the libertarian idea that a political system is just when it successfully secures the rights of individuals as understood within the Lockean tradition of (or the regime of individual liberty as conceived of by Adam Smith, John Stuart Mill, Herbert Spencer and other) classical liberals. I have contributed to the discussion as well. So, why yet another work in defense of libertarianism?

When a proposed 'paradigm' is not widely favored in a discipline, those who do find it promising need to advance their arguments – and apply them to innumerable problems and controversies – if their view is to achieve visibility and, perhaps, prominence. Proponents of the mainstream view are certainly not under any great pressure to hash out the implications of the minority view. Meanwhile, the mainstream positions gain constant support and exposition from think tanks, research centers and, most of all, academic scholarship. Thus, for example, wherever public finance is studied, tax policy will be a very well traveled area of discussion, while those who regard taxation as unsavory can expect little such academic work devoted to their ideas. So it is up to research centers and scholars supporting the contrarian paradigm to keep churning out the studies and the arguments that can give their position a chance.

There is another fate such fringe – or radical – positions must endure: the fate of being dismissed with offhand comments in major books and other publications, as if their contribution could be dispatched so easily. And it is my awareness of innumerable such nettling offhand dismissals that prompted me to work on the present book. The introduction addresses several examples of these cursory comments, while the body of the work takes up other topics that fail to be discussed from a libertarian standpoint in mainstream forums.

I wish to thank the publishers of *The Freeman*, *International Review of Social Economics*, *Economic Affairs*, *World & I*, *Academic Questions* and

Res Publica for the use of materials in this book that appeared in their journals. Jim Chesher, Douglas J. Den Uyl, Douglas B. Rasmussen, Randy Dipert, Nick Capaldi, Tom G. Palmer, J. Roger Lee and quite a few others deserve thanks for the many discussions we had that helped me to get clear on some of the ideas in this book. Some of these were developed and scrutinized in the course of my work as public policy advisor for Freedom Communications, Inc. of Irvine, California. I am grateful for the cooperation of many of the current and former associates of this company – in particular the late Jim Rosse, Sam Wolgelmouth, Ken Grubbs, Steve Greenhut, Cathy Taylor, Skip Foster, Steve Buckley, Ray Sullivan, Jennie Lambert and other editors and publishers of FCI's newspapers across the USA – for their very helpful criticism and challenges of my rendition of libertarian ideas.

I thank Freedom Communications, Chapman University, and the Hoover Institution for their continued support of my work. I also wish to thank David M. Brown for his editorial help.

People, I thought. These are people. Their general uniformity was interrupted only by their individual variety.

Steve Martin, *The Pleasure of My Company*

Introduction

Defending Libertarianism

> [P]olitical philosophy, when it has an impact on the world, affects the world only indirectly, through the gradual penetration, usually over generations, of questions and arguments from abstruse theoretical writings into the consciousness and the habits of thought of educated persons, and from there into political and legal arguments and eventually into the structure of alternatives among which political and practical choices are actually made.
>
> Thomas Nagel, 'Justice, Justice, Shalt Thou Pursue, The rigorous compassion of John Rawls' *The New Republic* (October 25, 1999), pp. 36–37

When I speak of defending libertarianism, I have in mind taking up various challenges of the position and showing why they are misguided or unfounded. Most of the chapters that follow address one or another more or less widely entertained charges against the fully free society. But some deal with issues that any political position needs to address, and still others consider certain controversies within the libertarian school of political thought itself.

Often, people who tend to be taken quite seriously simply dismiss libertarianism with a kind of wave of their intellectual hand, making only the briefest reference to some line of argument they are relying upon – as if it were axiomatic that the libertarian option can't cut it. I will show in this work that the libertarian alternative deserves better treatment and that these dismissals stem from wishful thinking that aims to hoodwink rather than rationally persuade. I will also take on some of the more developed criticism of libertarianism.

In our time libertarianism has gained notoriety, if not always respect. Not only is there a political movement afoot by that name across the globe – with academicians, pundits, publications, and think tanks helping to forge its ideas – but there are also libertarian and classical liberal political parties fielding candidates throughout the United States and elsewhere. Moreover, there is a rich literature of libertarian theory in nearly all the social sciences and humanities, even though in political theory proper it is almost exclusively the position of the late Robert Nozick that receives any serious attention.[1]

All this has led to public discussion of the substance of this political viewpoint, as well as some serious misrepresentations of it. The most clear-cut example of the former have been books and scholarly papers in which the position is briefly mentioned and dismissed; and of the latter, the charges leveled by some communitarians – for example, Thomas A. Spragens, Amitai Etzioni, Charles Taylor, Michael Sandel, and others – that libertarianism (or its previous incarnation, classical liberalism) rests on an untenable and indeed ridiculous rationalism, scientism and, especially, atomism.

According to this charge, libertarianism assumes human beings to be almost preternaturally self-sufficient and able to choose whether or not to take part in social life at all. In other words, libertarianism supposedly assumes that human beings are asocial atoms. The association of libertarianism with such atomism has been repeated so often that among certain thinkers it has become a mantra, in no need of elaboration or support.[2] This, what some call the rugged-individualist approach, deriving from the work of Thomas Hobbes, is taken to be the only one given in support of libertarianism.

Others claim that libertarianism is hedonistic; or that it lacks an honorable political creed; or that it cannot support patriotism; or that it does support patriarchy; or that it promotes recklessness toward the environment and crass corporatism, spawning business scandals.

More ingeniously, some claim that what libertarianism's philosophical underpinnings support is not a free-market, *laissez-faire* system at all but rather something libertarians routinely oppose: the welfare state. By this account, libertarians are confused.

As an example of these dismissive cursory attacks on libertarianism, consider Cass R. Sunstein's criticism of free-market economics:

> A familiar problem with unrestricted free markets is that they can produce pervasive injustice. A less familiar problem is that free markets often trap people, including the well-off, into wasteful and continuing struggles for better positions. It is in the very nature of the problem that even reasonable people may be unable to extricate themselves from those struggles without collective help. In the face of struggles of this kind, free markets should not be identified with freedom, properly understood.[3]

Did you get that? Not only is freedom unjust, but it isn't even freedom proper – a claim Marx made repeatedly in his own critique of classical liberal ideas:

> This kind of liberty [free competition] is thus at the same time the most complete suppression of all individual liberty and total subjugation of individuality to social conditions which take the form of material forces – and even of all-powerful objects that are independent of the individuals relating to them. The only rational answer to the deification of free competition by the middle-class prophets, or its diabolisation by the socialists, lies in its own development.[4]

Both of these are indeed pregnant assertions, even if in Sunstein's case they are offered as an apparently self-evident aside. His statement has the virtue of revealing the basis for much antagonism toward not only the free market or capitalism, but also toward the United States of America (which rhetorically, at least, stands for the free market). It also shows how persistent the Marxian conception of capitalism continues to be among American intellectuals.

The alleged 'pervasive injustice' of the free market has nothing to do with injustice as ordinarily understood. Injustice in the political realm involves the violation of individual rights – not, as some prominent theorists have claimed, unfairness or inequality or even indecency. To commit an injustice is to kill, assault, kidnap, rape, enslave, molest or steal from someone – to treat him or her other than is due to a human being as such. It is to burglarize someone's home or business or trespass on their property (including, some would argue, their intellectual property). All of this is prohibited and severely punished in the courts of a free capitalist society, which pursue justice when they function as they ought to. Cass Sunstein cannot be ignorant of this. So why is he saying that the free market by its nature produces injustice?

Because he uses the term 'justice' idiosyncratically or in a question-begging way. He deploys what has come to be prominent in academic political theory since the publication of the late John Rawls's *A Theory of Justice* in 1971, according to which 'injustice' in the sense of rights violation became influentially transformed into 'unfairness.' Rawls's famous motto, 'justice as fairness,' guides the thinking of the bulk of academics on political economic matters.[5] Here's where the question-begging comes in. It isn't that the free market does – or rather encourages – anything really *unjust*, only that it fails to provide everyone with what is '*fair*' or rather with what many academics believe would be right if only the world could be managed fairly. And what would that come to?

Accordingly to Rawls, taking justice as fairness requires that no one in a society possess more than another, except where that 'more' would also result in more for those who are the worst off – by giving incentives to producers, for example. This idea of justice as fairness makes sense because for Rawls, quite idiosyncratically, there is nothing anyone has that he or she deserves to have; let alone more than what others have.

The most fundamental reason for this is that Rawls discounts free will entirely. For him, 'Those who have been favored by nature, whoever they are, may gain from their good fortune only on terms that improve the situation of those who have lost out.'[6] To those who might protest, motivated by common sense and a long-embraced conception of justice, that this is to neglect the frequent justice of greater gains in a free market system and how those who create those gains are responsible for them, Rawls replies that the assertion that we 'deserve the superior character that enables us to make the effort to cultivate our talents is … problematic; for such character depends in good part upon fortunate family and social circumstances in early life for which we can claim no credit.'[7]

When social life is understood this way, everyone is seen to be a member of a team, equally significant and thus equally deserving or due equal consideration of his or her needs, wants, hopes, aspirations, capabilities and the like. One person's advance is determined by factors that might just as easily have promoted the advance of another. It is all a matter of luck. So to take the wealth from those who happen to have it and treat it as common to all makes perfect sense, except when some inequality could foster a common advantage.

Per Rawls himself, the free market is much more fair than other more collectivist economic orders. For while not everyone enjoys the same level of wealth in a free market, the discrepancies do tend to improve the lot of everyone. By Rawls's own standards, the free market, though unfair, can make people much better off than alternative and fairer systems.

But despite the prominence (and often exaggeration) of Rawls' ideas, 'fairness' is not the right standard of justice in a legal order. Because of that prominence, the libertarian idea, which takes very seriously the possibility and denies the injustice of numerous inequalities, is often given short shrift. Yet character is not, *pace* Rawls, mostly a matter of luck. It is instead the result of how persons act in the world and what they thus freely choose to make of themselves, very often in the face of major obstacles (including the lack of advantageous family circumstances). Yet this possibility is deemed naïve by many Rawlsians, probably because their understanding of the world rests on a rather strict determinism according to which none of us can really make any *bona fide* choices at all. Presumably, we are all driven or molded to be who we are. What we do is a necessary consequence of that molding, not a matter of choice.

Furthermore, the world is *inherently* 'unfair' – and, thus, 'unjust' in Rawls's (and Sunstein's) sense of the term. Some are born more beautiful, more talented, healthier, in better locations, in nicer times, and/or with greater material resources than are others. This is the main complaint of egalitarianism: nature itself is not 'fair', and never mind whether a moral concept such as 'fairness' can, strictly speaking, apply to nature at all. But somehow all ought to be made fair, via politics.

The paradox of how fully determined people, lacking any power of choice or *self*-determination, can remake the world seems not to bother most Rawlsians. In any case, contrary to what egalitarians believe, there is a significant kind of human equality in nature, at least most of the time: we are all faced with our lives to run. And how well or badly we do this will leave its mark on us for better or for worse. In this sense, we are all in the same boat. The beauties of the world can make a great mess of their lives, as can the rich and talented. Or they can do the best they can or just slide by in mediocre fashion. No human, at least not under normal circumstances, can escape the quintessentially human task of having to attend to life to have a chance at flourishing in it.

Nor is it the case that if some do enjoy advantages as a matter of luck others become justified in 'rectifying' this, engaging in evening things up, as it were. Someone's good health, numerous talents or great looks is no justification for taking from that individual what it gains and turning it over to someone less fortunate. At most it could occasion a moral imperative to share some of it, which is by no means facilitated by coercive wealth redistribution, quite the contrary.[8]

An unavoidable problem with any collective-coercive attempt to eliminate unfairness – a problem even from the radical egalitarian's own perspective – is that it introduces the most dangerous form of unfairness, namely, giving some people power over others. How do you equalize things without creating powerful equalizers? These equalizers must be armed, otherwise many of those who are deemed to be advantaged will not yield to the effort to be equalized. The only result must be some version of George Orwell's fable *Animal Farm*, in which although all animals are supposed to be equal, some end up far more equal than others.

What about the claim that 'free markets often trap people'? The fact is, we do often allow ourselves to develop bad habits when we are free. We splurge when we go shopping; we might not save enough money for rainy days; we purchase goods that we do not really have much use for simply because this is what we did before; we fail to be prudent as we buy or sell our labor and products; we indulge in numerous vices such as greed, gluttony, immoderation, intemperance, and so forth. Indeed, free men and women often fall prey to temptations like this.

Now all this is true but what of it? Arguably, the most addictive habit of all is political power. Thus the collective help that Sunstein recommends as a remedy for such temptations poses precisely the worst temptation of them all.

Instead, what we need is common sense, civility, friendly reminders, maybe a harsh talking to once in a while from friends, family, editorialists or social and religious leaders. Above all, the fact of our own individual responsibility for our own lives, and for the consequences of our choices, should be acknowledged and respected. The last thing we need to combat bad habits is for a bunch of people to arm themselves and impose their idea of prudent living on the rest of us by force. Such enforcers are exactly what a free society must seriously resist.[9]

The possibility of lapsing into bad habits is just the sort of risk that free men and women face all the time. We need not be victimized by it. Responsible conduct is evident enough in the area where Sunstein himself does so much of his work, namely, scholarship, which is relatively free of bureaucratic edict. In the realm of intellectual expression there is virtually no government regulation, at least not in the United States, in virtue of the First Amendment. Thus this sphere affords us an instructive illustration of how men and women who are free will likely fare. They in fact perform their share of untoward and blameworthy deeds, but they also produce extremely varied and worthy works. And they cope with all this in a (relatively) civilized fashion, namely, through vigorous criticism and without recourse to coercion and the activities of vice squads (although there is growing evidence of some of this in the name of political correctness). There aren't many conferences at which the participants take shots at each other aside from those that are verbal. Only if one believes men and women to be inherently impotent, merely impelled by circumstances beyond their control, will one be tempted to intrude upon them with one's utopian plan and prevent them from making their own plans. Yet, why blame anyone then, even those who allegedly perpetrate unfair manipulation via advertising or marketing? They, too, are helpless, after all, in carrying on as they do!

In two respects, the price of our capacity for free action is, indeed, eternal vigilance. We need to be vigilant both to keep our freedom safe from those who would act aggressively against us for various high sounding reasons, and also to deal responsibly with our precious liberty. In the first instance, of course, it is in response to people like Rawls, Sunstein, Nussbaum and all their followers, as well as those in government who carry out their interventionist task in the belief that they are acting properly, that we need to be vigilant. In the second instance, it is our own weaknesses and temptations that require vigilance from us.

The number of distinct stances that can be taken against individualism and the free market is quite wide-ranging and prolific – a tribute to the creative ability of humankind, really. Yet many of them boil down to the same assumption that along with freedom comes helplessness rather than empowerment. Some, for example, claim that while men may benefit from unfettered freedom – or at least middle-class men – women do not, or at least not as much. Martha Nussbaum charges: 'A simple "get the state off our backs" position may look attractive when we are thinking about the sex lives of middle-class men, but it is clearly inadequate to deal with the situation of women and other vulnerable groups. There is no consent where there is pervasive intimidation and hierarchy.'[10] Such a stance implicitly disparages the ability of women to join in voluntary efforts to fend off male 'intimidation and hierarchy.' While in some cases, when women are being coercively assaulted, Nussbaum is right;[11] she is wrong if she conflates these, as many feminists do, with cases such as insulting women or not paying them high enough wages.[12] Such equivocations invite the intrusions of the Nanny State, not the protection of women from those who would violate their rights. Furthermore, is there any good reason to think that if the culture embraces such intimidation, the state, with all its men, wouldn't also embrace it? In fact, to the extent that there is such prejudice, less centralized spheres of the culture could often offer ways to escape it. When relations are voluntary, options are expanded, not shrunk.

Other criticisms of libertarianism are less substantive and cannot be dealt with at any length in this Introduction. Some, in fact, are worth only a mention here because of their curiously hostile tone and *ad hominem* character. For example, social philosopher Alan Wolfe, in a discussion of the values of conservatism, states that the 'young and the childless are rarely conservative, but they are often libertarians. Libertarianism is a political philosophy for Peter Pan, an outlook on the world premised on never growing up … .'[13] Such comments – actually, they are best dubbed *slurs* – cannot be answered apart from noting that they serve to dismiss the substance of libertarianism, perhaps because the author has little or no interest in dealing with the arguments and so prefers the way of insults and intimidation. They do alert us to the distressing fact that some of the most prolific and industrious public thinkers are utterly contemptuous of the tradition of individual liberty, a fact that may be of greater concern today than it was a few decades ago. Since September 11, 2001, there has been much consternation about how others in the world not only misunderstand but actively resent, even hate, the central elements of Western liberalism, namely, its individualism, capitalism and at least rhetorical commitment to the ideal of individual rights to life, liberty and the pursuit of happiness. But the plain fact is that many in the United States of America do so as well.

There are many other challenges the libertarian must cope with, including some that focus on how certain prominent classical liberals, whose arguments are sometimes deployed to help support the libertarian position, did not advance a fully consistent or pure case for negative liberty. Thus, for example, Filimon Peonidis, a philosopher from Aristotle University of Thessaloniki, Greece, has argued that John Stuart Mill permitted major exceptions to his version of limited government. One area was education, another circumstances in which 'by the force of opinion and even by that of legislation' people's freedom appears to be limited – especially by media companies that present to their customers the fare the companies want them to experience.[14] In such cases, Peonidis argues, Mill would allow government to interfere. Ergo, the case for a complete *laissez-faire* in the media business must be unsuccessful.

Of course, Mill has never been a pure classical liberal, let alone libertarian, so a strenuous claim that he was inconsistent is somewhat beside the point. There has always been his famous, though usually misunderstood, example of 'paternalistic' interference, as when one prevents someone without consent from stepping on a bridge about to be blown up. (This, however, cannot reasonably be construed as an example of anti-libertarianism in his thought.[15]) More significantly, Mill argued for some measure of state redistribution of wealth as well as government monopoly for certain 'natural' monopolies such as public utilities. Mill's compromises with respect to individual liberty are well known and don't tell us whether some case might be made against such compromises. We can in any case note that 'hard cases make bad law,' so that while certain exceptions might be made to the principles of limited or minimal government as a matter of juridical discretion, they should not be officially encoded in the legal system.

Even apart from the work already extant in which libertarian ideas are developed and shown to have certain public policy implications, it is now time to mount a rebuttal to some of these assaults. This book aims to address many such charges and anticipates questions.

One fact about the intellectual defense of libertarianism to keep in mind is that not all elements of a *defense* of libertarianism need be elements of libertarianism *per se*, which is a political position barring coercion from human social life. Just why coercion should be barred from social life is a complicated matter. The best answer may emerge from various areas of philosophy, economics, sociology, history, and other disciplines. This is one reason that sometimes very different – though not all equally successful – defenses can be advanced for libertarianism. What I say here is, of course, not the last word, nor is it set forth as such. I believe my approach is more successful than many others, a matter in any case the reader will have to assess, however.

I hope that with the responses that follow on the record, the discussion of the libertarian position will be advanced. And perhaps also its adoption. Once the misrepresentations are cleared up, it will at any rate be possible to consider whether the position is sound on its own merits. For that is really what is most important about a political idea.

Notes

1 Robert Nozick, *Anarchy, State, and Utopia* (New York: Basic Books, 1974). This work by a Harvard University professor, educated at Princeton University and formerly someone with Leftist credentials, was an anomaly in the 1970s, even though it became widely discussed and even popular (winning, as it did, the National Book Award). Arguably Nozick broke through in part because of his pedigree, which is not to take away from his ingenious and brilliantly articulated arguments. But since Nozick did not return to political theory during the rest of his sadly short life – he died at 63 from stomach cancer – the discussion of libertarianism by the prestigious statists in the field ended with consideration of his original position alone. The likes of John Rawls, Ronald Dworkin, Thomas Nagel, and others who treat the topic paid attention only to Nozick and continue to do so. Yet dozens of other political theorists also became convinced of libertarianism and produced numerous works making a case for it. This suggests that a kind of Kuhnean sociology of knowledge phenomenon has been at work, with prominence of a position being treated as more important than substance.

2 Most notable among these is Amitai Etzioni, a prominent academic who has been a widely published popularizer of communitarianism, and Charles Taylor, a much more formidable critic of radical individualism and defender of communitarianism. See Amitai Etzioni, *The Spirit of Community* (New York: Crown Publishing Co., 1993) and Charles Taylor, *Philosophy and the Human Sciences* (Cambridge, England: Cambridge University Press, 1985), especially his essay 'Atomism.' See also Robert Bellah et al., *Habits of the Heart* (New York: Harper & Row Publishers, 1985).

3 Cass R. Sunstein, *The New Republic*, March 29, 1999, p. 45. It is odd how readily intelligent folks will dismiss freedom in light of the fact that when we are free, we do face some temptations that may result in regrettable consequences. People who are free are subject to all sorts of pressures, inclinations, habits and oversights. Yet, as public choice theorists have observed, getting 'collective help' – that is, government regulation – to prevent these is far more hazardous than letting free people deal with the problems in their own various creative ways. We can't get around the fact that human survival and well-being is a complex matter, and one that hinges most basically on our ability to make individual choices. You can't get it out of a box of Crackerjacks.

The trust in coercive power rests, probably, on the belief that to guarantee the achievement of a desired goal, brute force is the best approach (as when we finally slap a friend who is being hysterical). The libertarian admits that in personal relations such a technique may work now and then. The libertarian denies, however, that it is at all productive as a long-range approach to dealing with human problems. For more, see

Tibor R. Machan, *The Passion for Liberty* (Lanham, MD: Rowman & Littlefield, 2003), Chapter 3, 'Against Utilitarianism – Why not Violate Rights if it would do Good?'

4 Karl Marx, *Grundrisse* (New York: Harper & Row, 1970), p. 131. Marx, too, had no confidence in the creative initiative of free men and women as far as solving their personal and social problems is concerned. Instead, he thought we are captives of (mostly economic and technological) forces that act upon us and that these forces had to be met with even greater force, namely, that of the state. This has been a powerful legacy of not just socialist but modern liberal politics: when a problem arises, invoke the power of the state to solve it.

5 Even for Rawls 'justice' can have other senses. It's only that he had wanted to explore it as it relates to fairness.

6 John Rawls, *A Theory of Justice* (Cambridge, MA: Harvard University Press, 1971), p. 101. This idea is extensively developed in Serena Olsaretti, *Liberty, Desert and the Market: A Philosophical Study* (Cambridge: Cambridge University Press, 2004), suggesting that the thrust of the defense of the free market rests on the belief that all those who own wealth or assets deserve it. (I will return to this point in several sections of this book.)

7 Ibid. , p. 104.

8 See, Tibor R. Machan, 'Why liberty is necessary for morality,' *Think*, Issue Nine (Spring 2005), pp. 87–89.

9 Just how influential this line of thinking has become, consider the currently popular practice of legal prosecution of those who make available, via the market place, a source for yielding to the temptation to overindulge – in immoderate smoking, eating, and who knows what else. The thesis advanced by John Kenneth Galbraith, in his famous book, *The Affluent Society* (Boston: Houghton Mifflin, 1958), that consumers lack sovereignty, has made its impact by now into the legal order (as per Thomas Nagel's point at the beginning of this Introduction).

10 Martha C. Nussbaum, 'Experiments in Living' (review of Michael Warner, *The Trouble with Normal*),' *The New Republic*, January 3, 2000, p. 33.

11 Nussbaum suggests, quite properly that 'We need to protect people not only against physical force, but also against intercourse accomplished by threat or intimidation, and by the abuse of positions of authority. [Thus] a high school principal who said to a student "Pay me $500 or you will not graduate" would surely be convicted of a crime; but a principal who said "Sleep with me or you will not graduate" was acquitted of rape because the woman did not say "no." Extortionate offers should be criminal, Schulhofer argues, in sex as in other realms of life, whether we call such cases rape or criminal assault. And Schulhofer extends his analysis to a defense of sexual harassment laws in the workplace, and of professional bans on intercourse between doctors and patients lawyers and clients … . Warner never wrestles with these difficult cases. Had he spent more time confronting a wide range of feminist writings, he would have had to face the fact that law does not just compromise sexual autonomy, it also protects it. A simple "get the state off our backs" position may look attractive when we are thinking about the sex lives of middle-class men, but it is clearly inadequate to deal with the situation of women and other vulnerable groups. There is no consent where there is pervasive intimidation and hierarchy.' None of this warrants attributing to libertarians an attitude of 'who cares' since it is indeed mainly by dint of their conception of individual rights that such untoward conduct can come under legal scrutiny and resistance.

12 See, for example, Catherine MacKinnon, *Only Words* (Cambridge, MA: Harvard University Press, 1993).

13 Alan Wolfe, 'The Revolution that Never Was,' *The New Republic*, June 7, 1999, p. 41.

14 Filimon Peonidis, 'Mill's Defense of Free Expression – Its Contemporary Significance,' *Journal of Social Philosophy*, Vol. XXXIII, No 4 (Winter 2002), pp. 606–613.

15 See, Tibor R. Machan, 'Prima Facie v. Natural (Human) Rights,' *Journal of Value Inquiry*, Vol. 10, No. 1 (1976), pp. 119–31, for why there are extraordinary circumstances in which even the most basic rights may be *disregarded*.

INDIVIDUALISM AND LIBERTY

Chapter 1

Is It Responsible to be Free?

'Why all the focus on rights? What about obligations?' Or 'What makes rights supposedly more important than responsibilities?' This kind of question is often asked of those who consider the free society to be the best and most just.

It is misleading on many fronts, however. For one thing, it presupposes that while the questioner cares about moral conduct, the proponent of freedom and individual rights cares only about leaving people unconstrained and, presumably, unguided by anything other than what these unfettered persons (arbitrarily) choose. While it is true enough that some advocates of rights may also be advocates of arbitrary conduct, such a stance is far from logically mandated by concern for a *particular principle* of social morality, the principle of individual rights![1]

Indeed, quite the opposite. The requirements of exercising moral responsibility are what justify the concept of rights and the active defense of rights to begin with. We need a concept of rights to specify and safeguard the sphere within which we may function without fear of being routinely interfered with.[2] A responsible person not only asks that his own rights be respected, but also takes care to respect the rights of others – not primarily because he fears punishment but because he respects the peaceful choices of other individuals, values good relations with them and wishes to enjoy the benefits of the just society that are essential to his own flourishing.

A right is a kind of justified (social) moral claim. It does not exhaust the realm of moral claims or principles. But it is one of them. A right designates a sphere of freedom, a circumstance or environment in which one is authorized to act in a certain way.

If you have a right to use your company's printer, it means that nobody may stop you from doing so – at least not so long as you abide by any of the relevant provisos attending that right. You may have a right to operate it only when, say, nobody else is using it. And only during working hours. And only if you refill the paper tray if the paper happens to run out while you're doing a print job. But within the reasonable constraints that attend the right, nobody is justified in stopping you from using the printer.

Note, by the way, that the mere fact of possessing a right does not entail any obligation to exercise that right. Nobody is justified to point a gun at you to force you to print out a document merely because you are entitled to do so, just as no one can force you to occupy a house you own merely because you are entitled to do so. Rights that one gains by contract – such as the right to use the company printer – may, of course, have been granted only on the stipulation that the grantee then accepts certain obligations. But these obligations, even if fulfilling them depends on exercising the rights one has thus contractually gained, are not the same thing as those rights. It is not the possession of the right that in such a case obliges one to exercise the right, but the fact of the obligation (here, as a term of employment). This may seem like a painstaking elaboration of the obvious. But the distinction between a voluntarily accepted obligation and a coercively imposed one tends to get blurred in much discussion of our rights.

By the same token, having a right to vote means no one may stop you from voting if you choose to vote. It doesn't mean one is obligated to vote – not even that one necessarily has the personal responsibility to do so. After all, there may be no one or nothing worth voting for. Similarly, having a right to publish newspapers, to speak or to worship, means one is free either to do it or not do it. And even if one ought to vote or publish something, one has the authority to abstain. Free men and women have the right not to do what they should, so they may not be forced by others to comply with their moral responsibilities other than to respect everyone's rights.

A right pertains to what other people may do to one. It designates realms and circumstances in which you may not be coercively interfered with. A fundamental right – like the right to life, liberty, and the pursuit of happiness; that is, the right to make decisions and take actions as one sees fit, unmolested, so long as one does not tread on the same right of others – is a right to be enjoyed by all peaceful citizens within a community, and in virtue of the individual's humanity as such. A fundamental right is not an acquired right, in other words.

It is also not a made-up or fictitious right. Humans observe the basis for such fundamental rights in our own actual nature as conceptual, choosing beings. We observe that an environment of freedom is one in which beings like us can live right, and thrive. We can identify and theorize about such rights. But we do not invent them, just as we do not invent our own natures. In fact it would be foolhardy and counterproductive to try to concoct 'rights' out of whole cloth; for to the extent we attempt to practice them, such fabricated rights, by failing to take into account our actual nature, must work against our nature and undermine rather than support our way of living right.

Yet some people advocate and attempt to impose fictitious rights anyway. These fake-rights advocates are able to ignore or downplay the destructiveness of their efforts by focusing on only one aspect of the results. If I assert a phony 'right to medicine' and steal a bottle of cough syrup from you, use the cough syrup, and succeed in assuaging my cough, it is only by regarding the situation very selectively that I can say the fake right I have thus asserted 'promotes human living' on net. For I am ignoring a few things: about myself, about the person from whom I stole, about the kind of society I am promoting.

With respect to the person from whom I stole, I am ignoring the fact that he is now a victim of theft. The victim's own success at living well – well-being – cannot have been enhanced by what I did. Perhaps he would have given me the cough syrup voluntarily, had I asked. But I have deprived him of that choice. I have deprived him of the ability to make up his own mind about the matter and go by his own judgment. By my coercion, I have violated the fundamental social condition that he requires to promote his own life. (And I have also, perhaps, exacerbated his cough.)[3]

I am also ignoring something about myself: that by acting as a thug I undermine my own moral capacity to flourish in a social context. For human beings, rational animals, the means of proper survival is our faculty of reason; we are not the non-coughing animal, who survive mainly by not-coughing. If I reflect honestly on what I did, I cannot ignore the fact that the cough syrup was not mine to take, that it in fact belonged to someone else. But I can evade that fact. I can pretend that I acted as a rational, considerate human being, who had every 'right' to the cough syrup. I can pretend that my victim deserved what he received at my hand, and that, really, he too is better off as a result of my having robbed him. I can argue that it's a good thing if people, all people, treat each other as prey and simply take whatever they need, whenever they need it, simply *because* they need it. I can pretend that we'd all be better off in a society of looters instead of in a society of producers. I can pretend that all the good and complicated, life-serving man-made things like cough syrup come about by magic rather than by hard, rational effort.

I can pretend all these things and by so pretending undermine my capacity to reason, and thus my capacity to serve my own well-being – even as I invite the same kind of assault against my person that I have perpetrated against the owner of the cough syrup. I can erode my own self-respect and the respect for me from others. This is a very high price to pay for a little cold relief. We don't pay the full price if we do such a deed only once, in a moment of weakness or desperation, and repent and determine not to do it again. We do pay it more and more as we adopt such practices as a way of life. It is not in anyone's true, human interest to either become a career criminal or to live in a society of widespread mutual criminality. (Now and then it may appear otherwise but that's a mistake.)

Yet some people do advocate the adoption of such habits, and as a matter of formal social policy; and they even call this demand for institutionalized criminality a demand for 'rights.'

Why do people who advocate systematically violating the rights of others characterize these violations as acts of *respecting* rights? In part, it's because we have reached the stage of civilization at which actual rights have been discovered, are widely talked about, and have earned a certain enduring respect. These rights are still in force, and sustain our civilized life even as they are chronically contradicted and undermined. They are part of the ingrained cultural heritage of the West and certainly of the United States. The function of our government is explicitly to 'secure rights.'

So it is hard to argue outright, 'Let's enslave others. Let's run riot and destroy each other. No more rights!' And perhaps it is impossible for anyone posing as a friend of society to admit, even to himself, that this is what he is pushing for, at least in some degree. So those who oppose genuine rights seek to steal the respect accorded to them along with all the other things they're seeking to steal. It's not that they're against the rights that government was established to secure, they might say; it's just that they want to add more 'rights' to the list. Just as hypocrisy is the compliment vice pays to virtue, so the doctrine of pseudo-rights is the compliment welfare statists pay to genuine rights.

A pseudo-right to health care, welfare or social security implies that one is free either to obtain or not to obtain these benefits, that others may not prevent one from getting them. My right to health care means no one may stop me from obtaining such care if that is what I want. In this respect, the pseudo-right is similar, superficially, to an actual right. But actual rights do not inherently contradict each other as pseudo-rights do. Do I, as a taxpayer or doctor, retain a right to freedom over my actions or income if you are entitled to rob me or enslave me for the sake of satisfying your 'right' to health?

By contrast, respecting the right to speak out or to worship does not require me to do anything for (or to) people, only to avoid intruding on them. To recast these rights on the pseudo-right model, one would have to insist on the 'right' to enjoy the mass in one's home, even if that means legally compelling the church to send you a priest; or the 'right' to have your opinions published in somebody else's newspaper. If we rarely think of perverting freedom of speech and worship in these ways, it's precisely because we acknowledge the crucial value that these rights have in sustaining a tolerant society and enabling us to act in accordance with our own consciences in these arenas. We don't mess with these rights because they're too important. What we need to recognize is that *every* manifestation of the right to 'life, liberty and the pursuit of happiness' is too important to inflate out of existence with an ever growing list of pseudo-rights that always come at the expense of somebody else's rights and liberty.

The social attempt to protect our (genuine) fundamental rights through government entails provision for these fundamental rights. As per the Declaration of Independence, this is what government is supposed to be for: to secure our 'negative' rights. Such provision does, of course, involve expenses which need to be secured by some, but properly only voluntary, means. It is this fact – the evident cost of government – that has rendered the institution of taxation immune from properly harsh criticism. It is widely but mistakenly believed that without taxes to fund the governmental protection of rights, this protection is impossible. This isn't necessarily the case.[4] But even if taxes are viewed as an unavoidable means of 'positively' providing for the functions of government that protect our 'negative' rights, that would not then warrant extracting moneys from the citizenry to fund all manner of 'positive' pseudo-rights. With no moral basis shown for the enforcement of pseudo-rights, the government's revenues may be used only to protect actual basic rights. The government empowered to protect us from criminality may not engage in criminal conduct toward the very citizenry it is charged to protect.

Where do responsibility and obligation come in, if rights do not obligate us to devote all our time and resources to anyone who happens to demand them?

The concept of 'responsibility' pertains to our ability to make moral and rational decisions on our own, decisions for which we can be held accountable precisely because we choose them. Responsibilities, as ordinarily understood, are not a matter of law but of morality or ethics, of how we ought to live. They are everywhere in our lives. With any role we have assumed, that of friend, parent, corporate officer, cabby or athlete, we have, in effect, agreed to fulfill numerous responsibilities. But these need have nothing at all to do with laws.

Some responsibilities you have simply in virtue of being human and alive – for example, the responsibility to sustain our lives, the responsibility to understand and cope with the world around us. Other responsibilities are more specific, undertaken in the course of fulfilling the more fundamental responsibilities: the responsibility for a job, a house, a marriage, children. All of these are matters of choice. Some of these choices result in obligations. But if you hadn't made the choice, the obligations would not exist either.

The concepts of responsibility and obligation are allied, but obligation is the narrower concept; it means a responsibility that is binding, especially legally binding. The *American Heritage Dictionary* defines obligation as 'A social, legal, or moral requirement, such as a duty, contract, or promise that compels one to follow or avoid a particular course of action.'

A civilized person's sense of responsibility for his own well-being naturally subsumes respect for the rights of others that he hopes to receive for his own rights. But in a just society, respect for rights is not a matter only of mutual moral consideration and good will among responsible persons, but also of law and force – a matter of legal obligation. Such obligations, in a free society, are 'negative' in the sense that they prohibit rather than require certain conduct. They include, for example, prohibitions against the committing of violent crimes. Ideally, the legal obligation to respect rights only bolsters or codifies the moral responsibility to respect rights that every civilized adult person gladly accepts anyway. But even normally responsible people are not always so; more important, some persons, those we call thugs and criminals, chose to be irresponsible when it comes to the rights of others. The principle of self-defense justifies acting forcibly to resist such persons who would ride roughshod over the rest of us and enacting laws to guard against such conduct.

The proponent of the free society recognizes that there is a difference between a responsibility and a legal obligation, that these concepts are not co-extensive, that not everything you should do is to be done under threat of fine or jail. You may have a responsibility to be polite to people, or generous and charitable toward them when they are in dire straits. But statists assert that if people are in dire straits, you have an enforceable obligation to help them. They contend that you may be conscripted to help others. What they are arguing for is not akin to the obligations of a nurse or butler, who voluntarily accept work that requires them to become a kind of 'servant' of their employers; it is akin to the obligations of a serf, doomed by birth to a life of involuntary servitude.

No person should be manacled in this way for the crime of having been born. The guarantee of moral conduct desired by the critics of freedom does not exist. That doesn't mean in a free society you lack moral responsibilities, or cannot be evaluated with respect to how well you fulfill them. If you treat your friends callously, that's your choice, but you will be judged by that. You may lose a friend and gain a bad reputation. At any rate, you will be a bad friend. But there's no law, and ought be no law, that you must be a good friend. And thank goodness! If such a thing could be enforced it would tend to taint our friendships and leech them of the value they have for us only in virtue of being voluntary. Would we like to live in a society in which we were all assigned friends, and our designated friends had no choice but to meet with us for a certain minimum amount of time each week? Who wants to wonder whether his friends are behaving considerately because, otherwise, they might be fined or jailed?

Thus the notion of a dichotomy between rights and responsibilities is patently absurd. They entail each other. In fact, I can be *responsible* for making moral choices only if I am *free* to make moral choices. Only a social environment in which rights are routinely respected is conducive to the exercise of one's responsibilities in all areas of life. The flip side of the coin is also true: a social environment in which rights are routinely ignored or abrogated fosters irresponsibility – for it buffers those who behave irresponsibly from consequences they would otherwise suffer. Perhaps in a free society I can't rob the corporate offices of a tobacco company at gunpoint myself, without risking jail; but it seems that as society becomes less free, I can pretend I had no idea that smoking is hazardous to my health, blame my conduct on the tobacco companies, and commit the robbery via lawsuit, instead, and with no concern at all about being legally penalized for this theft. (This isn't to say that there aren't circumstances in which you might be legitimately held liable for harm to another, because of your own negligence. But deliberately ingesting poison that you know to be poison isn't quite in the same category as having a shoddily constructed roof collapse on you.) I might not be able to rob my neighbor at gunpoint to fund a personal project I care about, but perhaps the government will perform the coercive extracting of funds for me, through taxes, and hand me a subsidy. To the extent that a society's institutions enable such conduct, it rewards and fosters irresponsibility.

Under a political system of liberty, people are left alone to assume moral responsibilities for themselves. That's what freedom means. Human beings are different from the lower animals precisely in that we confront each other's complaints, demands, and requests in a civilized way, as opposed to growling and leaping. To be 'civilized' means to act without initiating physical force. When we say 'this is a civilized discussion,' we mean that people are not shouting at each other or shoving each other about; that they seek to persuade each other rather than bully each other. They are being civil. A civilized neighborhood doesn't have much crime or any oppressive laws – people do not deploy force while interacting with each other. Those who favor a fully free system simply endorse this ideal of civilization consistently and say that only in cases of self-defense is force warranted. All other matters must be handled through peaceful persuasion, or even peaceful pressure, but not by bullying and coercion. That, in any case, must be a rule of law, even if in rare cases, in emergencies, resorting to coercion could be justified.

Perhaps parents are at least sometimes justified in requiring a child to behave with the form of responsibility – to brush his teeth or to apologize for some wrongdoing, perhaps – even if the child assents only from fear of disapproval or penalty. It may be better for a child to at least mimic the form of responsibility, lest he never become acquainted with the idea at all. But this can only be an interim and unsatisfactory state of affairs. For if the child never does actually begin to assume responsibilities on his own, he never really matures. True responsibility is an expression of individual autonomy. It is not a matter of evading a sharp word or evading prison, but of considering for yourself what actions you should take, in light of the requirements of your own life and the standards that ought to guide you in living it. It means you are thinking for yourself. This thinking-for-yourself is how human beings survive and thrive.

A society which demands that you obey orders with respect to the alternatives you face instead of thinking them through on your own is not only depriving you of the benefits and pleasures of independent thought, but is actively undercutting your most basic means of survival as a human being. There is no greater responsibility than that of exercising your own capacity to reason. And doing so requires freedom.

Notes

1 I develop the underlying moral support for the free society in Machan, *Classical Individualism* (London: Routledge, 1998). How basic rights, including the right to liberty, rest on a sound ethics may be gleaned from Machan, *Individuals and Their Rights* (Chicago: Open Court Publishing Co., Inc., 1989). I should stress that there are defenders of a free society who do not advance the same argument and there are some who would insist that the principle of the individual's right to liberty that underlies such a society does not require defense (that is, that the ban on all aggression is self-evidently sound, even axiomatically true). See the works of such thinkers as Milton Friedman, Ludwig von Mises, David Friedman, Richard Epstein, Murray N. Rothbard, Loren Lomasky, and others for different approaches to defending the free society. Others, such as Douglas B. Rasmussen, Douglas J. Den Uyl, Eric Mack and Fred D. Miller, Jr. advance supporting arguments akin to my own.

2 There is no way to guarantee complete security from rights violations – sometimes the most that can be done is to punish violators and compensate victims.

3 Jeffrey Friedman, in 'What is Wrong with Libertarianism?' (*Critical Review*, Vol. 11, No 3 [Summer 1997]), claims (but does not argue) that 'all legal systems, including

libertarianism, coercively enforce rules that assign the 'ownership' of all persons and all bits of the world. Every legal system throws a net of coercion over the entire society it covers, prohibiting by force any deviations from its definitions of rights' (p. 428). This is also the thesis of critical legal studies, the neo-Marxist school of jurisprudence, which equivocates between coercion and plain force and holds that the protection of private property rights amounts to coercive imposition of arbitrary rules in favor of the ruling class. (See Tibor R. Machan, 'How Critical is Critical Legal Studies?' *Academic Questions*, Vol. 1, No 4 [Fall 1988], now reworked as Chapter 12 of this book.)

True enough, all legal systems deploy *force*, but not all force is the same. Thus those who defend themselves from violent attacks use force but do not initiate it, so theirs is by no means coercive force. Coercion is the sort of force that's invasive, that violates individual rights. And when a legal order and authority is constitutionally confined to using force non-coercively – defensively or in retaliation – it is not coercive. (For more on this, see Randy E. Barnett, *Restoring the lost constitution: The presumption of liberty* [Princeton, NJ: Princeton University Press, 2004].) Friedman's entire critique of libertarianism rests on this basic error of equivocating between force and coercion (which is to say, between actions or public policies that protect individual sovereignty and actions or policies that violate it). It is, also, a perfect illustration of bloviation and a startlingly convoluted effort at producing erudition.

Friedman also fails to appreciate, in his skimpy discussion of actual libertarian arguments against 'government interference in the market economy,' just how significant a role *prior restraint* plays in such policy. (For more on that particular point, see Tibor R. Machan, *Private Rights and Public Illusions* [Oakland, CA: Independent Institute, 1995], and 'The Petty Tyrannies of Government Regulation,' in M. Bruce Johnson and Tibor R. Machan, eds, *Rights and Regulation* [Boston: Addison-Wesley, 1983], pp. 259–88. This work contains many discussions of government interference, by libertarians and others. One is especially noteworthy, namely, J. C. Smith, 'The Processess of Adjudication and Regulation, A Comparison,' pp. 71–96. Unfortunately Friedman's discussion, despite its confident, even conclusive, tone, does not benefit from a consideration of arguments presented in these or similar works.) For a reply to Friedman along lines of the libertarianism of this work, see Tom G. Palmer, 'What is *Not* Wrong with Libertarianism: Reply to Friedman,' *Critical Review*, Vol. 12, No 3 (Summer 1998), pp. 337–58.

4 See Tibor R. Machan, 'Dissolving the Problem of Public Goods: Financing Government Without Coercive Measures,' in Machan, ed., *The Libertarian Reader* (Lanham, MD: Rowman & Littlefield, 1982).

Chapter 2

The Principles of the Declaration: Here to Stay?

Do the principles laid out in the American Declaration of Independence have lasting significance? Are they stable? Do they accord fundamentally with how we ought to live in each other's company no matter where and when we are? Do they accord fundamentally with our basic nature? Or are they applicable only to a given time and place?

Of course, the answer also depends on whether there is an enduring 'human nature as such.' Because what if our basic identity as human being does indeed change from town to town and era to era? Of course, it may be that in some far-flung era human nature could change in a drastic and fundamental way that we cannot now imagine. But this isn't what the controversy is about. It's about whether who we are as human beings has changed so fundamentally over the course even of a couple of centuries that the most fundamental political principles no longer apply, even if they did apply when originally formulated.[1]

One of the most influential critiques of the very idea of stable and lasting principles of political economy comes from Karl Marx. Marxism contended that humanity is on a kind of unknowing journey, at each stage of which different principles of political organization apply – just as different principles govern the development of an infant as versus a teenager. To try to live today by the principles that governed us, say 250 years ago, would then be a mistake, he claims.[2] Of course, not everyone who holds this view is a Marxist; but even non-Marxists have been influenced by the understanding of humanity and history that Marx did so much to propagate.

In deriving their political principles, the American Founders examined truths about human beings and society that they regarded as *enduring*. Only after these studies did the Founders affirm these as stable lasting ideas and ideals and encapsulate them in the Declaration of Independence. The Declaration is not a treatise on political theory but an announcement to the world of what the Founders held to be certain political truths, to be taken as self-evident in such a public announcement: namely, that all of us are created equal and are endowed by our creator with certain unalienable rights, among which are life, liberty and the pursuit of happiness; and that governments are instituted amongst us to secure these rights.

This was a revolutionary idea. In most lands, government was regarded as the ruler of the people, the sovereign. Kings were looked upon, at least officially, as endowed with divine rights entitling them to order their subjects to conform to their will, almost regardless of what that will might be. Even today, in civilized and advanced societies like Holland, Norway and Sweden and England, nationals are referred to as subjects. They are not officially seen to exercise an independent will of their own. By law or by public policy, they are subject to the will of the sovereign. This is true in many countries of the western world – let alone in realms ruled by sheiks and dictators.

The ideas summarized in the Declaration of Independence rejected and replaced that belief. The American Revolution is called a revolution because it removed power from the government and turned it over to individual members of the community. The conviction was that these kings are not basically different from you or me: they, too, are human beings. So why should we accept that they must have paramount authority over us? The Founders identified every person as a self-ruler, that is, as a citizen rather than a subject. This principle made the United States a revolutionary country, even if not all of its revolutionary ideas were successfully applied and incorporated into the Constitution, nor were all fully and consistently embraced.[3] The Constitution harbors many serious compromises of the principles of the Declaration. Southern states, for example, wanted slavery to be legal. Eventually slavery was abolished, at great and, some would argue, unnecessary cost. But for a while, the Constitution was not fully loyal to the Declaration. Nor are many of America's present laws strictly loyal to the spirit and letter of the Declaration of Independence.

Is there anything wrong with such contradictions, however? Some argue that times have changed and the Declaration has become obsolete. Must we now accept that the Declaration should be put on a shelf and treated as if it were a set of antique ideas or a 'living document' – one that, like an adolescent, is always in process of developing and does not embody any lasting principles?

Many aspects of society do change. The ways we now dress, the instruments we use, how we raise our children, our means of transportation, our cuisine. But are honesty, loyalty, integrity among these fashionable and easily outmoded things? Yet this is what many critics of our political tradition maintain: that everything is fashion. They argue for the proposition that just as with all these other ephemeral things, our basic political principles too must change. There is nothing permanent here, nothing sacrosanct, nothing worthy of our enduring loyalty.

To see the error here, it is important to distinguish between what is fundamental to human nature and what is not so fundamental. After all, it is *fundamental* human nature that the authors of the Declaration sought to account for and accommodate; they were not prescribing etiquette or dress codes. If human nature at the most fundamental level changes from era to era, the disparagers of the Declaration might have a point.

But they don't. Although practices and customs may change, basic human nature and human needs do not. In any era, for example, it is understood that parents have the responsibility to ready their children for adulthood. The specifics might change, but the general truth is universal. Anywhere and any time, there are certain norms that apply in virtue of the fact that the being whose life they are to govern is human. Nor should we be surprised by this cross-cultural stability of certain principles. Those who accept the basics of Darwinian evolutionary theory also generally accept that certain life forms develop and become stable and basically unchanging while they last. Thus stable lasting principles of botany, biology and psychology, as well as ethics and political economy, can be identified without in any way contradicting the tenets of evolutionary theory. The study of our civilization (brief in biological terms), too, confirms that our nature and the moral needs have persisted from age to age. We're still all homo sapiens here.

Principles of ethics and politics are not in all respects like the principles of gravity or photosynthesis, which cannot be violated. Laws pertaining to the bulk of inanimate and even much of animate nature are necessary and incontrovertible. In contrast, while moral and political laws spell out what is required, incontrovertibly, for human well-being, they can indeed be ignored. We *ought to* follow such principles but we have the freedom of choice to try to evade them.[4]

The situation is analogous to the principles of physical health. Even though consuming strychnine is bad for us, we are quite able to act, at least for a little while, as if it were not so. Both common sense and the criminal law accept our ability to choose wrongly by failing: we should refrain from stealing but some of us refuse to do so. Even our judges and supreme court justices can act wrongly and thus fail to make the law conform to the appropriate principles.[5]

I don't mean to imply by any of these observations that Americans have been chronically loyal to the principles of the US Declaration. There were periods in American history when there were just as many – and even more – violations of individual rights as there are now. Examples include slavery, conscription, the exclusion of women from the political arena, and failures to recognize the full personhood of women under the law. Such practices violated the very principles laid down by the Founders.

There is a cardinal difference, though, between today and the early years of our history with respect to the status of these principles: these principles were once of major public concern. Thomas Jefferson, Alexander Hamilton, John Marshall, Abraham Lincoln and others may not have agreed about them. But they did regard them as principles by which a human community ought to be governed. In our own time, however, what seems to concern most politicians is how to divvy up the proverbial pie. Today the idea has taken root that in some unexplained way *the country* has acquired a lot of wealth and that the proper business of government is to dole out this inexplicably acquired wealth, presumably 'fairly.' The preoccupation with 'fair' pie-divvying has largely superseded concern for justice and rights, not only in the minds of most political thinkers but also in the minds of many ordinary citizens.

Another source of violence against the country's founding principles is the fact that people are more concerned now about safety and security than about liberty. This concern is a manifestation of human nature, but not of any fundamental change in human nature! Panicky people tend to abandon concern for basic principles. It is not the only factor in the sociological mix, but it is an important one. It's mostly when one is in dire need that one is most tempted to commit an act of theft – even if one knows theft to be wrong. Similarly, when our security as a nation seems particularly threatened, people begin to think that maybe we should not abide by such principles as due process of law. Maybe we should instead treat everybody as guilty whether guilt can be shown or not, on the assumption that doing so will help make us more secure. Yet, paradoxically, once we think this way, the very idea of defending our freedom against enemies becomes moot insofar as we ourselves give up on our free system. What's the point of defending the American political tradition if you forsake that tradition in the very process of defending it?

Moreover, pitting the right to liberty against other values is a conceptual error of enormous magnitude. F. A. Hayek made it very clear why this is so:

> That freedom is the matrix required for the growth of moral values – indeed not merely one value among many but the source of all values – is almost self-evident. It is only where the individual has choice, and its inherent responsibility, that he has occasion to affirm existing values, to contribute to their further growth, and to earn moral merit.[6]

If we grant that there are indeed enduring principles of justice, grounded in human nature, then even in the most dire circumstances we should maintain our commitment to these principles, however much we might debate exactly how they apply in given circumstances.

The Founders spoke of unalienable rights – not intermittent or disposable rights that governments and others may ignore at will. True, on occasion in our early history major figures have also done so, including even Thomas Jefferson and, more significantly, Abraham Lincoln. The former compromised his philosophy of limited government when he undertook some of his policies, including the Louisiana Purchase, the latter when he suspended the writ of habeas corpus, the greatest protection a free country can offer its citizens against arbitrary search and seizure. But the sheer historical fact of such actions does not mean they are justified.

It is because our basic humanity doesn't change from year to year and place to place that we can still read the ancient authors such as Plato, Aristotle, Hobbes and the rest and recognize what they are talking about, even if we disagree with them. The historians, poets, novelists, scientists, explorers and jurists of every age continue to speak to us. Our shared humanity enables us to understand each other, and if we somehow managed to resurrect them, we could sit down and have a discussion. Maybe not about the Internet, but about raising children, friendship, politics, beauty, integrity and virtue. Whatever created us, whether God or evolution, once our species came into existence, its members shared a specific identity.

What is that identity? For one thing, all human beings, in all ages and places, are creative. We invent things. We manipulate our environment to make things better for us. We don't just rely on what surrounds us 'as is' like other living things. Plants and non-human animals survive and flourish by following the directions of built-in, hard-wired prompters of behavior, akin to what some of our own physiology follows. But most other living things are unable to exercise initiative to figure out how things are and how they might contribute to their lives. Only we can think, only we have the capacity to choose between right and wrong. And we properly credit and blame people for their freely chosen actions. We are able to abide by or neglect our needs or responsibilities. It's a choice; it's not hard-wired.[7]

Clearly, this aspect of our humanity is invariable, beyond any reasonable doubt. It has persisted from prehistoric times, when men and women began to fend for themselves by making complicated tools and designing their habitats themselves, to the birth of civilizations as they began to speak and write, compose music, embark on trade, and devise philosophies and theologies, all the way on through to the modern era with the development of movies, spaceships and computers. The forms of expression and invention have changed, but what endures is the fact of our creative capacity as such, and our need to be free to exercise it.

What the American Declaration of Independence gave eloquent voice to is the fact that certain basic principles of community life rest on these lasting and fundamental facts of human nature. Accordingly, those principles, too, are lasting and fundamental. They apply whenever and wherever humans congregate and seek to flourish, in Germany, South Africa, Afghanistan, China, Russia, or Madagascar, two thousand years ago and tomorrow. And even if they are openly rejected by the ruling authorities and perhaps even by most of the people. After all, human beings can be wrong – which is also one of our lasting and fundamental attributes.

What follows from this? To start with, that when Nazis kill Jews or Soviets kill kulaks or terrorists kill anybody, it isn't because they happen to live by different but equally sound principles of community life. Their different ways are not on the order of, say, preferring goulash to fish soup while others prefer fish soup to goulash. The political corruptions of those regimes are not even comparable to 'we like the impressionists and they like the surrealists' in art. Optional matters of taste or disputes over aesthetics are by no stretch on a par with matters of life-and-death ethical principles that immediately affect the ability of human beings to coexist with each other and even survive at all.[8]

When fundamental principles of human relationships are violated, by, say, genocidal murder – a massive and obvious denial of the human rights of the victims – this is fundamentally and objectively wrong. This is an 'easy case' ethically, because the action is so extreme and unambiguous. Any good person, even if not very knowledgeable about ethical principles, would recoil and call it wrong, based on the awareness any healthy human being would have of the value of human life.[9] The confidence to set forth a full ethical philosophy and to determine even complex or indirect implications is certainly possible as well, but must be earned through hard study and examination of history, philosophy, theology and through adherence in practice to the basic principles that have come to be discerned.

Armed with the knowledge that certain principles do hold firm, we know that it is proper to resist confidently and without apology when people assail our rights or even our very lives, as did the hijackers of 9/11. We know that it is proper to declare that those who consistently and persistently reject these principles are living a bad life and making evil choices. And if someone were to claim that such a moral assertion amounts to inappropriately imposing our standards on others, we would need to remind him that, among other things, being righteously indignant about the wrongness of moral claims is in itself an act of relying on moral principles thought to apply to everyone; in this case, the principle of an agnostic 'tolerance'![10]

The Declaration speaks of the rights to 'life, liberty, and the pursuit of happiness.' Let us assume that the immorality of murder is not in question. Everyone who respects the rights of others also has the right to be free from the forcible intrusion of others. Granted, this is not widely observed in practice, especially by governments. Nonetheless there is a moral-political equality among us, just as the Declaration of Independence states. It is grounded in the fact that as human beings, we require freedom to exercise independently our capacity to reason to further our own lives.

What about the right to the pursuit of happiness? It means that we are all entitled to conceive of what kind of life we should lead and then proceed to pursue that life without interference, unless in the course of doing so we violate the rights of someone else. It is not so much an addition to the right of liberty as an elaboration of why we all ought to be free. One might want to pursue farming, philosophy, Internet wizardry, racecar driving, or a combination of all these things. And it is up to each person whether to pursue these goals. The right to the 'pursuit of happiness' does not imply that everyone's conception of happiness is equally right or valid or sensible;[11] one could certainly misconceive what will make one happy and choose to live badly. It implies only that the road should be left open, a road which it is then up to each of us to travel.

Is the idea that the government's job is first and foremost to protect our rights as stable and lasting as the principles of rights themselves? Is even the idea of government something as basic as the rights the Founders thought it ought to secure?

Some contend that while it may be true that human beings have basic rights, the protection of these rights requires extensive government intervention in society. If everyone possesses not only 'negative' rights (that is, to life, liberty, and the pursuit of happiness), but also positive rights (that is, to health care, social security, fair treatment in the marketplace), then government's job is quite extensive. It will be obliged to work to secure provisions that are owed to all. Extensive taxation, wealth redistribution, social regimentation and the like would entail a nearly unlimited government rather than the limited kind sufficient to secure negative rights.

Others argue that precisely because of the above, governments are themselves illegitimate, immoral institutions and only anarchy is politically justified. Governments are now involved in regulating everything: tobacco farming, milk production, the building of sports arenas, drug consumption, and much more. This is true, of course, in most countries of the world, which do not rest their public affairs on the precepts of the Declaration of Independence. But this is also the case now in the United States, where the government has evolved into a universal social manager, with public policy expanded to handle everything that some sufficiently influential segment of the population wants government to handle. The seeds of this expansion were sown early in the republic's history, under the leadership of Alexander Hamilton's view of government. It accelerated after the Civil War and, even more so, under the leadership of such presidents as Woodrow Wilson, Theodore Roosevelt and Franklin D. Roosevelt, becoming nearly the default view since then.

In the meantime, the American government routinely fails to do what it was appointed to do, namely, be the peacekeeper within the realm in which it was instituted to secure our negative rights. Under such protection of our negative rights, citizens could and did undertake all the tasks now expected of governments, through various voluntary associations – churches, clubs, corporations, orchestras, and sports teams – with no one being conscripted against his will. The assumption was that we did not need the government to hold a gun to our heads to do the right thing, even if we do sometimes fail to do what is right. Who are politicians and bureaucrats, after all, to imagine that they may make that choice for us, as if we were children or invalids? The government is comprised of other adult human beings and thus whatever their proper task, it cannot include coercing us without our consent. But today, the 'negative rights' that actually do reflect basic human nature and the requirements of human flourishing are chronically violated and undercut by the attempt to secure the so-called 'positive rights.'

So, is it to be either a near-totalitarian government or no government at all? Some critics insist that the principles laid out in the Declaration are ephemeral. Social-political-economic principles, per Hegel–Marx, serve purposes confined to a given historical framework. For example, when the Constitution was framed, it stressed the need for the government to promote the 'free flow of commerce,' and for a new nation that makes very good sense. Laissez-faire or something close to it would, then, be the right public policy to follow. But in later eras, different tasks arose for governments that required substantial expansion of the scope of its jurisdiction and authority. In time, the massive bureaucratic regulatory system that has almost completely abandoned the task of securing negative rights has become the right system for the country. Yet if the Founders and their teachers were correct that the rights we have are based on our human nature, and if our human nature is substantially unchanged over the course of human history, then this historicist view of the function of government is wrong.

It is also wrong to believe that assigning to government the role of securing our negative rights is unrelated to the stable and lasting principles the Founders identified. If we do have the rights of life, liberty and the pursuit of happiness, and if the institution of government – that is to say, a legal order in which such rights are to be protected, updated, and maintained – is justified in order to secure them, then unless somehow those rights have been lost or our human nature has changed substantially, the task of government that the Declaration identifies would also remain stable and lasting.[12] But the argument that human nature has changed so radically – that we really are all children or invalids by nature these days, perhaps – cannot be persuasively made. Men and women had moral capacities and rights in 1776, and we have them now.

Notes

1 For a good and succinct statement of the issue, see Isaiah Berlin, 'A Letter on Human Nature,' *The New York Review of Books*, Vol. LI, No 14 (September 23, 2004), p. 26. Berlin distinguishes between a 'fixed' and a 'common' nature, rejecting the former (after identifying it with Rousseau and the position of innatism) but embracing the latter.

2 This, indeed, was Marx's central criticism of capitalism, namely, that it was propounded as a universal rather than a temporary political economic system. The best source for seeing his views about this is the posthumously published volume *Grundrisse* (New York: Harper & Row, 1970).

3 Thus while the Revolution disposed of the concept of 'subject' and, certainly, 'serf,' it left the policy of taxation, also conceptually contingent upon the feudal system, intact. See, Tibor R. Machan, 'No Taxation, With or Without Representation,' in Robert McGee, ed., *Taxation and Public Finance in Transition and Developing Economies* (New York: Springer Verlag, 2005).

4 For why the idea of free will is not unscientific, see Tibor R. Machan, *Initiative – Human Agency and Society* (Stanford, CA: Hoover Institution Press, 2001).

5 Indeed, for certain reasons having to do with the function of the supreme court in a democracy, justices are restricted to doing only case-by-case legal analysis. The general principles must emerge from these and may not be simply announced by the court.

6 F. A. Hayek, 'The Moral Element in Free Enterprise,' in Mark W. Hendrickson, ed., *The Morality of Capitalism* (Irvington-on-Hudson, NY: The Foundation for Economic Education, 1992), originally written for *The Freeman*, 1962.

7 There is much dispute about this. See, for example, Filipe Fernandez-Armesto, *Humankind, A Brief History* (Oxford, UK: Oxford University Press, 2004), who maintains that the dividing line between human beings and some other animals, such as great apes, is too blurred to be taken seriously for any normative purpose (such as assigning rights to humans but not to other animals). For a contrasting view, see Tibor R. Machan, *Putting Humans First* (Lanham, MD: Rowman & Littlefield, 2004).

8 Even the issue of whether artistic judgments are based on some fundamental standards of artistic excellence could be debated but I will leave that aside here.

9 For a discussion of how some ethical principles are seen to be common to us all, see Bernard Gert, *Common Morality: Deciding What to Do* (Oxford, UK: Oxford University Press, 2004).

10 Of course, to make such a criticism of such declarations is itself paradoxical since the criteria on which it relies will be treated as stable and worth observing for us all.

11 For more, see Tibor R. Machan and Douglas J. Den Uyl, 'Recent Work on the Concept of Happiness,' *American Philosophical Quarterly*, Vol. 21 (1984), pp. 1–31.

12 For why the anarchist arguments fail to show that any type of government must violate the very rights the Founders held it ought to secure, see Tibor R. Machan. 'Anarchism and Minarchism, A Rapprochement,' *Journal des Economists et des Estudes Humaines*, Vol. 14, No 4 (December 2002), pp. 569–88. See also Roderick Long and Tibor R. Machan, eds, *Anarchism/Minarchism: Is a Government Part of a Free Country?* (Burlington, VT: Ashgate, forthcoming).

Chapter 3

Justice, Self and Natural Rights

'A man is said to be just because he respects the rights (*jus*) of others.'

Thomas Aquinas

The intellectual arena is alive with arguments and controversies concerning a perennial moral and political problem, much more fundamental than whether one or another practice in our society is just or right. These controversies concern whether there exist basic standards for human personal and community life as such. Perhaps no such standards exist. In that case do various communities, cultures, regions of the globe or other groupings of people decide on such matters, with no objective standard to rely upon in the last analysis?[1]

Developments in Eastern Europe and the former Soviet Union, in South Africa, Nicaragua, Chile, China and other parts of the geopolitical sphere have thrust this question into virtually any thinking person's life. Can we judge the South Africans by objective standards or only those by which we happen to apply to institutions in North America or in Western Europe? Can we say that the Chinese or the South African government ought, in fact, to institute democratic processes or is that just a wish we happen to have that others simply do not share and have no reason to take seriously unless they wish to? Can we say with conviction and confidence that, for example, a more individualist system of economic organization is more suitable to human community life than a collective command system? Or is it all really quite relative and indeterminate how a human community should be constituted?[2]

My plan in this chapter is to defend the position in political philosophy that the right to liberty or negative freedom is the proper standard of justice in human community life. It will also be argued that in a good or just human community moral virtue is not only accidentally possible but is necessarily enhanced. Furthermore, it will be shown that this conception of political justice rests on an objective and at a basic level universalizable foundation. That foundation is naturalism, including naturalistic ethics and rights theory.[3]

My task will be somewhat laborious, since so much about the position I wish to present is currently in dispute. The first step will be to examine some metaethical and metapolitical challenges a naturalist approach faces in our time. Next a case for a sound (objectively valid) idea of human nature will be advanced, one showing that human life is teleological and normative –

it is goal-directed and involves moral responsibilities. From this it will be maintained that given the moral nature of human beings, political justice must be grounded in the effort to establish, maintain and preserve what our moral nature requires in a social-political-legal context. In conclusion some critical objections to this position will be taken up.

Current Philosophy and Naturalism

Before developing the case for the natural rights classical liberal position on justice, it is worth noting some metaethical and political problems that stand in the way of such a task. During the last two and a half decades, a lively discussion has ensued about natural law ethics. In the mid-twentieth century most prominent philosophy departments espoused some variety of noncognitivism. When one mentioned natural or human rights, one was quickly directed to read Margaret Macdonald's famous emotivist essay, 'Natural Rights,'[4] This was essentially an application of A. J. Ayer's logical positivism to political morality.

The philosophical climate has undergone some changes since. By now there does not exist a comparably firm orthodoxy in metaethics or metapolitics. Yet, even today the more prestigious philosophers and departments tend to look with disdain toward naturalist ethics and politics. What's more, the naturalist politics that we associate – albeit somewhat problematically – with John Locke has come under fire from several classical liberal and conservative political theorists from whom one might expect support.

Locke's natural rights theory has also been deprecated recently by some admirers of Plato's political thinking.[5] These thinkers essentially lump John Locke's political views with those of Thomas Hobbes, at least at the basic philosophical level.[6] A more recent line of criticism of the natural rights classical liberal stance is deeply skeptical and more broadly based.[7] It would avoid Platonism even more than natural law classical liberals or libertarians for the very reason that it finds fault with naturalism as such.[8]

The criticism of naturalism advanced from some of these positions will be taken up later. Let us see, for now, the position these critics believe justifies their disdain for naturalism.

Judging by some of its champions, it would appear that they find the idea of human nature without foundation.[9] Some of this is owed to the philosophical orientation of Karl Popper.[10] Just as positivists, such as Macdonald, as well as most Existentialist critics of the Platonic–Aristotelian tradition, these critics reject the concept of 'the nature of X' if it is supposed to involve anything that is not purely conventional. Accordingly, human nature is not objective but nominal and even historically or culturally relative and conditioned.

There is another recently revived doctrine antithetical to naturalism. This is political intuitionism, combined with the claim that one is able to reach substantive moral and political conclusions without any reliance on work in other branches of philosophy. This thesis of 'the independence of moral theory'[11] has had considerable influence. One need only read the major journals of ethics and political theory, where papers often begin with a claim about our 'considered moral judgments' and proceed from such intuitive beginnings to various moral and public policy conclusions.

In advancing a naturalist foundation for political justice, it would be imprudent to avoid confronting the metapolitical positions sketched above. A kind of Kuhnean result is in evidence from the widespread promulgation of these views. Most prominent ethicists and political theorists share this attitude. This is made evident, in a slightly different but not entirely unrelated context, by Russell Hardin, when he notes that 'Anyone who tries to defend an unvarnished right of contract for any two parties to do whatever they want to do under any circumstances will be met with vacant stares from most moral and political theorists today.'[12]

Naturalists in the classical liberal school aim at uncovering some objective ground that would enable us 'to defend an unvarnished right' to life, liberty and property – including, derivatively, freedom of contract (though not of the type caricatured by Hardin). Thus, not facing up to the challenges placed before naturalism by these various prominent theorists will render it impossible to make convincing advances. The paradigm of noncognitivist, anti-naturalist metaethics and metapolitics needs to be shown to be inadequate before the naturalist position can even gain a hearing. That will be my first task in this chapter.

Naturalism

Why is there so much skepticism about the idea of 'the nature of X'? The doubtfulness is similar to that which motivates deconstructionists in contemporary literary criticism. We can go all the way back to Heraclitus and, especially, his pupil Cratylus to locate the lineage of this school of thought.[13]

The skeptic's persuasiveness can be understood, given one version of naturalism that has *bona fide* historical roots. This is a troublesome doctrine. It could justifiably lead classical liberals and British conservatives – that is, those who are weary of leviathan for various reason (especially in the United States of America and in the United Kingdom) – to fear dogmatism and authoritarianism.

The naturalism in question, linked to the Platonic natural law tradition, posits the existence of transcendent, permanent or timeless, and perfect natures for every being.[14] Yet, with this Platonic idea of what the nature of something must be, we are stymied from the start. If to know 'the nature of X is a, b, and c,' would also require knowing that the proposition is a timeless truth, a temporal human being could not affirm this. Forever there would have to be doubt about any proposition affirming that kind of truth.

Therein lies one of the major objections to naturalism. I will argue, later, that the Platonist conception of what 'the nature of X' must mean is not the best way to understand what 'the nature of X' must mean. There is a neo-Aristotelian approach – which may be called, following Ayn Rand, contextualism[15] – that has a far better prospect.

Human Nature

If there is an objective moral foundation to the classical liberal system of polity, its earliest (albeit still halting and by no means fully consistent) expression is to be found in the natural rights theory of John Locke. Contrary opinion exists, of course – some claim that Thomas Hobbes is the actual grandfather of this polity.[16] But it is widely admitted, at least, that if this republic (the USA) rests on a normative political framework, it is that which was inherited from the political works of John Locke. Such other thinkers as Thomas Hobbes or Adam Smith either did not advance a sufficiently normative theory or did not exert sufficient (early) influence. Locke, as other thinkers, borrowed from others (for example, the Levellers). But he put together the most coherent position favoring the idea that each human individual is politically sovereign, in possession of basic rights that it is the proper task of government to secure.

I stress the normativity of the Lockean legacy because it is in Locke that we find the defence of such ideas as that every person ought to respect every other person's equality, freedom and independence and that each individual human being should have a sphere of personal authority accorded to him. The rights Locke claims everyone possesses are political norms, not, as in the case of Hobbes, innately prompted strategies for survival. Locke not only held – though he did not prove – that such social–political norms were binding on all persons in a human community. He also believed that these norms were themselves based on more basic edicts of personal conduct, namely, 'the law of Nature.' Individuals are free, in the sense that they, in adulthood, are able to bring it about on their own to follow these laws. 'The state of Nature has a law of Nature to govern it, which obliges everyone, and reason, which is that law, teaches all mankind who will but consult it, that being all equal and independent, no one ought to harm another in his life, health, liberty or possessions' (*Second Treatise on Civil Government*, Chapter II, Sec. 6).

Now the Lockean view has come under attack from both the Right and the Left.[17] The Right sees basic rights as mere individualist artifacts, invented in defiance of the much more reliable streams of tradition and custom that grow, through trial and error over the centuries, to become the most dependable devices for social living. The Left takes these rights to be (in Marx's phrase) 'insipid illusions,' beliefs produced so as to legitimize certain historically inevitable impulses of human beings at a given time period. They are mere rationalizations, not genuine philosophical–moral foundations.

The most severe damage to the doctrine of natural rights has arisen from the philosophical system that has given rise to the scientism found mostly in the social sciences. This view denies that a normative outlook on human community life even makes sense. It is empiricist and skeptical. It mostly yields conservative conclusions about politics since, in the absence of convincing guidelines for public policy, the best guide is the past – including class structures, coercive laws, and other edicts based on tradition and custom.

I will try to cast the Lockean perspective in a contemporary light, without losing any of its crucial features and power. I will spell out, in several paragraphs, what the natural rights perspective is. This will make it possible to judge whether dismissing it, as many philosophers and social scientists do, is warranted. The last section of this chapter will focus on some objections, advanced recently by utilitarians, skeptics, and historicists.[18]

Natural Rights in Outline

What is a natural rights theory? It is an answer to a question that arises in connection with human community life, namely, 'How, in the most general terms, should we (human beings) live with each other?' In particular, this answer rests on an investigation of human nature. The community in question embraces people who are unrelated – that is, may not stand to each other as kith and kin, friends, colleagues, and so on. Among family members, friends, colleagues, and so forth, special, narrower ethical principles could probably handle the problems a theory of natural rights aims to handle among human beings unknown to each other. But the situation of large human communities, with strangers as members, is familiar enough, so it isn't difficult to imagine why our question would arise. How should we interact with human beings as such, never mind other ties?

Now this question has been answered in very different ways, for very different reasons. I won't canvass all. It is probable that most people have some familiarity with them.

For example, one answer has been to model human community life on some such life in heaven – the city of God. Another has been to advise the community to ensure the equality of all of its members (at least in terms of crucial goods and services), or to purify the race, or to serve God, or to help the forces of history. These have all been defended, in elaborate treatises, as answers to the question addressed by natural rights theory, namely, 'How should we live as a community?'

Numerous questions that arise in the various areas of human inquiry have a bearing on the study of politics. This shouldn't really be surprising. Politics concerns the basic principles of human community life. The issue is certainly complicated by all sorts of factors about human beings: their relationships, environment, health, sustenance, goals and purposes, and so on. Political theory subsumes virtually all other fields of inquiry.

Here is the natural rights approach to answering our question. First we need to grasp some points about reality and our knowledge of it. Then we need to learn how we would best understand what is meant by such judgments as 'We should act so and so,' 'He should not act so and so,' 'This is good,' or 'This is evil.' The reason is that in politics we are, after all, concerned with how we *should* or *should not* act, as to the institutions we can support for governing communities. So we need to consider how to answer normative questions. So we need to explore the application of the ideas of 'should' and 'should not' to human conduct and, especially for our purposes, human institutions. For this we will first need to consider what is human nature and identify standards of personal, social and political norms – the realm of ethics or natural law – and whether it is even possible to speak of what individuals morally should do in their own lives and toward their fellows. We need, mostly, to consider the *framework* for good conduct within a social-political context, that is, what we ought to support as a *system of justice*, the basic principles of community life.

By following this naturalist approach, we will come to the topic of basic human rights theory, our main concern.

Some Basic Philosophical Issues

First, existence cannot be inherently confusing – we may be confused about it but it must make sense once closely studied. If this is denied, then all bets are off, not just in human affairs and the studies of them but in all realms of inquiry, including the denial itself. The words we speak, even as we affirm or deny anything, will lack clear and unambiguous identity and the meanings of our concepts will be indeterminate. This will include whatever we ourselves might wish those meanings to be as a matter of our intentions. For example, as we state that by 'rights' we only mean social devices invented by us, we will have to admit that these devices may or may not be what we want them to be. If reality is itself something in total flux, all the way to its most basic structure, our statement that this is so cannot be depended upon. It will mean nothing firm or stable. And, not insignificantly, in the realm of ethics and politics that will tend to imply that the powerful – by virtue of their power and not the clarity and truth of some ideas that justify some conduct – must rule, and no check on them, based on what is really right and wrong, is possible. So, insofar as we admit that we can make sense of even the minimum of our lives, we affirm that reality hangs together in a reasonably orderly fashion, at least at the most basic level.[19]

Moreover, we can know the facts above well enough. We can also know a lot more than that, if only we work hard to find things out. Knowing reality as it is is not impossible, as some people have claimed, provided we do not have an impossible ideal as a conception of what is meant by doing so. From what we have already learned we can infer that we can learn about reality. The task is one of finding out about it, through extensive and hard work.[20]

Among other areas of reality of the greatest interest to us is human nature itself, that is, what we are as human beings, quite apart from our individual identity, our special origins, gender, race, professional competence, and so on. These can be crucial in some contexts but for now what concerns us is human nature. The reason for this concern is that we are interested in how human beings should conduct themselves toward each other *qua* human beings, and that cannot be answered without knowledge of what human beings are simply as human beings. Once we have got a glimpse of human nature, as it were, we can then ask how considerations of 'should' apply in the case of human beings as such. And that provides us with the basic material needed to determine the norms of interpersonal conduct, that is, the norms of political life.

The point about the general integrity of reality is complicated but perhaps a clue or so would suffice so that it can be understood without much difficulty. Everything that exists abides by some very minimal principles, namely, those that pertain to existence itself. That is, just for being something, anything at all, whatever exists abides by certain principles, namely, the principles of existence – the necessary conditions for something being at all, whatever it is then identified to be. Those principles are, as might be suspected, very general in character, since they apply to everything, past, present, future, and even the possible. (The very possibility of the existence of something involves these basic principles.) And because of this generality, these principles have to be extremely broad in scope but limited in content, in what they imply. This is because – granted that all existence, necessarily, exists – there is a great deal of variety in all of what does exist.

The most basic principle of existence is that what exists must be something specific, something definite. A chair must be a chair, a table a table, a dog a dog, a person a person, an act of justice an act of justice. This sounds terribly broad, even 'empty', but that is because the point bears on everything whatever, so it cannot include very much in the way of variations. Things are what they are, and this is true about everything, contrary to what may appear to be true. However, there is quite a lot embedded in this point, the main thing being that no contradictory situations can exist in reality – that is, it cannot be the case that, for example, something both *is* a table and *is not* a table.

Perhaps a quick example will show how deeply we all need this point in our understanding of reality. Thus, when in a court of law some testimony is subjected to cross-examination, if the testimony is shown to contain contradictions – for example, someone is found saying both that he was in New York on 4 June 1988, and that he was not in New York on 4 June, 1988 – then we have found something terribly wrong with the testimony. The same would be the case if he said that he had a hat on yesterday afternoon and that he did not have a hat on at that time. Or that he is married to Susie as well as that he is not married to Susie. This is all wrong because such things simply cannot be.

Now this and some related considerations about reality inform us of the absolute requirement of keeping our understanding of reality consistent. There is a lot else we need, but this minimum requirement is entirely indispensable. Everything else about our way of dealing with reality requires that this central point be adhered to.[21] That is why, for instance, if a theory, say of natural rights, contains a contradiction, it cannot be considered even possibly right, let alone true. The same is clear of any scientific theory, a legal contract, or a plan of action. Reality does not tolerate – that is, embody – contradictions, that is, facts that are of one kind and not of that kind all at once in the same fashion.[22]

From the above remarks very little follows except for a few points already hinted at. Knowledge may not involve contradictions or inconsistencies. This general point about knowledge follows the general point about existence, because knowledge is our correct awareness or identification of existence, whatever else it is. The way we obtain knowledge differs from one area of study to others – for example, in history the records left to us, involving trusting others a great deal, give us knowledge; in biology experimentation with members of the same species of living beings, and our awareness of differences and similarities in the behavior of these members and their various parts, will provide us with knowledge; in sociology the careful observation of how groups of people behave and the interpretation of this observation by reference to our knowledge can be found in each case of knowledge, some in only a limited case, depending on what it is we study. This is important because sometimes it is thought that unless the knowledge in one field of inquiry abides by the standards of knowledge in all others, it is impossible that we have knowledge in the former.[23]

That is why some people think that we can have knowledge only in the physical sciences, because they believe that knowledge must always and exclusively rest on our awareness of physical properties and attributes. Here is why empiricism is so popular – because knowledge that is guided by the dictates of the empirical sciences is taken to be the only kind of knowledge.

But then we would rule out at the start any knowledge of whatever lacks strictly physical properties. And that would be a prejudice. Such prejudice is encouraged by theories of knowledge that require that all cases of knowledge be exactly like all others. There is no justification for this, even though it is a widespread view. (The same affects our problem with beauty or moral goodness – a theory demands that all things beautiful or morally good be identical, and we cannot confirm this, so it is concluded that beauty or moral goodness is purely relative, even subjective.) Yet just as there can be trees, equally healthy, that are very different yet still trees, so there can be knowledge, equally sound, yet different and still knowledge.

A few other, more special, points need to be made about knowledge. First, to know something is to have correctly concluded on the basis of the relevant evidence that something is the case (even if this means only that something is probably so and so, or that something is possibly so and so). Second, the evidence involved is something we may obtain by various means at our disposal – for example, simply looking; looking and touching; looking, touching, and hearing; looking, touching, hearing, and comparing to something else; and so forth. The minds we have, and our sensory organs, working together at our direction, is how we obtain knowledge. And even if we don't get knowledge immediately but only well-supported beliefs, even good or educated guesses, it is by way of the mind in its highly complicated ways of operation with the senses, that we get this much.

Basically, when we attempt to obtain knowledge we aim for knowing what is what and how something becomes (or became, or will become) another thing; why this has occurred and not that; and where things have occurred, and so on. In all our efforts we need to recall that contradictions are prohibited and that different kinds of evidence may have to be used to discover different facts about the world.

The above is extremely brief but necessary. From there we can take a very long jump to something much closer to what interests us here, namely, politics. What we need to turn to is a consideration of the place of norms in existence. We are familiar enough with knowledge about facts concerning inanimate and animate existence – rocks are hard, dogs often bark, penicillin can prevent disease, governments often wage war. These kinds of facts can be known without much debate about them, although very soon after we have come to admit that we know something along these lines, we find that other matters we might think we know are extremely controversial. But that is not what is at issue – controversy is a social problem that anyone who wishes to tell others what he knows (or claims to know) will encounter. First, we need to find out whether there is anything we know about controversial topics. Such a topic is the topic of norms, principles of human conduct. That Napoleon should have prepared his men better for the battle at Waterloo, or that Teddy Roosevelt should not have led the US into war, or that President Bush should have fought against inflation by refusing to print more money, or that one should respect the wishes of one's spouse when we consider where to live – all these are facts or alleged facts about which much controversy arises. Yet that is not the issue, but how we might come to know about these matters. The natural rights theory (which I find sound) answers this question by noting, first, that considerations of what one should or should not do pertain to considerations of what is good and evil. That which is good (and possible) for one to pursue is something one should pursue, and that which is evil (and possible) for one to pursue one should not pursue, to put the matter plainly. But this just shifts our problem.

How do we come to know what is good? Here we need to consider what 'good' means. It means the fullest realization of some particular thing as an instance of its kind – for example, a good peach is a fully realized peach, or a peach that has most fully completed the nature of being a peach. A good tennis game is a fully realized tennis game, or a tennis game that has fully reached the crux of a tennis game. The idea is not a very simple one, but whenever we appraise tomatoes, peaches, apples, chickens, parking lots, or whatever, we can learn whether we should praise it or criticize it by reference to the fact that the thing (or activity or whatever) in question has more or less fully reached its distinctive nature in the given case at hand. This tennis game is a good one if the players play by satisfying the central ingredients of tennis and whatever those ingredients imply for the particular game at hand. (The particular game at hand may require realizing the game somewhat differently from another particular game.) A good skiing slope or a good knife or a good source of light – all these pertain to how fully some particular case realizes the essence of what it is in its own instance. We don't always talk of a good this, a good that or a bad this, a bad that; but such expressions as 'great,' or 'neat,' or 'swell,' or 'far out,' or 'fantastic,' and numerous others make the same point for us, as do 'lousy,' 'rotten,' 'poor,' and so on. When we consider what good is most generally, it has to do with whether something has realized its nature in the case at hand. The nature of something – what it is that makes it the kind of thing it is – for example, a tennis game, a golf ball, or a Christmas tree – is the place or category it occupies in the most rational way of classifying attributes, properties, and whatever else we perceive about existence. This process yields our knowledge of trees, chairs, furniture, balloons, time, days, weeks, months, space, fields, meadows, galaxies, the mind, memory, imagination, an idea.[24]

There is nothing mysterious about the point that everything has a nature, since everything that exists is most successfully classified as one kind of thing or another, and it must be so classifiable for it to exist and for us to understand it and for it to be anything at all. (This follows from the previous discussion.) In the case of human beings, this all leads to the issue of the relationship between their action and being good. Being a good human being, like being a good anything, requires the fullest possible realization of human nature in the particular case of a given person. Thus we – that is, some widely read or heard human beings, at least – need to know what human nature is so we can tell what it is to be good at being a human being. In other words, some clear enough idea of human nature is required for anyone to be able to judge, with reasonable success, what it is to be a good human being.

What then is a human being as such, that is, what is human nature? This is where the naturalism of natural rights theory comes into full focus. Natural rights theory can produce an understanding of the rights human beings have by reference to an understanding of human nature. That is why they are called natural rights – rights someone has (or we are justified to ascribe to someone) by virtue of his or her human nature.

Human nature is the set of facts that are true of human beings just insofar as they are human beings, nothing else (for example, not as students, mothers, Germans, and those 25 years old, or as animals, objects, geometrical figures, and so on). What is that set of facts?

Without repeating my earlier points, it includes that human beings are animals (with a biological nature and all of what that involves) and capable of rational thought (that is, having the capacity to think in terms of principles, to think at the level of general ideas or concepts and what these imply). The ancient idea that man is a rational animal is still sound, although some of it, and what exactly it implies, has had to be modified in the light of our greater understanding of some of the issues involved. Still, the crucial point is that human beings are by nature animals and capable of rationality. A good human being would, then, be one who, speaking very generally (with all the very important details deliberately left out, so this can apply to everyone), is biologically healthy and fully alert (except, of course, when continued alertness requires rest). As to what this implies about how we should conduct ourselves personally and in public, we come to next.[25]

The first normative area we are concerned with is personal ethics – that is, the code or laws of nature that pertains to how we should conduct ourselves. By nature we live a most fully human life by being rational. We thus achieve well being on all possible levels (which excludes any interference that we cannot control). But here is the rub. To the best of our knowledge the bulk of the animate world behaves as guided automatically – for example, instincts, drives, reflexes, and so forth (given the environment surrounding it). Human beings, however, are not compelled by their inner drives, instincts, and so on, to behave as they do. To put the matter plainly, they are able to choose between genuine alternatives. Maybe some animals can, too. Those cases are rare enough not to pose a problem here. Human beings may also have some instincts, but this too is negligible. The point is that people in maturity are able to choose what they will do. (We are not discussing childhood, even adolescence, although a fuller discussion would have to consider those stages, as many other things.)

Now it is central that human beings enjoy the freedom that other animals lack just in the area of thinking. Human beings, unlike other animals, cope with reality mainly through the medium of ideas, theories, principles, concepts, and so on. To live, even to the minimum degree of viability, a solitary adult needs to figure things out, and then he can take the actions his life requires for sustenance. An adult, of course, can choose to wither away, to die, not to live, in which case thinking is not required for him. But we are not concerned about those human beings who do not choose to live and thus have no interest in the principles of human conduct, of human action, of human living. The norms we are interested in have application for us because we haven't got innate drives, and so on, to guide us in living; but if we will not live, then the norms are beside the point.[26]

The first point, then, about basic moral norms is that they are required only for the living. But this is inseparable – in the case of an investigation of the human good – from the fact that our capacity for thought needs to be initiated or put into effect by us. If we don't put thinking into effect, we merely coast or drift – usually on the opinions of others – voluntarily at the disposal of others. In the morality underlying natural rights theory, living requires thought, rational observation, reflection, consideration, recollection, assessment, evaluation, comparison, and so on. Without choosing this kind of activity we in fact also reject the requirements of human life, and to the extent that we fail to engage in rational thought, and so on, we are failing in the commitment we make when we choose to live, namely, to live as fully as is possible to us.[27]

For a rational being to choose life is to choose a rational life, and one that isn't rational just now and then. This is a choice one can renege on, but to that extent one will be less than a good human being. Not living in accordance with one's nature is to fail to be good. The requirements for being good, then, include, first and foremost, the exercise of one's rational faculty, something that human beings must do by choice. It is now clear that goodness is being in full accord with one's nature. That is the function or point of the concept, as it were. Thus, given our human nature – namely, being a rational animal – it is possible to understand what being a good human being is.[28] It is to be in full accord with the requirement of rationality and biological health. It is clear from an understanding of human nature that one's capacity for rationality, one's distinctive humanity as it were, is kept in force by choice.

So the first moral responsibility of any human being who has chosen to live is to be mentally alert, to think rationally, and to act accordingly.[29] This is a responsibility of each individual person. It is a matter of personal choice that one does what one should do, otherwise it makes no sense that one should do it. What one cannot help but do cannot be something one should do. Choice is of the essence of moral responsibility.

But this is not all there is to it. To live our lives according to our nature is the human good. Only individual human beings can make the act so as to achieve or neglect human moral good. Others cannot do it for them. All that can be done even for children is to provide them with good examples and shield them from gross errors.

Alongside the universal moral responsibility to live a human life rationally, there are endless diverse details. They are less crucial for now because they can vary. What will be rational for one person at one time need not be for another. Numerous general principles are pertinent outside the norm that we should think and act rationally. For example, it is generally rational to be honest, productive, generous, prudent, well-integrated, and courageous. These are the virtues one will find articulated by most moralists. What they differ on is what comes first and why. Suffice it to summarize that human life requires that a person live rationally because that is what living the life of a human being amounts to and that is to what a person commits himself when he chooses to live.

The natural rights theory outlined here is based on an ethical view in terms of which the morally good human life consists of a person living rationally. Success, excellence, or happiness (in the sense of full flourishing), as a human being, is best pursued by living in accordance with the requirements of one's nature as a rational animal.

What, if anything, does this tell us about human community life? That only a human community the fundamental organizing principles of which incorporate the basic facts of human morality can be said to accord with human nature, be conducive to human moral goodness and thus be characterized as just. Just communities are not those populated only by good human beings.[30] That could come about by way of accident: people might accidentally gather together and all at once be at their best, regardless of the organizational characteristics – constitution – of their community. A good human community is such that it makes moral goodness more than accidentally possible; indeed, it enhances human goodness. This is where natural rights surface.

The just political community is what it is because it accurately reflects the requirements of human nature within the context of community life – that is, it meets the requirements of morally sovereign individuals by means of respecting and protecting individual human rights to life, liberty and property.[31] These rights are the standards of justice for the organization of a human community – the criteria for how to establish, maintain and promote justice in community life.

That these negative rights can be the foundation of justice is disputed often on the grounds that justice requires greater activism, not merely protection from untoward acts. A just state or government would, accordingly, engage in certain promotional activities – legislate appropriate conduct, further the good behavior of its citizens, repair past social wrongs, and so on. How, then, could the administration of a system of basically negative rights – that is, protecting against murder, assault, robbery, fraud, embezzlement, kidnapping, and the adjudication of charges for the commission of such deeds – count as the maintenance of justice?

If one appreciates that adult human beings possess a moral nature, whereby it is crucial that they make decisions within their sphere of authority, circumscribed by their negative rights, then one can see why a just political and legal system would provide primarily protective rather than active or legislative policies. Given the naturalist basis of this idea of justice and given the idea of human nature that makes the best sense, it would appear evident that a just system must be engaged in securing peace and the respect of negative rights rather than promoting certain ends or objectives, something only individual choices may facilitate.[32]

Consider in contrast Rawls's conception of 'justice as fairness.' The central difference between the Lockean individual rights perspective and that offered by John Rawls is that for Rawls human beings are cast into situations from which they cannot extricate themselves of their own free will – even their moral character is determined by luck. Accordingly, it is not possible to envision human beings as autonomous, sovereign and morally responsible[33] and, therefore, in need of what Nozick has called 'moral space.'[34] Rather, all persons are in the same boat of having been cast into a situation quite apart from their choices or best alternatives. To remedy the unfairness that is experienced by them, justice is needed *via* the establishment of equality of circumstances.[35] This involves the active promotion of certain states of affairs, ends or objectives, as the substance of justice.

The Rawlsian conception of human nature is unjustified – it would be unable to explain the enormous advances human beings constantly make in their own lives, their successful creative accomplishments, even the philosophic and scientific innovations that characterize so much of human living. The kind of passivity ascribed to humanity by Rawls and his followers does not even square with how Rawlsians behave, namely, as creative political partisans of the down-trodden, the poor, and needy.

Instead of this passive conception, the institutions of a political community should rest on the more accurate view that human beings are by nature creative free agents, capable of self-direction in nearly any circumstance, except where political justice is not possible, for example, in the midst of an earthquake or when they are crucially incapacitated. The range of their creativity may not be identical, but in normal circumstances each person has ample opportunity to initiate the effort to advance his or her own life, to become more able to cope and to succeed at the innumerable tasks that may provide fulfillment to human individuals.[36]

Within the present framework, however, basic negative rights are the standards or principles of just human interaction that arise from nature.[37] Of course, conduct in line with these standards can give rise to rights that arise from contract, promises and familial relations. A child has rights which parents or equivalent agents must respect, and parents, too, have rights children must respect.[38]

Rights, then, are those principles which govern some of the basic relations between human beings, but their source may be varied. The most basic source of rights, however, is human nature which implies moral requirements for community life such that every person may be forced to abide by certain principles: it is everyone's natural right to be respected for what one is, namely, a human being, capable of choosing to live, to think, and to act rationally, and to interact by respecting the rationality of all others.

The rights to life, liberty, and property state these points somewhat cryptically, meaning:

1 since it is one's basic nature to be able to choose to live, one's life (as the outcome of one's essential human choice) is something no one other than the agent is permitted to terminate or take (except once the person is refusing to respect the life of another and elicits self-defensive action that may kill);
2 since the choice to live entails the commitment to think and act rationally, it is unjustifiable that others who have explicitly or implicitly[39] joined a community would be authorized to subvert one's liberty to make this choice (it would be the negation of another's humanity to subvert his choice between rational thought and action or irrational mental life and behavior);[40]
3 since rational choice should lead one to interact with others, who also will find it rational to associate with others, the association of individuals and

> the results of such association (for example, cooperation, competition, trade, bequeathal, and so forth) may not be violated.

All told, then, the rights to life, liberty, and property – not to be murdered, not to be assaulted or coerced, and not to be robbed or have one's property expropriated – are natural rights. They emerge because we are human beings, we have the power of choice, as such, to live and to flourish, and we should do so in societies. The crucial point is that natural rights theory rests on the moral nature of human life, on the requirement of each person to choose life and flourishing for him- or herself. The main complaint against this idea is that if another lives badly, neglects his or her life or suffers misfortune, help may be forced upon or demanded of him or her. But this is to destroy the human dignity of the person, however needy or earnest he or she might be. Nor may others force someone to engage in the sort of conduct often deemed to be honorable – namely, charitable conduct – since coerced charity is not charity but robbery. Those who urge such measures fail to observe the requirements of human nature. That failure only *appears* to be useful, helpful, necessary, moral, nice, unavoidable, and so on. Once these matters are carefully considered, the alleged welfare state is not really one that promotes welfare at all. It is impossible to be of value to human beings – promote their overall welfare – if one acts out of accord with human nature (except, perhaps, entirely accidentally).[4]

Let me summarize my points. First, natural rights theory aims to address the central question of political life, namely, what norms should guide us in our basic relationship to other human beings? Natural rights theory aims to answer this basic question by consulting nature, specifically human nature. It adheres to certain fundamental points about reality and our knowledge of reality, and it has a certain view about what goodness is, namely, the flourishing of something in accordance with its nature. With respect to ethics or how morally we should conduct our lives, the question is what human nature amounts to and how it may be fully actualized in an individual human being (which is to say, by an individual human being who possesses the capacity to realize this human nature consistently in his or her case). By choosing life and rationality, one commits oneself to act in a morally proper manner. A community is good – a just human community – if its principles are in accord with the moral requirements of human (personal and social) life. The libertarian political stance stresses the primary significance of human freedom or liberty ('negative freedom'), that is, the foremost significance of each person's right to liberty of conduct in the context of social or interpersonal conduct. Respecting the right – and taking measures to resist its violation – is warranted on the basis of the ethics and natural rights theory outlined in this discussion.

Some Points of Criticism

At least an outline of the case for the natural rights classical liberal position has been spelled out so as to secure the soundness of the very idea of human nature. The case for the objectivity of the moral foundations of a natural rights theory with libertarian content has also been sketched in sufficient detail so that the position can be plainly considered. It is now possible to take a critical look at some of the objections raised against the naturalist – that is, natural law, natural rights – stance of which the present position as a variant.

Let me turn first to a critic who combines two vital elements of contemporary conservatism, namely, a belief in the significance of tradition with a commitment to a utilitarian value theory. The former belief keeps such a critic close to some of the individualist features of the American polity since, after all, that polity has for more than two centuries embodied such features – that is, it has become traditional to embrace individualism in America. The latter is the view implicit in David Hume's anti-rationalist conservatism, whereby the values to be pursued by us find their overarching justification in their public utility. The only element of contemporary conservatism not directly present in this approach is religion; however, religion is presupposed within the traditionalist element, since by reference to tradition religion emerges as a vital feature of culture.

A conservative utilitarian criticism of the natural rights position involves the following points: it may be true that there are various necessary conditions that are required for human existence and flourishing or excellence. Yet it does not follow at all that from these (or from knowing these) it is possible to infer norms or virtues or principles of human conduct. (This is plainly a restatement of the is/ought gap thesis of David Hume and the subsequent empiricist/positivist movement in epistemology and metaethics.[42])

From this position it would seem both hopeless and undesirable to forge and sustain a free society or legal system by relying on natural laws or rights (whether in the Aristotelian/Thomistic or Kantian/Gewirth tradition). Assuming negative freedom is in most cases a good thing (that is, it is good when human beings do not intrude on each other's lives and properties),[43] there is reason to believe that within the framework of natural law or essentialist ethical and political thinking this good thing would be jeopardized. We are reminded of the historical fact that most thinkers who have supposed that we can derive 'oughts' from the 'is' of what human nature comes to, have promulgated ethical and political views that have given scant respect to negative liberty. Plato, Hegel, and Marx, to name but three outstanding figures, have all advocated holistic or totalist moral–political systems.[44] While that does not prove natural law or essentialist/naturalist views wrong, the critics would wish us to consider the matter as perhaps suggestive and warn those fond of negative freedom against the temptation to rely on anything like the naturalist tradition.

To put it more succinctly, conservative utilitarian critics of the natural law/natural rights position firmly cling to the Humean is/ought argument against the possibility of naturalist ethics and politics. So they claim that our better theoretical alternative is utilitarianism which does not insist on the full, uncompromising protection of negative rights and allows plenty of room for various paternalistic and welfare policies by governments of human communities.

Now every theory that is flawed needs in the end to be provided with a substitute that holds up. For merely lacking full adequacy – completeness and consistency – will not be fatal to a theory while no better one is available. Some critics of natural rights liberalism also defend – as well as consider problems with – the sort of ethical/political doctrine we may expect from a utilitarian or consequentialist approach. Here, following a prudent strategy of not denying the troublesome aspects of the view being favored, utilitarians pre-empt the sort of criticism of the positivist/utilitarian ethical/political stance which has led John Rawls and Robert Nozick, among others, toward its rejection. This is that the position does not guarantee public policies that are in perfect accord with our moral intuitions. For example, one major criticism of utilitarianism is that the pursuit of the greatest happiness of the greatest number (or the general welfare or Pareto optimality) may lead to policies in law and politics which are on their face morally intolerable[45] – solving the population problem by means of random killing, giving important and widely admired people (VIPs) organs from the bodies of those no one cares about, and so on.[46] Utilitarianism, thus, makes possible the justification of what would normally be considered moral callousness. And it is extremely doubtful that any theory can hope to justify such callousness.

But it can be replied that these impressions are essentially unjustified because the position won't generate any more callousness when carefully understood than would other ethical positions. In short, a utilitarian critic of the natural rights stance can hold that the theory provides us with better results in our efforts to understand our moral problems in life than does the natural rights theory. The reason is mainly that the latter view is philosophically flawed while the former is no worse when it comes to handling difficult moral problems.

Another criticism important to address comes from out and out skeptics. The objection to the present thesis advanced by some of these critics has three main parts. First, it claims that naturalism has been invalidated by contemporary empirical science.[47] This is especially true as far as the naturalist depends on some type of teleological thesis. Second, it finds fault with the attempt to develop a case for liberalism based on an ethics of individual flourishing, drawn from Aristotle. One such critic tells us, for example, that

> Writing in an age of mass democracy and wage-labour, Aristotle's latter-day liberal followers prescribe a life of bourgeois virtue – of thrift, industry, prudence and creative work. However one assesses these ideals, the salient point is that in

> each of them the content given to human flourishing is taken wholly from the conventional norms of the theorist's local culture. It is far from clear what is the claim on reason attributed to these ideals.[48]

He also maintains that 'The attribution to Aristotle of a belief in the moral centrality of choice-making (made by Machan and others) is all the more incongruous in that the belief plainly presupposes an affirmation of the freedom of the will which Aristotle does not make.'[49]

Third and last, the skeptical critic is doubtful about applying the ideals of classical liberalism to different cultures, thus denying their universalizability, certainly implicit in natural (human) rights theories. The critic can claim, for example, that the individualism involved in the West's political legacy will probably not – and certainly need not – apply to a tribal culture. Therein, the critic can point out, individuals – or, at least, their freely chosen goals, projects, tastes, desires, preferences, and so on – are not regarded to be important. Individuals are important only as members of the group.[50]

This is a point very similar to that made by certain historicist critics of the natural rights position. Their criticism of Western political thought centers on the alleged fallacy of seeking some stable, trans-historical foundation for political justice. They argue, implicitly at least, that standards of justice, goodness, and so on are going to have to be relative to given stages of human historical development.

The historicist objections of the natural rights tradition rest on the premise that the individualism implicit in the Lockean doctrine is false to the facts and is merely an invention of a certain historical period.[51] This criticism, reminiscent of Marxist objections to bourgeois politics and law, contends that the self or ego is an invention, something intellectuals created so as to rationalize certain public institutions and policies. Based on what we have learned from the history of ideas, political history, and cultural anthropology, we can see, the argument goes, that the idea of the individual self, the autonomous or sovereign person, is a modern contrivance, instead of a successful identification or true discovery of some fact about the human species.[52]

Of course when fully elaborated, this criticism goes on to maintain that human beings are by nature collective. It is maintained that the human individual is a part of a larger whole and thus the good life for the human being is never anything that is derivable from his or her nature as an independent, sovereign, morally equal being. Let me now take a look at these objections to natural rights.

Against Utilitarian Criticism

There are two lines of argument that I will suggest against the utilitarian position. First, I will refute the objections to naturalism. Second, I will argue that the position itself requires something of a naturalist foundation to be coherent and complete. Since what I have presented earlier – in my outline of the natural rights position – should provide the grounding of the refutation of these two criticisms, I will be somewhat brief.

The is/ought gap troubles moral philosophy only if we accept a questionable, albeit prominent, theory of what it is both to be something and to know something, as well as the belief that a rational argument must have a deductive form. Thus, first, the empiricism underlying this skepticism begs the question of what there can be – to wit, it holds that only beings which are capable of being sensed can be ascertained to exist.[53] This rules out any type of existence that could involve characteristics we associate with values and morality. Since the empiricist view is open to serious doubt and there is reason to believe that a more pluralistic ontology would be more sound – based on common sense and its integration into a logically coherent order of existence – the is/ought gap suggested by empiricism need not be accepted as binding on a serious effort to inquire into the issue of values.[54] Furthermore, the deductivism assumes that the formation of valid concepts could only proceed by way of deducing ideas from other ideas that fully contain them already – which basically denies any kind of growth of knowledge. So accepting the sting of the is/ought argument cuts much too deep – it undermines not just morality but all substantive (non-tautological) claims to knowledge.[55]

There is, of course, an additional problem with the subjective utility or positivist approach to understanding justice. This is that it leaves it entirely undecidable whether to embrace that theory. For, after all, whether a theory should be embraced is itself something of a normative question. The positivist – in economics or in law, not to mention in ethics – is, after all, advocating something. The positivist is addressing us with the proposal that what we ought to do is to embrace a theory about values and virtues that has it that values and virtues are all subjective, a matter of personal taste or preference. But then why would not the positivist's own theory come to anything more than something we ought to embrace if we like it but not if we do not?[56]

As to the suggestion some make that the natural law (that is, objective morality) position poses a threat to human ('negative') liberty, that is a justified concern only with an intricisist conception of values and moral goodness. This view has it that, in and of themselves, by virtue of certain innate traits of characteristics or properties, some items in nature are good, and they command support from those capable of seeing their goodness. The stress is on an enforceable, obligatory command which may be acted on by anyone, including someone who understands the command as it bears on another and can coerce this other's adherence.

The crucial difference between this intrinsisist conception of goodness and the present naturalist view is that the former omits from consideration the relational element of choice involved between a human individual and the values appropriate for him or her to pursue.[57] In other words, regardless of whether one chooses to act in certain ways, the mere behavior or movement furthering some goal can count as morally adequate in this intrinsisist framework, since that alone will satisfy the implication that the good should be pursued. Yet, of course, if 'ought implies can,' as it must, this intrinsisist view stumbles very badly. Having made someone behave so that this behavior promotes some goal has not succeeded in producing *moral* value, since the latter is dependent on *freely choosing* the appropriate behavior, that is, on acting rightly. It is clear, of course, that here there appears only a somewhat cumbersome technical difference between some authoritarian conceptions of moral and political virtue and the libertarian position presented above. But sometimes a lot hinges on small differences.

At this point I must discuss ethical and political anomalies since some utilitarians believe that their defense of the anti-naturalist/positivist stance is helped a great deal by recalling them. They seem to think that these sorts of cases cannot be handled by the natural law/rights position, which would be a failing since they evidently occur and need to be handled by us. If a moral/political/legal framework cannot guide us in this task, that framework is seriously flawed.

There are peculiarities about anomalous cases. These may cast them in a different light from that which favors the utilitarian position. To begin with, each anomalous case involves an emergency. That is to say, it places people in unique circumstances that no ethical theory is able to render manageable. Typical are desert island or lifeboat examples so often raised in judging ethical theories. Ethical theories are general guidelines for human conduct. Thus if they cannot handle the desert island or lifeboat examples, they must fail as ethical theories. So, even though it is argued, for example along Kantian lines, that honesty is a duty, if there is an imaginable case where it is not, the theory that so maintains must fail. Prudence is a virtue but sometimes one ought, first, to practice the virtue of courage. Moderation is good policy but clearly not always. It is not possible to find any kind of specific behavior or conduct, outside of following the very general policy of being rational, that will always be the right one for the situation, especially when the situation is extraordinary.[58]

One point to recall about natural rights is that they are supposed to guide the formation of law and government, not personal conduct. Natural rights are the application of ethics to public policy, so necessarily they apply only in circumstances where public life is possible. Some examples of the alleged inadequacy of natural rights theory as applied in practice presuppose that such rights are to guide conduct at the individual, personal level, thus they simply fail to appreciate the purpose of natural rights theory.

Libertarian natural rights theorists have taken their clue from John Locke who distinguished between situations 'where peace is possible'[59] as distinct from those where it is not. Rand, too, has addressed the issue of the relationship between circumstances in one's life that are exceptional and the moral position that is most suitable to human life in general. Are the principles or virtues that are to guide ordinary human conduct and relationships identical to those that might help with the bizarre? The same type of question may be asked of a scientific theory.[60] In all of its realms, especially in that which is open to choice (as that involving human beings), nature can confront us with odd cases in which principles designed to treat normal circumstances do not apply smoothly.

But there is also the consideration that some anomalies illustrate that moral wrongs of the past produced the character of the case such that we seem to be faced with a dilemma. Thus one might be persuaded that someone's rights should be violated so as to correct a previous wrong – as in affirmative action policies – and so accept the view that rights are not compossible.[61] And even though libertarian natural rights theorists have actually addressed the class of such cases, many utilitarians, following Hardin's lead, have not found their work compelling enough to indicate how they have gone wrong.[62]

The general thrust of the natural law/rights approach in handling anomalies may be summarized as follows: the purpose of ethics or moral systems is to provide for the guidance of human living, with political ethics and law to provide for the guidance of human life in the company of other human beings. To the extent that an ethical and/or political system helps achieve the purpose it naturally has – that is, the purpose assumed in asking the question that gives rise to it as one of the many competing answers – it is a sound system. But even a sound system of ethics and/or politics can face difficulties, so the question is whether one or another faces them more successfully – more comprehensively, with greater integrity, and so on.

What of the relationship between the ethical system and the political one (the principles of which would form a constitution or set of common laws on which positive law would most appropriately be made to rest in human community aimed at justice)? Ethics is prior to politics – how I should live is logically prior to how we should act together. So the relationship between ethics and politics is best seen in the light of the fact that each person, as an adult, faces questions of living concerning oneself logically prior to those questions of living with others who are strangers to oneself. (Of course, there are ethical questions pertaining to living with members of one's family, neighborhood, and so on; these are not political but social in the sense of pertaining to rather intimate or specialized yet close human interaction, not to the organizational principles of a large human community.) This is a matter of the ontology of the situation. That is, because one is the initiator of one's own behavior, in need of guiding one's conduct, one needs to have the answer to what one should do, how one should carry on *per se* before advancing to the problem of what one should do or how one should carry on *vis-à-vis* others. The ethical dimension of one's life has priority and the political is subsidiary to it, so when a conflict arises the ethical is decisive. (The political realm is nearly always subject to ethical or moral scrutiny, whereas political principles are not invoked in evaluating ethical principles.) For official representatives of the political dimension it may not be advisable to stress this publicly, of course, and as far as their own conduct is concerned, given their personal loyalties, the priority issue may not arise at all. (The point is well played out in Melville's *Billy Budd*.) The natural law is prior. The natural rights each person has *vis-à-vis* others (who are strangers to one but are members of one's human community) may on occasion have to be disregarded in the face of the responsibilities of natural law. Anomalous cases seem to me all explainable in terms of the naturalist stance just sketched.

Of course, this sketch immediately calls to mind some elements of utilitarianism's consequentialist character. There is one major difference, however, between utilitarianism's and natural rights theory's teleological position. Utilitarianism is entirely uncommitted to some definitive conception of the human purpose and, therefore, of the *summum bonum*. With the human good left essentially subjective, the question of moral right and political rights is also undecidable. The escape clause – namely, that what right and justice and the like come to is 'stipulated along the lines of Ulpian's maxims, or along Roman or Common law lines'[63] – just cannot make clear sense, in utilitarianism's own theoretical terms, of the assertion, for example, that there is 'a right or even the moral duty to be unjust to individuals in certain circumstances.'[64]

The point here is not to deny that difficulties can arise in reconciling principles of morality with principles of politics and law. There is some reason to doubt that such difficulties must turn into moral dilemmas for all normative frameworks.[65] There is no good reason to even identify basic human rights as *prima facie* rights just so as to accommodate the alleged conflicts that can exist between different basic human rights.[66] Wherever it is suspected that such difficulties face us, the proper course that would seem to me warranted would be to attend very carefully to the intricacies of the circumstances. (The positive law is itself indicative of this point, when we consider how it handles alleged wrongdoings in exceptional circumstances, such as those involving shipwrecks, famine, earthquakes, and so on.) Such cases tend to beg for the fullest possible knowledge of all the factors, since only then can we learn if the persons involved made full use of their faculties so as to arrive at the most rational – that is, morally most suitable, given the nature of man as a rational being – decision under the unusual circumstances. Sketching such cases won't suffice.

Some utilitarians give us the clue to the last criticism I wish to level at the positivist elements of the utilitarian stance. They inform us that 'The legal never exhausts the moral'. What we could learn from this is that the law has a narrower scope and might very well be aimed at guiding us through normal elements of our lives, with its very general and very few edicts, compared to morality which bears on every aspect of life under our volitional control.

Against Political Skepticism

Both of the central points advanced by the skeptic can be answered. First, Aristotle, as the representative of the objectivist and universalist stance in ethics and politics, is the first to admit that not everything that is morally right and wrong is universalizable, even though fundamental virtues may be. And in my own position, as well as in the positions of those who share it, rationality is the central virtue – just as in Aristotle, right reason fills that role. Other virtues are more contextual – which is entirely consistent with Aristotle and with an Aristotelian approach to moral theory. Moreover, all the virtues spelled out by 'latter day liberal followers' can be conceptually related to the original virtues spelled out by Aristotle. (Whatever is added, can be defended, as well, and this may simply show some learning in the field, not relativism at all.)

Second, Aristotle does address the issue of choice-making in his distinction between the intellectual and the moral virtues. The latter require choice – which makes sense, since morality involves self-responsible conduct or neglect, something that could not be without the capacity for choice.[67] Aristotle did have a doctrine of free will – only it was not a major aspect of his moral theory. He located freedom of the will in the process of deliberation. As Jeager notes, 'Aristotle's notion of free will is the exact complement of the notion of most perfect deliberation in the Epinomis.'[68] And David Ross notes that 'On the whole we must say that [Aristotle] shared the plain man's belief in free will but that he did not examine the problem very thoroughly, and did not express himself with perfect consistency.'[69] This suggests clearly that a conception of justice based on an Aristotelian understanding of human nature may include the idea that human beings have free will. This idea is, of course, central to the conception of human morality that requires a free society.

In the main, most skeptics do not bother to investigate these issues at any greater length[70] and thus it is not possible to argue with them. Suffice it to say that many of the skeptical claims advanced directly against natural rights theory are unsupported and some are evidently false.

We should add that, no doubt, a normative naturalist would have to invoke a teleological conception of human behavior – where else would the standards of right and wrong, good or evil come from? If by nature human beings are not destined – that is, it would not be more healthy or suitable or fitting for them – to be doing one thing rather than another, why insist that doing it is a good or right thing? The only alternative would be a theistic doctrine, which of course also embraces some variety of teleology and would, thus, come under similar fire from some allegedly devastating empiricist thesis.

However, there is no such devastating empiricism around, no decisive blow against teleology, and it is no surprise that one of those skeptics who directly attacks natural rights theory did not even offer a footnote to indicate why naturalists ought to abandon their project. Given all the new philosophizing about metaphysics, epistemology, philosophy of mind, and so on, one would have to be rather steeped in a discredited logical positivism to think that teleology can be dismissed so cavalierly and thus normative naturalism (that is, natural law and rights ethics and politics) swept away with ease. Furthermore, anti-naturalists are also afraid of free will, once again because of their scientism – thinking that somehow the belief in free will is anti-science, anti-empirical, anti-cool! Poppycock! No more so than many other doctrines and, by my lights, far less so than any other. Science is fully compatible with the free will idea.[71] Empiricism in epistemology need not be taken as decisive about anything.

Finally, there is that old saw about how natural law and rights theory is a danger to political liberty. It is odd that people so wedded to scientism and determinism would worry about political liberty – why not just say *que sera, sera*? But then to claim that having some idea of human nature must endanger human liberty is really difficult to fathom.

Presumably, as Popper argued in *The Open Society and its Enemies*[72] – and as virtually all of his followers argue – a stable idea of human nature authorizes us to force people to conform to the standards we may derive from this idea.

First of all, it is a curious position to take in philosophy or any other discipline that aims to learn the truth about the world that we shall avoid some theory if it has certain consequences we do not favor. That is precisely the ideological thinking so many believe liberals are guilty of. If learning about human nature does happen to justify coercion, so much the worse for liberty. That this seems unwarranted to me is not here the issue. What matters is that philosophers have to follow the argument, not evade those results they fear.

As another prospect, however, what if, as in the case of Locke and most natural law classical liberals, precisely the opposite is warranted by reference to what we learn is human nature? What if it turns out that human beings ought to live the sort of life that places them in a position of moral responsibility, thus precluding the forcible imposition of any but the most minimal standards (that is, protection of their basic rights so that justice may prevail and self-governing virtue can flourish)?

Even if there were any problem with naturalism along these lines, certainly noncognitivism or skepticism cannot help – if there is no reason for imposing standard *A* (which limits liberty because human nature so requires), surely there is no reason to impose standard *B* (which protects liberty because human nature requires). Without standards nothing can be concluded, either for or against intrusive action, but the right standards may give aid and comfort to the champion of liberty – which is just what I think is the case. (Some skeptics, for example, Gray, seem to exemplify this point.)

Maybe what is wrong is that naturalism is a morally demanding position, after all, and many classical liberals just don't want to hear about that. Let us all be free, they want to cry out, but they don't much want to know about what to do with their liberty. Never mind that no one has the authority to make them do anything within the Lockean naturalist tradition. They don't even want to know about what they might be morally obligated to do as free agents. (The problem is that often those who claim to know what someone ought to do, jump quite illogically to the conclusion that they are justified in forcing another to do the right thing. But this is wrong. What is also wrong, however, is the belief that being a free agent, sovereign or autonomous, means that the standards of right conduct are invented by oneself rather than derivable from an understanding of one's nature and who one is.)

The trouble with the skeptical defense of liberty is that it can boomerang right back at those with a preference for liberty – if it is no more than a preference. (This point is made astutely in Renford Bambrough.[73])

So natural law theorists need not be taken aback all that much by the dismissal they experience from Popperians and other skeptics. (Some of these, by the way, have stopped being great friends of political liberty.[74]) Once they have made the points I have hinted at here – and added some of the nuances one needs with each new incarnation of the basic skeptical thesis – it is time to move on to more constructive work. It should not have to be pointed out that the world could use a good deal of it now.

As we have seen, when skeptics claim that teleology is obsolete and that empiricism is the right theory of knowledge, they are off-base. Such a position is untenable, not to mention odd for a skeptic to embrace.

It is worth adding that for a long time mechanistic materialism had been the reigning metaphysics. It was believed, at least by secular philosophers, that here lies the foundation for the solution to many human problems. Thomas Hobbes placed all his hopes on this view, as did many others. Even Kant accepted that at least the phenomenal world – what science is concerned with – yields fully to the laws of mechanics. Only the mysterious noumenal world escapes it – though we are left in the dark as to just how this is possible.

But mechanistic materialism is not the favored ontology even in physics. Any of the varieties of reductionism is certainly not self-evidently true. Arguably, also, a much more pluralistic metaphysics – akin to what I outlined earlier – makes much better sense of what we find around us as well as within us in reality.[75]

This leads us to the following conclusions: if there are different kinds and types of beings – substances – that have a fundamentally irreducible nature, the explanation of how they behave could also be very different. Efficient causality – the mode of the action of one thing upon another that is favored by reductive materialism and physicalism – need by no means be the only form of causality. Teleological causation – such as we invoke when we explain much of human (but a good deal of plant and animal) behavior – cannot be ruled out.

It is a matter of discovery, not a fundamental metaphysical assumption, as skeptical critics of the natural rights position assume, whether we affirm the reality of one or another kind of causal interaction. And there is evidence enough pointing to self-determined behavior when human action is at issue not to dismiss this on the ground of some *a priorist* reductionism.[76] Similar points can be raised against the assumption that empiricism is the hands-down winner in the competition between theories of knowledge. Clearly, the empiricist theory itself is not capable of being shown true by reference to the standards of truth and knowledge its adherents propound. Instead, a view of knowledge I sketched above makes better sense, namely, whereby what is known has a decisive impact on the standards of truth and knowledge about that kind or type of being. It is our task to see to it that we keep tracking what is known as we make our claims to knowing this or that, as well as trying to find out more about it. This again yields a pluralism, this time in the theory of knowledge – there are some general criteria that all successful knowledge claims need to satisfy, but there are also criteria that are relative to the context of the different kind and type of thing known. Thus what will be known about musical harmony will be a category of knowledge for different reasons from what will be known about the war of 1812 or the number of consecutive 7s that may occur in the calculation of pi.

This pluralism and contextualism handles very well, I propose, the problems derived from the fact of cultural diversity, without requiring us to accept cultural relativism. It makes the justifiable versus the unjustifiable diversions possible to identify, based on certain stable enough, trans-historical standards of good, right and just.[77] The present natural rights approach would appear to manage that very well – it may explain why the 'human rights' approach has been so widely invoked in international criticisms of political and legal practices through the last several decades.[78]

Arguing with Historicism

The objections historicists make against natural rights have greater punch than those made by skeptics, who are usually hoist by their own petard.[79] One of them states

> there is no expression in any ancient or medieval language correctly translated by our expression 'a right' until near the close of the middle ages: the concept lacks any means of expression in Hebrew, Greek, Latin or Arabic, classical or medieval, before about 1400, let alone in Old English, or in Japanese even as late as the mid-nineteenth century.'[80]

This critic also construes individualism as basically wrong, referring to 'that newly invented social institution, the individual.'[81]

Plainly put, the historicists contend that stable, trans-historical principles of political life cannot be identified. Both human nature and our understanding of the world change constantly; what we know is known from a given historical perspective. Human nature itself changes because we look at the world differently at different historical periods; our minds are influenced by when we use them and the resulting 'knowledge' is, thus, conditioned, which does not yield stable principles of ethics, politics, economics or any other sphere of human concern.

Yet much of this is clearly wrong. The rest of it is subject to dispute on conceptual grounds.

There is evidence that the dominant language of human life in certain earlier periods of human history paid scant attention to the human self, to individuality, to the moral autonomy and political sovereignty of human beings. No doubt, Plato and even Aristotle considered human beings in their relation to other social wholes – the family, tribe, city, class, race, and so on. But what of this? Why should any such historical evidence be decisive in questions of ontology and, eventually, ethics and politics?

Conceptual development can be both gradual as well as uneven, radical, or dormant. If human beings possess the capacity to make choices, they may exercise it differently as they will, constrained by some factors but with plenty of elbow room to work in. Also, in the domain of human knowledge many false starts, misunderstandings, prejudices, and so on, are possible. To look to what in fact people believed throughout history is only one avenue of discovery as to what actually exists.

The claim that, since the dominant modes of belief had been different from some belief system being considered, the latter is flawed, simply won't settle the issue. In many sciences we find advances toward a more and more fully developed conception of some thing – the solar system, the atom, the liver, the human mind, and so on. To claim that since in the past there was little talk about a potentially infinite universe, that idea cannot be sound, would be quite out of order in astronomy or cosmology.

Similarly, it may be granted that in the past – say prior to the eleventh century – extensive or even sufficient moral concern for individual human beings as such had been negligible (though by no means absent). Most philosophers focused on the place human beings occupy in the social landscape and what this implies as to their proper behavior *vis-à-vis* some supposedly greater body. (But let us not forget that this same talk is prevalent today – for example, in Marx's phrase 'the organic whole [or body]' of humanity.[82])

Furthermore, a dialectical point needs also to be made against the historicist thesis. Such a thesis will backfire because it purports to be *correct* even while many disbelieve it. Most people who have written on these matters have thought that what they say is true, whether they have been right or wrong. They have not believed that what they believe is only true for some period of time, in some phase of human history. And the historicist must implicitly propose that the thesis about the temporality of the idea of the human individual is universally valid – that is, for example, in 10,000 years it should still be accepted as true that the idea of the human individual was only a temporary myth, not something true.[83] But if this fails to be the dominant view, should it be dismissed for that reason alone? I doubt that historicists would be so giving.

The dominance of some position may be due to many factors, including the obvious one that those who advanced it may have found it convincing, may have benefited from advancing it, may have focused their gaze too narrowly, and so on. The real issue is whether the view can hold its own against alternative positions. The task is for historicists and all others to get into the fray and argue it all out, not keep invoking historicism itself against some position.

Finally, the historicist position is false to the facts of its own promulgation. It is, after all, individual human beings who propound ideas, who criticize them, who stand apart from the rest with their doctrines and skepticism. This testifies to the individuality of the advocate, at least – a human being who can act independently, who can think for himself or herself, and whose kind of individualistic life may therefore require certain socio-economic-political conditions for it to flourish.[84] The natural rights position pays very close attention to just this scenario about human life.

Naturalism, Some Final Reflections

Perhaps the central thesis of this chapter should once again be stated, this time as simply as possible. It is that, because of the kind of beings they are and numerous other facts about their lives, it is more just for human beings to live in freedom than even in the slightest condition of slavery. Or, even more bluntly, free men and women live more justly as human beings, than do slaves. It is this thesis that I have been defending.

Despite the simple truth of the above claim, it is also true that the naturalist normative framework may be difficult to identify and work out. No doubt many have tried to erect it and have failed – though the mere lack of widespread acceptance of natural law/rights views is no proof of this. The main reason for much of the actual failure is not so much a matter of moral and political inadequacy but the flawed metaphysical and epistemological doctrines that have guided the enterprise of developing the naturalist position.[85] If we had heeded Gilbert Harman's idea, that 'We must take care not to adopt a very skeptical attitude nor become too lenient about what is to count as knowledge,'[86] especially in how we conceive of moral and political knowledge and what tests we expect claims to such knowledge and the underlying arguments to meet, the task of developing the naturalist position would probably have fared better.

A theory in any field of investigation is an answer to a question that human beings raise. Which theory is the best one may be determined by which of the ones proposed answers the question best, which is itself determined by what we want from an answer. In political theory we want an answer that helps us guide our organized community affairs with the least degree of inherent conflict, the most comprehensive applicability to such community life, and the facilitation of human living while in the company of other human beings to whom one is not intimately related.

Whether the present theory meets these criteria cannot be known without a comparative analysis. What may be valuable in this undertaking is entering a contending answer with a clearly important perspective, one that places the individual in the center of political affairs.

If we do not allow a fruitless idealism to stand in the way of identifying the best theory in this sphere of inquiry, we will recognize that nature is the best guide to how we need to cope with our human personal and community lives, a matter to which each of us pays heed quite naturally, after all.[87]

Notes

1 It is arguable that this exact problem was tackled by Socrates in his various discussions, namely, whether a firm standard of right judgment in matters of justice could be identified. See Leo Strauss, *Natural Right and History* (Chicago: University of Chicago Press, 1953). See also Tibor R. Machan, *Human Rights and Human Liberties: A Radical Reconsideration of the American Political Tradition* (Chicago: Nelson-Hall Co., Inc., 1975).

2 The way the alternative is stated or expressed is often one of the points in hot dispute. Interestingly, many of those who would deny that there are objective standards in any of these areas are, nevertheless, insistent on describing the dispute in ways they alone deem appropriate!

3 Although I will be dealing with the naturalist metaethics and metapolitics that I argue supports the classical liberal or libertarian polity of individual (negative) rights, it should be noted that there are philosophers who argue that naturalism does not support such a position.

The concept 'objective' should here be understood to mean 'capable of being demonstrated on the basis of evidence of existing (natural) beings, attributes, and so on.' It is a concept that need not be interpreted differently from how it is used in, say, instructions to a jury to be objective in their assessment of a case presented to them, that is, consider only what is evident to them – facts, valid inferences from them, and so on – and not permit their wishes, desires, or biases to undermine their judgment. Of course, what is at issue in the debate is whether such objectivity is possible to human beings. For more, see Chapter 1, notes 4 and 5.

4 In A. I. Melden, ed., *Human Rights* (Belmont, CA: Wadsworth Publishing Co., 1970). I discuss Macdonald at some length in my doctoral dissertation, *Human Rights: A Metaethical Inquiry* (University of Michigan Microfilms, 1972), as well as in, *Human Rights and Human Liberties*.

5 Strauss, *Natural Right and History*.

6 The one major exception is Harry V. Jaffa, who finds much in Locke that is philosophically valuable. See his *How to Think About the American Revolution* (Durham, NC: Carolina Academic Press, 1978). Others who tend Jaffa's way are Thomas Pangle and Michael Zuckert.

I should make it clear that while I treat Locke's political thinking as the precursor to the kind of classical liberal or libertarian position I defend, I do not mean to imply that Locke himself was a full-blown, uncompromised libertarian. Clearly Locke was willing to take political steps against atheists and others, for reasons we do not now need to consider. When I invoke either Locke, Aristotle or anyone else in clarifying the position I want to develop here, it is mostly so as to indicate some familiar basic similarities of approach, thus making it simpler to understand the present position. One cannot always say everything pertinent, so these indices are very useful.

7 Perhaps the most general attack on natural rights theory comes from Richard Rorty, for example, in his *Objectivity, Relativism, and Truth* (Cambridge, England: Cambridge University Press, 1991), p. 31. Rorty is a pragmatist/historicist who denies any trans-historical knowledge, even in the natural sciences. That his historicist claims are themselves purported trans-historical claims about how human beings cope with their environment does not seem to phase him much, yet they would appear to involve him in a flat out contradiction. I present a case for what might be termed a minimalist foundationalism in Tibor R. Machan, 'Evidence of Necessary Existence,' *Objectivity*, Vol. 3 (Fall, 1992), pp. 31–62. See also Tibor R. Machan, *Objectivity, Recovering Determinate Reality in Philosophy, Science, and Everyday Life* (Aldershot, UK: Ashgate, 2004).

8 See, however, note 14 below, for a strange affinity between Strausseans and Rorty and co.

9 See, for example, John Gray, *Liberalism* (Minneapolis, MN: University of Minnesota Press, 1986), and *Liberalisms* (London: Routledge, 1989). See also Larry Briskman, 'Skinnerism and Pseudo-Science,' *Philosophy of the Social Sciences*, Vol. 3 (Summer, 1981), and Norman Barry, *On Classical Liberalism and Libertarianism* (New York: St Martin's Press, 1989).

10 John Gray has gone through several changes in his political orientation, yet he has throughout remained a Pyrrhonist in his epistemology. His most recent hero in political theory is Michael Oakeshott.

Some have observed that Gray has changed his mind on several occasions concerning the merits of liberalism and related doctrines. Yet what has remained entirely unchanged in his views is his Phyrronism or skepticism concerning not only morality but any kind of knowledge claim. Ever since I have known Gray, we have argued about the same issue, namely, whether human knowledge is possible at all. And, of course, when one denies that it is, one is rather unconstrained about choosing political positions, since they can now be entirely a matter of one's alternating preferences.

Incidentally, the source of skepticism in Gray is not much different from what it is in other skeptics, namely, the misguided conception of what knowledge must be, namely, timeless certainty. What many take to be the limits of knowledge really amount to no more than the fact that knowledge isn't something else, namely, becoming what one knows. To complain that we know reality only as it appears to us or in its knowable aspect is to (a) attribute to reality features that have nothing to do with reality as such, namely, that it is known or knowable by us, and (b) confuse knowing reality with somehow acquiring it *in toto* into consciousness. For more on this, see my *Individuals and Their Rights* (LaSalle, IL: Open Court Publishing Company, Inc., 1989).

11 John Rawls, 'The Independence of Moral Theory,' *Proceeding and Addresses of the American Philosophical Association*, Vol. XLVII (Newark, DE: American Philosophical Association, 1975), pp. 5–22.

12 Russell Hardin, 'The Utilitarian Logic of Liberalism,' *Ethics*, Vol. 97 (1986), pp. 73–4.

13 For a very informative discussion, see Stephen Cox, 'Devices of Deconstruction,' *Critical Review*, Vol. 3, (Winter, 1989), pp. 56–76. For the more constructive case supporting the foundationalist approach to moral and political theory, see some of the contributions to the special issue on this topic, 'Rethinking Foundationalism,' in *Reason Papers*, No 16 (Fall, 1991). It bears noting that all the talk about Post-modernism, as if these doctrines hadn't been thought of prior to our times, is more of a press agent publicity stunt than fidelity to fact – so called Postmodern thinking is much better described as pre-ancient (pre-Socratic, pre-Aristotelian) thinking. Or rather, more or less developed versions of these ideas surrounding these issues have been around in every age, with more or less popularity. For Postmodernism in general, see Stephen Hicks, *Explaining Postmodernism* (Tempe, AZ: Scholargy Publishers, 2004).

14 Some Straussians seem to acknowledge the difficulty of establishing such foundations, yet insist on the need to look for them (at least implicitly – for example, Allan Bloom, *The Closing of the American Mind* [New York: Simon & Schuster, 1987], who eschews a thorough discussion of absolute or fundamental realities, even as he severely lambastes those who have given up on it and embrace some variety of relativism).

There has always been some question about just how genuine this Straussean endorsement is, since Leo Strauss has claimed that for *bona fide* philosophers it is OK to deceive the ordinary folk and, also, that few so-called philosophers are *bona fide*. See, for an interesting discussion, Carl Page, 'The Truth About Lies in Plato's Republic,' *Ancient Philosophy*, Vol. 11 (1991), pp. 1–33. Perhaps it is the search alone, and the fate of those who are committed to it, never mind what one finds, that Straussians see as significant, but it would be too dangerous to admit this to all and sundry. Some of those who have studied with Strauss have openly endorsed nihilism – for example, Harry Newman. (See, for a good summary, Paul A. Basinski and Harry Newman, 'Nihilism Challenged … and Defended,' *Claremont Review of Books* (Fall, 1985), pp. 26–28). Newman probably articulates openly the essential features of Rorty's thinking, as well, as he does those of all epistemological skeptics.

15 See, Ayn Rand, *Introduction to Objectivist Epistemology*, 2nd edn (New York: New American Library, 1990).

16 See, for example, Frank M. Coleman, *Hobbes and America* (Toronto, Canada: University of Toronto Press, 1977). See also Edward Andrew, *Shylock's Rights* (Toronto, Canada: University of Toronto Press, 1988), for an elaborate and especially virulent denigration of the Lockean idea of individual rights. Leo Strauss and many of his students maintain that while Locke is to be credited with laying the foundations for the American polity, there is not any substantial philosophical difference between Locke and Hobbes. See for example, e.g., Walter Berns, *The First Amendment and the Future of American Democracy* (New York: Basic Books, 1976). The basic argument of the Straussians is that since Locke's basic philosophy (metaphysics, epistemology) fails to cohere with his allegedly natural law ethics and politics, the latter is largely a rhetorical device for justifying certain special political objectives. This, incidentally, resembles closely the Marxist view, whereby not a concern for truth but one of vested interest accounts for the 'convictions' underlying the American polity. See C. B. Macpherson, *Possessive Individualism* (London: Oxford University Press, 1962). Cf., also, Andrew C. MacLaughlin, *The Foundations of American Constitutionalism* (Greenwich, CT: Fawcet Publications, 1961) and Jaffa, *How to Think About the American Revolution*.

Whatever motivations we may attribute to Locke, the crucial question is whether his basic argument holds up. And if it is possible to find a philosophical groundwork that gives the Lockean portion credibility, the Lockean theory may be in good shape. After all, every level of an edifice need not be designed and built by the same engineers.

17 I use these labels while aware of the controversies and fine distinctions stressed by those to whom they apply. Essentially, though, the Right supports spiritual welfarism or paternalism, urging government to act as soulcrafters (see George Will, *Statecraft as Soulcraft* [New York: Simon and Schuster, 1983]), while the Left supports economic or material welfarism or paternalism, urging the state to guard us against mismanaging our households. The dispute is probably at the metaphysical level, namely, about which is more important, our souls or our bodies. The present position sees the person as an integrated, multifaceted entity with a most fundamental need for self-directedness. See Tibor R. Machan and James E. Chesher, *The Business of Commerce, Examining an Honorable Profession* (Stanford, CA: Hoover Institution Press, 1999).

18 Although I discuss the views in terms of their philosophical characterization, I will cite particular theorists so that we can get a clear statement of the criticism rather than having to produce a statement that members of these schools could contend is a caricature. Those I will consider have addressed the natural rights position quite directly.

19 I note this because it is contested in contemporary metaphysics (most prominently by, for example, the late Willard Van Orman Quine, who advocated ontological relativism, or Richard Rorty, who simply denies that we can have *bona fide* knowledge of the nature of what exists – that is, of the foundation of knowledge). To claim, as some of these thinkers do, that all this proves is that for us reality must be consistent is to attempt something by their own thinking one cannot do, namely, gain an independent perspective of the relationship between reality and human understanding. In other words, the very enterprise in which such thinkers are involved belies their own doctrine's soundness.

20 Here, again, the view I am sketching is implicitly or explicitly contested by such philosophers as Richard Rorty and Paul Feyerabend. And their skepticism has direct bearing on whether the thesis I sketch below can be defended. Both seem to me, however, to be captivated by the mistaken notion that when we know *X*, we must be influencing *X* and this brings into question whether what we know is in fact *X* or *X*+our-impact-on-*X*. But knowing *X* is not influencing but grasping it, not attacking but embracing it, as it were. Part of the confusion arises from thinking that when we know *X* as it is, we somehow must have implanted into our knowing faculty the *X* itself, which of course does not happen – what is there is not *X* as it is but our knowledge of *X* as it is. Knowing *X* is not the same as being *X*!

This should also allay worries about knowledge having always to be final, complete, closed. In this connection it is still very instructive to read J. L. Austin, 'Other Minds,' in his *Philosophical Papers* (Oxford: Clarendon Books, 1961, and Barry Straud, 'Wittgenstein and Logical Necessity,' in George Pitcher, ed., *Wittgenstein* (Garden City, NY: Anchor Books, 1969).

21 Tibor R. Machan, 'C. S. Peirce and Absolute Truth,' *Transactions of the C. S. Peirce Society*, Vol. 16 (Spring 1980), pp. 153–61.

22 This metaphysical position is not without its challengers and there is ample literature on the subject. Yet all I want to point out is that a challenge is itself something and if one denies that the above holds universally, it is an open issue what the challenge itself must mean. Aristotle still had the best defense of the law of non-contradiction as a basic fact of reality, not just of our mode of apprehending it.

23 Tibor R. Machan, 'Epistemology and Moral Knowledge,' *The Review of Metaphysics*, Vol. 36 (September 1982). I discuss in this paper the nature of natures – that is, what it is to be the nature of something. I carry further this discussion in *Individuals and Their Rights*.

24 Here the naturalism of the present position emerges most distinctively. For more, see Machan, *Human Rights and Human Liberties* and Douglas B. Rasmussen, 'Essentialism, Values and Rights,' in T. R. Machan, ed., *The Libertarian Reader* (Totowa, NJ: Rowman and Littlefield, 1982), pp. 37–52. See also Machan, *Individuals and Their Rights*.

25 I develop at some length the case for this definition as I try to answer a challenge by M. P. Golding, advanced in his 'Toward a Theory of Human Rights,' *The Monist*, Vol. 52 (October 1968), p. 495, in, for example, *Individuals and Their Rights*.

26 The argument for this conception of free will advanced by Roger W. Sperry, in his more technical paper, 'Changing Concepts of Consciousness and Free Will,' *Perspectives in Biology and Medicine*, Vol. 9 (Autumn 1976), pp. 9–19. See also Tibor R. Machan, 'Applied Ethics and Free Will, Some Consequences of Independence,' *The Journal of Applied Philosophy*, Vol. 10 (1993), pp. 59–72, and *Initiative – Human Agency and Society* (Stanford, CA: Hoover Institution Press, 2000).

27 The choosing in question may perhaps be characterized better by the term 'initiating (of thought).' It is done, as it were, by willing – the person's most basic act of paying heed or becoming alert or focused in life, something the person needs to sustain and maintain as an individual commitment. When this choice or initiation of the process of awareness is abnegated, even partially or temporarily – except, of course, during required rest – the commitment to living a good human life is faltering.

28 Machan, 'Epistemology and Moral Knowledge.'

29 I am here drawing on the work of Ayn Rand, 'The Objectivist Ethics,' in *The Virtue of Selfishness: A New Concept of Egoism* (New York: Signet Books, 1964). See, for more, my 'Reason, Individualism, and Capitalism: The Moral Vision of Ayn Rand,' in D. Den Uyl and D. Rasmussen, eds, *The Philosophic Thought of Ayn Rand* (Urbana, IL: University of Illinois Press, 1983). I develop these ideas more fully in Tibor R. Machan, *Classical Individualism* (London: Routledge, 1998).

30 Plato's conception of justice is broader than the justice that can characterize a political community. The just state for Plato is really the perfectly good human community, one in which everything goes right. For the difference between Plato's conception of justice and that which is considered here, see Hannah F. Pitkin, *Wittgenstein and Justice* (Berkeley, CA: University of California Press, 1972), pp. 303ff. Consider, also, that in Plato's Republic what is at stake is not political justice as such but the nature of the just or morally, ethically good or excellent human being. Justice, in that context, is a more encompassing concept than in the context of political theory as an effort to conceptualize the best constituents of a large community or nation state.

31 Some, such as Siegfried van Duffel, claim that 'The idea that people are sovereign beings does not allow us to infer that they have an obligation to respect each others' sovereignty.' 'Libertarian Natural Rights,' *Critical Review*, Vol. 16, No 4 (2004), p. 371. Few if any libertarians hold that just being sovereign suffices to obligate one to respect the sovereignty of others. Van Duffel, while quoting a passage from my own book on rights, fails to examine how I, for example, argue for that obligation. Essentially I show that the moral responsibility to think, to conduct oneself as a rational individual, demonstrates to one 'who would,' as Locke might have put it, 'but consult one's reason,' that a regime of individuals rights is to one's rational self-interest. That, in turn, obligates one to abide by that regime and respect other's sovereignty.

32 I develop in detail the argument for the obligatory nature of these rights for human individuals in the context of their community lives, in *Individuals and Their Rights*. Since I argue from the basis of classical egoism or individualism, it may be significant to appreciate just how one may establish the obligation to respect others' basic rights from such a moral foundation. Chapter 7 concerns just this issue. See also Tibor R. Machan, 'Reply to Critics of Individuals and Their Rights,' *Reason Papers*, No 17 (Fall 1992).

33 John Rawls, *A Theory of Justice* (Cambridge, MA: Harvard University Press, 1971), p. 104. Rawls may, of course, reject this characterization of his position but it is very difficult to see how he can make any room for moral responsibility given his view that character itself is a function of luck, and so on. See, for more on this point *vis-à-vis* Rawls, Machan, *Human Rights and Human Liberties*, p. 167–8. Consider the following: 'The assertion that a man deserves the superior character that enables him to make the effort to cultivate his abilities is … problematic; for his character depends in large part upon fortunate family and social circumstances for which he can claim no credit.' One may wonder whether Rawls is fully aware of the deterministic implications of this claim. He may as well embrace B. F. Skinner's doctrine in *Beyond Freedom and Dignity* (New York: Bantam Books, 1971), in which the ontological foundations of ethics are explicitly denied. Yet for Rawls it is problematic, to sweep aside free will entirely, for then how could he argue, as he evidently does, that human beings ought to act in accordance with his conception of justice as fairness? If we ought to be fair, it must be true that we have the choice to be fair or not to be fair. If whether we possess the character to be fair 'depends upon fortunate family and social circumstances,' than we either will be or will not be fair and there is nothing Rawls or anyone else can do about the matter, nor can anyone blame people for failing to be fair or for failing to support institutions of fairness throughout society. Does Rawls wish to embrace the view that whether one supports, say, affirmative action or opposes it is irrelevant to one's moral virtue? It would have to be, however, if our family and social circumstances made us supporters or opponents of such policies.

34 Robert Nozick, *Anarchy, State, and Utopia* (New York: Basic Books, 1974), p. 57. Nozick has since writing this book rejected his libertarian views – see his *The Examined Life* (New York: Simon and Schuster, 1989), pp. 286–96, mainly on grounds that even if individuals require such moral space, as spelled out by means of their Lockean negative rights, they may be made to conform to certain public purposes we all need to share. 'The libertarian position I once propounded now seems to me seriously inadequate, in part because it did not fully knit the humane considerations and joint cooperative activities it left room for more closely into its fabric'(pp. 288–7). Nozick thought (for a while) that such considerations and activities need to be given symbolic expression via certain government projects that give it meaning as such. The libertarian who shares the concern with such common goals and meanings will stress, however, that when these are instilled in the membership of the community by force, they lose their significance and, indeed, *via* such coercion will undermine the chances of their realization. Forced belief and practice is alienating and saps the society of its lifeblood. (Nozick reaffirmed his libertarian views shortly before he died.)

35 Rawls, *A Theory of Justice*, pp. 101–102.

36 Rawls subsequently published *Political Liberalism* (New York: Columbia University Press, 1993), in which, as Stephen Holmes points out in his review (*The New Republic*, 11 October, 1993, p. 42), Rawls

> unexpectedly combines this [*A Theory of Justice*'s] argument [about social determinism] with its opposite. Alongside strong claims about unequal upbringing and the redistributions it implies, we now find the observation that people are 'responsible' for their character and desires, whatever disadvantages their social upbringing heaped upon them, and that 'those who surf all day off Malibu must find a way to support themselves and would not be entitled to public funds'.

I should at this point call attention to James Sterba's efforts to demonstrate that from a classical liberal or libertarian negative rights theory one can reach conclusions that would favor the supportive welfare state. I address this position in my responses to Galston and Sterba elsewhere.

37 Some, such as Heather Gert, in 'Rights and Rights Violators: A New Approach to the Nature of Rights,' *The Journal of Philosophy*, Vol. 90 (1990), pp. 688–94, have argued that rights are superfluous since all human wrongs can be reduced to injuring or harming people. As she puts it,

> To say that I ought not to punch you because it would hurt you is sufficient – there is no further need to invoke that alleged thing that is your right not to be punched or hurt. Clearly, much of what is to be taken into account is the harm caused by our actions and the significance we give to the harm. (p. 694)

Yet this is wrong – rights violations often involve depriving people of choices and some of these choices, if they had not been made, would have resulted in greater injury to the person than what resulted from the rights violation itself. Concerning some other aspects of what it amounts to violating rights, see J. Roger Lee, 'Choice and Harms,' in M. Bruce Johnson and T. R. Machan, eds, *Rights and Regulation* (Cambridge, MA: Ballinger, 1983), pp. 157–73. Interestingly Gert does not consider any libertarian analysis of rights – for example, those by Eric Mack, Jan Narveson, Lee, or Rasmussen and Den Uyl. This is not surprising since most of her analysis focuses on what are called positive rights, such as 'persons in underdeveloped countries' having 'the right to even a minimal amount of food'(p. 693). But then her essay ought to have been entitled 'Positive Rights and Positive Rights Violators.'

38 See, for more on this, Tibor R. Machan, 'Between Parents and Children,' *The Journal of Social Philosophy*, Vol. 23 (1992), pp. 16–22.

39 For why implicit consent is a binding commitment to a principle of social life, see my *Individuals and Their Rights*, Chapter 7.

40 This holds even for those few who may have no means available to them to further their lives *via* the protection of their right to negative liberty – for example, the utterly incapacitated poor – since those who do have those capacities ought to strive to preserve the general, unexceptional conditions of human flourishing, meaning they ought to maintain those rights that will help them to do so as human beings. (Incidentally, those thoroughly incapacitated are not usually the ones who violate negative rights since they are by definition unable to do such strenuous things. It is, thus, moot to argue that they have the authority to engage in such conduct. It is more important to consider why others, not so incapacitated, might have that authority instead of the responsibility to provide the remedies needed.)

41 That the welfare state now and then does help some people is not a counter-example here. Some people fall out of airplanes and live to write best-selling books about it. Moreover, the good done *via* the welfare state is demonstrably costly to those who were taxed so as to produce it; and that much of this cost ought not to be borne by them is not an implausible thesis. Yet, it is more likely that the welfare state supports those who manage it more successfully than those in whose behalf such support is supposed to occur. See, John Gray, 'Classical Liberalism, positional goods, and the politicization of poverty,' in Adrian Ellis and Krishan Kumar, eds, *Dilemmas of Liberal Democracies* (London: Tavistock Publications, 1983). Gray notes that studies have demonstrated that

> The greatest net beneficiaries from the welfare state in Britain have been the professional middle classes, whose political pull and social skills have enabled them to create and then exploit a vast range of services largely sustained by tax subsidies derived from the poorer majority. The largest net losers from British welfarism, on the other hand, have been the working poor and then victims of the artificial poverty trap created by the extremely high marginal tax rates to which they are subject (p. 180).

42 Ernest van den Haag, 'Against Natural Rights,' *Policy Review*, No 23 (Winter 1983), pp. 143–75. Appendix 1 of *Individuals and Their Rights* is a direct response to van den Haag's arguments.

43 This point, incidentally, is difficult to support philosophically without a natural law, natural rights underpinning. In other words, how do we tell, without reference to human nature, that freedom is a (non arbitrary) good thing for a human being living in a community?

44 Renford Bambrough, in his *Moral Skepticism and Moral Knowledge* (Atlantic Highlands, NJ: Humanities Press, 1979), disposes of the alleged conceptual connection between essentialist or objectivist moral theories and authoritarianism.

It does not follow from the true premise, '[I know that] *A* ought to do *X*' that 'Therefore, [I know that] someone ought to force *A* to do *X*.' The further premise, '[I know that] (For any *A* and for any *X*) If *A* ought to do *X*, someone ought to force *A* to do *X*,' would have to be true, as well. While there may be some cases such that if *A* ought to do *X*, when someone, say *B*, knows this, someone, say *B*, ought to force *A* to do *X* – for example, if *A* ought to respect the rights of others, and *B* is the government established to protect rights – it is certainly false that for all cases of '*A* ought to do *X*' this is so.

45 Strictly, to determine whether they are intolerable would require establishing a superior competing theory; yet moral beliefs need not all rest on explicit moral theories – there is a moral reality just as a physical, chemical, biological or legal reality known to most ordinary people and to violate those beliefs should not remain unexplained.

Ethical dilemmas may appear to occur once one takes a close look at a situation that pits two or more equally sensible moral beliefs against one another. One way this might be resolved is to establish an ethical theory that succeeds in rationally ranking moral principles. A way of evading the problem is to claim that the world is simply too topsy-turvy for us to find an adequate theory to make sense of it (for example, in the realm of ethics). An explanation of all this may involve the fact that no theory pertaining to dynamic matters such as human conduct could be final in its scope, so there will always be some areas yet to be integrated within a theory. Theories will at times need modification so as to accommodate this fact.

46 There is a more serious problem with the utilitarian stance, identified by Kenneth Arrow, in *Social Choice and Individual Values* (New Haven, CT: Yale University Press, 1962). The very ideas of rational choice and democracy (or liberty) combine to generate contradictory public policy. Furthermore, the idea of the greatest happiness of the greatest number is confused, based on the incommensurability of the two features to be quantified, namely, the universe of those who can be happy and happiness itself, so it would help to know just what exactly the value standard is that van den Haag is proposing. See, however, Chapter 2 in my *Private Rights and Public Illusions* (Oakland, CA: The Independent Institute; New Brunswick, NJ: Transactions Books, 1995), where I argue that no such problem faces a natural rights approach to social or public choice theory because it leaves a rationally delimited public scope wherein democracy is to function.

47 Gray, *Liberalism*.

48 Gray, *Liberalisms*, p. 258.

49 Ibid., p. 265, note 26.

50 Does this mean the individuals do not exist as individuals or are neglected as such? Presumably, for Gray's objection to go through, he would have to claim that a tribe is an individual or an organic whole, just as Karl Marx claimed that 'the human essence is the true collectivity of man' (in *Karl Marx: Selected Writings* [New York: Oxford University Press, 1977], p. 126) most likely because he regarded humanity an 'organic whole' (in *Grundrisse* [New York: Harper & Row, 1972]).

51 Alasdair MacIntyre, *After Virtue* (Notre Dame, IN: University of Notre Dame Press, 1981).

52 In *Individuals and Their Rights* I defend a conception of the human individual that withstands most of the more plausible critical charges made against individuals – for example, that it relies on an anti-social, atomic conception of human life. See also *Capitalism and Individualism, Reframing the Argument for the Free Society* (New York: St. Martin's Press, 1990). For a more fundamentally focused discussion of individuality, as it arises in metaphysics (*vis-à-vis* whether the entities populating reality are or could be individuals), see Jorge J. E. Gracia, *Individuality* (Albany, NY: State University of New York Press, 1988). In relation to the claim that within an Aristotelian tradition – including, especially, the politics that emerges from it – it is worthwhile to note that Aristotle's metaphysics may be more individualistic than is widely believed. See, in this connection, Henry Teloh, 'What Aristotle Should Have Said in Metaphysics Z,' *The Southern Journal of Philosophy*, Vol. 20 (Summer 1982), pp. 241–55. See also Emerson Buchanan, *Aristotle's Theory of Being* (Cambridge, MA: Greek, Roman, and Byzantine Monographs, 1962), p. 2. I further develop this conception of the human individual in Machan, *Classical Individualism*.

53 Machan, 'Epistemology and Moral Knowledge.' If radical or strict empiricism is correct, then knowledge of what ought to be done is of course impossible, since 'good' and 'ought to' are not radically (even though they could be commonsensically) empirical concepts.

54 For a discussion of the problems with the open question argument Moore advances against the naturalist metaethics, see Machan, *Individuals and Their Rights*, p. 94.

55 This development has, of course, occurred with the emergence of such views as those of Paul Feyerabend and Richard Rorty. There have always been intimations of it in the thinking of various relativist and historicist philosophers. See, Tibor R. Machan, 'Some Reflections on Richard Rorty's Philosophy,' *Metaphilosophy*, Vol. 24 (January/April 1993), pp. 123–35. See also Machan, 'Evidence of Necessary Existence' and Tibor R. Machan, *Ayn Rand* (New York: Peter Lang, 2000), Chapter 2.

56 The significance of this point may escape some but it should not, at least not if one is interested in consistency. At a recent conference an advocate of legal positivism was arguing how unwise it is for justices of the Supreme Court as well as legal scholars to

read the United States Constitution as if that document depended in the slightest on some notion of natural law. Professor Lino Graglia invoked David Hume's is/ought gap thesis and defended the positivist notion that all that justices ought to do is read the constitution literally, placing limits on majority rule only on very rare occasions – such as in the unlikely event that some legislature enacted a law barring women from voting. In such a case, of course, the Constitution is quite explicit: no legislature may do such a thing.

Now from a positivist position there is no justification for this heartfelt advice. Graglia may feel strongly about this matter but by the tenets of Humean moral skepticism the fact, say, that the Constitution grants women the vote does not prove that justices ought to invalidate any law that prohibits the vote. From the 'is' of what the Constitution asserts no 'ought' could follow, according to Hume, as to what anyone ought to do. (As to how best to understand Hume on this context, I would defer to those who claim that he was opposing only the extreme rationalistic efforts to deduce moral oughts, not the more common ones of drawing moral inferences from our understanding of human affairs.)

If the response were that, well, it is inconsistent to be a justice of the US Supreme Court and also refuse to uphold the provisions of that court, the answer is, so what? Why ought one be consistent? It is just some people's preference, is it not? Furthermore, neither does it hold, as many positivists maintain, that what ought to be honored in the law is what the people – that is, the majority of those who vote and their elected representatives – want. So what if the people want *A* (the 'is') and the justice honors not-*A* (the 'ought')? No objection can be made against this by legal positivists.

On the score of consistency, incidentally, if the positivists admit that at least the justices ought to be consistent in their decisions with the document they took an oath to uphold, it is then not much of a leap of logic for one to argue that they ought to be consistent with the implications of that document. For example, if the positivist accepts that the US Constitution endorses nearly universal democracy, and if democracy presupposes certain societal provisions – for example, the right to privacy, private property, political participation, freedom of speech, freedom of association, equal treatment under the law, and so on – the legal positivist would have to accept, also, that the justices ought to reject all those laws that render democracy inoperable. Are the provisions listed above good candidates for what democracy – and thus the US Constitution – requires? Well, democracy involves the uncoerced decision of a member of a community to select one of several alternatives to promote as a principle of community life. Without those provisions there is no such absence of coercion. If one has no right to privacy, private property, equal treatment under the law, and so on, then democracy is impossible – the voter lacks independence and will very possibly be threatened by any outcome of the selection process that does not favor the majority. The voter will be unable to retreat to his or her dominion to escape repercussions for voting against the majority. The voter may be treated differently from other voters if he or she is not part of the majority.

Thus, it appears, that even the most minimal normative content legal positivism accords to the process of law making and jurisprudence commits the positivist to nearly everything that natural rights theorists advocate. Most significantly, of course, the positivist has made it impossible for him or her to advocate any normative claim, including the claim that democratic decisions ought to be honored by justices. There is simply, for the positivist, nothing to be said in favor of what justices ought to do that one could not, with equal validity from the positivist framework, deny that the justices ought to do. And such a theory must simply be declared hopelessly fruitless, unworkable, void and null.

57 Rasmussen, 'Essentialism, Values and Rights' and Douglas Den Uyl and Douglas Rasmussen, 'Nozick on the Randian Argument,' in Jeffrey Paul, ed., *Reading Nozick* (Totowa, NJ: Rowman and Littlefield, 1981), pp. 232–69. In my *Human Rights and Human Liberties*, I put the matter as follows: 'There are no intrinsically beautiful or good or right things, only things that are good, right, or beautiful in relation to living entities for which things can be good, right, and beautiful in terms of purposes and goals' (p. 66).

58 This is what's so unreal about the kinds of cases that analytic philosophers use to test ethical principles – ones so ingeniously devised by, for example, Judith Jarvis Thomson. No theory of ethics – indeed, no theory of any kind outside perhaps metaphysics – should be held responsible for managing all imaginable cases.

Despite overdoing the testing of ethics by reference to such cases, some of those that are realistic should, in fact, be considered in the examination of an ethical system. When I suggest, for example, that courage might now and then conflict with prudence, I have in mind a case such as when a soldier must defend against an attack from the enemy but could easily imagine hiding instead. The act of defense would involve courage, the act of hiding would involve prudence. One needs to consider the proper hierarchy of ethical principles in order to handle such a case. That is just what would be done in the study of military ethics.

59 Quoted in H. L. A. Hart, 'Are There Any Natural Rights?' in Melden, ed., *Human Rights*, p. 61n. This appears to be a paraphrase of Locke's point, advanced in his *Second Treatise of Civil Government*, Book 2, Chapter 19, pp. 211–48.

60 This is part of the value of all the hoopla that has emerged from T. Kuhn's work in the philosophy of science. But see my 'Kuhn's Impossibility Proof and the Moral Element in Scientific Explanations,' *Theory and Decision*, Vol. 5 (December 1974), pp. 355–74, and Machan, *Objectivity*.

61 For a detailed discussion of compossibility, see David L. Norton, *Personal Destinies, A Philosophy of Ethical Individualism* (Princeton, NJ: Princeton University Press, 1976).

62 For example Mack, 'Egoism and Rights,' and 'Egoism and Rights Revisited,' *The Personalist*, Vol. 57 (Autumn 1977), pp. 282–87. See also Machan, 'Prima Facie versus Natural (Human) Rights', *Journal of Value Inquiry*, Vol. X, No 1 (1976), pp. 119–31.

63 Van den Haag, p. 49.

64 Ibid., p. 48.

65 Earl Conee, 'Against Moral Dilemmas,' *Philosophical Review*, Vol. XCI (January 1982), pp. 87–97.

66 See Machan 'Prima Facie versus Natural (Human) Rights.'

67 Here is a passage that illustrates Aristotle's view:

> Virtue is concerned with feeling and actions; praise and blame are bestowed on voluntary ones, pardon (sometimes also pity) on involuntary ones. To define and distinguish the voluntary and the involuntary is, therefore, essential if one is enquiring into virtue – and useful for legislators too, in connection with the assigning of honours and punishment.' (*Nicomachean Ethics* III. 1, 1109b30)

68 Werner Jeager, *Aristotle* (Oxford: Oxford University Press, 1934), p. 152.

69 David Ross, *Aristotle* (London: Methuen & Co. Ltd., 1964), p. 201.

70 It is worth noting that Gray makes much of two points against classical liberalism, namely, its subjective individualism and its aspiration to universalism. On the first point, Gray characterizes individualism in a strictly subjectivist way and this is clearly not necessary for classical liberalism. See, for example, my *Individuals and Their Rights*, *Capitalism and Individualism*, and *Classical Individualism* in which I develop what I have called classical or humanistic conception of individualism. See also Norton, *Personal Destinies*.

Concerning the non-universalizability of liberalism's principles, it is worth noting that while no doubt some implications of these principles may not be universally applicable – ought, after all, implies can, and some societal circumstances make no room for certain possibilities – the real issue is whether the basics are objective, not universal. Cultural diversity can be divided into the sensible contextually warranted and the morally and politically intolerable varieties. Without some sense of what is basically right, that distinction is impossible to make and we are left with having to accept the killing of wives in India for the sake of collecting a new dowry as simply a different cultural practice. Indeed, Gray's own effort to criticize cannot escape a certain measure of universalization.

After all, should someone in a given culture advance the thesis of universalizability. Gray would argue against such an individual. So his own criticism of the alleged cultural imperialism of classical liberalism cannot help but amount to a kind of cultural imperialism. So what we are left with is the question: which of these trans-cultural systems of standards or criteria is the sound one? We lack the option of engaging in the discussion without any concern for that issue, as Gray seems to think we may proceed.

71 Tibor R. Machan, *The Pseudo-Science of B. F. Skinner* (New Rochelle, NY: Arlington House, 1974) and *Initiative – Human Agency and Society*. See also Roger W. Sperry, *Science and Moral Priority* (New York: Columbia University Press, 1983).

72 (Princeton, NJ: Princeton University Press, 1953).

73 Bambrough, *Moral Skepticism and Moral Knowledge*.

74 John Gray has, at one point, identified himself with a rather forceful conservatism but later with the radical wing of the British Labour Party and a virulent form of anti-Western anti-individualism. See for example, his review of Adam Seligman, *The Idea of Civil Society* (New York: The Free Press, 1992), in 'Authority's Ghost,' *The New York Times Book Review* (September 13, 1992), p. 26. See also his *Straw Dogs, Thoughts on humans and other animals* (London: Granta Books, 2002).

75 I explore this in greater detail in my *Individuals and Their Rights*. The main point is that our encounter with the universe clearly suggests a great variety of types and kinds of beings and while in some cases we may be mistaken in the belief that there exists a difference of type or kind while it merely appears to be so, in other cases it is not reasonable to expect the success of a reduction, say, from musical harmony to physical matter or process, from self-awareness to brain process, from literary excellence to chemical events.

76 I have in mind, in particular, Sperry, *Science and Moral Priority* and Timothy O'Connor, *Persons and Causes* (New York: Oxford University Press, 2002). For a good selection of essays on this topic, see Timothy O'Connor, ed., *Agents, Causes, and Events* (New York: Oxford University Press, 1995). See, also, Machan, *Initiative – Human Agency and Society*.

77 'Trans-historical' is not the same as 'transcendent.' What trans-historical involves is the stability of certain standards of right and wrong throughout the history of a distinctive species of agents who must, given the kind of beings they are, choose their conduct. Some fundamental choices are going to be sound for them any time, any place, although many of the derivative decisions may differ due to historical variables. Thus, while it may turn out that certain virtues, such as thoughtfulness or right reason, will never be dispensable for a good human life, other moral alternatives, *vis-à-vis* parenting, citizenship, or familial loyalty, will vary from culture to culture or even more particularly.

78 It may be instructive, and should be taken into consideration in the assessment of the respective views, that the natural rights theory of Locke gave impetus to the eventual emergence of such documents as the United Nations Universal Declaration of Human Rights, certainly a trans-cultural instrument of moral and political influence. While this may not be a document that fulfills its task flawlessly, it goes a good distance toward stressing the propriety of such an approach. It is doubtful, indeed, whether Gray's multiculturalism – buttressed, at one point, with a reference to Paul Feyerabend's epistemological anarchism – can make any sense of any kind of criticism, even that which he engages in, not to mention those involved in chiding the former Soviet Union, South Africa, Chile, Iraq and other cultures for inhumanities.

79 In the last analysis skepticism is so nihilistic that it robs the proponent of the position of any justification for saying anything at all, even critical. Why should we, from a skeptical perspective, accept any meaning of the words being spoken?

80 MacIntyre, *After Virtue*, p. 69. For whether the historicist position, for example, of MacIntyre, is *historically* accurate about rights in particular, see Brian Tierney, 'Origins of Natural Rights Language: Text and Contexts, 1150–1250,' *History of Political Thought*, Vol. 10 (Winter 1989), pp. 615–46, and 'Conciliarism, Corporatism, and Individualism:

the Doctrine of Individual Rights in Gerson,' *Christianesimo hella Storia*, Vol. 9 (1988), pp. 81–111.

81 Ibid., 228.

82 Marx, *Grundrisse*, p. 33. For how well developed this idea has become, often not even clearly linked with Marx, see Catherine A. Mackinnon, *Feminism Unmodified* (Cambridge, MA: Harvard University Press, 1987). See also Alan Freeman and Elizabeth Mensch, 'The Public–Private Distinction in American Law and Life,' *Buffalo Law Review*, Vol. 36 (1987), pp. 237–57. It is instructive to note that if we are to understand philosophical arguments for natural rights along Marxist lines, such that they are designed, even if inadvertently, to serve some special or vested interests, this can cut deep enough to indict Marxism as well as other views that employ it. For example, arguably one likely consequence of implementing the anti-individualist, anti-individual rights position is to strengthen the power of the state or government over against the claims of citizens. In short, this position fosters state power. One might then hold, consistent with the Marxist analysis, that these arguments against individuals have as their ulterior motive nothing other than statism, the gaining of full or totalitarian legal power over human individuals. Yet the real question is not what motivates these views but whether they are right.

83 Here the point earlier made *vis-à-vis* skepticism about universal principles holds against historicists, also. These self-reflexive arguments are not without their serious punch, using, as they do, the common logical rule of substitution to test various claims. For more on these kinds of issues, see *Reason Papers*, No 17 (Fall 1991), 'Rethinking Foundationalism.' See also Machan, 'Evidence of Necessary Existence.'

84 For an interesting history of ideas on the concept of the individual, see J. D. P. Bolton, *Glory, Jest and Riddle, A Study of the Growth of Individualism from Homer to Christianity* (New York: Barnes & Noble, 1973). But see also John O. Lyons, *The Invention of the Self* (Carbondale, IL: Southern Illinois University Press, 1978).

85 See my 'Law, Justice and Natural Rights,' *Western Ontario Law Review*, Vol. 14 (Fall 1975), pp. 119–30.

86 Gilbert Harman, *Thought* (Princeton, NJ: Princeton University Press, 1973), p. 145.

87 I wish to thank Mark Turiano for his advice on the preparation of this work, as well as James Sterba for his criticisms. I believe the discussion has benefited considerably from discussing various features of it with James Chesher, Douglas J. Den Uyl, Gregory Johnson and Douglas B. Rasmussen.

Chapter 4

Individualism and the Vitality of Community Life

The owner of a famous theater in Fullerton, California makes plans to sell it. Residents scold him for sacrificing the interests of the community, and some even urge the local government to ban the sale.

In the neighboring town of Orange, a resident in a historic district plans to build apartments on land he owns. Upon learning of his plan, some residents urge the local government to prohibit it, saying the community will be ruined if the owner is permitted to proceed.

In Indianapolis, influential citizens want to institute random car searches to stem drug trafficking. They claim that opposing the drug searches amounts to pitting private interests against community interests; in which case, of course, the latter should prevail. In this case, the United States Supreme Court sides with those who argue that their individual rights should be protected.[1]

Do the rights and interests of the individual collide – fundamentally – with the rights and interests of the community? Is there an inherent clash between individual sovereignty and political obligation?

On the face of it, that there could be such a clash seems a bizarre proposition, notwithstanding the many disputes framed in such terms that we read about everywhere. Communities, after all, are made up of individuals. Individuals form a community in the first place to promote their own survival through cooperation with others. The purpose of a concept of rights is to define the constraints within which these individuals may peacefully interact in the social context they have developed. The community is not some separate entity unto itself, subsisting somehow apart from the very individuals it comprises.

Yet many who criticize libertarianism, especially from a communitarian or socialist viewpoint, claim that the inalienable 'negative rights' that libertarianism defends – negative in that they prohibit others from violating one's rights to life, liberty and pursuit of happiness – are figments of the imagination. According to such critics as Henry Shue, Stephen Holmes, and Cass Sunstein, only positive rights exist – in this case, the positive right to be protected from intrusions, a right assigned by governments. On this view, rights to life and liberty are merely entitlements to protection, and the government decides who receives these entitlements and when they receive them. A right not specifically assigned and protected is said to be a fictitious right.[2] Thus, the allegedly non-welfare rights defended by libertarians can be viewed as 'welfare rights too'; thus, 'all legal rights are, or aspire to be, welfare rights.'[3] And such welfare rights imply extensive political obligations: namely, substantive services to others that governments may enforce. These critics claim that since there are no negative rights after all but only positive rights, libertarians can hardly complain when other positive rights, like 'the right to be provided with health care,' are added to the bushel of enforced 'positive rights.'

The gainsayers of 'negative rights' might even be right – if the way to figure out the nature of rights were to play a linguistic shell game.

According to the classical liberal tradition,[4] a right is a social norm – a kind of justified norm – that should be recognized and respected even when it is not being protected by a government.[5] An innocent person should not be murdered even if nobody is preventing that person from being murdered; the norm is correct even if there is no institutional protection of that person in force as of yet, and even if that person lacks the means to protect himself during a given attack.[6]

In point of fact, the so-called 'positive right' to protection by government is *derived from* the 'negative right' to freely enter into a compact with those who would form the government – and, more fundamentally still, from the right to defend oneself, which would encompass the right to enlist the assistance of others toward that end.[7] A proper conception of rights is not arbitrary. It is derived from a sound understanding of human nature and the requirements of human survival in a social setting. Libertarians do not object to positive rights that derive from contract or compact! This is what the critics fail to appreciate. They regard government as a given, as simply there, seemingly without ethical antecedent; whereas libertarians regard government or any similar agency as instituted by free men and women so as to secure the rights we have by virtue of our very nature. The critics glide past the central questions and so misconstrue the very meaning and purpose of rights.

The nomenclature of 'negative' versus 'positive' rights muddies the waters somewhat. The right to liberty surely is 'positive' with respect to the individual's freedom of action that the right implies. Of course being able to exercise that freedom does not guarantee that one will obtain specific goods, like food, necessary for survival; it merely enables one to engage in the peaceful actions that may serve to acquire food. But for human beings, freedom of action is more important than food, because that is what we need to get the food and the other life-serving goods that applying our reason enables us to acquire. The right to liberty is also certainly 'negative' in that it enjoins others from coercively interfering with an individual's positive freedom of action; 'no' is a negative word. But the question here is whether such 'negative' rights as the right to life and liberty somehow conflict with the interest of the community or the individual's serious obligations to the community. Is the notion of such a conflict even intelligible?

Prominent thinkers such as Richard Rorty, Charles Taylor, Michael Sandel and Amitai Etzioni champion the idea of communitarianism. Some go so far as to claim that all persons *belong* to communities, arguing that the relationship of dependency between individual and community is akin to the relationship of one's limbs to one's body. The social 'body' is thought to be an ontologically prior and even superior sort of being, of which individuals are merely constituent elements, and as such possess no justified claim to sovereignty.[8] Some embrace his view explicitly, others implicitly as they speak of what 'we' do and think and say and how particular individuals need to accommodate what 'we' have determined.

In modern times there are few more prominent alleged conflicts than that between the individual and the community. The natural antagonism between the private realm of the individual and the public realm of the group has emerged as a central theme of modern political life. Such essay titles as 'The Challenge of Privatization in the Former East Germany: Reconciling the Conflict between Individual Rights and Social Needs'[9] hint at how easy it is to treat individual rights as inherently at loggerheads with the good of the community.

How did this situation come about? How did individual rights and the public interest come to be perceived as arch enemies – with the individual, all too often, cast in the role of expendable extra required to sacrifice his rights to the 'needs' of the group?

It is true that no individual has ever survived alone, utterly apart from others. Family, neighbors, tribe, village, city, country, and now even the world are interconnected and form a vital feature of the life of every individual human being. Who we are does have a lot to do with the groups of which we are members. Human beings are not born alone on desert islands and obliged to create civilization from scratch. We are born into human society and we inherit human culture. But the question is, does the benefit an individual can gain from society in and of itself confer upon 'society' (or particular other individuals claiming its mantle) a substantively limitless claim upon the individual?

In early times, especially before there was much reflective thought, let alone writing, there could only be fleeting challenges to the normal social bonds. Individuals took tribal rules and customs for granted, and probably had little opportunity or felt no great need to resist them in any persistent way. To the extent that such bonds were challenged, the challenge would have been swept aside without much controversy. The requirements of survival were too stark and pressing in the earliest days of our history for much consideration to be given to 'doing your own thing.' There had to be food, there had to be shelter, there had to be someone to placate the gods. Until humanity reached a certain complexity of civilization and attendant division of labor, it would have been pointless for a woman to revolt against having to prepare the meat – or for a man to revolt against having to catch it. The issue of survival was too stark and pressing and constant. So while individuality may well have been stifled as a matter of course in such circumstances, the stifling would not have been perceived as such, or at least it would have been tacitly accepted as reasonable and unavoidable. So in primitive social circumstances the issue of the individual versus the community could not arise with much force.

As creativity became more unleashed and the community expanded beyond family and tribe, the relationship of the individual and the community did arise. With the birth of political thought the focus was mostly on how communities should be administered – what civic virtues should be fostered – rather than on how to resolve any conflicts between individuals and the community. In ancient Chinese political thought, Lao Tzu, for example, voiced skepticism about the propriety of invoking the wisdom of the community.

But it is of course in ancient Greece that the questions arose most influentially for the West. With the life and death of Socrates, the potential clash of individual with community was starkly dramatized indeed, provoking the lengthy explorations of Plato. But this conflict is often misunderstood. It is usually regarded as one between Socrates and the mob of Athens, the individual and the community. But he did not challenge the group's supremacy. Rather, he aimed to steer it on a better course, and in fact defended the authority of the Athenian state to condemn him to death.

In Plato's dialogue Socrates, or at least the Platonic version of Socrates, explains to Crito why he will not take the chance to flee to save his own life: it is because he has accepted the state's general dominion over him as just, even if it acts unjustly in a specific instance. Socrates imagines that if he were to evade the sentence, the state would rightly demand to know why he would

> overturn us – the laws, and the whole state, as far as in you lies? Do you imagine that a state can subsist and not be overthrown, in which the decisions of law have no power, but are set aside and trampled upon by individuals? … Well then, since you were brought into the world and nurtured and educated by us, can you deny in the first place that you are our child and slave, as your fathers were before you? And if this is true you are not on equal terms with us; nor can you think that you have a right to do to us what we are doing to you.

The state would instruct him that 'he who has experience of the manner in which we order justice and administer the state, and still remains, has entered into an implied contract that he will do as we command him.'[10]

Socrates offers no counterargument – nor does Crito. The conflict here was thus between the values of Socrates and those of his critics, rather than between the rights of Socrates (the individual) and the rights of Athens (the community). The idealist metaphysics of Plato further supports the supremacy of the community. Just as in geometry it is the idea of the circle that is perfect, not any specific circle, so, for Plato, it is the universal idea or form of humanity which is transcendent, eternal, and perfect, while the shadows cast by this form – you, me, and the other guy – are perishable, imperfect, even base.

Even Aristotle's focus upon the status of the individual citizen is not so stark as his focus upon the need to administer the community properly. For the ancient Greeks it was primarily the duties or obligations of citizenship that took priority over concerns about individual rights or liberty. Individual rights do make a vital appearance in Aristotle but not so prominently as they do in the thirteenth century and thereafter, especially in the writings of John Locke and later libertarians.[11] We may disagree with these early reflections, but they raise the question we too must cope with: to what extent is Socrates – or any individual – entitled to dissent from the group? And to what extent is the group entitled to subdue the individual?

And what sort of community is at issue – just any at all, so that, for example, if an individual comes into conflict with the community of the Third Reich or contemporary Iran or the former Soviet Union, such a conflict too must be resolved in favor of the community? Or are only communities of a much smaller kind at issue, such as the family, tribe, clan or neighborhood?

The question is not whether in point of fact individuals and groups have often clashed. Groups can trample individuals, and criminal individuals can set themselves against 'society.' As well, the individual's chosen objectives may often be at odds with his own rightly understood interest. But the existence of such clashes among badly or mistakenly acting individuals is no proof that such clashes are inherent and necessary – no proof that the interests of the individual and those of the community are *fundamentally* at odds. The issue is whether the rightly understood and fundamental interests of one individual and those of other individuals in a society are *necessarily* in conflict. Why should they be?

Well-formed communities consist in the associations of these individuals in accordance with appropriate principles of governance. Communities are formed for the sake of the individuals the community comprises. So individual human beings, if good and rational, cannot be fundamentally opposed to a good and rational community. It is their vital support system. The answer to Rodney King's question – Can't we all get along? – is: yes. If we behave ourselves. Of course, persons will disagree also over the criteria of a good community, but neither does the sheer fact of disagreement show that the true fundamental interests of persons in the community are anything but consonant.

What makes for a good community depends on our nature, on that which distinguishes us from other living beings: our capacity for thought – our reason. Human beings can learn ideas and figure out how to apply these ideas to improve our lives. We govern this capacity by choice. We don't have to be conceptual originators to do so; we can pick up ideas from books, conversation, even the habits we see people adopting for reasons which are understood only tacitly. For human beings such learning and communicating, which cannot happen without society, is central to our flourishing and even to simple survival.

Along with all the creative and practical benefits of being able to share wisdom with others in society, we also gain all the psychic benefits that flow from love and friendship. In a radically splintered society we might gain some of these values in a scattered or incidental way. But the more peaceful, complex, and stable our community is – and the more moral and just it is

– the better able we are to exercise virtue, think and plan, and enjoy the fruits of our efforts. If indeed adult human beings are creative, self-determined and morally responsible agents, communities ought to accommodate this by governing in accordance with the individual's right to life, liberty and property, which alone can secure for us the best chance to achieve the kind of life we ought to live. Anything else would be less than suitable to the life of the individual.

We need society to live. But society can also kill us. It can kill us quickly or it can kill us slowly, by stifling and banning our individuality. We aren't guaranteed hospitable communities. A community may be freighted with bad customs, bad habits, bad laws – and, yes, bad people. Often we look back upon the societies of earlier eras with disdain for their failure to cherish the requirements of human flourishing. But while primitive societies may not have known about these requirements, the same cannot be said of the rulers of later societies who could know what kinds of institutions are appropriate, but who nonetheless imposed the opposite.

So we need to monitor our communities. We need to ensure they are healthy and suitable to us. And this is a matter of individual responsibility. To abandon a corrupt tribe is something an individual does as an individual, not as a member of some other tribe. Even the family, a community that many mistakenly consider to be morally prior to the individual – meaning that one is supposed to place the interests of this community ahead of one's own – is not immune to criticism and censure. When an abused child is incapable of protesting and resisting, others, judging the situation to be intolerable, may make just claims in his behalf and even remove the child from this community.

It is important to underscore that the individual is the *sine qua non* of this analysis. The individual comes first. Society exists because individuals need society – and because individuals constitute it. What makes a community suitable to its members is its embrace of the principles individuals need to prosper in the company of others. These principles are social norms – individual rights – that are secured by both law and custom, and in terms of which many peaceful approaches to life may be actualized with impunity. Because each individual has a fundamental interest in the success of society and in being nurtured rather than molested by it, each individual also has a fundamental interest in respecting these norms.

Thus, among reasonable persons there is no necessary clash of interests, not at any rate at the most fundamental level of social interaction. When less fundamental conflicts occur among such persons – for example, over the provisions of a contract – the antagonists respect their mutual interest in sustaining society by acceding to the legitimacy of contract and the results of any arbitration. When individuals thus recognize their mutual interest in sustaining a free, rights-protecting society, conflicts between them can go only 'so far.' To cross that boundary line is to become a criminal.

If no *bona fide* conflict exists between individuals and community, the conflict in particular cases must in fact pertain to the opposing purposes of individuals within a community. Conceptions of a proper community may also clash, certainly. Some notions of community would, if implemented, do chronic violence to individuality and individual rights. These might bar certain peaceful individuals from membership for some perverse reason. Or they might prohibit existing members – persons innocent of any crime – from engaging in peaceful but frowned-upon activities, like dancing, having gay sex, selling a property, or building a power plant. Such communities are not suitable to the life of the individual, or at any rate they are only partially or intermittently suitable. It is no surprise that the desire some may have to establish a community that victimizes certain members would clash with the desire of the victims to be left alone.

What is the greatest threat to the individual when the alleged conflict between the individual and the community gains credibility? It is the haste and ease with which some people then rush to coercively suppress practices they find objectionable. Abetted by compromised social institutions, such persons too easily abandon the principle of individual liberty and indulge the expediency of coercion. Plain criminals, too – only without the intermediary of government to obscure the nature of what they're doing – resort to violence when impatient to get something. Plain criminals, too, care little about the costs to the innocent of their invasive actions.

It is especially important to adhere to principled problem-solving in societies whose legal systems rely on precedence. If a principle is compromised once, and this compromise is affirmed as legitimate – and then affirmed again, and again – a precedent is established in accordance with which all kinds of violations of individual rights can be promoted and established. If freedom of speech has been curbed with respect to pornography, why not follow suit when it comes to cinema or talk radio? Every pushy do-gooder can see the pattern and leap to exploit it.

Rights-trampling communities are bad communities. And when folks say that human beings need to give up individuality or abandon their basic rights for the sake of the community, they are distorting the actual nature of the conflict. The actions of a gang are not consistent with the requirements of a viable community.

The community of human beings so understood, however, must not be imposed upon people – in the sense that persons must not be forced to remain in the community if they wish to leave. For this would violate their basic nature, their creative role in directing their own lives for better or worse. Human dignity requires that one be in charge of one's own life and be judged accordingly. And this is one reason why a free society, wherein we all enjoy what Robert Nozick has called our 'moral space,' is so vital.[12] When persons are dealt with in ways that negate their sovereignty and truncate their moral space, their humanity is thwarted; they are demeaned. At the same time, such persons demean themselves if they neglect to cultivate their lives by accepting and cultivating a good community. Yet that is an issue they must contend with themselves. It is the challenge we all face. To deprive us of that challenge

– to force us into or out of communities against our own will – is to violate principles of community life itself. That is the meaning of the political idea of 'the consent of the governed' and of the economic idea of 'the exit option.'

The myriad details of the kind of community required for human beings cannot be laid out in an unalterable blueprint. The complex institutions a good community requires must be discovered, handed down peacefully from generation to generation, rekindled when lost sight of, revitalized, attended to, heeded and honed. But whatever shape such community life takes, one element must be fundamental and enduring. And that is the goal of respecting and protecting the sovereignty of the individual. Individuals must have room to make their own moral choices: about what career to pursue, what people to befriend, what recreation to embark upon, what to worship. This is what the theory of individual rights is all about.

Let us put some of this in concrete terms now. Consider the common allegation that the needs of communities in environmental matters conflict with individual rights. If wildlife preservation is at issue, involving wetlands, for example, it often seems that here clearly community interest and private interest are at odds. But why should this be so?

Actually, it turns out that a regime of private property rights affords the best chance for conserving the resources that human beings require in the long run.[13] The tragedy of the commons or collective ownership is the main threat to environmentally sound public policy, whereas private property rights can often secure long-term care for resources.[14] So it seems that respecting and protecting the individual's right to private property, and developing measures that address environmental problems within such an infrastructure, leads to the best solutions. And this 'best' will be what suits both the individual and the sort of community in which individuals can flourish.

Of course it is true that an environmentalist might oppose a given development despite the long-term environmental benefits of a consistently enforced property-rights regime. He might simply have a personal preference in the matter. But why should the environmentalist's desire to see untouched a particular square of land trump the property owner's desire to build apartments on that land? A society that respects individual rights is not a society in which every longing of every individual is ratified and imposed on others – which would be impossible to do in any case – but one in which individuals are free to pursue their values in cooperation with others. Upholding the principle of individual rights, and upholding it uniformly, is the only way to avoid dog-eat-dog communitarianism.

Or consider pornography and prostitution, both of which are often regarded as cases in which the community's best interest conflicts with individual rights. But is it so?

In fact, if private property rights are not strictly protected, those trading in pornography and sexual services simply go underground. The desire for such services does not disappear but is expressed and satisfied in often seedier and more intrusive ways than might be the case if it could occur freely in places where it is accepted and looked for. The right approach is to protect private property rights and thus not to ban private trade, but to limit it to where it is wanted. Pockets of smut trade or prostitution that may develop can then be more easily prevented from invading the areas where people refrain from trading in such goods and services. Even on the Internet, in which sexual expression is often taken to an extreme, those who wish to protect themselves and their children from such matter are able to do so, using Net Nanny and other filtering services. The integrity of such pockets cannot be maintained, however, if communities are ruled not by individual rights but by majority will or dictatorship.

Let's return now to the Fullerton, California case of the proposed theater sale that some residents opposed as inconsistent with community interests. Both the residents and the owner have the same basic social requirements of survival which, as we've seen, includes respect for individual rights, one crucial form of which is property rights. To abandon a commitment to individual property rights in this case would be a very serious breach of principle and, ultimately, would thwart the public interest. With the principle abandoned, no other individuals in Fullerton could be secure in their property either – including those who would violate the property rights of the theater owner. To build nice theaters, individuals need to know they'll be able to sell them when that is to their advantage. Without this freedom, the value of what people choose to create – and the motive to create – is seriously hampered. Sure, some nice things, even colossal things, are built in tyrannical societies – for example, pyramids – but mostly at the expense of conscripted legions who receive nothing in return for their sacrifice. Only in free societies can individual rights and community values be well aligned – because only in free societies are the rights of all peaceful members respected as a matter of principle.

In the city of Orange, a resident wanted to build apartments on property of his located in a historic district. Other residents objected, preferring that the area remain unaltered. As in the case of the theater, an accommodation was certainly possible: but it would have involved spending money. If preserving the land were so valuable to 'the community' – or a certain subset of the community – why not make it to the owner's best interest to cooperate by offering him the necessary cash, instead of forcing him to sacrifice his rights? In some cases restrictive covenants can prevent such situations as well, with the original terms of sale of a property stipulating that no alteration of the architecture is permitted in subsequent sales.

The residents of the Indianapolis neighborhood demanding random searches to abate drug traffic must accept that prior restraint against innocent citizens is a serious breach of community standards for a free people. Allowing unreasonable searches isn't the way to solve the problem of drug abuse. But violating the rights of innocent people hardly exhausts the options of neighbors beleaguered by drug traffickers. Local groups could obtain voluntary consent for car searches, perhaps – with bumper stickers for the cars of those who go along with the plan, and ostracism and other pressure, short of violation of rights, for those who don't go along. Cars without the bumper stickers would then be subject to the special attention of neighborhood watch groups. Even if this particular plan proved untenable, other voluntary plans can surely be conceived, once those concerned put their minds to it.

A community which fails to respects the rights of its members is unworthy of admiration and loyalty. On the other hand, members of a community which does consistently respect rights can be proud of the fact that they solve their problems in line with standards of civility and humanity.

The governing norms of a society should accommodate human beings as they are and as they ought to be. But for us to be as we ought to be, we must have the freedom to make the right choices, which is to say we must not be coerced for any reason, unless we behave as criminals ourselves. An environment of freedom obviously makes it possible for people to make wrong choices, whether from error or immorality. Accordingly, a community properly suited for human beings is by its nature non-utopian – it cannot and does not guarantee that all will always be morally well. But this very freedom also provides the most fertile field both for moral education and for genuine moral choice.

The thinkers of ancient Greece were keenly aware that human lives are at once private and public. They philosophized on behalf of the personal excellence and moral character of every individual, yet they also knew that such excellence and moral development required engagement with the community. Hermits are rare birds indeed, and they lead impoverished lives; their meager flourishing is enviable only in comparison with the even more limited options of those who live under tyranny.

The Greeks saw no necessary conflict between the individual and the community. Broadly speaking, they were right. It is only when we regard individual aspirations as necessarily whimsical or irrational, and community goals as necessarily a function of arbitrary collective will, that such a conflict appears unavoidable. In truth, it is avoidable. In truth, we can all get along.

Notes

1 Supreme Court of the United States, CITY OF INDIANAPOLIS, et al., petitioners, v. James EDMOND et al. No 99–1030 (2000). But see KELO et al., petitioners, v. CITY OF NEW LONDON, CT, et al. No 04-108 (2005).

2 Stephen Holmes and Cass R. Sunstein, *The Cost of Rights: Why Liberty Depends on Taxes* (New York: W. W. Norton, 1999), p. 21. See also Cass R. Sunstein, *The Second Bill of Rights: FDR's Unfinished Revolution and Why We Need it More than Ever* (New York: Basic Books, 2004), which celebrates Franklin Delano Roosevelt's political promotion of the idea of economic rights. Of course, Sunstein is mostly reinforcing here his earlier work in support of the idea that government grants us rights, we haven't any apart from this, and thus if FDR or any other political chief sees fit to ascribe economic rights to citizens, that's really the end of the argument. See, however, Tibor R. Machan, *Individuals and Their Rights* (LaSalle, IL: Open Court Publishing Co., Inc., 1989), for a demonstration of the soundness of the Lockean negative natural rights approach and the basis for the idea

that what Sunstein and company, are proposing is a regime of involuntary servitude for those who are to be coerced to provide the economic benefits to which people supposedly have rights.

3 Ibid.

4 See Tibor R. Machan, *Classical Individualism; The Supreme Importance of each Human Being* (London: Routledge, 1998).

5 See Tibor R. Machan, ed., *Individual Rights Reconsidered: Are the Truths of the US Declaration Lasting?* (Stanford, CA: Hoover Institution Press, 2001), especially the essay by Tom G. Palmer, 'Saving Rights Theory from Its Friends.'

6 Such rights, though, are applicable for purposes of guiding the establishment of legal norms, not as personal ethical guidelines (as are such moral virtues as honesty, generosity, prudence, or moderation). For more on this, see Douglas B. Rasmussen and Douglas J. Den Uyl, *Liberty and Nature* (LaSalle, IL: Open Court, 1990). Rasmussen and Den Uyl spell out what they term a theory of meta-normativity, meaning a position as to how members of human communities ought to organize themselves, what principles their constitution ought to include.

7 The wording of the Declaration of Independence is instructive here: 'Governments are *instituted*... deriving their just powers from the consent of the governed' (my emphasis). For a thorough fleshing out of this idea, see Randy E. Barnett, *Restoring the Lost Constitution* (Princeton, NJ: Princeton University Press, 2004).

8 Richard Rorty, *Objectivity, Relativism and Truth* (Cambridge, England: Cambridge University Press, 1991), especially the chapter 'Solidarity versus Objectivity'; Charles Taylor, *Philosophy and the Human Sciences* (Cambridge: Cambridge University Press, 1985), especially the chapter, 'Atomism'; Michael Sandel, *Liberalism and the Limits Of Justice*, 2nd edn (Cambridge, UK and New York: Cambridge University Press, 1998); and Amitai Etzioni, *The Spirit of Community* (New York: Crown Publishers, 1993).

9 Thomas Raiser, in G. S. Alexander and G. Skapska, eds, *A Fourth Way? Privatization, Property, and the Emergence of New Market Economics* (London: Routledge, 1997).

10 Plato, *The Death of Socrates: Euthyphro, Apology, Crito, and Phaedo*, translated by Benjamin Jowett (New York: Fordham University Press, 1995).

11 Fred D. Miller, Jr, *Nature, Justice and Rights in Aristotle's Politics* (Oxford: The Clarendon Press, 1995). Compare to Alistair MacIntyre, *After Virtue* (Notre Dame, IN: University of Notre Dame Press, 1984). See also Brian Tierney, *The Idea of Natural Rights* (Atlanta, GA: Emory University Studies in Law & Religion, No 5, 1997). An elaborate philosophic defense of individual rights as based on human nature appears in John Locke, *Two Treatises of Government* (Cambridge: Cambridge University Press, 1960).

12 See, Robert Nozick, *Anarchy, State, and Utopia* (New York: Basic Books, 1974), p. 57.

13 The issue of private property rights has produced a great deal of consternation within the community of political philosophers and economists because some cases of property are not immediately determinate – property in water or air mass would be very clear cases in point. Even in the plain ownership of land the issue of how far up or down ownership extends can arise. Furthermore, there is always trouble about initial acquisition – how does it become established that someone owns, say, a region of territory? Would the Lockean answer that 'mixing one's labor' will serve this purpose well enough to suffice or is this too ambiguous or vague? If one puts a fence around some land mass, is that a case of 'mixing one's labor' so that the enclosed area constitutes the private property of this individual?

Libertarians are by no means sanguine about the difficulties but they do insist that there are clear enough cases of ownership – as when one finds a valuable piece of stone or catches a not yet owned wild animal or encircles a tree – so that the initial standards of ownership can be built upon and the legal procedures for dealing with more complex cases can be developed without needless worries. See, for more on this, James Sadowsky, 'Private Property Rights and Collective Ownership' in T. R. Machan, ed., *The Libertarian*

Alternative (Chicago, IL: Nelson-Hall Co., Inc., 1971), pp. 119–33. See also Tibor R. Machan, *Right to Private Property* (Stanford, CA: Hoover Institution Press, 2002).

There are also certain political philosophers who are now deploying the label 'libertarian' for a position that is essentially fundamentally unlibertarian, that is, opposed to the rule, the right to individual liberty, including the right to private property – that is, the right to act to obtain and hold valued items others must obtain permission to use. See, for example, Michael Otsuka, *Libertarianism Without Inequality* (Oxford: Oxford University Press, 2004). No one can own a label but it is dishonest and worse to attach one with a certain meaning to ideas with opposite meanings. See Tom Palmer, 'John Locke Lite, The strange philosophy of "left libertarianism",' *Reason*, Vol. 36, No 8 (January 2005), pp. 56–59.

14 For more on this, see Tibor R. Machan, *Putting Humans First, Why We Are Nature's Favorite* (Lanham, MD: Rowman & Littlefield, 2004). See also Tibor R. Machan, ed., *The Commons – Its Tragedies and Other Follies* (Stanford, CA: Hoover Institution Press, 2001).

Chapter 5

Economics and Human Values

It is a political question – a question pertaining to values. Is capitalism worthy of our support? Is it a basically just economic system, or should we support some fundamental alternative?

Many do believe we ought to support a system quite different from capitalism. The 'ought' of this proposition alone suggests that in exploring our topic, we are engaged in a normative inquiry. That is to say, we are concerned with the area of our lives in which we judge things to be good or bad, right or wrong.[1] Normative inquiries consider the standards needed to make judgments about what is the right thing to do. Political economy is, accordingly, a normative discipline.

Yet many people contend that normative judgments lack any cognitive merit – that is, that such judgments, because they supposedly do not pertain to any facts of reality, cannot be true or false but are a matter of mere preference. But if this is the case we cannot even approach our subject with any hope of seeing the truth.[2] Yet, the issue has to be faced even in defending a minimalist policy such as libertarianism, where what is being argued is that we all ought to respect the basic individual rights of everyone and the legal order ought to give protection to these rights.[3]

People clearly do think and live as if normative matters could be decided by attention to certain facts, and thus need not be left to mere subjective impressions or intuitions. This fact is not definitive, but it is suggestive. Even more suggestive is the fact that we cannot even conceive of going about our lives without resorting to value judgments. And if our value judgments lack any objective connection to reality, why are they so critical to keeping us alive and flourishing?

Moreover, even those who dispute the possibility that such judgments could be objective imply otherwise when they suggest we should not accept that value judgments can have an objective basis! Obviously, the judgment that normative judgments cannot be justified either can be objectively justified or cannot be objectively justified. If the former, the assertion that we ought not regard value judgments as at least possibly objective is self-contradictory. If the latter, by its own skeptical terms the assertion can have no grounding whatever in reality.

One can escape the morass of skepticism here by recognizing a couple of features about value judgments that enable them to be objective even if also personal and chosen. One is the fact that such judgments are conditional: they possess an 'if–then' character. To recognize that ingesting a certain dose of cyanide will kill you is not a value judgment about the act of ingesting the cyanide but a plain scientific fact. But to say 'If I want to sustain my life, I should not ingest the cyanide,' is to make a value judgment. Yet it is certainly just as true! The proposition is conditional. But its conditionality is so fundamental – identifying a basic alternative, namely, between living a life and not living one – that it escapes being arbitrary.[4]

To conclude that 'I should not ingest the cyanide' is to presuppose an ultimate value – life – the sustenance of which is not automatic and the value of which cannot be defended by reference to other values somehow 'outside' of life. The value of life has to be taken as a given or framework within which other values are defended. This may be what worries some of those who claim that values can have no objective basis: if the objective basis of one's values has to do with whether one's life is being fostered or assaulted, but life itself cannot be further 'justified,' what can validate normative judgments?

There is no other answer than the fact that such judgments are required if one is to survive and flourish. One cannot go outside of one's own life for a justification of values, because values are all about what can promote one's life. Values emerge only with the emergence of life. It is life that entails a possibility of something being good for or bad for an entity. As Karl Popper put it, 'values enter the world with life; and if there is life without consciousness (as I think there may well be, even in animals and man, for there appears to be such a thing as dreamless sleep) then, I suggest, there will also be objective values, even without consciousness.'[5] Or as Ayn Rand put it: 'It is only the concept of "Life" that makes the concept of "Value" possible. It is only to living entities that things can be good or evil.'[6]

It's the relationships that actually exist in reality which give rise to the *conceptual* relationships. Values in fact arise in the world when life arises, just as flying arises among living species when insects and birds come into existence. To further grasp this, we might compare values to the narrower normative field of medicine: only when life exists does health begin to matter. One cannot look 'outside' an organism for the standards of health relevant to it, just as one cannot look 'outside' an organism for standards of value relevant to it. In either case, only certain courses of action will promote the organism's life. The concepts of 'value' or 'goodness' are grounded in the concept of 'life.' Moral goodness may even be fruitfully regarded – in line with the thinking of such ancient Greek philosophers as Socrates, Plato and Aristotle – as a kind of healthfulness.

Life entails alternatives. With life there is the possibility of improvement or impairment, success or failure, thriving or faltering, continuation or extinction – and on many fronts, not only with respect to the organism's biophysical condition. These fronts become more complex as the organism becomes more complex. (For human beings, the question of what courses of action truly foster one's life can be extremely complicated indeed at times.) Life, unlike inanimate matter, cannot simply change its form in any manner and go on forever, in some form or other. Once life comes into being it can be preserved or destroyed. Life is a process the sustenance of which requires persistent effort by the organism. It is this very conditionality – and the fact that the organism itself must take actions that support its life and avoid actions that hamper or destroy its life – which makes values possible and makes them necessary.

Once we understand this fact, the questions become more specific. What are the requirements of flourishing for *this* organism as opposed to *that* organism? Our list of values for a particular organism depends on the kind of thing it is, that is, its nature. Knowing what it is to be a redwood tree enables the botanist to evaluate how a given redwood is doing; knowing what a beaver is enables the zoologist to evaluate the condition of a given beaver. At the broadest level, of course, the only specialized knowledge required to assess the vitality of an organism is the knowledge of what it means to be alive. If your plant is wilting and drying up, you may not know what the problem is, but you know something is wrong with its capacity to survive. If your four-year-old is listless and has a high fever, you may not know what the problem is, but know something is wrong with his capacity to survive. In principle, all living entities can be evaluated with respect to whether they are flourishing or deteriorating, though in many cases it may take a specialist to assess the condition in detail and determine causes.[7]

When it comes to human beings, one fact of our nature – our free will – adds a new dimension to values. We not only live and may or may not flourish at living, but we also, ordinarily, can choose the conduct that fosters or hinders such flourishing. It is our capacity to choose that gives rise to individual responsibility. For us, the issue of values is not only a matter of what is better and what is worse, but also whether we should (choose to) act according to certain standards. We must continually affirm our commitment to our own lives and to the values that sustaining our lives requires. By contrast, we wouldn't propose that a lion should or should not hunt, or that the deer should or should not try to escape when hunted. Such creatures have no choice about whether to act in such a way as to promote their own lives, but simply do so.

Only human beings can think and choose. Only human beings can consider not only whether to eat or run, but also what social institutions best enhance their lives rather than thwart or undermine them.[8]

These institutions should accommodate not only the aspects of our nature that we all share, but also those that differ from person to person. Human beings have much in common, but we are also individuals. Our individuality means that each person must make some 'ethical calls' in light of his own unique circumstances, capacities and goals, and not simply in light of universal principles applicable to all. A universal ethic might tell us that every capable person should earn his keep, but it cannot tell us that Joe should be a chiropractor rather than a dancer, or what kind of dancer, or whether he should dance full-time or part-time while also going to school. We are also members of various groups, our participation in which may require conduct geared to the purposes of that group – familial, professional, social, and so forth.

So our lives can be lived successfully or badly, and in many very different ways, though, when well lived, in mutually compatible ways. This is what has contributed, in part, to the widely held view that ethical judgments are subjective, that is, merely a matter of the individual's will, tastes, or preferences. In fact, though, the differences are due to the often unique attributes, circumstances, opportunities, and available information of each human individual. It is true that a person *can* act without sufficient regard for his own personal context, but the mere fact that he can is no proof that he must. A proper social system permits scope for all the nuances involved in making the choices individuals need to make if they are to flourish. Such a system respects and protects the freedom of all members of the society.

To summarize: the sheer fact of life – not only human life, but life everywhere around us – gives rise to the question, 'Is it good or is it bad?' with respect to the goal of surviving and flourishing. Different kinds of life will require different answers to this question. It's not just any life but life of a specific type that has to be sustained and guided if the organism is to thrive. And thus, when we are considering good and bad for, say, a banana versus a human being, we will get very different answers. But there is a common element, as well: very broadly speaking, the enhancing of the life of a specific organism is good with respect to that organism, and the destruction of it is bad.

If we accept then that values can be objective even if people may heatedly dispute them, what is the implication for economic science and the defense of capitalism? I contend that the objective normative framework we need to understand human life well is the same framework we need to understand economic science well, including conclusions regarding the free market or capitalism.

To suggest why, let me quote from Professor James Buchanan, 1986 Nobel Laureate in economic science and well known to classical liberals. In his book *The Limits of Liberty* he observes: 'Economics, the science of markets or of exchange institutions, commences with a well-defined structure or set of individual rights.'[9] Buchanan thus acknowledges that even to get off the ground, the *science* of economics requires the predication of a normative component, namely, a system of individual rights. For rights pertain to what *ought* to be the case, how people ought to act; not just what they do as a point of fact. The right to private property, for example, presupposes that every person ought to be left free by others to seek to hold, keep and dispose of items of value.

Accordingly, the very foundation of the free market economic system involves a normative component, contrary to what some other economists appear to believe. The set of individual rights and, more particularly, private property rights are at the foundation of the practical science of economics.[10]

One cannot even think of exchange or trade without the concept of the individual's rights to life, liberty or property. If one's life doesn't fall under one's own authority to govern, no part or result of one's activities (that is, labor or property) may be offered to others on mutually accepted terms. One may not give it away. One may not lend it or sell it. One may not hold on to it for oneself, or invest it, use it, abuse it, or bequeath it. One may not capitalize on it or save it for a rainy day. Nor may one lose it. If one hasn't got anything, there is no market in goods.

The viability of establishing terms of trade rests on possession of these rights. Absent the right to liberty, all the actions associated with trade – manufacture, invention, research, marketing, labor, and so on – would have to be performed at the mercy of everyone else, without whose permission one would be morally paralyzed. Rare is the society where trade has been completely eliminated, for people want to live and will take the actions they need to try to live, even when they have no legal sanction to take those actions. But we've seen how gray and tenuous life can become when rights of trade are legally banished, as for example in the Soviet Union: *free* trade persisted only on a black market; the traders had to skulk like criminals; and if they were caught, their fate depended on a commissar's whim.

The concept of rights, including private property rights, is normative in that it designates what people *are or are not authorized to do*. Professors Rasmussen and Den Uyl call rights meta-normative,[11] indicating that while possessing basic rights does not serve to guide one's actions in and of itself, it does set the stage for moral action within human communities by authorizing one to resist assaults by others or to employ a government or bodyguard for that purpose. A society of individual rights at least prohibits certain behavior, to wit, the behavior no one is authorized to engage in, and it authorizes resistance to that behavior.

All of this is very important for classical liberal, libertarian institutions and the proper understanding and analysis of the marketplace. Today, markets don't always have much legitimacy in the legal sense. In most societies the right to private property is seriously compromised, indeed, grossly violated, by the legal system itself, not only by criminals. So the theorist must mentally envision the consistent market process that he thinks should transpire (or at any rate, could transpire, in the absence of intervention) in order to analyze what must be the features and consequences of such a market process.

When the analyst of markets then goes on to propose that markets ought to be established and that trade ought be protected among free citizens, to be persuasive he must provide a normative justification – that is, he must argue that this is a good thing, which ought to be pursued. He cannot stop with his explication of what happens in markets in point of fact. He cannot simply try to smuggle in some standard of 'optimality' or the like while trying to sidestep moral questions. For without such a moral justification, it can be argued without much resistance that markets are a bad thing and that students of markets are no different from students of, say, criminal activities or diseases. Indeed, that is the opinion of many among Western intellectuals: that market activities are but expressions of greed, the immoral pursuit of wealth. And their unwarranted but often inadequately countered assertions have resulted in destructive public policy.

If it is not morally good to institute markets, there are all sorts of alternatives we might be morally required to embrace. The market is not an automatic system, like the weather or the rotation of the planets. It is, instead, a system established and maintained by choice – maybe a long series of philosophical, moral and political choices. This is so even though once markets exist, much that happens within them – for example, the emergence of various institutions such as money, rented and leased property, labor negotiations, and so on – happens not because some leaders decide that it should but because ordinary people act on their own initiative and insight, inadvertently producing various orderly processes as one consequence of their individual actions. The possibility of centrally unplanned, 'spontaneous' orders which *as a whole* are not chosen but which do result from many *individual choices* is a theme of many classical liberals, most notably F. A. Hayek.

In any case, the emergence of markets is not the inevitable consequence of impersonal historical forces. Indeed, markets are very difficult to establish and then protect from those who regard them morally odious, such as Marxists, fascists, democratic socialists, theocrats, anti-globalists, protectionists or anyone who cares little about whether he lives or dies. Legal institutions require human initiative to be sustained. At least some people in society, therefore – and the more the better – must guard against the corruption or destruction of these institutions. And for that it's necessary to show the worthiness of doing so.

I have argued that individual rights are an abstract or conceptual way of designating a sphere of authority for human individuals (as distinct from fenced-off territories, which are concrete). They are a sanction of personal sovereignty.[12]

In the feudal era, people who lived in a country were regarded as the *subjects* of the king. In the liberal era, however, they are regarded as sovereign citizens, with government as an institution serving delegated purposes that has no power to intrude on matters of life having nothing to do with criminal activity. Of course this is the ideal case; the liberal era is not so liberal now and hasn't ever been fully liberal. But sovereignty survives as a principle that is still often asserted against unwarranted governmental intrusions.

'Sovereignty' means independence or self-government, that is, ruling oneself rather than being ruled by others. It is only the concept of individual rights – which itself rests on the facts of individual responsibility and standards of right and wrong – that can justify such sovereignty and clarify the boundary lines of the sphere within which each individual is the sole master. Others who want to enter that area must ask for permission. If they have not obtained permission, not only are they doing something wrong, but those whose rights are being encroached upon are entitled to resist them.

That is why one has the moral and political authority to hire a bodyguard or a government – to protect one's rights. One is justified in warding off thieves, thugs, rapists, or murderers, and also in using the needed force to resist them.

One's life is for oneself to govern, not subject to the governance of others without one's consent.

But why is this true? That goes back to the issue of what sort of a being one is. I have espoused the naturalist doctrine that our nature as thinking, choosing beings requires that such spheres of individual action be honored if we are to survive and flourish as humans. By contrast, some argue for the legitimacy of rights not on the basis of human nature but simply as the result of social agreement. Professor Buchanan has in mind by 'a structure of well-defined rights' a set of rights agreed to or contracted into, an agreement that serves all of our interests if we are alike enough. But because such rights are not justified by reference to human nature and the implications of our nature, the contractual rationale for adhering to them is brittle.[13] If there is no ethical imperative requiring people to adhere to their promises, then no morally binding reason exists for them to live by the terms to which they have agreed. Furthermore, the advantages to be gained from such an agreement are specified only subjectively, so they can be changed at the whim of the agents. If one can hoodwink others and get away with it, there is nothing objectionable about doing so beyond the displeasure of others. The assumption of social contract theory is that most of us are not smart enough or devious enough to do that, so we will probably abide by the social contract.

The natural rights position, in contrast, holds that, quite apart from any agreement, those embarking on human community life have the right to their life, liberty and property – although agreements do come into the picture at some point, namely, when consent is given to be governed. For only a regime of rights can secure for everyone the personal sphere of jurisdiction within which choices about one's life can effectively and meaningfully be made. Basic rights themselves are thus not a matter of agreement. We discover them as needed social principles. They are an objective feature of the human social world.

When we study human beings we notice certain basic, defining facts about their nature. We notice their creativity, individuality, moral agency. We notice that some fail, some succeed, and many are somewhere in between as they proceed to guide their lives. Now we ask: 'what do all these facts tell us about the way we ought to live?' Well, they tell us clearly enough, to paraphrase John Locke, 'if we but think about it,' that everyone ought to be free and protected in his or her freedom.

Unfortunately, of course, not everybody thinks about this. John Locke and later normative classical liberal theorists have recognized that *reason has to be consulted*.[14] Its findings – including how we ought to act – aren't handed to us on a silver platter. This is a most basic responsibility of each human individual: to attend to the world and discover how best to live! However much help each individual receives from those who have thought about these matters already, even to grasp their meaning one must think for oneself.

Although Locke had a somewhat problematic theory of human free will, his political thinking presupposes that ordinary human adults are free to attend to the issue of how they ought to live and interact with others. Since some will, however, fail to do this and thus fail to act properly, governments are highly advisable so as to secure for everyone the basic rights of individual human beings. Those who are immoral in a way that intrudes upon the sovereignty of others pose a threat to the rest.[15]

Accordingly, if we but think about it, we will learn that we need some place where we are in charge as individuals; a sphere in which we can distinguish ourselves as the individual human beings that we are, despite our complex social entanglements. Without such a sphere, we are going to observe what economists refer to as *dumping*, although in a broader sense than they typically mean it.

In environmental economics, 'dumping' means transferring to others burdens that one incurs oneself, usually without anyone noticing – for example, when one drives down a road and people vulnerable to respiratory ailments are assaulted by the pollutants one's car emits. This dumping is possible when there are no clearly defined private property rights that require one to ask another person for his permission before making use of that person's domain. If one could do that, perhaps he would say, 'Yes, for $5000 a year.' Environmental degradation would contract severely if this were the legal norm or even merely accepted as the basic standard of environmental property law to which a community aspires.[16]

Some environmental cases are difficult. We have not developed a realm of property rights in the air mass. On the other hand, we are not even trying. Legislators and constituents, especially lobby groups, are only rarely even considering that option, because the principle of the right to private property is not prominently embraced. Even those who support private property tend to say, 'Well, it will emerge through evolution,' or 'It is a matter of social contract,' or 'There is no objective normative case to be made for such rights outside of their possible convenience, if that is how people feel or prefer things.' This is a mistake. In human affairs sound ideas need to be well grounded and actively promulgated – it isn't enough to wait for them to evolve. After all, bad ideas are also contending for acceptance.

The kind of dumping that is referred to in environmental discussions can be construed more broadly to subsume any forcible severing of the link between one's actions and the consequences, good or bad, of those actions. This is the kind of dumping that the welfare state facilitates: the widespread sharing of both individual burdens and individual achievements not because one chooses to do so, but because lawmakers require it.[17]

Such dumping narrows the scope of self-responsibility. It weakens incentives both to take care to avoid destruction and to go the extra mile to achieve something. Aristotle noted the effect of dumping on personal incentives some 2500 years ago:

> That all persons call the same thing mine in the sense in which each does so may be a fine thing, but it is impracticable; or if the words are taken in the other sense, such a unity in no way conduces to harmony. And there is another objection to

> the proposal. For that which is common to the greatest number has the least care bestowed upon it. Every one thinks chiefly of his own, hardly at all of the common interest; and only when he is himself concerned as an individual. For besides other considerations, everybody is more inclined to neglect the duty which he expects another to fulfill; as in families many attendants are often less useful than a few.[18]

It was also noted by Thucydides when he observed that,

> [T]hey devote a very small fraction of the time to the consideration of any public object, most of it to the prosecution of their own objects. Meanwhile, each fancies that no harm will come to his neglect, that it is the business of somebody else to look after this or that for him; and so, by the same notion being entertained by all separately, the common cause imperceptibly decays.[19]

Professor Garrett Hardin, the UC Santa Barbara environmental biologist, calls what's happening here *the tragedy of the commons*.[20] Hardin was referring to commonly exploited land, such as an over-grazed pasture, but the principle applies as well to any communally shared burdens and achievements, such as compelled under socialism or the welfare state. What is produced in such a case is a *moral* tragedy of the commons.

The facts of our nature as moral agents[21] indicate that a realm of individual rights, including private property rights, is indispensable to a form of community fitting for human life – a genuinely *human form* of community life. There are other forms of community life, evident, for example, in how bees or ants or wolves or antelopes live together. But fully developed human beings require that a sphere of private property rights be conscientiously and consistently protected.

We have considered some of the facts that justify the *system* of private property rights. But to determine who actually owns what is a distinct problem. Once one grasps the soundness of the general case for the system, one is still left with the problem of how we know, especially in cases of conflict, who ought to have what. This requires a good understanding of how private property may be justly acquired and the sort of process by which its ascription is to proceed within human communities where the problem of who owns what arises.

In John Locke's famous labor theory of property acquisition, mixing one's labor with something is supposed to be the way to tell who owns what. Such mixing, of course, includes buying a thing in the market, with honestly obtained income. It's a very broad concept. It's sophisticated. But is it sound?

I don't think it's sound enough. But here I can only hint at the kind of improvement the Lockean theory needs.

Professor James Sadowsky made a very good attempt at clearly spelling out the principle of property assignment.[22] His view is also implicit in the more general position on the nature of virtue spelled out by Ayn Rand. In this view the primary moral virtue is rationality – the use of human reason in a consistent and sustained fashion. And the goal is human success as per one's nature, including one's individuality. This position implies Sadowsky's (as well as Israel Kirzner's) entrepreneurial view of property acquisition, which is that something becomes one's private property after one assesses it as valuable and, accordingly, places borders around it in more or less complex ways for purposes of current or future use.

When someone has made a prudent judgment and acted on it in the wild or the marketplace, and has thus (at least purportedly) insightfully engaged with that part of reality that can have value, this person then appropriates the thing in question. Within established communities such acquisition generally arises through voluntary exchange. The appropriate kinds of exchange include even exchange that ultimately proves mistaken. The choice of a transactor to treat something as valuable is a determining factor of exchange, not any assumption of infallibility. (Exchange perpetrated by fraud, however, is not merely a 'mistaken' exchange from the perspective of the victim but a result of the violation of his rights; the kind of mistake fraud encourages could not have occurred if the defrauded person had received honest information.) Whether one buys stock in IBM or a toilet seat, it's the judgment that leads to private ownership, the judgment that this item will matter, that it has value for people. We know that an item belongs to a person when that person has made the judgment and done what is necessary to act on that judgment in a manner consistent with the rights of all parties.

The institution of private property rights – which is the fundamental basis of market transactions – thus depends on the ethically significant (if not always successful) act of judging what is best to do. This fact also provides the link between free markets and individual human responsibility. Without the concrete stuff private property rights can secure for us, there would be no determinate sphere of personal jurisdiction. Only within such jurisdiction is there a means to establish what falls within a person's realm of responsibility and what falls outside it. The ability to assign moral responsibility enables us to avoid the moral tragedy of the commons.

Yet, the particular or detailed elements and implications of the private property system – including how complex valued items are to be defined and how novel versions are to be integrated into the system – cannot be spelled out before we see how problems arising in relation to private property ownership and trade develop and are dealt with through negotiation and, finally, through the courts. Due process is what ensures, as much as possible, that the developing system is just and practical. Criticisms of Locke are justified mainly because he didn't spell out a procedure for maintaining a system or property rights reasonably intact and uncorrupted. However, others in the classical liberal, libertarian tradition have made up for this.[23]

It is the normative base of a system of private property rights that grounds the 'well-defined structure or set of individual rights' with which, according to James Buchanan, economics commences. It is here that normativity infuses the market – even if, in the course of economic analysis, the issue of how property rights are justified, how they ought to be ascribed in particular and complex cases, and how they can be sustained against assault may be set aside or taken for granted. The issue can't be set aside when it comes time to justify the system, however. Explication of market process is not enough. Morality and human nature have to be considered.

Some classical liberal economists and political theorists seem to be at odds with each other when they speak about property rights. Many economists, for example, advance what they refer to as the economic theory of property rights. When they use the phrase 'property rights' in this sense, what is being said from the point of view of political theory is not that you are buying and selling property rights. In order to commence buying or selling, you are assumed to have the right to private property. You can't buy and sell anything prior to having property rights. Rather, property rights in the economic sense pertains to *having legal title* to things, the legally protected power to decide about the disposition of something.

What needs to be stressed is that in my own discussion, 'property rights' is not used to mean legally protected powers *per se*. That's because, apart from considering the technical subject of how the market functions through the existence of such legally protected powers, we do need a justification of the broader set of individual rights that Professor James Buchanan says is at the foundation of the theoretical and practical science of economics, including the natural right of every individual to own property. It is this natural right, and antecedent to any legal protections that may be instituted, which I have sought to defend.[24]

Notes

1 Some normative matters pertain to the well being of plants and animals, the quality of human conduct and institutions, and the aesthetic attributes of objects. Other normative questions, though, bear on our choices – ethical and political ones, for instance.

2 I defend the cognitive nature of normative, especially moral, judgments in Tibor R. Machan, *Objectivity: Recovering Determinate Reality in Philosophy, Science, and Everyday Life* (London: Ashgate, 2004). See also Machan, *Individuals and Their Rights* (Chicago, IL: Open Court Publishing Co., Inc., 1989).

3 A free society is defended by thinkers with widely different orientations but all are united in supporting a legal order that stresses individual sovereignty, personal self-rule and social voluntarism. In the present instance the defense comes from a neo-Aristotelian philosophical position. For more, see Machan, *Classical Individualism* (London: Routledge, 1998).

4 For more on this, see Tibor R. Machan, 'Rand and Choice,' *The Journal of Ayn Rand Studies*, Vol. 7, No 2 (Spring 2006).

5 Karl Popper, *Unending Quest* (Glasgow: Fontana/Collins, 1974), p. 194.

6 Ayn Rand, *The Virtue of Selfishness: A New Concept of Egoism* (New York: Signet Books, 1964), pp. 15–16. Here Rand argues for a form of egoism best characterized as eudaemonist, wherein we ought to choose to do what will enhance our own good as individual rational animals. See also David L. Norton, *Personal Destinies: A Philosophy of Ethical Individualism* (Princeton, NJ: Princeton University Press, 1976).

7 For an analysis of how much of recent philosophy undermines these ideas, by virtue of innumerable false twists and turns that would take volumes to straighten out, see Stephen R. C. Hicks, *Explaining Postmodernism* (Tempe, AZ: Scholargy Publishing, 2004).

8 For a detailed examination of the issue of free will and defense of agency causation, its ontological underpinnings, see Tibor R. Machan, *Initiative – Human Agency and Society* (Stanford, CA: Hoover Institution Press, 2000), and Edward Pols, *The Acts of Our Being: A Reflection on Agency and Responsibility* (Amherst: University of Massachusetts Press, 1982).

9 James Buchanan, *The Limits of Liberty* (Indianapolis, IN: Liberty Press, 1985). See http://www.econlib.org/library/Buchanan/buchCv7c2.html. (7.2.6)

10 Although often deemed a social science, economics is in fact a practical science, more akin to engineering than to astronomy, given that it lays out the principles by which prosperity is best achieved in a social context. See, Tibor R. Machan, *Capitalism and Individualism: Reframing the Argument for the Free Society* (New York: St. Martin's Press, 1990). See also Amartya Sen, *Rationality and Freedom* (Cambridge, MA: Belkap Press, 2002).

11 Douglas J. Den Uyl and Douglas B. Rasmussen, *Liberty and Nature: An Aristotelian Defense of Liberal Order* (LaSalle, IL: Open Court, 1991).

12 Clubs, corporations, teams and other voluntary groups in a free and just society gain their sovereignty as legally recognized organizations from the sovereign choices of members. For the application of this idea to business corporations, see Robert Hessen, *In Defense of the Corporation* (Stanford, CA: Hoover Institution Press, 1979).

13 Tibor R. Machan, 'Why Agreement is not Enough,' *Philosophia*, Vol. 28, Nos 1–2 (2000).

14 What this means is debatable, but the wording Locke uses suggests that whether one makes use of one's reasoning capacity is in one's own power. Elsewhere in his writings Locke discusses free will extensively, although it is not clear that he is able to reconcile its existence with his own scientism.

15 There are libertarians who claim to be anarchists and to reject government as a morally acceptable institution. But they substitute something that is only nominally different, namely, defense or justice-insurance agencies. For a full discussion, see Tibor R. Machan, 'Anarchism and Minarchism, A Rapprochement,' *Journal des Economists et des Estudes Humaines,* Vol. 14, No 4 (December 2002), pp. 569–88. For more, see Roderick Long and Tibor R. Machan, eds, *Anarchism/Minarchism* (Burlington, VT: Ashgate, forthcoming).

16 I develop this further in Machan, *Putting Humans First* (Lanham, MD: Rowman & Littlefield, 2004).

17 For a general discussion, see Tibor R. Machan, 'Justice and the Welfare State,' in T. R. Machan, ed., *The Libertarian Alternative* (Chicago, IL: Nelson-Hall, 1974).

18 Aristotle, *Politics,* 1262a 30–37 in Werner Jaeger, *Aristotle* (Oxford: Oxford University Press, 1934), p. 152.

19 Thucydides, *The History of the Peloponnesian War*, bk I, sec. 141, trans. Rex Warner (London: Penguin Books, 1954), p. 120.

20 Garrett Hardin, 'The Tragedy of the Commons,' *Science*, Vol. 162 (December 13, 1968), pp. 1243–8.

21 The fact that we aren't always full moral agents – for example, infants, invalids, and all of us while asleep – does not call into question the general truth about us being such. Definitions are always 'for the most part,' as Aristotle noted, and one function of adjectives is to alert us to borderline cases, exceptions and such which are, nonetheless, properly classified under them. For more on this, see, Machan, *Individuals and Their Rights* and *Putting Humans First.*

22 James Sadowsky, 'Private Property Rights and Collective Ownership' in T. R. Machan, ed., *The Libertarian Alternative* (Chicago, IL: Nelson-Hall Co., Inc., 1971), pp. 119–33.

23 See, for example, F. A. Hayek, *Law, Legislation, and Liberty: A New Statement of the Liberal Principles of Justice and Political Economy* (London, UK: Routledge and Kegan Paul, 1982).

24 For over a century Marxists and others have claimed that scientific economics, so called, is in fact a kind of ideology, a not very well disguised means for the promotion of certain arbitrary class interests which are by no means universally valid. Neo-classical economists have fought against this vigorously – consider Milton Friedman's book *Essays in Positive Economics* (Chicago, IL: University of Chicago Press, 1953), wherein he states and proceeds to argue that 'Positive economics is in principle independent of any particular ethical position or normative judgment' (p. 4) – but in vain, for the reasons advanced herein.

Friedman and others seem to me to shy away from any normative component in economics because they embrace the notion – made prominent by David Hume in the eighteenth century but then reinforced by twentieth-century logical positivists like A. J. Ayer (*via* his very popular *Language, Truth, and Logic* [New York: Dover, 1936]) – that judgments as to what is good or bad, right and wrong are simply incapable of being shown true or false. This view itself rested on the widely championed epistemology of empiricism, in terms of which only facts that could be apprehended via the senses had credible status.

The Marxist charge, of course, is telling only against those who reject the factual nature of normative judgments. Since positivist economics necessarily embodies certain values – for example, that of prosperity and, *via* the exchange system, private property rights – denying this will appear to be disingenuous.

If, however, value judgments can be shown to be true, then whatever is infused with them, including economics, could well be given (or denied) objective support instead of simply resting on arbitrary human interest. Moreover, economics could well be the instrumental science or technology of human prosperity, just as medicine is the instrumental science or technology of health, which is a human value. Prosperity, as health, could, in turn, be shown to be an entirely justified objective for us to pursue, perhaps even as a priority when compared to other alternatives such as order, acculturation, health, environmental fitness (especially if the latter presuppose it for their flourishing).

Chapter 6

Finding the Rational Man

> Reason is not a simple tool for simplifying, nor is rational thought an intellectual monoculture. And this … is not a tragedy. The world does not relapse into helpless confusion just because things have more than one aspect and can be correctly described in more than one way. On the contrary, overlapping pictures taken from different angles provide the right way to get a reasonably unified notion of an object … .
>
> Mary Midgley, *The Ethical Primate* (1994)

> The first and the most direct use of rationality, it can be argued, must be normative: we want to think and act wisely and judiciously, rather than stupidly or impulsively. If the understanding of rationality is firmly tied to the systematic use of reason, the normative use of rationality is easily placed at the center of the stage.
>
> Amartya Sen, *Rationality and Freedom* (2002)

How has the concept of rationality been used, and abused, by many economists?

What the economists have done in the name of reason has left us with the very widespread and well-entrenched idea that reason is useful only for purposes of determining the most effective means to achieve various ends. As far as ends or goals are concerned – what are the good or right things to do – these should supposedly be relegated to such *non-rational* elements of our nature as desires, whims, instincts, drives, preferences, and cultural pressure. By conjoining these two beliefs – instrumental rationality and value-subjectivism – we get the curious and paradoxical result that all persons act rationally, all the time; it also follows that no one ever does anything wrong.

Professor Gary Becker, University of Chicago Professor of Economics and Sociology, won the 1992 Nobel Prize in economics for 'having extended the domain of economic theory to aspects of human behavior which had previously been dealt with – if at all – by other social science disciplines such as sociology, demography and criminology.' Becker is one of the earliest and perhaps most prolific among those economists who believe that what motivates human beings in the marketplace, namely, utility – that is, the desire to make a good (economic) deal – is exactly what motivates them everywhere else – when they make love, play with their children, go to church, or develop theories of social science. He is the most unabashedly imperialistic of the neoclassical school of economic analysis in whose view human rationality consists of acting effectively to satisfy one's desires or fulfill one's preferences. Only Gordon Tullock, of the George Mason University, co-author with James Buchanan of the classic *The Calculus of Consent*,[1] comes close. (A book edited by Gerard Radnitzky and Peter Bernholz, *Economic Imperialism, The Economic Method Applied Outside the Field of Economics*,[2] collects the writings of many supporters of this way of thinking.)

In recent years the Nobel committee has rewarded a good deal of the work resting on the economic approach championed by Professor Becker. In 1986 they gave the prize to Professor James Buchanan, who was credited for his pioneering work in applying economic (or 'public choice') theory to an understanding of the political process. Public choice theory holds, in essence, that we can best understand the conduct of politicians and bureaucrats if we regard their behavior as utility-maximizing. As Buchanan characterized the approach, 'Politicians and bureaucrats are seen as ordinary persons, and 'politics' is viewed as a set of arrangements, a game if you will, in which many players with quite disparate objectives interact so as to generate a set of outcomes that may not be either internally consistent or efficient.'[3] In some details Buchanan's views differ from those of the Chicago School, although it is not possible to briefly distinguish their views of the nature of rationality. (The crux of the difference is that Buchanan seems to locate individual rational action, following Hobbes, at the point of the inception of political society, not at each point of human decision making.)

A few years ago it was the late George Stigler who received the award for his similarly oriented work in studying government regulation. And earlier, in 1976, Milton Friedman, the head of 'the Chicago School,' was rewarded for his work along more general lines that many credit for laying some of the foundations for subsequent economic imperialism. All these scholars not only endorse a version of economic imperialism but are also champions of a largely *laissez-faire* economic order, one that is firmly linked with libertarianism. Their ideas, if found problematic, naturally call into question in the minds of most critics the libertarian policy itself.

Some of the most prominent participants in the discussion appear to understand by the concept of 'rational' nothing more than 'logically consistent.' For example, Amartya Sen, in explaining how the economists see it, tells us: 'Rationality, as a concept, would seem to belong to the relationship between choices and preferences, and a typical question will take the form: "Given your preference, was it rational for you to choose the actions you have chosen?"'[4] So, the term 'rational' is taken by most of these economists to describe the behavior in which one pursues a given objective in the most efficient way – that is, in the shortest possible time, with the least amount of disagreeableness involved.[5]

This is not the only way economists construe or misconstrue rationality. They make another claim that is difficult if not impossible to defend. For example, Ludwig von Mises, former leader of the Austrian school of economics, claimed that, 'Human action is necessarily always rational … .'[6]

As Richard McKenzie explains, 'Austrian "rationality" can be captured in the very general notion that people either know, or will learn within tolerable limits, what is best for them and will seek to improve their position in life, with no mention of what it is that is pursued.'[7]

Stigler apparently also thought that the economic way of understanding human behavior – to wit, that everyone acts rationally or maximizes utilities, all the time – is accurate: 'Man is eternally a utility-maximizer – in his home, in his office (be it public or private), in his church, in his scientific work – in short, everywhere.'[8] Gary Becker put it somewhat less directly when he said: 'The combined assumptions of maximizing behavior, market equilibrium, and stable preferences, *used relentlessly and unflinchingly*, form the heart of the economic approach as I see it.'[9] And in his 1975 Nobel acceptance speech, Milton Friedman put it as follows: 'Every individual serves his own private interest … . The great Saints of history have served their "private interest" just as the most money-grubbing miser has served his interest. The *private interest* is whatever it is that drives an individual.'[10] We are all doing what we do to achieve the subjective values that we hold: the great Saints are acting as they do to attain eternal salvation, the money-grubbing misers to achieve wealth. Which is pretty close to saying that we are all acting rationally (provided we do not slough off in our pursuits – although if our values were to change, that, too, might be the rational thing to do).

Is there a connection between the two positions on rationality? If one holds that (a) rationality is entirely instrumental, and holds, too, that (b) the ends of action are entirely subjective (that is, incapable of being evaluated objectively and designated as either rational or irrational), then everyone who pursues any goal at all is necessarily 'rational.' This is because anyone whose actions might be judged irrational could claim, plausibly, that his goals are such that the way he is acting constitutes the rational pursuit of those goals.

We have already seen that many economists see rationality in purely instrumental terms – they believe that only *means in the pursuit of ends* can be judged as rational (except insofar as we judge some person who uses such means in such terms). But do economists also think that the merits of goals or ends of action are subjective? Certainly the Austrian school has many prominent adherents who do.

Ludwig von Mises claimed, for example, that 'When applied to the ultimate ends of action, the terms rational and irrational are inappropriate and meaningless. The ultimate end of action is always the satisfaction of some desires of the acting man … . No man is qualified to declare what would make another man happier or less discontented.'[11] Don Ballente characterized the Austrian approach as being 'most distinct from mainstream economics in its thorough emphasis on the individual decision maker as the focus of scientific analysis. Yet with the values and motives of individuals being entirely subjective it is impossible for an analyst to pass judgment on the optimality of the individual's chosen actions.'[12]

Neoclassical economists also tend to embrace value-subjectivism. As Richard McKenzie explains, for these economists, 'No agreement is presumed with reference to subjective evaluations of "goods" because there is no basis for establishing what constitutes agreement. (What is "satisfaction derived from apples"?)'[13] And Milton Friedman himself suggests this subjectivist take on values when he states that

> The liberal conceives of men as imperfect beings. He regards the problem of social organization to be as much a negative problem of preventing 'bad' people from doing harm as of enabling 'good' people to do good; and, of course, 'bad' and 'good' people may be the same people, depending on who is judging them.[14]

I wish to argue, then, as follows: if the subjectivity of values – that is, of ends sought or goals pursued – is embraced by both the Chicago and the Austrian schools – the two schools most supportive of the free market and thus of the libertarian political economy – and both also view rationality as purely instrumental, it would follow that both must regard all human action as 'rational' or utility-maximizing, exactly as von Mises and Stigler state. Why? Because there is no way to deny that an action is rational if goals can always be imputed, so as to render the means currently being undertaken as intelligible and efficient with respect to achieving the implicit goal.

Say that I set out to get to New York City. Am I being rational in how I do this? That is, do I employ the most economic means within the shortest time? I do as follows: I drive my car and I take numerous detours, stop frequently, backtrack now and then, linger and bide my time. A friend notices this and claims that I am being somewhat irrational, as my means are inefficient with respect to my end. But I respond: I want to get to New York City just this way, slowly, biding my time, backtracking. So I am, in fact, being perfectly rational – I am doing what I want to do, what I prefer. If there is no way to assess whether getting to New York City rapidly is for me itself a rationally superior goal to, say, getting there slowly, then *any way of getting there will be rational*, even if I crawl there, and even if my purpose in getting to New York is to say goodbye to someone on his deathbed who could die at any moment. Clearly this cannot be right. In point of fact, however, what constitutes instrumental rationality actually cannot be determined without the prior determination of the comparative superior rationality of the objective being sought.

Economic imperialists believe that they are telling us something quite simple and true, namely, per Buchanan, that all persons in society 'are seen as ordinary persons.' And, as they understand it, ordinary persons are driven to advance their own lot – understood as whatever they prefer – on every front. Everyone is, to put it even more plainly, selfish. Greed is no sin but a fact of life, a natural drive. For the economists, however, such terms are misleading, since when pressed they will insist that they 'do not assume that people in all parts of their lives are motivated by selfish considerations, but also by "honesty," "justice," "love," and "friendship".' And, as Geoffrey Brennan and James Buchanan elaborate the point, 'the *homo economicus* model in no sense rules out the possibility that each individual may be motivated by certain ethical or moral concerns, as long as we can take it that such ethical conduct on the part of anyone cannot be presumed to benefit everyone else.'[15] It does rule out, however, that anyone's motives could be open to criticism, might be wrong. As Becker himself made clear, 'the heart of the economic approach [is] to include hatred, love, obligation, etc.'[16]

Implied in this position is an assumption that rational moral *choice* or *initiative* is absent from human life, as it is from the lives of dogs or giraffes. Everything is set. (Stigler once argued just this, holding that the world is exactly as it has to be – nothing is wrong or right with it, it merely is.[17]) Furthermore, when reference is made to ethics or morality, what is meant is some form of conduct that benefits other persons than the agent. Thus the economist tends to accept the neo-Kantian characterization of morality, to wit, that no action is morally significant – praiseworthy – if it achieves a purpose of the acting agent. They do not take ethics to be a framework of principles whereby one initiates conduct for good or ill that can be identified objectively as such, independently of the current feelings, desires, preferences of the agent who is acting. Ethics or morality for these economists means, instead, doing whatever benefits other persons, period; that is, altruism. But since such altruistic conduct is incomprehensible from the motivational (scientistic) viewpoint, morality does not really make sense as anything but the private, albeit perhaps unconventional, interests that some people happen to have (for example, the great Saints).

While these thinkers support free markets – on grounds, I believe, of their common sense realization that it has been the most productive in human history – it is crucial to realize that their support is not decisive and not what the free market requires, even strategically, in our time. Scientism might have been in great fashion at some times in the past but not so now, given all the understandable concern for guiding visions and values.[18] It is, thus, insufficient to argue for a political economic system by assuming – and that is all these economists do – that human beings are utility maximizers (even when they benefit others) and that the system of free production and exchange is most hospitable to how they must behave. That is because many criticisms of the free market rest on a far more detailed and complex conception of human behavior, one that includes reference to the basic capacity of human beings to initiate and make choices about what they will do. Furthermore, these criticisms assume that some standard of proper conduct is identifiable and should be followed, regardless of who is thus benefited.[19]

Despite their Nobel Prizes, the reputation of the free market as a just system has not gained a great deal from economic championing of this system from a 'scientific' point of view. What lukewarm popular support there is now for capitalism in mainstream intellectual circles – for example, by Jeffrey Sacks at Columbia and Janos Kornai at Harvard University – comes from the collapse of socialism in Eastern Europe and elsewhere, and even that level of support is waning by now. The economic advocates of free trade and the unregulated marketplace have had something to do with that collapse, of course, but they have also prompted a pretty strong backlash from critics – for example, George Soros, Paul Krugman, Joseph Stiglitz, and others – especially so far as extending the principles of the free, capitalist market throughout the globe (à la globalization) is concerned.

Of course, one problem about this attempt to support globalization is that there is something of a ruse afoot when it occurs. Suppose someone defined the game of golf in terms of riding in carts, wearing funny pants and large shirts, and occasionally using the various clubs to beat one's dog. Would this be fair? Chances are, someone who gave such a definition of the game would probably be on a campaign to disparage it, not to explain its true nature. So consider how the critics of globalization – legion after September 11 – deal with that far more important contemporary phenomenon – which, by the way, isn't all that contemporary (since in certain periods of the modern era globalization was in full advance).

These critics point to the fact that globalization is sometimes related to child labor; it can involve various strains of insidious nationalism, such as trying to whip a country's economy into shape by coercion; and it can involve some regional collusion (as with the European Union). Indeed, when so characterized – or, should we say, caricatured-globalization looks like a positive evil, instead of a promising method to promote economic prosperity and political liberty fostered by sensible political economists (beginning with, among others, Adam Smith himself).

Why would some folks hate globalization as it is properly understood and conceived? Why would they be so eager to distort its nature and paint it in a bad light? We could ask the same thing about those who would distort the nature of golf or marriage or education. Enemies of golf might think that too much money is spent on the sport, at the expense of their own favorite pastime. Enemies of marriage might wish to discredit it because they have failed at it royally and now wish to make some other kind of union respectable. Critics of education might want to have others believe that all there is to it is indoctrination in dogmas that the old want the young to accept uncritically because, well, they don't much like to learn and find intellectual effort unpleasant. So what might be some reasons for disliking globalization so that it is then mischaracterized to make it seem a menace to be destroyed?

For one, the removal of international trade barriers, the central theme of globalization, unleashes competition, which is the nemesis of entrenched industries and labor groups. It is like the American 'dream team' that was sent to the Barcelona Olympics: unbeatable for a time, but eventually other countries started to catch up, and the dream team could not continue to win without doing hard work to stay on top.

Industry, including labor, often would like nothing better than to achieve prominence in the market and then stay there effortlessly. There is much of this everywhere – including academic life, where many people wish to coast without keeping up, without doing anything past the point where they get tenure. When young Turks turn up, as it were, and challenge the old guard, this is not often received with welcome. In principle, academics are supposed to keep going and invite challenge and criticism from their colleagues, but there is corruption, as elsewhere, and it often issues in barriers to entry or refusing tenure to a challenging young teacher or scholar and so on.

This is one of several reasons why globalization is resisted – the motive is known as protecting one's vested interest, and members of many industries evidence it aplenty. Another one is the widespread belief that if markets are opened up and international commerce encouraged, this will eliminate or diminish national and cultural distinctiveness. There is something to this, though not much.[20] It does not take genius to see that the marketplace unites people on some levels but by no means on all; one can tell this from going to any mall and seeing the enormous diversity of shoppers and merchants. The majority accept the common medium of exchange and the ethics of commerce that should guide everyone, without any threat whatsoever to personal, cultural, or religious identity, nor, again, to our ubiquitous basic humanity. (Recall the remark from Steve Martin's novella, with which this book beings.)

Of course, there are some groups the practices of which conflict with the principles of free trade. If your tribe likes to enslave people, this will certainly be threatened by globalization, since slaves experience the harshest barriers to free trade of all. If the dominant male citizens in some countries treat women badly and wish to bar them from economic power, this, too, is going to be threatened by freedom of trade.

Perhaps one of the main sources of the objection to globalization is the widespread belief that living a good life is itself something of an affront! People should suffer here on earth, not enjoy their lives, and globalization promises many folks just the opposite – namely, prosperous living.

Under the guise of globalization, of course, some dirty practices are also possible, and some mistake this for the consequences of a real thing. For example, taking your firm abroad because there in the host country you can dump your soot into the atmosphere with impunity may appear to be consistent with freedom of trade, but it isn't. This should be a crime, because people are being assaulted, and freedom of trade cannot tolerate assault among trading partners. Globalization, in fact, should encourage the enactment of laws that protect life and property from assault, including pollution.

In fact, however, outside the discipline of economics, most academicians are hostile to capitalism, not simply globalization. They treat the greed that economists praise with disdain – one need only recall the 'hero' of Oliver Stone's movie, *Wall Street*, who espoused the doctrine that 'greed is good' and was roundly seen as a villain for this. One need only consider how the popular press has embraced the largely phony claim that the 1980s, guided by the free-market rhetoric of Ronald Reagan – who many of these economic imperialists advised – was a 'decade of greed.' Intellectual trends don't necessarily comport with every manifestation of popular culture, but anti-capitalist sentiment in academia is certainly simpatico with that of such movies and press reports.

It is my thesis that it is wrong to extend the approach economists take to understanding human behavior to every area of human life.[21] People do not simply calculate costs and benefits in terms of a certain set of preferences or goals. Indeed, they probably ought to do so more regularly than they actually do. I also argue that a rational approach to ethics would give support to such a recommendation – but not to the view that we already and necessarily engage in such cost–benefit analysis everywhere in our lives. We would all be better off if people did practice prudence more consistently as they embark upon their economic tasks. But they do not do so automatically. As the late Allan Bloom put it in his essay 'Commerce and "Culture,"' 'It is not true, as the moderns appear on the surface to say, that men in civil society are always motivated by utility, by self-interest … .'[22] As Stephen Breyer put it, in his review of Thomas Philipson's and Richard Posner's *Private Choices and Public Health*,[23] a book critical from an economic approach of government spending on AIDS research: 'Economics can wisely inform our efforts to attain our goals; but ultimately, if we prefer John Donne to Adam Smith, economists cannot prove us wrong.'[24]

Should we prefer reading literature to reading economics, if we cannot do both at the same time? The economists cannot help us with such choices, namely, those that we are most troubled by – what ends we should pursue. All we can get is some measure of wisdom about how to pursue the ends we already have. And, to add to the difficulty, there really is no 'we' here – no consensus – about those ends.

Now if the case for establishing and protecting the right to individual liberty, including in the marketplace, depends on such economic analysis, then so much the worse for freedom. Economics can, at most, suggest why free markets are useful for purposes of enabling people to strive for prosperity or well-being. But it cannot demonstrate that prosperity is something we ought to foster and place ahead of, say, equality, order, or revolutionary progress.

But can anything prove that we are right or wrong about our preferences?[25] Economic analysis can *contribute* to such a quest, by showing us the limits of the possible. Economics can confirm you can't get blood out of a turnip, as it were. It can tell us not to strangle geese that lay golden eggs. And this is the beginning of the story of the virtue of prudence.

One reason the market approach to understanding human conduct does make sense up to a point is that *within markets* – that is to say, when they go to market, when they enter into commercial relations – people do tend to focus on making a good deal with respect to previously determined desires and preferences. They do not deliberate about whether to get affordable – within-their-budget – food once they are *in* the grocery store but only *before* they go there; nor whether to hire a stockbroker after they have begun investigating who might be the best for them to hire; nor whether to take a plane trip after they have called their travel agent. Such decisions are made outside of the market and explain why markets are entered in the first place. Of course, even outside the marketplace, we have economic concerns. It is prudent to pay heed to our economic well-being even while embarking on such non-economic matters as going to church or getting married to one's beloved.

Once a person has chosen to obtain some good or service through the market process, he or she is likely to realize that there are probably several options available and search out the one that will secure the desired good or service at the lowest possible cost and effort. Such instrumental rationality is clearly important and without it there would be a great deal of waste in human life. Adjusting one's available means to the goals one wants to attain is indeed rational. But to understand why, we require more than what the economist gives us: namely, the view that human beings are automatically rational. For this view simply does not make sense of even the widespread *economic* irrationality we witness in the world, not, at least, without reducing the economic approach to vacuity.

Because rationality in economics is so often treated as purely instrumental, when human decision making includes considerations that seem unrelated to economics, many prominent economists argue that a proper scientific approach to those matters means bringing them within the rubric of economics. As Becker makes clear, economists do attempt to account for seemingly varied human motivation – for example, honesty, justice, love, friendship, and so on. But these accounts state that some people just have a preference for these such that when they abandon the quest for efficiency in some economic endeavor – for example, by giving up a good job in favor of letting a less-experienced good friend get it – they do this only because their skein of given preferences makes this necessary. Or if someone refuses to treat an employee unjustly in the course of seeking some economic objective, it is only because within his or her preference scale, treating employees justly occupies a prominent position. In the end, then, all decisions are economic decisions, after all; per Friedman, 'every individual serves his own private interest.' The data of these private interests are just brute givens that cannot be analyzed except insofar as they exist and are ranked with respect to other preferences.

This kind of reasoning was explored by Wittgenstein some decades ago. Bouwsma gives the following account of it:

> The hedonist says: 'Men desire nothing but pleasure.' … Obviously this is no empirical proposition. The hedonist does not find this out by going about asking people what they want. He has no statistics about this. And yet he knows very well that people want all sorts of things. So it isn't at all like: Everybody wants a motorcar. If someone wants a motorcar, then he wants pleasure, and if he wants to smoke or to write a letter, then he wants pleasure. Pleasure is another word for whatever anyone wants. In other words it's a tautology. Everyone prefers the preferable. So pleasure is the desirable, the preferable.

> But there is, of course, the illusion of having discovered something. How does that happen? Perhaps in some such way as this. Freud asked – in his own language: What is the essence of the dream? Then he inspected and noticed that a certain dream was a wish fulfillment dream. And another, and another. This was it. A man is hungry and dreams of feasting, is thirsty and he dreams of passing water. Some dreams are like this. This comes like a flash, a great light – an *aperçu* … . Concerning pleasure there is no doubt. Pleasure is desired and there is no question of 'Why?' or 'For what?' about it. When it is desired, the case is clear. And now the temptation is to say that when you desire an automobile, what you desire is automobile-pleasure, eating-pleasure, writing-pleasure, etc. The generalization, which was mistaken at the outset, compels this manner of speaking…. Pleasures are not all of the same kind. There are higher and lower. This is the mistake of the generalization breaking out into curious distinctions, or it proceeds to develop the absurdities of the calculus. We desire nothing but pleasure, but there are qualities of pleasure. Poetry-pleasure is better than pushpin pleasure.'[26]

To the charge of vacuousness Becker responds that the conclusions of the economic analysis 'would not be attacked so much if they were in fact vacuous.'[27] A better explanation than Becker's is that since such vacuity is put in service of capitalism, as well as some rather disturbing notions (for example, that crime or suicide or divorce is always 'rational'), and since the prominent economists offer no other support for this 'odious system,' most people find the approach not only fruitless but objectionable. They object not so much to a vacuous thesis as to the supposed dirty work done by it.

The economist's use of the concept of 'self-interest' is vacuous, yes, but the common-sense meaning of the term tends to be 'ruthless, callous, unthinking pursuit of one's own advantages in life.' Since this idea clashes with the most widely supported ethics, altruism, a system that treats self-interest in any version as respectable will be 'attacked so much' for that reason. It is not the alleged substance of what in fact is a vacuous notion but the ordinary suspicion of 'self-interest' that generates the criticism.

Becker does not appear to appreciate just how serious the opposition to capitalism is, regardless of how it is supported. But because the critic can plausibly argue that the economist is embarking on scientism and economic imperialism at the expense of common sense, he can more easily dismiss not only the economist's method but also his preference for the free market. Preferences are just givens, after all; they're data. And even if the critic of capitalism may be knocking down a straw man, the 'value-free' economist is supplying a lot of the straw.

Sen notes that in the economic or instrumental conception of rationality, paradoxes arise 'in a situation where the outcome depends on other people's actions in addition to one's own.' More important for our purposes, he also notes that morality 'would seem to require a judgment among preferences whereas rationality would not.'[28] This suggests that if the view of rationality embraced by the economist is left intact, there will be a gap between morality and rationality. Must we accept this? The puzzle arises because in the case of human beings the fundamental and distinctive capacity of using reason to flourish in life has been identified as central to the moral life. Plato, Aristotle, Spinoza, Kant, and others have, in their various ways, argued that to be moral, to live ethically, is to make conscientious use of one's reasoning capacity. If the economist's view is right, it would seem that being rational not only has little to do with but can often conflict with being ethical.

In and out of the marketplace, virtues other than prudence – in the narrow sense of looking out for one's economic well-being – may be equally important to practice or even take precedence. Courage, honesty, justice, generosity, and so forth at times outweigh prudence (in the sense of the choice to prosper). By denying our freedom to make a rational choice as to which of the numerous virtues we need to practice, economic imperialism is not only false to the facts but also demeans us. It suggests that we are *unable* to pay attention to anything other than the satisfaction of certain built-in or given desires or preferences. This creates the illusion that we carry on only as we must, *driven* by our preferences, regardless of the situation or what is at stake. No wonder, then, that some economists have argued that it's economic analysis which can make the best sense of the behavior of laboratory mice![29]

No doubt, nearly all aspects of human living involve economic considerations – some thought of cost and benefit as determined in the marketplace. But there are values one cannot reduce to such factors – friendship, love, truth, beauty, and, indeed, goodness. There is, then, the economic aspect of, say, the purchase of a Rembrandt. But the experience and understanding of the beauty of the work cannot be reduced to this. The same painting could be worth $5 at a garage sale (sponsored by some poor guy who doesn't realize what he found in his attic) and $5 million in an auction by Sotheby's. But if the same person were the buyer in both transactions, his aesthetic appreciation and eagerness to have the painting could be identical.

The Beckerian approach manages to subsume so much of human activity precisely because it is so open – indeed, vacuous. Every decision a person makes has to do with cost and benefit. But what will count as such for that person is purely subjective and could, in fact, change from moment to moment. Thus if a criminal prefers to steal Volkswagens instead of Rolls Royces, that is explained by reference to that criminal's preferences. But if another makes the opposite choice, that too is so explained – both wanting to maximize their values, satisfy their preferences. But this is not of much help in understanding thieves and how their kind of life comports with how human beings ought to live.

In the extreme case, if an economist can't 'reconstruct' the consideration at all in economic terms as he understands economics, he may go so far as to claim it does not exist. At the Hoover Institution, where I was a fellow in the mid-1970s, Aaron Director, a very prominent economist at the University of Chicago, argued that the concept 'true' has no meaning in economics; only 'useful' does. Truth seemed to be a pretty large concern to set aside as irrelevant or unintelligible. But whether that claim is itself true was not a polite question to ask, as I found out.

Despite the welcome support of free-trade measures in most commercial realms that the economist's thinking has generated among these famous economists, to defend and revitalize individual freedom requires more. A proper approach would concede that while economics can shed light on many aspects of human living, other disciplines must also be enlisted, lest we suffer an incomplete and thus misleading understanding of ourselves.[30]

What is rationality? Lest we fail at the outset in our exploration of the difference between the economic and ethical ideas of rationality, we need to defend, briefly, a way of going about answering the question.

All beginnings seem to pose the problem of needing support beyond their own framework or assumptions. But, as Aristotle and some others have argued, some starting points are indeed axiomatic or primary – one cannot dig any deeper and their truth is both inescapable and a support for other truths. Some matters, like the law of identity, really cannot be questioned or doubted with any hope of being understood, despite what some current schools of philosophy – for example, Richard Rorty's form of radical pragmatism – suggest.[31]

Why do we think that such ineluctable grounds of inquiry might be found? Because, to start with, we are here asking these questions and doing so by relying on (or suspecting that we do already rely on) some such grounds in many of our activities. Our mutual presence at the inquiry, our mutual interest in the problem at hand, our mutual ability to focus on the issue at hand, all affirm that our search is mutually grounded over time (indeed over several generations, considering the history of this inquiry). Denying this would make the search we are conducting unintelligible. Without some common ground, those of us who inquire about these matters would not be able to embark upon it at all. As Rand argues:

> A man's protestations of loyalty to reason are meaningless as such: 'reason' is not an axiomatic, but a complex, derivative concept – and, particularly since Kant, the philosophical technique of concept stealing, of attempting to negate reason by means of reason, has become a general bromide, a gimmick worn transparently thin. Do you want to assess the rationality of a person, a theory or a philosophical system? Do not inquire about his or its stand on the validity of reason. Look for the stand on axiomatic concepts. It will tell the whole story.[32]

There is indeed an axiomatic common ground that underlies what we do, inasmuch as even to deny that we are discussing the issue in mutually intelligible terms would be to affirm that such terms are indeed at work in the discussion. Once these grounds are uncovered, confusion and conflict in usage are more likely to cease, or at least be clarified and ameliorated. Of course no one is justified in expecting final guarantees, as we can go astray in innumerable ways often not anticipated.

'Rational' is a term with diverse and sometimes incompatible usage in both common and philosophical discourse. The term is used to characterize what we say and do, but, given the different meanings people attach to it, people will disagree about whether a given course of conduct is rational. Some tend to mean by 'rational' that, for example, one is 'in possession of his or her (uniquely human) conscious faculties.' Actions that are rational are then supposed to involve competent, unimpeded, undiluted use of these faculties. In this rendition of 'rational,' both means and ends of action can be subject to evaluation as either rational or irrational. As Sen put it,

> The first and the most direct use of rationality, it can be argued, must be normative: we want to think and act wisely and judiciously, rather than stupidly or impulsively. If the understanding of rationality is firmly tied to the systematic use of reason, the normative use of rationality is easily placed at the center of the stage.[33]

(Some matters, of course, would not be subject to such evaluation, namely, anything not capable of being placed under one's conscious control.)

Others employ the word 'rational' to characterize some action that leads efficiently to satisfactory results, to just what was desired. This, as we have seen, is often designated as the 'instrumental' conception of rationality – what counts as rendering some behavior rational is that the most effective (even technically up-to-date) means are employed to get from some starting point to some desired objective. The meaning here is the one that I have associated with the economists and that we saw endorsed by von Mises and attributed to most economists by Sen. It is to act consistently, being (formally) logical, internally consistent in one's course of conduct.

Others hold that 'rational' means whatever is widely accepted – conventionally agreed to – in the relevant community as the way to proceed. Or it is argued that this is the most one can expect to mean by the term, given the difficulties of defending more robust senses of it. On this view rational conduct or, less strictly, reasonable conduct, is that which conforms to the commonly adhered-to standards. (In the law the 'reasonable man' standard is sometimes taken to mean this.)

In certain contexts the conceptions described above will conflict. To take 'rational' as meaning both 'self-consistent' and 'widely accepted in the relevant community' is perhaps plausible, yet assumes that the relevant community prizes consistency. Charles S. Peirce verged on assuming this when he proposed his conception of truth as that which an *ideal* community's membership would accept. Richard Rorty seems to travel much further into the realm of parochial intersubjectivity when he construes objective knowledge to be no more than what an actual community agrees to. The intersubjectivist sense of 'rational' we find in the early pragmatists also clashes with 'rational' as characterizing 'action flowing from competent use of one's conscious faculties,' since members of the relevant group might not use their faculties competently.

Any inquiry or action presupposes the axiom of existence, that there is a definite something that exists.[34] So we must grant that our inquiry about the nature of rationality rests on the existence of some common framework arising from this axiom. But at this level the standard is extremely broad and will not help with such special areas of inquiry as economics and ethics.[35] What we are after in inquiring whether human goals and institutions are rational is a narrower common standard. That is why the decision theorists' or economists' rendition of 'rational' is of little use here. But could we use the other, intersubjectivist sense just discussed?

A common standard of rationality implies a framework for evaluating judgments and actions in every area of human endeavor, from the sciences to the arts and humanities to everyday personal life. It presupposes a shared capacity to identify the standard as indispensable, binding, and universal with respect to the context of the inquiry at hand. In judgments as such, independently of the specific subject matter (but not of any subject matter), the context would be seeking knowledge or learning what exists or ought to be done, or why. Given the purpose of gaining knowledge, there would be a common standard by which judgments or conclusions can be evaluated (at least concerning a minimum degree of success, so that, for example, willful contradictions are ruled out from the start). 'Rational' would thus mean abiding by such a standard.

Clearly, inquiry into the meaning of 'rational' produces at least two (but maybe more) mutually exclusive answers. Why should we select one over the other? Can we give an answer to this question without encountering vicious circularity?

If a proposed answer to the meaning of being 'rational' implies that it is impossible to make ourselves clear about what exactly the answer is, then the answer should be rejected. At this fundamental level of inquiry, accepting the criterion of internal consistency is necessary, for inquiries as such make no sense without it. Seeking solutions itself presupposes that the standard is fully applicable. Some conceptions of rationality do allow contradictory procedures in the same context to be rational. For example, when 'widespread acceptability in the relevant community' is used as a substitute for 'rational,' too many matters are left ambiguous to enable us to avoid avoidable conflict.

We cannot consistently and reliably make use of either the economic or the conventionalist idea of rationality. Both fail to provide us with any common ground. The economist and the conventionalist can take us closer to settling on common means or methods, but most often what concerns us are goals – for example, in guiding our own lives or in public policies that are being recommended to an entire nation.

We turn to the conception of 'rationality' as 'abiding by common fundamental standards for judging choices or decisions in some specific context.' When someone correctly asserts that '"*X* is right" is the rational evaluation,' he must mean that '"*X* is right" is established by reference to common standards of establishing truth in a given context.' We can already see that within the context of human conduct, one common standard is going to be human nature. We generally want to know what course of action will promote individual human well-being given the nature of the agent.

But we need to consider whether this result begs the question. If one believes that the method for establishing the proper meaning of 'rational' is itself employed because it is considered rational, then one will think the result empty (or, as I like to say when criticizing the economists, 'vacuous'). This is especially relevant in ethics, because human nature includes as a central feature the capacity for rationality. Although the concept of 'rational' here has a different sense from 'rational' as applied to the characterization of specific conduct, the two are not separable. That human beings are by nature rational means that one of their central, defining aspects is their capacity to think conceptually, to form ideas, theories, identify principles, consider long range plans, and so forth. And it is this very capacity that enables us to assess whether some course of conduct is rational, that is, conforms to principles that are based on relevant facts of reality including human nature itself.

We must now consider the concept 'choice;' a central component of rationality and human nature. The strong relationship between rationality and choice has been recognized by many philosophers, beginning with Aristotle (who identified as the central virtue of human life right reason and linked moral virtues to choice quite unambiguously), through Spinoza, Kant, Wittgenstein, Rand and Sen, among others. The relationship is worked out in detail by Boyle et al.[36]

When economists speak of choice, they usually mean a selection that is revealed through actual behavior, that is, the action or behavior of someone who is exposed to an existing range of alternatives from which some or one may be selected. The sense of the term in its strong relationship to rationality, however, concerns *initiating* action – as when we speak of freedom of choice or free will. On the decision theorists' or economists' idea of rationality, so long as a given long- or short-range goal is efficiently achieved, the selection that is made from the available alternative is rational *ipso facto*. On the conception of rationality developed above, however, the choice of a goal or end, too, could be either rational or not.

Given that a choice can involve both selection from among alternatives and the initiation of some (possible) course of conduct, which sense of the term is appropriate for our purpose? Since we are speaking of rational choice, we are concerned with both possible uses, as well as with uses that indicate both aspects of choice within one particular phenomenon. Thus, if someone chooses to learn to play an instrument, he would both initiate some available course of conduct and select from alternative kinds of conduct (for example, learning to play an instrument, learning skiing, taking a vacation).

Only where the possibility of initiating – that is, being the fundamental or first cause of – one's conduct exists can the possibility of non-instrumental rational choice arise.[37] This explains in part why it does not make sense to speak of a dog making a rational choice, although dogs *can and do make many selections*. (The prevalent economic conception of rationality would not rule out considering a dog's selection of one dog food over another a rational choice! Nor the behavior of computers. If internal consistency of behavioral pattern is the proof of rationality, these are the kinds of conclusions that flow.)

Even when a choice is made in the sense that a person makes a selection from among alternatives, initiation is involved. The judgment that forms the plan of action, as it were – or the intention – that culminates in the overt behavior, had to be initiated by the agent. To be sure, such initiative is often nearly automatic. For example, when a concert pianist performs, the behavior is guided by a rather grand plan the details of which are not individually intended. Instead, once the pianist embarks upon the performance, the rest largely follows; his instruction to himself is to call upon reserves of learning. Yet, even here a difference exists between someone who focuses intensely and someone who is merely drifting along. Certainly this would be evident enough when one pianist is drunk while the other is sober. But it is just as true when one pianist is lax in concentration, merely 'phoning in' the performance, while the other concentrates intently. So even when many automatic forms of skill and knowledge are involved in acting to attain a certain goal, focus often needs to be initiated and then sustained by choice.

Human action is inexplicable without a recognition of free will. The exact mechanism of the process cannot be considered here, although I would cite the work of Roger Sperry, who accounts for free will in terms of the human brain's composition as a self-monitoring organ that makes self-governance or self-determination possible.[38] Keeping all this in mind, we can propose as a definition of the concept 'choice': either the initiation of some course of conduct, or the selection from among alternatives, or both. Rational conduct, in turn, would mean initiation of a course of conduct, or selection from alternatives, or both, in accordance with a common standard appropriate to the context, the broadest of which is human life, that is, the human life of the individual agent whose conduct we are assessing. Accordingly, when we speak of rational action in the context of ethics, we are referring to what someone ought to do given the best information he can obtain about human nature and himself and given the alternatives confronting him.

It should be noted that when speaking of invoking principles in ethics, at issue is a process of emergence and reciprocal reinforcement. The most important ethical step for a person comes before any principles could be known to the agent. It comes when the agent initiates and sustains a thinking process that sets into motion an inquiry or search for understanding and knowledge. One must already be thinking to become aware of the truth and relevance of the principles of living (among other things). So the most fundamental principle of living is acted upon not from conviction or belief, but as a matter of one's (rational) will.

Fortunately, a child does not need to articulate why thinking clearly about things is beneficial to attain the benefits of doing so. (One hopes he receives appropriate guidance from adults whose lead he is inclined to follow until he is in a position to think about such principles explicitly.) It is the will to live that is the ignition of the rational process, which, in turn, brings to awareness more of what one requires for living and flourishing, including ethical principles or virtues. One will not become aware and apply these if one fails to think, or thinks only in a haphazard or narrowly focused way. A person, to be ethically good, will require the policy of rational thought to carry himself forward in an integrated fashion.

Whereas in economics the sort of rationality that is usually referred to concerns only select virtues, in particular, the virtue of prudence – whereby one, in essence, does not waste one's life on irrelevancies – this virtue is insufficient to guide someone to living and flourishing. It can, in fact, misguide one if the practice of other virtues is lacking. One can become, for example, a superbly 'rational' profiteer and be guilty of parental malpractice. Rationality in ethics has a far broader scope than rationality in any specific area of human conduct, be it commerce, art, science, politics, parenting, education,and so on. Although there is the likelihood that someone who is narrowly rational will eventually be irrational even within his or her narrow domain, it is at least possible to excel in such a domain, while seriously neglecting others by failing to focus properly when attending to them.

If, however, one has a balanced or integrated character, and sustains a consistent practice of all virtues, then one may well act exactly as the economist assumes we all act when addressing our commercial concerns. Thus, the economist's assumption that we act rationally is probably not far from the truth, especially when we embark on market behavior – both in the sense in which the economist means 'rational' (deploying appropriate means to achieve given ends) as well as in the sense in which 'rational' is best understood by ethics (choosing ends appropriate to the life-as-a-whole of the agent).

Now that the story is told in full, we can see that what the economist actually means (if only implicitly) by 'rational' is that *if we go to market, then we will most likely seek to make a good deal.* It is false, however, to assume that wherever we are, whatever we do, we are seeking good deals, since we may very well have other rational objectives that relegate making a good deal much lower in the totem pole of values than is ordinarily the case when we go to market. If, for example, one is embarking on identifying and acting upon what is true in economics or ethics or politics, that usually would rank as more important than making a good deal in the narrow sense – so that one would not, for example, sell out one's convictions in order to receive a higher salary, betray a friend to get a better job, and so forth. The economist *qua* instrumentalist cannot make judgments about such ends, or even fully explain why the market is conducive to such moral judgment-making.

At the same time, a rational person, one who is ethical through and through, will indeed often act rationally in the sense meant by the economist. An ethical individual does not squander his wealth and does seek to enrich himself to the degree that this is conducive with how he ought to live as a human individual. And this could, often, involve very sensible, conscientious attention to making a good deal in the market.

How would the instrumentalist reply to our concerns and distinctions? Milton Friedman feels obliged to put the words 'good' and 'bad' in quotation marks when it seems he cannot avoid referring to the kind of conduct and assessments that people normally regard as morally good or morally bad. A follower of Friedman might argue that a person who values his or her character has a different preference function from the one who values, say, a higher salary. Is that not all there is to the matter, rather than some kind of objectively demonstrable superiority we are justified in ascribing to the former person over the latter?

Given the way mainstream economics approaches the phenomenon of human behavior, this will be true just because someone does, in fact, act to maintain his or her integrity. Doing so will mean, for the economic imperialist, simply that the agent places personal integrity very high on his or her preference scale. 'Preference scale' means 'just what people select – first, second, third, and so forth – from among available alternatives as the act.'

Yet does this tell us anything? We already see what the person does. What we need to know is why he does what he does. Asking for an explanation means asking for some set of factors that help to understand why this action rather than some other was taken. As we saw from Wittgenstein's remarks, it is an illusion to believe that invoking preference talk supplies what is wanted here. 'Demonstrated preference' will always be demonstrated in every action. Yet one person will refuse to betray a friend in order to climb the corporate ladder because he has integrity and values friendship – even as another person in the same situation exhibits the exact same 'demonstrated preference' only because he fears blowback.

What is our more-informative way of viewing the situation? While it is dangerous to impute objective values to human beings without knowing about whom in particular one is speaking, and sufficient details about that person's situation, some principles apply across the board. This is indeed what ethical theories aim at: namely, to identify *general* virtues or principles of action that ought to guide us as we live our lives.

The rational egoist holds, for example, that in a world governed by the laws of identity and non-contradiction, maintaining an integrated character is of superior value to (nearly) anyone than obtaining a higher salary, if one is obliged to make a choice between these two alternatives. Indeed, it is nearly impossible to consider, without inherent confusion, how it could be better for a person to earn more money if doing so requires the person to sacrifice honesty, courage, self-respect, dedication to justice, or generosity of spirit. These attributes are part and parcel of the guiding system of human action; without them, the higher salary may end up serving hardly any purpose in someone's life. In other words, a disintegrated individual isn't even likely to gain rational advantage from increasing his wealth, because the use of that wealth to his best advantage is itself based on being someone with integrity.[39] Obviously, the manifestations of the contradiction may vary greatly, depending on the scale of the betrayal, whether one repents, how good one is at suppressing inconvenient thoughts about one's own conduct, and so forth. But one cannot scuttle or undermine the most basic moral requirements of leading a good human life without experiencing destructive consequences.[40]

If the pursuit of wealth is to be morally defended, it is exactly this wider, moral view of human rationality which one must accept.[41] When critics of capitalism and free market economics reject the *homo economicus* approach to human behavior, they hope to undermine much more. They believe, I think, that discrediting the narrowly economic approach will discredit a rational egoist approach to life as a whole, including the political principles that make it possible for citizens to exercise freely the virtues of a rational egoist in the company of others. The economist's futile attempt to defend his value-free approach to understanding human behavior plays into the hands of capitalism's and thus libertarianism's critics. Only if one first appreciates the soundness of the broader ethics of rational egoism can the more narrowly focused idea of economic rationality be defended. Because then we can see that even if the free market accommodates irrational conduct in the moral sense (that is, with respect to moral ends), the freedom of that market is nonetheless morally justified because only a *free* market can accommodate freely chosen rational and thus moral conduct in the broader sense.

For the benefit of those who see value in much of neoclassical and Austrian economics – and rightly – let me repeat that from the standpoint of the rational egoist, it is morally appropriate to act prudently in the course of market transactions. I have not been arguing against attending to means but only against attending to means as if ends could not be attended to at all! There is, of course, no guarantee that we will always act prudently and morally. Yet, because ethics is a matter of individual responsibility, even if one embarks on economic activity in an unbalanced, irrational fashion – so that one neglects other personal and social responsibilities or virtues – there is nothing that any third party is authorized to do about this, apart from attempting persuasion, ostracism, boycott and such, unless the irrational actor acts criminally, in violation of individual rights.

Contrary to much that is taught in business ethics courses across the world, attempting to interfere with unethical, irrational market conduct that involves no fraud or theft in fact removes ethics from the realm of economic life. Such 'market failures' are not remediable by means of regulation and interference. So-called remedies are, in fact, nothing less than ways to delete morality from the marketplace. Or more precisely, the kind of setting in which moral choices can be made.

The free society and free market – that is to say, libertarian politics and law – offer no guarantee of ethics and, thus, of rational conduct by its participants. But such a system is most hospitable to rationality, both in economics and in ethics, by imposing what Nozick called 'side constraints,' by means, for example, of the instrument of the law of property. By this means the irrationality that does occur both in economics and in the broader realm of ethics is likely to have the greatest impact on those who perpetrate it and those who freely associate with the perpetrators. At the same time, moral conduct is given the greatest possible encouragement and scope. No other system offers this kind of promise for a largely prosperous and ethical human community.[42]

Notes

1 (Ann Arbor, MI: University of Michigan Press, 1962).
2 (New York: Paragon House, 1987).
3 James Buchanan, 'Why Governments "Got Out of Hand",' *New York Times*, October 26, 1986.
4 Amartya K. Sen, 'Choice, orderings and morality,' in Stephan Korner, *Practical Reason* (New Haven, CT: Yale University Press, 1974), p. 55.
5 One important reason is that economists (*qua* social scientists) tend, in the main, to adhere to scientism and positivism, both schools holding that the only legitimate understanding of human behavior comes from the general view that every event, including human behavior, is caused by some prior event with no choice about the ends in which the behavior results. Those ends are given by tastes and preferences and reason has no role in assessing and guiding them. Reason cannot judge of ends that are for all intents and purposes fixed. Reason can only judge of means. See George J. Stigler and Gary S. Becker, 'De Gustibus Non Est Disputandum,' *American Economic Review*, Vol. 67(2), 1977, pp. 76–90. For a dissenting view of this understanding of human behavior, see Roger W. Sperry, *Science and Moral Priority* (New York: Columbia University Press, 1983) and Edward Pols, *Acts of Our Being* (Amherst, MA: University of Massachusetts Press, 1982) and a host of, for example, neo-Aristotelian philosophers.
6 Ludwig von Mises, *Human Action* (New Haven, CT: Yale University Press, 1952), p. 19.
7 Richard McKenzie, *The Limits of Economic Science* (Boston, MA: Kluwer-Nijhoff Publishing, 1983), p. 8
8 George Stigler, Lecture II, Tanner Lectures, Harvard University, April 1980. Quoted in McKenzie, p. 6.
9 Gary Becker, *The Economic Approach to Human Behavior* (Chicago, IL: University of Chicago Press, 1976), p. 8 (my emphasis.)
10 Milton Friedman, 'The Line We Dare Not Cross,' *Encounter*, November, 1976, p. 11.
11 Mises, *Human Action*.
12 Don Ballente, 'Subjective Value Theory and Government Intervention in the Labor Market,' *Austrian Economics Newsletter*, Spring–Summer 1989, pp. 1–2. As should be obvious, the *mainstream* economics being referred to is not that embraced by the Chicago School, including Friedman, Stigler or Becker, but by contemporary welfare macroeconomists such as Paul Samuelson, James Tobin or John Kenneth Galbraith.
13 McKenzie, p. 44; see also Stigler and Becker's classic paper, 'De Gustibus Non Est Disputandum' ('There is no disputing of tastes'). Some much harsher versions of the kind of fatalism that we find implicit in (but at times made explicit by) some economists' works is available in Edward O. Wilson's *Sociobiology* (Cambridge, MA: Harvard University Press, 1975) and Richard Dawson's *The Selfish Gene* (Oxford, England: Oxford University Press, 1976).
14 Milton Friedman, *Capitalism and Freedom* (Chicago, IL: University of Chicago Press, 1962), p. 12.
15 Geoffrey Brennan and James Buchanan, 'The Normative Purpose of Economic "Science",' *International Review of Law and Economics* (Winter 1981), p. 158.
16 Personal correspondence, March 15, 1993. Invoking selfishness to explain human conduct is very likely the result of the persistent scientism within economics, the need

to provide some causal factors that *explain* what people do. Some economists will go to any length to argue that even the most benevolent acts are, in fact, selfishly motivated. Once I drove through an intersection and when I saw in my rear mirror that several others were trying to make it through, I speeded up and later reflected on whether I did this from selfish motives. No, I was trying to be helpful to others with minimal regard for my own advantage (which, in any case, wasn't in need of attention just then). True, generosity is cultivated in part to foster a decent community for oneself, but on particular occasions this is not the thinking that lies behind acting kindly and considerately. (For more, see Tibor R. Machan, *Generosity; Virtue in Civil Society* [Washington, D.C.: Cato Institute, 1998].)

17 See George J. Stigler, 'Law or Economics?,' *Journal of Law & Economics*, Vol. 35 (2) (1992), pp. 455–68. See also 'Do Economists Matter?' in Stigler, *The Economists As Preacher And Other Essays* (Chicago, IL: University of Chicago Press, 1982), pp. 57–67, where he holds that what economists do hardly matters inasmuch as the self-interested motives of economic agents will drive all of them. This implies, incidentally, that all economists spawn their theories as a matter of their own utility maximization efforts.

18 See, John C. Moorehouse, 'The Mechanistic Foundations of Economic Analysis,' *Reason Papers*, No 4 (1978).

19 Perhaps the most magisterial effort to make this point was made recently, by Amartya Sen, himself the recipient of the Nobel Prize in economic science but also a formidable moral and political economist, in his *Rationality and Freedom* (Cambridge, MA: Harvard University Press, 2002).

20 See, Tyler Cowen, *Creative Destruction* (Princeton, NJ: Princeton University Press, 2002).

21 Arguably they take it because they believe it does in fact support liberty and prosperity. Yet by fostering an amoral conception of human social affairs – whereby no one can meaningfully claim that anyone is underpaid, anything is overpriced, any demand is perverse, and so on, other than as a personal opinion – this approach actually undermines the case for liberty and prosperity.

22 Allan Bloom, *Giants and Dwarfs* (New York: Simon & Schuster, 1990), p. 288.

23 (Cambridge, MA: Harvard University Press, 1993).

24 *New York Times Book Review*, March 6, 1994, p. 24.

25 Some political theorists have made note of the fact that certain defenders of the free society are not wedded to the *homo economicus* approach. For example, Bob Brecher writes:

> Perhaps the point may be best made by Tibor Machan, a writer who, while greatly sympathetic to liberal individualism, is unusually critical of the 'subjectivist, undefined, arbitrary, "do whatever you desire" idea of human values'. Unlike Flew, Machan is clear that 'persons often demand what is, in fact, very bad – even for themselves' and that 'something can be worthwhile to someone objectively, even if that person fails to recognize this'. His own incorporation of these apparently uncomfortable and illiberal observations into a scheme palatable to capitalism and individualism may not be convincing, but his observations nevertheless serve to clarify two important things. First, they show the power of the moral ontology of individualism. Second, they illustrate the need for those who oppose liberal individualism to propose an alternative, rather than to attempt what is anyway the hopeless task of debating 'real' or 'genuine' wants with liberal opponents.
>
> Some liberal opponents are so misguided as sincerely to suppose that their liberalism is neutral with respect to questions of the nature of human beings. Others, being of a moral libertarian frame of mind, nevertheless fail to understand that their purportedly anti-ontological or anti-metaphysical view – that these are non-questions – itself constitute just another such view, however untheorized. Here, again, is Machan:
>
>> The human essence, then, is the true individuality of every person. The bourgeois individual is the first occurrence in human history when men and women are not first of all members of a tribe or a clan or even a family, but are recognized for what is most essentially human,

> namely, self-responsibility. Bourgeois men and women belong by nature to no one; they are sovereigns, they are capable of using this sovereignty for good or for ill and they require a political community that pays relentless, sustained attention to this fact.

Flew, unlike Machan, supposes that the sovereignty of such individuals consists in the autonomy of their wants, which is why he allows himself to think that Galbraith's worry is about wants being socially produced, rather than about their serving as a moral or political bedrock. He is muddled by having to insist on the autonomy of individuals' wants at the same time as recognizing, as anyone must, that wants are socially created.

Flew is wrong about the autonomy of wants; and his notion of the individual, while properly liberal in being based on supposedly autonomous wants, is therefore necessarily incoherent. How this notion of the individual, which Machan rightly rejects, has come to constitute liberal 'common sense', and how it might be resisted, are the concerns of the rest of this book. First, however, a positive aspect of that common sense needs to be discussed, lest its power be underestimated … . (Bob Brecher, *Getting What you Want? A Critique of Liberal Morality* [Routledge, 1998], pp. 19–20).

26 O. K. Bouwsma (J. L. Craft and Ronald E. Hustwit, eds), *Wittgenstein, Conversations 1949–1951* (Indianapolis, IN: Hackett Publishing Co., 1986), pp. 58–60. The same point, essentially, was made later in Nathaniel Branden, *The Psychology of Self-Esteem* (Garden City, NY: Bantam Books, 1971).

27 Becker, personal correspondence.

28 Sen, op. cit, 'Choice, orderings and morality.'

29 Oddly, whenever corporate managers, say those of Enron, are accused of wrongdoing, it is rare to find anyone defending them as economic theory would dictate: 'They simply had no choice but to pursue profit as they deemed feasible.'

30 I address this topic more fully in Tibor R. Machan, *Capitalism and Individualism: Reframing the Argument for the Free Society* (New York: St. Martin's Press, 1990).

31 I have argued this in my papers 'Evidence of Necessary Existence,' *Objectivity*, Vol. 1 (Fall, 1992), pp. 31–62, and 'Some Reflections on Richard Rorty's Philosophy,' *Metaphilosophy*, Vol. 24 (January/April 1993), pp. 123–35. The first work became the basis of Chapter 2 of Tibor R. Machan, *Ayn Rand* (New York: Peter Lang, 2001), the second Chapter 1 of Tibor R. Machan, *Objectivity: Recovering Determinate Reality in Philosophy, Science, and Everyday Life* (London: Ashgate, 2004).

32 Ayn Rand, *Introduction to Objectivist Epistemology*, 2nd edn (New York: New American Library, 1990), p. 61.

33 Sen, *Rationality and Freedom*, p. 42.

34 Consider just this: any question about whether existence does in fact exist, whether there is something or other, whether reality is real – however this is put by whoever raises the skeptical inquiry – is itself something that exists, thus confirming the very fact that is being questioned.

35 For a detailed treatment of the axiom of existence, aiming to clarify and develop Ayn Rand's account, see Machan, 'Evidence for Necessary Existence.'

36 See, Joseph Boyle, G. Grise and O. Tollefson, *Free Choice* (Notre Dame, IN: University of Notre Dame Press, 1976). See also the essay by Anthony Bertocci, 'Personality, Free Will and Moral Obligation,' in William F. Enteman, ed., *The Problem of Free Will* (New York: Charles Scribner & Son, 1967). Finally, see also Midgley, *The Ethical Primate*.

37 For a discussion of this see Edward Pols, 'Rational Action and the Complexity of Causality,' *Journal of Theoretical and Philosophical Psychology*, Vol. 22, No 1 (Spring 2002).

38 See Sperry, *Science and Moral Priority*. See also Tibor R. Machan, *The Pseudo-Science of B. F. Skinner* (New Rochelle, NY: Arlington House, 1974), and *Initiative – Human Agency and Society* (Stanford, CA: Hoover Institution Press, 2000). A detailed philosophical exploration of human beings as causes of their own actions may be found in Timothy O'Connor, *Persons and Causes, The Metaphysics of Free Will* (New York: Oxford University Press, 2000).

39 Or, as the Bible has it, 'For what shall it profit a man, if he shall gain the whole world, and lose his own soul?' Mark 8:36

40 For a development of the rational egoist ethical position, see Tibor R. Machan, *Classical Individualism* (London: Routledge, 1998) and David L. Norton, *Personal Destinies: A Philosophy of Ethical Individualism* (Princeton, NJ: Princeton University Press, 1976).

41 For such an effort, see Tibor R. Machan and James E. Chesher, *The Business of Commerce: Examining an Honorable Profession* (Stanford, CA: Hoover Institution Press, 1999).

42 A version of this chapter, since considerably reworked, was presented at the 1994 Institute for Objectivist Studies Summer Seminar at Oberlin College, Ohio.

Chapter 7

A Positive Libertarian View of Government

Success makes you a target. As libertarians make headway in getting their ideas aired and published, both liberals and conservatives have been taking potshots at the libertarian conception of government.[1]

Conservatives Bill Kristol and David Frumm have been especially eager to denigrate a libertarian idea of a government with properly circumscribed powers and scope. They complain that such a view is insufficiently 'inspiring' – that citizens cannot rally around a conception of society in which government plays a strictly restricted role. They wonder how such a society would fare in the face of foreign enemies and how it could function as a world power. Governments must generate enough devotion, reverence and respect to garner the support needed to govern, they argue. They believe that a minimalist government, set forth as 'a necessary evil' at best, cannot earn this reverence and thus has no chance of survival, let alone flourishing.

But these critics lack a clear understanding, let alone full appreciation, of the libertarian view of government. In fact, libertarianism does have a positive, upbeat and frankly demanding view of government.

The function of a proper government is to secure certain individual rights, among them the rights to life, liberty and the pursuit of happiness; it is to safeguard these rights that governments are 'instituted among men, deriving their just powers from the consent of the governed.' That is the libertarian view of government. It is also the view of the American Founders, and there can be no more venerable or inspiring heritage.[2]

The just powers of government are whatever powers are needed to secure the rights in question without their violation in the process.

Libertarians would do well to invoke the Declaration of Independence as their rallying cry against paternalistic conservatives who have no idea what they wish to conserve in the American political tradition. It is libertarians who want to preserve the Declaration's positive vision of government as the great, honorable, and properly understood guardian of our rights. The moral virtues of such a government are vigilance, valor, honor, and integrity. If politicians actually possessed these moral virtues in our time, would that not be inspiring? Would it not earn the respect of the people at large – perhaps even of Mr Kristol and Mr Frumm? Certainly the chances are greater that such a government could earn legitimate respect than could a government which meddles constantly in all of our affairs, with all the attendant mishaps that provoke so much contempt from the public, and all the corruption that comes with having embarked upon unjustified public policies. What many people hate about government is not its virtues but its vices. These vices arise from its lack of integrity, its failure to fulfill and stick to its appropriate duties.

So-called 'libertarian anarchists' insist that even such limited government amounts to a kind of tyranny. They reason that because even a limited government functions by law as the only agency of rights protection and adjudication within a given jurisdictional region, it amounts to a coercive monopoly. But a government that keeps to its role as rights protector within a given jurisdiction region is no more a coercive monopoly than is a department store that must be exited so as to reach its competitors. Within its own territory, the department store is a 'monopoly,' just like millions of other businesses. But since they do not prohibit either departure or the nearby presence of a competing store, they are not a *coercive* monopoly.[3]

Governments operate within particular spheres – 'countries' – whose owners have consented at least implicitly to be governed by these institutions. Just across the border, another country with another government is free to exist as well; so long as emigration is possible, no coercive monopoly is involved. It is all akin to gated communities which one may leave at will, and the benefits of which one may enjoy so long as one pays one's way, although one would not, of course, be justified in demanding that one's home there be serviced by the owners of another gated community.

So, then, does the libertarian provide us with an inspiring vision of a legal system?

One should note, first of all, that it is reductionist to charge political thought with the mandate of forging a vision for all of society. Society is a huge and diverse group of individuals intertwined in innumerable complicated ways. These various individuals have diverse purposes; in their innumerable interactions they are united, optimally, by a common sense of civility, of respect for the rights of everyone. It is imperialistic to attempt to generalize the goals of one individual or group to others apart from the very general purposes of seeking to live a fulfilled, happy, honorable life in peaceful coexistence with others. That it acts to secure the right of its citizenry to do just this is part of what makes government an honorable institution, when clearly understood and uncorrupted.[4]

It seems to me that even libertarians who reject the very idea of government can support the limited conception of it that I have outlined. After all, every libertarian is committed to some sort of institutional defense of individual rights, whether in the form of a 'competing government,' a defense agency, a justice agency or some other rights-protecting 'firm.' For most of us, this limited conception means some version of government as an institution dedicated to conscientiously guarding individual rights.

How could anyone seriously believe that a government that resists becoming coercive and that carries out its job in accordance with due process – the requirements of justice – cannot inspire the citizenry of the society in which it operates? Only those who mistakenly expect government to be something it should never become – a parental authority – could chastise advocates of limited government for failing to endorse a regime that functions more as nanny than protector of individual rights. The kinds of respect and honor governments ought to expect from their citizens are probably akin to the respect and honor that referees or umpires would expect from everyone concerned with how a game is guided by its rule-keepers. What matters is honesty, integrity, professionalism, and dedication to outstanding service. Beyond this governments do not deserve to be cherished and receive, especially, subservience, which is what we may suspect Misters Kristol and Frumm are really hoping for.

Notes

1 Among libertarians there are those who consider themselves anarchists. Actually, this is misleading because these same libertarians also defend a legal system that provides, as they see it, all the justified functions and services of governments, only they are not monopolies. This, too, is somewhat confusing because while such legal systems are said to be 'competing' with others, they are also said to be entirely capable of dealing with crime and the problem of 'the court of last resort,' as well as the requisite military resistance to invasion or aggression against those who subscribe to the system (citizens).

For why this is really just a more rarified version of government limited to the use of retaliatory and punitive force – excluding all systematic coercive, initiated force – see, Tibor R. Machan, 'Anarchism and Minarchism, A Rapprochement,' *Journal des Economists et des Estudes Humaines,* Vol. 14, No 4 (December 2002), pp. 569–88.

2 That the Founders did advance the rudiments of a libertarian legal order is not fully appreciated, given how their revolutionary political achievements were by no means complete, having, for example, left slavery, confiscatory taxation, and other statist measures in place. See Tibor R. Machan, ed., *Individual Rights Reconsidered: Are the truths of the US Declaration of Independence lasting?* (Stanford, CA: Hoover Institution Press, 2001), especially the essay by Ronald Hamowy.

3 For the elaboration of the nature of a constitution of such a legal order, see Randy, E. Barnett, *Restoring the lost constitution: The presumption of liberty* (Princeton, NJ: Princeton University Press, 2004).

4 Some have proposed what might be called 'the cricket test' – or, depending on which country is in question, 'the baseball' or 'the soccer' test – whereby a loyal citizen would need to also root for that country's sports teams in international competitions. Absent such rooting, citizens are then deemed to be disloyal. Yet this is a mistake, since in matters of culture many citizens take sides on the basis of familiarity, tradition, fraternity. The real test is wherein lie the expectations of being treated justly as citizens, that is, persons with interest in proper legal adjudication.

Chapter 8

Liberalism and Atomistic Individualism

Criticism of Atomistic Individualism

A Fatal Flaw in Individualism?

Classical Liberalism has its Achilles' heel. It is its radical individualist foundations. If, as critics assume, absent the individualism, we cannot sustain the case for classical liberalism, it is doubtful that this social-political stance can withstand skepticism.

Radical individualism holds that human individuals are, first and foremost, unique, particular beings with just one concern, namely, to advance their own goals. This is why critics have said that such individuals are atomistic and asocial. Classical liberalism had often appeared to embrace this because of the new science of classical mechanics. It was a view that Hobbes admired so much that he went to visit Galileo in Italy to learn it from him. For Hobbes human beings, too, are versions of matter-in-motion, only more complicated in their configuration.

Flaws of So-called Hobbesian Individualism

Whether or not anyone actually held this Hobbesian, arid individualist view, what's crucial for us to know is what some of the liabilities the critics have ascribed to it are.

Atomism, of course, does not square with the individual histories of most human beings. They are born into families where they remain significantly dependent on other persons prior to any possible calculation of their own advantages. The idea that standards of good and bad are no more than tastes and preferences is offensive to the common-sense idea that there are some things that are good and some that are bad and that these are not all a matter of taste or preference, attraction or aversion. Furthermore, the assumption of subjective value, that is closely linked with this sort of individualism, left no standard by which human conduct could be subjected to criticism. All criticism is left groundless if the only thing that matters is whether people prefer or do not prefer something. Even bad logic becomes immune to criticism.

In ethics and politics, the atomistic individualism goes against the grain. Many economists, for example, would say that for them the freedom of a classical liberal society is something they prefer. There is not much else to be said, since they take all values to be subjective.

But what if some of us, perhaps unwisely, do not prefer it? What if after we express preference for these norms, we were to renege – what could be wrong with that? What of the supposed corrosive influence of all this, influence that is said to undermine community bonds, loyalty, honesty, decency, and the rest, especially in the realm of commerce which in the modern age is all pervasive? To say that this would imply that we prefer the state of nature, with its risks and horrors, may be true, but what of it? Is there anything objectively, morally wrong with such a preference? Those who champion such individualism, and the critics who pick on them as representatives of the classical liberal ethos, deny that from this perspective any moral fault could be assigned to such persons.

Already in John Locke intimations of a different kind of individualism are evident. What is this individualism and why does it have more than a fighting chance of being right? What, moreover, is wrong with the critics' case against individualism?

Individualism Under Assault

Individualism has a bad reputation, 'willingly sacrificing all other human values so as to cultivate ... a particular group of virtues – notably independence, courage and honesty.'[1] By association, so does classical liberalism and its political economic system of capitalism. This gives collectivist political systems and economies a clear moral advantage. As Susan Mendus puts it, the 'liberal commitment to independence – to achieving things on one's own ... is [factually] false ... [and] morally impoverished.'[2]

The targeted version of individualism is embraced, more or less intact, by neoclassical and Austrian economists. Its basic premise is that all human behavior is motivated by a narrow, subjective self-interest or utility maximization. Having shown this individualism to be untenable, the system closely associated with it, namely, limited government that stresses the basic negative rights of individuals is also taken to be discredited.

But the charges against individualism are open to serious criticism. For example, individualism need by no means embrace atomism, anti-social attitudes and policies, hedonism or moral subjectivism. Nor need limited government or a constitution of natural rights rest on the arguably fabricated version of individualism that the critics usually target.

Often the criticism of individualism, and its broader philosophy of classical liberalism, is reminiscent more of political propaganda than of scholarly exchange. Marx, for example, refers to it as an 'insipid illusion.' Alasdair MacIntyre regards liberalism itself as vile, nasty, and very harmful.

> [T]he Marxists' understanding of liberalism as ideological, as a deceiving and self-deceiving mask for certain social interests, remains compelling ... . Liberalism in the name of freedom imposes a certain kind of unacknowledged domination,

> and one which in the long run tends to dissolve traditional human ties and to impoverish social and cultural relationships. Liberalism, while imposing through state power regimes that declare everyone free to pursue whatever they take to be their own good, deprives most people of the possibility of understanding their lives as a quest for the discovery and achievement of the good, especially by the way in which it attempts to discredit those traditional forms of human community within which this project has to be embodied.[3]

MacIntyre has argued that individualism is an invention and individual rights are artifacts with no enduring, substantive moral significance.[4] Marx and MacIntrye, furthermore, consign individualism and liberalism to the status of ideologies serving some specific historical purpose – in the case of Marx, the purpose of facilitating social productivity.

MacIntyre and others have argued that individualism rests on no more than arbitrary preferences that happen to have been expressed in a given epoch of Western history. Marx put the point succinctly: 'It is only in the eighteenth century, in "civil society", that the different forms of social union confront the individual as a mere means to his private ends, as an external necessity.'[5]

So prior to the eighteenth century, presumably, the individual as a choosing entity, seen as having the right to choose his social relationships on the principle of the consent of the governed, did not exist.

John N. Gray, however, delivers the most virulent frontal attacks on individualism:

> [I]individualist cultures devour their own moral capital and slide into debt-ridden stagnation as individualism corrodes family life and long-term planning and investment. So, then, what ails the poor nations of the globe is individualism, plain and simple. Exactly how this is done is not made clear but one may gather that individualism is the sort of social philosophy that demoralizes us, robs us of our sense of community and destroys our generosity, charity and fellow feeling.[6]

In less harsh but equally damaging terms, Richard Rorty maintains that individualism is an ideology that in our era has come to be accepted, even though it is a mistake. As Rorty suggests of his own pragmatist-communitarian alternative, it

> takes away two sorts of metaphysical comfort to which our intellectual tradition has become accustomed. One is the thought that membership in our biological species carries with it certain 'rights,' a notion which does not seem to make sense unless the biological similarities entail the possession of something non-biological, something which links our species to a nonhuman reality and thus gives the species moral dignity.[7]

Rorty's point is that principles of social organization are a function of what a given community has chosen, collectively, to embrace, and therefore rights, specifically those of the individual human being, are unfounded. They lack cognitive significance. So when it is claimed that a person has such rights and none should violate them, there is no basis for that claim. All such claims tell us is that the view is one that some groups of people have embraced, while other groups have decided to accept some other view. So Rorty can say, in one of his many more popular writings, that '[We]cannot say that democratic institutions reflect a moral reality and that tyrannical regimes do not reflect one, that tyrannies get something wrong that democratic societies get right.'[8]

Given these harsh or drastic conclusions about the doctrine, let us get a clear idea of what individualism amounts to. Then we will look at the views of some particular critics of individualism. Finally, two types of individualism, atomistic and classical, will be distinguished and it will be shown that at least the classical version is superior to collectivist alternatives.

Essentials of Individualism

Mary Midgley makes the point that 'our own culture, in particular, has grossly exaggerated the degree of independence that individuals have, their separateness from other organisms, and also their degree of inner harmony.'[9] She continues:

> But these exaggerations do not affect the more modest facts that underlie them. Whenever people have to take decisions, the language of agency has to be used, and the reasons why it had to be invented constantly become obvious. The language of impersonal process, by contrast, can scarcely be used at all for many important aspects of human behavior and, when it is used there, it often serves only for fatalistic evasions.[10]

What are the modest facts that underlie an exaggerated individualism? One is a certain indispensable level of separateness of every person. A human being is an individual in part insofar as he experiences a measure of separateness – for example, that his death does not require the death of another human being. A human being dies by himself. Insofar as that involves the extinction of his identity in some important respect, he is an individual with a separate identity.

Another component is an element of self-directedness. Self-determination or free will is a part of individualism insofar as an individual is someone whose initiative – choices, decisions and actions – is instrumental in determining who he is and will become. Individualism regards everyone as something of a self-made person, even if only in a minimal respect, culminating in no more than acquiescence. Individuals have a determining, decisive influence on their own lives. The idea is that how a human being develops is not reducible to the influence of other people, of history, or even of their parents. They put forth the initiative or effort that will produce significant aspects of their lives: knowledge, character, conviction, skill, and other personal attributes.

To put it a bit differently, every human being is capable of engaging and, within different individual conceptions, more or less responsible to engage in creative reasoning: in figuring things out, learning about the world, and understanding it to some minimal but essential extent. Cognition, at least at the conceptual, idea-forming level, has to be generated by the person – it cannot be imposed. A person is not a container into which ideas are funneled or poured, or something that responds to various stimuli passively. There is an element of self-generated understanding, however minimal, on the part of the individual according to the individualist social philosophical tradition.

Individualism also upholds moral autonomy for human beings, in the sense that it identifies the individual as the source of morally relevant choice. The point is not, as Steven Lukes argues, that individualism involves a subjective autonomy that 'will eventuate in ethical individualism, the doctrine that the final authority of ethical behavior, values, and principles is the individual alone.'[11] What individualism requires is that the initiative to do what is right, or wrong, must come from persons and cannot be wholly explained by reference to external or causally structural forces, such as cultural or genetic ones. It is not others, nor the individual's DNA or environment that is held responsible for what the individual does. Thus, it is an essential point of individualism that it is the agent who makes the moral choice, whose input is the most vital one for whether he takes the morally right or wrong action. Indeed, all *bona fide* moral blaming and praising is implicitly individualistic.

Individualism pertains to what people are like and how they ought to be. In political matters, it propounds the sovereignty of each adult human being. It holds that ultimately the individual members of a polity are sovereign, not the polity itself – not its leaders, not its representatives, but its citizens. They are not subject to some other sovereign whose natural position or superiority – or divine selection – has come to entitle him or her to exercise power over them.

The political individualism with which this notion of sovereignty is associated is very much a part of American and, by now, the modern Western political tradition. Indeed, those of us who come to the United States from outside, from the very beginnings of our stirrings as Americaphiles, have associated America with this individualism precisely for that reason.

Finally, the notion of liberalism, which is also associated very much with the American political tradition, is related to individualism. This is a fairly sophisticated idea – although for many, virtually common sense – that individual negative rights to life, liberty, and property, are to be ascribed to every human being by his nature.

So, these six conditions, drawn from different branches of philosophy but comprising a reasonably cohesive doctrine, pretty much characterize individualism. A seventh might also have been mentioned – the metaphysical form of individualism which maintains that every being in an essential respect is a particular being. According to this, there are no general or concrete universal beings – no such thing as society or even family, let alone humanity or ethnic group or tribe, no such thing as the team or America, or blacks or whites, or women or men as such. Instead, there are a great many particular beings, although they can be of various specific kinds. But their actuality is individual.

The Platonist Criticism

If Plato's dialogues actually spell out a philosophical viewpoint – and that has been disputed – then we are forced to the conclusion that Plato favors the reality of concrete universals over concrete particulars or individual beings. Particular beings, you and I as manifest in this actual, visible world, are in some sense inferior, imperfect versions of the perfect concrete universal that is our type, just as a perfect circle, as defined in geometry, is superior to any actual circular being.

Thus it is human nature – the *form* of humanity – that has the elevated or noble status. Actual persons, who imperfectly participate in this form, are always inferior, and lamentably so. It is, accordingly, no accident that Western civilization has always had some disdain toward the body, whether it be in connection with work, sex, business, or material possessions. Such is the legacy of Plato.

It is anti-individualistic in that the individual is always an inferior part of reality. The truly elevated part of reality is the universal, the ideal. The criticism of individualism derived from this Platonic outlook is embodied in a comprehensive, philosophical view. In response, we would have to deal with at least some aspects of that point of view, to which we will return later.

Aristotle as Anti-Individualist

Aristotle is invoked as a more moderate anti-individualist. The whole does not have to be all of humanity as is implicit in a certain reading of Plato, but may be the family, polis, community, or some other limited group.

Because Aristotle identifies human beings as essentially social, it follows from his view that no individual can flourish apart from the realization of this communitarian good. There are many echoes of this view in our own time, what with the reemergence of communitarianism in the writings of Alasdair MacIntyre, Richard Rorty, Robert Bellah, and Amitai Etzioni.[12] There are certain elements in Aristotle's position, however, that stress individualism since he gives a prominent place to self-directedness, something that does not square fully with an exclusively communitarian conception of human flourishing.

Christianity vis-à-vis *Individualism*

The idea that each human being is a distinct, unique child of God and that the saving of each individual's everlasting soul is the task of the ethical life suggests crucial elements of individualism in Christianity. But there are also anti-individualist directions in Christian theology. St Augustine said that every part of the community belongs to the whole.' There also appear to be certain ways in Christianity in which the individual may be sacrificed at least for the purposes of the whole. When Jesus said, 'Compel them to come in' and was taken by some, such as the more zealous missionaries, to suggest coercing people to become part of the faithful, this was anti-individualistic because it implies the rejection of personal choice and responsibility.

Debate continues about whether Christianity is more supportive or less supportive of individualism – the theologians Michael Novak and Robert Sirico stress the individualist element in the American debate, while the Catholic Bishops tend to stress the collectivist element, whereby compelling people to help the poor, thus denying their free choice in the matter of practicing the virtues of charity and generosity, seems to be favored.

The Marxian Critics

Charles Taylor and C. B. Macpherson seem to follow Marx in their criticism of individualism. Both espouse a holistic view, to the effect that humanity is, as Marx said explicitly, an 'organic whole' on a historical march toward self-development or emancipation, when all will have reached their full, unalienated species-being.[13] Others who draw on this Marxian tradition mix it with Aristotle and communitarian ideas. Among the leaders of this group is Amitai Etzioni, a sociologist at George Washington University and editor of *The Responsive Community*. That journal has published essays criticizing libertarianism that the author associates intimately with radical, atomistic individualism. Taylor and Macpherson also maintain that individualism is necessarily tied to an atomistic view of the self, holding that human beings are quite self-sufficient, apart from society.[14]

These critics are clearly focusing on what Mary Midgley called an exaggeration of individualism. Its *homo economicus* version posits that everyone is a utility maximizer and social relations among human beings are entirely optional, neither biologically necessary nor morally required. It is taken in this approach that the human individual is in principle, essentially, an isolated self, akin to Robinson Crusoe on an island who just appears out of nothing but manages to survive and flourish. If another individual of this type shows up, say Friday, the two then face the option of engaging in mutual transaction, each having their personal, private, subjective preferences set, with no role played by ethics, their biological, psychological or social nature in this process.

The critics, including communitarians and neo-Marxists, have found this version of individualism quite false to the facts, sociologically, psychologically or ethically flawed. Because sometimes this model of human nature and human behavior is taken out of the realm of technical economics and used to make sense of political economy, when criticism is leveled at this type of individualism, it appears that individualism *per se* is felled by the blows that are delivered; but this move is quite hasty.

Feminist Critique of Individualism

Some radical feminists, especially Catherine MacKinnon, attack individualism, often from a kind of neo-Marxian perspective that has been transformed to embody feminist components. It is supposed to be classes, not the individual members of the classes, who matter politically and ethically.

For example, MacKinnon recommends, instead of talk about a woman's right to abortion, that the discussion be cast in the collectivist parlance of group power. Here, again, the group is looked upon as the greater reality than the individual. This line of reasoning follows one advanced two centuries ago by August Comte, the French father of sociology:

> Everything we have belongs then to Humanity … Positivism never admits anything but duties, of all to all. For its social point of view cannot tolerate the notion of *right*, constantly based on individualism. We are born loaded with obligations of every kind, to our predecessors, to our successors, to our contemporaries. Later they only grow or accumulate before we can return any service. On what human foundation then could rest the idea of right, which in reason should imply some previous efficiency? Whatever may be our efforts, the longest life well employed will never enable us to pay back but an imperceptible part of what we have received. And yet it would only be after a complete return that we should be justly authorized to require reciprocity for the new services. All human rights then are as absurd as they are immoral. This ['to live for others'], the definitive formula of human morality, gives a direct sanction exclusively to our instincts of benevolence, the common source of happiness and duty. [Man must serve] Humanity, whose we are entirely.[15]

This notion, it will be easily seen, harks back all the way to Platonism – the idea that humanity is a reality which stands over and above every individual or even every subgroup of humanity.

Radical Pragmatism

The idea that there is something on which our belief systems can rest, which can hold it firm, which gives it stability and reliability, is rejected by at least the more radical versions of pragmatism. That much all pragmatists have in common, including Charles Peirce, John Dewey, Willard Van Orman Quine, and Richard Rorty, just to mention the major ones.

Out of this position, Rorty advances the belief that when people do have some understanding, this rests on what is agreed to by members of different communities. In his famous essay 'Solidarity or Objectivity?' Rorty rejects the possibility of objective knowledge – the sort a person imagines he might get after hard work, research, and the clearing away of prejudices and preconceptions. It is a myth that people can know the world as it exists, unconditioned by the thinking that they do in coming to know it. They are able to keep a stable, apparently independent worldview intact only because their community supports them in this. They have their various communities, they belong to them, and in terms of what these communities give them, they formulate an understanding of the world.

Rorty goes so far as to indict much of our history of ideas, claiming that 'The tradition of Western culture which centers around the notion of the search for Truth, a tradition which runs from the Greek philosophers through the Enlightenment, is the clearest example of the attempt to find a sense in one's existence by turning away from solidarity to objectivity.'[16] This objectivity, if attainable, would make some elements of individuality possible: a person could, at least now and then, take an independent view of reality and thus perhaps criticize even his own community.

Rorty insists, however, that no such objectivity is possible because, as he puts it in another place, 'we should have to climb out of our own minds' in order to attain such a stance. Indeed, he thinks, following Ludwig Wittgenstein, that any question that suggests that we need to do this is meaningless, 'should not be asked.'[17]

There is no role for the individual, with his independent consciousness, to ascertain or to stand apart and criticize the community's viewpoint. Rorty fashionably invokes Wittgenstein in support of this epistemological thesis by way of the latter's well known 'private language argument.' It maintains that a certain type of empiricism is false, one according to which every individual gains sensory impressions of the world on which he then, individually, builds an understanding of reality by organizing, naming, and drawing inferences from these sense impressions.

Wittgenstein held that no individual could ever create a language since such a language could never admit of being corrected. If I create my own language, every name I apply is like a christening: necessarily right because it is an act of will, not a publicly correctable discovery. If I created a language all on my own there would be no way anyone could correct what I am saying and doing; no one could hold me responsible for making a mistake.

Wittgenstein, no simple thinker to interpret, is taken to have argued that the only way that language can be understood as a medium within which errors and corrections can be made is if we look upon it as a social creation. Neither the subjective certainty of Descartes' individual mind, nor that of the empiricists' subjective sensory impressions, can provide us with intelligible knowledge. Thus the argument is supposed to oppose individualism. Another statement of this view which Rorty advances was proposed nearly two centuries ago by August Comte:

> The man who dares to think himself independent of others, either in feelings, thoughts, or actions, cannot even put the blasphemous conception into words without immediate self-contradiction, since the very language he uses is not his own. The profoundest thinker cannot by himself form the simplest language; it requires the co-operation of a community for several generations.[18]

So Rorty supplements his pragmatist view of anti-foundationalism with Wittgenstein's private language argument, thereby disposing of the notion that any individual could ever take a cognitively independent stand from his community. In effect this means that true dissidents do not exist, there are only warring groups.

Some Answers to Critics

Was Plato's criticism a telling one? Not really. First, it is arguable that the realm of perfect ideas is a philosophical myth. It is not supposed to be some objective reality, one wherein actual ideals subsist as concrete universals, superior to individuals here in visible worlds. Rather, arguably, what Plato may have had in mind is that we should always have a set of standards to which we refer the actual, and in terms of which the actual world might be improved. This reading of Plato does not exactly endorse individualism, but it certainly softens the blow against it.

As to Aristotle, it would be best to focus on Aristotle's ethics as opposed to the frequent interpretation of his politics. Arguably, every individual has to be a member of a community but it is not necessary for the individual to be a member of one kind of community or to select one community over all others, or to flourish within one community rather than another. As Zeller puts it,

> Plato had demanded the abolition of all private possession and the suppression of all individual interests, because it is only in the Idea or Universal that he acknowledges any title to true reality. Aristotle refuses to follow him here. To him the Individual is the primary reality, and has the first claim to recognition. In his metaphysics individual things are regarded, not as the mere shadows of the idea, but as independent realities; universal conceptions not as independent substances but as the expression for the common peculiarity of a number of individuals. Similarly in his moral philosophy he transfers the ultimate end of human action and social institutions from the State to the individual, and looks for its attainment in his free self-development. The highest aim of the State consists in the happiness of its citizens. The good of the whole rests upon the good of the citizens who compose it. In like manner must the action by which it is to be attained proceed from the individual of his own free will. It is only from within through culture and education, and not by compulsory institutions, that the unity of the State can be secured. In politics as in metaphysics the central point with Plato is the Universal, with Aristotle the Individual. The former demands that the whole should realise its ends without regard to the interests of individuals; the latter that it should be reared upon the satisfaction of all individual interests that have a true title to be regarded.[19]

Zeller seems to me to make a convincing case, as do others who show Aristotle to be, as Miller puts it, a 'moderate individualist,' to contrast him with those, like Hobbes, who propose an extreme or radical nominalist version.[20]

As to the Christian criticism of individualism, it depends largely on how we are to appreciate the theological criticism of a philosophical position. Taking Christianity as a fairly straightforward doctrine, where it joins hands with philosophy, there appears to be no major conflict between certain crucial aspects of individualism and Christianity. Augustinian Christianity sees the individual as a moral agent with free will and the responsibility to live a virtuous life. Thomism draws on Aristotle and thus affirms the role of the individual ethical agent, since Aquinas takes seriously the place of the individual's moral choice or initiative, as did Aristotle. As such, there appears to be no major opposition between the main thrust of Western Christianity and individualism, especially if we add to this the distinctive Christian doctrine of every individual person's status as a child of God and as having the responsibility to achieve everlasting salvation by his own chosen deeds.

Because of its other-worldliness, it is troubling how Christianity would answer the question, 'Who is the I?' Is it possible to answer this in a way that is accessible to non-believers and non-Christians? And there is the related provision of the Bible already mentioned, namely, that the non-Christian might need to be forcibly brought to the faith. 'Compel them to come in' can be rendered in such a way as to lead to policies that would rob the individual agent of his autonomy in making the decision to aspire to the kingdom of God.[21] Similar problems can be found in other religious faiths, of course.

As far as the Marxian view is concerned, although it is now somewhat out of favor, as we will see in Chapter 16, many still embrace it. It even receives some support from scientists, such as the late Lewis Thomas and many ecologists who endorse the conception of humanity or the earth as an organic whole.[22] Marxism shares one clear-cut problem with all anti-individualist positions, namely, that it is contradicted by certain very evident facts on the part of every human being, including, especially, someone like Marx – an undeniably creative intellectual.

Intellectuals – and in our capacity as willing, intending, thinking beings, all of us – are nearly always engaged in original acts. We are not the kind of beings who can be entirely submerged as mere passive particles in some evolutionary progression of history. There is always the role individuals play in understanding human history, recasting and criticizing it, not to mention putting its lessons into practice.

Marx is an especially renowned example of a critical human individual who has a personal, self-determined impact on events. That is one reason the late Sidney Hook could not square the role of the individual in history with hardline Marxism. Marx by implication excludes himself, as a potent member of the historical drama, from his understanding of human affairs. This is a powerful argument against the Marxian conception of humanity as a collective entity: in being unable to accommodate people like Marx himself, it reveals a self-referential inconsistency in the system.

As to communitarianism, a telling critical point, as *The Economist* noted a while ago, is that it 'caricatures outrageously' the substance of Western liberalism, 'calling it a doctrine of economic atomism that pays no heed to man's social nature.' This, as the editors noted, 'is simply false.'[23]

Second, the communitarians have no way to decide to which community we owe our loyalties. Is it my fellow ex-Hungarians, members of the professional community in which I work, my neighbors, fellow tennis players, fathers, drivers of BMWs, travelers, fans of the blues or of Fred Astaire's dancing, libertarians, divorced men, or what? How is the communitarian to group us so that we can be understood fully, as who we are, by reference to *that* group? Etzioni's communitarianism offers no clue given that all his claims about the community rely on some obscure 'we' whose wants, choices, will or desires are to be satisfied. This is altogether too vague and systematically so.

Is anything better to be said for Rorty's version? Rorty talks about solidarity replacing objectivity, but with which group do we proclaim this solidarity? Wittgenstein does not help here either. He argued against radical empiricism, the notion that any single mind, faced with nothing but groupings of bits of sensory impressions – sense data – could come to know the world, to attain propositional or conceptual knowledge. There is nothing in Wittgenstein to deny a human being the independent ability to perceive some parts of the world. The private language argument does not tell against perceptual – only sense data based – knowledge.[24] And as we would anticipate, it is from simple ordinary experience and reflection that human beings begin to know. They perceive the world and are not simply told about it. So, even after they have mingled this knowledge with what they learn from others – including elaborate conceptual knowledge built on complex chains of concepts – they must take care, individually, to remain properly anchored, to keep their bearings.

Furthermore, the idea that knowledge begins with community runs aground when we consider just how this could happen. Communities have no brain – only their members do. So even if after centuries of human history the bulk of what any of us knows does come by way of what others teach us, it could not have been like that from the start. Nor is it always like that now – there are plenty of cases in which children stand their ground against their teachers, citizens against their leaders, those who try to indoctrinate or brainwash them and whose efforts often enough need to be and do get thwarted by individual resistance. But for Rorty and other communitarians, the heroic stance of the dissident is impossible – they are either deluded in thinking they are lone rebels or actually amount to lunatics.

Individualism: Atomistic or Classical?

There are forms of individualism (not of the type that much of the classical liberal tradition inherited) which can withstand the critics' assault.

The type of individualism being sketched here stresses the humanity of each individual. This humanistic, or classical, individualism recognizes that there is in nature a distinct class of beings we call human. This is to contrast such an individualism with one – assuming there ever was one the critics focus upon that was actually proposed – that claims the individual is a bare particular, that what are called natures are constructs invented by our minds.

So on the one hand we must acknowledge the inadequacy of atomistic individualism but on the other hand we can firm up the foundation for individualism *per se*. This can be achieved by noting that in a study of human nature – that is, by a careful examination of what it is to be a human being – we arrive at the conclusion that one of the crucial factors about being a human being is individuality.

In response to this, instead of saying, with Hobbes, that there is no human essence, we can say in opposition to both Marx and Hobbes that the human essence is the true individuality of man. That human beings are also essentially social does not render its individualistic nature void. But their social nature must always be understood alongside their individuality. Accordingly, for example, while human beings require community affiliation, they need to consent to it as adults, not have it imposed upon them. That is the great insight of classical liberalism and the rejection of this, the failure of collectivism.

The Case for A Classical Individualism

Platonism Rejected

One of the major objections to the idea of an objective or real nature of something has to do with Platonism. It was Plato's form of naturalism that had been most widely developed, embraced and utilized in, for example, natural law theory. Even in the tradition of natural rights there is often an allusion to a Platonist conception of the nature of something; but there is a very serious problem with this view of 'the nature of something.'

We need first to remember that, for Plato, the nature of anything is a timeless, unchanging, perfect form in another, timeless dimension of reality. We do have some plausible examples of this: when we study geometry we can, perhaps usefully enough, think of the perfect circle as being in a timeless, perfect, unchanging realm however we might actually understand the precise status of being of the figures geometers define. Euclidean geometry is a formal field, so at least there is a plausible case here.

We were left with two extremes: the radically skeptical idea that issues in nominalism and radical individualism, and the Platonic alternative of an unattainable, hopelessly utopian and ideal conception of human nature. Both lead to skepticism in the end.

Rethinking Essentialism

We should rethink essentialism or naturalism, not abandon it. When we talk about the essence or nature of something we are most sensibly talking about what that thing is, given the best, most reasonable way to classify our experiences. The classification that we thus make – on the basis of evidence we have gathered and which is limited to the context of our present knowledge – is stable enough, given that the world cannot just up and change without rhyme or reason. Even such a changeable being as we are, can be classified in terms of certain basic capacities that can be stable enough to guide us in our political and even perhaps in our personal lives. It can be just as stable as we can expect the world to be, just from our knowledge of history and from our common sense.

In other words, we need an approach to understanding the nature of things that both gives us stability as well as makes room for gradual change. The world itself, as we know it from common sense, demands just that. We can learn it from history, from science, from everything that we are aware of: nature is stable as well as changing!

The Stability of Human Nature

When we study *homo sapiens* over the 100,000 years they have been on this earth, we see that human beings do, indeed, have a stable nature as thinking animals – biological entities that have the distinctive facility to think and depend upon exercising this facility in order to make their way through and do well in life. Moreover this thinking capacity of human beings does not just happen to go into motion. It is one feature of conceptual consciousness that individuals must initiate – they must themselves start this process, otherwise they perish, unless they enlist the thinking of others, who have started it, as a substitute.

It is by their own particular initiative – circumscribed by their family backgrounds, traditions, habits, customs, environment, opportunities, climate, and so forth – that human individuals must confront the task of living their lives. So they face the task of implementing or establishing their individuality every moment of their lives. But it also quickly points to the social nature of human life – the very fact that they are thinking animals points to the fact that flourishing in their lives is utterly interwoven with their fellow human beings.

Individualism Humanized

Now how does all this help us out of some of the problems and paradoxes that critics of individualism tend to focus upon? For one, since we have now a viable, sound, or feasible conception of human nature – not timeless, yet having the stability to be expected of a view about the nature of things – we can identify some general principles we could count on to guide our lives. These principles are going to be general enough to apply over time to succeeding generations even if they will not be guaranteed to hold for eternity as earlier naturalists had hoped.

Of course, as Aristotle already recognized, the precise application of the general principles that rest on our knowledge of human nature may not be exactly identical in different situations, at different times. Being honest in the twentieth century probably requires applying the principles to telephones, call waiting, fax machines, and computers. Two hundred years ago people did not have the responsibility to be honest in just this way. So honesty, although it may well be a very general human virtue that we all ought to practice, will also have its very individual, regional, temporal, and culturally related manifestations. And so, too, with other virtues such as courage, prudence, or justice.

There can be very many general human traits of character that make for human excellence that we ought to practice. That these must be applied in particular circumstances does not imply at all that they have to be subjective, mere preferences or choices that we invent at a given moment. These could well be human virtues, so that, for example, trans-historically we could consider a person 400 years ago and if we discover that he is a liar we could say that he did something objectively, morally wrong.

A good example of misguided criticism of individualism may be found in Charles Taylor's previously mentioned essay 'Atomism.'[25] Here Taylor claims that ascribing basic negative rights to individuals necessarily presupposes atomism, the view that human beings are self-sufficient apart from society. He links this view to Hobbes and Locke. He tells us that

> Theories which assert the primacy of rights are those which take as the fundamental, or at least a fundamental, principle of their political theory the ascription of certain rights to individuals which deny the same status to a principle of belonging or obligation, that is a principle which states our obligation as men to belong to or sustain society, or a society of a certain type, or to obey authority or an authority of a certain type.[26]

To start with, contrary to Taylor's claim, even Locke identifies pre-political moral responsibilities, when he tells us

> The state of Nature has a law of Nature to govern it, which obliges every one, and reason, which is that law, teaches all mankind who will but consult it, that being all equal and independent, no one ought to harm another in his life, health, liberty or possessions …[27]

Locke clearly, unambiguously refers to 'a law of Nature' – which in this context means a system of ethics – that governs the state of nature, and 'obliges everyone.' Locke does not claim there is only one law of nature or moral principle. But he does say that such a law obliges us all, so Taylor is wrong to think that Locke begins his understanding of politics with individual rights. In the state of nature there are obligations or, to put it another way, moral responsibilities or virtue one ought to live by. Of those, Locke calls attention to the obligation that 'no one ought to harm another in his life, health, liberty or possessions.' This obligation Locke treats as indeed enforceable. But it is too weak for those like Taylor who want us to be society's possessions. The East German socialists precisely implemented this belonging when they regarded everyone who tried to leave them as embarking on a kind of kidnapping of part of the collective self.

Locke's obligation[28] means that we ought to abstain from killing, assaulting, kidnapping, robbing, and otherwise interfering with other people's choices, the failure of observing which would justify forcible defensive response. But other laws of nature – for example, 'everyone is bound to preserve himself' – may not be enforceable. Furthermore, 'when his own preservation comes not in competition, [he] ought as much as he can preserve the rest of mankind.' But this is not enforceable. It is a moral, freely chosen, obligation of charity toward others.

Locke also makes clear, using a quotation from 'the judicious Hooker' that human beings are by nature social: '[W]e are naturally induced to seek communion and fellowship with others.'[29]

Taylor laments that our choices are not always mature enough to guide us toward self-fulfillment and self-development so the obligation must be an enforceable one. But a moderate individualist would say, first, that assisting with the initial stages of self-development is the task of parents, not the state of strangers who have come to govern society; second, that ordinarily each of us, except for the very unfortunate, will be able to set himself or herself to the task of self-development, gaining help when in need of it from society, not the state; and, third, that self-development must amount to something highly individualized, so others will usually be unprepared to assist in it very much except in a voluntary, invited capacity. This fulfills every bit the necessarily social component of human nature with no need to extend it to coercive impositions that arise from seeing each of us as belonging to society.

It is important to note that Taylor equates 'a principle of ... obligation' with 'a principle of belonging.' The two are very easy to differentiate. A person may have the obligation to be generous or kind or helpful without belonging to those who would benefit from this. Only slaves belong and do service, not from their sense of morality or ethics but from the requirement to comply with the demands of those to whom they belong. Men and women who possess both free will and moral responsibilities do the right thing, including fulfilling their obligations, because they choose to do so. Taylor completely ignores this distinction between an enforceable and an ethical obligation. Because of this he never has to deal with whether the social nature of human beings is something they need to fulfill as a matter of their moral responsibilities or something they can be made to fulfill at the command of others.

Taylor also claims, along with MacIntyre, that prior to Hobbes and Locke there was no reference to rights, which is flatly contradicted by other scholars.[30]

Furthermore, there is the occasional serious ambiguity in Taylor's use of the concept of obligation. Are we to understand by that term a course of conduct that is mandatory and enforceable or one that is a matter of moral requirement? If it is morally required, a person needs to be free from the coercive interventions of others so as to fulfill the obligation. If it is mandatory, others may impose it upon the individual by force. But then no credit is due to the person who obeys and thus ostensibly fulfills the obligation. A mark of a virtuous person is to recognize that his nature requires, among other things, extensive social engagement which is a part of his self-development, and fulfillment of his nature. What it does not require is that such engagement be unconditional. Taylor does allow that there are 'certain theories of belonging … which hold that our obligation to obey, or to belong to a particular society, may in certain circumstances be inoperative.' But he discounts this exception and says that 'in theories of belonging it is clear that men *qua* men have an obligation to belong to and sustain society.'[31] Taylor makes too little of what is, after all, a rather important qualification on so-called theories of belonging. For if a person has the authority to withdraw from a perverse society, he will have the authority, also, to determine what criteria to use for this purpose. This is not an epistemological *carte blanche*, of course, but a serious moral responsibility to find out what kind of society is suitable to human flourishing.

Critics of individualism might consider that competing accounts of our nature need to be considered not only on the basis of how wildly certain elements of our nature might be exaggerated, but also on how exaggerating aspects of our nature in one way may be far more harmful than in another. Thus while it is true that individualism can be propounded in an arid fashion, this has been far less harmful than the similarly exaggerated collectivist accounts. Consider, as just one example, the Russian author Tatyana Tolstaya's observation, in an essay written for *The New Republic* magazine shortly after the fall of the Soviet Union, of the nature of one grandly horrid example of collectivist social organization:

> According to [collectivists] 'the people' is a living organism, not a 'mere mechanical conglomeration of disparate individuals.' This, of course, is the old, inevitable trick of totalitarian thinking: 'the people' is posited as unified and whole in its multiplicity. It is a sphere, a swarm, an anthill, a beehive, a body. And a body should strive for perfection; everything in it should be smooth, sleek, and harmonious. Every organ should have its place and its function: the heart and brain are more important than the nails and the hair, and so on. If your eye tempts you, then tear it out and throw it away; cut off sickly members, curb those limbs that will not obey, and fortify your spirit with abstinence and prayer.[32]

Tolstaya's choice of terms may suggest to some that this is an overstatement of the collectivist position. But is it, really? Marx himself refers to human society as 'an organic body.'[33] We have already seen that 'belong' is Taylor's preferred term. And St Augustine states that '… every part of the community belongs to the whole … .'[34] What else does this suggest but that human beings are component parts of some larger body and are, thus, ultimately not self-directed? Indeed, it means that some people – a majority, politburo, central committee, or dictator – will have that power, not that the whole body will exercise it in some kind of cohesive, integrated fashion.

With the smaller collectives, such as communes or convents, especially where voluntarily entered into, the probability of disharmony and instability will not be so great, precisely because such groups can very well reflect the main attributes of the individuals who comprise them. Even if such groups are established and maintained coercively, their configurations may well suit the individual purposes of their membership, making stability more likely. But that is less and less likely as the collective becomes larger.

The individualist idea can, of course, also be made to serve unsavory purposes, but never so readily and with such cataclysmic results as those of collectivism, small or large. Most importantly, however, individualism can be rendered in terms that are closer to the truth of the human situation, both actual human capacities and realizable human ideals.

It is quite true that individuals ought to form social ties, that they ought often to be loyal to their groups, that it is best for them to choose to be generous, compassionate and kind toward others. It is also true that mere individual initiative will not lead to full human flourishing, which is the thrust of Aristotle's observation that human beings are by nature social-political animals. Even thinking cannot get much beyond mere familiarity with, as it were, the surface of the world, unless it is enhanced by the kind of education that only many generations' combined individual effort can produce. Just as the argument for individualism shows that the individual is indispensable, it also demonstrates that the company of other individuals is essential to the flourishing of human life.

But it does not follow from any of this that individuals ought to be coerced, by others, to comply with the tenets of any given social arrangement. All that can be demanded of anyone is that he accept the protection, for everyone, of his moral space or personal moral jurisdiction – that is, the respect of our basic rights that make it possible for us to act on our own initiative. It is the hallmark of individualism that even what is dead right for someone to do must be a matter of choice. Without that, the very dignity of the human being – the capacity for a person to earn moral credit for doing what is right – is destroyed.

Alas, though this may be true, it is also the case that without sustained philosophical support, such common-sense ideas are quickly overwhelmed, first by doubt and then by sophistry. In that spirit, suffice it to note that there is now a serious change of direction, at least in biology, concerning the adequacy of the mechanistic, scientistic model for understanding behavior, not just human but animal as well. In neurophysiology and psychophysics conclusions have been reached that give solid support to the idea that human brains are exactly the sort that enable human beings to function as causal, governing agents.[35] Furthermore, it is evident that although there is a great deal of value in approaching much of the world along lines recommended by the methods of modern natural science, that method has been extrapolated too hastily to areas of inquiry where it fails to apply. The enthusiasm with social science and engineering, both spheres where individualism fares badly except in economics, seems now to have abated. What may well be the missing element is the type of moderate or classical individualism that has been defended in the present discussion. Surely this is suggested by the current tendency to abolish individual responsibility and to embrace the idea that we are all basically helpless in the face of our troubles.

In any case, the individualist stance is not by any means so out of line as some of its critics suggest; it could indeed be the exact opposite story, at the end of the day.[36]

Notes

1 Mary Midgley, *The Ethical Primate* (London, England: Routledge, 1994), p. 123.
2 Susan Mendus, 'Liberal Man,' in G. M. K. Hunt, ed., *Philosophy and Politics* (London: Cambridge University Press, 1991), p. 47.
3 Alasdair MacIntyre, 'Nietzsche or Aristotle?' in Giovanna Borradori, *The American Philosopher* (Chicago, IL: University of Chicago Press, 1994), p. 143.
4 Alasdair MacIntyre, *After Virtue* (Notre Dame, IN: University of Notre Dame Press, 1981).
5 Karl Marx, *Grundrisse*, (New York: Harper Torchbooks, 1971), p. 17.
6 John Gray, 'From Post-Modernism to Civil Society,' *Social Philosophy and Policy*, Vol. 10 (1993), p. 44.
7 Richard Rorty, *Objectivity, Relativism, and Truth* (London: Cambridge University Press, 1991), p. 31.
8 Richard Rorty, 'The Seer of Prague,' *The New Republic*, July 1, 1991, p. 37.
9 Midgley, *The Ethical Primate*, p. 103.
10 Ibid.
11 Steven Lukes, *Individualism* (London: Oxford University Press, 1973), p. 101.
12 Amitai Etzioni, *The Spirit of Community* (New York: Crown Publishing Co., 1993), Robert Bellah et al., *Habits of the Heart* (New York: Harper & Row Publishers, 1985).
13 Marx, *Grundrisse*, p. 39.
14 Charles Taylor, *Philosophy and the Human Sciences* (Cambridge, England: Cambridge University Press, 1985), pp. 187–210.
15 Auguste Comte, *The Catechism of Positive Religion* (Clifton, NJ: Augustus M. Kelley Publ., 1973), pp. 212–30.
16 Rorty, *Objectivity, Relativism, and Truth*, p. 21.
17 Ibid., p. 7.
18 Auguste Comte, *A General View of Positivism* (New York: Robert Spellers & Son, 1957), p. 246.
19 Eduard Zeller, *Aristotle and the Earlier Peripatetics*, trans. B. F. C. Costelloe and J. H. Muirhead (London: Oxford University Press, 1897), ii, pp. 224–6 (quoted in Fred D. Miller, Jr, *Nature, Justice and Rights in Aristotle's Politics* [Oxford, England: The Clarendon Press, 1995], pp. 200–201). For an individualist understanding of Aristotle's metaphysics, see Emerson Buchanan, *Aristotle's Theory of Being* (Cambridge, MA: Greek, Roman, and Byzantine Monographs, 1962).

20 See, for more on the measure of individualism and the natural rights of individuals in Aristotle's philosophy, Miller, Jr, ibid.
21 For more on this, see J. D. P. Bolton, *Glory, Jest and Riddle, A Study of the Growth of Individualism from Homer to Christianity* (New York: Barnes and Noble, 1973). See also Paul Zweig, *The Heresy of Self-love: A Study of Subversive Individualism* (Princeton, NJ: Princeton University Press, 1980).
22 Lewis Thomas, *Lives of a Cell* (New York: Viking, 1971).
23 *The Economist*, March 18, 1995.
24 David Kelley, *The Evidence of the Senses* (Baton Rouge, LA: Louisiana State University Press, 1986). Ironically, Kelley did his doctoral dissertation, on which this book is based, under the chairmanship of Richard Rorty at Princeton University. For an extensive discussion of Richard Rorty's anti-objectivism, see Tibor R. Machan, *Objectivity: Recovering Determinate Reality, in Philosophy, Science, and Everyday Life* (London: Ashgate, 2004).
25 Taylor, *Philosophy and the Human Sciences.*
26 Ibid., p. 188. For my fuller discussion of Taylor's position, see Tibor R. Machan, *Generosity: Virtue in Civil Society* (Washington, DC: Cato Institute, 1998).
27 John Locke, *Concerning Civil Government, Second Essay: An Essay Concerning the True Original Extent and End of Civil Government* (1690), Chapter II, 'Of the State of Nature.'
28 The term 'obligation' is a bit misleading since it suggests an enforceable moral – that is, a properly grounded legal – principle, yet outside of civil society no edict is yet enforceable other than self-defense.
29 Ibid.
30 See, for example, Tierney, 'Origins of Natural Rights Language: Text and Contexts, 1150–1250,' 'Conciliarism, Corporatism, and Individualism: The Doctrine of Individual Rights in Gerson,' *Christianesimo hella Storia* 9 (1988), 81–111; and Cary J. Nederman, 'Property and Protest: Political Theory and Subjective Rights in Fourteenth-Century England,' *The Review of Politics*, Vol. 58 (Spring 1996), pp. 323–44. See also Fred D. Miller, Jr.
31 Taylor, p. 188, note 1.
32 Tatyana Tolstaya, 'The Grand Inquisitor,' *The New Republic*, June 29, 1992, p. 33.
33 Marx, *Grundrisse*, p. 33.
34 St Augustine, quoted in Thomas Beauchamp, ed., *Ethical Issues in Death and Dying* (Englewood-Cliffs, NJ: Prentice-Hall, 1984), p. 103.
35 See the work of Roger W. Sperry, for example, his *Science and Moral Priority* (New York: Columbia University Press, 1983), as well as Midgley, *The Ethical Primate*. See also Edward Pols, *Acts of Our Being* (Boston: University of Massachusetts Press, 1982) and *Mind Regained* (Ithaca, NY: Cornell University Press, 1998).
36 A substantial portion of the material in this chapter is drawn from Chapter 14 of my *Classical Individualism* (London: Routledge, 1998).

LIBERTARIANISM *PER SE*

Chapter 9

Anarchists and Minarchists: Allies After All?

My purpose in this chapter is to discuss a controversy that has split a goodly portion of the libertarian political movement for quite a while. Since the very birth of the American political tradition, there have been those who have found fault with its idea of even limited government, claiming, in essence, that government in any form is morally suspect if not out and out criminal. I believe Lysander Spooner's criticism of the US Constitution,[1] not for any particular provision it includes but because it assumes that the consent of those of one generation can bind those in subsequent ones. It has continued more recently with the leadership of Murray N. Rothbard and is kept alive by a host of libertarian thinkers, including Walter Block, Eric Mack, John Hasnas, Aeon Skoble, Jan Narveson, John Sanders, and quite a few others. Other libertarians, such as John Hospers, Ayn Rand, Douglas B. Rasmussen, Douglas J. Den Uyl, Roger Pilon, Tom Palmer and I, have held the view that limited government is compatible with the full respect and protection of unalienable negative individual rights.

In this chapter I shall argue, in part, that the dispute is not as significant as many of the parties maintain and that, in any case, both factions of libertarians actually reject anarchism as that is understood in the classical anarchist tradition, namely, as the denial of any moral justification for law and legal enforcement. That tradition has been largely pacifist and hostile to any systematic law enforcement and agencies that would carry it out. So-called anarchist libertarians are very different from the usual Marxist or socialist breed of anarchists, as well. 'Anarchocapitalists' defend arrangements in society that serve the sole purpose of protecting individual rights, calling these 'defense agencies,' 'protection agencies,' or 'justice services'; they would not assent to the socialist–anarchist view that in a true anarchist society the 'surpluses' generated by capital would devolve to the laborers, private property would whither away along with the state, and so on.

Robert Nozick, who was identified as belonging with the minarchist faction in this dispute, opened his famous book on political philosophy, *Anarchy, State, and Utopia,* with a discussion of whether a libertarian society must necessarily be anarchist, as Murray N. Rothbard and others have claimed. Nozick concluded that even with full respect for everyone's individual rights, a society that attempted anarchism would 'back into' a minimal state.

Nozick argued that this backing away from a 'society without a state'[2] into minimalism occurs even if innocent persons afflicted by private efforts to defend individual rights – or to punish culprits for violating them – are compensated for their worries about negative side effects. He claimed there would still be persistent concern about such side effects among those not directly affected. 'Even under the strongest compensation proposal which compensates victims for their fear, some people (the nonvictims) will not be compensated for *their* fear. Therefore there is a legitimate public interest in eliminating these border-crossing acts [that is violations of the rights of some in the process of acting to punish rights violations], especially because their commission raises everyone's fear of its happening to them.'[3] Nozick concludes that in the resulting system, which I call a minarchist society, one legal order alone would prevail within a given geographical area. There would be a single administration of this legal order.

Nozick thus contradicts the claims of Rothbard and other libertarians that in a fully free society, one that respects and protects individual rights of the sort that Nozick (and Locke, and Rand, and Rothbard) regards as basic, competing legal orders and administrators could operate within the same geographical realm. He contradicts the claim that law could become an *enterprise* just like any other provision of services people might want.

When living in communities, dangers from others exist and it is *ethically* imperative to address these dangers. Government, rightly understood, is the institution that specializes in proper protection of individual rights. Thus it would be ethical to establish government instead of leaving the task of rights-protection to individuals and businesses that lack the training or mandated mission to protect rights properly, that is, via due process and without violating rights in the process of this protection. Indeed, this institution, government, is unique in human communities because protecting individual rights is not like other tasks (for example, producing and selling bread) in that its genesis is not peaceful interaction but the initiation of force and the required response. Thus politics *cannot* be reduced, without remainder, to commerce (which is *per se* peaceful), contrary to what individualist anarchists maintain.

I believe that both the individualist anarchists and the so-called minarchists – those who support a properly limited government – are right on key issues and also that their differences are only apparent.[4] In one respect, no competing legal orders would exist in a fully free society, while in another respect, competition among different legal orders (but all abiding by certain ultimate principles and procedures) would be the natural libertarian situation.

What is the anarchist–libertarian case for adjudication and law enforcement? And what is the minarchist case for the libertarian society's approach to law? How opposed are they to each other, really? I will argue that the two positions only appear to be different because of certain preconceptions about what a legal order must entail.

The fact that Nozick's treatment of this issue received such close attention from political philosophers and theorists – as well as economists and public policy scholars – suggests that there is more at stake here than merely settling an internecine squabble. With good reason. The dominant principles of Western liberal democracies are of two distinct types. One stresses individual sovereignty. The other stresses more or less extensive collectivism or communitarianism. According to the latter position, all able persons naturally owe provisions for those less able who are in dire straits, that is, the poor, helpless, injured. These provisions are to be obtained via taxation or universal service, both of which are, to use Nozick's words, 'on par with forced labor' and therefore rights-violating.

Whether either system can be stable, orderly, consistent and just in the policies it precipitates has been the subject of much debate.

One motivation for incorporating a substantial welfare provision into a fundamentally liberal order is the belief that without it, no reason can be found for supporting the traditional configuration of countries as political entities. In other words, only if all citizens have enforceable positive duties toward one another may a government be justified at all. If no such duties are involved in maintaining justice, perhaps the need for government could not be established. So, in a sense, one promise (or threat?) of consistent classical liberalism or libertarianism is that it would require the abolition of government altogether – including the very idea of a country. But not all libertarians consider this a sound inference from their agreement that all individuals have unalienable rights to life, liberty and property.

The libertarian view is that none may violate these and other properly derived individual rights. If one needs to protect these rights, one may do so oneself or hire others. As with all services, provisions may be offered by various parties and none may acquire a protected, legal monopoly. So the protection of basic rights may be provided to different individuals by different firms specializing in such provisions, and no exclusion of competing providers can be justified on libertarian grounds. This right of competitive provision supports the anarchist–libertarian idea of legal adjudication and enforcement.

The response from the minarchist side is often that such a system would in principle be chaotic and could more easily fail to provide decisive results than a minarchist system. Dissatisfied parties could always seek yet another trial court, employ yet another police department, switch to yet another appellate court, and so forth, so there would be no 'court of last resort' to issue a genuinely *final* or *decisive* judgment. The right of competition would entail a right to opt out of legal contexts that do not suit one *qua* consumer of law-and-order. Such a situation would render the legal system non-functional in a variety of cases where those involved wish to press on with their claims, or simply go home without abiding by the judgment.

Minarchists also argue that a legal system is essentially different from other kinds of provisions because

(a) it involves the use of force against those who haven't authorized this use (alleged criminals);
(b) there is a need for law prior to market transactions, so law itself is in a different category (politics versus economics), and
(c) one should not be a judge in one's own case (*vis-à-vis* self-defense in complex cases).

It is my contention that, contrary to appearances, the two camps of libertarians aren't actually opponents but rather emphasize different issues, ones through which a common ground (and a common system of justice) may emerge.

Government is a legal service institution (the actions or policies of which are backed by allegedly justified physical force and its threat). Since it is just the definition of government that's in dispute in this discussion, for now I will give only this rough characterization rather than a formal definition.

Anarcho-libertarians reject the government on the view that its very nature entails fundamental injustices (such as taxation or exclusivity of legal jurisdiction).[5] Legal services consist of enforcing laws, and laws are supposed to uphold justice. If, as libertarians contend, political justice consists primarily of respecting individual rights, then proper legal services involve adjudicating disputes about rights violations, overseeing the conviction of criminals, and providing for some of the police protection and military defense of people who live within the relevant jurisdictions, all in the effort to protect these rights.

Rights are the objective criteria by which just adjudication is to be conducted. Respecting rights fulfills the requirement of a civilized legal system whereby the rule of law rather than the will of human beings (as rulers) is followed. But anarcho-libertarians believe it is impossible for the government to achieve justice without also violating justice.

If the provision of legal services is to be just, they say, government must enjoy the full consent of the governed, not just the majority of those being served by it. (That consent may be explicit or, some have argued, implicit – based not only on overt but tacit agreement implied by one's actions.) But can even a properly limited government exist with the full consent of the governed? Some argue it has never done so and, indeed, cannot, for it is necessarily coercive, involving as it does the forcible monopolization of the legal services it provides.[6] To achieve justice, it is held, legal services must be provided in ways government cannot provide them, namely, absent any kind of initiated coercion.

Those who understand government to be unjustly coercive by its very nature can relate to Max Weber's definition:

> A state is defined by the specific means peculiar to it, the use of physical force. The state is a human community that successfully claims the monopoly of the legitimate use of physical force within a given territory. Politics, then, means striving to share power or striving to influence the distribution of power, either among states or among groups within a state.[7]

Notice that Weber talks here of the state as a human community, in the fashion of Hegel, Marx, Green and Bosanquet, rather than in the fashion of classical liberals such as Locke, Mill or Spencer. But many make use of this conception of the state to characterize government as an organization that monopolizes the use of force within some geographic area and raises its revenue through coercive taxation.[8] Tyler Cowen gives a slightly different definition of government or state, saying it is characterized by 'finance through taxation, claim of sovereignty, ultimate decision-making authority, and prohibitions on competitive entry.'[9] And John Hasnas tells us that 'What appears to be essential for an organization to be considered a state is that it monopolizes the basic policing, rule-making, and adjudicative functions in an identifiable area and funds these functions through taxation.'[10]

Our own concern here is not the nature of the state insofar as it is closely linked to the collectivist ideas of Hegel or Marx – the state as a holistic, organic community of human beings – but the nature of *government*, which is the institution established to provide legal services *for* human communities. As the American Declaration of Independence puts it, such 'governments are instituted among men, deriving their justice powers from the consent of the governed.' Here government is not a state, that is, not a human community of a certain type but an institution *within* such a community. The libertarian controversy concerns whether governments are necessarily in violation of basic individual rights, or can exist and function without necessarily doing violence to those rights.

Of course, political theorists debate the proper scope of legal services or governments more generally than libertarians do. Some would include the provision of a wide set of goods and services apart from the protection of individual rights. Indeed, some deny that such rights exist at all, and believe government should proactively mandate production of goods and services for various segments of the citizenry. Indeed, some argue that government comes before any rights – government being the grantor of rights, not the protector of them.[11] Here we are considering only the more specific controversy among those who share the classical liberal tradition that regards the protection of individual rights as the sole – or at most, the paramount – service that a properly conceived government or legal order provides: the controversy about whether, within a given region, only one or several providers of legal services might practically exist.[12]

As the Declaration of Independence put it, it is 'to secure these rights' that governments are instituted among men. But must there be some kind of insidious, rights-violating monopoly afoot were governments to proceed to carry out this task? Or might government be a monopoly of the benign sort that we find in the provisions of all goods and services? If the term 'monopoly' is construed with sufficient narrowness, even a barber shop enjoys a monopoly (over the barbering done at its exact location); as does any grocery store, amusement park, apartment complex or a gated housing community (and the various services provided or 'bundled' within). Could government be a monopoly that just happens to have emerged without anyone forcibly imposing it?[13]

To obtain the services even of a competing barber shop, one needs to take the trouble to go to a location other than the one where the original shop is located. So it is with all other competing providers other than those that deliver their service or product, such as some pizzerias or plumbers. Is government merely a larger monopoly of this kind? Or is its monopoly necessarily held coercively, by the violation of the rights of others who would also want to offer its services?

I have argued that governments may serve communities without any degree of coercion and without being a monopoly.[14] Jack Sanders claims I use the concept 'government' idiosyncratically, since it proposes that one can have such an institution without any measure of initiatory coercion.[15] Yet he argues that history shows that no government has ever existed that did not engage in extensive coercive activities.

One response[16] is that the concept of 'government,' not unlike that of 'marriage,' is rarely – perhaps never – instantiated fully or flawlessly. These are normative concepts and while it is important to learn whether instantiating them is realistically *possible*, it is not always decisive that they are rarely instantiated. So the *history* of governmental conduct is not decisively indicative of the *nature and morality* of government, any more than the history of actual marriage demonstrates whether marriages can exist *as they ought to*, whether as usually conceived they could be a proper arrangement between couples.

In classical liberal political theory as encapsulated in the Declaration of Independence, the concept 'government' is used in a way that suggests that it is compatible with respect for individual rights. John Locke, for example, not only deemed government compatible with such respect but believed it was needed to provide effective protection of such rights.[17] More recently, Ayn Rand and her students have argued that government *can* exist without taxation, a practice that Murray Rothbard and others see as inherently anti-libertarian. If indeed it is possible for government to subsist without taxation (and possible to show that it can), the fact that historically governments have always relied on taxation is not definitive. Just as the fact that no society has every been *fully* capitalist does not prove that a consistently free market is somehow inherently unworkable.

One matter that anarcho-libertarians rarely discuss, noted by David Kelley,[18] is the fact that such market institutions as corporations, partnerships, private businesses – and even plain one-shot trades – presuppose a background of law-enforcement, including protection of property rights and the integrity of contracts. Such enforcement must thus be fundamentally different from the provisions of other goods and services. J. Roger Lee has also raised this issue, charging that anarcho-libertarians commit a philosophical *category mistake* as they attempt to reduce all politics to economics. This may be symptomatic of some economic approaches to understanding human (social) life.

A rebuttal might assert, of course, that 'politics' is a category which is unjustly coercive by nature and thus inherently incompatible with justice; that all along, the belief that we require politics has rested on a misunderstanding: the notion that the use of initiated force is sometimes proper in human community life. Anarcho-libertarians see ample evidence for this belief among statists and tend to think that minarchist libertarians simply have not gone far enough in shedding this very bad habit of associating community life with coercion.

But the anarcho-capitalists get this wrong. Politics in a libertarian polity concerns, in part, *the need for using force against unwilling persons* who have, however, implicitly *asked for* it by way of their criminal conduct. It is not that a proper politics rests on the idea that *initiated* force – that is, coercion – is sometimes justified; it rests rather on the need to cope with (defend and retaliate against, and adjudicate disputes involving) such initiated force in special, appropriate ways (suggested by the concept of *due process* in criminal law-enforcement). Politics addresses the problem of dealing with involuntary or coerced human interactions – crimes, wars, and other forms of rights violation or violence.

To this it may be replied that even today there are arbitration agencies that provide legal services, so it must be possible to do so. Yet key here is that all such agencies are still subject to legal scrutiny by governments. Their customers may file complaints against them. They may be sued in regular courts.

The attempt to reduce all politics to commercial enterprises raises other concerns. Limiting the providers of rights protection and adjudication to the tasks aiming at this goal will be impossible without any rule of law at all beyond their own chosen procedures and laws. After all, why should an ordinary business enterprise decline to expand its activities, perhaps to providing social security services, unemployment compensation, wildlife preservation, or terrorist assassination? The enterprise might do such things on ideological grounds even if no profit is involved, provided its other services garner a large enough profit. Is a mafia to be tolerated as long as it offers 'protection'?

As far as I understand, the possibility of overstepping libertarian bounds and the need to prevent the same, pretty much puts these anarcho-libertarians in the camp of those who do, in fact, defend some form of government, albeit one that's supposedly free of the flaws of governments defended by socialists and welfare statists. It is a form of government rejected by those anarchists who want no laws at all to govern societies and who believe that communities will flourish through cooperation not overseen by any laws, only by personal moral vigilance.

Perhaps the most controversial question among those who want legal services provided solely for the protection of individual rights is whether governments need by nature be a *coercive* monopoly, in the sense of specifically banning competition – as is, say, the United States Postal Service's first class division – rather than a benign monopoly, like that of a privately owned apartment house or an air carrier (once airborne). In order for the USPS to retain all first-class mail service, a legal authority must prohibit anyone from offering an equivalent service, and they must have the power to enforce this prohibition. Such an enforced monopoly is coercive.

But a monopoly or near-monopoly is not coercive if it exists by virtue of overwhelming customer support – for example, Microsoft's dominance in the software industry.[19] A privately owned apartment house is a *de facto* monopoly in the same way in which any particular ownership constitutes such a monopoly, especially to someone else who wants that item in particular but cannot have it, since it is now owned by another. Prospective homeowners find themselves in this position when the seller closes a deal on the 'perfect' house with another buyer. Owners of a good may set terms of use for others, by, say, evicting renters who fail to abide by terms of a lease. A passenger air carrier becomes a *de facto* benign monopoly between ports of embarkation and disembarkation. While flying United Airlines from LA to NYC, one has no access to competitors *en route* over Kansas.[20]

In short, some provision of services, given the nature of the service, may only appear to be coercively monopolistic. However, since customers are aware of this and prior to entering the exchange can easily seek out competitors who are free to enter the market, the apparently coercive monopoly is not in fact such even when the service being obtained is one provided for a long period of time. My suggestion is that becoming a citizen of a country may amount to (provisionally) consenting to such long-term provisions of rights protection from a given government.

The service anarcho-capitalists envision being provided by non-coercive legal service agencies – as well as by governments that would protect individual rights only by operating within the terms of such rights – appears to resemble services provided by coercive monopolies. Citizenship is a long-term condition. One of its great benefits is, indeed, that it offers substantial predictability and objectivity – that is, the rule of law. But can there be *bona fide* competition among governments such that despite retaining some characteristics resembling those of coercive monopolies, they are in fact non-coercive? Governments of this apparently monopolistic type would be more like air carriers in transit rather than a postal monopoly.

Anarchist critics argue that no such apparent monopoly is necessary. They insist that one could simultaneously gain defense services from competing agents – shop for them on the model of shopping for home-delivered pizzas or plumbing services. The idea is that one could gain criminal legal services, as well as others of course, from one legal agent but then decide that one no longer wished that agent to be the provider and proceed to subscribe to another legal agency or enterprise within the same territory. In short, one could change one's citizenship as easily as one changes which pizzeria delivers one's pizza.

Put the question another way: could there be legal service provisions without countries? Could legal services be delivered to citizens without their having to move, or could they even be divided such that one agency offers police service, another prisons, another adjudication? Or is this impossible for the same reasons that it is impossible during a flight from Los Angeles to New York to enjoy the benefits of both competent service and of switching mid-flight to another carrier? Perhaps even the separation of distinct parts cannot work, just as it would not work for a patient in a hospital to get a bed from one agency, blood tests from another and nursing from yet another, without some common provider that coordinates it all.

Many minarchists dispute the notion that governments *must* be coercive (in the sense of being rights-violating, as opposed to using force while protecting rights), even though a proper government would naturally govern within a homogeneous region, like a country. They admit that throughout history, governments with jurisdiction over homogeneous regions have been more or less coercive. But they contend that this is neither unavoidable nor necessary. Just as marriages could be free of major flaws, although few in fact are, so too could governments be free of major flaws, including coercive policies like taxation or conscription or even banning secession.

Even in the Weberian conception of government, government is only a monopoly *per se*, not a *coercive* monopoly. When Weber says of government that it 'successfully claims the monopoly of the legitimate use of physical force within a given territory,' his characterization does not in itself imply that such a successful claim must itself issue a legal or coercively maintained monopoly.

The controversy between anarchists and minarchists over government institutions or 'services' takes place in a certain ethical context. We all assume that human beings *ought to* defend themselves against criminals and foreign aggressors. This is a view not shared by old-fashioned anarchists, those who reject all law-enforcement; but it seems uncontroversial among those libertarians debating the nature of limited government or legal services.

But if the division of labor is a sound principle, not everyone ought to do his own defending – it is quite complicated to do so, especially considering the appropriate due-process constraints of a free and civilized society. We ought, instead, to employ specialists. Government is a specialist in securing justice and the rule of law. But government is logically or conceptually a pre-market institution. It is required *for* the maintenance, elaboration and protection of the individual, including private property and rights.

Anarchists claim that it would be a violation of individual rights to have governments that aren't competing *within a given geographical region*, akin to how different pizza delivery providers compete in the same neighborhood.[21] It is true that just as one can move from one apartment house to another, one gated community to another, and one airline service provider to another (once a flight is completed), so one should be able to move from a legal jurisdiction to another. But one could not have certain crucial legal services – particularly those involving the criminal law – provided in the manner of pizza deliveries. The type of service being provided involves a long-term commitment to having one's rights protected and innumerable activities conducted within the framework of such protection, something that requires ongoing mutual access to courts, police services, and so on.

Of course, libertarian anarchists contend that if the competition among governments does not occur within the same geographical area, one is being unjustly compelled to take one's legal 'business' elsewhere, a violation of basic rights. They also seem to suggest that under their proposed scenario of competing governments there is no sustained risk of accused or convicted criminals switching jurisdictions midway through legal proceedings! Presumably, it would not pay, in the long run, for courts in adjacent or even remote jurisdictions to go against the judgments of competing courts. By theoretical fiat, then, in the anarchist world of the future all mafias and PLOs would disappear. All criminals would either be law-abiding criminals, or else helpless to set up and patronize their own 'defense agencies.'

This analysis rests, I believe, on the (economic?) assumption of the universally agreed-to utility of common standards in market services. Indeed, in free markets, providers do often converge on the standards they deploy for their customers – so that after the initial conflict between, for example, different VCR services, the market eventually settled for one over the other. VHS won out over Beta, and now DVD is winning out over VCR.

Justice, however, is not a utilitarian objective but a rights-based objective, aiming at settling disputes in individual cases, not over the long run. Even if in time the various courts would see the utility of adhering to common standards, at any given time they may well choose not do so (just as in a DVD world we continue to use VHS and even Beta). And this would be an obstacle to justice that is supposed to be swift and efficient *for individual citizens*.

Justice and property rights are not utilitarian objectives and not marketable ones. The functioning of enterprises *presuppose* property rights. In order to invest, trade, hire, fire, contract and do all those things enterprises are likely to do, those who embark upon an enterprise must have their right to private property and freedom of trade/contract *clearly (enough) defined* and *well (enough) protected* so as to carry on with their tasks. And the definition and protection of private property and related rights within a complex society requires objective law and its impartial enforcement. While the realm of politics may not be capable of yielding fully objective results, even in the judiciary of a free society, nor produce fully impartial enforcement of the law, it is explicitly committed to serving the individual good of all citizens *qua* rights-bearing citizens (the 'public good'), not various private interests whose special pleading tends to prevent such objectivity and impartiality.[22]

There is a threat of an infinite regress if law itself is understood as just one more form of enterprise. Your neighborhood has a barbershop, auto factory, farm, insurance agency, and brokerage firm; next on the block is your adjudicating firm. Whereas with the others there can be several on the same block, almost literally, with the adjudicating agency, especially *vis-à-vis crimes*, several different ones serving the community would pose problems, if we assume a context in which they are all independent and do not have to answer to a government with oversight power. Suppose one agency is hired by the barbershop, another by the factory and a third by the insurance agent.

And suppose some of these come into serious legal disagreements among themselves, involving basic rights violations, not mere contractual disputes. How is the adjudication to ensue? Will the plaintiff be able to secure the presence of the defendant in the same courtroom? Not if the defendant refuses to deal with the same adjudicating agency as the plaintiff.

More importantly, suppose there is a dispute between the adjudicating agency and some *other* adjudicating agency.

A Swiss-cheese conception of governments operating within the same territory – all possessing 'ultimate' authority to conclude disputed arbitrations – seems inherently unworkable (and has worked only sporadically through history – for example, in ancient Iceland). It is almost inevitable that if such 'competition' is attempted, it will, in some significant cases, generate irresolvable legal conflicts – not merely irresolvable in practical fact but in principle. For if two 'competing' legal authorities themselves dispute the outcome of a case, which one may trump the other? Who will adjudicate between the adjudicators? By theoretical stipulation they are not, after all, operating within yet another governmental framework, answerable to an uber-government or 'true' government that is authorized to resolve disputes between defense agencies by reference to a common legal framework.

The fact that such 'irreconcilable differences' could not be resolved even with the force of law – given the fact that both parties enjoy the same full right to exercise the force of law, as deployed according to their own separate standards – thus defeats the very purpose of law, namely, a means of just, individual-rights-respecting, systematic resolution of conflicts between parties who cannot or will not work out the conflict on their own. That is why we value the law and, however bitter and disappointed we may be, accede to legal outcomes even when a court does not rule in our favor. We sense, at least implicitly, what society must be like if courts did not have the power to definitively resolve passionately disputed cases in which both parties believe they are in the right.

Anarchists like Bruce Benson, author of *The Enterprise of Law*,[23] have answers to these questions, resorting mainly to interagency contractual agreements, as inspired by the model of international law.

In the international arena we have no binding court of last resort, yet often the World Court and similar bodies function quite successfully as adjudicators of disputes between parties with different citizenship and, indeed, between different countries. Why so? Because there are various motivations that impel the parties to come to a resolution, usually involving business disputes. Yet this does not always occur, and it is especially problematic where criminal law is concerned.

Different countries hold different standards of justice and reciprocity is often resisted. When Yugoslavia's past-president Slobodan Milosevic was indicted by an international court, compliance was not initially forthcoming because Yugoslavia did not then recognize the authority of the court, at least not within its own jurisdiction. When the presence of ex-Chilean dictator

Augusto Pinochet was sought in the Spanish courts, he had to be captured in England where he went for medical treatment. Chile did not cooperate with the Spanish authorities. And when Bertrand Russell and Jean-Paul Sartre established the international court in which the United States of America was indicted and, if I recall correctly, convicted of war crimes in Vietnam, the US government refused to respond.[24] And these are only the more visible cases. Thousands of others where international cooperation in criminal adjudication is absent understandably go unnoticed. Those, I think, may be deemed failures of the enterprise of law or at least the model of law as a sort of competitive enterprise.

On the other hand, one can embrace the enterprise model with some modifications; the point is that systems of adjudication need to be broadly integrated to be functional. To the extent that a Benson-type model works, it is because it resembles a true government; to the extent that it does not, it is because it does not sufficiently resemble a true government. If we consider, say, the United States, Canada, Mexico, New Zealand, Australia, Japan and all other countries as fora of dispute-adjudication, the possibility of changing one's residence or citizenship affords one something akin to benefiting from competition. Even within countries with a substantial federalist political organization there is the opportunity for benefiting from competition. New York, New Jersey, Pennsylvania, and so on – states of the United States – all compete for 'customers' of their adjudication services. Certainly we see such competition functioning vis-à-vis taxation, which in this context could be viewed as court fees. They vary. And parties to potential disputes will shop around to find the most efficient process at the lowest cost.

In this scenario, however, the fora wherein adjudication can proceed are large habitations, with thousands or millions of potential disputants signed up within the same homogeneous system. They are usually committed fairly long term and may leave only if they have a clean record and no adjudication pending that involves them. Moreover, within the system, various layers of authority operate, so that the appeal process is integrated and there is in principle a court of last resort – an ultimate arbiter.

In this sense, an adjudication service resembles some other enterprises in which one signs up for the long haul. Insurance services are like this, as are apartment rentals, car leasing and even marriages. Midway through the duration of the long-term contract, the option to exit does not exist or exists only at great cost. And this is because the very idea underlying these kinds of relationships between customers and service providers or trading partners, is that reliable, ongoing and predictable arrangements are of benefit to all of the parties.

Even within the same jurisdiction, many kinds of competition could be accepted, as long as there were a governmental structure that could resolve disputes among the competing 'governments.' There would be one actual government and any number of sub- or demi-governments – security guard firms, arbitration courts and the like. But if the State of New York found that a particular arbitration agency was chronically meting out injustice in violation of explicit arbitration contracts, the New York government could be justified in investigating the arbitration agency, ordering changes, and/or shutting down the arbitration agency. And the arbitration agency would not be free to say, 'Hey, butt out, New York State and/or federal government! You're just another defense agency on the block here; you play adjudication your way and we'll play it our way.' Rather, the private court would be obliged to submit to the judgment of the government.

Thus it seems that both the traditional conception of a homogeneous country and free and open competition could be secured, satisfying – one can always hope – the demands of both minarchists and 'anarchists' among libertarians. 'Anarchists' would have to concede the necessity of a robust ultimate arbiter in matters of legal enforcement; minarchists would have to concede that many forms of defense-service competition could coexist within a single regime if that regime (government) provides a means of that ultimate arbitration. It has always been my view that there is some misunderstanding about this matter among supporters of the free society. They need not be divided on it. So long as the commitment to respecting individual rights is unwavering, a resolution between the anarchists and minarchists, along the lines sketched above, is possible. This is so even though in some cases the parties carrying on the dispute seem almost to have a vested interest in not having it resolved amicably, of continuing to charge the other side with breaching fundamental principles of individual rights. That seems a sad mistake to me and distracts from the far more significant task of making the case for libertarianism in the face of innumerable *bona fide* statist challenges.

Notes

1 Lysander Spooner, *No Treason: A Constitution of No Authority* (Boston, MA: L. Spooner, 1867).

2 For the most recent publication of Murray N. Rothbard's libertarian–anarchist essay 'Society Without a State,' see Aeon Skoble and T. R. Machan, eds, *Political Philosophy: Essential Selections* (Upper Saddle River, NJ: Prentice-Hall, 1999), pp. 488–99. It also appears in J. R. Pennock and J. W. Chapman (eds), *Anarchism* Nomos XIX (New York: New York University Press, 1978), pp. 191–207, and in T. R. Machan, *The Libertarian Reader* (Totowa, NJ: Rowman and Littlefield, 1982), pp. 53–63. Originally published in *The Libertarian Forum*, January 1975, pp. 3–7.

3 Robert Nozick, *Anarchy, State, and Utopia* (New York: Basic Books, 1974), p. 67.

4 I indicated my stance on this issue in 'Ethics vs. Coercion: Morality or Just Values?' in Llewellyn H. Rockwell, Jr et al., eds, *Man, Economy and Liberty* (Auburn, AL: Ludwig von Mises Institute, 1988).

5 Rothbard discusses the issue in *The Ethics of Liberty* (Atlantic-Highlands, NJ: Humanities Press, 1982), pp. 162–3. For his definition, see p. 171, where he says,

> The State may therefore be defined as that organization which possesses either or both (in actual fact, almost always both) of the following characteristics: (a) it acquires its revenue by physical coercion (taxation); and (b) it achieves a compulsory monopoly of force and of ultimate decision-making power over a given territorial area.

6 Arguably though, not everyone's consent may be needed. Suppose I hire a bodyguard who consents to become my defender against all aggressors. Some person then attacks me and my bodyguard defends me from this attack, a course of conduct that may become violent toward the aggressor. Now, does it matter that the aggressor did not consent to my bodyguard's defending me? No. The aggressor in effect gives consent by taking an action that has as its natural, rationally-to-be-expected result, my defending myself either personally or through an agent. So, *does it matter that a government that acts purely defensively isn't consented to by, say, criminals or foreign aggressors?* This would be a government that does not coercively collect taxes, so consent would only be relevant to its getting hired and being paid voluntarily by those whom it defends. Payment could be in the form of premiums, as with insurance; or per-service, as with some attorney or dentist fees; or bundled with prices for various goods and services, as with payments for newspapers that also provide magazines on Sundays.

7 Max Weber, *Economy and Society: An Outline of Interpretive Sociology* (Berkeley: University of California Press, 1978), p. 56.

8 See, for example, Murray N. Rothbard, *For a New Liberty*, pp. 49–50 (1973); John Hospers, 'What Libertarianism is,' in *Liberty for the 21st Century*, p. 14 (Tibor R. Machan and Douglas B. Rasmussen, eds, 1995); David Boaz, *Libertarianism*, p. 187 (1997); Robert Paul Wolff, *In Defense of Anarchism*, p. 1 (1970); Ludwig von Mises, *Liberalism in the Classical Tradition*, p. 35 (1985).

9 Tyler Cowen, 'Law as a Public Good,' 8 *Econ. & Phil.* 249, 250 (1992).

10 John Hasnas, 'Some Reflections on the Minimal State' (unpublished manuscript).

11 Stephen Holmes and Cass Sunstein, *The Cost of Rights: Why Liberty Depends on Taxes* (New York: W. W. Norton, 2000).

12 For a succinct account, see Aeon Skoble, 'The Anarchism Controversy,' in Machan and Rasmussen, eds, *Liberty for the 21st Century*, pp. 77–109.

13 This is the kind of monopoly that Robert Nozick envisions as the dominant legal authority. See Nozick, *Anarchy, State, and Utopia*, p. 109.

14 See, Tibor R. Machan, 'Dissolving the Problem of Public Goods: Financing Government Without Coercive Measures,' in Machan, ed., *The Libertarian Reader*. I have also advanced some points in support of this position in Tibor R. Machan, *Individuals and Their Rights* (La Salle, IL: Open Court Publishing Co., Inc., 1989), Chapter 7 ('Individualism and Political Authority').

15 Jack Sanders, 'The State of Statelessness,' in Jack Sanders and Jan Narveson, eds, *For and Against the State* (Lanham, MD: Rowman and Littlefield, 1996), p. 286.

16 See Machan, *Individuals and Their Rights*, Chapter 7.

17 For a discussion of Locke and anarchism, see Stuart D. Warner, 'Anarchical Snares: A Reading of Locke's Second Treatise,' *Reason Papers*, No 14 (Spring 1989), pp. 1–24.

18 David Kelley, 'The Necessity of Government,' *The Freeman* 24 (April 1974).

19 Max Weber's definition of 'the State' does not specify coercive or non-coercive monopoly as characteristic of states or governments. Even Hasnas claims of the state only that it 'monopolizes the basic policing, rule-making, and adjudicative functions in an identifiable area.' This is ambiguous: the crucial issue is *how* a government comes to monopolize these functions: coercively, or by the consent of those to whom they are provided. Only when he adds taxation to the definition of the state or government does the coercive nature of such an institution become evident. But that is begging the question, just as Rothbard did when he made taxation a defining element of government.

20 It is instructive to note that dealing with travel providers is often frustrating in nearly identical ways to dealing with government agencies. Once one is on board or has signed up, changing carriers is very cumbersome and, given one's plans, nearly impossible and financially prohibitive. Those providing the service seem to be well aware of this, given how they tend to conduct themselves toward their customers. Not in all cases, of course. One can disembark from a London cab and find another easily enough, although it may be tougher when one is going to some remote region of the city (let alone some village in New Mexico).

21 There are some cases of quasi-Swiss-cheese type countries that might be pointed to as quite peaceful and operational, such as Baarle-Nassau/Baarle-Hertog. History has left us here with a territory composed of two municipal jurisdictions. The shape of this realm is unique: it belongs in part to Holland and in part to Belgium. The people are reported to be 'quite comfortable with the situation, even though it raises so many complicated and difficult problems that even the most brilliant jurists are puzzled.' For more on this see http://wings.buffalo.edu/philosophy/faculty/smith/baarle.htm. Arguably this shows their viability, although not superior efficiency, for purposes of administering a system of just criminal law. But in practice the residents can choose which taxes they must pay only by moving (in some cases, they will move the front door of their home or shop in order to take advantage of the more favorable tax code).

22 For why the goal of objectivity and impartiality is thought to be impossible to achieve, see James M. Buchanan and Gordon Tullock, *The Calculus of Consent, Logical Foundations of Constitutional Democracy* (Ann Arbor: University of Michigan Press, 1962), the work that advanced the theory of public choice, according to which public servants are just as utility-maximizing as market agents.

I dispute that this is a necessary feature of public service in any type of political order. It is, of course, *typical* behavior of public servants in what economists call a 'rent seeking' society welfare state. However, in a free, libertarian government such public or civil servants may well carry out their oath of office to defend the constitution because the constitution does not sanction special interest legislation and regulation. For more on this, see Tibor R. Machan, *Private Rights and Public Illusions* (New Brunswick, NJ: Transaction Books, 1995).

23 Bruce Benson, *The Enterprise of Law: Justice without the State* (San Francisco, CA: Pacific Research Institute for Public Policy, 1990).

24 More recently the administration of US President George W. Bush refused to accede to the authority of a World Criminal Court.

Chapter 10

Robert Nozick and the Libertarian Alternative

Like its more extreme brother, socialism, welfare statism has been tried and been found wanting.

Throughout much of the twentieth century an often-expressed and prominent political ideal haunting America and the rest of the West was hardly distinguishable from that of the former Soviet Russia or Communist China. The welfare state too, after all, aims at establishing, by means of government action, a conception of social welfare. It is distinguished from state socialism and communism only by its *means* for achieving its purpose and by the degree to which the alleged ideal is enforced. Thinkers like Rawls, Sen, Nussbaum, Dworkin, Sandel and so on all seem to favor a substantially egalitarian welfare regime because, in their view, things are unfair otherwise. They aren't concerned for the poor, *per se*, but about lack of equality, income gaps and the like. Certain concessions are made to the usefulness of retaining some human liberty, political democracy, and due process of law.[1]

But the quasi-egalitarian welfare state can no longer be advanced with complete self-confidence as a just system. Those who dream of building it have had to confront a troublesome reality: none of the citizens and groups who were to be satisfied with its policies is in fact satisfied. The welfare state is now seen to be but a somewhat more civilized version of Thomas Hobbes's state of nature – a war of all against all. In the wake of this development, the intellectual climate has shifted. One major development was the publication, in the early 1970s, of Robert Nozick's book, *Anarchy, State, and Utopia*,[2] which defends the social order of *laissez-faire* capitalism.

Nozick argues that justice, properly conceived, is best secured within the framework of the minimal state. He begins by assuming that all individuals have certain natural rights as identified in the tradition of John Locke's natural rights theory. Nozick does not defend this claim but argues that a social order developed with scrupulous respect for such rights best maintains justice. His argument takes the form of a transcendental deduction, postulating those principles which make sense of our moral intuitions respecting how human beings should live among each other. Having demonstrated that respecting individual rights will satisfy these moral intuitions, Nozick has shown, at least, that the principles are sufficient for a just system.

Nozick's recognition of the lack of moral foundations for his political position leaves it open to skepticism from critics like Samuel Scheffler,

Thomas Scanlon, and Thomas Nagel, who find fault with libertarianism on the grounds that Nozick's argument lacks moral foundations. My aim in this chapter is to reply to criticism of the Nozickian system. I will not, however, be defending Nozick's *argument* for that system.

Although the significance of his work has generated considerable interest in libertarianism, those inspired by Nozick to consider it have not gone beyond his own work, and appear to think that the shortcomings of that work represent shortcomings of libertarianism *per se*. But the theory of justice underlying the libertarian viewpoint may indeed have good support already.[3] At any rate, all interested parties should look beyond Nozick in their efforts to understand and perhaps develop a just political system. American citizens in general, and in particular those involved in politics and law, would also benefit from a reexamination of what is, after all, a powerful tradition in American politics.

The case for the free society offered by Robert Nozick relies on the possibility of identifying at least some very basic moral and political principles. Nozick is not a skeptic. Nor did John Locke consider his defense of the minimal state – a constitutionally limited republican form of government – as essentially pragmatic or utilitarian. He believed, with Nozick, that the form of society he advocated is proper for human beings; that is, it accords with human nature and that people *should* establish a society with a minimal state as the means of legal order, not that human beings would automatically do so. The idea of natural rights is, then, a normative one, meant to draw a distinction between rights that *happen* to be upheld by legal powers (sometimes referred to as positive rights) and rights that legal powers *ought* to uphold (natural rights).

In Nozick's view, the legal system of a free society would work to protect individuals against aggression from both domestic and foreign sources. But to determine what constitutes the sphere violations of which would represent aggression,[4] the system of natural rights is incorporated within a constitution administered with the consent of the governed (in whatever manner this can be achieved). At the heart of this system of natural rights is the right to property: the natural right of each individual to seek and obtain, as well as trade and bequeath, valued items found in nature and the market. The evolving legal structure based on this system would be a reflection of the detailed implications of these natural rights for the concrete affairs of men and women in the community.

It is evident from the above sketch that the society Nozick defends is similar to, though hardly identical with, the system practiced in the United States; his position stresses precisely those aspects of this system which are gradually being abandoned both in law and in the minds of those who forge America's institutions. Thus, it is no surprise that following the publication of Nozick's book many essays appeared which were highly critical of his position. Though I will not be considering many well-known Marxist critics,[5] some of these offering recent criticism no doubt echo ideas Marx and other prominent figures have popularized.[6] Many other critics make use of another and more recent anti-libertarian approach, that of John Rawls in his *A Theory of Justice.*[7]

Rawls argued that justice must be understood by reference to a hypothetical contract entered into 'behind the veil of ignorance' by individuals who know nothing of their individual attributes, capacities, prospects, and aspirations – but who nonetheless wish to devise a system of principles that accords with moral intuitions that (somehow) persist in this state of ignorance. Such a contract would omit considerations of what individuals want and have reason to expect and would focus only on some workable scheme consistent with conventional and widely held notions of right and wrong. It is not entirely clear whether the two principles that Rawls derives from this scheme – the principle of equal liberty and the difference principle – would have to be enforced by government, although in view of the paramount need for redistribution of benefits (and disadvantages) in his proposed system, it would be virtually impossible to exclude extensive governmental coercion from the system.[8]

Those who criticize Nozick from Rawlsian premises tend to stress precisely this alleged need for government to equalize benefits and hardships. But a free society limits the role of government to keeping the peace, and it encourages individual initiative without coercively interfering with personal and voluntary collective action; such a society thus neglects the second Rawlsian principle which allows social or economic inequality only if it benefits the least-advantaged social class. Rawls ignores the role of personal initiative in achieving desirable ends, treating such achievement as the result of nothing more than accidentally distributed natural assets (upbringing, fortune, genetic endowment or the like), and therefore as morally arbitrary. Rawlsians thus believe that the free society perpetrates an injustice by permitting individuals who do not deserve it to achieve disproportionate levels of well-being.

Another criticism issues from both neo-Marxists and neo-conservatives, who often chide the free society for failing to give official encouragement to the moral or spiritual dimensions of life.[9] On the libertarian view, the government of a free society would be engaging in unauthorized conduct if it tried to promote virtue in any way beyond what is entailed by acting to preserve and protect the individual rights of all. But such critics charge that peacekeeping and the resulting encouragement of private initiative is insufficient to maintain a decent social order.

It is true enough that neither John Locke nor Robert Nozick has developed a sufficiently robust moral theory to answer some of these challenges. Locke merely mentioned that all of us must abide by the law of nature, independently of positive or civil law. He not only did not develop fully enough an ethical position but in places explicitly endorsed a hedonistic view of values.[10] Nozick, for his part, arrives at the basic political principles of individual rights in a round-about manner rather than on the basis of clear-cut and articulated moral principles. He assumes these principles of rights and squares them with our moral intuitions, from which he concludes that his assumptions are sound. But moral intuitions can be used to support conflicting basic political principles – for example, those of both Nozick and Rawls.[11] So while certain intuitions may be ultimately sound, as philosophical investigators we cannot simply leave it at that but must learn what if any objective bases exist for them.

In any case, Locke and Nozick are not the only supporters of the free society. In our times, numerous works offer multifarious economic, sociological, historical, and philosophical support for the libertarian alternative. Not all scholars who have contributed to the discussion are equally prominent, of course. The critics are not simply attacking Nozick or Locke but the system of libertarianism itself. If they are to do a creditable job, they must confront these other efforts. Apparently taking Thomas Kuhn's thesis about the hegemony of received paradigms[12] as if it were prescriptive, the critics often argue only with those who have achieved prominence.

The central complaint about Nozick's position is that our moral intuitions warrant more coercive statism than his analysis permits.[13] This argument is well aimed at Nozick, who seeks to draw support for his rights theory from our intuitions. Consider, for example, his view that,

> Taxation of earnings from labor is on a par with forced labor. Some persons find this claim obviously true: taking the earnings of n hours labor is like taking n hours for another's purpose. Others find the claim absurd. But even these, if they object to forced labor, would oppose forcing unemployed hippies to work for the benefit of the needy.[14]

To this line of argumentation, which relies on what people tend to believe about various forms of conduct regardless of whether they have good grounds for their beliefs, Thomas Scanlon replies that

> even if the notions of forcing and voluntariness sometimes incorporate notions of rights, as Nozick's analysis of voluntariness suggests, they certainly do not always do so. Where they do not, it seems unlikely that we can settle the question of the moral acceptability of a form of treatment by appeal to intuitions about forcing and voluntariness. If these notions do incorporate moral principles, then such appeals to intuition are going to be suspect when these principles are themselves in dispute … .[15]

Another attack stresses the failure of Nozick's position as contrasted with the one he attacks. Nozick believes that any system of society that proposes to strive for collective end-states – for example, a particular distribution of wealth, or a specific quality of life – will encounter inherent contradictions in its policies, and will also violate even the degree of freedom that most egalitarians are willing to consider indispensable. This last is true because, given even that minimal level of freedom, citizens can begin to upset any achieved end-state with the amount of freedom they are allowed, such that to reestablish the desired end-state would require continually renewed, extensive force.

Thomas Nagel suggests that this scenario does not really present a problem:

> It only seems a problem to Nozick, and a further violation of liberty, because he erroneously interprets the notion of a patterned principle as specifying a distribution of absolute entitlements (like those he believes in) to the wealth or property distributed. But absolute entitlement to property is not what would be allocated to people under a partially egalitarian distribution. Possession would confer the kind of qualified entitlement that exists in a system under which taxes and other conditions are arranged to preserve certain features of the distribution, while permitting choice, use, and exchange of property compatible with it. What someone holds under such a system will not be *his property* in the unqualified sense of Nozick's system of entitlement.[16]

Yet another criticism of Nozick – this one directed against his minimal statism – argues that the delegation of authority as directed by a system of rights would not exhibit the smoothness Nozick assumes. Robert Paul Wolff criticizes the simple rights transfer approach:

> By analogy, in a simple rights-transfer, as when I hire a lawyer to close a real estate sale for me, there is a minute slippage or blockage in the rights transfer, due to the fact that my agent is also an independent human being. Because he is a person as well as an agent, there is a small but nonzero probability that he will exceed his authority, or get his instructions confused, or interpret a situation in a manner that I would not approve. There is also a nonzero probability that I will be unaware of the breakdown or agency, or will be unable to rectify it. Because Nozick focuses his attention on simple rights-transfers, where the probability of slippage falls below the minimal threshold of moral awareness, he fails to see that as the protective association grows, as the rights collected are transferred and retransferred, as my relationship to my so-called agent grows ever more attenuated, I will become less and less able to see my own will, my own moral agency, in the actions of the association's owners and employees.[17]

Finally, another line of criticism concentrates upon Nozick's methodology in *Anarchy, State, and Utopia*, asserting that he fails to pay sufficient heed to basic philosophical spadework. As Samuel Scheffler put it:

> Contemporary philosophers who choose to work within the natural rights tradition need to explicate their use of natural rights terminology. Given the metaphysical associations of the tradition, such philosophers must explain what they *mean* by assigning rights to people. They must, further, say something about the source of these rights, and they must deal with a variety of epistemic questions. How do we know what rights people have? What sorts of evidence justify us in believing that people do have certain rights but do not have certain others?[18]

Others find Nozick's method of 'argument from best explanation' unsuited to his subject matter.[19] Yet some consider him nothing more than an apologist for the kind of society that favors a given segment of the population (the rich) at the expense of others.[20]

Sundry tangential points in Nozick's work have also come under criticism, and I shall presently address one such.[21] First, however, let us consider each of the criticisms just recounted. In view of Nozick's silence on these critical points it seems appropriate to address the critics for another reason. After all, there is more than argumentative gamesmanship at stake here. Quite apart from the goings-on in academic circles, the political systems of the West – insofar as they approximate the system Nozick advocates – are under severe challenge, not only from totalitarians but also from those, like Solzhenitsyn,[22] who claim that Western liberalism lacks moral backbone, and from radical Islamic theologians and terrorists who hold that the West, especially the United States of America, is in cahoots with the devil because it fails to control against materialism and other vices.

I have contributed elsewhere to the philosophical case for the free society[23] in part by arguing[24] that the failure of John Locke has now been remedied in the work of David L. Norton,[25] among others. Norton's individualist ethical system supplies the Lockean idea of natural law (the moral system that exists independently of any legal code) with solid content. Of course this has some bearing on Nozick's argument, since he, too, relies on Locke's natural rights.

For Scanlon, it is not enough that we abhor various forms of coercion. But with Norton's full-blown ethical individualism at hand, distaste for coercion is not the only clue to its impropriety. The very underpinnings of ethical conduct, the freedom of choice to act, is undermined by it. (I have developed this point in various portions of this work, Chapters 2 and 7, in particular.) It is worth, however, spending some time on a particular aspect of this line of argument for libertarianism.

Many who champion human liberty make it clear enough that although ethics matters to every person's life, it isn't necessary to agree on it to defend the free society. They explain that without freedom of choice, when one behaves properly it has no moral significance. Only good conduct that is freely chosen is ethically or morally significant. So only a free society accords with our moral nature – anything else undermines it. Without the sort of liberty defended in free societies, the ethical life, however one might spell it out, must suffer.

There is, however, a feature of certain moral systems that will be significant in whether one considers violating individual liberty very tempting. Plainly put, if an ethical system amounts mainly to working for others – such as utilitarianism or altruism – it is more likely that for people to follow it they need the fear of repercussions, of sanctions. This means that encouraging people to be ethical will require coercion. Those who support vice squads hold this view.

Others, however, believe that when you act immorally, unethically, in the last analysis it comes back to haunt you. This might be called the boomerang effect endorsed in the tradition of Socratic–Aristotelian ethics: wrongdoing is self-destructive, whether immediately or in time – it will cost you at least what you might have gained by being good.

Other ethical positions, however, don't have this element about them. Doing the wrong thing is often seen as precisely self-promoting; others are likely to lose out. And so there is this temptation to break with the notion that 'ought' implies 'can,' meaning if you ought to do something, you must be free. Instead, the idea is that people must be forced to do the right thing; otherwise, they have no reason for doing it.

Of course, whether Socratic–Aristotelian ethics is right in holding that all wrongful conduct ultimately punishes the perpetrator, that virtue brings reward and vice causes loss, is widely debated. In this ethical tradition, called 'eudemonism,' extended famously by Ayn Rand, the idea is quite reasonable. Ethics concerns a set of principles by which one's life can flourish and thrive. So, if one does not act ethically, if one fails to be guided by moral virtues, one will pay dearly – one will be less happy, less fulfilled, less excellent as the human individual one is. So for those within this tradition of moral philosophy there is little risk in championing a fully free society. The bad guys will get their due even if no one punishes them for being bad, here or in an afterlife.

This is not so with utilitarianism, altruism, Kantianism and many religious moralities. The good guys are supposed to be good, just because, and won't be of their own accord, unless they fear the results. For Kantians it is because doing good is just how a rational individual must act – do not by any stretch of the imagination look for any rewards for it. Kant despised the idea that morality is supposed to have pay-offs. For utilitarians, the sheer value of maximum satisfaction, among those capable of being satisfied, is supposed to suffice to motivate good conduct on everyone's part, even if the individual were to be left dissatisfied. And, of course, for the altruist doing the right thing is just something innately good and it would be indecent to expect any personal benefits from it. As the philosopher W. G. Maclagan, wrote, '"Altruism" [is] assuming a duty to relieve the distress and promote the happiness of our fellows …. Altruism is to … maintain quite simply that a man may and should discount altogether his own pleasure or happiness as such when he is deciding what course of action to pursue.'

Perhaps it is persuasive enough to stress that no moral credit accrues, nor any moral blame, to someone who is being coerced. As a lover of individual liberty this is probably all that one can stress, without endorsing a specific moral system (which champions of the free society tend not to wish to do lest they chase off a lot of fellow travelers). But a good dosage of eudemonism will certainly help to convince folks that it is safe enough to have everyone be free, given that when they embark on any sort of personal or social malpractice, they will lose out even if no one lays in on them for it.

We can now return to discussing further the naturalistic conception of ethics and of rights. Worries about the reliability of moral intuitions need no longer trouble us especially in light of a systematic theory showing which moral principles are prior, which subsidiary, and so forth. There is such a theory, and indeed, there has been a good deal written about it for some decades. But academic philosophers have not examined it thoroughly enough to consider it worthy of confrontation.[26]

According to eudemonist individualist ethics, the flourishing of the individual human being as such is the highest goal at which each person ought to aim, and certain basic principles of conduct – notably the ethical virtues suggested by Aristotle and elaborated by others more recently – will serve as broad guidelines in this effort. It remains, of course, for the individual to make sure how they guide him or her in his or her particular circumstances. Here is where so many are tempted by relativism and subjectivism but needlessly. The objective application of universal basic principles in any practical science, including ethics, varies a great deal, while the principles remain the same. The idea is that when applied to the issue of the constitution of a human community as such – not a club or association or corporation or university but a human community – these basic moral principles imply the primacy of individual rights to liberty. That is because without such liberty, the moral life is severely impeded.

The Lockean natural rights are just those basic socio-political principles which, when established as a feature of a constitution, enable all members of a society to aspire to individual excellence without the fundamental threat of irresolvable conflict.

Of course, to make out the full case for this position does indeed require what Scheffler claims any natural rights theory requires, namely extensive philosophical analysis. Nozick may have thought the work already being done when he published was not well enough developed to make mention of them – or perhaps he had not yet become familiar enough with them to invoke them with confidence.[27] Nevertheless, Scanlon's objections are answerable.

Philosophers have argued that we can identify certain first principles that enable us to avoid resting an argument on an infinite regress.[28] It has also been shown that reductionism about the nature of existence is unjustified, so that room exists for such domains as the mental, the moral, and the political.[29] The compatibility of essentialism with individualism has also been demonstrated, so as to secure both objectivity and diversity in the normative theory that supports the free society.[30] The possibility of knowing moral truth has also been discussed in direct relationship to libertarian political theory. So Scheffler's criticism against Nozick is unjustified when wielded against natural rights libertarians. Nozick himself did not advance the kind of theory in which the philosophical underpinnings of his political assumptions required extensive discussion but other libertarians certainly did.

Nagel thinks Nozick should not worry about wholesale coercion. Since no one 'really' owns what he or she possesses, interfering with use, exchange, and the like cannot be regarded as coercive.[31] Replying to Nagel's attack on Nozick, however, requires a less extensive theoretical project than a close look at our contemporary world where the absence of protection of private property rights is a notorious cause of poverty and underdevelopment.

The issue of whether there could be anything like *absolute* entitlement is a red herring. The operative term here is entitlement. Being entitled to something *must* involve certain specifications as to what should be respected and will be protected in doing with that to which one is entitled, and what others may or may not do with that in the light of this. Nozick only stresses that in a system where various end-states *must* be maintained (that is, as a mandated feature of a social system), no such specification can be made, so that arbitrariness enters at all levels.

A condo owner might be entitled to the full use of her backyard as a vegetable garden, but not as a tennis court. So she has no 'absolute' or limitless entitlement to the backyard. But if she is entitled to use it as a vegetable garden and shortly after she plants her garden the state determines that its various end-states might be more efficiently pursued by prohibiting the garden, the entitlement is empty. Exactly this is what is going on with the current abuse of eminent domain laws, for example, when a firm like Costco in the USA is able to induce city officials to condemn private property so as to lease it to the large firm that offers more taxes to the city!

That Nagel fails to see the force of Nozick's criticism is his fault alone, for no one needs enlist a notion of absolute entitlement to show that coercive enforcement of various end-states is incompatible with *any* kind of entitlement, even the right to free speech. In the history of constitutional law the alleged entitlement to say and publish whatever one wishes (within the reasonable or at least clear-cut limits of certain laws against libel, obscenity, or incitement to riot) is really nonexistent. Businesses may not speak or publish by way of the electromagnetic spectrum if the government believes their doing so will upset some prescribed pattern or end-state (for example, by increasing smoking; hence ads promoting smoking are banned).[32] That is to say, even the entitlement conferred by the First Amendment is often treated as merely a *privilege*, revocable in exactly the fashion predicted by Nozick as characteristic of the welfare state and defended by Nagel and co.

Wolff's criticism of the simple rights-transfer approach seems on target if Nozick's approach is taken literally. But need one suppose that he conceives of actual cases of rights-transfer in the literal geometrical fashion his language suggests? All the physical sciences make allowances for errors in measurement, despite the fact that their calculations begin with idealized cases. So even if we left Nozick's approach intact, the elaborate rights-transfers in real life can withstand the tendency toward error, given institutions providing appropriate review and conflict resolution, for example, a court system.

But even if Wolff's criticism stands against Nozick, does it stand against the free society *per se*? Not really, especially in light of Wolff's demonstration that we can make ourselves aware of the problem of rights-transfer, and take it into consideration as we exercise our moral judgments and undertake risks. If there is a sound argument for undertaking these risks, then despite the chance of error, one might wish to undertake them. Indeed, it is because of the great probability of threats and acts in violation of a person's rights in the state of nature that one authorizes specialists to act on one's behalf, precisely for the purpose of reducing that probability. Nozick admittedly fails to demonstrate that one *should* take this relatively lower risk. He merely argues that, motivated by fear, people *would* take it. But other defenders of the free society show that the establishment of genuinely limited, non-coercive but purely defensive (and retaliatory) government with the function of protecting and preserving rights is objectively valuable, despite obvious risks.[33] Wolff's anarchistic objections, then, aren't enough to show that Nozick's system is unjustified even though they do point to certain weaknesses in Nozick's own argument for that system.[34]

Let me very briefly outline an argument in support of the objective value of a government which has as its functions the protection and preservation of individual rights. Even libertarians, those labeling themselves 'anarchists,' reject the *terms* of it but not its substance; since, they fully support defense agencies, justice agencies and the like, all of which are based on laws that aim to protect individual rights.[35]

Human beings are moral agents. They can flourish only when they make provisions for exercising moral choice. To do so, they must protect themselves by using science and technology to exercise control over inanimate nature and morally dumb nature (that is, creatures other than human beings). But in dealing with other human beings, who are capable by their own choice of either enhancing or obstructing one's efforts to live successfully, everyone must resort to different approaches from what they do to control non-human nature.

To treat others as if they were not moral agents is to fly in the face of reality.[36] To ignore the fact that they nevertheless can be obstacles in one's own life is to do likewise. The appropriate approach institutes a system for dealing with those who choose to engage in such obstruction. (By 'appropriate' I mean 'warranted by reference to the nature of human existence.') It should be kept in mind here that reference to human nature is meant to be taken quite literally, which implies that it is possible to know what every human being – other than crucially incapacitated ones for whom special provisions are made in the law – essentially is.

This is a crucial point in light of the widespread nominalism and radical (Rortyite) pragmatism that permeates contemporary intellectual life, whereby designating something as, for example, 'a human being,' is regarded as merely a convenient, expedient, or arbitrary decision with no possibility of objective support.[37] In other words, dealing with other human beings requires that we act with justice, and dealing with their obstruction of one's humanity – violations of individual rights – requires that we abide by due process. Thus, while a rock may be crushed if it blocks one's way, or a fly may be squashed if it is a nuisance, a person very likely to be guilty of theft, even of rape or murder, may not be killed, or indeed punished at all, absent a conviction by a court of competent jurisdiction.[38]

Government is an instrument for the administration of justice. As such, it is objectively valuable to each human being who lives amongst other human beings and for whom the administration of justice can become relevant.

Nozick's approach is very different from the one taken above. The former approach to political philosophy is Aristotelian in that it takes account of the proper ends of human life and evaluates whether proposed institutions enhance the achievement of such proper ends. Nozick seems to have wanted to follow more modern lines of argumentation, and he did succeed in showing that by methods very similar to those of Rawls, he could develop a political theory with very different consequences. Nozick uses the method of a detective whose aim is to explain the past. But the function of political theory is to guide our actions in the public affairs of the future.[39]

Some, following the Canadian Marxist C. B. Macpherson, try to show that Nozick is simply an apologist for bourgeois interests.[40] The charge is misconceived, swallowing as it does whole the notion that thinkers of a certain economic background are constrained to think along certain lines. Such a bourgeois theorist as Nozick supposedly cannot help but argue for capitalism – which, if true, makes it hard to understand why there are so many bourgeois socialists about.

The one interesting feature of this attack is that certain ways of understanding the free society tend to encourage it. When some economists with a free market orientation maintain that everyone acts with the sole motive of maximizing his or her private satisfaction (or of maximizing his or her utilities), the idea can turn upon the economists themselves, who can then be charged with merely wishing to secure their own satisfaction, even as they engage in economic analysis. As opposed to seeking truth – generally regarded as a possible and proper goal of scholarship – the economist insists we are all slaves of our elemental desire to be satisfied and fulfilled by means of acquiring material things, or whatever it happens to be that makes us feel pleased. Truth itself is merely incidental to this; some may be fulfilled by it, but others may be fulfilled by untruth. As the late Aaron Director of the University of Chicago's economics school once said, 'What's important is utility, not truth.' And for economists, 'utility' amounts to desire-satisfaction, regardless of what the desire may be. To assess or evaluate a desire is presumably pointless; as Stigler and Becker stipulate in a very famous essay: one cannot question desires.[41]

Because Nozick invokes, at least in part, the economic model of human action in his analysis of the development of a just social order, this kind of self-referential point can be legitimately scored against him.[42] But in the end, the debit has little to do with the substance of Nozick's theory. One must realize, as noted already, that Rawls starts by assuming a modicum of self-interest on the part of those who enter into a contract behind a veil of ignorance. Marx, too, assumed that, as directed by their economic conditions, members of different social classes would seek their own best advantage. Those who wish to argue with this general method of invoking the idea of self-serving motivation in analyses of social and political affairs, could do far better by taking on such philosophers as Thomas Hobbes, Adam Smith, and Karl Marx, than by zeroing in on those who make only a partial use of the idea.

A similar issue emerges in a comment by Thomas C. Grey:

> Radical libertarianism depends heavily on the rejection of the concept of human needs as distinguished from wants and preferences. See, for example, D. Friedman, *The Machinery of Freedom* 65 (1973). ('The word "need" should be eliminated from the vocabulary of political discourse,' ibid.) The notion that needs are simply wants which the speaker approves of and the related notion that wants are insatiable and infinitely variable together entail the rejection of any conception of a finite and discernible human nature as the basis for ethical argument. Yet if this conception is rejected, what is the non-utilitarian ethical basis for the rights which libertarians assert? Are not the protection of life, liberty and property against aggression important because of some essential human need for security against such intrusions?[43]

This is a formidable challenge but it ill applies to Nozick, or even to Friedman. After all, there is a difference between making talk of needs a part of political discourse and invoking some idea of needs in the preliminary analysis from which one might arrive at various political conclusions. In fairness to Grey, there certainly are some libertarian-oriented thinkers who would excise the concept of need from all discourse and substitute the concept of preference throughout.[44] Be that as it may, it is uncertain that the substitute Grey offers secures an ethical base for political discourse. Grey approvingly quotes Oliver Wendell Holmes:

> Sir Henry Maine has made it fashionable to connect the archaic notion of property with prescription. But the connection is further back than the first recorded history. It is in the nature of man's mind. A thing which you have enjoyed and used as your own for a long time, whether property or an opinion, takes root in your being and cannot be torn away without your resenting the act and trying to defend yourself, however you came by it. The law can ask no better Justification than the deepest instincts of man.[45]

But does this view accomplish what Grey wants? A normative or ethical justification of property rights must involve some well established theory as to what human beings *should* do. But Holmes is talking about what human beings *will or must* do, by force of instinct or habit, not by force of choice and moral conviction.

Apart from the inadequacy of Grey's alternative, does the libertarian alternative require reference to needs as Grey suggests? Not if a theory of ethical conduct and a theory of rights can be developed in support of the system. As indicated above, a theory of ethical conduct does exist that gives support to the natural rights theory that underlies the libertarian social/political system.

Given an understanding of the nature of man, one can show that the flourishing of human beings requires that individuals take certain kinds of actions on their own initiative to exercise their distinctive capacities, that they do so *by choice*. Given these capacities, we can learn what enables an individual human being to flourish, what it would be for any person to be a morally good human being – namely, the sustained exercise of these distinctive capacities, most fundamentally the capacity to reason. And since to exercise these distinctive capacities in a social setting requires that others abstain from acting aggressively toward one, it is naturally right that a society be governed by those principles that rule out such aggression.

Needs do come to play an important role in this theory. Because each person's life will be enhanced by taking certain actions, the requirements for those actions are *needed* by the actor. In this sense there will be requirements persons must satisfy both privately and publicly. Privately, for example, individuals will need to take the actions that enable them to flourish. Obstacles to this effort can come from three sources: their own unwillingness or inability, the limitations of the natural environment, and the limitations imposed on them by others.

Part of the natural environment to be taken into account is the moral autonomy of others. Thus personal ambitions must be satisfied without abridgement of the like peaceful ambitious conduct of others. The limitations others can impose on a person are the only ones that may be overcome by way of concerted forcible social action, and it is this group of limitations that the libertarian social/political system seeks to specify by reference to the theory of natural rights.

To demand of others that they eliminate the obstacles posed by nature – such as attacks by a virus or tornado – would be unjust. It would make them slaves to one's own purposes, compelling them to neglect theirs in the process. It is impossible for others to eliminate the obstacle of personal choice, of the lack of will to flourish. One cannot substitute another person's moral character for one's own; moral autonomy cannot be transferred like a property deed. Nor should anyone, given what his own human flourishing requires, want to demand such serfdom from others. To demand of others that they abstain from coercively limiting one's actions in one's own behalf is to demand that they abide by the conditions of mutually beneficial opportunities for self-advancement which they themselves also require as autonomous agents.

So Grey is unwarranted in claiming that the libertarian system neglects a theory of human needs that can inform our understanding of political life. The libertarian system can rest on a theory of ethics appropriate to human nature[46] and a theory of rights based on such ethics. This approach is non-utilitarian, just as Grey realizes it must be to avoid arbitrary state action. Specifically, the greatest happiness or good of the greatest number of human beings is not the goal of political organization within this theory. Nevertheless, the libertarian natural rights argument does note the beneficial consequences promoted by the libertarian system. This theory of the human good notes that by acting on certain principles it is more likely for human beings to succeed in their lives. In the political domain, these principles are the natural rights which require protection and preservation by a government confined by the dictates of this specific purpose.

Governments should not seek to achieve certain end-states such as equality, productivity, or the flourishing of science or the arts. But they should maintain certain conditions which will enable citizens, if they choose, to pursue various goals properly suited to them as human beings and as the individuals they are.

I should mention at least some additional points that are pertinent to thinking about the free society. One such point is related to the work of Professor Ronald Dworkin,[47] which is said by its author to be in the liberal tradition of legal and political thought, and yet aims to strike a blow at the central ideal of classical liberalism. Although he sounds as if he were advocating Lockean individual natural rights, Dworkin advocates the priority of procedural rights.[48] But he accepts the state as given, in no need of legitimization or justification, and consigns individual rights to the minor function of guarding against too much or arbitrary interference with citizens that has the purpose of achieving collective goals. Dworkin ridicules the libertarian conception of the right to liberty by citing the widely accepted powers of contemporary governments to curtail human liberty. He simply ignores the problem this raises with respect to slavery, a practice also once widely accepted, yet one we would hardly think could be sanctioned from Dworkin's position.

Dworkin's book of essays on rights theory, published in the late 1970s, is primarily concerned with technical legal philosophy. He does consider broader political issues, but simply evades all the difficult problems with and obvious objections to his position. What is interesting about him is that he has managed to publish a work on individual rights whose practical implications (for example, in matters of constitutional law) are almost diametrically opposed to those ordinarily associated with the tradition of individual human rights. He has also advanced a more comprehensive case for his egalitarian position in his book *Sovereign Virtue*.[49] Here he deploys an approach remarkably similar to that of Amartya Sen and Martha Nussbaum, except that instead of concluding in favor of libertarianism, he concludes in favor of a robust welfare state. The source of the difference is straightforward: Dworkin, as Sen and Nussbaum, is not much concerned with the social preconditions of morally virtuous conduct, namely, freedom from others' coercion.

In Chapter 20 I will address an argument by James P. Sterba, concerning welfare rights, that was recast against Nozick by Adrian Bardon, recently.[50] I wish to discuss it briefly here because Bardon brings up an issue that's central concerning the nature of basic rights, rights that would become the substance of a constitutional government. He argues that he has successfully 'cast doubt on that approach to rights' that holds that 'there are negative rights that cannot be outweighed.'[51] Bardon's way of saying this already shows how wide of the mark he is concerning the nature of rights. Rights aren't like other good things – ice skating versus, say, volley ball, dinner at home versus at a restaurant, a vacation in Hawaii versus one in Italy – to be weighed and measured and compared. It's a category mistake to think they are.

Consider a woman's right to be free of rape. Is this a right that might even conceivably be outweighed? No. It is a principle, a firm limit, which identifies the fact that women are free to do as they please with their own body (whether they deserve this or not) – they are sovereign authorities concerning how to live their sex lives, to whom they will give their consent to engage in sex, and so on. In contrast, Bardon's conception of rights raises the possibility that someone might weigh the woman's right to be free to govern her own sex life against, say, a desperate male's right to gain sexual satisfaction by using her against her will.

Of course, Bardon is concerned with property rights but he forgets that these, too, are rights to action, not rights to objects. As Ayn Rand makes clear,

> the right to property is a right to action, like all the others: it is not the right *to an object, but to the* action and the consequences of producing or earning that object. It is not a guarantee that a man *will earn any* property, but only a guarantee that he will own it if he earns it. It is the right to gain, to keep, to use and to dispose of material values.[52]

Rand also makes clear that earning isn't the sole means by which ownership can be established – we have a right to our hair or lungs without having earned these because to act to gain and to keep them, as it were, is part of the process of growing up and becoming ourselves. (Life itself is a process of self-generated *action* so that even the right to life is a right to a wide range of actions.)

Put another way, the right to private property is a right to acquire and to hold – which are both *actions* – various items no one has previously acquired and held or items which others have acquired and are holding are willing, freely, to part with (another action). So, in fact, private property rights are akin to rights to act freely – as when one acts to engage in consensual sex or work or recreation. In the case of property rights, one acts to engage in, as it were, consensual acquisition or holding of some items. (Notice, no one may impose ownership on another against his or her consent because of this right to freedom of actions such as acquisition and holding.)

Thus, property rights identify someone's sphere or range of freedom of action *vis-à-vis* items in the world, not unlike how the right to freedom of speech spells out spheres of freedom of action *vis-à-vis* verbal or written expression of ideas. Indeed, these latter presuppose the right to private property, for speeches need to be given some *place* to which one has a right or has gained permission from those who do, and writing takes places on materials (paper, blackboards, sand, computers, and so on).

Now it is true that others could well need the items someone has come to own by exercising the right to acquisition and holding, but since that exercise may not be interfered with, and interference with it would place others in the position of robbing the agent of his or her sovereignty, consent needs to be obtained in order to obtain even such desperately needed items. A need cannot be weighed against a right, any more than a wish can be weighed against a right. There can be no weighing involved – not between rights, nor between rights and needs – although a rights holder could weigh whether to hang on to what he or she owns, contribute it to the person in dire need or to some cause or project, or otherwise dispose of it in light of his or her weighing of the importance of these alternative possibilities. The weighing is not of different rights or different people's rights but of the importance of the goals to which one may contribute what one has the right to freely acquire.

Here is what would happen if the weighing were about rights. *Someone would have to do the weighing.* By what right would such a person weigh other people's rights? Would that person's right to weigh also be open to being weighed? By whom? The whole process would amount to a conceptual and public policy mess.

In fact, the role – or conceptual point – of basic individual rights is to remove from public policy, based on constitutional laws that rest on rights, the element of arbitrariness by basing decisions on self-consistent, compossible principles instead. The very conceptual point of rights within the sphere of social, political and legal policy is lost if they are subject to being weighed since they are supposed to be the rock bottom of decision-making – if I have a right to do X, this is the end of the story.

There is no such thing as 'weighing rights' – the idea is what philosophers call a category mistake, akin to talk about weighing, say, time or concepts. Indeed, to even consider weighing rights is to suggest that the importance of human beings, *vis-à-vis* their place in the citizenry, may be weighed against each other within the realm of politics, something that was abandoned once the idea of inherent status was jettisoned, finally, so no one could justly claim to be more important than someone else as far as the law of the land is concerned.

There are many other criticisms of the free society which could be considered. Marxists have done their hardest to discredit the system. Schweickart has argued that under capitalism it is unjustified to associate material benefits with desert because, after all, ownership confers much undeserved benefit on capitalists.[53] But he takes on only the economists who have tried to link productivity to benefits without much concern for the issues of moral philosophy. There are far better ways of establishing the link between virtue and success in a free society, such as by reference to a broader idea of what human success involves in addition to gaining economic benefits.[54] What the economist has to say is essential, just not the whole story.

Those who fault the free society for lacking a moral vision seem to want some promise of a utopia, something comparable to the Christian heaven or the communist earthly paradise; but of course, this is unavailable. A more sensible moral vision does emerge from reflecting on the free society, and Robert Nozick chose well to close his book with it.

> The minimal state treats us as inviolate individuals, who may not be used in certain ways by others as means or tools or instruments or resources; it treats us as persons having individual rights with the dignity this constitutes. Treating us with respect by respecting our rights, it allows us, individually or with whom we choose, to choose our life and to realize our ends and our conception of ourselves, insofar as we can, aided by the voluntary cooperation of other individuals possessing the same dignity. How *dare* any state or group of individuals do more or less.[55]

Notes

1 Not all contemporary political thinkers fit this bill. Some feminists, such as Susan Moller Okin, *Justice, Gender, and the Family* (New York: Basic Books, 1989), are egalitarian in other respects than the mainly economic. Okin addresses the libertarianism of Nozick in her book but is completely misguided about, for example, the labor theory of value, something Nozick himself embraces only tentatively and something that does not constitute a central element of my own defense of the right to private property. Okin confuses the productive and property-creating Lockean activity of 'mixing one's labor with nature' and the 'labor' of women as they carry to term a newborn. For the conception of private property rights, one that completely eschews the idea of 'mixing one's labor,' that figures in my own defense of the fully free, unregulated, unregimented society, see Tibor R. Machan, *The Right to Private Property* (Stanford, CA: Hoover Institution Press, 2002). This work develops the theory along lines sketched by Ayn Rand, James Sadowsky, and Israel Kirzner. See, most pertinently, James Sadowsky, 'Private Property Rights and Collective Ownership' in T. R. Machan, ed., *The Libertarian Alternative* (Chicago, IL: Nelson-Hall Co., Inc., 1971), pp. 119–33.

There is an even more fundamental defense of private property rights found in Samuel C. Wheeler III, 'Natural Property Rights as Body Rights,' in Tibor R. Machan, ed., *The Main Debate* (New York: Random House, 1987), pp. 272–89. Curiously, although in print since the publication of this work, by a prominent house, Wheeler's argument hasn't attracted the attention of critics of libertarianism such as Okin and Olsaretti. That may be because Wheeler's case does not rest on any notion of desert or the mixing of labor with nature. Critics of private property rights have, of course, always had trouble with private assets such as one's limbs, eyes, kidneys, beauty, health, and so forth, none of which need be deserved but all of which are nonetheless clearly one's own. If these, or their use, give rise to further assets, they too seem clearly to be no one else's but the person who has them. Indeed, a feature of the libertarian approach taken here is that the onus of proof should not be on those who possess valuable stuff, including one's own talents and other assets, but on others who propose to lay claim to them. (See, for more, Tibor R. Machan, 'Liberty vs. Coercion: the Burden of Proof,' *The Freeman*, January 1974, pp. 35–38.) The point is that although one may not deserve what one has, that by no means justifies others' confiscating it from one unless some prior obligation exists, which is what is generally wanting in the critics' case.

Okin stresses that she objects to Nozick's refusal to treat women and men differently for political purposes, and on this score she would find me guilty as well. However, this is clearly because Okin chooses to politicize all social problems, which is precisely what the form of libertarianism being discussed here opposes. Such a totalistic political theory, found, for example, in the works of most Marxists, fails to acknowledge that many, many social problems are such as not to involve the kinds of violation of individual rights that constitute coercion. It is only where coercion is present that political solutions are appropriate, although, admittedly, some feminists, Okin included, stretch the meaning of 'coercion' so far as to justify innumerable paternalist public policy measures.

2 Robert Nozick, *Anarchy, State, and Utopia* (New York: Basic Books, 1974).

3 Outside academia Ayn Rand has made the most comprehensive contribution to this effort. See Ayn Rand, *Capitalism: The Unknown Ideal* (New York: New American Library, 1967). For several valuable discussions by academicians, see Machan, ed., *Libertarian Alternative*. See also Eric Mack, 'Egoism and Rights,' *The Personalist* Vol. 54 (1973), pp. 5–33. In Tibor R. Machan, *Human Rights and Human Liberties* (Chicago, IL: Nelson-Hall, 1975), written during 1970–74 and so without the benefit of Nozick's work, I offer a synthesis of various strains of argumentation in support of a free society.

4 See F. A. Hayek, *The Constitution Of Liberty* (Chicago, IL: University of Chicago Press, 1960).

5 See, for example, M. Harrington, 'The Misconception of Society,' *Commonweal*, Nov. 7, 1975, at pp. 534–6; David Schweickart, 'Capitalism, Contribution and Sacrifice,' *Philosophical Forum* Vol. 7, (1976) pp. 260–76. The standard attack on libertarianism from Marxist circles is best represented by C. B. Macpherson, *The Political Theory Of Possessive Individualism* (Oxford, England: Clarendon Press, 1962). For more discussion of Marxism, see Tibor R. Machan, *Marxism: A Bourgeois Assessment* (Lanham, MD: Hamilton Books, 2005).

6 See, for example, Lawrence A. Scaff, 'How Not to Do Political Theory: Nozick's Apology for the Minimal State,' *Arizona Law Review,* Vol. 19 (1977) pp. 193–219.

7 John Rawls, *A Theory Of Justice* (Cambridge, MA: Harvard University Press, 1971); Nozick's book had its genesis in a paper, included in *Anarchy, State, and Utopia* as Chapter 7, published as 'Distributive Justice,' *Philosophy & Public Affairs,* Vol. 3, 1973–4.

8 See Ernest van den Haag, *Liberty: Negative or Positive,* I *Harvard Journal of Law and Public Policy*, Vol. 63 (1978), pp. 70–71.

9 See Daniel Bell, *The Cultural Contradictions Of Capitalism* (New York: Basic Books, 1976); Michael Harrington, *The Twilight Of Capitalism* (New York: Simon and Schuster, 1976); Irving Kristol, *Two Cheers for Capitalism* (New York: Basic Books, 1978).

10 John Locke, II *An Essay Concerning Human Understanding* 2 (Oxford, England: The Clarendon Press, 1706).

11 See note 11 in Chapter 3 for more.

12 Thomas S. Kuhn, *The Structure of Scientific Revolutions* (Chicago, IL: University of Chicago Pres, 2nd edn, 1970).

13 See, for example, Samuel Scheffler, 'Natural Rights, Equality, and the Minimal State,' *Canadian Journal of Philosophy*, Vol. 6 (1976), pp. 59–76.

14 Nozick, *Anarchy, State, and Utopia*, p. 169.

15 Thomas Scanlon, 'Nozick on Rights, Liberty, and Property,' *Philosophy & Public Affairs,* Vol. 6 (1976), p. 14. That is to say, Scanlon isn't accepting Nozick's dispensation with a defense of individual rights other than by way of the 'argument to the best explanation.' He wants to see an argument that establishes that we do have the rights Nozick only assumes we have. Unfortunately, Scanlon, as many others, is guilty of the scholarly sin of stargazing – as if no one but a star such as Nozick has produced arguments worthy of consideration, thus missing the arguments advanced for individual rights by others (Eric Mack, Roger Pilon, Jeffrey Paul, myself and others).

16 Thomas Nagel, *Libertarianism Without Foundations,* Vol. 85 (1975), *Yale Law Journal*, p. 147.

17 Robert Paul Wolff, 'Robert Nozick's Derivation of the Minimal State,' *Arizona Law Review,* Vol. 19 (1977), pp. 23–24. This entire issue of *Arizona Law Review* was devoted to articles critical of Nozick's book.

18 Scheffler, p. 62.

19 For example, Scaff, pp. 193–211.

20 Ibid. This is not precisely what Scaff tells us but by calling Nozick's work an apology and by invoking a sort of Marxian meta-analysis of Nozick's methodology he does suggest that Nozick was really speaking for some particular ideological interest group rather than attempting to establish the truth about human political life. While Scaff does not provide a Marxian critique of Nozick, others have provided such a critique of classical liberal thinkers. See Macpherson, *Political Theory Of Possessive Individualism*

21 See Thomas Grey, 'Property and Need: The Welfare State and Theories of Distributive Justice,' *Stanford Law Review*, Vol. 28 (1976), pp. 877–902.

22 *See* Alexander Solzhenitsyn, *Two Addresses* (1976); 'A World Split Apart,' *Imprimis*, Vol. 7 (1978), pp. 1–6 (Harvard Commencement Address, 1978).

23 Machan, 'Law, Justice and Natural Rights,' *Western Ontario Law Review*, Tibor R. Machan, 'Human Dignity and the Law,' *Depaul Law Review*, Vol. 26 (1977), pp. 807–32 and *Objectivity: Recovering Determinate Reality in Philosophy, Science, and Everyday Life* (UK: Ashgate, 2004), especially Chapter 7, 'Richard Posner's Pragmatic Jurisprudence.'

24 Machan, 'Natural Rights and Morality.'

25 David L. Norton, *Personal Destinies: A Philosophy Of Ethical Individualism* (Princeton, NJ: Princeton University Press, 1976).

26 I have in mind the philosophy Ayn Rand developed, Objectivism. For a succinct presentation, see Tibor R. Machan, *Ayn Rand* (New York: Peter Lang, 2001), and for a more detailed one, see Leonard Peikoff, *Objectivism. The Philosophy of Ayn Rand* (New York: Dutton, 1991). Rand, however, is a novelist who turned to philosophy in part to explore the possibilities for ideal types in the romantic novel. While her own works have not appeared in scholarly periodicals, her views have come to the attention of philosophers. See, for example, Luther John Binkley, *Conflict of Ideas* (New York: Van Nostrand, 1969); Doug Den Uyl and Doug Rasmussen, eds, *The Philosophical Thought of Ayn Rand* (Chicago: University of Illinois Press, 1983) and, especially, the *Journal of Ayn Rand Studies*.

27 Nozick himself explained to me in the Spring of 1976, while I visited his home (in Brighton, MA, I believe it was), that he wanted to show that views very different from those of Rawls could be derived using an essentially similar philosophical method. Thus his book might be regarded as a sophisticated rhetorical move which enables him to go on to develop his arguments further.

28 See Douglas B. Rasmussen, 'Aristotle and the Defense of the Law of Contradiction,' *The Personalist*, Vol. 54 (1973), pp. 149–62.

29 As a sample of such work within the Aristotelian tradition of non-reductionism naturalism see, Tibor R. Machan, *The Pseudo-Science of B. F. Skinner* (New Rochelle, NY: Arlington House, 1974), Roger W. Sperry. *Science and Moral Priority* (New York: Columbia University Press, 1983), and Hillary Putnam, *Word and Life* (Cambridge, MA: Harvard University Press, 1994).

30 Norton, *Personal Destinies*, pp. 25–27.

31 In a subsequent work, Thomas Nagel and Liam Murphy, *The Myth of Ownership* (New York: Oxford University Press, 2003), try to justify this view, without success. Ownership is no myth – it is in evidence throughout the globe, as is its violation – theft, robbery, embezzlement and such, based on laws that are themselves based on the principles, more or less faithfully, of private property rights. It is, of course, a moral relationship such that it signifies that those who own X are justified to use and dispose of it without others' interference. It derives from their ownership, first and foremost, of their lives and the priority of their taking care to thrive in this life with the aid of whatever is available to them from nature that none other has acquired and, subsequently, via commerce. See Tibor R. Machan, *The Right to Private Property* (Stanford, CA: Hoover Institution Press, 2002) and 'A Defence of Property Rights and Capitalism,' in Brenda Almond, ed., *Introducing Applied Ethics* (Oxford, England: Blackwell, 1995). A neo-Lockean defense

of the right to private property comes from James Sadowsky, 'Private Property and Collective Ownership,' in Machan, ed., *The Libertarian Alternative*.

32 I have in mind the ban on cigarette advertising in the broadcast media.

33 See, Tibor R. Machan, 'Anarchism and Minarchism, A Rapprochement,' *Journal des Economists et des Estudes Humaines*, Vol. 14, No 4 (December 2002), pp. 569–88. For why funding government does not require coercive measure, any more than, say, funding health care or education does, see Tibor R. Machan, 'No Taxation, With or Without Representation,' in Robert McGee, ed., *Taxation and Public Finance in Transition and Developing Economies* (forthcoming).

34 If we keep in mind, however, that Nozick's objective was to show that an argument akin to one deployed by Rawls in favor of massive wealth redistribution gives ample support for prohibiting such wealth redistribution – that is, for a limited government libertarian polity – this turns out not to be a failing on Nozick's part but a misunderstanding of what can be expected from his book.

35 See, for example, Murray N. Rothbard, *Power and Market: Government and the Economy* 2nd edn (Kansas City, KS: Sheed Andrews and McMeel, 1977), especially Chapter 1, 'Defense Services on the Free Market.'

36 The reality at issue is that persons are moral agents and ends in themselves, not available for others' use without their agreeing to that use. This is not a self-evident reality, yet a reality nonetheless.

37 For a defense of this 'essentialist' approach to what the nature of something is, see Ayn Rand, *Introduction To Objectivist Epistemology* (New York: New American Library, expanded 2nd edn, 1990). See also Tibor R. Machan, *Individuals and Their Rights* (Chicago, IL: Open Court Publishing Co., Inc., 1989). See also, Machan, *Objectivity* (a work that addresses several skeptics about objectivity, including regarding whether the natures of things can be known objectively). It is rather odd that those advancing these arguments expect others to have confidence in their findings about how human beings relate to the world cognitively, while denying that prospect to all others on grounds that no such arguments can be advanced at all!

38 Consider the following from Harry V. Jaffa, *Equality And Liberty* (New York: Oxford University Press, 1965):

> [T]he doctrine in the Declaration of Independence of the self-evidence of the difference between man and other species, and its absolute moral significance, is *the* premise of the laws of nature and of nature's God. This premise, it is true, has been gravely questioned by scientific developments since the eighteenth century. However much the course of science may, as it must, raise theoretical doubts concerning this and every other premise of human thought, it remains the necessary moral and political premise of everything we call human and decent (p. 16).

For a discussion of why, despite numerous claims to the contrary, there is no reason to suppose that the course of science *has* called into question, at least thus far, the moral and political premise of the free society, see Roger W. Sperry, 'Mind, Brain and Humanistic Values,' in John R. Platt, ed., *New Views Of The Nature Of Man* (Chicago, IL: University of Chicago Press, 1965); Theodosius Dobzhansky, *The Biological Basis Of Human Freedom* (New York: Columbia University Press, 1956); Machan, *The Pseudo-Science* and *Initiative – Human Agency and Society* (Stanford, CA: Hoover Institution Press, 2000). Essentially, in spite of the mere fact that entities do not remain firm in the fashion of timeless, perfect Platonic forms, it doesn't follow that they are all in a Heraclitian flux. For many centuries – approximately 100 – the human species has been as we now know it, with only minor changes in height and other inessential human attributes. This is no different from how biology, botany, physiology and other life sciences offer up quite stable principles that guide serviceable practices. Politics, in a sense, is one of these life sciences pertaining to the way human communities ought to be organized (the difference between, of course, the 'ought' element).

39 For a critical discussion of Nozick's methodology from the broader philosophical perspective of the present author, see, for example, Tibor R. Machan, 'Nozick's Geometrical Libertarianism,' *Occasional Review*, Vol. 6 (1977), pp. 167–87.

40 See, Scaff, 'How not to do Political Theory,' p. 5.

41 Director made the remark to a group of scholars at the Hoover Institution at Stanford University about 1976, when I was a national fellow there. The prominent *homo economicus* view is laid out in detail by George Stigler and Gary Becker, 'De Gustibus Non Est Disputandum,' *American Economic Review*, Vol. 67 (1977), pp. 76–90. See also Milton Friedman, 'The Line We Dare Not Cross,' *Encounter*, Nov. 1976, at p. 11: '[E]very individual serves his own private interest .. . The great Saints of history have served their "private interest" just as the most money-grubbing miser has served his interest. The *private interest* is whatever it is that drives an individual.' See, for an extensive discussion of analyzing the infrastructure of human community life along *homo economicus* lines, Richard A. Posner, *Economic Analysis of Law* (Boston, MA: Little, Brown, 1992). For a discussion of the problems facing such arguments in support of a free market, see Machan, 'Some Normative Considerations of Deregulation,' *Journal of Social, Political and Economic Studies*, Vol. 1 (1979), pp. 363–77, and 17.

42 When addressed specifically to Nozick's argument, Scaff's criticism is on target. Some of Nozick's language makes it appear that he adheres to the *homo economicus* conception of human beings. But Nozick was attempting to enter a discussion begun by others in the philosophical community, for example, Rawls, who had already employed this language. After all, the individuals behind 'the veil of ignorance' are uniformly self-interested in just the (ambiguous) sense in which the *homo economicus* model conceives of them.

43 Grey, 'Property and Need,' p. 898.

44 Posner, *Economic Analysis of Law*.

45 Oliver Wendell Holmes, 'The Path of Law,' *Harvard Law Review*, Vol. 10 (1897); p. 477.

46 The form of ethical egoism (or individualism) that provides sound support for a theory of natural rights (within the Lockean tradition but without its problems) is identified as classical egoism, stressing its Aristotelian naturalist foundations. See Tibor R. Machan, 'Recent Work in Ethical Egoism,' *American Philosophical Quarterly*, Vol. 16 (1979), pp. 1–15 and 18.

47 Ronald Dworkin, *Taking Rights Seriously* (Cambridge, MA: Harvard University Press, 1977).

48 Ibid.: 'The constructive portions emphasize an idea that is also part of the liberal tradition, but that has no place in either legal positivism or utilitarianism. This is the old line of individual human rights … '(p. vii).

49 Ronald Dworkin, *Sovereign Virtue* (Cambridge, MA: Harvard University Press, 2002).

50 Adrian Bardon, 'From Nozick to Welfare Rights,' *Critical Review*, Vol. 14 (2000), pp. 481–501.

51 Ibid., p. 496.

52 Ayn Rand, *Capitalism: the Unknown Ideal*, p. 322.

53 Schweickart, 'Capitalism, Contribution and Sacrifice.' For a very extensive critique of this line of argumentation, associated by the author with Robert Nozick and a few other libertarians, see Serena Olsaretti, *Liberty, Desert and the Market* (Cambridge: Cambridge University Press, 2004). It is worth noting that books critical of libertarianism tend, mainly, to discuss Nozick's case and are usually published by very prominent university presses – Oxford, Princeton, Chicago, Harvard and so on. In this connection it is worth noting that when W. W. Norton published a book titled 'The Passion for Equality,' I proposed to them a book to be titled 'The Passion for Liberty.' Norton's editors didn't even wish to look at the plan for the book but turned it down cold. (It was subsequently published by Rowman & Littlefield.) I am not privy to the motivation for the recurrent phenomenon of prominent presses publishing repeated critiques of libertarianism. But the evaluation process of such projects may leave something to be desired – mainstream scholars are consulted, most of whom are critical of libertarianism, and they turn down

proposals, while they favor those that are critical. As a case in point, Blackwell publishing company once considered my manuscript, 'Individuals and Their Rights,' and while one reader liked it, Professor Alan Ryan reportedly sent in a one line rejection: 'Do we really need yet another defense of the God given right to private property?' (I was made aware of this some time later by a friendly reader for Blackwell.)

54 See, for example, Rand, *Capitalism: The Unknown Ideal,* Chapter I; and Sadowsky, 'Private Property.'

55 Nozick, *Anarchy, State, and Utopia*, pp. 333–4.

Chapter 11

Will Technology Make Us Free?

Why do many cyber-enthusiasts believe that elements of the e-conomy – namely, the kind of trade and other activities associated with the Internet – will fundamentally aid the cause of individual liberty?[1] Can encryption, for example, set us free (or hide us) from the tyrannical reach of governments? Or is such confidence ultimately the result of a misguided and scientistic faith in technological tools at the expense of vigilance about how they are employed?[2]

At least since the scientific revolutions of the sixteenth century we have tended to expect an awful lot from scientific and technological progress – often too much.

The inclination actually goes back to the optimistic rationalism of the Greek philosophers. In ancient Greece it was the philosopher Democritus, as well as his very scantily recorded predecessor Leukippus, who proposed that the world is made up of one thing, namely, atoms. Democritus also held to the empiricist doctrine that perception amounts to recording copies of the tiny atoms and thus gaining understanding of the real world. Once the laws of atoms were identified, all else could be understood and explained. We may call this the first scientistic temptation. It is a view that is very tempting to adopt because it appears to conform to the requirements of science, which include analyzing everything into its smallest components and learning why it all behaves as it does by reference to how these smallest components behave.[3]

I am, of course, begging an important question by calling this view a temptation, implying thereby that it is mistaken, even blameworthy, albeit often yielded to by philosophers and other thinkers. Perhaps it is right to try to get to the simplest of all entities and thus produce the simplest of all explanations! Perhaps greater complexities would then be easy to grasp. But such an approach is a kind of shortcut that avoids the difficulties of a more pluralistic conception of the world, one in which different principles may govern different kinds of beings. To determine this, we cannot start with theory that presupposes a monistic view of causation in the world. We must look at the world and observe how different kinds of entities actually behave.

While the ultimate roots of scientism and materialism may be found in the ancient world, two early modern thinkers figure most prominently as promoters of this view, namely, Thomas Hobbes and Francis Bacon (an early employer of Hobbes). Bacon's reductionism, inductivism and scientism – and the vision he laid out in *The New Atlantis* of a technological utopia ruled by experts ('The end of our foundation is the knowledge of causes, and secret motions of things; and the enlarging of the bounds of human empire, to the effecting of all things possible') – are arguably the true ancestors of Marxist 'scientific' socialism as well as of later technocratic visions. (Bacon was rather hostile to real science; for example, he did not welcome the news that the Earth revolves around the sun.)

Although Bacon is not considered in academic circles an important philosopher in our time, his influence on both Hobbes and general thought is very important. For example, consider the seventeenth-century statist and founder of econometrics Sir William Petty – whose descendent the 2nd Earl of Shelburne created the 'Bowood Circle' (Richard Price, Joseph Priestley, Jeremy Bentham, and James Mill). Petty tried, in various different ways, to make politics a science after the manner of mathematics. The Bowood Circle cannot be simply summed up as 'statist,' but there was a strong rationalist element in their work – and both the rationalism and the statism can be traced back to Petty. Even the collectivist side of John Stuart Mill is rooted in this tradition (that is, more than the influence of Harriet Taylor was at work here).[4]

The major promise of the Hobbesian philosophy is that henceforth we will be able to control the causes that impel human beings to behave as they do and thus develop what Skinner would call a technology of human behavior. Thomas Hobbes advanced the modern version of the view of Democritus when, inspired by the scientific work of Galileo, he proposed that there is nothing in the world but matter-in-motion, and that all the distinctions, differences and varieties we seem to perceive in reality are just nominal – exist 'in name' only. Now that we know that all human behavior is based on the same principles as the behavior of the most fundamental materials of the universe, matter-in-motion (for Bacon the 'secret motions of things' and for contemporary physicists' strings), we presumably should be able to organize society 'correctly' and almost if not quite as easily as we get the eight ball into the corner pocket.

Here, too, the temptation to reduce everything to just one kind of thing – to learn the laws of that one kind of thing and assume one has arrived at an explanation of all other kinds of things – had not been resisted. The hope was that just as with the inanimate portions of nature, wherein understanding leads to the ability to control, so it would be with human nature. We would understand what we are and then apply this understanding, just as social engineers envision it, successfully and benevolently manipulating human affairs.

As I have argued elsewhere, real science (including technological development) is based on human creativity.[5] This understanding does not mesh with the mathematical determinism of some visions of modern technology – that is, certain forms of technocratic politics and general society. Such mathematical determinism – also known as reductive materialism – indiscriminately applies the principles of classical physics or mechanics to all realms of inquiry, especially the realm of social and political life. It is the view sometimes dubbed the grandfather of classical liberalism and one that is evident in the works of such disparate contemporary thinkers as B. F. Skinner, Karl Marx and James Buchanan.[6] In his books *Beyond Freedom and Dignity* (1971) and *Science and Human Behavior* (1968), psychologist Skinner claimed to have identified a technology of human behavior by confining himself to elements of human life that are observable, eliminating all references to mental or internal entities such as feelings, mind, purposes, intentions, memories or thinking. Of the last, Skinner said it is best understood as 'the probability of verbal behavior,' making it, thus, quantifiable and subject to scientific study.[7]

Many thinkers, eager to find some intellectual framework that would offer a sure-fire solution to the troubles facing human communities, regarded these efforts with hope. Indeed, it is arguable that the Hobbesian approach (reinforced by Hume's empiricism and logical positivism, as well as the emerging idea that there must be an unbridgeable gulf between facts and values) spawned the later flourishing of the social sciences. Following the diminished intellectual and especially philosophical reputation of the moral and religious views of human life, the mantle of (specifically physical) science became a must for any discipline to gain respectability.

The scientistic perspective was even enlisted to rationalize a classical liberalism that, you would think, rests most comfortably on a view of the human being as a free agent.[8] While Hobbes combined his reductive materialism and radical individualism with what to him seemed a highly efficient absolute monarchism, those who followed in his steps got wind of a version of public choice theory and realized that instead of trusting some monarch, it is the marketplace that should be entrusted with working most naturally and efficiently.[9] In Newtonian space, what moves most efficiently is whatever encounters the least resistance or friction. From this, it is not a very long leap to the idea that human behavior should not be burdened with regulations, regimentation, interference and whatever else could stand in its way blocking or impeding self-improvement.

More recently, scientism has supported high expectations from the development of the computer. As John Searle put it,

> these strong feelings may come from the conviction of many people that computers provide the basis of a new sort of civilization – a new way of giving meaning to our lives, a new way of understanding ourselves. The computer seems to provide, at least, a way of explaining ourselves that is in accord with the scientific worldview and, perhaps most important, the computational theory of the mind expresses a certain technological will to power.[10]

But he added, 'I believe that the philosophical importance of computers, as is typical with any new technology, is grossly exaggerated. The computer is a useful tool, nothing more nor less.'[11]

Despite the apparently seamless move from the mechanistic conception of the universe to a deterministic conception of human life, upon close inspection the plausibility of this viewpoint crumbles.[12] Consider, for example, that human beings often err in conceiving of the way things are. Indeed, that is just what those who embrace the mechanistic idea claim about those who disagree. Yet, it is very difficult, if not impossible, to make sense of this phenomenon of making a mistake, let alone of thinking badly, within the mechanistic, deterministic framework. Other living things do not make such mistakes. The very idea of truth versus falsehood makes little sense unless there is freedom to err. The ability to choose between right and wrong presupposes that one is not being compelled by antecedent forces to do what one is doing – that one can in fact choose freely between alternatives, and might have chosen otherwise.

In addition to this elementary problem, the deterministic view of human life cannot explain the sources of all the diversity in how human beings live and what they believe – including human beings who come from similar backgrounds and encounter similar influences. It is fairly simple to understand such diversity and variety in the framework of a view that regards human beings as having free will. Their freedom makes all the variety possible: in art, culture, politics, philosophy, religion, cuisine and the rest. But if human beings are hard-wired, it is hard to understand why they would ever act with willful irrationality or self-destructiveness, as human beings sometimes do.[13]

Nor can the uses and abuses of human technology itself be understood by the mechanistic viewpoint inspired by that technology. As we know, at least by the evidence of the twentieth century, human beings are far from having solved their political problems via the materialist or physicalist approach, whether in its Hobbesian, Marxist or positivist incarnations. Looking to any (hard) scientific and technological advance as the primary means of securing social institutions, including liberty itself, is a mistake. At the heart of this conclusion is the simple fact that all tools human beings develop, intellectual or otherwise, may be used for good or ill. That is as true of the Internet and encryption as it is true of gunpowder.

One prominent classical liberal presented a case a while back for the potential of the liberating power of encryption,[14] claiming that once this technique has been perfected, the state will lose most of its power. A skeptic from the audience noted,[15] however, that not only is the state busily at work breaking all the encryption codes but that it also, as a last resort, could sabotage such evasion of its powers by simply shutting off the electricity. This is not to say that a lock on your door won't prevent many attempts at home invasion, but that no home dweller is immune to a really determined cohort of intruders.

In addition to the unreliability of technical devices for purposes of securing our liberty, depending on them to achieve that end can undermine the personal resolve needed to protect individual rights. Furthermore, the belief that technology can deal with the threat of tyranny can lead to what we might call a soulless approach to politics. In other words, devices are treated as the means for doing what requires human thought and passion and commitment to values. When people trust in gadgets as the exclusive means by which their individual liberty is secured, their focus on vigilance and other civic virtues is likely to wane. Science and technology will solve the problem, so why bother with self-improvement?

All in all, what is needed is the fullest possible acknowledgement of the insight that the price of liberty is indeed eternal vigilance. Although the emerging technological tools and devices can all be used to facilitate such vigilance, without the personal commitment of the citizenry, those tools will be insufficient. Since such commitment is a matter of individual choice or initiative, it is unreasonable to expect any guarantee of advance.[16]

None of this is to deny that very positive results may emerge from the invention of the Internet and other tools produced via science and technology. But these must not be confused with the kind of measures needed to secure and maintain the infrastructure of a free society, measures that can only come from the sustained efforts of human beings.[17]

The unpredictable human factor is what most crucially determines whether a technology will be used for good or ill. We can say that the defense of liberty does gain some advantage from new technologies – as does the state in its efforts to find new ways to control us. But the ability to offer a positive alternative to scientism and to other rationalizations of statism is far more pivotal. To win a war of ideas, you above all need ideas, and the will to defend them.

So, actually it is freedom that will promote technology, not so much the other way around. That's because having the right to liberty respected and protected promotes human creativity and its fruits.

Notes

1 Examples of this belief abound. See, for example, *Internet Computing Online*, a magazine that features articles making this case. See Ian Clarke, Scott G. Miller, Theodore W. Hong, Oscar Sandberg and Brandon Wiley, 'Protecting Free Expression Online with Freemart,' January/February, 2002. See also Yacine Atif, 'Building Trust in E-Commerce,' January/February, 2002. For more along these lines, see the materials posted at http://www2.epic.org/reports/crypto1999.html.

2 For a discussion of whether the Internet is a gadget or tool, see http://www.j-bradford-delong.net/OpEd/virtual/technet/An_E-conomy.html.

3 Science, in turn, brings the unambiguous fruits of technology, thus embodying a promise that's difficult to resist.

4 I thank an anonymous reader at Ashgate for some of the points included in the early passages of this chapter.

5 Tibor R. Machan, *The Pseudo-Science of B. F. Skinner* (New Rochelle, NY; Arlington House Publishing Co., 1974), and *Initiative: Human Agency and Society* (Stanford, CA: Hoover Institution Press, 2000). For a somewhat ambivalent contemporary argument in support of a view closer to Thomas Hobbes and Francis Bacon, see Philip Ball, *Critical Mass: How One Thing Leads to Another* (New York: Farrar, Straus and Giroux, 2004).

6 Many more could be included among those who propose that a reductionist program can be fully successful. Among economists, for example, there are Gordon Tullock and the late Nobel Laureate, George Stigler. See, Gerard Radnitzky and Peter Bernholz, eds,

Economic imperialism: The Economic Approach Applied Outside the Field of Economics (New York: Paragon House Publishers, 1987).

7 It is a question begging, of course, to designate the methods of one of the sciences – or even of a group of them, often referred to as the hard sciences – as the scientific method. Different sciences may well require different methods and some disciplines that the former view may dismiss as unscientific may then also qualify as sciences, albeit with methods of study quite unlike those of, say, physics.

8 It is vital to realize that there were other approaches by which classical liberalism had been defended; for example, the normative or moral tradition of natural law and the Christian tradition of individualism. For more on these, see Tibor R. Machan, *Human Rights and Human Liberties, A Radical Reconsideration of the American Political Tradition* (Chicago, IL: Nelson-Hall Co., Inc., 1975), and J. D. P. Bolton, *Glory Jest and Riddle, A Study of the Growth of Individualism from Homer to Christianity* (New York: Barnes & Noble, 1973). It is mainly because of the new prestige of the natural sciences after the fourteenth century that the positivist version of classical liberalism gained more impact. This is not all that different from what happened among the critics of classical liberalism, such as socialists. As against the humanistic socialism of Charles Fourier, it is Karl Marx's scientific socialism, so-called, that emerged as the most prominent.

9 Often, following Hayek, the case against all-powerful government is made on grounds of the lack of sufficient knowledge needed to coordinate human (and, of course, economic) activity from above. It is, in fact, impossible to gain the requisite type of knowledge, namely, the local information of individuals who know their own needs and circumstances better than anybody else. For a good summary of the issues, see F. A. Hayek, *The Fatal Conceit* (Chicago, IL: University of Chicago Press, 1991).

10 John R. Searle, *The Mystery of Consciousness* (New York: NYREV, Inc., 1997).

11 Ibid.

12 Two recent books develop this theme in detail: John Searle, *Rationality in Action* (Boston, MA: MIT Press, 2001) and Stephen Toulmin, *Return to Reason* (Cambridge, MA: Harvard University Press, 2001).

13 This is especially problematic, by the way, for environmentalists who blame or praise us for how we treat the environment even as they deny basic differences between human and other animal life, all the while wishing to remain purely scientific as well.

14 David Friedman has advanced this position in no uncertain terms, for example, at a symposium at the Cato Institute. Many others who champion classical liberal, libertarian politics have a similarly hopeful outlook regarding the potential for securing liberty by these and related means. See, for example, *Laissez-Faire City Times*, an Internet publication many of the writers and editors of which see the Internet along these lines.

15 This incisive skeptic was the author.

16 See Tibor R. Machan, *Initiative – Human Agency and Society* (Stanford, CA: Hoover Institution Press, 2000).

17 A more elaborate discussion of this topic may be found in Toulmin, *Return to Reason*. See also Tom Sorell, *Scientism: Philosophy and the Infatuation With Science* (London, UK: Routledge Ltd., 1991). For some of the serious obstacles to Internet-based advances toward liberty, see Yaman Akdeniz, Clive Walker, and David S. Wall, eds, *The Internet, Law and Society* (London, UK: Longman, 2001). A very fruitful if somewhat ambiguous discussion of some of these matters can be found in Ball, *Critical Mass*.

Chapter 12

How Critical is Critical Legal Studies?

> For Barney had never questioned the nature of his right to the swimming and the fishing, the boats and the blue summers, which he had described so confidently to the stranger. His ignorance of human misery had been consigned to him with as much loving care as an inheritance … .
>
> Peter Matthiessen, *Partisans*[1]

In 1987 and 1988, controversy abounded over the failure of two law professors to obtain tenure at Harvard Law School.

The professors, Clare Dalton and David Trubek, were exponents of the legal philosophy known as Critical Legal Studies (CLS). It is generally believed that the denial of tenure had to do with the teaching and scholarly practices they engaged in, as shaped by that legal philosophy. In Spring of 1988, Harvard president Derek Bok decided against tenure for a third professor of the school, whose fate had been in limbo during the affair.

The fracas over Critical Legal Theory at Harvard goes back to the 1970s, when its adherents, aka 'Crits,' tried to dismantle the basic legal training of the law school. By 1990 or so, Bok and his allies would largely defang the insurgency, but the Crits continue to maintain a strong if minority presence at the school, as they do at institutions across the academic landscape.[2]

If one judged by the complaints of certain of the school's members – for example, Professor Robert W. Gordon in his essay, 'Law and Ideology,'[3] – one might get the impression that Crits are ostracized at the important schools and gain entry only in some of the less prominent institutions of legal learning, if anywhere. In fact, Crits tend to protest too much – quite a few are very well situated indeed, much better situated than the natural law advocates in jurisprudence, not to mention those who actually defend the object of the Crits' hostility, capitalism. CLS is well represented in law schools at Cardozo, Georgetown, Miami, Rutgers, Stanford, SUNY Buffalo, UCLA, Yale, and – yes, most of all – Harvard! Major figures in the movement have included, at least until recently, Duncan Kennedy, at Harvard; Mark V. Tushnet, at Georgetown; Mark Kelman and Robert W. Gordon, at Stanford; and Richard Michael Fischl, at the University of Miami.

Evidently the CLS scholars harbor quite ambitious expectations for the impact of their thinking on legal education in the USA. So when a few of their brood fails to gain tenure at Harvard University – a place where many professors in many fields do not receive tenure either, even after having been 'given the privilege' of teaching and working there for the initial years of their career – CLS leaders see this as unjust and ideologically motivated.

Yet exponents of competing radicalisms – for example, members of the radical political school of thought that favors pure capitalism, libertarianism – for the most part have yet to reach even the lower-level plateau from which they can grouse about not yet having gotten tenure at Harvard; and this is true regardless of publication and teaching record. In academe, it is not enough to produce good work. A kind of aristocracy exists (an aristocracy of prestige, not of talent), so that the *status quo* is more entrenched in academia than elsewhere in our society. When it comes to radicalism, this *status quo* is much more Marxist than *laissez-faire* capitalist.

What do the aggrieved scholars who inhabit the field of 'Critical Legal Studies' believe? And is there any substance to the charges of unfair treatment?

What they believe is that American political-legal institutions are hopelessly unjust, hopelessly biased in favor of people who have no justification for being so privileged. They object not merely to the corruption of institutions that may at root be sound, but to basic elements of American law as such, including the institution of voluntary contract and the protection of the right to private property. In and of themselves, such institutions constitute fundamental injustices in the system, say the Crits.

The Critical Legal Studies school of legal education and scholarship is a direct challenge to individualist social and political thought. Crits argue that the supposedly impartial institutions of bourgeois individualist law are anything but. Quite the contrary, they say: individualist law is itself an ideology, a framework of administering law and public policy that is biased in favor of certain special interests, namely, the propertied classes.

The Crits often take as their foil the view that such legal institutions are *neutral* – mere neutral efficiency begetters, at least when operating optimally. But the dichotomy between 'neutral' and 'biased' ignores the possibility of a view of law that, while hardly 'neutral' toward the principles of justice it embodies, advocates that they be applied in an objective and universal fashion – to protect the fundamental rights of all, equally. That is a substantive ethical understanding of the legal system that need not presuppose that all agents invoking the law must lack self-interest, or even be guided solely by enlightened self-interest, or never err. (There is certainly a lot of unprincipled maneuvering to *violate* the rule of law within the law's own framework, for instance.) But accepting as they do the neo-Marxist, Postmodernist notion that objectivity and truth are not even possible – that perceptions of reality must always be mediated by alleged class or racial or other collective interests – the Crits would hardly be persuaded by a view of property-rights-protecting law as valid even if fallible.

CLS scholars are of course not monolithic in their thinking, but they do share a basic approach. While some focus on the content of the law or propose reforms to it, in general the school is not so much concerned with advocating changes in the US Constitution or the various Criminal Codes as with stressing certain methodological issues surrounding the teaching of law – especially at the more 'elite' institutions such as Stanford, Harvard, UC Berkeley, and Yale laws schools (although their methodological concerns still have a definite, if only implicitly acknowledged, bearing on constitutional and legal issues).

CLS promotes a very suspicious – 'critical' – attitude toward the legal system governing the society the laws of which the professors are supposed to teach. Indeed, it is appropriate to say that the Crits *challenge* law rather than *teach* it. But that is not too surprising, given their wide-ranging rejection of even the possibility of objectivity; to hold such an assumption *ipso facto* exempts oneself from any obligation to survey a field objectively.

CLS scholars embrace several ideas that are not entirely distinctive to them – for example, that there is really no specialty such as *legal* reasoning: reasoning in the law is pretty much the same as in any other field, fraught with the same pitfalls, subject to the same biases, tacit assumptions, and so on. Crits also tend to make the point, shared by many others who reject legal positivism, that the law is part of the culture and cannot be treated as some autonomous institution. Judges are better off if they do not expect that the law can be understood apart from an understanding of the larger society in which it operates.

At first blush one might think that CLS is a stepchild of the legal realist movement. And there is indeed a conceptual link between CLS and legal realism insofar as Crits stress the instrumental function of law, its role as a vehicle for advancing certain (possibly hidden) causes. More important, however, is the CLS's alliance with the Frankfurt School of critical theorists, a neo-Marxist offshoot that emphasizes the need for the constant (Marxism-informed) re-examination of society's institutions and of the conditions required for such constant scrutiny.

According to the Crits, the legal system is contaminated by (largely bourgeois) assumptions that spawn injustice. Most fundamentally – in the very structure of the politically propagated rights that undergird them – the laws manifest class interest; for no good reason they tend to favor property owners and employers over those without property and employees. And even where these principles of law do not intrinsically favor the powerful interests, if they are not properly scrutinized during the educational process – especially at law schools where the prominent jurists of tomorrow are being trained – the result will be persistent uneasiness about whether any connection between justice and law obtains in our society. Crits admit that extant law undergoes change – for example, they note that tenants and employees now have more rights than in the past. Yet they are nonetheless appalled by 'how legal training produces its mind numbing paralysis – how even left-liberal students trained by left-liberal teachers end up drained of energy and hope for social change.'[4]

CLS scholars sometimes also endorse what Rutgers political science professor, Benjamin Barber, has called 'strong democracy.' That is, they want the democracy that they admit obtains at the political levels of our society to become woven into other aspects of culture as well: economics, science, education, and so on. Here, again, Critical Legal Studies is not original – Professor Paul Feyerabend, a philosopher of science at UC Berkeley, has argued pretty much this view in his *Science in a Free Society.*[5]

But CLS brings some of these 'radical' ideas to bear not just on the law but also on legal education *per se*. CLS professors teach not only constitutional law or jurisprudence but also tax law and property law, and use the classroom podiums to criticize what they take to be the unexamined underpinnings. They play the part of Socrates, of impartial gadflies asking the tough questions of the citizens of that unselfconscious polis that is the United States of America.

When one inspects the standards CLS professors invoke in their critical activities, however, one soon notices that their Socratic skepticism is quite lopsided, and hardly cuts equally harshly at all the presuppositions of our legal system. They certainly don't take much of a scalpel to their own implicit assumption that they are entitled to carry out their sweeping criticisms in a context in which such unabated criticism amounts to a breach of contract, a failure to do what they have been hired to do: namely, teach the profession of law. But no very incisive analysis is required to unveil the agenda of Critical Legal Studies. Its practitioners champion socialism and debunk capitalism, every chance they get.

In his *Tikkun* article, Robert W. Gordon goes to bat for Crits victimized by unjust discrimination at the hands of bourgeois law faculty. Among the villains are the most conservative and liberal colleagues of the Crits. Claiming, essentially, that CLS is merely a method of challenging all the tacit assumptions underlying 'legal discourses [that] are saturated with categories and images that for the most part rationalize and justify in myriad subtle ways the existing social order as natural, necessary, and just,' Gordon chides those who are fearful of Crits.

First, Gordon attempts to distinguish Crits from Marxists who regard the law to be 'an infernal machine for the projects of the ruling class, albeit one full of tricks and devices that can sometimes be turned back upon its makers.' Second, he argues that the law needs the scrutiny of the Critical Legal school in light of the enormous impact on it by those schools of law and economics (for example, Professor Guido Calabrese and Judge Richard Posner) which argue that a value-free economic analysis supplies a valid picture of how our legal system works. Gordon thinks Crits are able to show the underlying hidden assumptions of this bourgeois legal theory, and that it yields vacuous explanations and aims to rationalize the existing legal order. Third, Gordon baldly asserts that 'people with identified left-wing associations have always had trouble finding and holding on to jobs,' contending that Crits, like so many others on the left, are unjustly treated in academe, especially at law schools.

The *New York Times*, in its report on the Harvard Law School controversy, quoted some poignant passages from 'Some Realism About Critical Legal Studies,' an important essay by Crit law professor Richard Michael Fischl published in *The University of Miami Law Review*.[6] Fischl offers numerous good illustrations of the Critical Legal Studies approach. Professor Gordon's more journalistic piece seems to draw heavily on this article for its own examples.

During his course on labor law, Professor Fischl asks his students questions that he believes unearth the assumptions underlying much of American law, especially as it relates to private property and business. In one especially illustrative passage, Fischl recounts his approach to teaching the laws governing the relationship between employer and employee:

> Near the beginning of my course on labor law, I engage my students in the following dialogue: Picture an employee who works for a company that produces widgets. One working day, this employee builds four widgets and, at the end of that day, tenders to her boss an amount in cash equal to the cost of the necessary materials and their procurement, the reasonable rental value of her workplace and tools, and the approximate cost of other managerial expenses. She then leaves the shop and takes the widgets with her, planning to sell them and keep the profits.

After this, Professor Fischl asks his students what will happen. He reports that some say the employer will sue the employee on grounds that the employee has committed theft. He goes on with his account as follows:

> I then ask why the *employer* is not guilty of the same misconduct when he pays the employee a reasonable 'rent' for her labor, keeps the widgets for himself, and sells them for his own profit. There is more stirring and murmuring, until someone finally says, 'Because the widgets belong to the employer – the law says that they're his property.' Why should that be, I ask. After all there is nothing 'necessary' about permitting the employer to 'rent' the worker and keep the widgets; why not structure the relationship the other way around? When someone objects that, if we did that, 'then we wouldn't have capitalism,' I reply that that's exactly my point.[7]

So, per this, the law's protection of the employer's property is entirely arbitrary – there is nothing 'necessary' (that is, justified or right) about it. Gordon refers to the same employer–employee issue and also insists that, contrary to what other teachers seem to convey, the relationship is not a 'natural' one. He then also lays out the allegedly hidden ideological assumptions of the law – unveiling how it is merely a means of rationalizing injustices.

It does not seem to be relevant for either of these champions of a supposedly *critical* approach to law that the initial agreement between employee and employer might well have been made with the clear and mutual understanding that the employee would be paid a salary or wage for his skills and effort and that the employer's ownership of the produced widgets is acknowledged and indeed fully agreed to in advance by the employee. Would admitting this mutual knowledge and mutual agreement be crediting employees as a class with too much awareness of their circumstances – too much ability to choose how they interact with employers? Is it possible that the Crits rest their challenges on unspoken assumptions of their own, for example, about the impotence and ineptness of employees?

The truth is that the very arrangements that Fischl and Gordon claim capitalist-generated law treats as 'necessary,' are, in fact, quite optional – and are openly taught as such in many law courses. Both Fischl and Gordon could have described the situation of work under capitalism such that the worker is not seen as a victim nor the owner as a robber baron – nor the law as some arbitrary instrument in the hands of the latter. They could have explained that the market is a place where workers are indeed sovereigns (as opposed to being wards of a state that allegedly 'protects' – that is, 'regiments' – them by setting terms of trade for them). They could have reminded their students that in the market, workers often *choose* not to become entrepreneurs but to remain employees, so as to be free of certain kinds of responsibilities; whereas owners – as novelists, movie stars or industrialists – often enough earn their wealth.

Fischl and Gordon could have admitted to their students that the law in our supposedly employee-trampling society happens to make possible many different kinds of agreements that can also be honored. Some people rent a building, perform work there, collect earnings for this work and pay rent to the owner. Others buy a building and go into business for themselves. Others form cooperatives. Yet others form communes and leave it at shaking hands. As Robert Nozick has ably observed, capitalism is the one system under which innumerable 'experiments in utopias' are possible – a system much more open than that predicated as ideal by the socio-economic theories underlying Critical Legal Studies.

Fischl and Gordon could have reminded their students that one can draw up many very different agreements with companies that want work done for them. One, of course, involves employment for a wage or salary. Another involves signing on as an independent contractor. Some persons freelance, dealing with several 'employers.' As for the property issue, it's a red herring: most of American law does not stress property relations so much as the integrity of various agreements or contracts (which implicitly acknowledge rightfully owned property, of course, and the right of the owner to contractually dispose of it as he sees fit). Contract is what is central, and contract law shows perhaps the most respect to all parties involved – certainly more than whatever legal apparatus is available in socialist economies, where the state dictates terms and all parties must simply follow orders (a fact that somehow eludes the critical faculties of CLS faculty).

Ironically, many of the institutional hurdles in the path of these various market arrangements arise not from the law as a guardian of capitalist processes but from the various tax codes and regulations – for example,

National Labor Relations Board rulings – that prevent people from becoming independent contractors, partly because labor unions do not welcome this phenomenon. But, in line with their own barely hidden assumptions, the Crits don't count the beneficiaries and officiators of the government's regulatory empire as members of an oppressing class.

A conscientious, fair accounting of the law and its social context would have had to at least acknowledge such alternative interpretations. That would have been the genuinely critical, open attitude. But the Crits give no sign of attempting to acquaint students or readers with the idea that capitalism treats workers as full human beings, just as capable of undertaking prudent strategies in the market as are the owners of capital who need them (and who risk suffering great losses) to make this capital marketable. So to make it appear that the laws in our quasi-capitalist system impose an arbitrary, coercive, unjust organization of production that favors some special class of persons – employers – the 'scholars' of Critical Legal Studies must load their examples. The implication is that some other system – socialism is the 'natural' candidate – would do much better.

It seems that Critical Legal Studying requires not only the excavation of 'hidden' assumptions, but the burying of facts.

How, one might ask, is the Critical critique of capitalism different from the Marxist critique of capitalism from which it is laboriously distinguished? Well, it isn't, much, except that Marx argued that these 'infernal arrangements' could not be ameliorated until a total revolution succeeded in abolishing capitalist institutions and ushering in socialism, while the Crits seem to think that it would be nice to hasten the process by inventive pedagogy. They resemble the champions of Critical Race Studies, who offer a rationale for wholesale lawlessness in the name of protesting the allegedly thoroughgoing racism of Western European institutions of law and government.

Critical Legal Studies, then, contrary to its repeated denials, seems more ideologically than critically motivated. Perhaps there are exceptions; two prominent cases do not tell the whole story. Yet it must be noted that neither Fischl nor Gordon have any genuinely critical attitude to report in their supposedly authentic descriptions of the CLS view of legal relations under our mixed system.

The point here is not the particular facts of the nature of the labor market, that is, whether, as Professor Fischl observes, the 'distribution [of wealth and economic power] is a *choice* – not a "natural" or "necessary" phenomenon.' Whether that is so is worthy of fair debate. Fischl seems to regard the 'choice' about social arrangements as largely a top-down kind of choice. Perhaps, instead, the distribution of wealth or economic power follows the lines of historical choices made by people, with some exceptions that unfortunately cannot be remedied without abandoning the system altogether. But you would never know there could be reasonable argument about these matters from perusing the accounts of Fischl and Gordon.

Despite their boast of being – unlike their targets – beyond ideology – the Crits veer very close to orthodox Marxism in their view that roiling beneath the surfaces of the various systems of ideas in society – law, religion, politics, philosophy – there must be some kind of insidious hidden agenda orchestrated by the economic powers that be. Those who have perceived this truth, in turn, are duty-bound to carry out the revolution whenever they get the chance. Throughout academe, sociologists, economists, and philosophers inspired by Marxism or neo-Marxism have behaved accordingly, including the Crits. The bourgeois bogeyman may be thus effectively dispatched, but not without also making a casualty of academic objectivity.

Yet – Crits and their more orthodox Marxist brethren might ask – aren't neo-classical economists and their law and economics brethren in law schools doing exactly what the Crits do? To be sure, even if the law and economics gang could be found guilty of some of the same offenses the Crits commit, that only proves that those offenses are not confined to the Crits. It does not vindicate the Crits. But let us look at the law and economics school briefly and see if their sins are indeed comparable.

The law and economics school of jurisprudence roughly holds that the law – especially case law – is largely an expression of economic rationality – or, at any rate, that law would make the best sense if it could be directed toward that objective. For example, law and economics scholars regard many of the decisions reached in case law – dealing with anything from the sentencing of trespassers to the assessment of tort damages – as expressive of a kind of utilitarian calculation, implicitly aiming for a Pareto-optimal resolution. Some of the economics and law-school organizations, such as Dean Henry Manne's center at George Mason University School of Law, hold seminars for judges and invite noted economists – for example, Herold Demsetz, Armen Alchian – to explain the economic interpretation of law. And a few of the leaders of this school – such as Richard Posner – are now sitting judges.

In contrast to the Crits, though, these scholars do advance a substantive – not wily 'critical' – thesis. They do not claim to be promoting a neutral scrutiny of our legal system, to be merely hunting for hidden assumptions, with no theses of their own to advance. Quite the contrary. They spell out a very clear, usually jurisprudential doctrine, and engage in extensive debate as to whether it is correct (for example, in Posner's book, *The Economics of Justice*[8]). And they do not lack detractors – many of them from the philosophical community, publishing their critiques in such journals as *Philosophy and Public Affairs*.

Most law and economics scholars actually believe that their approach is value-free – as do many psychologists and historians who by no means have any kind of ideological agenda (even if one might agree with the Marxists that a normative message is still inadvertently conveyed *via* this so-called value-free education). Yet that is a different matter, since there is nothing conspiratorial about the economists' approach. In fact, it would be reasonable to take the teachings as merely a broad conditional proposition: if you want a country to prosper economically, then follow such-and-such approaches to legal reasoning, adjudication, plea bargaining, public policy, taxation, international trade, and so on. If you don't want the country to progress economically, or if you feel that other values are a more pivotal consideration, the economic approach to law will have serious limitations.

No one would wish to argue that there should be no room in our law schools to explore and debate the kinds of issues proponents of Critical Legal Studies are concerned with. No professor should be denied promotion for introducing skepticism into his or her courses or scholarship; but when such skepticism is allowed to overthrow legitimate legal training altogether, the question becomes very different.

And the apparently typical cases of Critical Legal Studies pedagogy do raise doubts about whether CLS is a *bona fide* critical perspective. It seems much more like a means of advancing a political agenda. Professor Fischl paints a selectively callous portrait of the market and suggests some supposedly benign, compassionate, egalitarian alternative. Professor Gordon does no better.

Even if their point about open criticism and self-reflection could be taken at face value – which, as we have seen, they can't be – the Crits miss the point of an education in the law. There is, after all, a time and a place for everything. The practice of throwing every class in law school open to unbounded and critical debate may be properly revolutionary, but it is not a conscientious fulfilling of the task at hand. The bulk of the courses even in the 'elite' schools are largely training grounds for assisting people in their legal affairs in this society, not for either trying to change the world into some (allegedly) ideal version or guarding students against the possibility of resting some of their practical preparations on misguided premises. Worthy as these goals may be, they cannot displace the professional training that is the main purpose of the curriculum. There is ample opportunity in most (and especially the better) liberal arts universities and colleges, attended by students prior to entering the best law schools, to confront the big questions about the philosophical, moral and political assumptions underlying the law in our society as well as alternative societies.

Most law school courses are on the order of professional training sessions. Prospective lawyers go to law school just as others attend conservatories, schools of industrial design, architecture, pharmacology, business or engineering. They want to learn a trade, a craft, a profession; if they are to succeed, their professors must convey to them the nuts and bolts of that trade, not perennially question whether the nuts and bolts even exist, or should exist. In engineering schools one does not use a course on structural design to explore the metaphysical question of whether any objects really exist in reality or whether a principle of design today will also apply tomorrow. A marriage and family therapy masters program does not include extensive speculation about the value of family life, merely explorations about how to keep families functioning. When medical colleges do not give equal time to the African witch doctor's 'methods,' are they mistreating their students? One can argue that if they spent time on such materials they could and even should be sued for malpractice! The law is a no less important field to the health of a society and its members.

As for the law schools themselves, most have particular courses – usually under the heading of 'Jurisprudence' – in which the topics the Crits revere could be covered. But to allow these topics to swamp the syllabi of courses on contract law, agency law, labor law, criminal law, would be counterproductive *at that* time and in *those* courses.

It is a curious thing for skeptics to try to infiltrate such schools and, when rebuffed, protest that they have been treated unjustly. After all, even Socrates would not be welcome in the kitchen, challenging recipes when dinner is about due; or at a building construction site, grilling the foreman about whether the laws of physics really hold. No, he would be well advised to conduct his inquiries in a setting where the central objective is in fact to consider the broad philosophical issues that bear on human life and the ways and means of organizing a community.

But none of my own observations should be taken to mean that competent law professors, who in fact do prepare their students to handle expertly the American legal system – for example, for some possible client – should be penalized for advancing radical ideas in their various publications, provided they also keep up the scholarship that will make them good professors. There is room even for considerable advocacy on the part of professors without having to give up *bona fide* scholarship and instruction, even when the line between the two is not simple to establish.

Well, all this may strike one as simple common sense. Why then do the Crits urge what could reasonably be construed as disruptiveness?

Probably because their agenda is revolutionary not only in the pedagogical but in the political sense of that term. Here again they betray a distrust for the people the teaching of whom they have chosen to take up as a career. And they cannibalize and distort the basic ideas of the very 'ideology' they deride, namely, the classical-liberal notion that from a wide-ranging critical discussion will flow the best understanding of a subject matter. This, after all, is a central tenet of the conceptions of education of John Locke and John Stuart Mill, an understanding of the value of discourse that was developed in conjunction with the championing of social and political individualism.

If we are really in favor of open and various discourse, we should also keep in mind a possibility even more radical than what Crits talk about, namely, complete privatization of education. One reason for the dismay with not just American legal education but American education as such is that in this society we have a somewhat complex combination of publicly funded but largely democratically administered education. That is true from the elementary school level all the way to post-graduate studies. Even our 'elite' private universities are very powerfully wedded to the state – hip-deep in grants from various government agencies and departments.

In such a climate it is not a surprise that all education will tend to reflect contemporary political orthodoxy. And to the extent that the political arena is beset with confusion, lack of direction, mediocrity, so too will much of formal education. (In Europe, where the state is even more directly involved in education, there is, however, not such a strong democratic impact on the field. The momentum from the past, with its tradition of exclusive, aristocratic education, has managed to persist in many – but not all – education institutions even in the midst of the gradual trend toward political democracy.)

With all their affected skepticism of regnant orthodoxy, one has to wonder why the Crits haven't questioned the advisability of the virtually total politicization of education. If there is anything that would achieve the goals to which Crits give lip service – namely, diversity and ongoing rethinking of institutions – it's a totally privatized educational system.

But, alas, that kind of laissez-faire free-for-all wouldn't mesh with the Marxist program.

Judging by the reports of two of their own prominent defenders, the Crits have two counts against them. One is that they are merely parading themselves as uncommitted and fair critics – whereas in fact they are pursuing an agenda of academic sabotage. Second, whether or not their rhetoric of criticism is authentic, it betrays a misunderstanding of the very nature of law school education.

For these two reasons the suspicions many law schools have about the Crits seem to be warranted. Individual cases are legitimately scrutinized with such concerns in mind.

So what then should law schools and universities do when scholars use classrooms as political platforms? Scholars can have firm viewpoints, even skeptical ones. The issue at the various law schools must be whether the purpose of legal education is enhanced. Are professors teaching what they have been hired to teach – or are they working to steer their students in what they take to be the more important but actually irrelevant subject for study? If the latter, then promoting the teacher, even if in some ways a brilliant thinker and scholar in the areas that interest him or her, would not be a responsible course. Academic freedom does not include the right to change at will the curriculum of a law school to that of political philosophy or revolutionary ideology.

If this is what Clare Dalton and David Trubek were guilty of at Harvard, former president Bok was right to deny them tenure.

Notes

1 Peter Matthiessen, *Partisans* (New York: Viking Press, 1955).

2 See Bruck Brower, 'The Law School and the Law: A "Benthamite" dean lets a hundred legal flowers bloom,' *Harvard Magazine*, January–February 2000; reprinted at http://www.Harvard-magazine.com/issues/jf00/law.html.
3 Robert W. Gordon, 'Law and Ideology', *Tikkun*, Vol. 14 (1988), pp. 15–16.
4 Ibid., p. 16.
5 Paul Feyerabend, *Science in a Free Society* (London: New Left Books, 1978).
6 *University of Miami Law Review*, Vol. 41 (1987), pp. 505–11. Professor Fischl authored a follow-up of sorts, 'The Question That Killed Critical Legal Studies,' *Law & Social Inquiry*, Vol. 17 (1992), pp. 779–83
7 Fischl, p. 527.
8 Richard Posner, *The Economics of Justice* (Cambridge, MA: Harvard University Press, 1981).

Chapter 13

Should You Apologize?

Moral Concepts, Groups and Facts

Are there some facts that are presupposed in apologizing and forgiving? What are they? Could we apologize and forgive without them?

The way I plan to go about discussing these questions needs to be addressed briefly before I begin. I take it that when an idea, theory, or principle gains its meaningfulness from others on which it rests, conceptually, then if those other ideas are false or confused, those that rest on them are called into question. It is, of course, possible that some other source of support could be found for the original ideas. But the burden of showing that such ideas exist and are meaningful and true lies with those who wish to defend the idea, theory, or principle in question. If, for example, the concept of 'intention' rests on the idea of mental action and it turns out that no mental action exists, then for the time being 'intention' has to be given up as a sound idea, at least until its foundations are reconstituted.

The questions on which I will focus arise in connection with certain social-political-legal problems, such as the rectification of past oppression by some against other citizens of a country as well as apologies offered for the commission of such past oppression. Even if most of these citizens are deceased, as are the perpetrators of the oppression against them, it is sometimes argued that a country as such owes an apology for the oppression, as well as that the descendants of the oppressed might and sometimes ought to forgive the country for the oppression their ancestors suffered. Sometimes these issues are linked to consideration of reparation or compensation, from members of the group that oppressed to members of the group that was oppressed.[1]

Anyone who regards the idea of collective guilt or culpability objectionable, and I count myself among these, needs to have an account available of these sorts of matters that is substantially individualist.[2] For example, in Western liberal legal systems the sins of the parents do not serve to condemn the children; the vices of some members of an ethnic group do not transfer to others. If some Jews were complicit in killing Jesus, other Jews aren't deemed guilty, not in virtue of also being Jews, not unless the tenets of the religion dictated the original killing and current worshipers fully embrace those tenets. Even then, they would not be guilty of the killing itself, only of sanctioning the killing. Also, children do not inherit the debts of parents unless they are also willing members of a corporation or firm that has incurred and is still obligated to pay the debts.[3]

Some take this very seriously and have been faulted for being unable to make clear sense of any references to the intentions, actions and responsibilities of groups. For example, the view that Christians inflicted upon thousands of people the torments of the Inquisition, that Germans are responsible for the murder of millions of Jews, and that France or Britain or Iraq perpetrated some kind of military action against some other country – all these would appear to be problematic from the standpoint of those who deny group culpability and guilt.

For this reason it will be of some use here to consider what facts if any underlie such concepts as 'guilt,' 'apology' and 'forgiveness.' First, for these concepts to be meaningfully deployed, they require some matters of fact of which we can be aware and from which these concepts are formed. Otherwise assertions about whether one owes others an apology and whether one may be forgiven for what one is apologizing for could not be shown to be true (or distinguished from denials). 'I apologize for having insulted you,' and 'I forgive you for having insulted me' could not be true, meaningful assertions without certain facts being the case, such as being responsible for the insult.

In short, something about human beings must make it possible to think and speak of making decisions, choosing courses of conduct, failing to act properly in order to speak truly of someone having the obligation – or duty or responsibility – to do something, including, apologizing for some conduct. Similarly, there are preconditions for it being the case that someone can or should forgive someone else. Apology, forgiveness and the like have, thus, certain ontological preconditions; and if these are unfulfilled, the application of such concepts turns out to be groundless (because they lack the requisite conceptual base[4]).

The situation is analogous to there having to be atoms for there to be molecules; if no atoms exist, then no molecules can exist either, not, at least, as they are now understood. Or for Jesus Christ to have existed, there must be a Christian God and have been a Virgin Mary and if not, there could not have been a Jesus Christ (not in the relevant, Christian sense). Of course, it is not impossible, in the sense of being self-contradictory, for molecules to exist without atoms, nor for Jesus Christ without the Virgin Mary, only that is quite irrelevant.[5]

In relation to apologizing and forgiving (among other morally pregnant activities), if no one can choose to do something wrong or right, then to apologize to or forgive someone for having chosen to do what is wrong in the ordinary sense in which we mean these terms can make no sense. One might refashion the concept in some way, such that 'to apologize' would be consistent with unavoidably having done something untoward – say, by having the concept mean 'to lament' – but that would no longer be the apology we know and associate with people doing wrong things and regretting and wishing to be forgiven for having done them.[6]

Let me illustrate just how preconditions, along the lines I am suggesting, are required in another domain, namely, in connection with ascribing criminal responsibility to persons. To wit, H. L. A. Hart tells us, in connection with culpable negligence, that

> [N]o satisfactory account of what it is which makes 'conduct' voluntary or involuntary, capable of covering both acts and omissions can be given in [the] terminology of 'states of mind' or 'mental attitude.' What is required (as a minimum) is the notion of a general ability or capacity to control bodily movements, which is usually present but may be absent or impaired. … It is important to pause and note that if anything is 'blameworthy,' it is not the 'state of mind' but the agent's failure to inform himself of the facts and so getting into this 'state of mind.'[7]

The idea here is that one must have the capacity to bring about conduct that produces culpability. So it would have to be up to the individual to bring such conduct about, something one could do or refrain from doing of one's own initiative. In traditional terms, culpable conduct presupposes free will. If one had no freedom of choice to do or not to do what turns out to be wrongful actions, it would make no sense to claim that one should or ought not to have done them.[8]

It is, however, only individual human beings with minds that are capable of forming or omitting to form conscious intentions guided by conceptual understanding that fit this condition. That is to say, human beings make judgments as to the desirability of certain complex actions, such as taking someone else's belongings, for which they are then responsible. The human mind, with its capacity to form general ideas – that are not a perception of some state of affairs that pre-exists in nature – uses the capacity to become volitionally aware by forming such ideas, based on perceptual evidence and on inferences. One can choose to think – to form complex conceptual propositions – or choose not to do so. This is clear enough from the fact that some persons do and others fail to become aware of how they ought to act and when they do not, their ignorance is no excuse. They could have become so aware.

For example, persons who fail to appreciate that an individual's color, race, national origin or gender is no grounds for attributing to that individual either favorable or unfavorable moral characteristics are morally responsible for what they come to believe as a result. That, indeed, is the source of culpable, blameworthy racism or similar prejudice, namely, a judgment that precedes evidence or proceeds hastily or carelessly.

Without such a capacity to either attend to the facts or fail to do so, no responsibility could be ascribed for holding prejudicial views such as those held by racists, sexists or bigots. So in, for example, a Skinnerian world, for contrast, the facts about human nature would be such as to render any moral responsibility – including the basis for an apology or for forgiveness – unfounded since in such a world this capacity for freedom of choice that brings moral responsibility into existence would be no more well grounded than, say, would be the casting of spells or the invocation of spirits in a naturalistic world.[9]

Some might dispute this on the grounds that certain determinists do retain the use of concepts such as 'responsibility' or 'punishment.' But they do not mean by these concepts what is meant as we use them in our day-to-day moral and legal discourse. So such transmogrifications do not suffice to refute my point – they amount to wishing to eat one's conceptual cake and have it too. Since for Skinner and other determinists (for example, Daniel Dennett whose compatibilism is but a will-o'-the-wisp[10]) – be they hard or soft ones – our behavior is prompted by the interaction of the environment and the organism with no choice or initiative available to the agent – nor any standard of right and wrong the agent might then choose or fail to choose to act on – concepts presupposing the possibility of choice have no basis.

So, while it is true enough that many champions of deterministic accounts of human behavior assure us that their view makes ample room for ethics, morality, personal responsibility, blame, praise, apology, forgiveness, punishment and atonement, among other institutions and phenomena, their reasons seem to be that (a) they know how well these ideas are interwoven with human affairs and so without them their theory would lack realism and (b) they alleged that all these concepts mean something other than what they are normally taken to mean. Thus by 'punish' they do not mean 'meting out untoward treatment in response to an avoidable wrongdoing' – as the normal criminal law and ordinary ethical thinking would have it – but something along the lines of 'act so as to prevent future performance of this kind.' Skinner himself was forthright about all this when he rejected, instead of merely recasting, the sense of such concepts as 'freedom,' 'dignity,' 'regret' and 'choice' in his various works.[11]

Second, not only is it the case that without certain ontological propositions being true there would be no way to ground conceptually a claim to having moral obligations and, correspondingly, if those are not met, having the moral responsibility to apologize.[12] The very idea of moral misconduct – although not bad, undesired, unhealthy or even revolting *behavior* – would be impossible, provided we mean by 'moral misconduct' actions that one has undertaken of one's own initiative and for which one is, therefore, responsible (one might not have taken those actions but chosen to take them).[13] Culpable malpractice, too, in the law, would have to be given up as a correct account of how some people act.

The moral dimension of human life assumes personal responsibility to make the right choice from among various alternative courses of conduct – or, in other words, free agency or will – on the part of human beings who aren't crucially incapacitated.

Morality Without Facts

Let me give a quick example. Peter Singer is a very prominent defender of animal liberation and substantial sacrifice in behalf of the world's poor. He embraces a utilitarian approach to substantive ethics. Yet he is also an advocate of noncognitive metaethics. Popular sentiment or private intuition is what he produces to ground his beliefs that animals must be included in a utilitarian calculus and that most Westerners ought to give up a great deal of their wealth to help others around the world.[14]

Not surprisingly, Singer does not really take his own advice seriously, either as far as his own conduct is concerned nor as far as what he believes others ought to do.[15] And why should he approach matters otherwise? He has no basis on which to claim that his utilitarianism is or even could be morally binding on us. Public opinions as well as intuitions vary a great deal, from person to person, culture to culture, and era to era. Hindus firmly believe that cows are sacred while Christians believe that human life is sacred. In the eighteenth century the public flogging of children was intuitively held to be a fine thing; today, it is held to be barbaric.

What Makes Apologies Work?

As with moral responsibility – which, if it is real, often can issue in the justified ascription of blame and praise for deeds done by persons – so it is with apologies. Both presuppose some facts about human beings that are in serious dispute. To put it plainly, those who apologize must have certain attributes in terms of which their offering a *bona fide* – or even disingenuous – apology makes sense. Meaningfully demanding an apology from, as well as granting forgiveness to, someone similarly presupposes certain facts about human beings without which the moral point of view would be a bogus one.[16]

For example, to apologize is both to accept responsibility for a wrong done that the agent could have refrained from doing and to seek forgiveness from those who have been wronged by what was done. This is why it is problematic to accept an apology issued in behalf of persons who have not actually accepted responsibility or sought forgiveness, as when a spouse apologizes for a mate or a parent for a child. If an agent hasn't acknowledged wrongdoing and does not seek to be forgiven for this, no one else can do this for the agent. All that such 'apologies' can amount to is a profession of dismay or lament.

Nor is saying 'I am sorry' sufficient for an apology because it could mean merely that one is dismayed or laments what has happened without taking any responsibility for it. Very often when one hears of someone's mishap or loss, one says, 'Oh, I am very sorry.' This could express merely that one feels badly about what happened without suggesting contrition for it. Of course, sometimes 'I am sorry' is used as an apology; but it need not be so meant or taken.[17]

Those, however, who apologize implicitly admit to possessing free will – or what I have been calling initiative throughout this discussion.[18] Free will, initiative or agency implies that it is we who normally cause our conduct and might not have caused the conduct that is (deemed to be) wrong or right. If we lack this capacity, so that instead what we 'do' is an unwelcome happening – akin to an earthquake, tornado or bug bite – apologizing and wanting forgiveness make no reasonable sense.

It would not make sense to expect an apology from inanimate matter, plants or non-human animals. If a dog bites or a rock falls on someone, the idea that an apology is now due – other than from some possible human agent who contributed to such a result – is nonsense (other than in Disney movies or fairly tales, both of which enjoy poetic license). These all behave as they naturally must, although it is arguable that some animals possess a measure of free choice and even moral sense (something I will not discuss here). However we best put their situation, the crucial point is that none of the above possesses, as a central feature of their nature, the capacity for moral responsibility. Why? Because none can be the cause of its own significant actions, nor apprehend or grasp how it *ought to* act.[19]

Moral Objectivism

Another assumption of apology and forgiveness – as well as all morally pregnant concepts – is metaethical cognitivism or objectivism. That is to say, that what is right and wrong must be knowable. What we ought to do is a fact about how we relate to the world properly, not merely a matter of some people's wishes, desires, hopes and the like. Judgments concerning how one ought to and ought not to act must be something that can be established as true or false.[20] If this is not so, apologies and other moral notions would be arbitrary, *ad hoc*, and groundless in the sense in which people speak about them. If I can apologize without being responsible for the wrongness of what I have done, this is certainly something different from what we ordinarily mean by an apology. Such perverse uses of the concept of 'apology' would render the sincerity of an apology or forgiveness, for example, impossible, just as the 'truth' of a dream or fantasy is impossible to tell.

Some very crucial institutions in most societies presuppose that human beings can know what is right and this is knowledge (of certain kinds of facts) about human life. In short, if human life is truly value free – that is, if concepts of right and wrong, good and evil, guilt and innocence, worth and unworthiness, blame and praiseworthiness and many other concepts with ethical presuppositions are wholly inapplicable in human life, just as many in the social sciences used to assume – this would make apologizing something entirely odd, unrelated to our common moral universe.[21] And in the case of apologizing for injustice or other misconduct toward others, the denial of the capacity of human beings for free agency would be a cruel hoax, as well. It would underscore the view of those who perpetrated and continue to defend the unjust actions and institutions involved that in fact, realistically speaking, no injustice had – indeed could have – been done, so that nothing needs to be apologized for and no forgiveness needs to be sought.

Assuming Individualism

Finally, a version of moral individualism is also presupposed by moral concepts such as 'apology' and 'forgiveness.' It is supposed to be human individuals, not groups, who do what is morally wrong and for which they could and sometimes should apologize, otherwise the offer of an apology by someone – an individual – would be disingenuous. It is human individuals who possess the capacities of mind – resting on their individual brains and faculties – by which they can produce beliefs and actions for which they may need to apologize and which might be forgiven by other individuals.[22]

There are serious philosophical and related schools of thought that attempt to deny this because they share Karl Marx's belief that 'The human essence is the true collectivity of man.'[23] This then leads to treating human affairs not as the product of individual choices or initiative but of class tendencies. It is, by Marx's lights, humanity that actually acts – goes through development processes independently of the subjective features of human consciousness.[24] (I refer here to Marx instead of more recent proponents of such a view because of his prominence and influence and because a good deal of contemporary discussion of collective responsibility and guilt is derivative of his sort of class or collective analysis.) But we may appreciate one of the central problems with that idea, namely, that all such beliefs and arguments are themselves what individual human beings develop, hold, and advance, and in connection with which they criticize one another, claiming that those who disagree are individually wrong for doing so. That may be seen as the most elementary form of individualism implicit in human intellectual discourse.[25]

Arguably, some may wish to have it both ways, admitting some measure of individual responsibility for conduct yet also holding responsible – that is, blame or praise – human collectives (as when a corporation or even a country is the focus). 'Germany caused the Second World War,' or 'The Jews killed Christ' or 'Muslims are the terrorists' would be examples of such attributions. According to the present approach, however, these kinds of claims are at best short cuts, loose talk, and cannot be literally true.

It may also be claimed that people who speak for groups, such as governments or corporations, can apologize and seek forgiveness even if those who perpetrated the moral evils at issue are no longer alive. This is an interesting idea, especially in the wake of British Prime Minister Tony Blair's apology for Britain's conduct during the Irish famine, the US government's compensation of Japanese Americans for their unjust internment during World War II, and several Swiss corporations' payment of large sums to relatives of Holocaust victims.

Exactly how to render all these sensible is not an easy task but one account that squares with moral individualism focuses on the fact that in each of these cases the transfer of legitimacy – of governments and corporations – involved, in part, a willing assumption of responsibility for the organization's past actions. If I join the KKK, I, in a serious sense, become supportive of its past deeds, and once they are acknowledged to have been vile, I need to apologize for having been supportive of them. And to clear the name of the organization, its leaders would need to place it on record as having regretted the organization's past deeds. In a crucial sense, then, we are still concerned with how individuals see themselves and their actions and their willingness or lack thereof to accept responsibility where that is warranted. That the language is often somewhat hazy testifies to the fact that these matters are difficult to sort out, especially for purposes of issuing simple, straightforward statements to the public at large.

Conclusion

I would suggest that the several presuppositions I mention above – free will, moral objectivity and moral individualism – render apologies, forgiveness and similar aspects of our moral lives well grounded. Putting it a bit differently, that human initiative exists, that moral knowledge is objective and that individualism is a sound social theory all point to the conclusion that when, in the ordinary sense of these terms, human beings apologize and when they forgive one another's wrong deeds, this is something that fits properly within their lives and is not some illusion, myth or ruse – or something in need of being recast into language that no longer means what we ordinarily take it to mean.

What may be most controversial about the above approach is that moral individualism strongly suggests that apologizing to those one could not have wronged is probably mostly – though perhaps prudently – ceremonial. At worst it may be a case of capitulating to collectivist prejudices and thereby perpetuating some of the conditions that led to the injustices that required an apology in the first place. Accordingly, the conclusion here reached is that collective as well as retrospective apologizing is ill founded.[26]

Notes

1 Other issues may also be involved, such as assigning guilt to all members of a group for the deeds of some of its members. Can current managers of a corporation be faulted for the deeds of past members, as is suggested by apologies offered by current managers of some Swiss banks for the deeds of past managers? Can current members of ethnic groups share the blame for the deeds of past members? Could they owe an apology to those who descend from the victims? Several volumes deal with these and related matters, including Larry May, *The Morality of Groups* (Notre Dame, IN: University of Notre Dame Press, 1987), Peter A. French, ed., *Individual and Collective Responsibility* (Rochester, VT: Schenkman Books, 1997), Larry May and Stacey Hoffman, eds, *Collective Responsibility: five decades of debate in theoretical and applied ethics* (Lanham, MD: Rowman & Littlefield, 1991), Sandra L. Bloom, *Bearing Witness: Violence and Collective Responsibility* (Binghampton, NY: Haworth Press, Incorporated, 1998).

2 Some communitarians, such as Michael Sandel, dispute the very existence of individuals as being ontologically prior. See Sandel, *Liberalism and the Limits of Justice* (Cambridge: Cambridge University Press, 1982). Their thesis is that a self is inherently collective or communal so that everyone is a bundle of persons, the one whom we ordinarily think of as the individual plus various more or less intimate others. But see, in response to his idea that selfhood is ontologically flexible, John Haldane, 'Individuals and the Theory of Justice,' *Ratio* XXVII 2 (December 1985), pp. 189–96. See also Tibor R. Machan, *Individuals and Their Rights* (LaSalle, IL: Open Court Publishing Company, Inc., 1989) and *Classical Individualism* (London, UK: Routledge, 1998).

The central idea of individualism isn't atomism but that there is one, unitary self who is the source of significant action, an individual will, as it were.

3 Accordingly, comparing demands for contemporary white persons' reparations to contemporary black persons' for slavery and segregation from whites with reparations to Jews from certain German corporations, such as banks operating in Switzerland, is a category mistake.

4 For bachelors to exist, there must be adult male human beings. If there aren't, then no bachelors can be, not in the sense in which the concept is now deployed. The concept of bachelorhood presupposes the valid concept of adult male human being.

5 It is true that there might be – that is, it is logically possible for there to be – molecules without atoms and Jesus Christ without a Virgin Mary, whatever that is supposed to state. However, I am not interested in logically (that is, formally) necessary truths here, although some do speak of 'the logic' of a concept. I am concerned that the conceptual base of certain ideas be identified and not forgotten as those ideas are deployed.

6 Such refashioning of language was a prominent feature of B. F. Skinner's *Beyond Freedom and Dignity* (New York: Viking, 1971).

7 H. L. A. Hart, *Punishment and Responsibility* (New York: Oxford University Press, 1968), pp. 142–43.

8 For more on this, see Tibor R. Machan, *Initiative – Human Agency and Society* (Stanford, CA: Hoover Institution Press, 2000). In this work I explain why Frankfurt type refutations of alternative possibilities are not telling. They are, essentially, contrived and gain their thin plausibility from highly exceptional language uses.

9 Skinner, *Beyond Freedom and Dignity*. Cf., Tibor R. Machan, The *Pseudo-Science of B. F. Skinner* (New Rochelle, NY: Arlington House Publishers, 1974).

10 Daniel Dennett, *Elbow Room: The Varieties of Free Will Worth Wanting* (Cambridge, MA: MIT Press, 1984).

11 For how Skinner recasts these and related concepts, see Skinner, *Beyond Freedom and Dignity*, *Science and Human Behavior* (New York: The Free Press, 1965), 'Behaviorism at Fifty,' in T. W. Warin (ed.), *Behaviorism and Phenomenology* (Chicago, IL: University of Chicago Press, 1964) and 'Answers for my Critics' in Harvey Wheeler (ed.), *Beyond the Punitive Society* (San Francisco, CA: W. H. Freeman and Co., 1973),

12 My remarks here rest on the conviction, not argued for here, that concepts are formed by reference to facts of reality. In short, I am invoking a realistic understanding of concept formation. See, for more on this, Edward Pols, *Radical Realism* (Ithaca, NY: Cornell University Press, 1998). See, also, Ayn Rand, *Introduction to Objectivist Epistemology*, exp. 2nd edn (New York: NAL Books, 1990).

13 There are those who argue that moral responsibility is possible without it being the case that the agent could have done otherwise. I address this compatibilist view in *Initiative*. Briefly, compatibilism robs morality of its central feature, namely, that the agents of morally significant conduct had the capacity to avoid doing what is wrong or to do what is right. If compatibilism is true, then only good behavior is possible, not morally right conduct that depends on choice.

14 See Peter Singer et al., *Animal Liberation,* 2nd edn (New York: The New York Review of Books Collection, 1990) and *Practice Ethics* (London, UK: Cambridge University Press, 1993).

15 See Peter Berkowitz, 'Other People's Mothers,' *The New Republic*, January 10, 2000. Berkowitz makes note of the fact that despite Singer's proclamation that the very old ought to be allowed to die and the resources to keep them alive ought to go to help those who suffer poverty and deprivation, Singer himself has spent extensive resources on helping his own elderly mother.

16 As Nagel puts it, 'The concern with what one is doing to whom as opposed to what happens, is an important primary source of ethics that is poorly understood.' Thomas Nagel, 'Equality,' in Thomas Nagel, *Moral Questions* (Cambridge: Cambridge University Press, 1979), p. 115. I take it Nagel here is reminding us of Kant's famous dictum, '"Ought" implies "can".'

It has been suggested by one critic that the view that moral responsibility is predicated on some sort of free will is a minority position and that there are many different senses of this idea that can be made to fit within determinist or compatibilist theories. As I note above, this may well be due to not wanting to depart from reality too obviously as one advances one's philosophical views and because the concepts of 'responsibility' have been radically recast. Another reason is that determinist – even soft determinist and compatibilist – views are widely deemed to be consistent with what the philosophers take to be the requirements of science, so despite their willingness to make room for the ethical life, they are also beholden to the scientific account of human life. Not willing to do what Kant did, namely, to divide reality into the noumenal and phenomenal regions, they simply concoct a so-called compatibilist position. As noted, Skinner was more forthright and simply tossed the moral realm altogether, thereby preserving consistency albeit at the expense of ordinary realism. If this sounds somewhat judgmental or moralistic, in suggesting as it does that some people perform dubious theoretical moves so as to satisfy incompatible goals, well, that is merely one way of understanding the point. But why would that be so outlandish? When scientists tried to reconcile the findings of astronomy with a given cosmology, they were accused of constructing bogus epicycles. Even if one may have problems with discerning motives, the fact should suffice that this was a dubious move. Other such efforts are no less culpably carried out.

17 Arguably, one source of concern about former president Bill Clinton's response to being accused of wrongdoing with Monica Lewinsky is that he would usually only say, 'I am sorry for what happened.' It is very possible that this was done at the advice of legal counsel so as not to legally implicate Mr Clinton. Saying, 'I apologize for what I did' would very possibly have run the serious risk of implicitly admitting guilt, which, given his problems with Paula Jones, could have been quite costly. 'I am sorry for what happened' leaves open whether I am responsible.

18 Machan, *Initiative,* and Tibor R. Machan, 'Applied Ethics and Free Will,' *Journal of Applied Philosophy,* Vol. 10 (1993), pp. 59–72.

19 For a discussion of this issue, see Tibor R. Machan, *Putting Humans First, Why We Are Nature's Favorite* (Lanham, MD: Rowman & Littlefield, 2004).

20 I develop the case for this claim in some detail in Tibor R. Machan, *Objectivity – Recovering Determinate Reality in Philosophy, Science, and Everyday Life* (London, UK: Ashgate Ltd, 2004).

21 Machan, *Initiative*. This was the gist of A. J. Ayer's logical positivist view of morality in *Language, Truth, and Logic* (New York: Dover, 1936).

22 For more on this, see Machan, *Classical Individualism*. For a view that embraces a form of collective guilt and debt, see Randall Robinson, *The Debt, What America Owes to Blacks* (New York: Dutton, 1999). Matters can get complicated but the general idea I would propose is that any liability be dealt with similarly to how tort law deals with it. Individuals, or their voluntary associations such as corporations and the like must be found liable. That is the approach that was taken *vis-à-vis* Swiss bank and German corporate debts to survivors of the Holocaust and their offspring, as well as to Japanese Americans who were interned in the USA. It is problematic, also, just how abrogation of US Government Treaties with Native Americans – that is, Native American tribes – can

be adjudicated once all the parties to the treaty have died. For this, a fully developed sound theory of tribal and political identity over time may be required.

23 Karl Marx, *Selected Writings* (New York: Harper & Row, 1970), p. 126. Others, not necessarily completely in agreement with Marx, uphold a similar view. See, for example, Charles Taylor, *Philosophy and the Human Sciences* (Cambridge: Cambridge University Press, 1985), where in several chapters he writes of people *belonging to* society or some other group.

24 Marx, *Selected Writings*, p. 417.

25 For more, see Tibor R. Machan, 'Individualism and Discourse Ethics,' in *Classical Individualism.* For a very detailed discussion of ethical individualism, see David L. Norton, *Personal Destinies, A Philosophy of Ethics Individualism* (Princeton, NJ: Princeton University Press, 1976).

To appreciate the individualist point, the following may be of some help here:

> Language often obscures truth. More than is ordinarily realized, our eyes are blinded to the facts of international relations by tricks of the tongue. When one uses the simple monosyllable 'France', one thinks of France as a unit, an entity. When to avoid awkward repetition we use a personal pronoun in referring to a country – when for example we say 'France sent her troops to conquer Tunis' – we impute not only unity but personality to the country. The very words conceal the facts and make international relations a glamorous drama in which personalized nations are the actors, and all too easily we forget the flesh-and-blood men and women who are the true actors. How different it would be if we had no such word as 'France,' and had to say instead – thirty-eight million men, women and children of very diversified interests and beliefs, inhabiting 218,000 square miles of territory! Then we should more accurately describe the Tunis expedition in some such way as this: 'A few of these thirty-eight million persons sent thirty thousand others to conquer Tunis.' This way of putting the fact immediately suggests a question, or rather a series of questions. Who are the 'few'? Why did they send the thirty thousand to Tunis? And why did these obey? … Empire-building is done not by 'nations' but by men. The problem before us is to discover the men, the active, interested minorities in each nation, who are directly interested in imperialism, and then to analyze the reasons why the majorities pay the expenses and fight the wars necessitated by imperialist expansion.

Parker Thomas Moon, *Imperialism and World Politics* (New York: The Macmillan Company, 1930), p. 58.

26 The exception may be that derivatively – that is, when one speaks for others who have appointed one as their representative or spokesperson – such apologies could have merit. For a discussion of why it is wrong to seek rectification of all past wrongs from someone or another now, see Christopher W. Morris, 'Existential Limits to the Rectification of Past Wrongs,' *American Philosophical Quarterly*, Vol. 12, No 2 (April 1984), pp. 175–82.

Chapter 14

Between Parent and Child

Are we forgetting about the kids?

Critics sometimes say that libertarians don't pay enough attention to social issues as compared to political issues, nor to certain gray areas in the political arena, for example, the morality and legality of abortion or assisted suicide and, especially, the legal status of children.[1]

Now it is true that most libertarian theorists have thus far been preoccupied with fundamentals, but understandably so. The very idea of a fully free society is anathema to most other political philosophers. Even if most contemporary political philosophers would also take issue with full-fledged socialism or communism, their statism inclines them to be less dismissive of such ideological systems – which are, after all, only extreme variants of their own views.

Some libertarians have addressed the ticklish questions of abortion. But they have also argued that abortion *per se* is not a concern of libertarian justice – that what is of concern is the point at which someone becomes a rights-bearing human being. Should this turn out to occur immediately after conception, so be it, and this is the point at which rights ought to be enforced; but if this occurs later, then so be it also.[2]

I will not revisit those topics here. I note them to distinguish them from others even more remote from politics: topics in social philosophy such as the proper view of gambling, drinking, adventure, commercial speculation and so forth; and the topics of applied ethics (business, medicine, science, athletics, and so on). Libertarians do have something to say about these, though not necessarily *qua* libertarians. Yet, as the following discussion illustrates, there are affinities between libertarian politics and libertarian treatments of such a topic as the proper, ethical relationship between parents and children.

We take it for granted that there are moral dimensions to the parent–child relationship. Such concepts as parental authority, child abuse, and the duty to obey suggest as much. We also distinguish between the legal and the moral dimensions. For example, we refer to the legally enforceable duty of child support or to children's rights that may be protected by law, as opposed to a parent's moral responsibility to teach values or the child's responsibility to help around the house.

How do these moral components of the parent–child relationship arise? So what if children are begotten by parents? How could this obligate parents to do anything in particular? And what if the child refuses to obey his parents? What is wrong with that aside from a kind of recklessness inviting inconvenient parental repercussions?

Certainly much of the law across the civilized world affirms the obligations of parents and children. But the sheer fact that these obligations are widely upheld isn't enough to explain and validate the morality of the relationship. When children challenge a parent, or a parent contemplates how to deal with his children, such questions need to be answered independently of the law. And much of family life is carried on behind closed doors in any case, so that mere legal guidelines cannot suffice to steer people in the right direction. A family life that proceeded by continuously consulting the law would surely be an impoverished one. And any legal code that attempted to predetermine all the moral paths a parent and child may take would be an impoverished – or overly presumptuous and intrusive – legal code!

So let's explore, as moral questions, what children owe their parents and what parents owe their children, and why.

Parental authority and its limits may be understood by answering the question: 'What would my child reasonably have wanted me to do for (and to) him once he has become an adult?' Then we may take it that upon accepting the role of parents one has agreed to deal with one's children according to the prospective answer to this question.

Would a grown person wish that his parents had guided him in certain fundamental ways when he was young? Would he wish for some sternness in this guidance – for example, that the parents refuse to let him take up smoking, require him go to bed at a reasonable hour, insist he do his homework? Suppose a child has discernible musical talent. Would the adult who had been this child have wanted her parents to apply reasonably stern discipline about developing this talent? If so – and if what parents ought to do is rear their children to grow into mature and fulfilled adults – then this would inform them about how they ought to rear their children.

The same would hold with respect to general moral standards and mores as with measures pertaining to individual development. Parents or guardians owe their children what the adult version of the child would rationally propose they should have done. (Notice that this requirement of rationality precludes any demand for the impossible – for example, what would have been unfeasible economically or otherwise.)

A crucial element of self-development is the ability to become who one will be by choice, not because one has been molded into what someone else has decided one will be. This (what we should call a) rational-reconstructive approach to child-rearing does justice to a human being's essential autonomy or free will: if we keep in focus what the adult version of our child would want us to do about his development, we seek to recognize the role of autonomous choice early on, if only in a surrogate fashion. We, as parents, stand in for the adult version of our child and thus give the child a kind of self-direction. As the child develops we encourage as much independent decision-making as we can reasonably countenance.

This approach also encourages the necessary amount of moral teaching from parents. A grown person would not reasonably desire that he had been brought up without regard to sound moral standards. Since moral teaching involves disputed precepts – especially if complete moralities are being taught rather than just common-sense moral principles – parent moral teaching would always have to be somewhat provisional, with parents aware that someday the child will likely challenge their teachings. Parents must thus be prepared to defend them by reference to reasons that can be understood and eventually evaluated (as opposed to the easier but less enlightening 'Because I told you so!'). Mere indoctrination or indifference to moral issues would constitute, at least in part, neglectful child rearing.

As to what children owe their parents, the issue might be approached by way of considering what parents need from children to make a feasible household and a developing child possible. A child should obey parents because this is the child's best option for development – so long as parents are endeavoring to promote that child's development. Since children, especially very young children, are not able to assess this well, the general prescription 'Obey your parents' makes sense for most parent–child relationships. But if and when the child-rearing experience ceases to be the best alternative – for example, if unnecessary beatings occur, or wildly irrational moralities are promulgated – and the child or someone representing his interest can grasp this, obedience is no longer owed and the child is justified in leaving to seek a better situation. Since a child won't always understand what his situation is, let alone possess the wherewithal to escape it, some kind of public awareness of a parent's child-rearing techniques must be available to remedy any abuses. Thus if a child is persistently hidden from public view, that may be prima-facie grounds for closer public scrutiny of what is happening in a particular family.

What about such matters as religion and politics? Here rearing would have to involve handing down some values but with the understanding that these are going to be available for personal choice later in the child's life. It would not be rational to expect parents to avoid imparting their values to their young – indeed, it is part of their responsibility to do this. But it is sensible to expect, also, that parents make it evident to a growing child that as they grow up it is reasonable for them to assess on their own the values of the parents, hopefully in a spirit not of blind rebelliousness but of genuinely independent thinking. The way to forestall the former (if possible; it isn't always) is to encourage and expect the latter. (Some of this will require adjustment during the adolescent years when young people are most probably especially focused on gaining an independent consciousness of ideas, values, goals, tastes and preferences.)

By projecting what children would have wanted for themselves as children once they become adults, we also assume that even while still growing up, children want to be successful adults and therefore want their parents to rear them for such success. Is the assumption rational, even if a kid bridles against reasonable discipline and counsel? Yes; and the child's assent to this doctrine is communicated by the interest he takes in living. 'Do well by me since I have embarked on the project of living well – something you, my parents, ought to have expected of me once I joined the human race.'

It seems, then, that a kind of teleological ethics makes the best sense of parental authority and children's obedience. Given the rational assumption that children would want to be brought up in certain ways, the conditions for such rearing are authorized for parents to secure, and even impose. And they also provide the limits to which parents may go.

There is a final topic to be considered. Clearly, children are not without rights – indeed, including some specially emergent positive rights (for example, to be fed). First, they have the rights that adults do – to life, liberty and the pursuit of happiness – albeit the exercise of these rights occurs through the judgment and help of parents. A child is a dependent being and thus lacks the full sovereignty that is required for the independent exercise of one's basic rights. Yet, even as young human beings, children do possess the rights of human beings through the guidance of their parents. They may not be killed, assaulted, stolen from, and so forth. But what they do with their lives, what actions they take, and how they dispose of their property or seek their happiness is all largely under parental supervision. That supervision, in turn, must conform to the provisions implicit in our earlier discussion about parental obligations. If there is clear and present danger that children are not being provided for, law officers would have the authority to investigate.

From the time a child is born – perhaps even earlier, depending on how the dispute over when personhood truly begins is best resolved – the child's citizenship would be recorded and all the protection to which he is entitled would also be provided. Because of the special status of children as dependants, those entrusted with the protection of their rights would have a certain legal leeway toward parents that is not accorded to them with respect to adults without children.

Parents properly expect their government to enforce the contract they have entered into on both sides. Their parental authority should gain official support; their abuse of it, official rebuke. In turn, runaway kids – at least those who have not yet reached a certain threshold of independent capacity – should be returned home, provided no evidence of child abuse is available. Laws should not ordinarily protect children as if they were independent, mature agents in cases where they inappropriately behave as adults – for example, by purchasing certain goods and services, entering into contracts, and so on. Everyone ought to be on notice that children are dependents and may not be counted upon to act otherwise.

Some measure of autonomy is due every normal child, who evolves from a state of total dependency through stages of gradually lessening dependency. Children are not zoo animals, to be barred from exploring the neighborhood or making contact with others. Furthermore, because children have been invited into the lives of their parents, and because they *are* children and not adults (indeed, in the beginning, helpless infants), parents have committed themselves to provide for them. May public authority back this commitment? Yes, because when people have children, they enter into a compact with them. This may be difficult to appreciate because it is a unique relationship, one that is possible only with human children. Since parents choose to have children, and since children are dependents for most of their childhood, parents can only be understood as making a promise to supply what their children need to grow up. And thus to such parental support the children are entitled.

Apart from these considerations, which bear on the way a libertarian order would address the parent–child relationship, there is one other problem worth addressing here. It has to do with the difficulty of dealing with irresponsible childbearing, something that is rampant in many societies.

Those who prize a free society as I have been discussing it, one wherein the legal system concerns itself first and foremost with protecting individual rights – keeping the peace and fending off attacks from enemies – have a very tough problem to overcome in the fact that millions of people who have no business doing so keep having children. The problem arises because in a truly free society persons may not be prevented from acting freely unless they have committed crimes against others. Prospective parents who fit this description are, therefore, quite free to engage in sexual unions and these unions often bring children into the world. But many such prospective parents cannot afford to have children and quite a few proceed to rely on the government to provide the children with their basic necessities, including day care, education, and medical services. (Others will forgo their own proper development in life because they realize what awesome responsibilities they have assumed.) When the children depend on the state, withdrawing government-provided services does not deprive the parents but the children of what they need to flourish in life. And children have nothing to do with getting themselves into this kind of fix, relying on others to furnish them with what they need to live.

Accordingly, when champions of individual liberty advocate cutting government's size and scope, they are faced with a very serious obstacle. This is the understandable concern we all have for the innocent children who have been brought into this world by irresponsible parents. It is difficult to accept policies that would lead to children having to suffer, even if those who have the children brought this about, not those who want government to stick to its appointed task – to secure our rights.

How can this problem be faced in a way that does not put innocent children at grave risk?

Of course, in a free society there would be many institutions ready to take up the task of caring for children and others who are helpless without support. Even in a welfare state there are hundreds of such institutions, so if government did not offer this help by taking it from others who aren't responsible for these individuals, there would most likely be even more if government got out of the way. But there cannot be any guarantee that every child would be taken care of. Indeed, not every child is taken care of even when government becomes their guardian. But when government – which has the use of force at its disposal to transfer resources to those who need and want them – isn't available, it looks as if this amounts to cruelty or callousness.

Never mind that it is cruel enough to demand by force of law that responsible taxpayers, who have kids only when they are willing to care for them, provide for kids they did not produce. But it is also undeniable that most folks who aren't loyal to the ideals of liberty believe that helpless children and other incompetents should not be left on their own. And they are willing to enlist the force of government to do what they should be doing if they are sincere in their concern for such children and others, namely, provide them with help out of their own pockets.

In light of this, some would just abandon the ideals of a truly free society. They would accept at least the level of government expansion and expense, apart from its rights-protective mission, required to save the kids.

But with this concession to expanded government the floodgates are opened for sure. There is no end of people who would use that precedent to then lobby for government support of transfers to what they deem to be vital projects – as, indeed, they do in the welfare state all the time. How else do we explain that tobacco farmers, failing car companies, airlines without passengers and thousands of other clients march to Washington and other centers of government to demand they, too, be provided with funds taken from taxpayers who haven't been guilty of producing their losses? It is because once some segment of society, even if it is just helpless kids, get government aid, everyone starts thinking, 'Hey, there's stuff there for us, if we get there fast enough via our representatives in Congress.'

My reason for raising this issue here isn't to join up with those who will give up on the ideal of a truly free society because some problem seems intractable. It is very doubtful whether the welfare state solves this problem, given how many kids go unattended and are merely cared for in perfunctory ways. Rather, I want to point out that there will always be something that a good theory does not fully address. There will always be something we will need new thinking to solve. The task of interpreting essentially sound principles to cover problems is neverending. Yet decisions need to be made, and they can be better or worse even if never final and perfect. Here, too, the perfect tends to be the enemy of the good! In this case, too, there are suggested solutions in need of serious consideration so as to save freedom from those who would toss it aside at the slightest provocation. Adoptions, for example, could be made far easier and that would probably hold out a great deal of hope for helpless kids, hope that is now barred because of the red tape and obstacles to adopting kids. And there are probably other options, not yet thought of, that would emerge, were we to insist that liberty may not be breached even in heart-wrenching circumstances.

Still, here is a matter that needs a solution that can also be made to fly with the general public – in other words that doesn't upset ordinary sensibilities – otherwise we are left with a powerful excuse and great pressure to give up on liberty.

Notes

1 See, for example, my own books: *Liberty and Culture: Essays on the Idea of a Free Society* (Buffalo, NY: Prometheus Books, 1989), *A Primer on Ethics* (Normal, OK: University of Oklahoma Press, 1970), *Generosity*, and *Classical Individualism*, and, co-authored with Jim Chesher, *The Business of Commerce: Examining an Honorable Profession* (Stanford, CA: Hoover Institution Press, 1999). Books I have edited touching on the subject include *Commerce and Morality* (Lanham, MD: Rowman & Littlefield, 1988), *Educating the Human Individual* (Stanford, CA: Hoover Institution Press, 2000), and *Morality and Labor* (Stanford, CA: Hoover Institution Press, 2000).

2 I have argued elsewhere that without a developed cerebral cortex no human being can exist as such, so that the point at which killing the fetus becomes homicide is around the 24–27 week of pregnancy. Prior to this time, what pro-life champions refer to as 'unborn babies' are in fact fetuses, *potential* human beings or infants. The development of the full organism occurs in stages, including a phase during which it exists potentially but not yet actually, just as do trees, butterflies, and so forth. Members of Libertarians for Life, mainly Doris Gordon, Edwin Vieira, Jr, and John Walker, differ. See their many essays on the web site www.cris.com/~Bwjass/lfl/litlist.htm.

Chapter 15

Should Ads for Hazardous Goods be Banned?[1]

Libertarians are rather brazen about the freedom of the market place, although not more than they are about freedom of speech, religion or other human activities. They decry paternalistic public policies and see them as doing violence to people's fundamental rights.

Nowhere else is this more evident than in how libertarians approach the trading of hazardous products and services. Even such goods as hard drugs are thought of by libertarians as something people ought to be free to trade, provided they are informed about what it is they are buying and selling. For example, when the sugar substitute cyclamate was taken off the market because in some experiments when rats were fed large dosages they died, many libertarians facetiously proposed to have the product sold as rat poison. That wouldn't deceive anyone, so it should not be banned.

Cigarette trade has recently been the focus of much criticism – several states and the federal government have reached enormous settlements with tobacco companies that were accused of causing massive health hazards and out-and-out illnesses, despite the fact that those who fell ill had been warned of tobacco's dangers. One of the early casualties of the war against tobacco was cigarette advertising. So I shall use this as a token of the kind of bans that libertarians consider unjust and indicate why they view the matter in that light.

The American Medical Association has often and successfully called for a ban on the advertising and promotion of all tobacco products. A new wave of debate on interpreting the Constitution and on the nature of advertising followed and, indeed, has already been concluded.

In this discussion I intend to sidestep the 'public policy' and strictly legal approach to the topic and focus instead on what is less discussed basic moral and political values. I consider the main values embodied by our Constitution to be basic moral values as well. Central among these values are liberty, limited government, and natural or human rights. I also take it that these values are not subject to majority rule. This point was clearly expressed by the US Supreme Court when it stated in *West Virginia State Board of Education v. Barnette* (1943) that

> The very purpose of the Bill of Rights was to withdraw certain subjects from the vicissitudes of political controversy, to place them beyond the reach of majorities and officials, and to establish them as legal principles to be applied by the Courts.

> One's right to life, liberty and property, to free speech, a free press, freedom of worship and assembly and other fundamental rights may not be submitted to a vote; they depend on the outcome of no elections.

The particular issue here is commercial speech and its deserved but by now frequently neglected protection under the First Amendment. Tobacco advertising is a clear and aptly controversial example of the principle I wish to address. It is a useful case because, as with the exercise of the right to freedom of speech in general, a principle is at issue. Tobacco advertising can serve as a good test case since in this case the exercise of this right is very much derided throughout society. A similar case was pornography and the most famous test had to do with the publication of *Hustler* magazine and its publisher Larry Flynt – a motion picture, *The People vs. Larry Flynt*, actually chronicles that case quite accurately. Flag burning, too, is often seen to serve as such a test case, although it isn't so clear-cut because burning a flag is by no means obviously a case of speaking out on a topic (whereas advertising tobacco and publishing a magazine are clearly cases of speech as the First Amendment's language makes clear).

Virtually all attacks on liberty, including the liberty to express various viewpoints, ideas, theories, beliefs, appeals, requests, and so forth, rest upon a basic moral error. This is the error of confusing basic rights with what is morally or ethically right.

The effort to ban commercial speech about tobacco products is one of the purer examples of this error. If we assume, for the sake of argument at this point, that it would be right for people to stop smoking, we have, as yet, said absolutely nothing about the rights of the case. It may turn out that coercing people to quit smoking, restricting their access to tobacco products or information about such products, violates their rights. The paradox here is that in the pursuit of what is right, one may do what is morally wrong! A similar case can be made about banning gambling or pornography, even prostitution – all these are arguably morally objectionable, at least under certain circumstances, yet banning them is arguably a violation of the unalienable right to liberty mentioned in the Declaration of Independence and arguably referred to via the Ninth Amendment of the US Constitution.

The reason for the paradox in all these cases of banning conduct is that the particular way in which the 'good' (or right thing) in question is pursued may conflict with another good that takes priority.

All social moral principles are not created equal. Some are more fundamental than others. What is characteristic of rights is that, almost by definition, they are foundational or basic. Other social values must give way to them in cases of conflict. We can see this in everyday speech. It makes perfect sense to say, 'It may not be right for someone to do (or believe) this, but he or she has every right to do so.' This is also expressed routinely when one hears it said that 'I disagree with what you are saying but will defend your right to say it.' When what someone is saying is morally objectionable and is, therefore, disagreeable, that is where the priority of the right to say the thing is clearly illustrated.

But what rights do we have? Some rights seem to be dictated by common sense. The 'right' not to be harmed seems to be one of these rights. If this is a right, shouldn't tobacco products or information about such products be restricted or banned?

Unfortunately, common sense is not always accurate. There is in fact no basic 'right not to be harmed.' The reason for this is twofold: people can voluntarily undertake risks, and people can have their rights violated without being harmed. In the first case, people voluntarily pursue dangerous activities all the time. They take on dangerous jobs, pursue dangerous sports, drive cars, and so on. What we expect in such situations is that the people involved have some conception of the risks they are undertaking – not that they be free from harm. In the second case, if the government restricts my freedom to speak on behalf of a cause I do not believe in, I have not been harmed, but my rights have been violated. In the end, then, rights and harms are not necessarily connected.[2]

In a similar vein, rights and government have no necessary connection with each other. Some people mistakenly believe that rights are what the government allows us to do.[3] But if this were true, it would make no sense to say that governments can violate people's rights, something they have done quite often throughout human history and continue to do around the world. Since, as the American Declaration of Independence so clearly notes, we are 'endowed … with certain unalienable rights,' we can possess rights that were not given to us by government and which government cannot legitimately take away. It is under the monarchical conception of government that it makes sense to think of rights as grants of privileges, since in such a system the monarch owns the realm and gives permission to do some things to its *subjects*.

The Declaration of Independence was written to abolish the monarchical idea of politics and maintained that individuals in society are in the position of having sovereignty in contrast to government possessing it. And the first ten Amendments were designed by the American Framers to protect us from government infringement of rights we were said to possess 'by nature.'

Basic Rights

The Amendment that concerns us here is the First, but the principle behind all of them is the same: people have basic rights independent of governments. This principle further reinforces our claim that a fundamental error occurs when one confuses rights with what is right. For what one discovers about basic rights is that they represent liberties, and liberty implies the possibility of choosing a 'wrong' course of action as much as a 'right' one. This point is clearly evident in freedom of speech cases where many wrongheaded causes and ideas are allowed to have their say with the same degree of legitimacy as those that are closer to the truth. Our basic rights, therefore, must be understood as essentially liberties; and these liberties are given political expression through Constitutional guarantees against government interference.[4]

The main remaining issue here is whether people can have their liberties restricted in the name of 'paternalism' – using the power of government to protect us from ourselves. But in a free society, if paternalism has a place at all, it would arise only where information about alternatives was suppressed and thus lacking. But clearly such is not the case with tobacco products and their use and hasn't been for decades.

Of course, I am not arguing or conceding that smoking is the 'wrong' that must be protected by our distinction. Whether someone's smoking qualifies as wrong conduct is certainly not a simple matter to decide.[5] Even if in some cases it is clearly wrong to smoke, there can be many others when it is not. Yet some certainly regard smoking in this way; and it is useful to recognize that even if one concedes the point about the 'wrongfulness' of smoking, no foundation has yet been laid for waiving basic rights or Constitutional protections. (I leave aside the issue of secondhand smoking for now because [a] there is much scientific doubt about it, and [b] even if it does harm to some persons, unless they are subjected to it under duress and not of their own free will, there is no reason to ban it.[6])

In one notable case, the Federal Trade Commission (FTC) charged the R. J. Reynolds Tobacco Company with running a false and misleading advertisement ('Of Cigarettes and Science') on the health effects of cigarette smoking. The FTC believed the advertisement to be deceptive because R. J. Reynolds had interpreted a government study on the causes of heart disease in a way that was not detrimental to smoking. The FTC lost the case because the judge ruled that the advertisement qualified as noncommercial speech, since no prices, brands, or products were mentioned. Had prices, brands, or products been mentioned, the FTC would have had the power to regulate the advertisement under the limited First Amendment protections granted to commercial speech.

The question arises, however, as to why R. J. Reynolds would not have enjoyed full First Amendment protection even if it had mentioned its own products?

In the last few years, the courts have given commercial speech secondary status with respect to First Amendment protection. Although the courts clearly protect the right to advertise, they nevertheless subject advertisers and producers to the myriad of government regulations.

The secondary status of commercial speech is the inevitable result of trying to reconcile free speech with a regulated economy. But this reconciliation is conceptually unstable. It assumes, on the one hand, that economic activities can be divorced from communication and information about such activities. Since these two cannot be separated, the right to free speech is compromised in an attempt to retain the government's power to regulate voluntary economic transactions. On the other hand, the reconciliation assumes that the right of free speech applies to some categories of speech and not others. Commercial speech needs to be wrenched from other forms of speech to make this argument fly, yet no logical and legal ground can be found for this in the US Constitution.

'Private' v. 'Public' Speech

The main way of trying to separate commercial from noncommercial speech is to argue that the latter is 'public' speech while the former is 'private' because it serves some private interest. This distinction is used to argue that the court has gone too far in allowing First Amendment protection of commercial speech. The First Amendment, these critics claim, was meant to cover cases of public speech, not private. They would agree with us that it is incoherent to grant commercial speech only partial protection, but their solution is to afford commercial speech no First Amendment protection at all!

The distinction between public and private speech is simply not viable. In the first place, it is typical for those who object to First Amendment protection of commercial speech also to fail to object to government regulation of the economy. But if economic matters were purely private, the government could have no 'public' interest in regulation; and it is the supposed public interest of government in economic regulation that refutes the claim that commercial speech is a purely private affair.

In addition, those who speak are seldom, if ever, as disinterested as the concept of 'public' speech would lead us to believe. Groups which have causes to advance in the name of the 'public interest' have at stake precisely the same things as corporations do in their advertisements: organizational growth, jobs, visibility, competitive advantage (relative to other groups with a cause), and the like. Individuals, too, seldom make disinterested public pronouncements, especially on controversial issues of public policy (for example, taxes and zoning changes). If the First Amendment is not designed to protect self-interested speech, there is precious little that it does protect.[7]

Finally, speech, by its very nature, is public, since it is communication. And advertising is most certainly public because it is addressed not to particular individuals but to unknown members of the public. We should abandon the distinction between private and public speech and accord commercial speech the same full First Amendment protection given to all speech.

Does it now follow that advertisers can make any false or fraudulent claim they wish about their products? The answer here is no, because there is a significant moral difference between making a promise and expressing a belief. The informational components of advertisements can plausibly be construed as an initial statement of terms between seller and buyer. This is why it is legitimate to hold advertisers accountable to some degree for the truth of their ads. Expressions of belief, on the other hand, do not function like promises, because no one is called upon to deliver a good according to the stated terms. No one has the right to defraud another. But to say that hardly justifies intrusive governmental regulation of commercial speech.

If the R. J. Reynolds advertisement had included accurate product information, the ad could not be held morally and legally culpable. The court should have ruled in Reynolds's favor, even if they had included product information as part of the advertisement. The court's attempt to dodge the issue by calling the Reynolds advertisement 'noncommercial' may have been convenient, but it leaves commercial speech vulnerable to attack.

In this respect, the court has strayed even wider of the mark in its recent ruling in Posadas, a case that arose in Puerto Rico in which once again the court distinguished between commercial and other types of speech, a distinction that is inexcusable despite the specious claim that the 'original intent' of the First Amendment was to cover only political speech. In fact, however, the precise meaning of the First Amendment concerns any kind of speech whatever, and a law must be interpreted to mean what it says – legislative intentions are too diffuse and varied for us to be guided by them (and, in any case, they are discerned by reference to the meaning of the terms used to indicate them, not the other way around).

It is true that the First Amendment does not unequivocally grant protection to commercial speech, but that is irrelevant – it certainly does not bar such protection either, just as it does not bar protection for religious, philosophical, ideological, poetical, or any other special kind of speech.

If this is not sufficient, as it should be, we should also recall here the Ninth Amendment which says that 'The enumeration in the Constitution, of certain rights, shall not be construed to deny or disparage others retained by the people.' This Constitutional provision can only be understood as wisely extending protection to many matters not explicitly mentioned or foreseen by the Founders. So when the First Amendment is coupled with the Ninth, one must assume that commercial speech is still speech and hence Constitutionally protected. When we also add to all this that the Fourteenth Amendment requires that 'No State shall … deny to any person within its jurisdiction the equal protection of the laws,' it becomes clear that a ban on any kind of honest advertising would constitute a form of discrimination against people in business *vis-à-vis* other professions, activities, and forms of speech. In short, the principles embedded in the Constitution clearly favor the argument for full Constitutional protection of commercial speech.

Nevertheless, the argument persists and is a simple one: cigarettes are 'lethal' products while the images conveyed by cigarette ads in no way convey this danger – indeed the opposite message is conveyed. The consumer is therefore deceived into believing that cigarette smoking is acceptable, attractive, or without risks and hazards. This argument, however, is nothing but a version of the old shibboleth that advertising itself is inherently deceptive.

Advertisements are said to be inherently deceptive because they 'selectively emphasize' certain features of a product to make the product appear more attractive. Since this technique ignores or de-emphasizes other features, the consumer is deceived. The moral conclusion many draw is that since advertising is deceptive, and deception is morally wrong, advertising is morally wrong.

But the case for 'generic deception' depends upon there being something wrong with presenting something in a positive light and upon the likelihood that people are unaware of the type of message being delivered. Neither condition can be satisfied.

There is nothing wrong with presenting something in its most attractive light. We do this all the time. On our résumé we do not list the jobs we lost or the failures we had. In our personal grooming we take care to look attractive and hide our 'flaws.' As to the nature of the message, what is generic to advertising is precisely the effort to present something in its most attractive light. Since attractive presentation of information is virtually what we mean by an advertisement, it is nonsensical to claim generic deception when one confronts an advertisement. Selective emphasis does not violate the canon of truthfulness *per se*, because the basic truth conveyed by advertising is that when you see it you expect to see the item portrayed in its best light. And surely there are (some) attractive people who use tobacco products.

After examining basic moral and Constitutional values, one is forced to conclude that the tobacco industry is on the side of principle in its opposition to the AMA. It is obvious that banning or restricting commercial speech about tobacco products ignores basic rights and liberties and opens the door to further coercive control of speech.

What is perhaps less obvious is the damage already done. That Congress and the media could take a proposal like the AMA's seriously, and indeed that well-educated medical professionals could be so completely ignorant of the meaning of liberty, signifies a national crisis of understanding of our own heritage of political liberty. Furthermore, the *ad hoc* attitudes of the present court concerning commercial speech offer little hope that this crisis will be remedied from this quarter.

Yet in the end, what is very disturbing is how insulting all this is. Despite continual subjection to claims about the evils of tobacco, people are being told that they are too incompetent to make up their own minds about these products. The damage that has already been done is reflected in the fact that we take such insults on a daily basis. The libertarian insists that this trend must be reversed and the insults must be identified for exactly what they are. It is a first, but necessary, step in preventing the world from filling up with fools.

Notes

1 An earlier and shorter version of this chapter appeared in *The Freeman*, December 1987, Vol. 37, No 12 co-authored by Tibor R. Machan and Douglas J. Den Uyl and the latter's contribution remains part of this chapter.

2 For a very illuminating discussion of this, see J. Roger Lee, 'Choice and Harms,' in M. Bruce Johnson and Tibor R. Machan, eds, *Rights and Regulation* (Boston, MA: Ballinger Books, 1983).

3 This is what is argued by Stephen Holmes and Cass Sunstein, *The Cost of Rights* (New York: W. W. Norton, 1999).

4 The best contemporary discussion of how what is right by nature differs from what rights we have by nature occurs in Leo Strauss, *Natural Right and History* (Chicago, IL: University of Chicago Press, 1952), although Strauss is not very supportive of the case for natural rights.

5 See, for more on that, Tibor R. Machan, 'Morality and Smoking,' in David Benetar, ed., *Ethics for Everyday* (New York: McGraw-Hill, 2001). Also see Douglas J. Den Uyl, 'Smoking, Human Rights, and Civil Liberties,' in Robert D. Tollinson, ed., *Smoking and Society, Toward a More Balanced Assessment* (Lexington, MA: Lexington Books, 1986), pp. 189–216.

6 For more on this, see Tibor R. Machan, 'Coping with Smoking,' the *Newsweek* Education Program, *More Controversial Issues* (New York: NewsSource Unit, 1996).

7 It needs to be noted here that a confusion is inherent in our system because of the public ownership of the electromagnetic spectrum over which most commercials are broadcast. When one owns something, one has the authority to manage it or assign the management to those one prefers. Radio and television broadcasting is regulated by the Federal Communications Commission 'for the public' and this group may well hold that there will not be advertising for cigarettes – or for gambling, prostitution, hard liquor, and so forth – on public property. As with the former Soviet Union's publication, *Pravda*, the government here is the editor, as it were, and may not acknowledge any need to accord others the right to have their own say about various matters.

HARD AND SOFT STATISM

Chapter 16

The Ideology of Death that Will Not Die

> The idea that a social system might move, that is, regress, from a supposedly superior, historically advanced socialist to a supposedly outmoded capitalist mode of production was inconceivable for Marxist theoreticians.
>
> Paul Hollander[1]

Why weren't we happier about it than we were?

Shortly after the collapse of the Soviet empire, Martin Anderson – head of President Ronald Reagan's transition team and a top advisor to Reagan during the early years of his administration – spoke to the conservative Philadelphia Society. Anderson lamented that Americans were not as euphoric as we ought to be given what had just transpired. The West had won the Cold War. Capitalism was fully vindicated. The theories of Ludwig von Mises and Frederick A. Hayek, two premier economists who had long defended the free market system and predicted that communism would fall, had been confirmed in practice.[2] The world had seen a demonstration, albeit at great and unnecessary cost, of the hopelessness of socialism. We seemed to have witnessed the beginning of the end.

So why were we not cheering that this destructive experiment was at last over? Why were there so few celebrations?

I had a chance to speak with Anderson following his talk. What I suggested was that true believers do not give up. They merely rephrase, reformulate, reanalyze, back and fill. And since human minds can be extremely clever in bailing themselves out and rationalizing their failings, it was certainly reasonable to conclude we will by no means see any substantial retreat on the part of socialism any time soon. The fall of the Berlin Wall and the spinning off of former Soviet satellites were certainly good things and cause for optimism. But such optimism needed to be tempered, for they did not represent the final curtain on the socialist ideology.

Conveniently enough for those who don't want to relinquish it, Marxism comes with readymade escape clauses. Like any robust theology, a comprehensive system of ideas such as Marxism is prepared to cope with many social developments. Consider how the Roman Catholic Church has managed to accommodate even the most radically secular developments in Western culture – for example, evolutionary biology – without ever giving up its fundamental theology; it rests on principles sufficiently capacious and elastic to enable nearly any adjustment to inconvenient discoveries of reality.

Perhaps the most one can expect is that new renditions of the Marxist position will carry a new label. Indeed, we are today being asked to consider such milder versions of the position as communitarianism, economic democracy, and market socialism. But it is not hard to find full-throttle assaults on the market characteristic of Marxism.[3]

Karl Marx was above all a visionary. From his earliest writings we can detect his collectivist moral vision, one that affirmed the ultimate significance of humanity as a concrete being. It is only when we devote ourselves to humanity that we will find true happiness, he wrote in his high school separation essay.

> When we have chosen the vocation in which we can contribute most to humanity, burdens cannot bend us because they are sacrifices for all. Then we experience no meager, limited egoistic joy, but our happiness belongs to millions, our deeds live on quietly but eternally effective, and glowing tears of noble men will fall on our ashes.[4]

And in this belief Marx never wavered even as he claimed to become a scientific socialist and to abandon the moral point of view.[5]

What Marx was willing to revise was his effort to convince others of his vision. For some time he believed he might employ the traditional techniques of moralists who attempted to convince people to follow the righteous path. But as he became better informed about the sweeping influence of (pseudo-) scientific thinking – that is, of scientism – he turned away from his earlier approach to embrace what he called 'scientific socialism,' an outlook positing the necessary development of humanity toward communism. In this new approach, communism ceased to be an ideal and become what Marx called a 'real movement.'[6]

It is not my concern here whether Marx was sincere. Clearly one can convince oneself of the need to think differently about some aspects of the world in an effort to bolster other aspects of one's thinking. In any case, over time Marx reverted less and less to the utopian socialist approach, while never relenting in his belief in the superiority of the socialist way of life. He began arguing that the socialist polity must come about regardless of what anybody does, as a result of the ineluctable working out of social laws. Marxism, in short, is flexible enough to incorporate the recent developments in Eastern Europe and sustain the belief that socialism is indeed still the best mode of community life.

In a 1883 preface to the Russian edition of *The Communist Manifesto*, Marx explained how socialism might be instituted in Russia despite the backwardness of its economy. Marx said it would be possible if the revolution served as a 'signal' to the proletariat of the West. 'If the Russian Revolution becomes the signal for a proletarian revolution in the West, so that both complement each other, the present Russian common ownership of land may serve as the starting point for a communist development.'[7] Marx had earlier discounted the prospect of any socialist revolution not premised on the full development of capitalism. Such a revolution, he argued, would do little else but 'socialize poverty.' Why? Because prosperity, wealth, economic growth all depended for their fullest development on the constituents of a capitalist political economy.

For Marxism, humanity is an organism, akin to a human individual as we ordinarily understand one. In *Grundrisse*, Marx even calls humanity an 'organic whole' or 'body,' in which place he also refers to the ancient Greeks as humanity in its 'childhood.'[8] Marx had always been a collectivist in the sense that he took humanity to be a concrete universal indeed, perhaps even a concrete individual. He regarded individual human beings as 'species-beings.' For him, this meant that they were mere parts in the larger organism of humanity.[9] Whatever there is of individualism in Marx's views, it certainly can mean no more than that the flourishing of any individual person is entirely dependent on the flourishing of humanity as a whole.[10]

One important ingredient of this collectivist humanism is the notion that the species must undergo stages of development. It experiences infancy, childhood, adolescence, a young adulthood, and eventually a mature adulthood. Furthermore, just as with individual human beings, humanity must pass through its various stages of development in the proper sequence, lest it suffer various imbalances or anxieties. A person who skips adolescence – because, say, she must deal with war or otherwise be obliged to become a young adult too early in life – will suffer certain maladjustment that will probably result in various adversities throughout her life. Indeed, this is presupposed in our understanding of what psychologists can do for us, namely, help us recover from such a maladjustment-inducing early life.

In Marx's mature understanding of humanity's development there is no place for skipping the various stages of political economy. Tribalism, feudalism, capitalism, socialism and communism must all come about in proper sequence. The Soviet experiment, insofar as it never seriously expanded beyond the borders of Greater Russia, from a Marxist point of view must be seen as futile, even little more than a fraud. In Marx's view, Russia never underwent capitalism; and without successfully absorbing Western capitalist countries that had undergone that stage of humanity's development, there was no justification for seeing it as ready for socialism. (It is important to consider, in this connection, that Soviet imperialism was a necessary adjunct to the Soviet Union's claim to be a faithful institution of Marxian revolution. Without successful imperialism, no such claim could be borne out from within the Marxian framework.)

Accordingly, when the Soviet empire collapsed in 1989, arguably, in Marxian terms, it amounted to no more than the fall of a major, traditional, semi-feudal, colonial power. The claim that it represented a flunked experiment in standard-template communist development would have to be categorically denied. All that had been attempted was some variety of the command economy or feudal mercantilism. Whatever claims were being made linking the USSR to Marxian socialist revolutionary developments would have to be taken as at best ignorant wishful thinking or, more likely, evasive deception, even as it managed to provide certain guidelines to how the USSR was being run from the Kremlin.

What about current developments in the region? From the Marxist viewpoint these developments are now more closely on course than in the past. As with most such empire-building experiments throughout the world, once the empire collapses because of various economic and other pressures, there is initial disintegration and eventually gradual bourgeois development. This is certainly a plausible scenario for what is happening in Russia in the early twenty-first century.

It is crucial to keep in mind that dialectical or historical materialism is unlike mechanistic or reductive materialism with respect to the laws of motion that characterize it. Whereas, mechanistic materialism proposes that change occurs in a rigidly predictable, mathematically precise fashion, dialectical or historical materialism is more akin to biology, geology or, as Marx himself put it, natural history. Accordingly, there is no promise in Marxian theory – as distinct from some of Marx's imprudent activist projections – concerning the arrival of capitalism or socialism or communism in humanity's future. Just as psychology does not offer rigid predictions concerning the development of a given individual, so dialectical materialism does not propose a timetable for the future stages of humanity.

Current indecisive experimentation with free-market structures throughout the former Soviet bloc is thus fully consonant with Marxian theory. Just as familiar bourgeois developments did not occur in some fixed, rigid fashion, so the future of capitalism and socialism is likely to see flexible developments.

So, at least, could a Marxian approach be sketched with respect to recent world events. Indeed, when supporters of liberal democratic capitalist societies express amazement at why Marxists across the globe haven't laid down their intellectual armaments, I am always amazed by their amazement. It is, first of all, an unrealistic expectation from a psychological viewpoint. Our experience with Catholicism should have taught us that much, with the Vatican managing to be in tune with nearly everything science and history has to offer, however much it may seem that its theology would be overburdened by it all. It is also unjustified in terms of what the Marxists have offered, indeed, in terms of what Marx himself told us.

Nevertheless, I want to argue that this Marxian thesis should be abandoned, but not because of what happened in the Soviet Union and elsewhere in the world, for all these events could have been anticipated by any conscientious Marxist. Each could have agreed with Ludwig von Mises's and F. A. Hayek's analysis of the futility of expecting a socialist system to accommodate the demands of economic efficiency. Marx would never have claimed that one can substitute socialism for capitalism, quite the contrary. And given human nature under the capitalist phase of humanity's development, all the arguments about the impossibility of calculation under socialism should have been fully acceptable to Marxists. But there is a way to avoid the problem in the Marxian view. To avoid the problem we need the 'new man', who certainly has not made its appearance in humanity. This fully altruistic, entirely socialized human being is not going to expect the kind of efficient economic organization that Mises and Hayek had in mind when they criticized socialism. The 'new man' must be the kind of human being who constitutes the citizenry, otherwise there will not be proper motivation to achieve 'from each according to his ability, to each according to his needs.' This 'new man' would be so fresh off the assembly line that no standard economic analysis could appreciate the workings of the society, economic or otherwise, based on the nature of this 'new man'. Marx was very specifically vague on the issue of what communism would be like, precisely for this reason. We cannot tell just yet. Let's wait until the 'new man' shows up, and then we'll fill out the analysis.

So Marxism has an 'out,' a way to explain all failings of socialism-as-practiced here-and-now.[11] But it is all wrong.

There are many reasons, but chief among them is his false view of man's essential nature. Marx inherited the scientistic and deterministic aspects of his philosophy from Hegel. Hegel had argued that although human beings are subjectively free – that is, capable of making choices in their lives – at the aggregate or holistic level, history is determined. We may only know this retrospectively but it is, nevertheless, true. A professor of mine once explained this form of determinism by comparing it to how, although you are free to make any move you want to in a chess match with Bobby Fisher, it is given that he will beat you anyway. Flail away against the tide all you want, in other words; the tide will still wash over you. No matter what you do, reason works out its necessary development through human social, political and economic history. The laws of countries, their customs and so forth are the manifestation of this progress of Reason (or Idea).

Marx took a somewhat different metaphysical view of it all but retained the determinism. And it is entirely unclear how either Hegel or, especially, Marx could find room for free will in human existence; the 'actions' of groups and nations are, after all, made up of the actions of individuals. (Yet in the Marxist view even the individual, except of course the Marxist theorist,[12] must fall sway to class logic, seeing the world through the lens of his economic interest.)

Determinism is an untenable and self-defeating proposition even for Marxism with all its illusory wiggle-room. I have elsewhere developed a case for the existence of free will,[13] however, and for now merely conclude: despite the appearance that Marxism is theoretically capable of handling recent developments in Eastern Europe, ultimately an individualist view of historical causation makes better sense of these events.

The fact may be difficult to accept, especially in the modern age when problem solving via science and technology is such a great expectation. But when it comes to human existence, there is free will to contend with, not merely inadequate knowledge of natural chaos. The social sciences must not aim to produce theories and engineering programs that fail to take this fact into account despite the temptation to write it off as an illusion because the underlying metaphysics that many scientists and philosophers assume rules out free will and human agency.

Marxism has been and will continue to be influential not because it is true but because a great many human beings have a yearning for it to bring about what it promises, namely, a guaranteed harmonious community life for us all. It offers a mythos and a towering abstract edifice, rationalizing antagonism to capitalism, an anti-capitalism they are loath to give up no matter how dramatically the destructive consequences of any form of wide-scale economic interference with the market may be demonstrated. People choose to believe or not believe on grounds that may be sound or unsound – it is really up to them. We cannot erase this fact of choice from our lives and it will do us good to keep it in mind. It would reduce the cynicism produced by the glaring failure of utopianism that offers the panacea of resolving all human problems by means of the impersonal workings of history. It would put human individuals back into the role of decision makers, with all the attendant risk and benefits that this entails.[14]

Notes

1 Paul Hollander, 'Why Communism Collapsed in Eastern Europe,' *Society*, 30 (Jan/Feb. 1993), p. 41.

2 This was admitted by Robert Heilbroner, 'After Communism,' *The New Yorker* (September 10, 1990), p. 92, who had been an avid defender of a version of Marxism for most of his career: , 'Ludwig von Mises … had written of the "impossibility" of socialism, arguing that no Central Planning Board could ever gather the enormous amount of information needed to create a workable economic system … . It turns out, of course, that Mises was right … .'

3 But see also such unreconstructed Marxian offerings as Andrew Bard Schmookler, *The Illusion of Choice* (Albany, NY: State University of New York Press, 1993), in which the author basically reiterates Marx's thesis that liberal individual liberty is nothing but a fraud – 'the most complete suppression of all individual liberty and total subjugation of individuality to social conditions which take the form of material forces.' Karl Marx, *Grundrisse*, trans. D. McLellan (New York: Harper Torchbooks, 1971), p. 131.

4 L. D. Easton and K. H. Guddat, eds, *Writings of the Young Marx on Philosophy and Society* (Garden City, NY: Anchor Books, 1967), p. 39.

5 This is the idea that human beings ought to conduct themselves in certain ways, that they ought to make certain kinds of choices based on standards of right and wrong. Marx had been a socialist of this kind – a utopian socialist – prior to championing a historical determinist approach that appears at first glance to abandon the moral viewpoint.

6 Karl Marx, *Selected Writings*, ed., D. McLellan (London: Oxford University Press, 1977), p. 171.

7 Ibid., p. 417. Some dispute that ideology guided the Soviets at all, preferring some kind of socio-economic explanation for all that happened there. See, for a good discussion, Martin Malia, 'The Archives of Evil, Soviet Studies after the Soviet Union,' *The New Republic*, Vol. 231 (November 29 and December 6, 2004), pp. 34–41. See also Igal Halfin, *From Darkness to Light* (Pittsburgh, PA: University of Pittsburgh Press, 2000), and *Terror*

in My Soul (Cambridge, MA: Harvard University Press, 2003) for a defense of the impact of Marxist ideology on Soviet history.

8 Marx, *Grundrisse*, p. 33, and *Selected Writings*, p. 359.

9 See ibid., p. 126, where Marx states that 'The human essence is the true collectivity of man.'

10 Some, such as H. B. Acton, *What Marx really Said* (London: Macdonald and Co., 1967), have detected a kind of individualism in Marx, albeit not at all the kind we commonly identify with capitalism. See, for more, Tibor R. Machan, *Capitalism and Individualism* (New York: St. Martin's Press, 1990).

11 It is one of Karl Popper's valuable insights that this way of thinking is unfalsifiable. See *The Poverty of Historicism* (Boston, MA: Beacon Press, 1957).

12 Marx wrote:

> Theoretical communists, the only ones who have time to devote to the study of history, are distinguished precisely because they alone have discovered that throughout history the 'general interest' is created by individuals who are defined as 'private persons'. They know that this contradiction is only a seeming one because one side of it, the so-called 'general', is constantly being produced by the other side, private interest, and by no means opposes the latter as an independent force with an independent history – so that this contradiction is in practice always being destroyed and reproduced.'

Selected Writings, p. 183.

13 Tibor R. Machan, *Initiative – Human Agency and Society* (Stanford, CA: Hoover Institution Press, 2000). See, also, Edward Pols, *Acts of Our Being* (Amherst, MA: University of Massachusetts Press, 1983) and Roger W. Sperry, *Science and Moral Priority: Merging Mind, Brain, and Human Values* (New York: Columbia University Press, 1983).

14 I develop the major themes of this view in Tibor R. Machan, *Classical Individualism* (London: Routledge, 1998).

Chapter 17

Libertarianism and Conservatism

In the United States of America, libertarianism is often bundled with conservatism, mainly because many conservatives aim to retain the ideas of the Founders who had been near to libertarianism and its philosophical ancestors, such as John Locke.[1] However, the two are in fact quite distinct and on some levels opposite each other – for instance, methodologically conservatism tends toward anti-rationalism.[2]

In recent years libertarianism has nearly come of age. There are now detailed developed theories supporting this position.[3] Numerous organizations – academic associations, lay societies, 'think tanks,' and a political party – compose the libertarian 'movement.'[4] Disputes, too, abound among those who would unhesitatingly identify themselves as libertarians.[5] Both systematic and off-hand attacks on libertarianism emanate from various intellectual, political, journalistic, social and other circles.[6] The opportunity to publish works discussing the positions pro and con now exists beyond the limited range of a few 'in-group' publishers.[7] Academic courses in politics and philosophy often cover the subject matter.[8] And the language of day-to-day politics now exhibits signs of the influence of libertarianism (as distinct from more traditional American political ideals).[9]

Libertarianism is, to a considerable extent, a theoretical extension of crucial concepts found in the American political tradition – for example, liberty, consent, rights, equality, due process – so the position is not a radical challenge to the American tradition. (This may be disputed by some, of course, depending on whether they regard the American political tradition as distinctive in its libertarian or in some other elements.)[10] As such, libertarianism is properly associated with aspects of American conservatism. Many American conservatives cherish institutions and practices that reflect libertarian ideals or principles. So American conservatives are concerned with maintaining or supporting some institutions to which libertarianism gives theoretic support. In practical terms this has led to frequent coalitions between conservatives and libertarians – for example, in their advocacy of the protection and preservation of the free market, defense of the institution of private property, support of a legal system that respects personal responsibility and places severe restrictions on the power of (at least the federal) government.[11]

Yet it is clear that often many conservatives are not comfortable with libertarianism despite agreements on some of the practical issues. Conservatives tend, on the whole, to be anti-rationalistic in their methodology.[12]

Libertarians, in the main, have high regard for reason – for uncovering objective and true principles from which to derive subsidiary political and legal principles and infer various practical policy recommendations or prohibitions.[13] Some embrace an empiricist rationalism, some a Cartesian, and yet others an Aristotelian/Thomistic variety, but virtually all consider the reliance on the human mind and what it can discover about reality as something to be encouraged, not demeaned.[14]

More particularly, the principled adherence to individual liberty – for example, the right of every individual to live by the judgments he or she makes and to be free from the imposition of others concerning his or her conduct affecting his or her life – has led libertarians to support resistance to all political and legal measures (in various ways, depending on circumstance) that aim at imposing upon human beings a way of life they individually reject.[15] Conservatives do not share, in the main, I contend, such a *principled* commitment to liberty and would refuse to apply this (putative) principle to many cases that a libertarian clearly would. Thus the latter would enjoin the regulation of entertainment by public authorities, even in cases deemed tasteless – for example, topless dancing. Conservatives would consider such public policy permissible – at least at the community level.[16] Other examples abound, but in general, I would say, conservatives tend to deny any *principle* of liberty in the first place, and they would very likely dispute some of the basic aspects of libertarianism, including some crucial elements of arguments usually advanced in support of the doctrine.[17]

It is my aim to show in this chapter that some of the points persistently raised by conservatives with respect to libertarianism can be met. For example, I will indicate that considerations of social morality and standards of community conduct are by no means ruled out for libertarians, who attend to them in a principled but voluntary manner. In this I will stress the point that political authority is ill-suited for purposes of preserving and upgrading the moral climate of a human community. Libertarians contend that politicians are not moral leaders!

My aim is not to seek out the most extreme versions of conservative thought, nor to attempt to explain and justify the more bizarre renditions of 'libertarianism' that some conservatives focus on in their scrutiny. Every point of view has its most implausible as well as its blandest versions, and an honest confrontation with it must avoid focusing on either of these. (Thus, there are 'libertarians' who really amount to plain old-fashioned utopian anarchists; and there are other 'libertarians' who make so many concessions to statism that their position is indistinguishable from those in which liberty is demeaned.) The same could be observed about practically any point of view in virtually any area of controversy. The crazy and bland versions simply aren't worth the time in an honest intellectual examination. It seems that it is most advisable to select a reasonably formidable, distinctive, yet not impossible statement of the view one selects for scrutiny, so as not to build into the version obvious seeds of destruction.

Let me explain a few important points about libertarianism. It is, first of all, a political doctrine. It should be distinguished from the following three categories: 'metaphysical libertarianism' related to the problem of the freedom of the will;[18] 'social libertarianism,' namely, the view that concerning voluntary human activities and associations everything not involving coercion is equally proper, morally correct, immune from valid moral criticism, rebuke, ostracism, and other forms of opposition and condemnation;[19] and 'moral libertarianism' or libertinism, namely, the view that all freely chosen conduct has *equal* merit from the point of view of what is right and wrong in human behavior.[20]

Different arguments have been advanced in support of political libertarianism, but the doctrine itself is a claim to what is permissible for human beings to do toward each other by means of the aid of force or its threat, nothing more. This claim has been the result of different arguments, some of which are unsound, others invalid, but some indeed theoretically adequate for showing that in human communities force should only be used – in all of its extremely complicated manifestations, possibilities, and threats – for the purpose of protecting and preserving human individual liberty, nothing else.[21] Whether this conclusion can be established, whether it is proper to look to reasoned arguments and theories to establish conclusions bearing on political life, whether any considerations might supersede a conclusion so established (for example, requiring that although liberty should be furthered politically, something besides politics requires its neglect in certain circumstances) – are relevant issues. But let us be very clear about the principal fact: libertarianism is a claim about the scope of permissible force or threat of force among human beings, including human beings who constitute the governing administration of a given human community. It is a political claim or theory and not some other, however much it may presuppose a variety of other, nonpolitical claims.[22] If one assumes that this claim itself embodies the suppositions of its various arguments, then one prejudices one's criticism against a wide variety of libertarian thought. After all, the same conclusions can be derived from different sets of premises. This is an elementary point of logic. And even if some arguments for liberty are inadequate, it does not follow that none better are available. Indeed the doctrine on which all libertarians are in agreement has been defended on various philosophical grounds.

These and other points need to be kept in mind in order to appreciate what is at stake in the discussion of libertarianism. But there is another point that has especially direct bearing on the discussion of this political outlook. Unlike most others, libertarian politics, in particular, may not be assimilated into non-political ideas and ideals. It is distinctive precisely in its firm specification concerning the scope of politics in human life, namely, with the point that liberty is the paramount value to be sought by way of politics. The rest of human existence needs to be developed in an atmosphere of freedom, with all the creativity and ingenuity available to human beings In these areas there may exist firm standards. But experimentation may also be proper.

Political principles, stated explicitly, must however guide the most awesome and dangerous instrument of human interaction, namely physical force. Such force is permissible and useful only in repelling force, not in building character, love, faith, scientific knowledge, and so on.[23]

Libertarianism is not addressed directly to these other spheres of human life because the method of politics cannot be extended to these spheres with moral and practical legitimacy.

What are some arguments for libertarianism? Actually, as far back in recorded intellectual history as Lao Tzu in the East[24] and Alcibiades in the West, certain libertarian ideas are clearly detectable. In Xenophon's *Memorabilia*, the young Alcibiades shows Pericles that only that concept of law is valid which precludes the use of force except for retaliatory and defensive purposes. Aristotle discusses the views of the sophist Lycophron who believed that the function of government is to guarantee mutual rights;[25] he also confronts the city planner Hippodamus who thought that only conduct wrong in itself – insult, injury and homicide – should be prohibited.[26] Later on in the West, William of Ockham developed certain ideas about natural rights that stress the requirement for moral choice in every man, thus limiting the range of human interaction.[27] Locke explicitly asserts that each individual is to be regarded as free and independent of the authority of others (in maturity, obviously), and may be subjected to elaborate legal government only with his own consent.[28] Mill thought that liberty should be protected and preserved wherever none has harmed another, mainly so as to secure progress.[29] Spencer advocated natural rights on the grounds that human evolution clearly points to a system of such rights as most in conformity with evolutionary progress.[30] Albert Nock did not believe that the moral nature of man could be preserved without his liberty being protected.[31] Ludwig von Mises believed that the economic activities of society could not continue in a most effective and sensible way unless a free market prevails and the price structure is permitted to serve as the means of communication.[32] Ayn Rand thought that the proper end of human life, to be pursued by each individual in accordance with standards of rationality, could not be voluntarily sought by everyone except in a free society based on the rights of man.[33] Robert Nozick holds that the assumption of individual rights within a human community is the best assurance we have that the structure of that community will not violate our moral precepts and intuitions.[34] And there are varieties of the libertarian argument beyond these more or less prominent versions.[35] Virtually all of these thinkers have contributed to the libertarian political tradition, even if, as in the case of Mill, Spencer, and some others, they did not remain libertarians even to the degree to be expected from them in their own times.[36]

Among contemporary representatives of these different strains of libertarianism, all agree with the central libertarian ideal, namely, that none should initiate force against another. But a division among libertarians beyond some of the more theoretical issues has bothered many conservatives. This is the split on the issue of government. The anarchist libertarians, led by the late Murray N. Rothbard, whose libertarianism rests on the two traditions of Lockean natural rights and Austrian economics,[37] hold that governments by definition initiate coercion, so they are incompatible with libertarianism. 'Limited government' libertarianism, found mainly in the writings of Ayn Rand, John Hospers, and Robert Nozick, conceives government along lines consistent with libertarian principles – for example, without the power to tax and for the primary purposes of protecting individual rights.

It is difficult to comment on the substance of the controversy. It goes on at the present in full force and involves claims and counterclaims of considerable complexity. Moreover, in my view, anarchist libertarians are only seeming anarchists.[38] They use language that appears to condemn a government with exclusive jurisdictional authority within a given community (and in a given area that is homogeneous and makes the enforcement of law therefore possible). What anarchist libertarians deny is that governments have any legitimate authority to exclude alternate contenders in the task of protecting and preserving the rights of individuals. Those libertarians who advocate government claim that while such exclusion appears to be arbitrary and unjustified, and often has been throughout history, there need be nothing arbitrary about it when properly understood.

The appearance of the language of anarchism in libertarian circles has led conservatives with libertarian leanings to become fearful and suspicious. Some even claim that consistent libertarianism leads to anarchism and the denial of anarchism is a minor inconsistency that one must simply accept. (Milton Friedman seems to believe this, in contrast to David, his son, who has argued for anarchist libertarianism, though from a framework different from Rothbard's.[39]) In general, those who find the institution of government important in society, even if cut down to its appropriate proportions, have regarded libertarianism with suspicion because of the anarchist rhetoric, if not substance. Anarchists of the Kropotkin or Bakunin varieties, on the other hand, have made clear that they regard 'anarcho-libertarianism' as a fraud, since by their doctrine the institution and protection of private property requires some kind of legal authority, government, or similar institution in society.[40]

Conservatives have always found government important, but have not liked the drift toward totalitarianism evident in contemporary statist trends. They have stressed the inefficiency of most (federal) statist undertakings but have eschewed, I believe, a principled rejection of statism. Generally stated, conservatives in the United States would leave to a federal government the job of military protection even if this might involve conscription, extensive foreign alliances, and foreign intervention. They would leave to state, county, municipal, and even more localized governmental/community bodies concerns such as upholding standards in education, science, art, and entertainment. Moreover, conservatives do not object to a free market. But they would place fewer aspects of human life at the disposal of market transaction and decision than would libertarians. Take the area of the arts or entertainment, for instance.

where we may properly classify as corrupt such offerings as pornographic novels and movies. Conservatives would welcome here, let alone permit, a local government's imposition of regulations excluding or restricting the production, sale, and purchase of such items that fit within a definition of pornography (arrived at by the consensus to be used in communities – involving quasi-democratic and quasi-aristocratic methods).[41] Although conservatives would deny that obscenity and pornography are indefinable, as modern liberals have maintained, they would not try to define these by some rationalist argument but would leave the matter to the customs and traditions that have come to prevail in the area where the concerns arise.[42]

The conservative is concerned more with having certain standards of conduct insisted upon, whereas the libertarian is concerned more with avoiding any semblance of imposition, not to mention coercion, in human community life. The more this is all they focus upon, the more the two will find each other in disagreement, indeed in hostile camps. But this is to stress extremes. Credible versions of libertarianism and conservatism in America remain allied on numerous important fronts. To make this evident, I will spell out several rarely observed aspects of libertarianism. Misunderstanding about these cannot but serve to undercut the goals of both. It is possible that even after all the clarification, important differences will remain. Yet no one need be extremely concerned about this. Even a moderate individualism will call to mind that many of the differences among human beings only appear to be about principles. More often they stem from idiosyncrasies, not unimportant but still personal peculiarities – that is, the irreducible individual differences among human beings that have slipped into abstract theoretical reflections without clear notice.

The area where conservatives appear least to understand libertarianism concerns the issue of moral standards, especially in the area of social ethics. Here no outright coercion is at stake, yet conduct may be evident to the community at large and influences can make themselves felt to sensitive individuals or those who are especially vulnerable. In short, it is in the area of social standards that conservatives have the most trouble with libertarianism, apart from the more philosophical matters of rationalism, theism, modernism, and so on, even if these are not entirely separate. As former Secretary of Education William Bennett has written,

> our society now places less value than before on what we owe others as a matter of moral obligation; less value on sacrifice as a moral good; less value on social conformity, respectability, observing the rules; and less value on correctness and restraint in matters of physical pleasure and sexuality. Higher value is now placed on things like self-expression, individualism, self-realization, and personal choice.[43]

(This was, of course, written before it was revealed that Bennett has been an unrestrained, profligate gambler.) He is also quoted as having said that

'Unbridled capitalism is a problem. It may not be a problem for production, but it's a problem for human beings. It's a problem for the whole dimension of things we call the realm of values and human relationships.'[44]

Conservatives, then, are inclined to fear the commitment libertarians show for the regime of individual liberty, not less so than some on the Left, such as Michael Sandel, Amitai Etzioni and other communitarians. Both conservatives and communitarians are willing to compromise on liberty so as to have the government address various social issues such as drug abuse, prostitution, sexual promiscuity, lack of service to others and so forth.

But how are social issues to be addressed for the libertarian? A libertarian draws a pretty sharp distinction between government, society, and the individual.[45] A government bears on everyone's life in a society and acts *for* everyone. It may thus act only in accordance with principles that apply to all, namely, regard for the individual human rights of each person.[46] In society, however, while all must at least abide by these principles, there are numerous other valid concerns. Different individuals, with different kinds of backgrounds, convictions, religious faiths, cultural habits, professional aims, temperaments, talents, and so forth, will develop a great variety of social relations. Are there standards which would warrant either promoting or discouraging and undermining certain kinds of social relations? Might one not insist even on their being prescribed or made illegal, respectively?

For instance, while someone like Bennett might not endorse alcohol prohibition, he would claim that prostitution, sexual frivolity, sacrilege, abuse of parental authority, or drunken binges are not socially desirable and ought to be dealt with by way of public policy and government regulation.

For the libertarian it is clearly unjustified to advocate laws against these practices. But might not one maintain that, for example, all else being equal, homosexuality is less healthy and admirable a form of sexuality than heterosexuality? Could not one maintain that when it comes to artistic exhibitions, the presentation of a festival of 'porno flicks' should far from merit the same respect as a festival of the plays of Shakespeare? One might even go further and vociferously condemn divorce, pre-marital sexual relations, and avant-garde literature, all as a matter of standards and taste.

Is it possible for libertarians to do this? Mustn't they be silent on these topics in the light of restricting themselves to matters of politics, which to them means only the defending of human liberty? Surely such a merely negative approach is inadequate for these purposes. If this follows from libertarianism, is it not then in fact deficient for coming to terms with human community life? Would not all those activities one should regard as wrong, debasing, degrading, vile, vicious, and so forth, barring those that involve outright coercion, have to be regarded by libertarians as perfectly acceptable? Would not silence about the quality of such social matters imply official approval? Would it not follow that if there is permission, from the point of view of the law, to produce, sell, and purchase pornography, the law would in fact be promoting the same? Does it not follow that in giving official protection to the purveyors of bad social practices in the name of individual liberty – for example, when a federal court gives the First Amendment as grounds for prohibiting a town mayor from closing the doors of a movie house that is showing pornography – one is clearly endorsing conduct that is socially improper and is at once undermining the currency of liberty?

These and many other questions, put in more or less fair and intellectually honest ways, have been posed to libertarianism by conservative writers. Not every libertarian would be able to answer these questions (and their logical kin) to the satisfaction of many conservatives. Because, however, many who write on the topic have either omitted to research whether libertarians have answered these questions satisfactorily or have simply picked on select and very narrow libertarian texts to show that libertarians are not up to the task, an attempt to answer these questions here will be of some use.[47] The answers I can give will be reflective enough of at least a prominent line of libertarian theory so that they can safely be regarded as 'libertarian answers.'

Libertarian political theory implies that a government functions properly when it upholds justice in human relations by the standard of natural human rights – as initially developed in John Locke's *Second Treatise* and given more depth and scope by contemporary libertarians.[48] Such a government would fulfill both the ancient and the modern role of state, namely, the encouragement of virtue and the promotion of peace and prosperity. The former would be achieved by securing liberty for all, which is a necessary condition for the virtuous life in society.[49] If one acts because of coercion or its threat, one cannot make moral choices. A legal system in which freedom is not protected and preserved prevents individual moral responsibility. So government that protects and preserves human freedom encourages individual moral responsibility and human virtue. Such a government also makes possible the development of peaceful means by which to achieve various personal and social goals. One of these social goals is the promotion of improved conditions of life. And while in libertarian theory no one has a natural *right* to have welfare or prosperity provided by others, it is implicit within the theory that advancement in the arts, sciences, education, leisure, material wealth, and psychological health – are all valuable elements in human life, even if not in equal measure to all.

Libertarian political theory holds it as a violation of the nature of man to engage in coercive dictation of other people's social practices, sexual habits, religious affiliations, and so forth. Nevertheless libertarianism does not preclude other means for advancing social goals. Some of these are close voluntary substitutes for outright coercion. Moreover, parental responsibility in a free society (along libertarian lines) would not preclude the use of physical force against a child within the dictates of reason. A child is normally incapable of making rational decisions concerning its behavior and could, unless at times forcibly yet reasonably forbidden from doing so, place itself in severe danger. This form of coercion is not excluded in libertarian theory.

Coercion among normal adults is forbidden, with exceptions allowed only if they have been properly defended in a court of law guided by rational rules of evidence and libertarian principle (incorporated in the common and constitutional law).[50] Voluntary approaches to social direction, in the variety of ways we refer to as ostracism, rebuke, boycott, and so on, are available for use to everyone and anyone. These ways can be developed into massive and severe instruments of social control and change. It would be quite illegitimate to dismiss these methods as ineffectual, especially in light of the entirely ineffectual character of coercive efforts to promote or stifle personal and social development. The libertarians cannot and will not give the false promise that coercion will guarantee the rooting out of evil and the promotion of good. The libertarian is prepared, however, to spell out realistic non-coercive prospects of achieving these ends. Outside the government's proper peace-keeping and retaliatory functions, there is ample room for the libertarian to introduce non-political means so as to cope with the problems and challenges of personal and social life.

Let me stress this again. Libertarianism is a political theory, an answer to the natural and central political question: in accordance with what basic principle(s) should a human community be organized? Never mind now that such a (rationalist) approach *appears* to assume that one can simply create society. Libertarians realize well enough that social systems emerge and evolve, but they also realize that a crucial factor in this evolution is precisely how this question is answered by human beings. So the libertarian is interested, *as* libertarian, in offering for serious consideration his basic principle as the content of a community's legal system or constitution. Contrary to what critics of the free society have said, be they Marxists such as Marcuse and Fromm or conservatives like Burke and Kristol, the principles of liberty do not preclude a broader ethical framework. These principles of liberty are, as it were, the political tip of a very large iceberg which represents a general philosophy of existence and human life. True, in a complete philosophical system politics is not independent from other elements. But it *is* distinguishable, so that political ideas may in turn be supported in isolation from their underpinnings.

The broader ethical framework that gives backing to libertarian political principles has not been fully attended to in the past by prominent classical liberals and libertarians, mainly because ethics itself has always been viewed as giving license for coercion.[51] If you know what Johnny should do, you may coerce him, even if it isn't little Johnny but mature John whom we are considering now! Marxists have certainly tried to convince us that if we know what is objectively socially useful, we may establish a state and make everyone's conduct conform to this. In an intellectual atmosphere in which this association between virtue (or principles of morality) and coercion prevails, it is no surprise that advocates of liberty remain silent about virtue.[52] Whether it be satisfaction of the will of God, the provision of some secular (hypothetical) social contract, the utilitarian provision for the greatest happiness of the greatest number, or the ushering in of the culmination of the historical dialectical progress, in each case such value theories have allowed for, even required, coercing people to achieve the value in question.

It is a widely held view about values that only if they are intrinsic – as it were, present *within* what is to be valued – are they objective. This tends to support the view that an individual's choice of the behavior that is worthy is not central to the merits of this behavior, so that the liberty of the acting individual is thus regarded as negligible.[53] This has at times fostered the dichotomization of human virtue (that is, the human good) and individual liberty (that is, the choice to act virtuously).

It is not then surprising that those who have, perhaps only through common-sense reflection, perceived the importance of liberty – for example, economists, who are always being criticized for not giving enough heed to morality[54] – would not eagerly embrace the moral point of view and indeed proclaim their own concerns or discipline value-free. Under the perspective that the value which some state of affairs or end or behavior embodies is the goal to be achieved – not our own moral excellence, which only we as individuals can achieve – the understanding has emerged that people may be forced to do what needs to be done to achieve the good. It is the state of having *reached* the end that is morally relevant, not the process of having lived *by* seeking it or some other self-perfecting approach. This view has been devastating in the modern age.

So one main reason conservatives distrust libertarianism is that they have focused on the political results of a comprehensive philosophical outlook that has libertarianism as its political theory, namely, the view that liberty should be protected and preserved. But there is much more to this outlook. Libertarianism is only a small, politically relevant portion of it, unlike classical liberalism that preceded it.[55]

The broader framework underlying libertarianism is in the tradition of Aristotelian philosophy. This is the best broader framework; not, however, the only one offered. (I assume that we are concerned with a formidable defense, not with incomplete, sloganized versions.[56]) The main Aristotelian ingredient is metaphysical pluralism, which means roughly that reality does not have to be, nor is as we can clearly perceive, one kind of thing, but has the potential for manifesting itself in numerous ways. There is a monism, too, in this metaphysics, namely, that certain basic principles govern the *whole* of reality including all distinctive realms and features of it.[57] Along the lines of such a basic view, the emergence of value considerations can make sense. Ethics, politics, aesthetics, and so forth are all intelligible without having to introduce something perplexing and untenable, namely, supernaturalism.[58]

When life emerges in reality, objective values emerge too. The living have a lot to lose by dying. And in the case of human life, value considerations take on a *moral* component because individual human beings are *responsible* for identifying the values that will sustain and improve their lives – that is, because of the phenomenon of free will.

Since we are responsible – like it or not – for living well or badly, we must eschew any substitute for this responsibility lest we shed our very humanity in the process. Thus political liberty. The philosophy that underlies the robust theory of libertarian politics can be seen, thus, to secure a natural – as distinct from a supernatural – place for objective personal, social, and political norms. And this is just one feature of libertarianism that conservative critics have denied.[59] They have focused on the fact that many arguments for liberty – going as far back as Taoism and as close to our time as the position of Professor Milton Friedman – have been based on moral skepticism.[60] Yet there have also been other arguments, which critics have not discussed in detail and are still discussing only when the famous among us make them, even if only incompletely.[61]

It would not be surprising, however, that arguments for what to many appears as a very good idea are usually incomplete. The identification of principles in any domain of reality is gradual, rocky, evolving. Man is not omniscient and often makes tragic detours seeking the truth. This is ever more so when we reach realms involving norms, the difference between right and wrong, good and evil. In normative areas there is often great resistance to the process of careful, objective study. One should expect this from those who would be identified as failures were the truth known even incompletely, and sometimes from those with good will but eager to caution us about dogmatism and, in politics, about authoritarianism or the temptation many human beings have to claim a monopoly on the truths of ethics and politics.

Today the libertarian political principle does, however, enjoy the support of a reasonably well developed, rational philosophy. It may, with some risks stemming from necessary brevity, be summarized as follows: once an individual chooses to live, that individual has committed himself to living well or properly, namely in accordance with his nature; libertarianism is the political theory which best takes into account man's nature, namely, his essence as a free, rational living being whose conduct can only be made morally worthwhile by the individual himself by sustaining his commitment. This kind of life, with all of the diversity and universality it entails – based on the broad human and highly specialized individual and other characteristics every individual possesses – is what should be chosen by each individual. This kind of life involves an array of human virtues (honesty, productivity, prudence, courage, fortitude, justice, self-respect, and so on), but these virtues must be sustained and practiced by choice and their precise interpretation must be adjusted to the individual's own case. For our purposes it is crucial to note that this kind of life is not owed to anyone; it entails no other obligations than those freely chosen by the individual, even if it is true that once chosen these obligations should be fulfilled, and even if it is true that some of these obligations should be chosen by an individual because of his humanity and individual identity. And all of this is to take place in the world we are familiar with, involving numerous implications bearing on various aspects of reality (for example, parenthood, friendship, career plans, political concerns, ownership, professional tasks, and so forth). So as to achieve such feats as a matter of individual responsibility, it is necessary that everyone enjoy the freedom in society that human beings can insure for each other without in any way being required to become indentured to others. Therefore, the free society, via the respect of everyone's naturally derived rights to life, liberty and property, is the best political order for every human being.

Concerning the social elements of a mature libertarian political theory – numerous implications may be identified. Those, however, are very specialized because of the volatile nature of human circumstances. Nevertheless, a few claims that have been made as to the social philosophy of libertarianism need attention.

For example, some maintain that libertarianism presupposes a hedonistic ethic. This is not true – it presupposes an eudemonistic individualism, as can be discerned from what has already been said here.[62] Is libertinism implicit in the advocacy of liberty as the highest political principle? No – libertarianism only prohibits the *forcible* squelching of indecent conduct, not its vigorous criticism, opposition, boycott or denunciation in peaceful ways. A preoccupation with material wealth is supposed to be implicit in libertarianism. But there is no requirement in that political doctrine to the effect that human beings ought to strive for material wealth, even if ordinary prudence would be expected from anyone as regards his material needs and wants. Nor is libertarianism anti-religious. Nothing in the doctrine requires the forfeiting of religious worship, although, it is true, the argument underlying libertarian politics stresses the rational identification of reality, thus by implication, fundamental reliance on faith for purposes of understanding ethics and politics is eschewed. And libertarianism is often said to presuppose a mechanistic materialistic conception of human nature. This is equally misguided. The pluralistic metaphysics that forms the basis of the philosophy in support of libertarian politics does not prejudge in favor of mechanistic materialism, even if some economic libertarians lead one to believe this by virtue of their particular social science methodology.[63]

No doubt, even a robust philosophical case for libertarianism, as outlined here, will conflict with several of the main tenets of contemporary conservative thought. For example, a rather optimistic view underlies the libertarian doctrine, in contrast to the view some leading conservatives have advocated. But this optimism is by no means committed to the doctrine that man is naturally or automatically good, but only to the view that man *can* be good by his own sustained effort. When conservatives claim that man has a 'proclivity toward violence and sin,'[64] the libertarian would have to object. Neither argument nor historical evidence supports this claim. Only a very selective, sensationalist or journalistic view of human history omits from consideration the considerable degree of human virtue and good that permeates human existence – if mainly away from the limelight. But the libertarian rejects the modern liberal, secular utopian view of man's perfectibility (by the rational organization of society or the dialectics of history). Man is perfectible, but only by his own sustained disciplined effort. And if this be optimism, the libertarian will have to plead guilty. What the libertarian is concerned with *qua* libertarian is to make possible – not to falsely guarantee – for each human being to aspire to goodness in his own circumstances, admitting that this aspiration may be neglected. And this is not utopianism.

There is another, less fundamental but quite emotion-packed issue on which libertarians and conservatives are frequently in serious disagreement, namely, foreign policy. The foreign policy of a free society, as its domestic policy, stresses the social primacy of liberty. This amounts to a strict foreign policy of *defensivism*, as explained in an essay by Professor Eric Mack.[65] Some libertarians insist on an isolationist foreign policy, but that cannot be derived from the libertarian political framework, contrary to their contentions.[66] As to the implications of libertarian defensivist foreign policy for the conduct of the present American government, this is a very complicated matter, but not unmanageable. Libertarians have not developed the specialization for purposes of answering the numerous particular policy questions the present American government faces, but they are, quite justifiably, very suspicious of the wisdom of the *status quo*. In my view the few libertarians who have made contributions to this area of concern have remained far too abstract and have succeeded mainly in raising questions, not in answering them.[67] Still, it is not an exaggeration to maintain that conservatives would find libertarians too complacent about the threat of international communism, just as libertarians find conservatives too complacent about the threat of domestic authoritarianism in the wake of a policy of virtual Wilsonian imperialism. The point that should be admitted is that some very serious thinking needs to be done to discover – instead of dogmatically to assert – what a free society's foreign policy implies for those who are seeking to establish such a society from within a mixed society such as America is today.

To conclude, let me recall here some thoughts expressed by an individual whom some conservatives have called upon to give support to their anti-libertarian concerns.[68] The late Leo Strauss made numerous relevant points regarding the issues surrounding the present discussion, but three are especially germane. First, Strauss identified the good life for man as 'simply the life in which the requirements of man's natural inclinations are fulfilled in the proper order to the highest possible degree, the life of a man who is awake to the highest possible degree, the life of a man in whose soul nothing lies waste.'[69]

He also believed that: 'political freedom and especially that political freedom that justifies itself by the pursuit of human excellence … requires the highest degree of vigilance.'[70]

And finally he held: 'There is no adequate solution to the problem of virtue or happiness on the political or social plane.'[71]

If we put these three ideas together – which, it seems to me, do give expression to Strauss's own views (as rare as this is in his writing) – we will arrive at the libertarianism I have been speaking of throughout this discussion.

This libertarianism is, put plainly, the view that the task of politics is liberty, nothing more or less, and the task of virtue, human excellence or happiness, is a task that only the individual on his own can strive to fulfill either alone or in personal and voluntary association with others, never by force or coercion.

Notes

1 See, for several discussions of this, Tibor R. Machan, ed., *Individual Rights Reconsidered: Are the Truths of the Declaration of Independence Lasting?* (Stanford, CA: Hoover Institution Press, 2001).

2 This is clear in what Edmund Burke tells us, namely,

> Men have no right to risk the very existence of their nation and their civilization upon experiments in morals and politics; for each man's private capital of intelligence is petty; it is only when a man draws upon the bank and capital of the ages, the wisdom of our ancestors, that he can act wisely.

Quoted in Kenneth M. Dolbeare, *Directions of American Political Thought* (New York: John Wiley & Sons, Inc., 1969), p. 11.

3 For example, John Hospers, *Libertarianism* (Los Angeles, CA: Nash Publishing, 1971), *Human Rights and Human Liberties* (Chicago, IL: Nelson-Hall, 1975); Robert Nozick, *Anarchy, State, and Utopia* (New York: Basic Books, 1974); Ayn Rand, *Capitalism, The Unknown Ideal* (New York: Signet Books, 1967); Murray N. Rothbard, *Power and Market* (Menlo Park, CA: Institute for Humane Studies, 1971). Rand denied that she was a libertarian, yet her political principles were those of libertarianism and her work is frequently cited in libertarian literature as providing a basis for libertarianism.

4 For example, CATO Institute, Washington, D.C.; Institute for Humane Studies, Fairfax, Virginia; Center for Libertarian Studies, New York, New York; The Reason Foundation, Santa Barbara, California. None of these organizations is in political affiliation with the Libertarian Party and they are all educational, non-profit outfits.

5 Some of the subjects of serious dispute include whether government is consistent with libertarianism, whether libertarian principles give support to the claim that abortion should not be illegal, whether isolationism or some other form of principled foreign policy – for example, defensivism, as explained by Eric Mack, 'Permissible Defense,' *Reason*, 8 (July 1977): pp. 26–31 – is proper from a libertarian point of view. On abortion, see *Reason*, 9 (April 1978).

6 The list is very long indeed. Examples may be found in the pages of *Commentary*, *National Review*, *The New Republic*, and *The Nation*, as far as general readership magazines are concerned. Scholarly criticisms, especially of Robert Nozick's libertarian arguments, have appeared in *Philosophy and Public Affairs*, *The Public Interest*, *Political Theory*, *Canadian Journal of Philosophy*, *Modern Age*, *The Intercollegiate Review*, *Journal of Philosophy*, *Ethics*, *Human Rights*, and many other publications.

7 See note 5. Among major publishers who have issued works on libertarian thought are Basic Books, Macmillan Publishing Company, University of Chicago Press, Open Court, and Prentice-Hall.

8 For example, at Harvard University, University of California at Berkeley, Stanford University, Princeton University, University of Southern California, and many other prominent universities libertarianism is regularly covered in philosophy, economics, and political science courses.

9 No other political doctrine emphasized the concept of human rights as libertarianism. But libertarians have popularized the idea of victimless crimes, decriminalization, tax resistance, deregulation, and restitution for victims of crimes. The language of academic

political theory has adopted many of the ideas found in Robert Nozick's work, although it is doubtful that this indicates any substantive decline in the leftist orientation of academic humanists. Here Nozick's own prominence and philosophical competence accounts for the development of libertarian-flavored discussions.

10 We may recall here the Jaffa/Kendall and Jaffa/Bradford debates in conservative intellectual circles.

11 Any attention to libertarian and conservative publications will reveal just how often such writers as Yale Brozen, Henry Hazlitt, Milton Friedman, William Rickenbacker, and William Niskanen have appeared in both of their pages, usually expressing concerns with the topics mentioned.

12 For example, Russell Kirk, *The Conservative Mind from Burke to Eliot*, (Chicago, IL: Henry Regnery, 1953), Arianna Stassinopoulos, *After Reason* (New York: Stein and Day, 1978), and M. E Bradford, 'A Better Guide than Reason: The Politics of John Dickinson,' *Modern Age*, 21 (Winter 1977), pp. 39–49. In most conservative criticisms of reason it is Cartesian or mechanistic rationality that is at issue. Moreover, not only conservatives but many others consider this version of rationality inadequate. See for example, Paul Feyerabend, *Against Method* (London: NLB, 1975) and F. A. Hayek, *Law, Legislation, and Liberty* (Chicago, IL: University of Chicago Press, 1973), vol. 1. For a most formidable criticism of the form of rationalism at issue here, see Michael Oakeshott, *Rationalism in Politics* (New York: Basic Books, 1962), although it would be very risky to categorize Oakeshott's position here. Kirk, in his later work, *The Politics of Prudence*, edited and with an Introduction by Mark C. Henrie (Wilmington, DE: ISI Books, 2004), explicitly criticizes libertarians for failing to practice 'the art of the possible.' That is like criticizing abolitionists for failing to practice the art of the possible. Come to think of it, though, thinking such as Kirk's would probably consider the abolitionist movement unrealistic and, therefore, misguided, too.

13 For a prominent thinker who has often been considered more of a libertarian than a conservative, though welcome in both intellectual traditions, F. A. Hayek appears to join conservatives and Michael Oakeshott in being suspicious of reason but only in the constructivist sense. Other libertarians cannot be aligned in this respect with great precision, but many with an ethical argument for the free society would regard themselves as Aristotelians or Thomists, while those with an empirical bent may be regarded as very respectful toward Humean or positivistic empiricism. For more on this, see my *Human Rights and Human Liberties*, pp. 258–64, passim.

14 But note that their conception of reason is significantly different from what most conservatives consider narrow.

15 For example, libertarians oppose any law, *qua* legally enforceable measure in human community life, that prescribes personal or social moral principles or rules – including those that are valid and true – and that prohibits their violation. Thus it may be wrong to engage in premarital sexual intercourse but when done with full consent, it may not be prohibited; and though it may be morally right to publish books with taste and moral awareness, a publisher may not be forced to do so (or punished for not having done so). The complications of a nation with massive public facilities – run at taxpayers' expense and given state direction – cannot be discussed here, although libertarians are far from unaware of them in their various writings. See, for example, the thirty-seven essays in Tibor R. Machan, ed., *The Libertarian Alternative* (Chicago, IL: Nelson-Hall, 1974) and twenty-one more in Tibor R. Machan, ed, *The Libertarian Reader* (Lanham, MD: Rowman & Littlefield, 1982). See, also, Douglas B. Rasmussen and Tibor R. Machan, eds, *Liberty for the 21st Century* (Lanham, MD: Rowman & Littlefield, 1995). It should be noted that forbidding the violation of side constraints – that is, the violation of individual rights – does not amount to 'the prescription of personal or social moral principles or rules' but to the protection of the sovereignty of individuals in a free society.

16 The evidence may be found in the widespread support such regulatory proposals have received in various elections from conservative voters and political representatives.

17 Bearing directly on politics, the rejection of the rationalist approach often results in the rejection of the so-called absolutist versions of the principles of the free society. See, for example, Walter Berns, *The First Amendment and the Future of American Democracy* (New York: Basic Books, 1976).

18 For example, C. D. Broad, 'Determinism, Indeterminism, and Libertarianism,' in *Ethics and the History of Philosophy* (London: Routledge & Kegan Paul, 1952).

19 See note 15.

20 Many conservatives believe that the secular bent in libertarian theories necessarily presupposes the subjectivist ethics of libertinism. Also, they object to the humanism often implicit within libertarianism. See for example, David Ehrenfeld, *The Arrogance of Humanism* (New York: Oxford University Press, 1978). The classic rejection of Locke's libertarianism may be found to be based on the alleged egoism of Locke. See for example Leo Strauss, *Natural Right and History* (Chicago, IL: University of Chicago Press, 1953). Strauss, unlike most conservatives, is more critical of the narrow Hobbesian egoism than of egoism *per se*. For a type of ethical theory that stresses the importance of the individual and would serve well as the moral underpinnings of libertarianism, see David L. Norton, *Personal Destinies, A Philosophy of Ethical Individualism* (Princeton, NJ: Princeton University Press, 1976) See also my 'Recent Work in Ethical Egoism,' *American Philosophical Quarterly*, 16 (January 1979), pp. 1–15, and 'Review of *Personal Destinies*,' *American Journal of Jurisprudence* (1979), pp. 213–26.

21 For a discussion of what counts as an adequate theory in this and other realms of inquiry, see my 'Rational Choice and Public Affairs,' *Theory and Decision* 12 (September1980); pp. 229–58. Since no man can reasonably aspire to produce a final, unchangeable understanding of a reality that is dynamic and by no means finished, only open-ended theories can be considered even plausible, let alone adequate, especially in the human sciences. But certain criteria do apply which require a theory to be consistent and fair to the facts.

22 One might consider that the theory of evolution is a biological theory, even though its validity presupposes numerous facts in chemistry, physics, epistemology, and so on. The fact that Darwin did not address all the issues in these fields with bearing on his own sphere of concern does not detract from the truth of his views.

23 Force, even in its petty versions – for example, government regulation (which former President Ford called 'petty tyrannies') – is the enemy of creativity, imagination, and flourishing. An active being's primary faculty, namely, his reason, and all of what relies on it, are undercut when force is interjected. This is why slavery, massive or minute, simply cannot work as well as liberty, as the Nazi and Soviet experiments demonstrated.

24 *The Way of Lao Tzu* (Indianapolis, IN: Bobbs-Merrill, 1963).

25 Aristotle, *Politics* III.9, 1280b 10.

26 Ibid., 111.7, 1267b 38.

27 William of Ockham, *Opus Nonaginta Dierujm*, Chapter 65.

28 John Locke, *Second Treatise on Civil Government*, ed. J Gough (Oxford: Oxford University Press, 1956).

29 John Stuart Mill, *On Liberty*, ed. C.V. Shields (Indianapolis, IN: Bobbs-Merrill, 1957), p. 66. The progressivist character of Mill's thought is explained in Gertrude Himmelfarb, *On Liberty and Liberalism* (New York: Knopf, 1974).

30 Herbert Spencer, *The Principles of Ethics* (Indianapolis, IN: Liberty Classics, 1978).

31 Albert Jay Nock, *Our Enemy, the State* (Caldwell, ID: Caxton Printers, 1946).

32 Ludwig von Mises, *Socialism* (London: Jonathan Cape, 1936).

33 Ayn Rand, 'The Objectivist Ethics,' in *The Virtue of Selfishness: A New Concept of Egoism* (New York: Signet, 1964).

34 *Nozick*.

35 For the individualist anarchism that has been stressed by some as an essential part of the libertarian tradition, see James J. Martin, *Men Against the State* (Colorado Springs, CO: Ralph Myles, 1970) and Murray N. Rothbard's *For a New Liberty* (New York: Macmillan,

1973) and *Power and Market*, which present a compilation of Lockean and Austrian economic arguments for anarchist libertarianism.

36 By this remark I aim to stress that there is nothing odd about regarding someone as part of a tradition even if that individual's views are not exactly expressed in contemporary terminology.

37 See note 35.

38 See my *Human Rights and Human Liberties*, pp. 143–60. In my work I discuss several versions of anarchism, including the views of Professor Rothbard. To date, however, discussions of Rothbard's position have centered on Nozick's arguments against anarchist libertarianism. See the essays in *The Journal of Libertarian Studies*, 1 (Winter 1977). For my own assessment of the debate, see Tibor R. Machan, 'Anarchism and Minarchism, A Rapprochement,' *Journal des Economists et des Estudes Humaines*, Vol. 14, No 4 (December 2002), pp. 569–88.

39 David Friedman, *The Machinery of Freedom* (New York: Harper and Row, 1973). For Milton Friedman's explicit view on this issue, see Joe Cobb, Tibor Machan, and Ralph Raico, 'An Interview with Milton Friedman,' *Reason*, 6 (December 1974).

40 See several letters to the editor of *Penthouse* magazine, March 1974, in response to an essay about Professor Rothbard by Samuel Blumenfeld in *Penthouse,* November 1973. See also Sam Wells, 'Anarcho-Capitalism is Not Anarchism, and Political Competition is Not Economic Competition,' *Frontlines* 1 (January 1979).

41 For example, see Irving Kristol, 'Pornography, Obscenity, and the Case for Censorship,' in J. Feinberg and H. Gross, eds, *Philosophy of Law* (Belmont, CA: Dickenson, 1975), and Walter Berns, 'Free Speech and Free Government,' *The Political Science Reviewer*, 2 (1972), pp. 217–41. In this as in other of his writings, Berns insists on associating libertarianism with the doctrine that truth is relative; yet no such doctrine underlies libertarianism, quite the contrary, considering that libertarians insist on the universality of the truth of the principle of liberty. (Nor, as Berns insists, do libertarians embrace the legal philosophy of Oliver W. Holmes, Jr, who was a pragmatist and completely eschewed the doctrine of natural law, one of the most often cited theories in support of libertarianism. For more on this, see Tibor R. Machan, *Objectivity: Recovering Determinate Reality in Philosophy, Science, and Everyday Life* [London, UK: Ashgate, 2004], especially Chapter 7, 'Richard Posner's Pragmatic Jurisprudence.')

42 Gary North, 'Pornography, Community, Law,' *National Review*, 25 (August 31, 1973).

43 William Bennett, *Index of Leading Cultural Indicators* (New York: Simon & Schuster, 1994), pp. 8–9.

44 Quoted in David Wessell and John Harwood, 'Market Economy Begins to Reach Further Into Government, Society,' *The Wall Street Journal Interactive Edition*, May 14, 1998.

45 On a microcosmic level this distinction would be reflected in, for example, referee, game, and player, in basketball, with only the first having a claim to authority for using force. See Albert J. Nock.

46 This is explained further in my *Human Rights and Human Liberties*, Chapter 4.

47 For some rather clear examples of offhand references to libertarianism, see Stephen J. Tonsor, 'Liberty and Equality as Absolutes,' *Modern Age*, 23 (Winter 1979), p. 8; John P. East, 'Leo Strauss and American Conservatism,' *Modern Age*, 21 (Winter 1977), p. 18. See especially Ernest van den Haag, 'Libertarians and Conservatives,' *National Review* (June 8, 1979).

48 It is Leo Strauss and his students who teach the view that Locke's work is not actually *bona fide* political philosophy. See Michael P. Zuckert, 'The Recent Literature on Locke's Political Philosophy,' *The Political Science Reviewer*, 5 (1975), pp. 271–304.

49 For more on this, see my *Human Rights and Human Liberties*, p. 137, and 'Some Consideration of the Common Good,' *Journal of Human Relations*, Vol. 18, No 3 (1970): pp. 979–94. See also Frank S. Meyer, *In Defense of Freedom* (Chicago, IL: Henry Regnery, 1962), Donald J. Devine, *Does Freedom Work?* (Ottawa, IL: Caroline House Books, 1978), and, especially, Douglas Den Uyl, 'Freedom and Virtue,' *Reason Papers*,

5 (1979), pp. 1–12. A somewhat similar view is defended in Alan Gewirth, *Reason and Morality* (Chicago, IL: University of Chicago Press, 1978), although Gewirth believes that capability, too, is a necessary condition of morality and therefore one has a right to welfare (that is, the provision of such capabilities by others). For some objections to this and a discussion of a variety of human rights theories, see my 'Some Recent Work in Human Rights Theory,' *American Philosophical Quarterly*, 19 (January 1982), pp. 61–72.

50 A specifically libertarian theory of law has obviously not been developed to the extent other theories have, although the works of F. A. Hayek, Bruno Leoni, Richard Epstein, John Hospers, J. Roger Lee, Randy Barnett, and others offer many insights as to the foreseeable elements of a distinctively libertarian legal code. Since the American political and legal traditions are very close to some crucial aspects of libertarianism, legal theory in America would be of much help in the development of a libertarian legal system.

51 A very good example of this is found in Lord Devlin, The *Enforcement of Morals* (Oxford: Oxford University Press, 1959). In earlier times, with the close relationship of state and church, the moral commandments were often tantamount to legal edicts. For an argument for liberty which accepts that if one knows that another is doing wrong (or not doing right), one should interfere, see Cobb, Machan, and Raico, 'Interview with Milt Friedman.'

52 The Founding Fathers' greater concern for liberty rather than virtue may be appreciated along the present line of analysis.

53 No one quite announces the matter this way, but various doctrines of what *true* liberty means – namely the freedom from hardship, from hunger from physical or spiritual suffering (even if it does not mean the freedom from the interferences of other human beings) – amount precisely to this view.

54 Irving Kristol, '"When Virtue Loses All Her Loveliness" – Some Reflections on Capitalism and the "Free Society,"' in *Two Cheers for Capitalism* (New York: Basic Books, 1978).

55 Classical liberalism may properly be regarded as far more than political theory such as libertarianism, since it is philosophically broader involving ideas about the nature of man, God, value, science, and so on. Although libertarianism may indeed be defensible from a very specific philosophical perspective, it is not itself that perspective.

56 Unfortunately critics of libertarianism focus only on the slogans, or those renditions that emanate from very prominent circles, regardless of how complete and comprehensive these may be. See my 'Considerations of the Libertarian Alternative,' *Harvard Journal of Law and Public Policy*, 2(1979), pp. 103–24, where I examine critical discussions of Nozick's work and try to provide some of the theoretical replies to Nozick's critics based on a libertarian view that is much broader than his.

57 For more on this, see my 'Reason, Morality, and the Free Society,' in R.L. Cunningham, ed., *Liberty and the Rule of the Law* (College Station, TX: Texas A & M University Press, 1979).

58 Moreover, the political theory that presupposes supernaturalism is theoretically flawed by begging one crucial question of political life, namely, by what principles should a human community be governed? To answer that it is to be discovered by revelation, the people who do not experience it will be left automatically in the position of having to accept the words of those who do. The naturalist approach, which relied on man's essential (natural) capacity to reason, begins political inquiry in such a way as to make it possible for everyone to learn the answers.

59 See note 41, Berns, 'Free Speech and Free Government,' p. 237. The argument runs as follows: prominent thinkers who have advocated what are political theories in the libertarian tradition have asserted the relativity of truth, but truth is not relative even by the implications of their own theory, therefore, libertarianism is false. But this argument is fallacious. It assumes that if 'P implies R' is true, but 'P' is false, then 'R' is false. Yet it has been argued, I believe successfully, that 'S implies R,' and 'S' is true, therefore 'R' is proven. We may regard 'P' as the view that truth is relative and 'R' as the libertarian

political theory, while 'S' is the view that man has a moral nature so he must choose his own moral excellence. Assuming that both 'P' and 'S' imply 'R', it won't do to keep refuting 'P' in order to refute 'R'.

60 For Friedman's view, see Cobb, Machan, and Raico, 'Interview with Milton Friedman.

61 I am referring to the extraordinarily widespread discussions of Nozick's work, in contrast to the much more comprehensive works of Ayn Rand and Eric Mack. For Mack's work, see his 'How to Derive Ethical Egoism,' *The Personalist*, 52 (Winter 1971), pp. 735–43, 'Egoism and Rights,' *The Personalist*, 54 (Spring 1973), pp. 5–33, and 'Egoism and Rights Revisited,' *The Personalist*, 58 (Summer 1977), pp. 282–8. See also essays by Eric Mack, John Hospers, John O. Nelson, James Sadowsky, Nathaniel Branden, and me in Tibor R. Machan, ed., *The Libertarian Alternative*.

62 See David L. Norton, *Personal Destinies*, for a detailed exposition of this ethical position. I should not leave the impression, however, that Norton is a libertarian I simply contend that his eudemonistic individualism provides a correct foundation to libertarian political theory.

63 I have in mind scholars associated with the University of Chicago department of economics, noted for their strict reliance on positivist or empiricist methodology and its presuppositions.

64 Russell Kirk, *The Conservative Mind*.

65 Mack, 'Permissible Defense.'

66 R. A. Childs, Jr, editor of *Libertarian Review*, has advocated what he calls 'noninterventionism' in American foreign policy, *Libertarian Review*, 8 (January 1979), p. 25, but there is no reason at all to accept that libertarianism implies this. Defensive military action can easily require foreign intervention, even in the affairs of countries that are not the direct enemies of a free society (for example, when such countries are unjustifiably complacent about military threats against them *and* such threats, pressed in identifiable actions of course, are also threats against one's own free country). The war against Iraq has been a bone of contention between many conservatives and many libertarians – probably best illustrated by how those at the Heritage Foundation and those at the Cato Institute would deal with this policy. For my own general account for the proper stance on the topic, see Tibor R. Machan, *The Passion for Liberty* (Lanham, MD: Rowman & Littlefield, 2003), Chapter 13, 'Military Defense of a Free Society.'

67 See, for example, Murray N. Rothbard, 'Soviet Foreign Policy: A Revisionist Perspective,' *Libertarian Review*, 7 (April 1978); pp. 7–23.

68 East, 'Leo Strauss,'.

69 Leo Strauss, *Natural Right and History*, 2nd edn (Chicago, IL: University of Chicago Press, 1970), p. 127.

70 Ibid., p. 131.

71 Strauss, 'Restatement on Xenophon's Hiero,' in *On Tyranny* (Ithaca, NY: Cornell University Press, 1968), p. 194.

Chapter 18

Socialism Redux on the Horizon

It is the most widely championed opponent to libertarianism in our time.

Soon after the election of Bill Clinton, sociologist Amitai Etzioni, a professor of sociology at George Washington University and signatory to Bill Clinton's list of 'economists' supporting his presidential campaign, published a letter of complaint in *The New York Times*. He chided those who objected that various Clinton appointees lacked proper training in the science of economics. Particularly cited was Robert Reich – former advisor to Michael Dukakis and then a professor at the John F. Kennedy School of Government of Harvard University and now University Professor and Maurice B. Hexter Professor of Social and Economic Policy at Brandeis University and at Brandeis's Heller School of Social Policy and Management – who became Clinton's labor secretary for a spell and had been trained not in economics but in law.

Professor Etzioni was named in 2001 by Judge Richard Posner as among the top 100 American intellectuals when measured by academic citations. He is a leader of the communitarian movement, and a prominent figure in the field of socioeconomics, which is a hybrid of sociology and economics. He is an advocate of these ideas that I can only dub as new excuses to crowbar American economic policy in the direction of democratic socialism. Certainly communitarian Etzioni is highly critical of the teachings of mainstream or neoclassical economics. According to him, this field involves entirely unrealistic assumptions, namely, those embodied in modeling and mathematical analyses, including perfect competition and full equilibrium.[1]

Etzioni argues that because of such unrealistic assumptions, mainstream economics misguides people so that they embrace free markets and supply-side macroeconomic policies. Since, however, the basic tenets of neoclassical economics are wrong-headed, it cannot be that the proposed free markets and supply-side public policy would be healthy for the American economy. Instead we must adopt the approach championed by the socioeconomists and the communitarians. For the sake of the well-being of communities we must accept a good deal of government intervention in the economy, even if some individuals are inconvenienced thereby.

But Etzioni's laments about the alleged errors of neoclassical economics in his letter and books like *The Moral Dimension* and *Public Policy in a New Key* infer way too much from the shortcomings of neoclassical methodology; he believes that any (at least, any free-market) conclusions produced by those using such methodology are also wrong-headed. Complaining about efforts at privatization in former Soviet colonies, he writes in the letter that to 'urge post-Communist societies to shift to raw capitalism is to ignore the inherent social instability (which led all Western countries to welfare capitalism) of such a system, and to invite social tensions that are explosive and will contribute to removing both democratic institutions and the drive to capitalism.' He has been joined in this prognosis by billionaire George Soros and by many other writers on the left (for example, Robert Kuttner).

In indicting the free market for lacking social stability Etzioni caricatures classical liberalism or libertarianism as being supported by nothing but the *homo economicus* or atomistic conception of human nature.[2] There is indeed such an atomistic conception extant; it is derived from Thomas Hobbes's idea of human nature, which is derived in turn from his nominalist view of anything's nature.[3] Yet it is only the neoclassical defense of libertarianism which invokes this abbreviated conception of human individuality, and only with regard to the modeling of market behavior. There are, indeed, some economists who embrace an imperialist position, that is, who attempt to subject all human affairs to economic analysis.[4] But that is not by any means the dominant idea underlying the libertarian view of political life. Etzioni believes he has conquered the citadel, but he has merely blasted a single poorly laid brick.

The modeling and mathematical analyses that neoclassical scholars conduct are most promising for the understanding of a free market and of what might be expected from government intrusions upon market activity. As Nobel laureate Milton Friedman has explained, the model is to the actual world of human economic life what theoretical physics is to the actual world of physical events.[5] If people would only keep this in mind when they infer public policy from the results of the analysis, things would not go astray. This approach may not be fully adequate to understanding human economic life. It has, however, offered some valuable insights and explanations of, for example, why command economies, government regulation, debt financing, minimum wage legislation, rent control and similar government boondoggles fail. Furthermore, it is by no means the only way classical liberals and libertarians approach their analysis of human community life. Economic imperialism is not even fully embraced by most neoclassical economists, let alone by all those who find the classical liberal polity a sound way to organize the basic legal structure of human community affairs. Many free-market economists (specifically, of what is called the Austrian school), reject mathematics altogether as a tool of economic understanding (except in quantitative reports of historical events).[6]

Thus, even if the neoclassical approach is flawed, it does not follow that free markets and supply-side policies also are. They may well be justified on other grounds – for example, because freedom is generally better for human beings than the involuntary servitude championed by communitarians. They don't describe it in those terms, of course; they prefer to disguise their goal by deploying such adjectives as 'responsible' to describe their ideal – as if the persons being socially engineered can act responsibly when forced to behave as others think they should. A problem with examining the communitarian thesis is that nearly all those who speak for it use the locution of 'we want,' 'we desire,' 'we prefer.' While no doubt this is true of some of the citizens in a community, it isn't true of them all and that makes a big difference to the type of public policy implications that follow. Perhaps the most basic element of the communitarian stance is just that it refuses to acknowledge this fact, namely, that it is unjustified to speak in terms of 'we' when in fact only 'some' agree to some measure of what communitarians favor as constitutive of community life.

In any case, despite some of the excesses of the neoclassical school of economics, in a free society we are safer in their hands than in the hands of the socioeconomists. The former mostly wish to understand the economy and set the limits to government involvement in it, so government is roughly analogous to an honest judge who does not distort his adjudicative function.

It is true, as already noted, that neoclassical economists do sometimes claim more power for their approach than it actually possesses. For example, Professor Gary Becker, the 1992 Nobel Prize winner in economics, claims to be able to understand nearly all aspects of human community life – including family, marriage, crime, and suicide – by applying the methods of economic science.[7] Yet what social science avoids such imperialism altogether? And Etzioni's alternative, the discipline of socioeconomics and what emerges from it, namely, communitarianism, are a confused mess because of its reliance on the admittedly small-scale yet clearly still distinctively collectivist social analysis.

Communitarianism thus serves as a cover for reintroducing various ideas of mercantilism and command economics following the demise of outright socialism.

Robert Reich and Professor Etzioni, both members of this 'new' school, in fact favor the old-fashioned polity of social democracy. According to social democracy, 'we' – namely, those in power in Washington and other headquarters of government who deem themselves authorized to speak and make policy in the name of everyone – may dictate to us all what is important for 'the community', by which they mean, of course, their own vision of what the community ought to do and look like. They are hostile to the idea that the best communities are those made voluntarily, by the members of the community, rather than those that have been imposed by someone from above. They treat the 'community' as some sort of organic body, as if adults are intrinsically incapable of exercising personal sovereignty, and thus would tolerate extensive subjugation of the citizenry in the name of community values. Just as, for a conservative like William Bennett or George W. Bush, the concept 'family values' justifies the imposition of various forms of private and social conduct on possibly unwilling persons, so the concept 'community values' justifies similar impositions in the realm of economic life for the communitarians. It's one reason that conservative figures like

David Hume and Edmund Burke are heroes to both the conservatives and the communitarians.

Do not misunderstand these points. Communitarians are *not* socialists of the Marxist–Leninist variety. They have learned at least this much: trying to regiment a very large society in virtually every respect is a hopeless dream. Yet as a dream it does remain, albeit in scaled down form, for communitarianism aims for such an objective within smaller collective units, such as cities, towns and villages (as per Hillary Rodham Clinton's book, *It Takes a Village*[8]). Yet the major feature of communitarianism is shared by those greater collectivist sociopolitical utopias, namely, the negative one of demeaning the idea of individualism.

Communitarians stress how thoroughly bound up we all are in society. We cannot think, talk, or live our lives except as members of a community. We are thoroughly dependent on other people, so that there is little which can be left to individual discretion. And here is where things turn ugly. Etzioni, whose book *The Spirit of Community*[9] is a pop manifesto of communitarianism, illustrated this in a letter to the editor of *Reason* magazine, which gave a rather critical review of his work. Etzioni protested the reviewer placing the term 'public' in quotation marks, claiming that those who are not 'extreme libertarians' will 'acknowledge that the free market will not attend (or not sufficiently) to some goods – basic research, for instance. Because the yield of basic research is available to one and all, those who heed only private interests will rationally free ride.' Guess he's not privy to the research budgets of Google, Microsoft, et al.

This is the familiar idea that many widely desired goods that can be enjoyed by persons other than those who paid for them will on that account alone not be produced by free men and women at all. Therefore, freedom must be restricted, say the communitarians. People must be taxed to the hilt in order to make them pay for such production. They must be made to serve these goals involuntarily, even if they would rather devote their efforts and wealth to something else.

That kind of assumption is exactly what motivated the Marxist–Leninists, of course. The public just does not know what is good for it – suffering as it does from 'false consciousness' – so the state must force it to behave properly, to support industrialization, agricultural collectivization, uniformity in the arts, education, and sports, and whatever other straitjackets the socialists deemed vital to the common good. Communitarians are now revamping this argument, most often regarding environmental and community values – for example, conservation and social stability, respectively.

Yet the ploy doesn't wash. There are few genuine public goods. Is basic research one of these, as Etzioni claims? What does such research focus on? *Cui bono*?[10]

AIDS research benefits, first of all, those who are at risk. Others have no stake in it except indirectly: as a means to avoid various levels of risk, out of concern for friends in the high-risk groups, or out of concern for the overall quality of a community. But we all have such an indirect stake in nearly everything positive that people do. That, in turn, would imply, given Etzioni's line of thinking, that we should all be forced to contribute to the production of *everything*. Indeed, the communitarian view thus collapses into outright socialism, the thesis that is founded on the idea that we are all first and foremost social beings (or, à la Marx, 'specie' beings), and that such concepts as individual rights are mere ideological efforts to disguise this beautiful fact about us. Communitarian premises therefore rationalize the tyranny we have witnessed as a result of the last century's national and international socialism, the feudalism of earlier centuries, and even tribalism, the most primitive form of political life human beings can experience.

In fact, 'basic research' and similar notions are nothing if not broad and vague, and Etzioni and company use them carelessly, making it possible thereby to provide support for socializing all sorts of scientific activities, with all manner of beneficiaries. Consider the fact that not even roads can be very accurately characterized as public goods; certainly one could treat them as private without radical change. In some places there are private turnpikes as well as private roads (for example, in Disneyland, retirement and other residential villages). Environmental efforts, too, are often deemed to be public measures, whereas in fact they often serve strictly private concerns. Public schools, public parks, public beaches, public forests, and, indeed, nearly every other realm now designated 'public' are, indeed, private or special-interest projects in support of which the rest of us are placed into involuntary servitude. Meanwhile, the few *bona fide* public projects like crime prevention and national defense – that is, the protection of our individual rights, the very purpose of establishing a government – get neglected.

'If the Sierra Club is fighting for untrampled ski slopes for its members,' states Etzioni in one missive, 'it is acting as a special interest group. If it is acting to preserve clean drinking water for one and all, it is acting on behalf of the public.' Appealing as it may sound, this is wrong. Even skiing can be made out to be a general good, if one frames it in terms of its health benefits and other desirable social consequences. And clean water, in turn, is a 'public' good only for those who drink from the taps (when such water is provided through a government – hence 'public' – utility), not for those who drink from privately distributed bottles.

The only truly public good is the protection of individual rights. Human beings are too differentiated, too individual to be lumped into a homogeneous group with respect to virtually any possible endeavor, except insofar as each adult requires freedom to exercise his own sovereignty.[11] So, *pace* Etzioni, the reason 'public' should often be placed in quotation marks is that it does not really mean what it says. Most 'public' goods are in fact private goods that are being gained on the backs of an over-taxed, over-regulated citizenry.

The Etzionis of our world want to regiment not only the economy but also society as a whole, although they are willing to do it starting with one small community; hence their fascination with such programs as spot checks of automobiles in crime-ridden areas, programs that gradually establish the public policy that whenever enough folks in a community have a worry, they may violate anyone's rights in a usually futile effort to remedy the worry.

Consider, for example, that the goals which Etzioni claims make it desirable to move from 'raw capitalism' to the welfare state have been far from achieved through the welfare state. To the contrary, in America, the welfare state has spawned more social instability and tension than we find in the near-capitalism of the early history of this country (excluding the obvious case of the unambiguously vicious and *anti-capitalist* institution of chattel slavery).

Communitarians could benefit from careful study of Charles Murray's analysis of the nature of state paternalism in books like *Losing Ground*.[12] But Etzioni's one reference to Murray attempts to tar him with the brush of economic reductionism, placing Murray's complex cultural and social-psychological analysis on the same footing as the curious and problematic tautological approach to the understanding of community adopted by Becker and Posner.

In fact, though, it is communitarianism which is reductive. The approach reduces ultimately to nothing more than warmed-over socialism, albeit with all kinds of disclaimers. It has proven to be a destroyer of economic performance and humane living conditions in communities across the globe.

Capitalism and individualism, although not utopian, promise solutions that are clearly far superior. The communitarians have much to learn not only from the vital lessons of recent history but also from the growing and improving literature of classical liberal social analysis.

Notes

1 In the earlier discussion of economic rationality I give my own critique of neoclassical economics which, however, does not jettison that school's support for free market economics, something that clearly does not sit well with communitarianism.

2 The publication Etzioni edits, *The Responsive Community*, devoted a two-part essay to this effort in 1992, Thomas S. Spragens, Jr's paper, 'The Limitations of Libertarianism.' As Professor Aeon Skoble makes plain in his poignant deflation of this effort, 'Another Caricature of Libertarianism' (*Reason Papers*, No 17 [1992]), the piece is a medley of straw man arguments, as are most of Etzioni's not so subtle efforts to tar and feather individualism and classical liberalism. (Oddly enough, a similarly inaccurate and ignorant analysis is offered by someone who has seemed to be a friend of libertarianism, namely, Richard Cornuelle, in 'New work for invisible hands,' *Times Literary Supplement* (April 5, 1991), reprinted some months ago by Cato Institute's *Policy Journal*.)

3 I discuss this in detail in Tibor R. Machan, *Classical Individualism* (London: Routledge, 1998) and critically assess it in my *Capitalism and Individualism, Reframing the Argument for the Free Society* (New York: St. Martin's Press, 1990) as well as in Chapter 3 of this work.

4 See, for a collection of works that discuss this, Gerard Radnitzky and Peter Bernholz, eds, *Economic Imperialism: The Economic Approach Applied Outside the Field of Economics* (New York: Paragon House Publishers, 1987).

5 Milton Friedman, *Essays in Positive Economics* (Chicago, IL: University of Chicago Press, 1956).

6 The most comprehensive non-positivist account of the economics of capitalism may be found in George Reisman, *Capitalism, A Treatise on Economics* (Ottawa, IL: Jameson Books, 1996).

7 Gary S. Becker, *The Economic Approach to Human Behavior* (Chicago, IL: University of Chicago Press, 1976) and Gary S. Becker et al., *Economics of Life: From Baseball to Affirmative Action to Immigration, How Real-World Issues Affect our Everyday Life* (New York: McGraw-Hill, 1998).

8 Hillary Rodham Clinton, *It Takes a Village* (New York: Simon & Schuster, 1996).

9 Amitai Etzioni, *The Spirit of Community: Rights, Responsibilities, and the Communitarian Agenda* (New York: Crown, 1993).

10 For more discussion on whether the free market is capable of supporting such research, see Tibor R. Machan, *Liberty and R&D* (Stanford, CA: Hoover Institution Press, 2002).

11 I develop this point in Tibor R. Machan, *The Pseudo-Science of B. F. Skinner* (New Rochelle, NY: Arlington House Publishing Co., Inc., 1974).

12 Charles Murray, *Losing Ground: American Social Policy, 1950–1980* (New York: Basic Books 1984).

Chapter 19

Two Philosophers Skeptical of Negative Liberty

> On pain of living a life that's seriously immoral, a typical well-off person, like you and me, *must* give away most of her financially valuable assets, and much of her income, directing the funds to lessen efficiently the serious suffering of others.[1]
>
> Peter Unger

In this chapter I am going to discuss two very prominent political philosophers who have chimed in powerfully on contemporary discussions of classical liberalism. One of them is Amartya Sen, who is a Nobel Prize winner in economics but also is a very active philosopher. He is currently at Harvard University but used to be the Master of Trinity College at Cambridge University in England.[2]

Sen is a very respectful critic of classical liberalism, not one who just brushes it off or treats it disdainfully. He taught at Harvard University when the late Robert Nozick was teaching there, and they co-taught a course for six years. When Nozick died, Sen gave a eulogy at his funeral.

The other philosopher is Martha Nussbaum, member of both the law and philosophy faculties of the University of Chicago and a prolific author of books in ethics and political theory, as well as an active public policy advocate on the international front, championing mainly women's and egalitarian causes.

As for Sen, he is prominent in the area of developmental economics as well as in his critique of neoclassical approaches to values. His most recently published book, *Rationality and Freedom* (2002),[3] contains quite a few of his powerful criticisms of market economics. He was very respectful of Peter Bauer and they often agreed on what developing countries need in order to emerge out of their underdeveloped state.

Sen is what may be called a meta-economist; someone very concerned with the underlying assumptions of the discipline. For example, he has advanced an interesting critique of the tendency on the part of many economists to write off all values as preferences. He argues that there are various ways in which the word 'preference' can be used, not merely the one many economists focus on. His ideas in this and other areas are very challenging.

In particular, however, when it comes to the concept of freedom – political-economic freedom – Sen deploys both a version of the positive freedom theory

– namely, freedom as 'freedom to,' meaning being free to attain certain ends by virtue of having the resources to do so – as well as the idea of freedom found in classical liberalism, that dubbed 'negative liberty' – which means being free from coercion by others. Indeed, somewhat problematically, he often lumps these two senses of 'freedom' together without alerting us to which he has in mind. This may be due, in part, to his stress on the form of negative liberty that leaves people free, *via* the democratic process, to enact public policy measures that secure positive freedom. Yet Sen is quite explicit in rejecting libertarianism and its conception of freedom. 'In terms of its informational basis, libertarianism as an approach is just too limited … it also neglects the most basic freedoms that we have reason to treasure and demand.'[4]

What basic freedoms does Sen have in mind? Those that are made possible by confiscating resources from those who own them and providing them to those who lack them but could make very good use of them. The example that is perhaps most pertinent is what is provided by way of Good Samaritan Laws – for example, medical assistance to an injured person whose freedom of movement, of getting ahead in life, is seriously impeded by way of some accident or mishap and who would lack the capability to carry on a normal life. Similar, more massive, examples that Sen focuses upon include famines, disasters, poverty, and lack of employment. The freedom involved is what has been dubbed 'positive freedom' and it involves a demand, as Sen recognizes, on the resources, labor and talents of others whether or not they choose to provide them.

One thing we discuss in political theory is just what kind of freedoms there are. In the last fifty years or so (but starting much earlier with such writers as Thomas Hill Green), there has been a discussion as to whether freedom is best understood as a condition of not being interfered with or rather as a power to achieve something. Is it *freedom from* other people's interference or is it *freedom to* achieve a certain goal?

Many people who support the welfare state, or the larger than classical liberal role for the legal system and government, tend to accept the notion of *freedom to* as an enabling condition due to someone from others and to be secured by government. So that those, for example, who are poor (although nobody is interfering with them or contributing to their poverty by limiting their negative liberty *via* trade restrictions or property rights violations) and, therefore, unable to achieve certain goals it is deemed by many that they ought to be able to achieve, are not free in this positive sense of the term. Even though no one is preventing you from flying to Russia, if you can't afford to fly to Russia but it would be good for you to fly there, then you are not free to fly to Russia and those who might enable you to do so are deemed to be depriving you of your freedom. More pertinently, even though no one has deprived you of economic liberties – for example, to produce goods and services, to enter into contracts with others – the valuable goal you might pursue of obtaining health care or old age retirement is unavailable to you, thus limiting your freedom to flourish in your life.

This sense of freedom is very often deployed by people within the modern liberal political tradition. Yet many of them have some affinity with the classical liberal school but they believe that classical liberals unjustifiably and thus unwisely neglect this important kind of freedom. They hold that this freedom is required in society – the freedom to achieve various goals that are good for people, such as education, health insurance, or social security. Some even argue that unless classical liberals acknowledge that at least the poor and deprived have a right to such positive liberty, their own theory of individual negative rights is incomplete. For example, University of Notre Dame philosophy professor James P. Sterba argues that for those entirely unable to act to advance themselves while enjoying their negative right to freedom that right is utterly meaningless – it cannot, thus, be reasonable for them to abstain from some violations of other's rights to such negative liberty, especially property rights. And they believe that once it is accepted that a government ought to protect our positive freedom or liberty, room will need to be made for a lot more interventionist public policy such as wealth redistribution and economic regulation that most classical liberals would favor.

Why does Sen think that this freedom is equally important – if not even more so – as the negative freedom requiring that people not intrude on one another? Part of the reason is the underlying conception of human nature. What that conception is makes a big difference to the sort of freedom one will champion. If one believes that, as a rule or for the most part, human beings who are not being interfered with by others have the capacity (with some help from intimates, of course) to secure for themselves what they need so as to flourish in their lives, then one is going to emphasize being *free from* interference because the central condition that an adult needs to flourish is not to be oppressed by other persons – that is to say, not to have others constrain them. In short, human beings in society require, first and foremost, their sovereignty.

Once oppression stops, normal adults can get innumerable tasks accomplished, various goals achieved – maybe not all at once, not all equally effectively, but nonetheless with considerable promise. The major obstacle to our advancing in life, based on this idea of human nature, is other peoples' interference (as identified by a theory of rights violation or freedom abridgement). Once that is fended off, prohibited, or penalized by law, people will have the chance to exercise their initiative – their capacity to make the necessary moves to improve upon their lives – and flourish in life. Thus they don't need to have others conscripted to serve them – they will find mutually acceptable ways to attain their peaceful goals.

That, certainly, is the main theme of classical liberalism, with some variations on the specifics depending on which classical liberal is talking. Having barred coercion or initiated force, the human potential to get things done successfully is unleashed; therefore, the idea that people ought to be forced to support each other is opposed and taken as the main impediment to their flourishing in their community existence. Of course, even for classical liberals, there are some exceptional cases where people are incapacitated or in a state of emergency such that they will probably need help, but the classical liberal, who champions freedom from interference, tends to maintain that even in those emergency cases free men and women will come to the assistance of those in need. There, in short, will be voluntary organizations, service groups and so on, so there is no need or justification to get government to meddle in these affairs – society is enough, politics is not necessary, to cope with exceptional cases or emergencies.

Those, however, who believe that human beings are ill-equipped to get ahead on their own – that they are either too ignorant, too weak, too poor, or in some other way deficient to pursue a fruitful life – will hold that being free from interference by others is not enough for human flourishing. Sen is amongst those. When he uses the words 'development as freedom' – for example, in the title of one of his most prominent books – the word 'freedom' there means not just the classical liberal freedom of not interfering with people, but it means a condition of being enabled by the legal order – first *via* the negative right to freedom to vote and then the positive right to wealth redistribution – to escape their poverty, ignorance, or sickness, and to move ahead *via* such support from others. To make this possible, it is necessary to conscript others who are already well enough enabled to do work for those in need, *ergo* extensive systems of confiscatory taxation in systems of justice that characterize the welfare state or democratic socialism. Those so conscripted may not want to contribute to this goal; they may want to do something else – either productive or wasteful – with their lives. But it is taken to be a matter of justice that they must be made to yield to the conscription and expropriation that is required to secure these benefits for the needful.[5]

The matter may be discussed in terms of either freedom or rights. So there are then positive and negative freedom or rights advocates. The classical liberals tend to embrace the notion of negative freedom or rights whereas welfare statists and socialists are more sympathetic to the positive freedom or rights position. The idea for classical liberalism in either cases is that no one is justified to intrude on the lives, liberties and property of anyone else who hasn't given permission for this to happen, which implies that there is a prohibition against others entering one's sphere without one's permission. (The exact specifications of such a sphere are to be established by various ethical and legal proceedings.)

On the other hand, those who accept the notion of positive freedom or rights – or the right to capability – tend to think that everyone in need must be provided by those able to do so with goods and services. That is to say, just for being a human being, especially in modern societies, one who is deprived is entitled to other people's support, especially when one lacks such support relying only on one's efforts and those who would voluntarily help out. In other words, if unable to support oneself, that *ipso facto* imposes a duty on capable others to provide the support.

That is the positive freedom or rights thesis, and that's where we get the notion that in a modern welfare state one has many entitlements to such things as social security, education, a minimum wage, health insurance, prescription drug benefits and the rest. In order to secure these entitlements – in order to get one's freedom or rights to these protected – the government may tax those already sufficiently well off and make sure that those in need are supplied with support.

Again, when discussed in terms of rights, there is an assumption underlying the negative rights position that as long as someone's negative rights are respected or protected – that is, one's right to liberty, property, freedom of religion, freedom of speech – one is going to be able to cope and flourish in one's life (perhaps with a little help from one's friends or various voluntary agencies). This is because the only thing that significantly impedes the governing of one's life – that is, one's sovereignty – is other people intruding on it. Here, too, exceptions are by no means denied but voluntary assistance is deemed by champions of negative rights to bail out those in special need or facing emergency situations. The best solution to lacking what one needs is to go to work and produce what will alleviate it. If one hasn't got a job, one is supposed to find one in the marketplace where many offers of employment are anticipated. If one lacks an education, one is supposed to get one or rely on one's guardians or parents to provide it since they have taken on this responsibility, not one's neighbors or fellow citizens.

Again, the classical liberal, libertarian idea is that young human beings are quite capable of growing up with the support of those who thoughtfully invited them into their lives – parents, guardians, and so on – and they will eventually be able to supply themselves with whatever satisfies these needs. And those in desperate straits will find support without having to violate the negative rights of anyone.

Some people are obviously more adept at coping with this task of self-development and with obtaining voluntary support from others and some are even luckier because their parents are richer or they are prettier or healthier or whatever than are others. The idea of human nature underlying negative rights, as with the idea of negative freedom, is that, providing one isn't interfered with by others who have the choice to abstain from such interference, one is going to be more or less able to secure for oneself what is necessary for a reasonably prosperous, healthy, flourishing life.

In contrast, the positive rights – just as the positive freedom – view tends to be supported by a passive conception of human nature. People are rather inert and helpless, even when nobody is intruding on them and nobody bothers them. They will basically remain poor even if the obstacles others' intrusiveness creates for them are removed – for instance, slavery is abolished, conscription is banned, criminal interferences of all kinds are stopped, and the confiscation of the fruits of their labor and luck is stopped. Despite all this, the positive rights position assumes they will probably not escape poverty, ignorance, social insecurity and so forth. (Harvard University's John Rawls, the twentieth century's most prominent political philosopher held to such a passive view of human nature, arguing that we are molded to be who we are, including the virtues or character traits we will possess. He was reputed to be in agreement with the behaviorist conception of human nature advocated by his colleague B. F. Skinner.)

This position sees human beings not so much as active, creative, productive, self-motivated and forward-moving but as nearly fixed in a certain state or circumstance and moved only by prompters from their environment. So unless others are forced to support them, which is to say, to provide them with necessary goods and services, they will most likely remain where they are, that is, undeveloped economically, psychologically, educationally, and any other way pertinent to human flourishing.

Oddly enough, in the history of the thinking about human nature there are certain classical liberal views concerning that concept which support the positive freedom or rights position. Many classical liberals with a scientific bent of mind – which to quite a few has meant a classical mechanistic or reductive materialist viewpoint – reject the idea of free will, for example. They embrace the idea that people are complex objects being moved by various factors in their environment or genetic make-up. Only if those factors are there will they be moving forward. On their own, they are not able to do that because there is no room for initiative in their metaphysics or scientific outlook. (It is for this reason, mainly, that the concept of entrepreneurship, which presupposes the capacity for taking the initiative in economic problem solving, is difficult to make room for in neoclassical theory. This is also where the Austrian School seems closer to the more humanistic rather than the scientistic tradition of social science.)

A good many people of the modern age have this view of human beings – that we are only moving because we are being moved – on our own, we would remain static, we would not make any progress. This clearly comes from classical mechanics, where any object's motion is a matter of momentum or being moved by something else. For many classical liberals with this scientistic bent of mind, then, the notion was that everything naturally moves forward, so what is needed is the removal of obstacles, including government interference and regulation.

But others took a different approach. For them the idea was that the state needs to spur people into action because otherwise people will languish inertly. We lack personal initiative or the freedom of will to get things moving on our own. This second idea of the conception of inert human nature tends to support the positive rights and positive freedom idea, whereby what is important politically is to arrange things in such a way that people are given support because without it they are not going to make progress or flourish. It is this that lies behind much of the thinking that we find in, say, John Maynard Keynes when he admonishes government to stimulate employment. Yet it is also part of supply-side thinking, which focuses on stimulating production!

So for the issue of whether there is to be a genuine, *bona fide* free society and marketplace, the decisive issue is, 'What conception of human nature is actually right?' Are we self-movers, self-governors, and sovereign beings to at least a substantial enough degree that we can thrive in peace? Is our freedom *from* oppression sufficient enough to achieve a progressive forward-moving economic system? Or do we need aggressive support from above?

Now a paradox of the latter idea is that if we do need this support because people lack initiative, how do people administering public policies – that is, those in government – possess it in sufficient measure that they can change things for the rest of us? That's always an interesting question. Why are people who move into a bureaucratic office suddenly enabled to make all kinds of moves in society that are progressive, helpful, proactive and creative while those whom they are serving in society are not?

There's another source of the positive freedom or rights thesis, more of a moral position than one about human nature. This is that we all belong together, form a kind of team – what according to Marx appears as the specie-being thesis. This is the view of society as a family, clan, or tribe. Like a team, if a member isn't quite up to snuff, other members need to pitch in, even come to this member's assistance to enable the person to resume a productive role within the group. If there is someone in the family who is not proficient at self-help or self-government, the morality of familial relations requires that other members of the family pitch in.

Many people who support the welfare state believe that we ought to look at society like this, that we are all together in the same boat and if somebody is in need of certain support, it is not just a matter of generosity, charity, or compassion to help them but of a legally enforceable obligation. In this framework one isn't really being oppressed when forced to provide for somebody. Instead one's debts are being collected – *via* taxes and such – so the needy in the tribe or clan can be supported. Anyone refusing to provide that support is simply to be made to do the duty he or she owes (as a matter of social contract or natural obligation).

A lot of people have a frankly collectivist view of society, whereby individuals are not deemed to be sovereign – rulers of their own lives – but are natural team members. Not only Karl Marx but also his French near-contemporary, Auguste Comte, embraced this idea, as do such neo-Marxists as Charles Taylor. Communitarians tend not to be completely clear on this but judging by their frequent denunciation of individualism, their caricature of it as 'atomistic,' they too may be included among those who hold at least a moderate collectivist position and posit enforceable obligations we owe to the group to which we 'belong.' They hold that our legal obligations extend to everybody on the same team.

The question is, 'Is this outlook correct? Is it sound?' If it is, the positive liberty or rights position gains considerable support.

Sen seems to think it is – at least, to a significant extent. The freedom he believes is needed for development includes the positive type, whereby the successful members of society may be compelled to do service for the less than successful ones even though they have done nothing to make the latter badly off. By this stance, we are all in the same boat; and so when people need help, the rest have a legal obligation to help. The needy are due this help, and those able to provide it may be forced by legal authorities to do so even when they have goals of their own that don't coincide with this. But their own 'egoistic' or 'individualistic' goals are not as important as their 'cooperative' obligations, given the underlying idea of human social relations. Here is the source, also, of the incessant concern with fairness or impartiality, as if society were the family dinner table at which the primary moral issue is to treat every member with equal concern. (A very good example of thinking along these lines may be found in Ronald Dworkin, *Sovereign Virtue*.[6])

Many embrace some version of this view – it is very prominent and it flies squarely in the face of the classical liberal idea of a just polity, wherein one is one's own master and has the right to decide what to do, for better or for worse, even if considerable inequality in wealth and other values results from this regime of free choice. (The late Robert Nozick made the point emphatically, in his process theory of justice which he placed in opposition to John Rawls' end-state theory which stressed the importance of 'justice as fairness.') In the classical liberal regime, if one does not chose to give help to needy people, one may – but need not – be stingy, greedy or otherwise morally remiss but nobody is authorized to coerce someone to do anything for anyone else. Ethical conduct has to be a matter of one's own free will.

The classical liberal position, of course, includes a kind of moral individualism – where even though it is recognized that individuals often have moral responsibility to others, those have to be carried out voluntarily. If you carry out an obligation to help somebody because somebody else makes you help the other person, that doesn't make you a good human being; it doesn't make you generous or charitable nor does it render your conduct morally proper. Basically if that is how it transpired that you behaved generously or charitably, you did this because you were afraid to go to jail and so you complied with the order to come up with the required support. This means, within the classical liberal tradition – especially its normative version – that one's moral nature is now being impeded because one is not free to make choices – you are not accorded the right of freedom of choice as a moral agent must be. (This idea comes through most clearly in Kant's motto that 'ought' implies 'can.')

Sen, to a significant degree, and those even more egalitarian who share his views, deny all this; we don't have a right to our lives, at least not an unalienable right that authorizes us to fend off those who would conscript our labor and confiscate our property so as to feed the needy (and fund all those who administer the redistribution that this policy entails). Our lives belong to a considerable extent to society, race, clan, tribe, nation or humanity. He testifies to this in several of his works but perhaps most influentially in his discussion of famines and how mere negative individual rights – to liberty, private property and so forth – fails to serve those most in need under such dire circumstances.[7] His discussion is extensive but boils down to the lament that when there is extensive demand for food, even if it is in plentiful supply, its price will rise and those in the greatest need won't be able to afford it. *Ergo*, governments must regulate the price, prevent gouging, protect the right to capability.

A very good example of someone who fully embraces the idea of enforceable obligation to others, mentioned earlier in this work, is Comte, the 'Father of Sociology.' Comte was going to reform religion to base it on a secular rather than a supernatural foundation without losing its moral substance that we are obligated to serve others or society (because throughout we have been bequeathed all these values). So when we come into this world, we are already obligated to everybody to repay a great debt (never mind that debts are owed to those who provide others with goods which others willingly accept on specific terms). By Comte's light we do not have the freedom of choice according to this view but are, instead, indebted in such a way that legal authority is authorized to extract payment. As Comte has it, the moment we are born we are burdened with these obligations that can be imposed on us by law. That is another way to support the welfare state.

> Everything we have belongs then to Humanity… Positivism never admits anything but duties, of all to all. For its social point of view cannot tolerate the notion of *right*, constantly based on individualism. We are born loaded with obligations of every kind, to our predecessors, to our successors, to our contemporaries. Later they only grow or accumulate before we can return any service. On what human foundation then could rest the idea of right, which in reason should imply some previous efficiency? Whatever may be our efforts, the longest life well employed will never enable us to pay back but an imperceptible part of what we have received. And yet it would only be after a complete return that we should be justly authorized to require reciprocity for the new services. All human rights then are as absurd as they are immoral. This ['to live for others'], the definitive formula of human morality, gives a direct sanction exclusively to our instincts of benevolence, the common source of happiness and duty. [Man must serve] Humanity, whose we are entirely.[8]

Sen seems to accept this at least part of the way, although he is ambivalent because he also favors a substantial role for free-market solutions to problems. And he is also far more of an individualist, insisting that men and women require room to govern their own lives. (Sen's work on the issue of ethnic identity versus rational choice – regarding *who* any person really is – is very supportive of a classical liberal point of view.[9]) Yet, when certain types of needs arise, market solutions are no longer sufficient for Sen. Still, he supports, for example, liberalizing institutions, the infrastructures of various third world countries. That liberalization involves, in large measure, the classical liberal's unleashing of people's energies, thereby making countries prosperous and successful just as many classical and neoclassical, including Austrian, economists have envisioned this since and even before Adam Smith.

But it also involves making it possible for voters to support the enactment of wealth-redistribution public policies.

So Sen is one of the 'third way' thinkers, neither a socialist, nor a capitalist but in the middle, like welfare statists – or 'market socialists'. They defend a certain measure of negative freedom or rights, but they don't want too much of it; they value a certain measure of coercion – although they do not admit that this is what they value as they call it positive liberty, rights, or capability – but they don't want too much of this either. Sen is probably one of the most prominent, intelligent advocates of this position, which he has dubbed the 'capability approach' and which is now an international movement very prominent, for example, on the worldwide web.

The classical liberal's answer to that is, in essence, that trust in the government's method of solving social problems, namely, coercion, is tragically misplaced. If human beings aren't generally going to be kind, generous, and charitable of their own volition, as they are exposed to peer pressure and their own conscience, then there are scant grounds for believing that those administering governments are going to be that way. Governments are institutions administered by people subject not less but more to the temptation to skirt their moral responsibilities since they possess awesome powers with the law backing them. (Here is where the Left's refrain about the alleged power of corporations misses the point: without the backing of government, those corporations would only have economic power, which is to say, the admittedly considerable ability to promote, but always peacefully, their goods and services to sovereign consumers.)

The paradox Sen and others with faith in government's efforts to achieve a desirable distribution of benefits and burdens is that if you don't trust other people in their free market or private sector operations to do what is right – for example, to be kind, helpful, and otherwise supportive of those who are in need – why trust those in government who possess a shield against accountability for their moral failings, called 'sovereign immunity' in certain legal systems? Public choice theory goes a very long way toward demonstrating that the priorities of bureaucrats and politicians, even before entering 'public service,' quickly start centering on advancing their own special objectives. Which is quite natural, given that the system in which they serve the idea of the public interest, and thus of public service, is so bloated and confused that only special or vested interests are left to work for. The classical liberal advances, in contrast, the far more modest notion of the public interest, namely, the protection of individual negative liberty or rights for all those who are being served by a legal system. This is a genuine public interest since all citizens are benefited from such protection. As Hayek made the point,

> That freedom is the matrix required for the growth of moral values – indeed not merely one value among many but the source of all values – is almost self-evident. It is only where the individual has choice, and its inherent responsibility, that he

has occasion to affirm existing values, to contribute to their further growth, and to earn moral merit.

In particular, concerning the problem of the dire poor in, say, the circumstances of a famine, Sen seems not to be concerned about the fact that those who engage in what might be construed as gouging – or who are charging what the market will bear for the food they have available – are within their rights to do this. No enforceable obligation exists to provide food for those in dire need of it, although out of charity or generosity such food as is needed may very well be provided. That there are many in need of the food does not entitle them to it, any more than if someone needs help with some emergency in his or her home it justifies going to the neighbor with a gun to conscript the needed labor or skills. There are considerations other than need, such as personal sovereignty and autonomy, that trump any effort to extract involuntary servitude from others. Calling the provisions 'capability rights' does not disguise the fact that such capability is being obtained at the cost of violating the negative rights of those who are to provide them.

What appears to give plausibility to Sen's position, and indeed the position of those championing the welfare state be this within a country or globally, is the sentiment of sympathy and concern. But such sentiments do not establish any rights to other people's even desperately needed services.

The other thing, even more significant, that has distinguished classical liberals is that they believe human nature does not in fact support welfare statism. Human beings need mostly to be free from intrusiveness and from oppression and whatever help they require must, therefore, be obtained voluntarily. Despite the widely promulgated idea that food is more important than liberty, that coercive measures to feed them must come before the luxury of individual liberty could be afforded, unless men and women are free, they will hardly be able to produce food for themselves and their loved ones. What they produce will, instead, be confiscated and redistributed so they will generally find their work given direction by others, usually to ends that do not support their own well-being.

In a condition of freedom, when their rights are respected and protected, men and women will be able to discover how to improve their lives; even if they have a very slow start with it, even if some struggle will have to be involved, this is the most reliable way to have a society that will prosper best, one where people can have their needs best met, leave ignorance and poverty by becoming reliant on their own initiative and the initiative of their family members, neighbors, friends and those who would trade with them for mutual satisfaction (which is most likely to lead to mutual benefit). In other words, political solutions are not the answer to social problems for the classical liberal, whereas it is for the welfare statist. The two differ most decisively on their conceptions of human nature. And the argument on that issue is quite heated in our time – whether people have, for example, consumer sovereignty or can easily be made dependent upon corporate manipulators, whether they can choose to become obese or habituated to smoking or using credit cards or whether these matters are out of their control.

Let me now turn, somewhat more briefly, to another very prominent supporter of the kind of polity Sen advocates. Sen's frequent co-author and co-worker, Martha Nussbaum – co-author of some of the essays in Sen's famous book, *Rationality and Freedom*[10] – advances a defense of the welfare state on an explicitly Aristotelian basis. This is interesting for me, especially, and to some others who support classical liberal thought from a neo-Aristotelian position – say, to the late Ayn Rand and Murray N. Rothbard, to Douglas B. Rasmussen and Douglas J. Den Uyl, Fred D. Miller, Jr, and Eric Mack. These all believe, along with Aristotle – as well as Nussbaum – that there is a right and wrong way to be and act based on a proper understanding of human nature (or essence). They too hold that an objective list of human moral virtues spells out the ethics we ought to practice so as to most likely lead a successful human life.

This is not an odd view at all. Without a conception of human nature, mainly along Aristotelian lines, one cannot make out a case for a universal ethical system, based not on sectarian views but on what is accessible to all people, namely an understanding of what, in essence, we all are and what it takes to live our lives best in the most general terms. Thus many thinkers still rely on this aspect of Aristotle – updating him a little, adding some modern elements, excluding some ancient ones (for example, his elitism, his endorsement of slavery and the differential treatment of women, and so on).

So how do Nussbaum and these Aristotelian classical liberals differ? How does Nussbaum end up favoring the welfare state and egalitarianism while the others consider these unjust?

Probably the most important reason is that Nussbaum believes that Aristotle's apparent endorsement of the state's cultivation of our moral virtues – of inducing us to do the right thing – is the right way to understand politics. Aristotle is also taken to be something of a communitarian who favored the interest of the *polis* to which the interest of its citizens may be sacrificed, if need be.

Aristotle had roughly this doctrine: as people grow up, at first their parents habituate them to practice the moral virtues they will need to lead an excellent human life, one that is devoted largely to making the *polis* a success. After reaching maturity, however, the rest of society and, as most understand Aristotle, even the government, takes over this task. (There is a debate afoot as to whether Aristotle really meant for the state or members of one's community to properly carry out the 'virtue-making' policies. Fred D. Miller, Jr, has argued for the latter idea. And there is also debate about whether Aristotle saw the *polis* as having priority over the citizens who constitute it.) So Aristotle is seen by Nussbaum and by others as a supporter of the paternalistic welfare state because he has a proactive view of government as far as fostering the moral virtues of the citizenry.

One source of support for this paternalistic view of Aristotle is that he discusses the ideas of the sophist Lycophron, whose position is quoted very cryptically in the *Politics* to the effect that the proper role of government is 'a guarantee (or guarantor) of mutual rights.' Aristotle rejects this, arguing that the government – or is it the community? – must do more, not merely protect rights. This is akin to the current debate between welfare statists and classical liberals.

Nussbaum embraces the welfare statist understanding of Aristotle and even takes it quite a bit further. Based on an Aristotelian conception of human nature, she advocates a more egalitarian *world* government. This world government or global public policy agency isn't only to support moral virtue but substantially order our way of life by enforcing public policies that equalize conditions in society which are a source of acrimony, upheaval, and instability. (In this, Nussbaum is joined by such non-Aristotelian political philosophers as Peter Unger and Peter Singer.)

One matter that seriously differentiates Nussbaum from the classical liberal Aristotelians is that the latter do not believe that moral virtues may be enforced. They need to be practiced as a matter of choice, voluntarily, because they are accepted as a matter of conviction, not from fear of punishment and other coercive methods. (Recall the point above made by Hayek about negative freedom being 'the matrix required for the growth of moral values.') Yes, it is vital to be morally, ethically good but only free men and women are actually qualified to embark upon that project. Moral virtues such as generosity, moderation, prudence, and honesty are all to be practiced because one chooses to practice them, not because one is regimented to behave in line with them. (Only justice, in its political sense, may be subjected to enforcement because justice involves keeping proper borders intact between people, preserving their respective sovereignty or autonomy.)

Nussbaum's mistake, as the classical liberal sees it, involves destroying morality and demoralizing society in the haste to reach a particular state of affairs that she deems proper – economic and similar equality among people. Even if this were the highest ethical objective, it certainly may not be the highest political one. That must fall to securing everyone's right to liberty which, then, makes it possible for everyone to freely practice the moral virtues, perhaps including the measure of generosity and charity – *via* various private acts and organizational policies (giving, embarking on philanthropy and so on) – that will achieve the desired equality. But it is all compromised if people are forced to part with their labor and wealth to achieve this. Furthermore, the desired equality among them will also be seriously compromised by empowering some of them to engage in this forced collection and then redistribution of wealth. This must, as Robert Nozick showed so clearly with his famous Wilt Chamberlain example, lead to a substantial police state.[11]

I leave aside for the moment the issue of whether the egalitarian ethics of Nussbaum has merit.[12] Suffice it to say that Sen and Nussbaum are the kind of defenders of the welfare state – or more – with whom it is possible to join issue, although whether they would actually engage in the discussion with a fully open mind is difficult to tell. (It is difficult to tell who is able to do that, once they have gone through much of their lives laying out what they take to be a solid enough case for their convictions.) Still, whether addressing Sen and Nussbaum directly or only those who pay close attention to their views, classical liberals need to come to terms with both of these thinkers because they are very highly respected by the scholarly community, write with finesse as well as verve, and, correspondingly, are studied widely by the young scholars and intellectuals who are preparing to become influential in how members of society will think about ethics, politics, and public policy. Indeed, arguably these two thinkers are today the most influential in global public policy and classical liberals ignore their work to the great peril of the prospects of their own ideas and ideals.

Notes

1 Peter Unger, *Living High and Letting Die: Our Illusion of Innocence* (London: Oxford University Press, 1996).

2 I know Sen reasonably well because he was a guest lecturer at the Department of Economics of UC Santa Barbara, where I taught in the early 1980s, and we befriended each other and have stayed in touch.

3 Amartya Sen, *Rationality and Freedom* (Cambridge, MA: Belknap Press, 2002).

4 Amartya K. Sen, *Freedom as Development* (London: Oxford University Press, 1999), p. 67.

5 There are those who maintain that taxation amounts to no more than collection of payments due. Say you wish to sell antiques, so you rent space in a building owned by someone and agree that whenever you make a sale, some of what you fetch goes to the owner. Professor Craig Duncan, my co-author of *Libertarianism, For and Against* (Lanham, MD: Rowman & Littlefield, 2005), claims this is analogous to the nature of taxation. The country is like the building. 'The building's owner … charges vendors a percentage of their sales intake – say, 20 percent – as payment for the opportunity to sell from one of the building's stalls… . The owner is not stealing [the vendor's] money when he demands this sum from [the vendor].' According to Professor Duncan this is how we ought to understand taxation, not, as I argue, as extortion by some members of society (the government) of the rest who live and work there. But the analogy is a bad one. No one owns a free society. No one who lives in a free society is provided with the opportunity to strike up a deal with some owner of that society or to choose from among different owners of societies in which he or she might live and work. Instead, people would be born into a free society where others, including their parents, relatives, or guardians, own homes, places of work and so on. Other people – the government – would not have the authority to coerce them into paying them 'taxes' and to put them in jail if they refuse to pay up, with no chance of bargaining about the percentage, of whether to pay a flat fee (whether they win or lose in their various commercial endeavors), a percentage of some possible take and so forth. All of these latter options are, however, possible when an antique seller rents a stall from someone who owns a building where customers may seek out vendors. But free societies, unlike the place where an antique vendor may or may not rent a stall, are not anyone's property. Professor Duncan does, however, correctly describe societies that are not free. In a feudal system, for example, the king or tsar or other monarch owns the society. In a dictatorship the dictator is the owner. In fascist societies the leader in effect owns the

society. And in democracies that aren't governed by a constitution that protects individual rights the majority owns the society. These owners then charge a rent from those they permit to live and work on their property. That kind of system is, indeed, the natural home of the institution of taxation. Such societies are also the natural home of serfdom, where others than those who own it live and work only when permitted to do so. They have no rights other than those granted at the discretion of the owners. Both serfdom and taxation arise naturally in societies that are owned by someone. In free societies, however, no one owns the society. Individual citizens may or may not own all kinds of things in such free societies – land, apartments, family homes, farms, factories, and innumerable other items that may be found before human beings have expropriated them from the wilds or what has been produced by or traded back and forth among the free citizenry. Of course, in complex, developed free societies the citizenry will most likely have instituted a legal order or government, based on the principles of freedom – individual rights to life, liberty and property, for example. And they will probably have instituted some means by which those administering such a system will be paid for their work – user fees, shares of wealth owned, a flat sum, or something more novel and unheard of (for example, contract fees). Citizens can come together, roughly along lines of how the original American colonists came together, and establish a legal order or government that will be empowered, without violating anyone's rights, to provide for a clear definition, elaboration, and defense of everyone's rights. Then, once such a group of citizens has come together and instituted a government with just powers – powers that do not violate but protect individual rights – the proper funding of the work of such a government can be spelled out. What is crucial here is that such funding must occur voluntarily, namely, as the kind of funding that does not violate anyone's rights. Unlike the case Professor Duncan gives us, where someone has prior ownership over the various items in society that can be owned, in a free society ownership is achieved through various types of free action. This includes coming upon something unowned and appropriating it – land, trees, lakes, whatever – or being given in trade various things by others or, again, being born into the world with various assets or attributes that may well be used to create wealth through production, use or exchange. A truly free society, then, does not belong to anyone but is a region or sphere wherein individuals are free to come to own things. It is one within which those who live there are free to embark on actions that involve, among other things, the acquisition of property. That is part of being free, not being coerced by others to give up what one has peacefully acquired, not being prohibited by others from embarking on various actions, including peaceful acquisition (including production and trade).

In short, a free society is based on principles of individual rights, not on having gained permission from prior owners of the society on analogy with how a renter of a stall in an antique mall comes into possession of that stall. In free societies ownership is a right everyone has by his or her nature as a human being and it isn't granted as a privilege by a prior owner.

6 Ronald Dworkin, *Sovereign Virtue: The Theory and Practice of Equality* (Cambridge, MA: Harvard University Press, 2000).

7 Amartya Sen, *Choice, Welfare and Measurement* (Cambridge, MA: MIT Press, 1982), especially Chapter 16, 'Equality of What?'

8 Auguste Comte, *The Catechism of Positive Religion* (Clifton, NJ: Augustus M. Kelley Publ., 1973), pp. 212–30.

9 See Sen's short pamphlet, *Reason Before Identity* (London: Oxford University Press, 1999).

10 (Cambridge, MA: Harvard University Press, 2002).

11 Robert Nozick, *Anarchy, State, and Utopia* (New York: Basic Books, 1974), argued that if economic egalitarianism, *via* wealth redistribution, is a requirement of justice, then if large numbers of people pay even small amounts to someone with exceptional skills who they want to see exhibit these skills, then there would have to be frequent forcible redistribution of wealth since those with such skills would be far wealthier than others.

That, in turn, would imply a substantial police state with the powers to forcibly redistribute wealth, something that would itself be extensively un-egalitarian.

12 For more on that issue, see Tibor R. Machan and Craig Duncan, *Libertarianism, For and Against* (Lanham, MD: Rowman & Littlefield, 2005) in which I critique democratic liberalism for its elevation of fairness to the position of justice.

Chapter 20

Does Libertarianism Imply the Welfare State?

James P. Sterba contends that libertarianism, if true, would imply the welfare state – a polity markedly different from the one proposed by libertarian theorists and one that most explicitly repudiate.[1] Sterba contends that unbeknownst to themselves, various libertarians are laying out arguments that support just such a welfare state;[2] not the polity of negative individual liberty but, instead, that of substantial positive liberty.[3]

His argument, in summary, goes as follows: libertarians defend negative liberty because they claim that only if citizens possess such liberty or the right to it, can they act as *bona fide* moral agents. Yet there are many cases of individuals in society who, despite the protection of their negative liberty or the right to it, would not be capable of making significant moral choices because they are too poor to flourish, or even set out on a path of self-direction, let alone self-improvement.[4]

Sterba holds that it would be unreasonable to require the poor to sacrifice the liberty not to be interfered with when receiving the 'surplus' resources of the rich necessary to meet their basic needs. But since it would *not* be unreasonable to require the rich to sacrifice the liberty not to be interfered with when using their surplus resources for luxury purposes, the rich may be morally required to make such a sacrifice. Furthermore, what people are morally required to do is what is either reasonable to *ask* everyone affected to accept or, in the case of severe conflicts of interest, reasonable to *require* everyone affected to accept. So the right to life and property endorsed by libertarians actually support a right to welfare.[5]

In effect, Sterba asks the well-known rhetorical question: how free can someone be who has no means to exercise liberty? And if one isn't free to act, how can one be a *bona fide* moral agent? 'Ought' implies 'can,' so without that ability, there can be no moral agency. It would presumably thus be unreasonable to hold that the poor have the moral responsibility to act in such a way as to abstain from accepting the surplus wealth of the rich. And it would be equally unreasonable to hold that the rich have no moral responsibility to provide for the poor. It would be wrong to resist having their surplus wealth taken from them for the poor – for example, *via* taxes.

Sterba concludes that the libertarian must grant that at least some people in any society have a 'right to welfare,' the protection of which government is properly established to secure.

But only if there would *typically* be many poor who are innocent and also incapacitated in a libertarian community would it follow that there would be many people unable to choose any other course of action, if they are to survive, than grabbing from other people what doesn't belong to them. For if the poor got that way because of their own choices, then they didn't have to become poor. If they are not incapacitated, they have the means to flourish other than stealing the wealth of others. (Consider that even in the massive disaster such as the recent tsunami in Southeast Asia, thousands of people freely chose to help and there are many other options for the needy apart from looting and robbing those who have 'surplus' wealth.)

The libertarian argues that the right to liberty, when respected and protected will typically enable people to flourish (though it does not guarantee that they will). They can then try to do what is morally right. Thus only the right to negative individual liberty should be respected and protected; although, of course, decency should manifest on innumerable fronts. But critics, like Sterba, claim that within a libertarian system many people would simply have no chance for self-directed flourishing:

> [W]ho could deny that most of 1.2 billion people who are currently living in conditions of absolute poverty 'lack the opportunities and necessities to satisfy their basic needs?' And even within our country [USA], it is estimated that some 32 million Americans live below the official poverty index [$14,000 per annum for a family, $7,000 per annum for an individual], and that one fifth of American children are growing up in poverty. Surely, it is impossible to deny that many of these Americans also 'lack the opportunities and resources to satisfy their basic needs.'[6]

Sterba needs to argue, as he does, that in a fully libertarian system massive poverty would ensue – it would be the *typical* situation for there to be great masses of deserving poor people, ones who through no fault of their own are unable to thrive. Libertarians, not surprisingly, dispute this. They counter that the most prosperous and otherwise beneficial societies are also those that give greatest respect and protection to negative individual rights. In turn, they hold that where poverty is widespread, negative individual liberty is, in the main, left unrespected and unprotected.[7] Libertarians base their view on both economic analysis and history, including what they take to be a sound understanding of human nature (which some of them consider only implicitly). They argue that it is the protection of negative individual liberty that provides the most suitable and hospitable social climate for the creation of wealth.[8]

A libertarian does not typically claim that an hospitable climate for wealth creation *guarantees* the economic success of all; but those who are poor would have either failed of their own accord or been the few unfortunate people who are innocently incapacitated and *also* do not enjoy the benefit of the generosity, charity, and compassion of others. Those are two quite massive and historically unsupported assumptions.

In a free society, there is no reason to think that there would be many such persons, at least compared to the numbers one can expect in societies that don't protect individual rights. Thus, even the most well-known opponent of capitalism, Karl Marx, was aware that unless human nature itself changes and the 'new man' develops, socialism could do no more than to socialize poverty, that is, make everyone poor. Which is a way of conceding that the free market is indeed the best social system to generate prosperity. (And Marx was indeed clear about regarding capitalism as the most productive of such systems so far in human history.)

One reason libertarians believe this is that they recognize that the lack of firmly respected and protected private property rights creates a mammoth tragedy of the commons. Persons empowered to foist their burdens on others who have not consented to accept the burden are less likely to try to steer clear of such burdens to begin with. Those coerced to share their achievements with others are less likely to pursue such achievements in the long run. This kind of tragedy of the commons and attendant dearth of incentives to produce is rampant under socialism, with predictable and by now extensively chronicled costs in prosperity *and* freedom.[9]

No political economies other than substantially capitalist ones have fared better in reducing poverty. The few which have done well enough – for example, Singapore – do so because of the capitalist elements they permit and despite massive political and other social failures. Overtly socialist economies have seen the curtailing of civil liberties, institution of forced labor and involuntary servitude, regimentation of the bulk of social relations, arrested scientific and technological progress, censorship of the arts and other intellectual endeavors, and so on.[10]

The United States and other Western liberal capitalist societies are still the freest, with many of their legal principles giving at least considerable expression to classical liberal, near-libertarian ideas. They are, at the same time, the most generally productive (and creative, culturally rich) of all societies, with their wealth aiding in the support of hundreds of others across the globe. This, of course, is not uniformly true, so there are serious exceptions, including widespread impediments to free trade such as protectionism, favoritism and state monopolization of some economic activities.

Barring impossible-to-conduct controlled socio-political-economic experiment, such historical evidence is all we can adduce to examine which political economic system produces more prosperity. No one can seriously dispute that the systems with discernable libertarian or capitalist features have fared much better than those that veer in the direction of statism, including some of Europe's major countries.[11] But Sterba disputes it, and he has an answer to the above. In reply to another discussion of mine of this matter, he tells us that:

> Machan, seeking to undercut the practical force of my argument, has contended that when we compare economic systems to determine which produce more

> poverty, 'No one can seriously dispute that the near-libertarian systems have fared much better than those going in the opposite direction, including the welfare state.' Here one would think that Machan has the US in mind as a 'near-libertarian system' because earlier in the same paragraph he claims 'America is still the freest of societies, with many of its legal principles giving expression to classical liberal, near-libertarian ideas.' Yet apparently this is not what Machan thinks since in a footnote to the same text he says, 'It is notable that the statistics that Sterba cites … are drawn from societies, including the United States of America, which are far from libertarian in their legal construction and are far closer to the welfare state, if not to outright socialism.'
>
> Obviously, then, Machan is surprisingly unclear as to whether he wants to call the US a near-libertarian state, a welfare state or a socialist state. Yet, whichever of these designations is most appropriate, what is clear is that the poor do less well in the US than they do in the welfare liberal or socialist states of Western Europe such as Germany, Sweden, and Switzerland. For example, 22.4% of children live below the poverty line in the US as compared to 4.9% in Germany, 5% in Sweden, and 7.8% in Switzerland, and the US shares with Italy the highest infant mortality rate of the major industrialized nations. The US also ranks 67 among all nations in the percentage of national income received by the poorest 20% of its population, ranking the absolute lowest among industrialized nations. Accordingly, the success that welfare liberal and socialist states have had, especially in Western Europe, in coming close to truly meeting the basic needs of their deserving poor should give us good reason to doubt what Machan proclaims is the superior practical effectiveness of 'near-libertarian states' in dealing with poverty.[12]

Okay. I didn't make clear that the term 'near-libertarian' should be read in the context of how much further from libertarianism are such systems as those in Asia and Africa and most countries in other periods of human history. But when one draws on evidence from the United States, it is vital to keep in mind that our society is indeed a welfare state, with many watered-down libertarian legal and economic elements that contribute to what ails some people in that society. These include minimum wage laws, protectionism, price supports for and subsidies to failing firms and entire industries, welfare, foreign aid, and so forth, all dependent on that major impediment to justice, confiscatory taxation (a relic of feudal times).

Having disposed of this quibble let me address the numbers Sterba cites by calling upon the charitable and generous help of other libertarians, all of whom have read Sterba's comments. As one of them states: 'My own response would be to note, among other considerations, that Western European unemployment is routinely terribly high, which suggests that there are greater troubles there than in the United States, except perhaps in some special areas, stemming from the severe curtailment of freedom in the labor markets.'[13]

To evaluate the relationship between the protection of negative liberty – for example, property rights, religious freedom, freedom of expression – and the condition of the poor, requires special analysis. For example, what have the poor done to avoid poverty but allegedly could not do because of negative liberty; or, how many would be poor were it not for (a) protection of negative liberty or (b) protection of positive freedom (for example, taking from the rich in taxes and transferring some of the wealth to the poor – with the cost of the transfer being, of course, lost).

In international affairs, there are other matters to consider: Sweden, as well as other European countries, for example, has had a fairly robust welfare state until recently, but now is suffering from very serious economic shortfalls. Why? And when it did have a robust welfare state, did it not benefit from American military defense provisions against the USSR that it would have had to fund from taxes that were instead now available for welfare payments? And although Sweden has been a robust welfare state, it has no anti-trust laws curtailing big business, which gives it certain unfettered competitive conditions lacking in the United States that have economic consequences that make it better off. Furthermore, the explanation of the malaise Sterba documents in America is arguably something other than the semi-libertarian attributes of the US economy.

But I am not confident in any case that consequentialist arguments can decisively establish the superiority of one system over another. Indeed, because human beings are free to choose, they may do less than their best in a free society, at least some of the time. Coercive systems, in turn, may at times scare them badly enough so that they work harder – the Nazis and Fascists of Germany and Italy, and even the Soviets, proved that under a tyranny one can achieve some economic results, when all the might of the state is directed to those specific results (no matter what the costs are to the balance of economic life). But these instances hardly suffice to make them better systems than free societies in which perhaps the trains don't always run on time (at least not government-subsidized Amtrak trains).

What about the claim that 'the US shares with Italy the highest infant mortality rate of the major industrialized nations'? Libertarian scholar A. R. Rutten addresses the charge by first noting that infant mortality is the ratio of the number of children who die to the number of children who are born. Because of medical care, many of those who would die at or before birth survive in the United States. Thus, the denominator in 'infant mortality' in the US includes many children who aren't in that denominator elsewhere. However, since they are, almost by definition, high-risk babies, a lot of them end up dying soon after birth. *Voila*: higher infant mortality! (Indeed, the infant mortality rate will be higher as long as greater proportions of the 'extra' babies die than of the 'ordinary' babies. Given the problems facing them, this seems almost inevitable.)

Put another way, it is dangerous to compare these statistics across countries because they really are not measuring the same things. There are people in the US statistics who just do not make it into the statistics in other countries. Moreover, it is hard to 'correct' the data so that they do measure the same things. For instance, you don't want to compare births per pregnancy across countries, since that also includes the number of pregnancies that are aborted. And, since abortions are often in response to fears about the health of the infant, you cannot just take them out of the mix, since they include some potentially sick infants.

Sterba also contends that the poorest segment of the American population receives less of the 'national income' than the poorest segment of the population in other countries. I do not know whether this is true. If it is, part of the explanation may lie in the inability that many people in other countries encounter in attempting to rise very far above poverty – for example, in many African countries it is nearly impossible to hold on to one's wealth, given the inept and corrupt system of private property protection. It is impossible to keep track of wealth distribution. Percentages do not tell the whole story. We need to ask: percentage of *what*?

Another contributor to the discussion, Professor Stephen Cox, proposes that we consider two countries each containing a million people. In Country A, the average income is $1000 a year. The top 20 percent of the population earn an average of $2000 a year, for a total of $400 million. The middle 60 percent earn an average of $833 a year, for a total of $500 million. The lowest 20 percent earn an average of $500 a year, for a total of $100 million. So the lowest 20 percent of the population earns 10 percent of the national income of $1 billion.

In Country B, the average income is $30,000 a year. The top 20 percent of the population earns an average of $50,000 a year, for a total of $10 billion. The middle 60 percent of the population earns an average of $30,000 a year, for a total of $18 billion. The lowest 20 percent only earn an average of $10,000 a year, for a total of $2 billion. So the lowest 20 percent of the population earn 'only' 6.67 percent of the national income, which is $30 billion. Yet somehow the lowest income tier in County B is doing a lot better than the lowest tier in Country A.

Country A could be compared to Haiti while Country B could be compared to the United States. The question is, 'Which country would you rather live in, even if you were among the poorest 20 percent of the population? The one that allows you to survive more comfortably or the one that allows you to quote a more intimidating statistic?'

Moreover, chimes in Professor Jan Narveson, statistics about how many people live 'below the poverty line' are meaningless until we know what the country in question decrees to be the 'poverty line.' European countries draw these lines at more reasonable levels than we do. 'Poor' doesn't mean actual-poor in North America; it means, rather, that the official, reported family income of the individual in question falls below some percentage of the average. By such a criterion it is logically necessary that any country with any income distribution other than absolute equality would have to have a lot of 'poor' people, whatever the official percentage is decreed to be. But presumably, Sterba is interested in substance – in a family's ability to obtain 'basic needs' – things like food, transportation, as well as VCRs, multiple TV sets, air conditioners, and the other conveniences of modern life. The American poor do very well on all those fronts, and better, by far, than the poor elsewhere.

The American 'poor' (those with a family income below the officially decreed poverty line) have the highest incidence of car ownership in the world, even by comparison with the entire population of other countries, not just the 'poor' of those countries (with the single exception of Germany). They have a higher incidence of two-car ownership than any other country, including Germany. They have by far a higher incidence of indoor plumbing, water services, refrigerators, and cooking ranges than any other country in the world. Their nutritional figures don't differ significantly from those of any other 'class' in the US, including the rich. Officially poor US households, with 0.56 persons per room, were less crowded in 1987 than the average West European household in 1980. By contrast, the average Japanese household has 0.8, the average Uruguayan 2.1, the average Indian 2.8 persons per room. (Remember, again: these are comparisons between US poor and average other persons overall, not other-country 'poor'.) Nearly a third of US 'poor' had microwaves in 1987 (it's undoubtedly far more today); almost a third had two or more color TV sets. The average American poor person is more likely to own a color TV than the average person in France, West Germany, or Italy. Eighty-one percent had telephones. American poor in 1987 spent an average of 80 percent as much on food as the median American household, and 32 percent of that was spent in restaurants! The average American poor person consumes more meat than the average citizen of any other country, except perhaps Canada.

Chris Sarlo, at the end of a very careful, fair, and exhaustive study, concludes, that it is almost certain that less than 2 percent of Canada's population lives in poverty. This is taking into account the costs of balanced nutrition, housing, sanitation, transportation needs, and so on. He notes that senior couples who own their own home outright and have a family income of $14,000 are accounted 'poor' by the Canadian statistical profile, an absurdity. By world criteria, such a couple would have to be accounted comfortably off; their real income is far above the median for the world, for example. It is the same general story as in the US.[14]

When first established in the early 1960s, the US poverty income threshold for a family of four was nearly 30 times greater than the median per capita income in the entire world. The American Census Bureau's survey of consumer expenditures shows that low-income households spent $1.94 for every $1.00 in income reported to the Census. Further, the Census ignores the entire US welfare system when calculating incomes of poor Americans. Since most of those 'poor' get Food Stamps, Medicaid, and so on, this makes a huge difference. In 1987, the unreported income of the 'poor' per family ran to about $9000; adding that to their average reported incomes doubles the figures, roughly – leaving the American poor with a median income almost equal to the average income in all of Canada in that year, I believe. This is far higher than any other country in the world.[15] Thomas Sowell also points out that the American 'poor' in year x tends to contain an almost entirely different class of actual individuals than in year $x + 10$, or $x - 10$.[16]

Narveson adds that

> Jim Sterba, like most writers trying to make an issue about the condition of the 'poor,' has been taken in by the official figures, and not even by any means all of those. He does not take seriously the political interest that officials have in exaggerating reports of poverty and any other evil that politicians think they can use to sell political programs for 'rectifying' those evils to the people whose votes they seek.
>
> It can still plausibly be argued, by the way, that if there had been no American welfare system at all, the American 'poor' would still be even better off today, even in purely material terms, than they are, taking their government benefits into account.[17] The point is that there is no substance to the claim that America is a country with a vast 'poor' population.[18]

Another libertarian contributor to this discussion, Professor George Selgin, an economist, observes that even allowing that the official statistics on poverty cited by Sterba are accurate given the definitions used, one has to consider the underlying definitions before drawing any policy conclusions. For example, it is well known that official US poverty statistics define poverty in terms of monetary earnings: a family that earns less than X dollars per year is said to be below the 'poverty line.' Such a definition (which is contrary to both economic theory and common-sense notions viewing poverty as a stock concept, referring to a low level of 'wealth') is problematic in two respects. First, many individuals (retired persons especially) live on very modest annual money earnings, yet have substantial wealth, for example, they own their houses outright. Quite a few such persons are very misleadingly included among the 'poor' in official statistics.

'Income' measures of wealth also do not include real or in-kind transfer payments, for example, the value of subsidized housing, food stamps, and so on. This last fact points to an irony in conventional 'anti-poverty' measures because the state defines poverty in terms of low *monetary* earnings but addresses the poverty problem mainly through in-kind transfers. It logically follows that the 'war on poverty' can never succeed! No matter how much you subsidize housing and consumption *via* real transfers, the beneficiaries remain just as 'poor' according to official statistics. Moreover, any increase in the welfare roles represents an increase in poverty even if the persons affected consume just as much as before!

Selgin wonders: 'Could it be that welfare bureaucrats like this arrangement, which assures that there will always be a poverty problem to keep them gainfully employed?' Perhaps. But even if this cynical view isn't justified, the fact remains that official poverty statistics have to be taken with a grain of salt.

One can also, however, stipulate for the sake of argument that the numbers are true and ask whether they actually mean anything. The single greatest predictor for children living in poverty is whether they are living in a single-parent household headed by a female (which is 90 per cent of all single-parent households). The US has a significantly higher rate of single-parent households (9 percent) compared to Denmark (4 percent), Sweden (3 percent), Germany (7 percent).

There are two significant contributors to the higher rate of single parent households. One is divorce. The divorce rate per 1000 married women is 21 in the United States, compared to 11 per 1000 in Canada, 13 in Denmark, 2 in Italy, and 12 in the UK. The second contributor is the incidence of teenage motherhood, which is much higher in the US than in any European country or Canada. As to infant mortality – when you compare rates in industrialized countries it's a pretty useless statistic. The infant mortality rates in Europe, the United States, Australia, and Canada cluster between 6–8 per 1000. The rate in the US was 7.9 in 1995. It was 7.1 in Australia, 6.9 in Austria, 8.4 in Israel, 7.0 in the UK. Such infant mortality statistics need to be compared to Africa, where most rates are over 100, and to South America, where in Argentina the rate is 28.8 per 1000 and in Brazil 57.2 per thousand.

So the rates in 'Western' countries are actually quite low. Add to this the high rate of teenage pregnancy in the United States (teenage pregnancies have higher infant mortality than 20–29 year old pregnancies) and the US rate looks quite good. Then add the fact that, as discussed earlier in this paper, in this country a baby born at 26 weeks will be treated as a 'live-born' infant. Most countries don't even attempt to treat infants with that degree of prematurity. So infant mortality, which seems like a simple statistic, is in fact rather complex. Unless one compares similar populations – age, income, prematurity – one is comparing apples to oranges.

We must also consider the fact that in most European countries the 'basics' cost a lot more than they do in the United States. Elsewhere, things like food and clothing are more expensive and require a greater fraction of income to buy. As reported by professor Eleftheria Maratos-Flier, of Harvard's Medical School,

> Worldwide, Americans spend the lowest percentage of total private income on food – 8.3 percent compared to 15 percent in Denmark, 16.3 percent in France, or 19 percent in Switzerland. The amount of time it takes to buy a 'standard meal' is 2:35 hours in Washington DC, compared to 5:20 in Paris, 3:52 in London or 4:42 in Rome. So maybe these countries re-distribute income 'better.' But if it takes more income to buy necessities the redistribution may not be all that helpful.

Professor Randy Holcombe, an economist, notes that yet another little factor to consider is that the United States is a large and heterogeneous country being compared to smaller and more homogeneous countries. Income inequality is greater in Europe overall, for example, than it is in Germany, Switzerland, Italy, or any other individual nation. Conversely, there is less income inequality in California, Ohio, Mississippi, or Arkansas, than there is in the United States as a whole. When the poverty line is drawn by comparing those at the bottom end of the income distribution to the rest of the distribution, larger and more heterogeneous populations will have more apparent poverty simply because of the way the statistics are compiled.

It does not appear, then, that Sterba has used his statistics very wisely, certainly not with sufficient refinement to make a convincing case for the position that countries with greater government welfare services than what is available in the United States of America have thereby attained a better standard of living, especially for those whom Sterba calls their poor. Indeed, his unwarranted assertion defies common sense. The number of people attempting to gain entry into the United States continues to be considerably higher than those aiming to emigrate to other societies. *They* know where the money and opportunities are.

There is another point to be stressed, though, which is that in a libertarian society – indeed, in any society – for some people being relatively poor may not be that big a liability. Not everyone wants to, or even ought to, live prosperously.[19] For some individuals, a life of comparative poverty could be of substantial benefit. Contenders would-be monks, hobos, 'starving artists' and the like, who despite the protection of their negative liberty do not seek economic prosperity, at least not in preference to other important objectives. Among the citizens of a libertarian society, then, we may find some who are poor but who are not, from their own perspective therefore, worse off than the rich. This is not hard to understand provided we do not regard economic prosperity as the sole index of well-being.

At one point Sterba suggests that libertarians may not care sufficiently for the poor because they do not see the need to affirm as a principle of justice the right to welfare. As he puts it: 'Machan seems reluctant to take the steps required to secure the basic needs of the poor.' He then asks, somewhat puzzled, 'Why then does he balk at taking any further steps? Could it be that he does not see the oppression of the poor as truly oppressive after all?'[20] Although Sterba's question is confusing, it may be worth addressing the point he seems to be driving at.

Libertarians are certain not theoretically required to be callous or uncaring where the cultivation of care is warranted, although libertarianism, as has been stressed throughout this book, is concerned with political issues not with every challenge life has to offer. As human beings libertarians may well be every bit as much and even more committed to generosity and charity than are others, especially those who wish to leave these matters to public policy and thus distance themselves from personal involvement and effort. Compassion *via* the government is not true compassion but via coercion.[21]

But it is true enough, as many libertarians would contend, that being poor in and of itself does not necessarily warrant being cared for, just as being sick in and of itself does not warrant being cared for – especially if the sickness is the result of self-abuse, gross negligence, or is the condition brought about by the actions of a thoroughly evil person. Moreover, suppose there are other tasks someone ought to pursue rather than help those in need? A good bit of humanity, for example, is occupied with scholarship, science, child-raising, education, and the arts, rather than the tasks that people like Mother Teresa take up as their full-time concern. Unless a strict code of altruism is the right ethics by which we ought to live, compassion is not an all-consuming virtue displacing every other consideration of life.

In short, being poor in and of itself does not justify special consideration.[22] Being in need of what it takes to attain one's well-being can warrant generosity and charity from others, if the need is a matter of natural misfortune or injury from others. But poverty does not always constitute such neediness. Justice requires that we examine individual cases, not merely mandate a blanket response to an undifferentiated class of persons, 'the poor,' among whom individual circumstances may vary greatly.

Sterba may also underestimate what Marxists might call the objective generosity or charity of libertarians. If one considers just how much greater the long-range prospects for economic well-being are for everyone within a libertarian political economy, the libertarian could well be regarded as the political theorist with the greatest concern for the poor (as measured by the actual consequences of his doctrine). It is more benevolent to treat people as if they are capable of attaining prosperity than to treat them as if they are inherently inept at it; more benevolent to foster institutional conditions in which they will be much better off than they would be in any dependency-encouraging welfare state.[23]

James Sterba has not shown that libertarianism implies the welfare state. He has failed to appreciate the analytical and historical context within which libertarianism is argued. He has also failed to appreciate that although in some cases a person might not be morally required to respect the rights of others – for example, in a rare case of helpless destitution, one could forgive a desperate person for stealing an apple off the fruit stand – nothing follows from the exigencies of such life-and-death circumstances regarding the rights that everyone in society has by virtue of being a human individual living in a community of other human individuals. As Den Uyl and Rasmussen so carefully argue, the polity of negative individual rights is a meta-normative system or, in other words, a political framework, within which human beings normally would and should pursue their highly varied flourishing.[24] It does not function to solve all human problems, not even moral ones. It is flaw of much utopian thinking, as Plato appears to have taught, to expect politics to provide solutions to the challenges of human living.[25]

We all face many problems, *vis-à-vis* our health, economic solvency, educational development, romantic aspirations, artistic fulfillment, scientific progress, recreation and so forth. Life is in part a struggle. These specific problems cannot and should not be addressed by legal coercion however urgent they may seem and however tempting it may be to use the force of the state to solve them. The law employs the concept of 'unnecessary force' to indicate when police officers sacrifice due process out of urgency or over-enthusiasm. Political theory, too, needs to acknowledge and work to combat this temptation. The few emergency circumstances in which we do not find the conditions. To quote Locke, 'where peace is possible'[26] – and in which there may thus be a moral requirement to disregard the negative rights of others – do not justify systematic abrogation of the system of justice that does, in fact, best suit human beings in their communities.

In response to some of what I have written on these matters, Sterba has claimed that I do indeed accept the 'theoretical thrust' of his 'argument that a libertarian ideal of liberty leads to a right to welfare.'[27] This is wrong. What I have argued for, quite independently of anything Sterba has said on the subject,[28] is only that there are rare cases in which some innocent person who is in dire straits may properly disregard individual rights to property. Such a person on rare occasions may be justified in taking from another what he or she needs if that is the only way to survive at all.

Following the work of John Stuart Mill, Ayn Rand[29] and Eric Mack,[30] I have argued that when conditions make the respect and protection of rights impossible, morality can require one to disregard rights.[31] Rights are not ethical primaries. They are based on more fundamental moral principles. In my view, classical egoist ethics is sound and gives rise to individual rights to life, liberty and property. But when community life – peace – is impossible, then emergency social ethics come into play.[32]

This idea is not novel. Mill, for example, argued that a person's liberty may be disregarded on rare occasions, as when he or she is about to step, unknowingly, on a collapsing bridge. Common sense also attests to this – it may be proper to restrain someone who is hysterical so as to prevent his harming himself or doing other wild things.

But none of this constitutes *carte blanche* for violating rights or for so-called welfare rights. As the saying goes: hard cases make bad law. A society would not be just for incorporating the ethics of emergency into its legal system. And the circumstances in which last-ditch courses of action are adopted should be those in which truly no other alternative – say, offering something in trade or simply asking for help – can serve to fill the need.[33]

In a free society in which property rights and other individual rights are protected in principle, such alternatives expand and proliferate. In unhampered markets, entrepreneurs find new, better and cheaper ways to empower people all the time, and certainly those with the most limited resources or capacities are among the chief beneficiaries of such innovation. If shut-ins who ten years ago had great trouble earning a living can now pay their bills thanks to PCs, PayPal and eBay, that is no thanks to welfare-state-enabled violence against the rights of others; it's thanks to markets and the rights-protecting institutions of the free society that foster and reward the innovation and production of others.

It is true enough that if the world were such that the respect and protection of individual rights engendered general unhappiness, including poverty, then libertarianism would be kaput. It is also true enough that if pigs had wings, perhaps they could fly. But such assertions are no proof that we live in a world in which pigs can fly and libertarianism is wrong.

Furthermore, if, conceivably, libertarianism were wrong, it does not follow that the welfare state would be right. The right to welfare is in effect a right to involuntary servitude from other persons. Even if people are in dire straits, let us say in deadly straits, it does not follow that they acquire rights to the lives and labors of other persons – to enslave others. This is so even if the lives and labors in question are rich ones – constituting what Sterba likes to call 'surplus wealth,' an undefined term if ever there was one.[34]

It seems to me that the welfare state – indeed, the claim that people have a right to welfare (that is, provisions from others who do not choose to offer them) – needs a defense that does not piggyback on the theories of socialism, feminism, libertarianism or any other position in political theory. This effort to derive welfarism from other systems is, as far as I can discern, a dead end. That is not to say, however, that a concern with how unfortunate but decent people might fare in a free society is misguided. It is vital that both the rights of individuals to make their own significant choices in life and their prospects for prosperity and happiness be addressed in a detailed political treatise.[35]

Notes

1 The one exception might be Jeffrey Friedman, the editor of *Critical Review* who embraces what he calls 'post-libertarianism,' an uneasy hybrid of libertarianism and the welfare state intimating that political ideas need to be defended on purely consequentialist grounds and that sometimes the protection of the right to individual liberty may not yield the best possible consequences for society.

2 Eric Mack has presented his views in various papers and collections of essays (for example, in Tibor R. Machan, ed., *The Libertarian Alternative* [Chicago, IL: Nelson-Hall, 1973], *The Libertarian Reader* [Lanham, MD: Rowman & Littlefield, 1982], and Tibor R. Machan and Douglas B. Rasmussen, eds, *Liberty for the 21st Century, New Essays in Libertarian Thought* [Lanham, MD: Rowman & Littlefield, 1995]); Rasmussen and Den Uyl present their position in *Liberty and Nature, An Aristotelian Defense of Liberal Order* (LaSalle, IL: Open Court Publ., 1990); my own case is to be found in *Human Rights and Human Liberties* (Chicago, IL: Nelson-Hall, 1975); *Individuals and Their Rights* (Chicago, IL: Open Court Publishing Co., 1989); *Capitalism and Individualism* (New York: St. Martin's Press, 1990) and *Private Rights, Public Illusions* (New Brunswick, NJ: Transaction Books, 1995); Jan Narveson lays out his arguments in *The Libertarian Idea* (Philadelphia, PA: Temple University Press, 1991). And Robert Nozick explains his (later modified or amended) reasons for libertarianism in *Anarchy, State, and Utopia* (New York: Basic Books, 1974).

3 Sterba has advanced his views in many forums, including his introduction to a book he edited, *Justice: Alternative Perspectives* (Belmont, CA: Wadsworth Publ. Co., 1991); several papers for scholarly journals such as *The Journal of Social Philosophy*, *Social Theory and Practice* and *Ethics*; his contribution to the volume he organized, *Morality and Social Justice* (Lanham, MD: Rowman & Littlefield, 1995); another volume he edited, *Social and Political Philosophy* (Belmont, CA: Wadsworth Publishing Co., 1995); and his single author volume on political philosophy, *Contemporary Political and Social Philosophy* (Belmont, CA: Wadsworth Publishing Co., 1995). Some of these discussions are repeated nearly verbatim, although when others respond Sterba attempts to address the new or reiterated twists in their arguments.

4 In many of his essays, some of which included responses to my criticism of his earlier rendition of his thesis, Sterba makes ambiguous use of the concept of 'liberty.' For example, he says in one: 'My contention is that in such situations [where negative rights cannot be secured because, to quote H. L. A. Hart's paraphrasing of John Locke, it is not a situation "where peace is possible"] the liberty of the poor has moral priority over the liberty of the rich despite the fact that the rich usually have the power to enforce a resolution favoring themselves.' James P. Sterba, 'A Brief reply to Three Commentators,' in Christopher Gray, ed., *Philosophical Reflections on the United States Constitution* (Lewiston, NY: The Edwin Mellen Press, 1989), p. 197. Is this negative or positive liberty? It seems to be positive liberty in the case of the poor, negative liberty in the case of the rich. The poor have negative liberty in that no one is preventing them from pursuing their ends – this is done through their unfortunate circumstances (poverty, illness, ignorance, and so on). What they lack is positive liberty – that is, being enabled to do what they want or ought to. Yet Sterba seems oblivious to this ambiguity, making it appear that the liberty the poor lack is the sort that he favors violating when it comes to the rich. Indeed, Sterba's focus should be on whether the rich really own what they are said to have property rights to, not on liberty at all. He seems to believe that when some lack what they (really badly) need, they mysteriously come to own what others have but do not (really badly) need.

5 James P. Sterba, 'Reconciling Conceptions of Justice,' in Sterba, *Morality and Social Justice*, pp. 7–10.

6 Sterba, *Morality and Social Justice*, p. 15. There is little discussion in Sterba's work of why people are poor or otherwise experience circumstances that afford them little or no opportunities for flourishing. Many libertarians would agree that many who face such circumstances make significant contribution to their plight; certainly in societies where opportunities and resources are generally abundant. Of course, libertarians draw a sharp distinction between those who are in dire straits through no fault of their own, and those who fail to act in responsible and possible ways that could extricate them from their adverse living conditions. In the philosophical literature that draws on the legacy of Marx and Engels and their followers, this distinction is not easy to make, since in this tradition human behavior is taken to be *determined* by a person's economic circumstances, into which persons are simply deterministically deposited. So one is bound by one's situation and cannot make choices that would overcome them. More generally, in modern political philosophy there has been a strong tendency to view human beings as passive, unable to initiate their own conduct, moved by innate drives or environmental stimuli. Thus those who are well off could not have achieved this of their own initiative, nor could those who are badly off have failed in significant ways. Accordingly, all of the poor or badly off, be they victims of others' oppression, casualties of misfortune or products of their own misconduct, are regarded alike. It is not clear how much Sterba's reasoning may be under the influence of these considerations. But he appears to view life as largely a zero-sum game.

7 As to many of Sterba's allegations about the situation in the United States of America, see W. Michael Cox and Richard Alm, *Myths of Rich and Poor* (New York: Basic Books, 1999). These allegations, that innocent poor people in America are going hungry and cannot meet their basic needs, give intuitive support to Sterba's position that a largely capitalist society – what I have called a 'near-libertarian' system – is not prosperous enough to be considered healthy or beneficial to people. Of course, that, even if true, would not defeat libertarianism. Comparative analyses would be necessary and even those are not decisive.

Suppose that some systems lacking the respect for and protection of individual liberty flourish in certain respects (Mussolini makes the trains run on time, Hitler builds fabulous Autobahns, no one goes completely hungry in Cuba or some such thing). It could still be the case that the presence of respect for and protection of individual liberty is indispensable to justice, even more so than the production of health and welfare.

8 Here most libertarians would invoke views drawn from philosophies of human nature, action theory, motivational psychology, and so on. In the main, libertarians embrace the

position that when human beings are not being subjugated, they tend to work toward their improvement, regardless of where they are on the continuum between destitution and abundance. Libertarians differ on the details, of course, with some subscribing to a neo-Hobbesian idea about what leads people to act, while others subscribe to a view of agency drawn from Ayn Rand and others. Some embrace the Hayekian notion of natural evolution. Or some combination of these ideas. None accept what seems to underlie many statist positions, namely, that most people are congenitally passive, even when they are not kept in subjugation. On this statist view, neither the lazy poor nor the greedy rich can be credited or blamed for their economic position in life. Nor, of course, can those who resist Sterba's analysis be blamed for possible moral blindness (which doesn't prevent Sterba from implicitly making this charge about libertarians!) – since they, too, presumably are the way they are because of circumstances beyond their control.

9 See, for more on this, Tibor R. Machan, *Private Rights and Public Illusions*.

10 See note 8.

11 It is notable that the statistics Sterba cites are drawn from societies, including the United States of America, which are far from libertarian in their legal construction and are far closer to the welfare state, if not to outright socialism. It is surprising why Sterba does not consider that perhaps what accounts for those statistics is *insufficient* freedom, given that there is ample historical evidence for the detrimental impact of socialism on economic conditions around the globe. Seeing, then, that socialism does not improve the general welfare and that the welfare state leaves a great many people badly off, it would seem natural to push for more negative individual liberty if one is to achieve the kind of results that Sterba desires.

12 Sterba sent his last comments to me via email in June, 1996.

13 Anonymous reply to email query for comment on Sterba's claim, to which several libertarian scholars have responded.

14 See, for more on this, Chris Sarlo, *Poverty in Canada* (Vancouver, BC: Fraser Institute, 1992). See also Chris Sarlo, 'The Politics of Measurement,' *Fraser Forum*, September 2003, pp. 29–30. For a detailed analysis of the issue being discussed here, see James D. Gwartney and Robert A. Lawson, *Economic Freedom of the World, 2004 Annual Report* (Vancouver, BC: Fraser Institute, 2004), the latest in a series of comparative analysis of the impact of political economic systems on the economic conditions of people across the world.

15 See, for more on this, Robert Rector, 'How 'Poor' are America's Poor?' in Julian Simon, ed., *The State of Humanity* (Oxford: Blackwell, 1995).

16 Thomas Sowell, *The Vision of the Anointed, Self-Congratulation as a Basis for Social Policy* (New York: Basic Books, 1995), in which Sowell notes that 78 percent of the individuals in the lowest 20 percent in some year were in the middle or even upper classes 10 years later.

17 In terms of 'spiritual' welfare, that is, real psychic well-being in other respects, there is no comparison. In the hard-core cases generated by the American welfare system, which reinforces the destruction of the family, production of illegitimate children, use of hard drugs, violent crimes, and so forth, genuinely poor people in most of the world are probably much better off. But that's another matter.

18 These were posted on the 'libprof' list on the Internet. The comments by the other libertarians cited here also came from a discussion conducted on that list during the month of June, 1996.

19 This is obvious from the fact that in some religions it is a mark of virtue to renounce wealth. In some cultures, in turn, alternative objectives are deemed to be more significant than seeking wealth so lack of wealth cannot be construed as any kind of failing there – it is, rather, a deliberate choice.

20 Sterba, 'From Liberty to Welfare,' *Ethics*, Vol. 105 (October 1994), pp. 64–98, note 34. Of course, Sterba begs the question when he asserts that the steps he recommends are the ones 'required to secure the basic needs of the poor.' When one considers that the positive right to welfare Sterba advocates comes to nothing less than the legal institution

of forcibly taking from people what they have obtained through their own work and/or voluntary exchange – that is, coercion – it is clear that Sterba claims that theft ought to be legalized for certain cases. That would encompass stealing from formerly poor people who have struggled hard to secure their basic needs and more than their basic needs. The libertarian disputes that this is sound jurisprudence or public policy. A national policy of subjecting all those who do reasonably well in their lives to involuntary servitude seems the farthest thing from what is required to help the poor. Instead structural reform, encouraging work and occasional charity, would appear to be more productive and moral all around.

21 For more on this, see Tibor R. Machan, *Generosity, Virtue in Civil Society* (Washington, DC: Cato Institute, 1998).

22 This may account, in part, for the indignation some poor people feel when they are offered help. Their dignity has been offended, for they know that their poverty follows from their conscious or implicit choices, ones they believe are best suited for their lives and which may indeed be fully justified for them. (This attitude was often exhibited by those who used to be called 'hobos.') Others may know that they are making progress and are capable of emerging from poverty if only left alone to do so. Or they may simply believe that they are responsible for their own lives and, even if just scraping by, don't want to become dependent on others unless emergency requires it.

23 Sterba fails to appreciate the difference between meaning (or intending) to do good and actually doing good. His implied charge gains its moral force from what seems to me a misunderstanding of morality along certain Kantian lines according to which what counts is how intensely one cares or wants things to turn out well, never mind whether they will actually do so. So-called tough love, for example, which is concerned with consequences, often in opposition to *showing* care and considerateness, has no place in such a moral framework.

24 Douglas J. Den Uyl and Douglas B. Rasmussen, *Liberalism Defended: The Challenge of Post-Modernity* (Northampton, MA: E. Elgar, 1997).

25 For more on this, see Leo Strauss, *Natural Right and History* (Chicago, IL: University of Chicago Press, 1950).

26 Quoted in H. L. A. Hart, 'Are There Any Natural Rights?' in A. I. Melden, ed., *Human Rights* (Belmont, CA: Wadsworth Publishing Company, Inc., 1970), p. 61, n.2.

27 James P. Sterba, 'Progress in Reconciliation: Evidence from the Right and the Left,' *Journal of Social Philosophy*, Vol. 28 (Fall 1997), p. 102. It might be worth pointing out that there is little 'Right' in the formal ideological sense about libertarianism. The Right as I understand it is conservative, even reactionary, and has traditionally rejected many of the tenets of libertarianism, even its principled adherence to the right to private property and free trade. Think of Pat Buchanan's vociferous opposition to free trade, or Edmund Burke's and Russell Kirk's criticism of individualism, a central feature of the libertarianism at issue here. Indeed, by some accounts libertarianism is 'Left' because it is closer than traditionalist conservatism to Enlightenment ideas that champion reason and science. Of course, some writers may express a combination of both inclinations.

28 See note 17, above.

29 Ayn Rand, 'The Ethics of Emergencies,' in *The Virtue of Selfishness, A New Concept of Egoism* (New York: Signet Books, 1961).

30 Eric Mack, 'Egoism and Rights,' *The Personalist*, Vol. 54 (1971), pp. 5–33, and 'Egoism and Rights Revisited,' Vol. 58 (1977), pp. 282–8.

31 In an undated radio interview, posted on the Internet [October 23, 1997], Ayn Rand is quoted as having said that

> I would say that *you would have the right* to break in and eat the food that you need [were you to land from a shipwreck in front of someone's closed but well-stocked house], and then when you reach the nearest policeman, admit what you have done, and undertake to repay the man when you are able to work. In other words, you may, in an emergency situation, save your life, *but not as 'of right'*.

[My emphasis.] In these statements Rand seems to contradict herself – however, both the placing of her second reference to rights and essay 'The Ethics of Emergencies' indicate her position by showing that what she has in mind is that one is morally justified ('right' with respect to the standard of one's own survival) to disregard the rights of others in such emergencies, but that it is not a matter of having *the right* to violate the rights of others. A similar point is raised by John Locke with regard to the status of rights when 'politics is impossible.' Douglas B. Rasmussen and Douglas J. Den Uyl, in *Liberty and Nature,* propose to clear up any confusion arising from the apparent conflict of moral justification by way of the concept of meta-normativity, one that characterizes the moral status of political principles.

32 See Tibor R. Machan, *Classical Individualism* (London: Routledge, 1998). Sterba, too, seems to embrace a form of egoism. He says it is unreasonable to demand of someone in dire straits that such a person respect the rights of others to their property – or 'surplus wealth.' This relies upon certain elements of a classical egoist position, according to which individuals ought first and foremost to strive to flourish in their lives and may make use of other persons, their wealth, and so forth, if there are no alternatives left. But one cannot then subvert this insight by making it a principle of society that actually systematically undermines rights and the conditions required for individuals to prosper, as a Sterba-defended welfare state would do.

33 Indeed, I argued this point some time before Jim Sterba and various libertarians began debating this issue in the journals. See my article 'Prima Facie v. Natural (Human) Rights,' *Journal of Value Inquiry,* Vol. 10, No 1 (1976), pp. 119–31. See, also, Mack, 'Egoism and Rights.'

34 It is very risky, philosophically, simply to borrow a concept from Marx while omitting the rest of the Marxian edifice. Thus the concept of 'surplus wealth' makes sense in the context of Marxian economics, with its theory of exploitation, concepts of human nature, economic determinism, alienation, revolution and so forth all attached. But one can't try to skip past the controversies implied by all those fundamental principles and latch onto a derivative principle as if it were self-evident.

35 I develop some of these points in my most recent discussion of Sterba's position, 'Does Libertarianism Imply the Welfare State?' *Res Publica*, Vol. III, No 2 (Autumn 1997), pp. 131–48, much of which forms the basis of the earlier sections of this chapter. Sterba and I have also debated these issues at Vanderbilt University in October 22, 1997, and March 24, 1999.

The issue concerns the importance of both the protection of the right to individual liberty (and other, derivative rights) and the prospect of well-being for all in a just human community. It is fair, I think, to believe that much of Western liberal-democratic-constitutional-republican politics touches upon this matter. How can people secure within their communities the protection of their basic rights to life, liberty and property while not promoting a callous, ungenerous way of life for anyone who is not deserving of it? It's a legitimate concern but, unlike Sterba, I find the answer in the principles and practice of ethics and culture in a free society, not in forcing others to do one's purportedly charitable bidding. (See, in this connection, Machan, *Generosity*.)

Chapter 21

Democracy in Public Life and Corporate Management

This chapter concerns the encroachment of democracy into too much of our social life, especially corporate commerce, and we will need to outline some relevant history.

But before that, in this discussion 'corporation' is used as a short term for 'business corporation.' I will not be referring to corporations such as charities, churches or things like that, but only about business corporations. What I want to discuss is how has there been so much success with the effort to put corporate business under a kind of democratic rule.[1] We would generally not think of placing the press or religion under democratic rule and yet it seems to be perfectly acceptable to millions of Americans (not to mention people abroad) that corporations ought to be governed not by those who own them, but by society at large in some sense.

We have to go back a little bit and remember that commerce itself has not had a very good reputation. For as long as I can remember, when I read about human thought, starting with Plato's *Republic*, on to Aristotle, then on to the Bible and to Thomas Aquinas, and so on, we have always had intellectual consternation about the role of commerce in human society. For example, in the *Republic*, Plato pretty much consigned the merchant, the tradesman, to the lowest rung of humanity. So much so that in the *Republic*, it is impossible, in the ideal city, for someone who is a merchant to ever lead a noble life – the good human life is impossible to the merchant. If you move quickly over 400 years to the Bible, you have to remember that the only time that Jesus ever got violent is when he ejected the moneylenders who exploited the Temple. But of course, many other people exploited religion – be they thieves, adulterers, or child molesters – all kinds of sinners go to church and use the church for their illicit purposes – but Jesus only picked on the moneylenders. It did not give commerce, especially commerce involving money, any kind of high moral standing in the Christian tradition.

In Aristotle, who followed Plato, there is a small concession. You can find commerce to be valuable, but only instrumental – only as a means to higher purposes – like giving to charity, promoting religion or advancing other noble causes. Commerce and commercial agents in and of themselves do not do the right thing. They always contribute to the right things through commerce, but commercial activities, *per se*, are never good.

Only with Aquinas does the Christian church begin to have a more tolerant view of commerce; and even there, it is not completely wholehearted. Usury begins to be less of a sin in Aquinas. What is unusual with him is that he begins to recognize that the market may be the best means to determine what a just price is. Prior to Aquinas, the notion of a just price was common; and it was generally believed that somehow it could be determined by theological speculation and even enforced by the state. But according to Aquinas the closest you can come to determining the just price (which was later discredited as a concept) was through market transactions. Presumably people on the ground, as it were, had the requisite knowledge and moral sensibilities to reach an understanding of what things should cost, how much people should be paid for work, and so forth. This role of the market as a place for discovering the right solutions to various problems of human interaction began with Aquinas.

We move on to the modern era and commerce becomes business. People now begin to realize that you do not just engage in what we might call amateur commerce but can guide commerce with some professional savvy or understanding. Just as once there could be amateur medicine, and later those with special skills, the doctors, so there could once have been amateur commerce and later a new group, business people. These are the people whom we are talking about nowadays – business professionals – who are like doctors in the field of health care: professionals in business may be said to be experts in wealth care.

For a long time the idea of commerce was treated with disdain by much of Christian civilization. One of the reasons that Jews were pressured into the business world was that they did not have the same kind of prohibitions against wheeling and dealing that Christians did. As a result, a great deal of business fell into the hands of the Jews who were virtual nomads – or displaced persons – in Europe and did not belong to local communities. The prohibition against commerce, and especially against making interest from lending money, did not apply to them as strongly as it applied to the Christians.

Also, once Aquinas had Aristotle's works translated into Latin from the Arabic, and thus reintroduced Aristotle's friendly attitude toward the physical world *via* his embrace of science, the Christian world began to be more accepting toward conduct and institutions that made life successful and prosperous on earth. Thus, about the time of the fourteenth and fifteenth centuries it began to dawn on monarchs that commerce had one useful value. It could generate wealth – and wealth to them was not so much to enhance the welfare of the population, but to feed armies and support conquest.

In time, in support of this goal, many monarchs established joint-stock companies, the predecessors of corporate business. These gave a monopoly position to certain people who would then establish corporations and even protected them against disasters through limited liability. That is one of the reasons that in England the corporate 'Inc.' is 'Ltd,' which signifies limited liability status so that the owners would not have to shoulder the burden of their misfortunes and misdeeds. Some of the liability would fall on the king and on insurance companies and society in general so that companies could undertake risky businesses like transporting materials on the sea, or engaging in mining – endeavors that routinely faced hazards.

This was the origin of the idea that many people from the left who look upon commerce today – for example Ralph Nader – find something objectionable about corporate business, namely, because they enjoy protection against the full burden of their possible misdeeds or mishaps. If a ship sinks, people die, and property gets lost they are only responsible to restore so much of it. That is why they needed the involvement of the monarch. Their limited responsibility was not something that was established by contract but by royal edict.

A significant crucial element of the American Revolution was that, by way of the Declaration of Independence, it changed the relationship between government and those who fell under its jurisdiction. Prior to the American Revolution, the official understanding (although there were rumblings against this) was that society had a pyramidic structure, with a king as head either fully empowered or with limited powers. Everyone else was a subject – meaning ultimately subject to the will of the monarch or the monarch's court or government. This is the exact reverse – at least in principle – of the political ideals sketched in the Declaration of Independence. There, sovereignty belonged not to government but to the individual human beings of the country – citizens – who had unalienable rights. Whoever wished to interact with citizens could do so only with their consent.

It is difficult to appreciate just how radical this idea is, even today. Most people cannot or refuse to grasp it. Only those who are convinced of the validity of the classical liberal tradition of political and social philosophy take it very seriously. The rest of the world finds it pretty much unbelievable either because they grew up in a hierarchical family and then moved into a hierarchical society with social structures or because they would like to be of the ruling class and realize that taking individualism seriously, resting a legal system on it, stands in the way of that.

One of the more optimistic aspects of the classical liberal, libertarian movement is that it's up against a very long tradition of abuse of individual rights and it is only in the last 300 years – and in terms of the age of humanity that is a very short period of time – that the notion of individual sovereignty and, thus, severely limited government, has gained some measure of official standing. Before anyone else may act invasively – be that a dentist, a doctor, or a politician – they have to get the consent of the person involved.

This was recognized in the US Constitution with respect especially to the press and religion. Unfortunately, the Constitution did not recognize it with respect to commerce and indeed many other endeavors and so their professionals are widely regimented by government regulatory agencies.

To be precise about this, in Article 1, Section 8, the interstate commerce clause, commerce is treated as part of public policy. Public policy at that time was very friendly toward commerce, aiming toward the promotion of the free flow of commerce. It did not, however, say what it ought to have, namely, let's keep our hands off commerce altogether, just as we must keep our hands off the press or religion. Because it was an activist – managerial rather than *laissez-faire* – public policy, anything that influences public policy could ultimately gain influence over the government's attitude toward commerce.

As the adherence to the idea – widely but not by any means uniformly held by America's early leaders – that what is best is if a non-interventionist government became less firmly accepted, the courts began to allow democratic influences on almost everything other than the press and religion. Perhaps the major turning point came with Justice Oliver Wendell Holmes, Jr's dissenting opinion in the Lochner *v.* New York case. Here is how Holmes made his case:

> The liberty of the citizen to do as he likes so long as he does not interfere with the liberty of others to do the same, which has been a shibboleth for some well-known writers, is interfered with by school laws, by the Post Office, by every state or municipal institution which takes his money for purposes thought desirable, whether he likes it or not. The Fourteenth Amendment does not enact Mr. Herbert Spencer's *Social Statics*. The other day we sustained the Massachusetts vaccination law. Jacobson v. Massachusetts, 197 U.S. 11. United States and state statutes and decisions cutting down the liberty to contract by way of combination are familiar to this court. Northern Securities Co. v. United States, 193 U.S. 197. Two years ago we upheld the prohibition of sales of stock on margins or for future delivery in the constitution of California. Otis v. Parker, 187 U.S. 606. The decision sustaining an eight hour law for miners is still recent. Holden v. Hardy, 169 U.S. 366. Some of these laws embody convictions or prejudices which judges are likely to share. Some may not. But a constitution is not intended to embody a particular economic theory, whether of paternalism and the organic relation of the citizen to the State or of laissez faire. It is made for people of fundamentally differing views, and the accident of our finding certain opinions natural and familiar or novel and even shocking ought not to conclude our judgment upon the question whether statutes embodying them conflict with the Constitution of the United States.

Holmes added this crucially important point of jurisprudence, one that is the rule now rather than the exception:

> I think that the word liberty in the Fourteenth Amendment is perverted when it is held to prevent the natural outcome of a dominant opinion, unless it can be said that a rational and fair man necessarily would admit that the statute proposed would infringe fundamental principles as they have been understood by the traditions of our people and our law. It does not need research to show that no such sweeping condemnation can be passed upon the statute before us. A reasonable man might think it a proper measure on the score of health.

To claim that only laws that 'a rational and fair man *necessarily* would admit that the statute proposed would infringe fundamental principles,' (my emphasis) is to declare that majorities or their representatives may do anything they want, since *nothing at all* can meet that condition. Indeed, in this tradition not even the First Amendment to the US Constitution is secure against legislative fiat.

Anyway, the policy against government interference with commerce became weaker and weaker. What transpired is that after the political leaders and the members of the US Supreme Court no longer took it as their public policy priority to promote commerce, they began to hold that commercial enterprises or businesses follow an agenda that the public demands. After all, Congress was empowered to regulate interstate commerce. So, in this respect, Ralph Nader actually has it right – that there is a kind of argument (which I call the 'creature of the state' argument) supporting the notion that in US law corporate commerce does not enjoy the kind of freedom that people in the press or religion does.

Let us get clear on this: if a legislature proposes that a government regulatory body oversee religion, that would immediately find courts striking down the idea even if it had majority support. The same holds regarding professional journalism. There are some gray areas here – mainly when it comes to the relationship between the press and criminal trials and, perhaps, *vis-à-vis* religious practices that violate other individual rights – but basically those are the two most absolutist libertarian principles of the American legal tradition. None of that exists with respect to business and commerce nor with respect to the institution of the right to private property.

Because robust business is so dependent upon a legal infrastructure that recognizes the right to private property, business subject to government regulations – be this democratic or non-democratic – enjoys less freedom than members of the press or religious institutions. Needless to say, this is a form of unjust discrimination – it clearly violates the principle of the Fourteenth Amendment, as Holmes' remarks showed so clearly. One might say, Justice Holmes 'dost protest too much.' As a result of the victory of Holmes's dissent during the New Deal, we now have a situation where, legally speaking, there is hardly any defense – except the traditional momentum – against the incursions of democratic procedures toward the regimentation of business by politicians and bureaucrats. There are some courts that change their attitudes – they begin to see that if governments start regulating business too much, it may in fact involve assuming greater powers for the state than the founders meant for them to have.

However, it is not a well-entrenched legal tradition in the US to give people in business the sort of strict protection to proceed in their avenues of development, ventures or entrepreneurship as people in journalism do. Consider, for example, insider trading – it is illegal by virtue of the rules of the Securities and Exchange Commission, yet there is nothing wrong about it unless it involves fraud or failure to perform one's fiduciary duties. Those infractions could be handled within the criminal or contract law. What is at issue there is not insider trading but that people stole or violated the client–professional code of conduct.

Insider trading, as such, actually has to do with what many in the field of business ethics complain, namely, that it is unfair. In other words, insider traders rely on some information that is not yet public, to gain an advantage in the marketplace. This is widely believed in business ethics circles throughout the country to be morally wrong because it involves taking advantage of information that not everyone possesses. Ideas such as the imperative to be fair, to compete on a level playing field, not to cash in on special advantages – these are what lie behind the condemnation of insider trading.

Yet the same attitude is not shown to journalism. Think about the widely sought after and praised activity of scooping – as when, say, *The Washington Post* scoops *The New York Times*; it would be absurd to claim, 'That's unfair!' Instead, journalists get Pulitzer Prizes for scooping. Yet, the very opposite attitude holds when it comes to business. The source of this, amongst other things, is the perverse tradition that not even in US law, which is most hospitable to commerce relative to other countries, is there a full measure of protection of private property rights and of the sovereignty of business professionals.

One telling point against business is that major corporations are getting this extra measure of protection through limited liability. So government regulation is simply a means by which this unfair advantage is offset.

However, there is nothing sacrosanct about limited liability; it could be done away with. Then protection would be given to corporate business *via* limited liability law – you take your risks and you get what is coming to you as a result. There would be no special protection for such entrepreneurs any more than for anyone else in the society.

Justice requires that the government be removed from its proactive role in the field of business. It should not have a policy of promoting or opposing business; it must be neutral toward it as it is toward religion or the publishing of newspapers. It ought to keep its hands off and then we will see where business goes, with the enforcement of the criminal law as its only guide to legitimate conduct.

The idea is not all that shocking. Why not see government, which is an expert at wielding force, as having only a defensive or retaliatory role in social life? Why is this so difficult to grasp – after all we do tend to accept that ordinary force, such as beating people up, slapping them, holding them down or making them leave an establishment against their will, may occur only if they have themselves engaged in violent conduct. Otherwise we must deal with people in a civilized, peaceful fashion. So, when the government is deemed necessary, the purpose for which it must exist must itself be such as to justify the use of force, namely, resisting crime or foreign aggression. That is the expertise of government, its *raison d'être*.

In the last several decades of the twentieth century many countries in the world began to adopt relatively free market policies, at least in some economic spheres. This has enabled working people, including business, to become globally competitive. That also means that no longer can workers and business in the original semi-free market societies command the prices and wages they once could.

Sadly, many people now believe that for the US to remain as far ahead of the rest of the world as it used to be, there is a need for a proactive protectionist business policy from government instead of simply allowing a free market society to take care of the problem by relying on human ingenuity and adaptability. Yet, people will continue to be entrepreneurs; they will reinvent themselves to engage in novel enterprises that those in other countries are not embarking upon. In short, they will more than likely find ways in which to prosper – they do not need a managed state to guide them in that direction. Unfortunately, that idea is not being promulgated by sufficient numbers of teachers, let alone politicians and bureaucrats who are only glad to take up the task of managing the economic and other affairs of others.

So now we have a society in which the purpose of businesses is beginning to be altered through the implementing of public policy. Instead of just allowing businesses to do whatever they want to do, justified by the confidence that on the whole they will tend to discover and do the right thing, now they are being legally required to engage in various tasks that the leaders believe need to be accomplished. This includes not only adhering to various rules and regulations that promote domestic business and worker interests, but, also, the rectification of social wrongs such as cleaning up the environment, remedying the lot of members of minorities and generally taking up socially responsible projects.

We now have the spectacle of one of the most prosperous free societies in the history of humankind being urged by many leaders to be ruled by the democratic management of its business sector. Not only is democracy supposed to set the goals of business enterprises but, even within the firm, there is to be democratic organization.

There is no easy way of reversing such a destructive and unjust trend. It is not an easy task to direct (or redirect) an entire country toward the principles of individualism and natural inalienable human rights, in part because in America, especially, there has always been the problem of its history of slavery and other social wrongs – it brings to mind changing the course of an aircraft carrier. One may assume that this is especially problematic for a society whose legal system is very ambitious and has always been promoted with self-righteousness. Such a society is likely to receive far more criticism and skepticism than those that simply plod on and make no claim to being special. In a country like America, there will always be a stark blemish on the country's history because of slavery. So while some carry on saying such things as 'In the good old days when we were free,' that is offensive, and rightly so, to those millions of people whose ancestors suffered enslavement. One can only say, justifiably, 'when white people were free', but not 'When we were free.'

Note

1 In this chapter I do not provide a full enough discussion of democracy. I have done that in Chapter 10, 'The Democratic Ideal,' in my book, *The Passion for Liberty* (Lanham, MD: Rowman & Littlefield, 2003). For a full-length exploration of democracy, see William N. Nelson, *On Justifying Democracy* (London: Routledge & Kegan Paul, 1980).

CONCLUSION

Chapter 22

The Dependence of Equality on Liberty

False assumptions can hinder an investigation. It is often assumed, for example, that the political ideals of liberty and equality are in inescapable, natural conflict.[1] A great many political decisions in contemporary democracies are, in large measure, aimed at producing equality by limiting liberty, short of extinguishing liberty completely.[2] Nevertheless, the conditions of a good human community, properly understood, do not require compromising either liberty or equality.

To understand fully the conditions of a good human community we must examine the nature of human beings and the nature of community.[3] Many of today's political thinkers are deeply skeptical that we can identity human nature or what is objectively good for human beings insofar as they are members of a community.[4] Yet, we cannot adequately understand political affairs if we fail to understand the nature of moral and political excellence and what constitutes a good or just human community.[5] My own position, as developed in this book and in other works, is that in good human communities both liberty and equality would be fully secured.

Fortunately, human nature is not a will-o'-the-wisp. It can be identified by a careful examination of ourselves and those like us throughout human history. Let me reiterate here some of the points covered in earlier portions of this work before I go on to a discussion of the relationship between liberty and equality.

A fairly clear conception of human nature has emerged throughout history, despite debate surrounding the issue.[6] It is evident that human beings are distinguishable as animals with the capacity to think, the capacity to initiate the process of conceptual consciousness. The activities, creations, inventions, worries, emotions, institutions, failings and the entire history of people are best explained by reference to the fact that they are capable of choice and thought.[7]

We rarely find people in total isolation, yet we can consider what the worth of community life would be to someone with the option to join a society.[8] This analysis can lead us to answer the question of what kind of community would be best for us.[9]

We share with lower animals the value of life. But we lack their ability to pursue the sustenance and improvement of our lives automatically. Instead, we can choose to learn general principles by which to guide our actions toward successful living. It is this choice to engage in directed (rational) thought that distinguishes us from other animals. For humans, the right course of conduct to follow for human beings is always the rational course. Only the exercise of reason enables a person to reach excellence in life, to succeed at living.[10] The moral point here is very general – each person ought to pursue success in life, and to do this should think clearly to the degree of his capacity. Many specific virtues follow from this for private and social life; although some will apply less at one time or place than others,[11] the virtue of being rational, *per se*, is always relevant.

Now we can ask, given this fact, what kind of community is right for people. Surely, it is one in which the life proper to persons – the moral life – can flourish? And surely the legal framework of such a community *must* respect – which implies also that it will guide the protection of – the proper conditions of moral existence, above all the liberty of each and every person. Right conduct cannot be produced by force. It must be up to the agent to choose to engage in it. And because we are able to refrain from abridging the liberty of others, and because such abstention is proper for human life in society, we *should* all refrain from abridging the liberty of others. The liberty of all will not guarantee, but is a necessary condition for, everyone's excellence. Individuals must produce their own success in life, but they require freedom in order to do this to the extent possible to them.

Complete details of what liberty in community life would look like and how it would be defended are beyond the scope of this chapter. But the structure would resemble that of the classical liberal model.[12] My argument for it differs from what Locke, Mill or Spencer produced. But as they envisioned, a good human community would consist of a legal system that specifies the liberty of all and enables the administrators of a properly instituted government to protect and preserve that liberty. Perhaps not 'perfect justice,' but at least properly conceived political justice, can be achieved through the legal system of such a community.[13] Its basic principles would consist of the natural rights each person possesses to life, liberty, arid property, that is, the pursuit of a successful life on earth. All of these rights, and derivative contractual rights, would involve strict requirements of protection and preservation in a good human community.

Clearly, extreme egalitarian, socialist or communist goals, of whatever political persuasion, could not be pursued *politically* within such a community. The law would not permit the imposition of such equality. Nor would it tolerate a spiritual or economic welfare state.[14] Government would not be acting properly in seizing people's property, whatever the goal; what it requires for its own operation would have to be purchased in the market! As extreme as this may seem, the establishing of such boundaries and restraints is nonetheless the proper approach to instituting a lawful government.

Prohibiting the use of coercive force to achieve egalitarian equality – of either a Leftist or Rightist variety – does not imply either the absence of *political* equality or the impossibility of achieving egalitarian economic or religious goals in the community. However, the coercive imposition of economic or spiritual equality is both unjust and practically impossible.[15]

In contrast, forcible maintenance of political equality – consisting in equal protection and preservation of the natural rights of each citizen – is both just and possible.[16]

In a just legal order, characterized by the officially authorized protection and preservation of the rights of each individual, equality finds a central place. The legal system regards all persons as equal in the crucial and only relevant respect of their human nature. Each individual is treated as a moral agent, an end-in-himself, and not as a prospective tool for the advancement of goals he has not willingly chosen to pursue. Each person, in such a framework or system of laws, possesses moral dignity, the *capacity* for moral excellence.[17]

By incorporating principles of natural rights into the legal framework, those who administer the law ensure that equal justice will be systematically pursued.[18] Individuals differ from each other in many respects and share certain characteristics only with larger or smaller subgroups of the entire society, but they all are moral agents, responsible to live an excellent life within their own contexts. Natural rights specify what is right for each individual *qua* human being in a social context – not what is right for nurses *per se*, students, fathers, women, Italians, cooks, and so on.[19] But if one is not thwarted in functioning as a human, thus moral, creative, and productive being in a society, one is also able by that very fact to function in any of these more specific capacities, so long as one's efforts are peaceful.

A good human community treats human beings as equal in the only respect relevant to political existence. Of course in various areas of life one can also reasonably value equality of treatment: when it comes to how a professor treats his students, a father his children, a dorm supervisor his residents, a sales clerk his customers. But for purposes of political justice the only relevant equality is equality under the law, which preserves and protects the natural rights of each citizen. To strive politically for universal equality of any other kind is to strive for what is impossible and therefore wrong to pursue.[20] To attempt it would be to abandon the distinctive purpose of political institutions, the pursuit of justice for all within a social context. The function of politics, and, thus, government, is to aim for justice for all citizens, not for the special values and benefits people can obtain in various subgroups of society through voluntary cooperation. (Other types of inequality are very much a part of nature; they would and do exist independently of anyone doing anything to anyone else. Thus to attempt to remedy these would not amount to rectifying an injustice. At most it would involve forcibly extracting requirements of generosity or charity from some toward others.[21])

Many see the idea of political equality outlined here as insufficient when compared with the popular, egalitarian view of equality. But that view assumes, among other things, that justice is achieved when we can all be observed to be equally well off. Attempting to achieve such economic equality is not proper for human life in view of the inadequacy of the framework in which human distinctions are attributed to human agency rather than (a) natural accidents and (b) personal choices; *making* us all equal would be to rob us of our moral equality, the natural right to strive for our success in life in our own fashion, depending both on what and who we actually are.

Egalitarians are concerned mostly with distributive justice. Aside from the fact that coercing someone to be part of such redistribution – by conscripting his or her labor or confiscating his or her resources – in and of itself implies a lack of equality of political status for all, the view that justice consists of equal division of wealth is false. Consider, for starters, the simple reality that those with different desires, goals, aspirations, talents, and age want and are capable of achieving different economic conditions. The wealth of a J. Paul Getty might be a great nuisance to someone whose main concern in life is to write the great American novel or to experience the conditions of existence available in isolation on a tropical island. (Winners of the lottery sometimes report that they are more miserable since winning it!)

It is not clear why many very influential philosophers, such as Sen and Nussbaum, have accepted the view that equality in economic conditions is always good, as well as worthy of forcible imposition. Equality is good only if human beings are, by nature, best off by being equal to each other with respect to the attribute, status or condition in question. Economic status is by no means the highest priority in human life, let alone within the law, nor is one's education, social position, or housing conditions, however important these may be. What is central to each individual is the opportunity to excel morally, to make the best of life within the context of one's age, location, talents, and many other highly diverse factors.

It is possible to be misled about the advisability of universal economic equality by the significance of equality in special contexts – for instance, family life or certain kinds of games. But other conditions could also be mistaken for universal values on similar grounds. For instance, stability, harmony, order, and safety are just a few conditions we could value in certain contexts without elevating them to the status of the political *summum bonum.*

To the extent that we are citizens of a country, we are entitled to be treated as equals under the law, for the legal authorities of such communities serve citizens (or should) in the capacity of protecting and preserving their right to liberty. Here equality is of value as it relates to the legitimate function that a legal authority or government has in our lives, namely securing the general good, and everyone's right to liberty. When more than this is attempted, for example, by attempting legally to establish equal pay for equal work, a minimum wage, or educational equality, they abandon their proper task and create a welter of irresolvable conflicts, a veritable Hobbesian war among all vested interest-groups.

When a state subsidizes special goals – child care, moon projects, symphony music, auto safety, faith-based charities, or the abolition of various personal vices – it is perceived as having a procedural duty to give equal treatment to all. Thus when some special projects and groups receive special legal aid, others who do not will consider themselves deprived of their due.

When, say, government gives subsidies or special legal protection to agriculture or loans to the airline industry, by its procedural duty to give equal treatment to all citizens it is obliged to provide subsidies to all other segments of society. (Of course, the fact that great need for help exists in the airline industry or in agriculture does not imply that such help is needed elsewhere or must be provided at all.) When married women receive special help to obtain jobs from airlines, then another special group, for example, obese men, will also demand it, *ad infinitum*. These are not predictions but merely observations about the logic of political dynamics. Given the procedural features that must attend governmental action purportedly predicated on equal treatment of all citizens, when governments undertake improper functions the same procedures must be followed – or else the idea of equal treatment of all citizens must be abandoned. These conflicts and contradictions can be avoided. Instead of engaging in charity, governments should confine their work to preserving and protecting natural human rights equally for all.

Liberty and equality, in the respect in which these are possible conditions and valuable features of a human community, are not only compatible but mutually dependent on each other for the purposes of maintaining political justice.[22] Misunderstanding of the nature of equality, as fostered by egalitarian political theories, has led to the denial of this fact. Though the job of uprooting that misunderstanding and promulgating a rational view of the relationship between liberty and equality may be a tough one, the quality of our human communities nonetheless depends, in part, on how successful we are in persuading concerned citizens that both are essential to a just community.

Notes

1 See Sidney Hook, *Pragmatism and the Tragic Sense of Life* (New York: Basic Books, 1975), especially Chapter 5, 'Absolutism and Human Rights,' pp. 79–98. See also Gregory Vlastos's 'Justice and Equality' in A. I. Melden, ed., *Human Rights* (Belmont, CA: Wadsworth Publishing Co., 1970), pp. 76–95. Of course, there are those who deny such a conflict but to do so they embrace a conception of human rights dubbed 'positive rights.' For more on this see Chapter 19, 'Two Philosophers Skeptical of Negative Liberty.'

2 For a good discussion of how this has resulted in Britain's political conditions see Robert Moss, *The Collapse of Democracy* (New Rochelle, NY: Arlington House Publishers, 1976). Almost all liberal democrats or social democrats aim for some such fusion. See the works of Amartya Sen and Martha Nussbaum discussed in Chapter 19.

3 A clear argument for this requirement is given in Leo Strauss, *What is Political Philosophy* (Glencoe, IL: The Free Press, 1959). I develop such an account in Tibor R. Machan, *Individuals and Their Rights* (LaSalle, IL: Open Court Publishing Co., Inc., 1989).

4 Relativism and subjectivism concerning not only normative matters but even the hard sciences is so prevalent that hardly any documentation is required. For the former, consider the claims of most of those in the social sciences; for the latter, the recent popularity of Thomas S. Kuhn's conception of the paradigm-dependence of any scientific claim, in *The Structure of Scientific Revolutions* (Chicago, IL: University of Chicago Press, 1962), and

Richard Rorty's view that truth is community dependent, in his *Objectivity, Relativism and Truth* (Cambridge: Cambridge University Press, 1991). Cf. Tibor R. Machan, *Objectivity, Recovering Determinate Reality in Philosophy, Science, and Everyday Life* (Burlington, VT: Ashgate, 2004).

5 Excellent beginning for this task may be found in Hanna F. Pitkin, *Wittgenstein and Justice* (Berkeley, CA: University of California Press, 1972), and Barry Stroud, 'Wittgenstein and Logical Necessity,' in George Pitcher, ed., *Wittgenstein* (Garden City, NY, Anchor Books, 1967).

6 See Tibor R. Machan, *Human Rights and Human Liberties* (Chicago, IL: Nelson-Hall, 1975), as well as Machan, *Individuals and Their Rights*, for a discussion of this and several other related issues.

7 For an elaboration of this, see Tibor R. Machan, *Initiative – Human Agency and Society* (Stanford, CA: Hoover Institution Press, 2000).

8 So-called 'state of nature' analyses deploy this method. Among libertarian political philosophers this is best developed in Jan Narveson, *The Libertarian Idea* (Philadelphia: Temple University Press, 1989).

9 See Thomas Hobbes, John Locke, Immanuel Kant, John Rawls, Robert Nozick, David Gauthier, and Jan Narveson for somewhat similar yet also distinctive 'social contractarian' approaches.

10 The claim here is, of course, terribly controversial, yet true in the sense that there can be truth concerning such issues. The Aristotelian naturalist ethical position is still the theoretically most adequate alternative available to us. Moral skepticism, in turn, is not only a defeatist position but quite baseless, because its major support, strict empiricism, collapses into solipsism.

11 Cf. Tibor R. Machan, 'Law, Justice and Natural Rights' in *Western Ontario Law Review*, Vol. 14 (1975).

12 See my discussions of this in various of my books, as well as in such essays as 'Reason, Morality, and the Free Society,' Robert L. Cunningham, ed., *Liberty and the Rule of Law* (College Station, TX: Texas A&M University Press, 1979).

13 Consider Robert Nozick, *Anarchy, State, and Utopia* (New York: Basic Books, 1974), especially Chapter 7.

14 Often people overlook the fact that both the Left and the Right tend to promote a welfare state of sorts, though with different criteria as to what constitutes welfare – for the Left it tends to be mainly economic well-being or capability, for the Right it is mainly spiritual or a certain version of moral well-being (preparatory of everlasting salvation in the afterlife).

15 Nozick, *Anarchy, State, and Utopia*. Of course, the late Robert Nozick is by no means the only one who has shown this – see, also, Murray N. Rothbard, *Egalitarianism as a Revolt Against Nature and Other Essays*, 2nd edn (Auburn, AL: Ludwig von Mises Inst., 2000).

16 Machan, *Human Rights and Human Liberties* and *Individuals and Their Rights*.

17 To appreciate the difference between naturalistic worldviews which deny this and those which affirm it, see B. F. Skinner, *Beyond Freedom and Dignity* (New York: Knopf, 1971), and Tibor R. Machan, *The Pseudo-Science of B. F. Skinner* (New Rochelle, NY: Arlington House, 1974). There are disputes, of course, about the exact political implications of this idea of human dignity – see, for example, Tibor R. Machan and Craig Duncan, *Libertarianism, For and Against* (Lanham, MD: Rowman & Littlefield, 2005).

18 The idea here is to take the 'oath of office' of members of the government far more seriously than we tend to do at present.

19 See my papers 'Human Rights: Some Points of Clarification,' *Journal of Critical Analysis*, Vol. V, No I, pp. 30–39; 'Prima Facie versus Natural (Human) Rights,' *Journal of Value Inquiry*, Vol. X, No 2; 'Law, Justice and Natural Rights.'

20 For a discussion of the pursuit of utopias in a free society, see the last section of Nozick, *Anarchy, State, and Utopia*. As to whether it is wrong to pursue what one knows to be an impossible dream – no, unless one has something better to do, which is almost always.

21 For more on this, see Tibor R. Machan, *Generosity, Virtue in Civil Society* (Washington, DC: Cato Institute, 1998).

22 For a very instructive discussion, see Roderick Long, 'Equality: The Unknown Ideal,' http://www.mises.org/fullstory.aspx?control=804

Chapter 23

Why Agreement Is Not Enough

Agreement can be very nice. Wouldn't it be wonderful if we could all just get along? But much depends on what it is we're supposedly agreeing to – and maybe a little bit, too, on whether we ever actually agreed to anything at all.

Social compact theories seek to explain the rationale for or genesis of social or political norms – or even the norms of personal conduct – in terms of what we 'as a society' supposedly agree to. But a contract is, strictly speaking, a legally enforceable agreement. Social contracts, being pre-legal in nature, are better classified as compacts, and that is the term I will use.

In the realm of personal conduct, social compact theory is a version of conventionalist metaethics – according to which right and wrong is whatever folks traditionally agree is right and wrong, rather than something that can be objectively determined. In the realm of social, political or legal norms, social compact theory contends that the proper principles of community life are those that either actual or hypothetical participants in a community *agree* to be legally bound by. For social compact theory, it is agreement alone that underlies the principles guiding social-political life.

I will argue here that any sound political system requires not only agreement (and not necessarily universal agreement, at that) but also logically prior, non-conventionalist ethical principles, or, at any rate, some sort of natural drives (like a drive for self-preservation). I dispute the notion that social compacts by themselves can *establish* binding norms of any sort whatsoever, norms that can be demonstrated to obligate one to act one way or refrain from acting another way.

Nothing follows morally from the fact that everyone within a group has agreed to abide by certain guidelines unless the agreement itself enjoys normative force. (After all, what if they all agree to march across the river as a gang and beat up or kill some innocent, just for the fun of it? Surely the act does not become morally obligatory merely because everyone in the group has assented to it?) Nor can this compact derive its moral significance from a prior compact, which must then derive *its* moral meaning from an even earlier one, and so on, *ad infinitum*. Unless there is some independent norm that can underlie an agreement, the agreement fails to obligate morally (although of course it may, practically speaking, be imposed by dint of physical threat mustered by a majority against all others). Agreements as such can have moral force only if *promising* as such has moral force, regardless of any other consideration.

One could also hold that an inborn motive or drive impels those party to a compact to live by it. Then the norms are binding not because of the agreement *per se* but because the agreement *had* to be made (so as to respond to fear of death, secure safety, or preserve life), then *had* to be followed by the self-interested parties to it. This proposal may or may not be plausible, but it is at least an attempt to explain the strong motivation to abide by the compact. Yet, many political theorists seem to hold that even absent any prior ethical norm or natural drive impelling the requisite behavior (at least among normal parties to the agreement) a social compact can set up binding and enforceable guidelines.

After my critical remarks I will now sketch an approach to establishing social or political norms that captures some of the appeal of social contract theories while offering a more robust and plausible basis for them. Social compact theories, I argue, *implicitly assume* that prudence is a moral virtue (or at least a natural drive) that we ought to (or will be motivated to) cultivate and in line with whose dictates we ought to (or will) agree to the provisions of a social compact.

For thinkers like Kant and Rawls, the alleged contractual basis for the legitimacy of law and government is supplemented by the very strict requirement that the resulting norms be self-consistent. But once this requirement of internal consistency is isolated and set aside, what remains of the social compact that could provide a foundation for social norms and law is both meager and inadequate.

To be sure, one might argue that self-consistency is naturally demanded of every theory – that it is a meta-theoretical criterion which virtually goes without saying. But if such self-consistency is not inherent in a system that rests on agreement but is, rather, itself a distinct normative requirement, then it seems evident that normativity – the relevance of value judgments – cannot easily be omitted from any sphere of human concern.[1]

Still, must rationality be a prerequisite for any social compact? After all, it might be possible for a particular group to reach a consensus on irrational rules of governance; and many irrational groups do in fact exist. The world is rife with organizations that embrace irrational ideas as their guiding principles. Terrorists, Nazis, and skinheads might each establish their rules on the basis of nothing but agreement, without these rules having any legitimate moral force. (Though even here, a moral doctrine of some kind or another, however crude or indefensible, usually motivates the program, for example, the notion that the purported racial superiority of the group's members justifies harassing or destroying the members of other races – a moral claim of sorts.) That the purposes sought by way of such irrational rules cannot be conscientiously and consistently acted upon, is, of course, much of my point: something more than sheer agreement is needed to establish viable and coherent social compacts, let alone morally binding ones.

To deny that rules spawned by a social compact resting entirely on agreement can be irrational flies in the face of history and common sense. To claim that these principles have moral force simply because they have been agreed to implies that they have moral legitimacy simply because they have been agreed to. Yet we criticize such groups precisely because they clearly *lack* moral legitimacy. The lynch mob may feel that it is justified, but we know that it is not. And we would not indict a person for breaching an agreement who, after a change of heart, proceeded to violate the norms of the Nazis or the Mafia, flouting their compact.

Yet Kant explicitly alleges that the 'idea [of social compact] alone enables us to conceive of the legitimacy of the state.'[2] He stipulates that the social compact is a 'mere idea of Understanding, which has, nonetheless, its doubtless (practical) reality.'

> [It] obligates every lawgiver to advance his statutes so that they could have emerged from the united will of the whole people, and to consider every subject, as regards his desire for citizenship, as though he had been party to accepting that will. For that is the basis of the legitimacy of every public enactment.[3]

New life has been breathed into this idea by John Rawls, whose hypothetical social compact is said to have been formed behind 'a veil of ignorance.'[4] There are other more Hobbesian versions of social compact theory, but among contemporary political philosophers the Kant–Rawls version enjoys prominence. Yet, their theories are not free of normative presuppositions either, and thus do not qualify as pure social compact theories. Both Kant and Rawls import certain norms into the social compact; norms that delimit what can count as a *bona fide* compact. For Kant, a strict rationalism – the will to reason – is part of the contract. For Rawls, it is his insistence on a 'reflective equilibrium' among basic intuitions that favor fairness, including respect for the principles of self-consistency. So for both thinkers the compact is generated by much more than sheer agreement.

Hobbes may be a better representative of pure social compact theory. According to Hobbes, when scarcity and congestion reach a critical mass in the state of nature, the self-interested motivation of individuals drives them to convene and reach a consensus. They then devise certain rules of social life, to be enforced by a monarch or government that is empowered to impose strict sanctions against law-breakers. At this point everyone forfeits all of the 'natural rights'[5] he had possessed in the state of nature, save for the right to resist being killed.

The Hobbesian theory does not specify the content of the rules, though it assumes the rules would aim to maintain the peace and preserve human life. For Hobbes, the only public good is peace, and there is no stipulation as to the moral content of the rules to which we assent for the sake of achieving it. In the Kantian–Rawlsean version of social compact theory, however, more is required of the agreement than the mere laying down of rules – they must be rational and fair.

Why is the Hobbesian conception so appealing, especially among supporters of the Enlightenment-based, liberal tradition of politics? Because it seems to offer an empirically-based, hence 'scientific' explanation of the origin of preferred laws, without the necessity of enlisting messy and perhaps controversial moral values. Even Kant embraced as much for the so-called phenomenal world, the world in which the practical task of politics is to be realized – for example, in his discussion of how people pursue happiness as a matter of natural necessity.

The notions that human action must be explained by reference to deterministically compelling motives (as distinct from purposes, which are goals set by us, not powers driving us willy-nilly); that morality is mainly a social invention; that people lack freedom of the will, at least from the scientific, practical point of view; and that their conduct is neither morally right nor morally wrong except as a matter of their relationship to certain social goals – all these and related assumptions are thought to accommodate liberal goals of anti-authoritarianism and scientific respectability.

According to the empiricist-scientistic viewpoint, prior to being driven to be bound by 'their own' decisions, members of a social group cannot be bound by moral standards. By this understanding of human life, it is not true that people ought to live one way rather than another, and that they are capable of individually discerning what the moral way is even apart from whether anybody agrees. Such an 'ought' would imply that they have the capacity to do otherwise, that they possess free will and are able to initiate their own conduct, without needing to be forced into a particular course of action by others. Instead, according to the empiricist view people are inclined, or rather driven – naturally motivated and determined – to act as they do. *Contra* Frost, there is no road less traveled by; we take the only road open to us.

For advocates of this position, the idea that one can 'cause' one's own conduct is simply incoherent. And therefore (if morality is deemed possible at all, within a determinist framework), free will cannot be a necessary ingredient of morality; 'ought' cannot really imply 'can.' To be moral means simply to behave in accordance with certain rules, even if one had no ultimate choice but to do so. On this view, Hobbes, albeit a mechanistic materialist, may legitimately espouse a moral system. For to do so implies only the promotion of certain kinds of behavior and the discouragement of others. The success of that advocacy may depend entirely upon deterministic factors, one of which is the advocacy itself.

With the demise of the classical idea of natural law – the view that human life has an end and that freely chosen, self-caused right conduct ought to and can further this end – the thesis of a hypothetical social compact seemed to present the best chance of resurrecting some shard of respect for moral and legal principles.[6] But eager as some might be to sweep the whole matter under the carpet, the issue of the nature of morality, including social norms, persists. Are we in fact driven to conform to social norms under certain optimal circumstances, or can we choose to comply with such norms on our own initiative (which suggests the possibility, too, of evaluating those norms and finding them wanting)?

If the only hope for some semblance of moral and political standards arises within a deterministic framework, the function of a moral or political norm will be taken over by an instinct or innate motive. For Hobbes, that innate motive is fear, self-preservation, or survival. The drive to survive is what propels people to form a social compact – even if Hobbes felt obliged to hem and haw as to how a deterministic account of this drive amounts to 'morality.' (Philosophers often try to splice concepts that do not really jibe.) Any incidental iteration of the familiar language of ethics notwithstanding, however, at root the Hobbesian system is an effort to dispense with morality altogether. The vision of man is that of mechanistically impelled 'matter in motion,' not purposeful, volitional consciousness.

But whether one proposes natural-law-based morality or innate-drive-based 'morality,' the social compact in and of itself cannot subsume the full measure of normativity often imputed to it. That is why both Kant and Rawls invoke much more than mere universal agreement in their efforts to extract from the compact moral and legal standards that can be considered binding. Rawls believes that the compact must be confirmed by intuitively acceptable moral conceptions placed in rational equilibrium.[7] He also introduces the idea of the 'veil of ignorance' to establish a basis for (collectivist) consistency. It seems that everybody in society who is party to the hypothetical compact 'would' agree to a Rawlsian scheme of redistributionism if only suitably protected from knowledge of their own natures and potentials. And so Rawls stipulates that the parties are thus blindfolded. Agreement will be thwarted if the contractors possess important individual characteristics, so with a wave of his metaphysical wand Rawls strips all the contractors of individuating characteristics. Consent is thus generated by the (ill-informed) intuitions Rawls imposes on the pre-individuated contractors.

Why is a mere agreement not sufficient? If no other source of norms is available – as is especially true in the case of Rawls – why not simply insist that norms come from brute human choices, be they rational, self-consistent, irrational, illogical, arbitrary, or whichever?

I think the reason this road is blocked for Kant and Rawls is that they both reject any sort of metaphysical or ontological grounds for morality. Rawls was very clear about it in his Eastern Division APA Presidential Address when he averred that 'much of moral theory is independent from the other parts of philosophy.'[8] Kant, too, locates morality in the hermetically sealed land of pure reason, *sans* external foundations: 'Every action is right which, in itself, or in the maxim on which it proceeds, is such that it can coexist along with the freedom of the will of each and all in action, according to a universal law.'[9] In the social realm, Kant enjoins us to 'act externally in such a manner that the free exercise of the will may be able to coexist with the freedom of all others, according to a universal law.'[10] An example of what he means: 'If a man and a woman have the will to enter on reciprocal enjoyment in accordance with their sexual nature, they must necessarily marry each other; and this necessity is in accordance with the juridical laws of pure reason.'[11] (One suspects that 'pure reason' might be abetted by the social mores of the day.)

In the case of Rawls, the attempt to deny the dependence of personal and social morality on other branches of philosophy also fails.[12] There is no way to explicate the meaning of 'rational' without consulting the philosophy of mind, questions of ontology or metaphysics, the subject of free will versus determinism, and so forth. If, for example, being rational implies, as Kant suggests, that an agent is free to make choices and to initiate his own conduct, this alone is enough to make a difference with respect to the ethics and politics that human beings ought to adopt. While it is true that in many ordinary human circumstances rough-hewn common sense can advance the discussion with sufficient clarity and precision, under certain skeptical assaults this will not suffice (and even unselfconscious common sense implicitly relies upon assumptions about the nature of reality, the possibility of objectivity, and the like). We all manage to deal with the physical, chemical, sociological and economic realities that surround us for a good while without resorting to specialists, but at certain points we find we must rely on them. So too with ethics and politics. Common sense is the beginning, not the end, of inquiry.

It might also be argued that for social compact theories, each person appraises proposed social morals on the basis of his or her own interest, given the interests and powers of others. So if one's acceptance of some point of philosophy, say in metaphysics, affects one's interests in a way that calls for a new ingredient in the social compact, that may well be defensible, and will be added to the list of points being negotiated. An example might be the need for free inquiry in the society – that is surely a plausible item. So it is tossed into the hat. But does this desire for free inquiry become part of the discussion because some metaphysical fact implies the benefit of such inquiry? Or because disagreements between parties about what indeed are the metaphysical facts spawn the practical question of how these differences are to be socially dealt with both in negotiating the compact and in the affairs of the resulting society?

Yet if there are some facts of any kind, including metaphysical or ontological facts, that permeate social life – for example, the fact that all human beings are sovereign agents and that their agency is a precondition of a moral life – these facts and their ethical implications cannot be contracted away, nor will they wither away. Such provisions will be a necessary part of a coherent human social life whether they are itemized in the compact or not. To the extent that they are violated, human life and the potentials of human life will be hindered.

Suppose that the members of totalitarian societies (or tribes) can be somehow regarded as having signed the social compact that ordains the soul-stomping regimentation to which they must meekly submit every day. The totalitarian regimes would still be way out of line, morally, no matter how many signed copies of the agreement there might be, no matter how many bows a chief receives. Or let's say it is a feature of the social compact that some people in society will be slaves. In parts of Ghana, for example, young virgins are forced to become sex slaves of priests, purportedly to atone for the grave sins of some family member. And maybe everyone party to this compact in such a Ghanaian sub-society really believes this. Nevertheless, coercive sexual subjugation of innocent virgins violates a basic requirement of human life, the need of each individual to choose, himself or herself, how he or she will live.

Slavery is a basic violation of one's humanity. Social compacts that ignore this fact must fail (as must the theories based on such compacts), but not because they violate either their own explicit terms or some procedural protocol. They fail on moral grounds. The agreement itself fails to comply with the principles it ought to comply with. A compact cannot be morally self-justifying; it cannot confect its own ethic from scratch, solely within its own asserted boundaries. It must consult a wider moral and metaphysical context.

Immanuel Kant attempts to secure the foundations of morality in pure reason, removed from that impossible field, metaphysics. This attempt itself relies upon a kind of metaphysics, but of a tortuous sort. What we do see in Kant, though, is that social compact theory rests on requirements of how human beings ought to act that do not themselves rest on agreement, that is, that are valid independently of any consensus about them. The particular moral principles Kant thinks govern human life may not be the ones we indeed ought to live by, but it is clear at least that some such principles are needed if social compacts are to be morally palatable.

No matter what kind of social compact theory we are addressing, whether Kantian, Hobbesian, or Rawlsian, it is always reasonable to ask the common-sense moral question of whether what people willed – whether behind a veil of ignorance, in unison, or at some great convention – *should* have been willed by them.

Now, some might argue that the very point of making agreements, normally, is to settle something. If asking the above question amounts to reneging on a done deal, we should have heard about the question a bit sooner.[13]

But this assertion makes the very point against which it is attempting to protest. Where does this judgment that 'we should have heard about it sooner' come from? It's a claim based not in a prior compact but in something more fundamental, some natural law or objective moral principle. If someone agrees to do X and later disputes the force of the agreement, it can well be said: 'You ought to have considered your doubts earlier.' But could this 'ought' itself rest solely on some prior agreement, in turn empowered by an 'ought' stipulated by a still prior compact, and so on, *ad infinitum*? If not, the moral force of the compact must be grounded in something outside of itself, in moral truths we know and take heed of apart from what we are agreeing to in the compact itself. (Here we need to keep in mind that agreeing to something that imposes burdens on un-consulted third parties – other than the 'burden' of abstaining from aggression – is perverse not because there is an agreement against such a procedure but because consent is fundamental in adult human relationships … whether the propriety of this consent is agreed to or not.)

When someone in the state of nature thinks about entering a social compact, it makes sense for her to ask, 'Ought I to join in the search for some way of solving our problem?' The ability to ask the question suggests the availability and relevance of standards that could help one make the right choice. This foremost standard one would want to consult is called prudence: the virtue of taking good care of ourselves, including when we embark upon social life. (Rawls himself admits that some such standard might be discovered but regards it as obstructionist to wait for it.[14])

It would not be cogent for the determinist to insist, on the basis of his view that entering the compact is a matter of being driven by fear to do so, that such a question cannot arise. For if we are indeed determined to behave as we do, this will be just as true after the social compact comes into existence as it was before. So no judgments as to what we ought to do will be applicable now, either. What if one's sundry urges motivate one to ignore the agreed-upon compact? On deterministic premises, a social compact has no more moral weight than any other moral stricture. One will just do what one must, and there is nothing morally to be said for or against it.

But if 'ought' does imply 'can' after all, then this, too, is a fact that is true both before and after the social compact. And then it is also true that, prior to the compact, there can be standards of ascertaining what one ought to do.

A recent example of social compact theory is advanced by Jan Narveson in his *The Libertarian Idea*.[15] He argues that

> the principles of morality are (or should be) those principles for directing everyone's conduct which it is reasonable for everyone to accept. They are the rules that everyone has good reason for wanting everyone to act on, and thus to internalize in himself or herself, and thus to reinforce in the case of everyone.[16]

But this is problematic because it builds into the social compact the requirement of reasonableness, even though, as we have seen, agreement need not be reasonable at all.

The normative requirement that we ought to be reasonable cannot be assumed as automatically constitutive of agreements and, thus, of social compacts. After all, some prospective signatories could ask, 'Why should we be reasonable?' Granted, this may seem like a silly, even incoherent, question. Yet it is certainly one that has been raised by philosophers and, especially, literary and religious figures. It may not be reasonable to have faith in God but many believe that faith is just what we ought to have. It may not be reasonable to indulge one's momentary feelings or passions thoughtlessly, yet there are famous figures throughout history who have promoted just this notion. (And many of the rest of humanity who have acted in accordance with it.) Why are they wrong, if they are? Why should we obey the advice of Socrates to follow reason instead of fancy? There are reasons why we should follow reason, even if the validity of reason itself is self-evident.

The contractarian stance does not answer the question but simply takes the indispensability of reasonableness for granted. As Narveson puts the point,

> Those who insist on being unreasonable aren't being metaphysical drop-outs; they are simply being sociopaths, and social contract theory explains very succinctly how to deal with such people: no contract, nothing is disallowed, and you do whatever you think necessary, period. If the 'unreasonable' don't like that, then they have their answer to the question, 'why be reasonable'.[17]

Yet, it is philosophically impoverished to provide this kind of answer to all those who have championed unreason. Such people may be wrong without being sociopaths. Indeed, if only sociopaths defended unreason, all the efforts by certain philosophers and others to rebuff, for example, the postmodernist zeitgeist, with its very large dosage of irrationalism, would be pointless.[18] There would be no need to dispute all those who have maintained that being reasonable is somehow sectarian, biased, or an expression of Western prejudice; only the frothing madmen of insane asylums would be babbling such notions, not tenured professors.

Of course, it might not be easy to reorient irrationalists toward reason. But that the effort is made suggests both that many who are capable of being reasonable choose not to be so, and that many advocates of reason see some hope of convincing some such champions to become reasonable (perhaps by appealing to the modicum of reasonableness they do exhibit). And at the least, an articulate defense of reason can help inoculate those who are disposed to be reasonable against the sophistries of those who are not so disposed, as well as guide us directly in the living of our own lives. While some aspects of why it is right to be reasonable are obvious to men of good will, not everything about reason or being reasonable is equally obvious.

A full defense of reason would explain that we are by nature rational animals; that nature, in turn, is a rational order (in the sense of being ruled by the laws of identity and cause-and-effect), not some random, chaotic mess; and if we are to deal with nature successfully, it is vital that we be reasonable. These conclusions, in turn, need to be supported as well – a full philosophical case would show why they are true, not simply taken for granted. And for that purpose it isn't sufficient to rely solely on common sense.

There are other problems with contractarianism, too, among them the fundamentally fully egalitarian stance its champions often adopt. The parties to the contract are viewed as having equal standing. Yet why should this be so? What if some are born with superior sensibilities and thus are in a better position to decide what rules ought to guide all of us? Or favored by the Gods?

This egalitarian assumption needs to be defended, not just assumed, yet social compact theories typically inaugurate their theorizing with the assumption that parties to the compact possess an equal measure of required sensibilities (like prudence and self-regard) or other attributes (like talent and intelligence). In the case of Rawls, as we have seen, a 'veil of ignorance' had to be deployed – blinding participants in the compact (and also, Rawls may have hoped, his readers) to any relevant particulars.

Furthermore, if prior to the compact certain ethical standards already bind us, then it may well be that certain social compacts are ill-formed and should never have been entered into. Indeed, given that social compact theory is often invoked to justify laws or systems of rules that reach far into the future, after all actual and 'hypothetical' participants in the agreement are long dead, one can easily raise the question of whether posterity is obliged by the contractual provisions. Should American citizens be loyal to the US Constitution, for example? How about the Charter of the United Nations? Or the laws that arise from the Hobbesian or Rawlsian social compact? Could there not be moral grounds for dismissing some of the provisions of these and other social compacts? Are such grounds themselves valid only because some later assembly of citizens have affirmed them? And what's the status of the documents that amend old compacts: do these new amendments qualify as social compacts, too? If they do, why is that so? How do we handle folks who disagree about that?[19]

These are objections to social compact theory that need to be addressed. I do not believe they can be, successfully. The question that remains then is whether and where the social compact approach is still required, given its shortcomings and given that from different philosophical perspectives it would not be necessary. I believe its power rests mostly on the scientistic, non-normative understanding of human conduct whereby we are driven to act as we do by inborn psychological dispositions that we cannot resist as a matter of choice.

Once, however, the theoretical veil of empiricism and scientism is lifted, I think the appeal of social compact theory would be narrowed considerably. In other words, while agreement may be important for the purposes of implementing certain principles, it is not agreement *per se* that would make these principles the ones we ought to adopt for the purposes of community life. Agreement is important, for example, with respect to conventions that equally well implement the same valid principle – even if another convention might have been equally viable. If you don't like the convention that red means 'stop,' you are still, and properly, culpable if you endanger others by interpreting red to mean 'go.'

But the orthodoxy of empiricism, in abandoning any hope for metaphysics, lacks philosophical as well as, for the time being, cultural force. The field is thus wide open and new beginnings can readily be forged.[20] A reconsideration of the Greek conception of human nature, specifically the Aristotelian conception, would provide greater promise for grounding justice than any such truncated approach as social compact theory.

Now comes the $64,000 question: why do social compact theorists reject this approach to grounding politics and law? For Narveson the answer is easy:

> There are people out there, apparently, who don't agree with the Greeks about how to live – or anyway, don't seem to. Aristotle is telling us how to be happy, and if he's right and we genuinely disagree, then we shall be unhappy. So what? What business is it of [anyone] whether I am unhappy?[21]

But the same objection can be raised about the results of the social compact! 'There are people out there, apparently, who don't agree with the drafters of the social compact about how to live – or anyway, don't seem to.' Big problem, isn't it? There are indeed people out there who do not agree with Narveson about how we ought to act toward one another as human beings, as fellow citizens, as neighbors. We are, after all, not living in the fully free society laid out in Narveson's social compact. And what's so bad about that? So what if we are not free? We simply won't be able to do as we want to, right? We're simply living under a social compact forged in accordance with values alien to our own. Can we still say that, agreement or disagreement aside, there is good reason why *in fact* freedom is better than, say, being sexually subjugated by the local parson … or escorted to the gas chamber?

But as soon as the Narvesonian theorist agrees that there is *some* reason, having to do with the value of human life, for seeking to institute, preserve and protect a free society, he has exited the confines of self-justifying agreement.

There can be no short cut here. It is just as much a philosophical and social hassle to agree or disagree with Narveson or other social compact theorists as it is to agree or disagree with Aristotle. Yes, it would be nice if we could all just get along and see eye to eye on everything with easy good will and mutual understanding, without ever having to sweat out an argument. But part of the reason we do philosophical work is to try to convince people of that which they do not already believe. Social compact theory cannot escape the problems we face as a result of our disagreements. If it could, social compact theory would have long since produced the results Narveson believes flow from it: namely, widespread agreement about the value of individual liberty and the resulting protection of that liberty throughout human societies.

Theories of all kinds will encounter skeptics. We still need to know which of them is best. If it turns out that people in fact ought to strive to be happy and promote their own lives, then that is a premise to which our thinking about how to live must attend. Certainly, it must be attended to when we consider what kind of communities are best suited for us, since those that ban us from pursuing our happiness will fail us just for that reason. It is no accident that the American Founders concluded that a free society is the one most conducive to the pursuit of happiness, and that they ought, therefore, build the kind of legal order that would best protect that freedom.

All this does not mean anyone can *impose* a vision of how to live on anyone else, nor even that anyone is authorized to try, apart from erecting obstacles to imposing such visions.[22] One's business in learning how we ought to live is just that: to learn it and to do it and, maybe, once in a while, explain it to others. But once one has learned it, one can continue to try to figure out the implications of this view for social and political life. And it turns out that the political framework that makes the pursuit of happiness possible also makes possible the rejection of that pursuit.

In any case, the defense of liberty inspired from within a neo-Aristotelian moral and political libertarian philosophy does seem to hold out philosophical promise. Aristotle's naturalism abandoned the Platonic aspiration for timelessly fixed natures from which eternal standards of good and bad, right and wrong, may be derived. He supplies us with an alternate, more robust conception of what is meant by 'the nature of X,' one that can produce a revitalized naturalistic ethics.[23]

An understanding of human beings as free, responsible agents provides us with norms we ought to apply in our own lives. Human beings are at their best when they freely, of their own initiative, actualize their potential to live rationally. This is an ontological foundation for the ethics that the social compact theory presupposes without argument. It implies, furthermore, that insofar as we are social beings who require some type of community, we face the question of what kind of community will be most hospitable to our task of living the right way. The standards of such a community are, among other ingredients, the natural rights that all members will be required to observe and will not be able to violate with impunity.

The social contractarian feature of this way of thinking of political norms includes, most prominently, what an economist might call the ultimate exit option: no one may be coerced to remain part of the community. At some level, the consent of the governed *is* required for government to have authority to administer the (just) laws. But no one may 'consent' to governmental deeds that would be immoral to perpetrate in private.

So what remains of social compact theory is, indeed, very important: namely, the value of freely reaching agreement among human beings, and the justifiability of certain kinds of efforts to reach it. When a sufficient number of participants in the polis can and do in fact agree on how to maintain and preserve appropriate standards of social justice (as well as on who should administer the effort), something crucial to the lives of the participants is achieved – the conditions for proper social intercourse. The compact provides, as well, the political will to enforce the conditions.

Human beings do not always do what is right *vis-à-vis* their fellows. To impress them with the need to abide by the proper norms, force is sometimes necessary. Such force would be ineffective if the political will did not exist to back it. If, as the classical liberal tradition holds, the proper norms provide individuals with jurisdiction over their significant actions – with, that is, sovereignty – responsible individuals will be the first to become involved in political action.

It is not enough to learn the true principles of justice; it is also vital to apply them. And applying them is not possible without widespread (not necessarily universal) agreement – to wit, a social compact or contract. The compact and the institutions and processes it generates are to be the method by which political norms are upheld and enforced in society. That method – in the Western legal tradition referred to as 'due process' – is itself always open to evaluation. When consent secures due process, something enormously valuable is secured: the prospect of success in the maintenance of justice.

Social compact theory fails as the first word about social and political norms. A social compact cannot suffice as *the* grounding of how we ought to comport ourselves in each other's company. Our agreement, and the means of implementing our agreement, can be very important. But mere agreement does not establish what is socially or politically right. For that we also (and more fundamentally) need a clear, if general idea of how we ought to live.[24] And then, yes, we can all get along.

Notes

1 Indeed, even when one considers discussions such as this one, one of the first questions that comes to mind is: 'Is the author right or wrong in dealing with this topic?' It seems to arise quite apart from any *agreement* about standards.

2 Immanuel Kant, *Metaphysical Elements of Justice*, trans. John Ladd (Indianapolis, IN: Bobbs-Merrill, 1965), p. 80.

3 Immanuel Kant, *Werke* (Berlin: Bruno Cassier, 1914), Vol. 6, pp. 380–81 (my translation).

4 John Rawls, *A Theory of Justice* (Cambridge, MA: Harvard University Press, 1971), p. 36.

5 Hobbesian natural rights are, strictly speaking, non-normative – unlike Lockean ones – but a feature of the life-sustaining innate drives of those in the state of nature. Some will dispute that Hobbesian rights are non-normative but at the price of neglecting a crucial element of morality, namely, the capacity to freely choose whether to take one or another action. Such 'moral' theories are actually at most theories of value or good, not theories of rightly or wrongly chosen conduct.

6 For a survey, see Shirley Robin Letwin, 'Modern Philosophies of Law,' *The Great Ideas Today* (Chicago, IL: Encyclopedia Britannica, 1972), pp. 105–53.

7 John Rawls, 'The Independence of Moral Theory,' *Proceedings and Addresses of the American Philosophical Association* (Newark, DE: University of Delaware, 1975), p. 5.

8 Ibid.

9 Immanuel Kant, *The Philosophy of Law*, trans. W. Hastic (Edinburgh, 1887), reprinted in *Great Books of the Western World* (Chicago, IL: Encyclopedia Britannica, 1952), vol. 42; p. 436.

10 Ibid., p. 398.

11 Ibid., p. 419.

12 Tibor R. Machan, 'A Note of Independence,' *Philosophical Studies*, 30 (1976); pp. 419–22. Natural law and rights theories achieve what the veil of ignorance aims for, namely the securing of moral equality, but only for the purposes of understanding political life. They focus on human nature, something we all share, but not at the expense of ignoring individual differences or pretending that they do not exist.

13 Narveson noted this in personal email exchange (December 1996).

14 Rawls, 'The Independence of Moral Theory,' p. 21.

15 Jan Narveson, *The Libertarian Idea* (Philadelphia, PA: Temple University Press, 1989). Another prominent social contract theorist is Tristan Engleheart, a specialist in bio-ethics and author of several books on the topic.

16 Ibid., p. 131. Narveson appears to be talking here about 'the principles of morality,' yet in the earlier mentioned personal email correspondence he states that 'social contract theory is quite obviously only aimed at interpersonal rules which are indeed "norms of community life."'

17 Ibid. Personal email correspondence.

18 For example, Steven Hicks, *Explaining Postmodernism* (Tempe, AZ: Scholargy Custom Publishing, 2004).

19 Similar difficulties face pure democrats – if majority rule *establishes* the soundness of legal or political principles, how would one defend these principles to those about to embark upon participation in the democratic process?

20 As an example, consider Edward Pols's recent book, *Mind Regained* (Ithaca, NY: Cornell University Press, 1998), which argues for a fundamental reconsideration of the scientistic, empiricist, and behaviorist orientation concerning theories of mind as well as the foundation of human moral life. In particular, the work mounts a frontal assault on the belief that teleological explanations of human action are unfounded – a belief underlying accounts of the normative dimensions of human life framed solely in terms of drives and motives.

21 Narveson's email.

22 This is why a constitution of individual rights does not require full explicit consent of all those who live under it, any more than one requires the consent of a mugger to defend oneself against attack. See, for more on this, Randy E. Barnett, *Restoring the Lost Constitution* (Princeton, NJ: Princeton University Press, 2004). This is also the best reason for why the military of a free country is not authorized to carry out wars of liberation, as *per* President George W. Bush's grand plan to liberate the world from tyrants. For more, see Tibor R. Machan, *The Passion for Liberty* (Lanham, MD: Rowman & Littlefield, 2003), Chapter 13, 'Military Defense of a Free Society.'

23 See Tibor R. Machan, *Individuals and Their Rights* (LaSalle, IL: Open Court Publishing Company, Inc., 1989). See also Tibor R. Machan, *Classical Individualism* (London: Routledge, 1998).

24 For a full treatment, see T. R. Machan, 'Individualism and the Problem of Political Authority,' *The Monist*, 66 (1983); pp. 500–16 (which is also Chapter 7 of, *Individuals and Their Rights)*. Why, for example, would it be wrong to contract for the use of some third party who has not consented? Because that party has rights and, regardless of any contractual determination, it is wrong to violate rights.

The concept of 'meta-norm' is advanced by Douglas B. Rasmussen and Douglas J. Den Uyl, *Liberty and Nature, An Aristotelian Defense of Liberal Order* (LaSalle, IL: Open Court Publishing Company, Inc., 1991). It means those norms the function of which is – in organized human communities or systems of justice – to enable other norms, those which directly guide action, to be freely and well practiced.

Chapter 24

Against Fairness

Everyone has been told that life isn't fair and generally it is deemed unwise to insist that we all get the same breaks – good health, good looks, a pleasant region in which to live, parents who are responsible and loving, as well as well off, and the rest of what is generally hoped for by most. It is, however, also argued by some that what most of us really want isn't happiness at all but comparable advantage, the condition to be as well off as the next person, at least.[1]

Some prominent political thinkers – for example, Rousseau – have made the more serious argument in support of a very strong moral, even political, imperative that people – in a society or throughout the world – must be treated fairly, as basically equal and with equal benefits and burdens for them all. Among those today who promote this idea explicitly is Kai Nielsen,[2] Ronald Dworkin,[3] and Peter Unger.[4]

The policy implication of this view is extensive and continuous wealth redistribution. No one has the right to keep extensive assets, for example, that he or she came by either *via* hard work, good luck, or the contributions of others. A beautiful model, especially, who gains considerable wealth because millions of others wish to pay to see her, for example, is to be taxed extensively and the funds taken from her are to be spread out to others who do not enjoy this advantage, who are disadvantaged. Even a very hard-working executive, paid a large salary with bonuses because he or she has successfully put a corporation on a firm economic footing, may not keep these earnings but is taxed progressively – not proportionately – and the funds are to be redistributed by politically appointed bureaucrats (though not before they are paid for this work quite handsomely). Someone who is lucky and wins a huge amount of money in a lottery must also part with a substantial portion of his or her winnings and that, too, will be redistributed. As Unger puts the point, 'On pain of living a life that's seriously immoral, a typical well-off person, like you and me, must give away most of her financially valuable assets, and much of her income, directing the funds to lessen efficiently the serious suffering of others.'[5]

All in all, the ideal of fairness or equality doesn't even allow the sort of differences in wealth and poverty that would remain after the familiar taxation policies of most welfare states – they do not go far enough, the champions of these ideals such as Unger argue. There are various philosophically interesting reasons offered why this ideal really is a political imperative and why the law ought to be guided by it. One reason is hinted at in John Rawls' discussion of whether people deserve the wealth they obtain in market transactions.[6]

Rawls claims that they do not because none of us really earns anything since we are basically socially conditioned to be hard-working, entrepreneurial individuals.[7] Our ambition or effort really isn't something we cultivate in ourselves so that we should be rewarded for it. It is entirely accidental who will be ambitious and who will not, so leaving it at the original distribution that comes from voluntary exchanges must be unfair. Nagel, explaining a possible global implication of Rawls's position, tells us that 'The accident of being born in a poor rather than in a rich country is as arbitrary a determinant of one's fate as the accident of being born in a poor rather than a rich family in the same country.'[8]

But Rawls himself rejects this implication because, as Nagel explains,

> The important point for our purposes is that Rawls believes that this moral principle [of fairness] against arbitrary inequalities is not a principle of universal application … . Rather, in his theory the objection to arbitrary inequalities gets a foothold only because of the societal context. What is objectionable is that we should be fellow participants in a collective enterprise of coercively imposed legal and political institutions that generate such arbitrary inequalities … . One might even say that we are all participants in the general will. A sovereign enterprise for mutual advantage.[9]

So, some kind of collective or state decision, in which of course not all take part – as in, say, the decisions of the Rotary or Elks Club, where a good deal of wealth redistribution goes on with full consent of all members – authorizes this equalization process within a given society.

Why is this a sound idea? No clue other than the assumption, entirely unproven, that such collective decisions (*via* the Rousseauian general will) are just. Yet this is hardly a proof of the Rawlsian justice as fairness stance. As David Gordon points out, 'Nagel fails to see this obvious point because he regards the sovereign state as the only way, under modern conditions, for people to escape from a Hobbesian condition of anarchic violence.'[10] As with other egalitarians, such as Dworkin, the state is a given and requires no moral justification. In consequence, its scope, too, remains unlimited other than by the collective or state decision process.[11]

The second argument in support of fairness rests on intuition: many feel deeply that it is simply natural for us all to share in the common wealth of society – we know this to be so intuitively. But this argument is a really bad one and I will not spend much time on it other than to note that intuitions are notoriously unreliable guides to what we ought to be doing. As the writer W. Somerset Maugham pointed out, 'intuition, [is] a subject upon which certain philosophers have reared an imposing edifice of surmise, but which seems to me to offer as insecure a foundation for any structure more substantial than a Castle in Spain as a ping-pong ball wavering on a jet of water in a shooting gallery.'[12] Ernest W. Pettifer makes clear, in the following passages, why Maugham is right:

> To us today the revelations of the legal murders and cruelties connected with the trial of children are revolting. We have become so habituated to the kindly and even anxious atmosphere of the Children's Courts, that it is hard to believe that the full ceremonial, the dread ordeal, of the Assize Courts could have been brought into use against little children of seven years and upwards – judges uttering their cruel legal platitudes; the chaplain sitting by assenting; the Sheriff in his impressive uniform; ladies coming to the Court to be entertained by such a sight – the spectacle of a terrified little child about to receive the death sentence which the verdict of 12 men, probably fathers of families themselves, had given the judge power to pass.[13]

In short, intuitions are in constant flux and, based on them, slavery had to have been fine in one age, not in another, as with the abuse of women and children and prisoners of war, to name just a few areas wherein we clearly seek for moral stability but aren't provided with it by intuitions. Intuitions – or as they are better known, common sense – can be an initial clue to where the truth lies but it cannot be decisive.

Yet another argument is a serious challenge to individualism and individual rights. It maintains, along the lines we already saw in Nagel, that people are by their very nature parts of a larger whole – society, tribe, humanity, the ethnic group or the community – and so belong to a group the members of which are owed loyalty and solidarity from them. Socialists like August Comte and Karl Marx held this view, as do some contemporary communitarians like Charles Taylor. These thinkers insist that the classical liberal polity rests on the false belief in atomistic individualism. This holds that we are independent, self-sufficient beings who can do without society altogether and for whom social relations are entirely optional. Such a view is similar to what some economists work with as they analyze market relations, but critics claim classical liberals rest all their ideas on it.

This ant-colony/beehive notion of human social life gains some support from the Aristotelian idea that we are all essentially social. But to take it to where socialists and communitarians do is an extreme leap. It denies that individuals can form ideas of their own, govern their own lives in the light of these ideas and be responsible for the result. Others should not be burdened if they live in misguided ways. And it is wrong to believe that we are obligated to shoulder burdens and share rewards, as if we did belong to some natural club or tribe. But fairness or equal treatment does follow if we do, so this idea is often invoked to support the redistributionist state.

In fact, though we are social beings, there is an essential individuality to our lives as well, and this demands that we enjoy sovereignty in how we live, rather than involuntary servitude to people with whom we did not chose to associate. As such, it is not unfair at all to be better off than others – they aren't owed our lives and labors, contrary to how egalitarians think.

Concerning fairness or equality, one reason in our time that these seem such ubiquitous imperatives is that in a reasonably abundant society children grow up being treated rather fairly by parents who owe all of them (in the family) decent treatment. Just as a teacher is supposed to attend to all of his or her students – having in effect made a promise to all of them to serve them with his or her skills – so parents have basically promised their kids to treat them equally well, provided they have the wealth to do so.

But all of this is highly conditional and by no means basic – it is the *responsibility* to keep the promise to provide service or good rearing that is. Yet having grown up with the justified expectation, based on the promise, of equally good treatment or fairness from parents and teachers, it makes some psychological sense that this expectation would be extended to governments that claim to be providers for their citizens – not just providers of equal protection of their basic rights to be free, but of whatever governments (politicians) promise (in a welfare state, for instance).

Yet this expectation is misguided for two reasons: the government is not a parent, and governments should not attempt to provide citizens with everything they would like.

The Rawlsian case is a bit more complicated because it rests on a very controversial yet widely championed idea in our time, namely, determinism. This is the idea that all people behave as they must, based on the factors that impel them to do so. Whether because of genes, evolutionary forces, peer pressure or whatever, there is a widespread idea, drawn from extrapolation from classical physics, that none of us is free and responsible and thus deserving of either gains or losses. It's all a matter of accident.

Paradoxically, however, from this picture, based on a deterministic view of human life, a moral conclusion is drawn that is incompatible with determinism: namely, that we all ought to work to fix the accidental distribution of benefits and harms, gains and losses, by means of a political order that is guided by fairness. Since 'ought' implies 'can,' this imperative cannot be reconciled with determinism.

But, just as Kant believed that a deterministic (phenomenal) world coexists with a (noumenal) realm where choice is possible, so Rawls and his followers embrace this two-world picture, one in which determinism rules, and another in which freely chosen moral and political conduct would remedy matters and where those opposing such remedies are to be morally faulted for their stance.

These last points not only indicate the paradoxical nature of the Rawlsian-based fairness imperative but also undermine it. It turns out that we are after all, moral agents and we can act in ways that make us morally deserving, quite possibly even deserving of greater wealth than what others, lacking such desert, obtain.

Furthermore, there is a *non sequitur* in this version of the fairness imperative: just because one doesn't deserve some portions of one's assets, it doesn't follow that others may take them from one. One doesn't deserve a lot of things which others have no authority to take from one – say, an extra kidney, a good second eye, one's good looks or talents, and so on. And many of these assets are possessed by individuals with no one seriously considering taking them without their consent; yet these are serious sources of inequality – life's many instances of unfairness, if you will – inasmuch as those who lack them often desire and could benefit from them a great deal. A homely person would want quite badly to be beautiful; someone without any musical aptitude may eagerly desire it, and someone who lacks athletic prowess might want to gain and benefit from it considerably.

Yet, even if we were to leave the matter with intuitions, it is clear that few would claim that their intuitions tell them they could deprive those who possess these advantages. Such intuitions do not seem to be the province of most people and tend to be induced by a prior embrace of certain moral notions. The focus on wealth redistribution, in any case, is not matched by any similar focus on other assets that would enrich people who lack them. Whatever advances those lacking the assets might make in their lives is pretty much left to various types of initiative, including generosity, charity, and ingenuity.

For these reasons – probably among others that have to do with the debilitating nature of trying to implement an egalitarian regime – the fairness imperative is grossly misguided. It is also impossible, since in the effort to accomplish the massive redistribution of benefits and harms, those who take on this task obtain an inordinately greater measure of power over others. That, in turn, is the most insidious inequality or unfairness that a human community can contain.

Notes

1 This, roughly, is the theme of Richard Laynard, *Happiness, Lessons from a New Science* (New York: The Penguin Press, 2005). But see also Helmut Schoeck, *Envy: A Theory of Social Behavior* (New York: Ardent Media, Inc., 1966; Indianapolis, IN: Liberty Fund, Inc., 1987).

2 Kai Nielsen, *Equality and Liberty: a Defense of Radical Egalitarianism* (Totowa, NJ: Rowman and Allanheld, 1985).

3 Ronald Dworkin, *Sovereign Virtue: The Theory and Practice of Equality* (Cambridge, MA: Harvard University Press, 2000).

4 Peter Unger, *Living High and Letting Die: Our Illusion of Innocence* (New York: Oxford University Press, 1996).

5 Ibid., p. 134.

6 John Rawls, *A Theory of Justice* (Cambridge, MA: Harvard University Press, 1971).

7 Ibid., p. 104. Rawls believes that the assertion that we 'deserve the superior character that enables us to make the effort to cultivate our talents is … problematic; for such character depends in good part upon fortunate family and social circumstances in early life for which we can claim no credit.'

8 Thomas Nagel, 'The Problem of Global Justice,' *Philosophy & Public Affairs*,' Vol. 33 (April 2005), p. 119.

9 Ibid., pp. 127–8.

10 David Gordon, 'Indifference to the World,' *The Mises Review*, Vol. 11 (Spring 2005), p. 9.

11 Thus, a country may have a limited monarchy or democracy, or an unlimited or absolute one, but these are not requirements of justice, only those of the general will.
12 W. Somerset Maugham, *A Writer's Notebook* (Baltimore, MD: Penguin, 1967), p. 325.
13 Ernest W. Pettifer, *Punishments of Former Days* (East Ardsley, England: EP Publishing, Ltd., 1974), pp. 35–6.

Epilogue

Libertarianism asks: what are the most basic principles of community life, of interacting with one another as human beings? What are the minimal but indispensable prerequisites of moral coexistence among the members of a society? When other persons are encountered, how must they be treated – and what actions are they entitled to take if such treatment is not forthcoming?

Of course, there is much more to living than abiding by basic principles of human interaction. There is much we do that pertains to ourselves alone – choosing a career, selecting flowers for our gardens, pictures for our walls, what to eat for breakfast, and so on. There is much we do that pertains specifically to our own families, friends, clubs, and other associations. The activities of our lives are not strictly political matters, but they exist within the framework established by politics. In pursuing our lives, we are obliged to respect established political principles (when those principles are just). When we engage in sports, commerce, science, and the like, we are obliged to do so without violating the rights of others. None of us must use unwilling people for medical experiments, steal our breakfast, or plagiarize another's novel or scientific report.

Besides such requirements, which may be enforced in order to uphold the conditions of civilization, a great deal else must be heeded in order to live well. Although these principles of good living may not be political matters as such, they can and often do relate to politics.

Our political ideas and ideals will be largely guided by our nature as human beings. Politics also depends on some psychological facts about us. Nor is it independent of various physical laws of nature: it is impossible, for example, for two persons to occupy the same space at the same time. Sociology, economics, history and other disciplines all concern what may be of political importance. One need only consider that the age when someone may take part in political decision-making or reach maturity with respect to criminal responsibility will have an impact on political matters. The ecology of our lives – what can spell a danger to us in our relationship to our environment – will also bear on politics and law.

The libertarian does not deny the reality of gray areas and borderline cases. Not all questions can be resolved with Solomon's axe. But neither is the libertarian reduced to skepticism therefore, thinking that the tough cases make it impossible for us to figure out what we should do altogether or, more pertinently here, what are our basic rights.

The story of how we must interact in human communities is not a finished one – it cannot be. People create so much, some of it quite new and unanticipated, and the rest of reality, too, proceeds to unfold in often unexpected ways. So the necessity of extending our principles, adjusting them to new facts, refining and tweaking them as our understanding is improved or amended, is simply a fact of life. An instrument like a constitution must not be framed in terms that pretend to be final. It must be given support by way of the forums of case law. When wisely framed, its terms need not be either ambiguous or impossible to extend to future problems.

What the libertarian claims is that respect for human nature – the freedom of men and women to think and to govern themselves unmolested, with their individual sovereignty intact – is the best policy to foster in human communities. This is the principle I have defended in these pages.

Index

abortion 215, 221
Acton, H. B. 239
Alcibiades 244
altruism 169
Amendment
  First 5, 171, 225, 226, 228, 248, 307
  Ninth Constitutional 224, 228
American Medical Association 223, 229
American Revolution 22, 305
anarchists 244–5
  Bakunin 244
  Kropotkin 245
Anarchy State and Utopia vii
Anderson, Martin 233
Animal Farm 5
anti-rationalist conservatism 46
apology 203
Aquinas, Thomas 303, 304
Aristotelian 24, 47, 181n. 29, 244, 250, 318 n. 10, 330, 337
Aristotle 52–3, 56, 62 n. 22, 68n. 67, 90–91, 107, 108, 130, 137, 170, 280, 303, 304, 331–2
  ethics 134, 142
Arrow, Kenneth 65n. 46
atomism 2, 8n, 135–6, 139, 211n 2,
Austrian School 98–9, 100, 274
Ayer, A. J. 95n. 24

Bacon, Francis 185–6
Ballente, Don 99
Bambrough, Renford 65n. 44
Barber, Benjamin 193–4
Bardon, Adrian 176
Barnett, Randy E. 81n. 7, 332n. 22
Bauer, Peter 269
Becker, Gary 97, 99, 101, 106, 173, 263, 266, 267
Bennett, William 246–7, 263
Benson, Bruce 157
Berkowitz, Peter 212n. 15
Berlin Wall, fall 233
Bernholtz, Peter 266
Berns, Walter 258
Bible 270, 303
Bill of Rights 223
Bloom, Allan 60n. 14, 104
Bok, Derek 191, 201
Bowood Circle 186
Brecher, Bob 117–18n. 25
Brennan, Geoffrey 101
Breyer, Stephen 104
Buchanan, James 86, 89, 92–3, 98, 100, 101, 187
Buchanan, Pat 300
Burke, Edmund 254, 263, 300
Bush, George W. 161n. 24, 263, 334 n. 22

Calabrese, Guido 194
Canada 291
capitalism 2, 101, 233, 287
Catholic 233
Chamberlain, Wilt 281
Chicago School 98, 100, 116 n. 12
children
  legal status of 215
  rights 218
Childs, R. A. 259
Christianity 130–31, 135, 204, 304
Clinton, Bill 212, 261
Clinton, Hilary 264
coercion 7–8
Communism 233, 275
communitarian 2, 72, 234, 264–5
community life 44
compact, social 319
Comte, August 132–3, 275, 277, 337
conquest, armies 304
conservatives 241
Constitution, U. S. 22, 27, 305, 307, 330
contemporary conservatism 46
contextualism 34
corporations, business 303

Cowen, Tyler 151
Cox, Stephen 60n. 13, 290
Cratylus 33
Critical Legal Theory 191

Darwin, Charles 23
Dalton, Clare 191, 201
Declaration of Independence 21, 23, 25–6, 81n. 7, 121, 151–2, 224, 225, 305
Democritus 186
Den Uyl, Douglas 81n. 6, 87, 280, 297, 300, 334n. 24
Dennett, Daniel 206
determinism, mathematical 186
Dewey, John 132
Director, Aaron 107, 173, 182n. 41
divine right of kings 22
drugs, illegal 223
Duncan, Craig 282–3n. 4, 283n 11
due process 331
Dworkin, Ronald 163, 176, 276, 335, 336

economics, statistics 290–92
egalitarianism 314, 329, 337
eminent domain 171
England 304
entitlement 171, 273
ethics 41, 168–9
Etzioni, Amitai 8n. 2, 72, 131, 247, 261–6
eudemonism 169, 170
evolutionary theory 23
existence 37

fairness 333
Feyerabend, Paul 61n. 20, 194
Fischl, Richard M. 194–7
force, moral 321
force, normative 321
Ford, Gerald 256
forgiving 203
Fourier, Charles 190n. 8
free-market economics 2, 6, 101, 103
free society 164
free will 207, 210, 251
freedom
  basic 270
  negative 45
Friedman, Jeffrey (*son of Milton*) 244, 297n.1
Friedman, Milton 95n. 24, 98, 99, 100, 114, 183n. 41, 244, 251, 262
Friendman, David 174, 190n. 14
Frost, Robert 324
Frumm, David 121

Galbraith, John Kenneth 9n. 9, 116 n12
Galileo 186
Gauthier, David 318n. 9
Gert, Heather 64n. 37
Getty, J. Paul 316
Gewirth, Alan 258
globalization 102–3
goals, liberal 324
good, definition 39
Good Samaritan 270
Gordon, David 336
Gordon, Robert W. 191, 194–7
Graglia, Professor Lino 66–7n. 56
Gray, John 60n. 10, 64–5n. 41, 68nn. 70 and 74, 127
Green, Thomas Hill 270
Grey, Thomas 174–5, 180
guilt, collective 203

habeas corpus, suspension of 24
Haldane, John 211n. 2
Hamilton, Alexander 27
Hardin, Professor Russell 33, 91
Hart, H. L. A. 205
Hasnas, John 151, 160n19
Hayek, F. A. 24, 88, 190n. 9, 233, 236–7, 255, 278
Hegel, Georg 46
Heilbronner, Robert 238n. 2
Hicks, Steven 332n. 18
Hippodamus 244
Hobbes, Thomas 2, 24, 134, 137, 139, 163, 174, 185–6, 262, 323–7
Hobbesian 316, 323, 330
Holcombe, Randy 293
Hollander, Paul 233
Holmes, Oliver W. 174, 306
Holmes, Stephen 80, 229n. 3
  positive rights 71

Holocaust 203, 209
Hook, Sidney 315n. 1
Hospers, John 244, 254
human nature, fundamental 22
Hume, David 187, 263
  anti-rationalist conservatism 46

individualism 305, 309
  conditions 129–34
infant mortality 289
innate drive 325, 330
Inquisition 204
insider trading 307
Internet 189, 190nn. 14, 17
Islamic radicals 168

Jacobsen v. Massachusetts 306
Jaffa, Harry V. 59n. 6, 182n. 38
Jefferson, Thomas 24
Jesus 131, 211n. 5, 303
Jews 203, 204, 211n. 3, 304
justice 172–3

Kant, Immanuel 55, 107, 111, 169, 276, 318n. 9, 321–7, 338
Kelley, David 152
Kelman, Mark 194
Kennedy, Duncan 191
Keynes, John 274
Kirk, Russell 255, 300
Kornai, Janos 101
Kristol, Irving 121, 258
Krugman, Paul 102
Kuhn, Thomas 67n. 60, 180, 317n. 4
Kuttner, Robert 262

laissez-faire 163, 192, 306
Lao Tzu 74, 244
law
  civil 165
  of Nature 139
  positive 165
Laynard, Richard 337n. 1
Lee, J. Roger 152
legal protections 315
Letwin, Shirley R. 333n. 6
liability, limited 304, 305, 308
liberalism, Western 7
Libertarian Idea 328
liberty
  negative 270, 285
  positive 270–71, 285
Lincoln, Abraham 24
Lochner v. New York 306
Locke, John 50, 59n. 6, 61n. 16, 69n. 78, 89, 91, 94n. 14, 139–40, 163–6, 168, 200, 314, 318n. 9
  individualism 126
  natural rights theory 32, 34
Lockean 241, 244, 248, 296, 298, 301, 333n. 5
Louisiana Purchase 24
Lukes, Steven 129
Lycophron 244, 280–81

Macdonald, Margaret 32
Machan, Tibor R. 59nn. 1, 4 and 7, 61n. 17, 62nn. 23 and 24, 65n. 46, 66nn. 52 and 53, 68–9n. 75, 80n. 2, 117n. 25, 179n. 1, 180nn. 3 and 5, 181nn. 29, 31 and 33, 182n. 37, 189n. 5, 190n. 8, 211nn. 2 and 8, 212nn. 19–22, 213n. 25, 229n. 1, 254, 283n. 11, 287–8, 297, 299, 300, 301, 304, 317–18nn. 3–7, 333nn. 12 and 22–4
MacIntyre, Alasdair 125–7, 140
Mack, Eric 253, 254, 280, 296, 297n. 2, 300
MacKinnon, Catherine 132
Macpherson, C. B. 131, 173
Malia, Martin 238n. 7
Maratos-Flier, Eleftheria 293
Martin, Steven 103
Marx, Karl 2, 21, 46, 57, 126, 127, 131, 141, 164, 173, 174, 187, 209, 213n. 23, 234–8, 239n. 12, 275, 287, 301, 337
  Grundrisse 9n. 4, 238n. 3, 239n. 8
Marxism 21, 135, 192, 233, 249
materialism
  dialectical/historical 236
  mechanistic/reductive 186, 236
Matthiessen, Peter 191
Maugham, W. Somerset 334, 338n. 12
May, Larry 210n. 1
McKenzie, Richard 99

Melden, A. I. 317n. 1
Melville, Herman
  Billy Budd 51
metaethics 321
metaethical cognitivism 208
Midgley, Mary 97, 128, 131
Mill, John S. 7, 186, 200, 244, 296, 314
Miller, Fred 134, 280
Milosevic, Slobodan 157
monarchs 304
moneylenders 303
Moon, Parker T. 213n. 25
moral
  autonomy 174
  definition 322
  individualism 209, 210
  objectivity 210
  requirements 44
  responsibility 211
Morris, Christopher 213n. 26
Moss, Robert 317n. 2
Murphy, Liam 181n. 31
Murray, Charles 266, 267

Nader, Ralph 305
Nagel, Thomas 163, 167, 170, 171, 181n. 31, 212n. 16, 336, 337, 339nn. 8 and 9
Nanny State 6
Narveson, Jan 290, 292, 318n. 8, 328, 329, 330–31
Natural Rights essay 32
Natural Rights theory 35–45
'natural' law 324
'natural' rights 45, 315
naturalism 31
Nelson, William 310n. 1
New Deal 307
Newman, Harry 60n. 14
Nielsen, Kai 335, 339n. 2
Nock, Albert 244
Norton, David 168, 213n. 25, 259
Norton, W. W. 183n. 53
Novak, Michael 131
Nozick, Robert vii, 1, 8n. 1, 43, 47, 63n. 34, 77, 115, 147–8, 163–78, 179n. 1, 180nn. 15 and 20, 181n. 27, 182nn. 34 and 39, 183, 244, 245, 254, 255, 269, 276, 281, 283n. 10, 297, 318n. 15
Nussbaum, Martha 6, 163, 176, 269, 280–82, 316, 317n. 2

objectivism 208
obligation 17
  parental 217–19
Okin, Susan Moller 179n. 1
Olsaretti, Serena 9n. 6, 183n. 53
oppression 203
Orwell, George 5
Otis v. Parker 306
Otsuka, Michael 81–2n. 13

Page, Carl 60n. 14
Peirce, Charles S. 109, 132
Peonidis, Filimon 7
Pericles 244
Pettifer, Ernest 336, 340n. 13
Petty, William 186
philosophers 325
Pinochet, Augusto 157–8
Pitkin, Hannah 316n. 5
Plato 24, 32, 46, 56, 60n. 14, 62n. 30, 74, 107, 130, 134, 137, 295, 303
Platonic natural law tradition 33
Platonism 132
political institutionism 32
Pols, Edward 334n. 20
Popper, Karl 32, 84, 239n. 11
  Open Society and its Enemies 54
pornography 246–7
Posadas 228
positivism 132
Posner, Richard A. 182–3n. 41, 194, 198, 266
post-modernist zeitgeist 329
poverty line 291–2
pragmatism, radical (Rortyite) 172
Pravda 230
principles, abandonment of basic 24
products, hazardous 223
property 177
punishment 206

Quine, Willard Van Orman 61n. 19, 132

Radnitzky, Gerard 266

Rand, Ayn 34, 61n. 15, 84, 91–2, 93n. 6, 108, 111, 169, 177, 180n. 3, 181n. 26, 182n. 37, 244, 245, 254, 280, 296, 300
rape 177
Rasmussen, Douglas 81n. 6, 87, 280, 297, 300, 334n. 24
Rawls, John 3, 47, 63n. 33, 163, 173, 181n. 34, 273, 276, 321–7, 330, 335, 338, 339nn. 6 and 7
  discounting free will 5
  justice as fairness 3, 43
Reagan, Ronald 103, 233
reasonableness 329
Rector, Robert 299
Reich, Robert 262, 263
Reisman, George 266
Republic, Plato's 303
responsibility 17, 206
Revolution, American 22, 305
rights
  basic 225
  contractual 13–14
  fundamental 14
  natural 164, 170
  negative 27–8, 176
  positive 27, 164
  principle of individual 13
  vs. pseudo-rights 14–16
  women's 177
Robinson, Randall 212n. 22
Roman Catholic Church 233
Roosevelt, Franklin Delano 27, 80n. 2
Roosevelt, Theodore 27
Rorty, Richard 59n. 7, 61n. 19 and 20, 72, 108, 109, 127–8, 132–4, 136, 172, 318n. 4
Ross, David 53
Rothbard, Murray 147, 152, 159n. 5, 245, 254, 280
Rousseau, Jean-Jacques 335, 336
Russell, Bertrand 158
Rutten, A. R. 289

Sacks, Jeffrey 101
Sadowsky, James 91–2
Saint Augustine 131, 141
Samuelson, Paul 116n. 12
Sandel, Michael 72, 163, 211 n. 2, 247
Sarlo, Chris 291, 299
Sartre, Jean-Paul 158
Scaff, Lawrence 180n. 20, 183n. 42
Scanlon, Thomas 164, 156, 170, 180n. 15
Scheffler, Samuel 163–4, 167, 170
Schmookler, Andrew Bard 238n. 3
Schweikart 178, 183n. 53
Searle, John 187
Selgin, George 292
Sen, Amartya 97, 98, 106, 109, 111, 163, 176, 269, 272–9, 282–3, 316, 317n. 2
Shelburne, 2nd Earl 186
shibboleth 228
Shue, Henry
  positive rights 71
Sierra Club 265
Singer, Peter 206, 207, 281
single-parent household 292–3
Sirico, Robert 131
Skinner, B. F. 63n. 33, 186, 206, 211nn. 6 and 11, 212n. 16, 274
Skoble, Aeon 266
slavery 22, 23, 327
Smith, Adam 102, 174
sociopaths 329
Socrates 59n. 1, 74, 328
Solzhenitsyn, Alexandr 168
Soros, George 102, 262
sovereignty 88
Sowell, Thomas 291, 299
speech, commercial 223–6, 227, 228
Spencer, Herbert 244, 306, 314
Sperry, Roger 112, 181n. 20
Spinoza 107, 111
Spooner, Lysander 147
Spragens, Thomas 265
Stassinopoulos, Arianna 255
Sterba, James P. 64n. 36, 176, 285–97
Stigler, George J. 98, 100, 101, 117n. 17, 173
Stiglitz, Joseph 102
Stone, Oliver 103
Strauss, Leo 60n. 14, 253, 300, 317n. 3
Stroud, Barry 318n. 5
subsidies 316–17
suicide, assisted 215
summum bonum 316

Sunstein, Cass R. 2–3, 80, 229n. 3
  positive rights 71
supernaturalism 250
Supreme Court, US 306, 307

Taoism 251
Taylor, Charles 8n. 2, 72, 131, 139–40, 275
Taylor, Harriet 186
Theories, Social Compact 321
Theory of Justice 3
third parties 327
'Third Way' 278
Thomas, Lewis 135
Thomson, Judith Jarvis 67n. 58
Thucydides 91
tobacco 223
Tobin, 116n. 12
Tolstaya, Tatyana 141
totalitarian regimes 326
Toulmin, Stephen 190n. 12
Trubek, David 191, 201
Tullock, Gordon 98

Unger, Peter 269, 281, 335
US Constitution 22, 27, 305, 307, 330
US Supreme Court 306, 307
usury 304
utilitarianism 169
  value theory 46

van Duffel, Siegfried 62n. 31
von Mises, Ludwig 98, 99, 100, 109, 233, 236–7, 238n. 2, 245

wealth, redistribution 335
Weber, Max 150–51, 160n. 19
  concept of government 155
welfare state 163, 176, 219, 220
West Virginia State Board of Education v. Barnette 223
Wheeler, Samuel 179n. 1
William of Ockham 244
Wilson, Woodrow 27
Wittgenstein 105, 111, 114, 133–4, 318n. 5
Wolfe, Alan 6
Wolff, Robert 167, 171–2, 180n. 17

Xenophon 244

Zeller, Eduard 134

Henry Jones, Lloyd George a John Williams (Brynsiencyn) yn Stryd Downing yn ystod y Rhyfel Byd Cyntaf.

(Llun a hawlfraint Archifdy Gwynedd)

YR ATHRO ALLTUD

Syr Henry Jones

1852–1922

E. Gwynn Matthews

ISBN 0 7074 0310 3

Dymuna'r cyhoeddwyr gydnabod nawdd Cyngor Celfyddydau Cymru.

Paratowyd ar gyfer y wasg gan
Y Ganolfan Astudiaethau Addysg
Prifysgol Cymru Aberystwyth

Clawr blaen: *Henry Jones a Thŵr Prifysgol Glasgow.*
Llun Henry Jones gan J. Bowman, Glasgow.
Tŵr y Brifysgol gan George Gilbert Scott a'r meindwr gan John Oldrid Scott.
Llun Gwasg Prifysgol Glasgow.
Clawr cefn: *Y Cwm – cyn adnewyddiad 1998.*

Argraffwyd a chyhoeddwyd gan:
GWASG GEE, LÔN SWAN, DINBYCH.

I Hywel a Rhodri

CYNNWYS

Rhagair		vi
Cydnabyddiaeth		vii
Talfyriadau		ix
Rhan 1	**GYRFA SYR HENRY JONES**	
Pennod 1	Cymru 1852–75	3
Pennod 2	Yr Alban 1875–82	13
Pennod 3	Dychwelyd i Gymru	22
Pennod 4	Athro ym Mangor	32
Pennod 5	Dychwelyd i'r Alban	48
Pennod 6	Athro yn Glasgow	63
Pennod 7	Y Cymro Alltud	81
Pennod 8	Cysgodion	92
Rhan 2	**ATHRONIAETH SYR HENRY JONES**	
Pennod 9	Rhyddfrydiaeth Newydd mewn Crefydd	103
Pennod 10	Yr Athronwyr a'r Beirdd	113
Pennod 11	Cymdeithas, Cenedl a Gwladwriaeth	123
Pennod 12	Rhyddfrydiaeth Newydd mewn Gwleidyddiaeth	130
Pennod 13	Dinasyddiaeth Dda	137
Pennod 14	Y Gymynrodd	147
Llyfryddiaeth Fer		152
Mynegai		156

RHAGAIR

Y llun enwocaf o Syr Henry Jones yw hwnnw ohono yn sefyll yn Stryd Downing gyda Lloyd George a'r Parchedig Ddr John Williams, Brynsiencyn. Saif y tri fel trindod yn cynrychioli safiad y genedl Gymreig y tu cefn i'r Ymerodraeth Brydeinig ar awr ei hangen. Mae Lloyd George yn cynrychioli Rhyddfrydiaeth Cymru a John Williams yn cynrychioli Ymneilltuaeth Cymru, ond beth a gynrychiolir gan Henry Jones? Er ei fod yn Rhyddfrydwr ac yn Fethodist Calfinaidd, nid fel lladmerydd y naill achos na'r llall y safai ef yno. Cynrychioli addysg oedd ef, a gwnâi hynny fel arloeswr addysgol ac fel Athro cadeiriog mewn athroniaeth.

Mae cyfraniad athroniaeth i feddylfryd y cyfnod hwnnw a gyrhaeddodd ei uchafbwynt ffrwydrol yn 1914–1918 yn hynod bwysig, ac ni ellir iawn gloriannu'r agweddau a fynegwyd gan arweinwyr crefydd, gwleidyddiaeth a diwylliant yn ystod y rhyfel heb fod yn ymwybodol o ddylanwad yr athronwyr arnynt. Er diwedd y bedwaredd ganrif ar bymtheg yr oedd deallusion Cymru wedi dod i gysylltiad â'r tueddiadau diweddaraf mewn athroniaeth yng ngholegau Prifysgol Cymru a'r colegau diwinyddol ar raddfa ehangach nag a welwyd erioed o'r blaen. Drwy gydol y cyfnod allweddol hwn o ddatblygu addysg uwch yng Nghymru Idealaeth oedd yr athroniaeth mewn bri, ac i'r Cymry Henry Jones oedd ei phroffwyd.

Nid oedd trafod athroniaeth mor gyfyngedig i'r ddarlithfa ag ydyw heddiw. Rhan o'r rheswm dros hynny yw fod â wnelo Idealaeth yn uniongyrchol â pholisi cyhoeddus, a bod gan ddynion fel Henry Jones ddawn arbennig iawn i gyfathrebu gyda'r cyhoedd yn gyffredinol. Ymgais yw'r gyfrol hon i egluro ei gyfraniad ef i fywyd cyhoeddus ei oes. Nid yw'n ymdriniaeth academaidd o'i athroniaeth. Ceisiwyd ei gyflwyno mewn ffordd a fydd yn apelio at unrhyw un sydd yn ymddiddori yn hanes Cymru, a bydd yr amlinelliad o'i athroniaeth mor ysgafn â phosib. Cyffyrddir â'i syniadau crefyddol, ond ei syniadau gwleidyddol fydd o ddiddordeb pennaf. Gan fod ei holl lyfrau allan o brint ers talwm iawn ceisiwyd rhoi'r cyfle iddo lefaru eto drwy nifer helaeth o ddyfyniadau Cymraeg a Saesneg.

Dylid egluro bod yr Idealaeth Hegelaidd a goleddai Henry Jones â'r fath arddeliad wedi marw'n llwyr gydag ef a'i gyfoeswyr. Darfu fel pe na buasai. Ond nid yw unrhyw angau'n derfynol. Ar ddiwedd yr ugeinfed ganrif daeth athroniaeth Hegel unwaith eto i amlygrwydd, gyda mwy o lyfrau'n cael eu cyhoeddi arno heddiw mewn blwyddyn nag a gaed mewn degawd ganrif yn ôl. Mae nifer o resymau dros hyn, ond un ohonynt yw datblygiad cymunedaeth fel adwaith beirniadol i ryddfrydiaeth mewn athroniaeth wleidyddol gyfoes. Dros nos, fel petai, daeth gwaith yr hen Idealwyr Prydeinig o ddiddordeb eto. Nis atgyfodir, ond gellir dysgu oddi wrtho. Mae'n amser priodol i edrych o'r newydd ar Henry Jones ac i gyhoeddi'r cofiant Cymraeg nas cafwyd hyd yma.

E. Gwynn Matthews
Prifysgol Cymru, Bangor
Calan Mai 1998

CYDNABYDDIAETH

Yn 1985 cefais fy rhyddhau o ddarlithio am un tymor i ddarllen ac ymchwilio fel y dymunwn a dewisais wneud astudiaeth o waith Syr Henry Jones gan fanteisio ar y cyfle i ymweld â Phrifysgol Glasgow. Mae fy nyled yn fawr felly i Bwyllgor Gwaith Rhanbarth Gogledd Cymru o Gymdeithas Addysg y Gweithwyr (fy nghyflogwyr ar y pryd) am roddi tymor sabothol i mi, ac i'r Cyfarwyddwr, Rufus Adams, am gefnogaeth a charedigrwydd cyson. Wedi i mi ymuno â staff Prifysgol Cymru, Bangor, bu fy mhennaeth adran, Alwyn Roberts, yn fy annog i fwrw ati i gyhoeddi.

Derbyniais gymorth sylweddol yn Glasgow gan nifer o swyddogion y Brifysgol. Yn bennaf yn eu plith rhaid i mi ddatgan dyled fawr i'r Athro R. S. Downie am ei ddiddordeb ac am ei gymwynas fawr yn rhoi cymaint o ddefnyddiau gwerthfawr i mi ar fenthyg. Rwyf yn ddyledus hefyd i Lyfrgellydd y Brifysgol ac i Guradur yr Hunterian Art Gallery, Glasgow. Hoffwn ddiolch i Archifydd y Brifysgol a'i staff am gymorth, ac iddo ef a theulu William Boyd am ganiatâd i ddyfynnu o bapurau personol Boyd. Cefais wybodaeth werthfawr hefyd gan Lyfrgellydd Llyfrgell Mitchell, Glasgow.

Bu cyfeillion ym Mhrifysgol Cymru, Bangor, yn gymwynasgar, yn enwedig Tomos Roberts, yr Archifydd, yr Athro J. Gwynn Williams ac Ifor Jones. Rwyf yn ddyledus iawn i'r Athro Hywel Teifi Edwards am dynnu fy sylw at ddarlithoedd Henry Jones i Gymdeithas Cymry Lerpwl, darlithoedd allweddol bwysig o safbwynt deall ei syniadau am genedligrwydd, ac rwyf yr un mor ddyledus i David Boucher, Prifysgol Cymru, Abertawe, am dynnu fy sylw at bapurau perthnasol yn y Llyfrgell Genedlaethol na fyddai wedi dod i'm sylw oni bai am ei garedigrwydd ef. Diolchaf i Lyfrgellydd Coleg Harris Manceinion, Prifysgol Rhydychen, am gael hyd i lawysgrifau a defnyddiau printiedig defnyddiol, ac am wneud fy arhosiad yno yn un mor ddymunol. Gosododd staff Llyfrgell Deiniol Sant, Penarlâg, fi yn eu dyled yn llungopïo erthyglau mewn cylchgronau prin.

Cefais gymorth sylweddol iawn gan gyfeillion yn Aberystwyth. Bu staff y Llyfrgell Genedlaethol yn barod eu cymwynas wrth i mi weithio drwy Gasgliad Syr Thomas Jones a chasgliadau perthnasol eraill yn Adran y Llawysgrifau. Darllenwyd y teipysgrif gan yr Athro Tom Roberts a chan fy nghyfaill Walford Gealy, y ddau gynt o Brifysgol Cymru, Aberystwyth. Heb eu sylwadau hwy byddai'r gwaith yn llai cymen o lawer. Mae fy nyled yn wir fawr i Glyn Saunders Jones o Ganolfan Astudiaethau Addysg, Prifysgol Cymru Aberystwyth am iddo estyn ei gefnogaeth a'i nawdd i mi ar awr dywyll. Y Ganolfan sydd wedi paratoi'r gwaith ar gyfer y wasg ac mae ôl trylwyredd a manylder Marian Hughes yn amlwg drwy'r cyfan. Bu Gwasg Gee yn gynnes yn eu cefnogaeth ac ni phallodd ymdrechion Thomas Alun Williams i sicrhau nawdd i'r llyfr. Yr wyf mor falch eu bod wedi llwyddo i fedru dwyn y gyfrol i olau dydd a hynny mewn modd mor lân ac effeithiol. Mawr yw fy niolch i Gyngor Celfyddydau Cymru am eu cymorth ariannol ac am iddynt ei estyn mewn pryd i'r llyfr gael ei gyhoeddi yr un diwrnod ag agoriad swyddogol 'Y Cwm', cartref Syr Henry Jones yn Llangernyw, fel amgueddfa ddeniadol a chofeb deilwng i'r athro alltud.

Mae un agwedd ar astudio gyrfa Henry Jones wedi rhoddi llawenydd arbennig iawn i mi, sef fy ymwneud â chymdogaeth Llangernyw. Bûm yn diwtor athroniaeth ar y dosbarth W.E.A. yno am nifer o flynyddoedd (tair ohonynt yn trafod gwaith 'eu hathronydd hwy eu hunain'), a chefais y fraint o arwain mintai i Brifysgol Glasgow lle pery atgof byw a chynnes o hyd am yr athrylith o Langernyw. Nid anghofiaf i na hwythau groeso twymgalon Mrs Birtwhistle i'w chartref, sef Noddfa, tŷ Henry Jones yn Tighnabruaich, a chymwynasgarwch y cyfeillion a agorodd gapel Kilbride yn unswydd i ni gynnal cyfarfod teyrnged wrth y bedd. Fe'm cyfoethogwyd gan gyfeillgarwch cymaint o gyfeillion newydd ym Mro Cernyw. Haedda un ohonynt, sydd yn wir yn hen gyfaill ers y chwedegau, sylw arbennig, sef John Hughes, Y Graig. Ef yw Cadeirydd Ymddiriedolaeth y Cwm ac ni fu pall ar ei frwdfrydedd a'i weithgarwch yn cynnal y weledigaeth o weld amgueddfa deilwng yn y Cwm a chael cofiant Cymraeg i Henry Jones. Mae ei gymwynasau yn rhy niferus i'w rhestru yma, ond mae'n gwestiwn a fyddwn wedi gosod pin ar bapur heb ei gefnogaeth cyson, a gwerthfawrogaf yn fawr ei gyfeillgarwch ef a'i briod Mona.

Erys dau gymwynaswr arall, sef Rhodri a Mair. Trodd Rhodri lawysgrif Rhan 1 yn deipysgrif ddarllenadwy. Darllenodd Mair ddwy deipysgrif o'r gyfrol gyflawn gan ystwytho brawddegu clogyrnaidd a thacluso mynegiant blêr, heb sôn am gwestiynu ystyr ambell draethiad! Mawr yw fy nyled i'r ddau, ac i'r teulu oll am oddef i mi gyd-fyw cyhyd gyda Henry Jones.

E. Gwynn Matthews

TALFYRIADAU

BPRT	Henry Jones, *Browning as a Philosophical and Religious Teacher*, Glasgow 1891. Cyhoeddwyd gyntaf gan Maclehose ac yna gan Nelson. Dangosir rhif tudalennau argraffiad Nelson mewn cromfachau.
DB	Henry Jones, *Dinasyddiaeth Bur ac Areithiau Ereill*, Caernarfon 1911.
FTE	Henry Jones, *A Faith that Enquires*, Llundain 1922.
IOJ	Henry Jones, *The Idealism of Jesus*, Llundain 1919.
IPC	Henry Jones, *Idealism as a Practical Creed*, Glasgow 1909.
JMJ	Papurau Syr John Morris-Jones, Archifau Prifysgol Cymru, Bangor.
LL	H. J. W. Hetherington, *The Life and Letters of Sir Henry Jones*, Llundain 1924.
LlGC	Llyfrgell Genedlaethol Cymru.
OM	Thomas Jones (gol.), *Henry Jones, Old Memories*, Llundain 1922.
PC	Henry Jones, *The Principles of Citizenship*, Llundain 1920.
TCEL	T. I. Ellis (gol.), *Thomas Charles Edwards Letters*, Ail Gyfrol, sef Atodiad *Cylchgrawn Llyfrgell Genedlaethol Cymru*, Cyfres III, Rhif 4, Aberystwyth 1953. Nodir rhif y llythyr, nid y dudalen.
TJ	Papurau Thomas Jones, Llyfrgell Genedlaethol Cymru Dilynir y ddwy lythyren gyntaf gan lythyren sy'n dynodi'r adran, rhif sy'n dynodi'r gyfrol yn yr adran a rhif arall sy'n dynodi'r ddogfen yn y gyfrol.
WFSR	Henry Jones, *The Working Faith of the Social Reformer*, Llundain 1910.
YA	Papurau Mrs Yale, Llanbedrog, Llyfrgell Genedlaethol Cymru.

Rhan 1

Gyrfa Syr Henry Jones

Dadeni Syr Henry Jones

Ai yn y gogledd oer
Dan rug yr Alban bell
Y rhoddwyd llwch fy mrawd
I lechu yn ei gell?
Draw, draw o fryniau'r wlad
A garai'n fwy na'r byd;
Ai dyma derfyn eitha'r daith
Ar ôl y gwaith i gyd?

Na, na os gadael wnaeth
Hen Gymru – fryn a dôl,
Pan gladdwyd ef, fe ddaeth
I Gymru yn ei ôl.
Mewn anfarwoldeb gwyn
Yr erys yma mwy
I ysbrydoli meibion mad
Y wlad a'u maco hwy.

Mae'n eiddo i ni yn awr,
Ar ôl y trinoedd trwch;
Nid oes o dan y grug
Yn unig ond y llwch.
Mae'r ysbryd sy'n bywhau
Ar fryniau Cymru lân,
Mae'r proffwyd yma mewn mawrhad
I godi gwlad y gân.

Llew Tegid

Pennod 1

Cymru 1852–75

Yn nhrymder nos, a phentrefwyr gonest Llangernyw wedi mynd i glwydo ers oriau, ymlwybrai'r plismon lleol yn bwrpasol drwy'r llan yng ngoleuni'r lloer. Cyfeiriai ei gamre tua bwthyn bychan ar gwr y pentre. Ar ysgafn droed aeth heibio'r drws ffrynt a throi am dalcen y tŷ lle'r oedd estyniad bychan, ac oedodd am ennyd i wrando ger y ffenest. Yna'n ysgafn, ond yn fwriadol iawn, curodd ar y ffenest a gwrando drachefn. Gallai glywed sŵn siffrwd oddi mewn, a chyda gwên fodlon ar ei wyneb, dychwelodd at y ffordd fawr gan droi tuag adref am ei wely. Digwyddai'r ddefod fach hon yn feunosol ym misoedd hydrefol 1870.

Gweithdy crydd o'r enw Elias Jones oedd yr 'estyniad', a'i fab ieuengaf, Harri, oedd yn disgwyl curiad y plismon ar y ffenest am un o'r gloch bob bore. Ers misoedd yr haf, yr oedd Harri, llanc yn tynnu am ei ddeunaw oed, wedi bod yn cysgu yn y gweithdy wedi diwrnod o waith, ond yn codi ar y curiad i ddechrau gweithio ar ei lyfrau ysgol o un o'r gloch y bore tan amser brecwast. Gyda'r llyfrau yn hytrach na'r lledr y gorweddai dyfodol Harri. Yn ystod ei yrfa byddai'n esgyn i gadair prifysgol, yn cael dwy ddoethuriaeth, yn cael ei ethol yn Gymrawd o'r Academi Brydeinig, yn cael ei urddo'n farchog, yn derbyn Medal Aur y Cymmrodorion ac yn derbyn gwahoddiad y brenin i fod yn Companion of Honour. Ond yn fwy na hyn oll, yn ystod ei oes yr oedd yn eilun ei bobl. Dangosodd Henry Jones fod modd i werinwr Cymraeg a Methodistaidd godi i safle o anrhydedd dirfesig, a hynny drwy ei ymdrechion ei hunan. Yr oedd yn cynrychioli blaenffrwyth y cynhaeaf toreithiog hwnnw a roddai i Gymru arweinyddiaeth Ryddfrydol ddisglair erbyn troad y ganrif.

Pan fentrodd yntau ddweud hanes ei ymdrech aruthrol i sicrhau addysg (iddo'i hun i ddechrau, ac yna, weddill ei oes, i eraill) mewn hunangofiant, sicrhawyd ei le yn oriel arwyr y genedl. *Old Memories* yw teitl y gyfrol, ac mae'n glasur. Llwydda i bortreadu'n fyw iawn gymdeithas wledig yng Nghymru tua chanol y bedwaredd ganrif ar bymtheg, ond mae'n cyfleu hefyd yn effeithiol iawn lwyredd ymroddiad yr awdur i addysg.

Ganed Henry Jones yn Llangernyw yn yr hen Sir Ddinbych ar 30ain Tachwedd 1852 yn fab i Elias Jones a'i wraig, Elizabeth Williams (gynt). Crydd oedd Elias Jones, ond pobl y tir oedd y cyndeidiau ar y ddwy ochr. Diflanasai'r tŷ lle ganed Harri rywbryd cyn iddo ysgrifennu ei hunangofiant, ond cafodd ei fagu mewn bwthyn o'r enw 'Y Cwm', a saif hyd heddiw. Dau dŷ bychan yn sownd yn ei gilydd oedd 'Y Cwm' mewn gwirionedd, gyda dwy ystafell ym mhob tŷ, un i fyny ac un i lawr. Yn yr hanner agosaf at Gapel y Cwm (M.C.) yr oedd rhieni Elizabeth yn byw, a da hynny, oherwydd doedd dim digon o le i bawb gysgu yn hanner y Jonesiaid!

Y mae'n anodd iawn i ni ddychmygu sut y gallai un ystafell, ddeg troedfedd sgwâr, weithredu fel cegin, ystafell fwyta a lolfa i deulu cyfan. Yr oedd Elias ac Elizabeth, eu tri mab a'u dwy ferch yn trigo yn yr un ystafell hon. Ni allent fwyta gyda'i gilydd ynddi. Yn ôl yr hunangofiant, y ddau fab hynaf, William a John, a gâi ginio gyntaf, am hanner dydd; yna Elias ac un neu ddau o'i gyd-weithwyr; yna'r gweddill, gyda Harri yn aml yn bwyta ar ei draed neu, ar y Sul yn enwedig, yn eistedd ar y rhiniog gydag un o'r lleill. Collwyd y ddwy ferch, un ohonynt yn blentyn. Cysgai Harri a William yn llofft tŷ nain drws nesaf. Gan fod y gegin yn rhy fach i osod y crud ynddi, fe'i cedwid yn y llofft, gyda darn o gortyn yn disgyn ohono drwy dwll yn y llawr i alluogi Elizabeth i'w siglo o'r gegin heb orfod dringo'r grisiau cul a serth bob tro!

Ar bwys hanner y Williamsiaid o'r Cwm yr oedd tŷ pobi lle'r âi'r plant weithiau i gadw'n gynnes, ac wrth hanner y Jonesiaid o'r tŷ yr oedd yr estyniad bychan, sef gweithdy'r crydd. Cawn ddisgrifiad byw o'r gweithdy yn *Old Memories*, ac mae'n amlwg mai hwn a'r capel oedd y dylanwadau ffurfiannol pwysicaf ar Henry Jones y plentyn. Yn wir, ei nod mewn bywyd pan oedd yn blentyn oedd bod yn grydd ac yn flaenor! Un ffenest isel, yn wynebu tua'r de, oedd i'r gweithdy. Eisteddai Elias Jones a'i gynorthwywr yn wynebu'r ffenest a'u cefnau at wal y gegin. Roedd ganddynt le i ymestyn led braich wrth bwytho. Ar y dde iddynt, ym mhen draw'r gweithdy, safai gwely bychan a ddefnyddid fel sedd esmwyth gan ymwelwyr neu gwsmeriaid, ac ar y chwith iddynt yr oedd dau ddrws, y naill gyferbyn â'r ffenest yn arwain i'r gegin, a'r llall gyferbyn â'r gwely yn arwain allan. Ar yr ochr honno hefyd roedd gan y postman sedd, oherwydd rhwng cludo'r llythyrau i lawr o Lanrwst yn y bore a dychwelyd gyda'r llythyrau a bostiwyd yn ystod y dydd gyda'r nos, gweithiai gyda'r crydd, gan arbenigo mewn esgidiau merched. Wedi iddo adael yr ysgol yn ddeuddeg a hanner mlwydd oed yr oedd lle wedi ei neilltuo hefyd i Harri i ddysgu crefft ei dad.

Yr oedd yn brentis gweithgar a deheuig. Yn wir, yr oedd yn bwythwr cywrain ers ei blentyndod. Cofiai gyda balchder y diwrnod hwnnw pan ddaethai ei dad i'r ysgol i'w gludo adref i wneud rhyw orchwyl oedd yn gofyn am bwytho rhy fanwl i'w ddwylo mawr ef. Y mae ar gael hyd heddiw esgid plentyn o'i waith. Mae'n waith anghyffredin, ac efallai yn un o dasgau swyddogol ei brentisiaeth. Chollodd o erioed mo'r grefft. Fe'i cysurai ei hun pan deimlai dan warchae fod ganddo alwedigaeth arall i syrthio'n ôl arni pe collai ei swydd academaidd. Ar ei ymweliad olaf â Chymru, ychydig fisoedd cyn ei farw, darganfu ei hen fedrau eto. Mewn llythyr at ei fab, Hal, dywed:

I visited a couple of old fashioned shoemakers here this morning – two brothers, both old men, going at cobbling in my father's old way, and living an uncommonly simple and innocent, and I fancy quiet and useful life. I made a 'blaen llinyn' just to see if I could put the twist and the bristles on, as of old. It came automatically back, Hal! I wonder sometimes what the net sum of my gains are as the result of scrambling from the shoemaker's seat to the professor's. But I'd do it over again Hal, if it came my way.[1]

Yng ngweithdy'r crydd profodd yr urddas dynol hwnnw a gyfyd o fedru ymfalchïo yng nghynnyrch ein llafur. Yno roedd perthynas gweithiwr â'i gynnyrch ac â'i gyd-ddyn, boed feistr, gwsmer neu lafurwr, yn gwbl ddynol a llawn parch.

There are few, if any, pleasanter scenes in the world than those presented by the little workshops of the country shoe-makers and tailors, there, master and man sit together side by side, talking freely with one another about anything and everything; for they sit quite near each other, and the strain of the work is not so heavy or constant as to prevent either conversation or singing.[2]

Efallai i'r teimlad hwn o barch at feistr, at was ac at waith ei wneud yn emosiynol amharod i gofleidio sosialaeth. Darganfu resymau deallusol hefyd dros wrthod sosialaeth, ond gorweddent ar gynsail profiad.

Un arall o brofiadau plentyndod oedd yn gyfrifol am ei berthynas amwys â Methodistiaeth Galfinaidd. Plentyn ifanc iawn oedd ef pan gyrhaeddodd Diwygiad '59 Langernyw, ac nid oedd ei atgof o'r digwyddiad yn gwbl hapus. Chwarae yn yr ardd rhwng y bwthyn a'r capel oedd Harri pan glywodd seiniau o'r oedfa a arwyddai'n ddiamheuol fod diwygiad yn gwawrio y tu mewn. Meddiannwyd ei feddwl ifanc gan y syniad fod yr Ysbryd Glân wedi dewis dod i Langernyw pan oedd ef yn absennol o'r oedfa! Ofnai nad oedd ymhlith yr etholedigion!!

Manifestly my Calvinistic upbringing was thorough; and even then the main joists of my creed were being laid, and by other hands than my own.[3]

Serch hynny, mae'n cydnabod ei ddyled i'r capel, ei aelodau a'r bywyd diwylliannol oedd yn gysylltiedig ag ef, dro ar ôl tro. Disgrifiodd y dylanwad hwnnw fel y 'most subtle and also the most universal'[4] a fu arno. Anodd gweld sut y gallai pethau fod yn wahanol gan fod holl ddyddiau'r wythnos, ac eithrio dydd Sadwrn, yn golygu treulio amser yn y capel. Y drefn arferol oedd: nos Lun, cyfarfod gweddi; nos Fawrth, cyfarfod Rhodd Mam; nos Fercher, cyfarfod canu; nos Iau, seiat; nos Wener, cyfarfod y gwŷr ieuanc. Prin bod amser i gael gwynt ar y Sul! Dyma amserlen arferol Harri ar y Saboth:

[1] TJ/U/3/221.
[2] OM, tt. 35–36.
[3] OM, t. 53.
[4] OM, t. 48.

8:30	–	9:30	cyfarfod gweddi i'r gwŷr ieuanc;
9:30	–	10:30	pregeth neu gyfarfod gweddi cyhoeddus;
10:40	–	12:00	Boreol Weddi yn eglwys y plwyf;
12:00	–	1:00	cinio;
1:00	–	2:00	cyfarfod darllen y gwŷr ieuanc;
2:00	–	3:30	Ysgol Sul;
4:00	–	5:00	te;
5:00	–	6:00	cyfarfod canu;
6:00	–	7:30	oedfa bregethu;
7:30	–	8:00	seiat.

Oni bai am yr holl gyfarfodydd hyn, ni fyddai teulu'r Cwm wedi gallu byw heb sathru ar draed ei gilydd yn y gegin fach. Ac yn sicr, nid oedd Harri yn cael y drefn yn orthrymus, i'r gwrthwyneb yn wir. Yn ei hunangofiant mae'n disgrifio blaenoriaid ac athrawon Ysgol Sul Capel y Cwm gydag anwyldeb. Hwy, wedi'r cyfan, a blannodd ynddo'r dwyster a'i symbylodd i blymio i ddyfnderoedd athroniaeth yn ddiweddarach yn ei fywyd. Cyfarfodydd y capel, yr eisteddfodau lleol a'r Penny Readings a roes iddo ei ddawn ymadrodd enwog.

Bu'r Penny Readings yn foddion i'w gyflwyno i ddiwylliant Saesneg, a hynny'n fwy llwyddiannus o lawer na'r ysgol ddyddiol. Yn wir, nid oes gan *Old Memories* air da i'w ddweud am Ysgol Llangernyw. Yr hyn a nodweddai'r oruchwyliaeth yno oedd ofn a bryntni. Yr oedd mwyafrif y plant dan lach am ddau reswm, eu henwad a'u hiaith. Cawsai eu hymneilltuaeth ei difrïo a'u Cymraeg ei chosbi dan gyfundrefn sarhaus y Welsh Stick. Dioddefodd John 'y Cwm' yn enbyd dan law'r prifathro, ond o'r herwydd yr oedd yn arwr i'w gyfoedion. Oherwydd ei allu cynhenid, llwyddodd Harri i osgoi'r gwaethaf yn bersonol, ond gyda chwerwder, serch hynny, y cofiai ddyddiau'r ysgol eglwysig, Seisnig. Eithr yn y Penny Readings, a gynhelid gyda'r nos yn yr ysgol, anghofid am wahaniaethau enwad ac iaith.

Mae'n amlwg mai'r prif ysgogiad y tu ôl i sefydlu'r Penny Readings oedd nifer o Albanwyr a ymsefydlodd ar nifer o ffermydd yng nghyffiniau Llangernyw. Dan lywyddiaeth Mr Sandbach, y sgweiar, byddai'r cyfarfodydd yn gyfrwng adloniant, megis canu, adrodd ac actio, yn y ddwy iaith. Yr oedd William, John a Harri yn gantorion lleol o fri (bu William a John yn eu tro yn codi canu yng Nghapel y Cwm), a swynodd canu Harri un o'r gwragedd Albanaidd, Mrs Roxburgh o Gae'r Llo, i'r fath raddau fel y penderfynodd roddi hwb diwylliannol iddo. Gofynnodd i Elias Jones ei anfon i'w gweld, a phan gyrhaeddodd dywedodd wrtho nad oedd crefft y crydd yn addas iddo ef, ac y dylai anelu at fynd i'r coleg i'w gymhwyso'i hun ar gyfer y weinidogaeth. Er iddi wybod nad oedd gobaith i Elias Jones gynnal un o'i blant mewn coleg, gwyddai Mrs Roxburgh hefyd nad oedd tlodi wedi llwyddo i rwystro bechgyn o gefndir cyffelyb i Harri rhag esgyn i bulpudau'r Kirk. Bid a fo am y nawdd materol, credai hi mai ei galwedigaeth oedd dyrchafu golygon y llanc pedair ar ddeg oed oedd â deunydd rhywbeth amgenach na chrydd ynddo. Anogai hi ef i ddarllen yn gyson bopeth a allai, ac eithrio gweithiau Thomas Carlyle! Ni lwyddodd i ysbrydoli Harri, ond ymlwybrai ef yn wythnosol i Gae'r Llo i ddarllen Saesneg, trafod a chanu gyda Mrs Roxburgh, ac ni adawai hi i unrhyw ofynion eraill darfu ar ei 'gwaith mawr'.

Yn y diwedd, ei bwriadau hi a orfu; ond nid fel canlyniad i'w hanogaeth hi, os ydym i gredu'r *Old Memories*. Yn ôl ei hunangofiant, cael rhyw dröedigaeth ar ffordd Damascus, neu Lanrwst yn hytrach, wnaeth Harri pan oedd ef a'i gyfaill Tom Redfern wedi mynd i weld rhyfeddodau Wombwell's Menagerie a oedd yn ymweld â'r dref honno. Bachgen o Helygain oedd Tom, a ddaethai i Langernyw fel *pupil-teacher* i'r ysgol; yr oedd ef a Harri yn gyfoedion o gyffelyb anian.

Yn Llanrwst cyfarfu'r ddau â Sam Roberts, perthynas i Harri. Wrth iddynt fynd heibio rhyw lanciau a oedd yn cadw reiat y tu allan i un o'r tafarndai digwyddodd Sam gyfeirio atynt fel cymheiriaid Harri. Tynnu coes oedd bwriad Sam, ond yn anfwriadol cyffyrddodd Harri i'r byw. Mewn fflach gwelodd mai tebyg fyddai ei dynged yntau, oni wnâi rhywbeth ohono'i hun. Yr oedd anogaeth gyson Mrs Roxburgh wedi bod yn cronni yn yr isymwybod, mae'n amlwg, oherwydd yn sydyn fe'i meddiannwyd gan weledigaeth newydd, ac ar y ffordd adref y noson honno ymdynghedodd Harri a Tom, ar lan afon Collen, gyferbyn â thai Tangraig, y byddent ill dau ryw ddydd yn raddedigion.

Doedd gan 'run o'r ddau y syniad lleiaf sut i wireddu'r fath uchelgais.[5] Y cam cyntaf i Harri oedd hysbysu ei rieni o'i agwedd newydd tuag at ei ddyfodol. Ni wyddent hwy pa ffordd i droi, mwy na Harri ei hunan. Heb fodd i dalu am addysg, ofer oedd gobeithion y prentis crydd. Yn annisgwyl, fodd bynnag, daeth llygedyn o obaith. Digwyddodd Elizabeth Jones a Mrs Parry, gwraig y gof, fynd i angladd ym Mhandy Tudur. Cyn troi yn eu holau am Langernyw, taith o tua dwy filltir, gwahoddwyd y ddwy am baned o de gan John Price, prifathro Ysgol Frytanaidd y Pandy. Yn ystod y sgwrs dros de cyfeiriodd Elizabeth at anesmwythyd ei mab. Yr oedd John Price eisoes yn ei adnabod ef a'i frodyr gan i'r tri ohonynt ddisgleirio yn ei ddosbarthiadau sol-ffa. Gan gofio, efallai, mai canlyn y wedd a wnâi John Price yn ifanc, trodd Elizabeth ato a gofyn, "Fedrwch chi ddim gwneud athro ohono fo?" Gwyddai'n burion am amgylchiadau materol teulu'r Cwm, ond er bythol glod iddo cytunodd i gael sgwrs â'r bachgen. Y bwriad oedd rhoi tri mis o ysgol iddo yn y Pandy, lle'n wir yr oedd mainc arbennig i lanciau a weithiau ar y ffermydd fanteisio ar ychydig o addysg estynedig pan oedd patrwm tymhorol gwaith ar y tir yn caniatáu iddynt gael eu rhyddhau dros dro.

[5] Graddiodd Redfern ym Mhrifysgol Caer-grawnt lle bu'n fyfyriwr yng Ngholeg Clare. Cafodd ei ordeinio i weinidogaeth Eglwys Loegr ac fe'i dyrchafwyd yn un o ganonau Llanelwy. Bu'n Rheithor Dinbych am flynyddoedd.

Pan aeth Harri draw i weld Price, yr oedd ganddo gynllun arall ar ei gyfer, sef addysg am gyfnod amhenodol am dri diwrnod yr wythnos, a gweithio fel crydd am y tri diwrnod arall i dalu am ei gadw. Cipiodd y cyfle'n eiddgar, a dechreuodd ar unwaith ym mis Mai 1869 gan ailgydio yn ei addysg ar ddyddiau Llun, Mercher a Gwener yn ysgol Pandy Tudur. Ei nod oedd ymgeisio am un o ysgoloriaethau'r Frenhines a fyddai'n ei alluogi i ddilyn cwrs dwy flynedd o hyfforddiant yn y Coleg Normal ym Mangor ar gyfer dilyn galwedigaeth athro. Safodd yr arholiad ym mis Tachwedd 1870 gan weithio'n gwbl ddiarbed yn y cyfamser. Anodd oedd cael y llonydd angenrheidiol yng nghegin fach y Cwm i wneud gwaith llyfr, felly âi Harri drws nesaf at ei nain i weithio, neu dro arall byddai'n mynd yn ddirgel i seler y sgweiar yn Hafodunos, lle'r arferai ei frawd ofalu am y gwres canolog dros nos, a chael yno dawelwch a chynhesrwydd. Dechreuodd godi'n fore iawn i astudio cyn i weddill y teulu godi, a mynych y deuai Tom Redfern i daflu graean ar ffenest ei lofft i'w ddihuno tua phedwar o'r gloch y bore. Pan geisiodd Harri wneud yr un gymwynas i Tom, cafodd flas tafod gwraig y llety! Fel y ciliai'r haf, fodd bynnag, yr oedd yn rhaid chwilio am gynllun arall. Gan fod John yn paratoi ar gyfer arholiad garddio fe drawyd ar syniad fyddai'n hyrwyddo efrydiau'r ddau frawd fel ei gilydd. Dibynnai'r cynllun ar ganiatáu i'r bechgyn gysgu yn y gwely bach yn y gweithdy! Ar derfyn dydd, tuag 8 o'r gloch, fe âi Harri i'w wely tan un o'r gloch y bore, tra gweithiai John. Yna am un o'r gloch byddai'r brodyr yn cyfnewid lle, gyda Harri yn gweithio tan amser brecwast. Ysywaeth nid oedd cyfansoddiad John yn ddigon cryf i ysgwyddo'r baich, a gorfu i Harri ddal ati ei hunan. Dyma pryd y trefnwyd i'r plismon guro ar ffenest y gweithdy am un o'r gloch y bore ar ei ffordd adre er mwyn gwneud yn siŵr fod yr efrydydd ifanc yn codi i ddechrau ar ei waith yntau. Yna, gyda bwrdd bychan o'i flaen a'i draed wedi eu plannu mewn clytiau o ledr i'w cadw'n gynnes, gweithiai â'i holl egni nes clywed sŵn hyfryd y llestri'n cael eu hwylio gan ei fam ar gyfer brecwast, a dechrau diwrnod arall llawn o waith yn yr ysgol neu'r gweithdy. Ddeng mlynedd yn ddiweddarach, adroddodd Henry Jones hanes yr ymdrech mewn llythyr at Cadwaladr Davies, cofrestydd cyntaf Coleg y Gogledd, gyda'r bwriad o ysgogi eraill i sicrhau gwell cyfleusterau addysg ar gyfer pobl ifanc a oedd yn dyheu am y cyfle, ond bod amgylchiadau yn drech na hwy.

> Many have worked more constantly, but few have worked more intensely. I have found kindness on every hand always, but had I failed in a single instance I should have met with entire bankruptcy. Failure would have been ruinous. Make use my friend, of any or all the facts. I have had a kind of melancholy pleasure looking back upon them. I thank God for the struggle, but would not like to see a dog try it again. There are scores of lads in Wales who would creep up, but they can't. Poverty has too heavy a hand for them.[6]

[6] TJ/U/2/6.

Glynodd Harri wrth y cynllun hwn er iddo gael cynnig llwybr haws. Yr oedd Mrs Sandbach, Hafodunos, wedi cynnig ei gynnal yn y dosbarth rhagbaratoadol yng Ngholeg Hyfforddi Caernarfon, ond coleg Anglicanaidd oedd hwnnw, ac nid oedd Harri am droi ei gôt er mwyn mantais bersonol. Dyna paham, efallai, y gwrthododd y person, yn ddiweddarach, roddi llythyr o dystiolaeth i'w gymeriad pan oedd yn cofrestru ar gyfer yr arholiad am Ysgoloriaeth y Frenhines. Bid a fo am hynny, daeth o'r arholiad yn argyhoeddedig ei fod wedi methu. Yr oedd am ailgynnig eto'r flwyddyn ganlynol, ac yn y cyfamser am weithio fel athro di-hyfforddiant mewn ysgol breifat i fechgyn yn Ormskirk.

Prin ei fod wedi cael amser i sychu ei drwyn yno pan ddaeth gair i ddweud ei fod wedi llwyddo yn yr arholiad a'i fod mewn gwirionedd â'i enw ar ben rhestr y Dosbarth Cyntaf. Bu'r prifathro yn ddigon hael i'w ryddhau o'i swydd ar unwaith, ac yn y Coleg Normal y treuliodd y ddwy flynedd nesaf. Bu'n fyfyriwr cydwybodol, er iddo fod yn amlwg mewn ambell 'brotest' yn erbyn y 'drefn', ac yn ôl *Old Memories* bu'n hapus yn y coleg. Cyfyng iawn oedd yr hyfforddiant; dim ond digon i alluogi dyn i gyflwyno addysg elfennol i blant heb ymdrech i ymestyn y myfyrwyr eu hunain. Ar ddamwain, ac ar ei liwt ei hun, y gwnaeth un o ddarganfyddiadau pwysig ei fywyd yn llyfrgell y coleg. Digwyddodd agor copi o *Sartor Resartus* Thomas Carlyle, ac wedi dechrau darllen, cael y llyfr yn un cyfareddol. Ar waethaf rhybudd Mrs Roxburgh, daeth yn edmygydd mawr o waith Carlyle.

Rhaid dweud bod y llyfr a'i swynodd gymaint y dydd hwnnw yn un enbyd o anodd o ran arddull, ffurf a dysgeidiaeth. Yr oedd Carlyle wedi astudio llenyddiaeth ac athroniaeth yr Almaen, a gwnaeth yr Idealaeth a nodweddai feddwl yr Almaenwyr argraff ddofn arno. Cyflwyna *Sartor* y darllenydd i 'Athroniaeth Dillad' sy'n seiliedig ar y syniad mai haenau allanol yn unig yw'r sylweddau materol sy'n gorchuddio realiti ysbrydol. Ymosodai Carlyle ar fateroliaeth ac ar unigoliaeth yr athroniaeth empeiraidd a rhyddfrydol a nodweddai'r meddwl Seisnig. Er na wyddai Henry Jones hynny ar y pryd, byddai yntau ymhlith yr huotlaf i ymosod ar y pethau hynny hefyd maes o law.

Ar derfyn ei gwrs coleg, llwyddodd i ennill y safle uchaf yn yr arholiadau, a disgwyliai gael cynnig ysgol gan y Prifathro yn unol ag arfer y cyfnod. Pan gafodd alwad i'w ystafell agorodd hwnnw'r sgwrs drwy ddweud nad oedd am gynnig ysgol iddo, a heb oedi i gymryd ei wynt, atebodd Jones gyda dicter fod ganddo grefft, a thrannoeth fe'i cafwyd yn ei ôl yn y gweithdy yn Llangernyw yn gwisgo ffedog ledr! Ond ymhen ychydig wythnosau dyma gais iddo fynd i weld y Prifathro eto, a'r tro hwn cafodd hwnnw gyfle i egluro mai bwriad awdurdodau'r coleg oedd ei wahodd i fod yn diwtor dros-dro yn y coleg, a dyna'n wir oedd y bwriad pan alwyd ef i'r cyfweliad cyntaf. Teimlai Henry Jones gywilydd ohono'i hun. Dyma enghraifft gynnar o'r dymer wyllt a fyddai'n peri anawsterau iddo yn ei ymwneud ag awdurdodau academaidd. Deuai ei fyrbwylledd â gofid iddo yn y dyfodol. Fodd bynnag, bu'r cyfnod byr fel tiwtor yn un pleserus. Cafodd gyfle i fwynhau cymdeithas yr ystafell gyffredin uwch, ac yn arbennig felly gyfeillgarwch Mr Thomas ei hen athro mathemateg, a hefyd ymddiriedaeth y myfyrwyr dan ei ofal. Rhagflas oedd hyn o ansawdd y bywyd y deuai'n gyfarwydd ag ef yn ddiweddarach yn ei fywyd.

Rhyw dri neu bedwar mis yn unig a dreuliodd fel tiwtor yn y Normal. Yn gynnar yn 1873 cafodd gynnig swydd ysgolfeistr ym Mrynaman mewn ysgol a godwyd gan y meistri haearn. Dyma brofiad cyntaf y gwladwr o gymdeithas ddiwydiannol, glòs. Yr oedd wrth ei fodd. Cafodd ei dderbyn yn gynnes a'i barchu gan gymdogaeth y glo a'r dur. Ymserchodd yntau yn y plant a'u teuluoedd, a darganfod am y tro cyntaf efallai fod ganddo ddawn anghyffredin i gyfathrebu, yn enwedig gyda phlant. Ni chollodd y ddawn honno. Pan oedd yn hen ŵr barfog, wedi treulio oes yng nghymdeithas ysgolheigaidd tair prifysgol, byddai plant bach ysgol gynradd Tighnabruaich yn edrych ymlaen yn eiddgar am ymweliad a sgwrs ganddo. Byddent yn codi ar eu traed ac yn cymeradwyo'n frwd.[7]

Bu'n llwyddiant mawr gyda'r rhieni ym Mrynaman, mae'n amlwg, oherwydd cododd y nifer ar gofrestr yr ysgol o 190 i 430 mewn dwy flynedd, ac yr oedd yn rhaid dyblu maint yr adeiladau ar fyrder. Yr oedd yr awyrgylch yn yr ysgol hon yn gwbl wahanol i un ysgol Llangernyw! O fantais fawr iddo oedd ei ddiddordeb a'i dalent gerddorol. Roedd canu yn ei waed ef a'r plant, a'r tadau hefyd! Deuai'r rhai fu'n gweithio'r nos at ddrws yr ysgol am 3.30 o'r gloch i ymuno yn y canu. Perswadiodd ei ddau frawd, William a John, i'w ganlyn i Frynaman i'w gynorthwyo fel athrawon anhrwyddedig, ond dim ond John a arhosodd. Roedd gan y ddau ynni, brwdfrydedd, gwreiddioldeb a chyfuniad o hiwmor a disgyblaeth wrth lywio'r ysgol. Yn ôl tystiolaeth Harri, yr oedd John yn athro wrth reddf. Yr oedd y plant yn ei hanner addoli ac yn dysgu'n rhwydd dan ei arweiniad. Ond yr oedd ei ddulliau yn gwbl anghonfensiynol! Un diwrnod aeth Harri i weld beth oedd yn gyfrifol am y rhialtwch a ddeuai o ystafell ddysgu ei frawd. Er syndod iddo gwelodd fod tri o fechgyn yn 'marchogaeth' ar gefn tri o'u cyfoedion, a'r athro a'i ddisgyblion yn mwynhau pob munud. Pan holodd yr ysgolfeistr ei gynorthwy-ydd beth oedd yn digwydd, yr ateb a gafodd oedd eu bod yn dysgu mathemateg!! Cyfrinach llwyddiant y dull newydd oedd fod y tri bachgen a gafodd y marciau isaf am eu gwaith yn gorfod cario'r tri a gafodd y marciau uchaf o gwmpas yr ystafell ar eu cefnau. Er gofid i'r plant mae'n siŵr, penderfynodd Harri fod y dull 'modern' hwn o ddysgu mathemateg yn rhy wreiddiol i'w gymeradwyo gan Arolygaeth ei Mawrhydi.

Yn ôl un o'i gyn-fyfyrwyr yn Glasgow, William Boyd (gŵr a gafodd yrfa nodedig ei hun fel addysgwr) nid oedd yn cymeradwyo cosb gorfforol.

[7] Tystiolaeth lafar un o'r disgyblion, Miss Douglas o Tighnabruaich.

> He was deeply indignant at the practice of corporal punishment in schools. On one occasion when a vigorous controversy on the subject was going on in a Glasgow evening paper, he was greatly shocked when I told him that a very considerable amount of strapping went on in practically all the Elementary schools of Glasgow. 'A blow struck at any child,' he said with passionate earnestness, 'should reverberate through the whole school.' I ventured to suggest that there were times when corporal punishment might be the least of various evils, but I could not convince him of that, so I turned the talk to his own experience of teaching. 'How did you manage for discipline,' I asked, 'did your pupils always behave themselves?' 'Generally,' he said, and a glint came into his eyes which I had once or twice seen turned to very good purpose on students disposed to be unruly, and I understood. Then the tention (sic) relaxed and he chuckled in a way he had. 'I had ways of my own with them,' he said, and proceeded to tell me how he had dealt with some very dirty boys who had persisted in coming to school unwashed after admonition. He made them bring a tub of water into the classroom and scrub themselves before the class. And there were no more dirty boys after that![8]

Fe allai ambell un feddwl fod ei ddull o ddysgu glanweithdra yn greulonach na chosb gorfforol, oherwydd fod elfen o sarhad yn y driniaeth. Mae clwyfo'r teimladau'n greulonach na brifo'r corff. Mae lle i gredu ei fod yn sylweddoli hynny, oherwydd pan edrydd ef hanes y twb ymolchi yn *Old Memories* mae'n dweud, "If a boy showed signs of breaking down, I spared him at once."[9] Efallai fod plant hefyd yn medru synhwyro pan na fydd malais yn y drin. Beth bynnag, ni ddylid edrych arno fel modernydd ym mhob dim. Fel y gwelai Boyd, gallai fod yn geidwadol iawn ar ambell beth.

> Another subject on which he had strong opinions was the wrongness of sex instruction. In the course of the memorable address, which he delivered to the common meeting at the first Secondary Education Congress in Glasgow … he deprecated such instruction in a sentence or two. Afterwards, he expanded his views to me. 'My Father,' he said, 'never spoke to me of these things, and I am glad he did not.' Though personally I disagreed with this view, I did not attempt to argue, because Sir Henry was not a man to argue with on matters about which he felt deeply.[10]

Ym Mrynaman, fel yn Llangernyw, yr oedd bywyd y capel yn bwysig i Harri. Wrth gydgerdded gydag un o'r blaenoriaid i'r seiat yng Nghapel Moriah, datgelodd yr ysgolfeistr yn gyfrinachol nad oedd yn ystyried y swydd honno fel ei wir alwedigaeth. Ei nod oedd bod yn weinidog. Nid yw darllenydd *Old Memories* yn cael ei baratoi mewn unrhyw fodd am y gyffes hon, ac ni chawn wybod pa bryd na phaham y daethpwyd i'r penderfyniad hwn. A oedd Mrs Roxburgh wedi'r cyfan am weld ei bwriadau ar ei gyfer yn cael eu gwireddu?

Prin fod rhan ddefosiynol y seiat drosodd cyn y cyhoeddodd Daniel Evans, o'r sêt fawr, 'gyfrinach' Harri ac yn y fan a'r lle dyma benderfynu hysbysu'r Henaduriaeth a gofyn iddynt anfon cennad i gymryd llais yr eglwys ar briodoldeb yr ymgeisydd ifanc am y weinidogaeth! Pan ddaeth y gennad, y Parchedig Thomas James o

[8] TJFU/4/124.
[9] OM, t. 109.
[10] TJFU/4/124.

Lanelli, bu'n gyfrwng i ddangos iddo ei wir alwedigaeth a thrawsnewid ei fywyd. Tynnodd ei sylw at Ysgoloriaeth Dr Williams a gynigid i ymgeiswyr am y weinidogaeth gyda'r enwadau anghydffurfiol i'w galluogi i astudio ym Mhrifysgol Glasgow. O'r diwedd felly, yr oedd cyfle i ennill lle fel myfyriwr mewn prifysgol. Ymddiswyddodd fel ysgolfeistr ym mis Mai 1875 gan ymroi'n llwyr i'r paratoadau ar gyfer yr arholiad am ysgoloriaeth yn yr hydref.

Yr oedd y fathemateg a ddysgasai dan Mr John Thomas yn y Coleg Normal yn sylfaen odidog ar gyfer maes llafur yr arholiad, ond yr oedd yn amddifad o Roeg a Lladin, dau bwnc gorfodol ar gyfer yr ysgoloriaeth. Methodd â chael cymorth unrhyw athro o ysgol ramadeg i'w hyfforddi yn y clasuron, ond bu gweinidog newydd ei gapel, y Parchedig Thomas Lloyd, yn efrydu am flwyddyn ym Mhrifysgol Glasgow, ac felly aeth Harri i aros gydag ef yn y ffermdy lle'r oedd yn lletya er mwyn manteisio ar ei gymhwyster prin yn y ddwy iaith. Buan iawn y goddiweddwyd yr athro gan y disgybl! Yn y cyfwng hwnnw bu'n ffodus i ddod i gysylltiad â Joseph Llewelin Thomas, myfyriwr ifanc o Rydychen a oedd yn byw rhyw ddwy filltir i ffwrdd, a hwnnw a fu'n ei baratoi yn y clasuron hyd at yr arholiad.[11] Gweithiodd Harri'n ddibaid o chwech y bore tan hanner nos drwy gydol yr haf, a phregethu bob Sul yn y capeli lleol. O'r diwedd daeth dydd yr arholiad, a chyda'r addysg a roes iddo'i hun fel ei unig gynhysgaeth, llwyddodd i ennill ysgoloriaeth. Yna roedd yn rhaid sefyll arholiad yn y Brifysgol, ac er mawr ryddhad iddo llwyddodd i adnabod y darn Groeg i'w gyfieithu ar y pryd fel rhan o lyfr cyntaf yr *Iliad*, un o'r unig ddau lyfr Groeg a ddarllenasai erioed! Trwy lwyddo yn yr arholiad hwn yr oedd yn cael osgoi gwneud y cyrsiau rhagbaratoadol a dechrau ar unwaith ar gyrsiau gradd.

Cyrhaeddodd yr Alban ym mis Tachwedd 1875 ar drothwy ei dair ar hugain oed, cryn bum mlynedd yn hŷn na'r lliaws o'i gydfyfyrwyr. Yn gefn iddo, yr oedd y profiad o fyw fel myfyriwr yn y Coleg Normal. Yr oedd yn aeddfed i fanteisio ar gyfle mawr ei fywyd.

[11] Nid oes sôn am Thomas yn *Old Memories* nac yn *Life and Letters of Sir Henry Jones*, Hetherington. Datgelodd Thomas y cysylltiad, a rhai atgofion am Jones (ond nid ei enw ei hun) yn y *Western Mail*, 6.11.1924. Mae'n mynegi'r gobaith y byddai awdur cofiant Cymraeg i Jones rywbryd yn y dyfodol yn dewis cyfeirio at y cysylltiad. Mae'n dda gan y cofiannydd presennol wneud hynny rŵan, bron dri chwarter canrif yn ddiweddarach!

Pennod 2

Yr Alban 1875–82

Yr oedd bod yn fyfyriwr ym Mhrifysgol Glasgow yn brofiad pur wahanol i'r hyn a gawsai Henry Jones yn y Coleg Normal. Nid oedd yn byw mewn coleg yma fel y gwnaethai ym Mangor, ond mewn llety. Yr oedd ef, ac ysgolor Dr Williams arall o'r enw William Bell, yn rhannu ystafell gefn yn Willowbank Street, nid nepell o'r Brifysgol, lle gofelid yn ofalus amdanynt gan Mrs a Miss Work. Dim ond er Tachwedd 1870 yr oedd y Brifysgol wedi bod ar safle Gilmorehill yn y rhan hon o'r ddinas, ac roedd yr adeiladau syber (a gynlluniwyd gan Syr George Gilbert Scott am hanner y gost o godi gorsaf St Pancras!) yn dal heb eu cwblhau pan gyrhaeddodd Henry Jones Glasgow am y tro cyntaf yn 1875. Serch hynny, yr oedd y Brifysgol yn sefydliad hynafol iawn â'i hanes yn ymestyn yn ôl at 1451. Nid hon oedd prifysgol gyntaf yr Alban. Sefydlwyd honno yn 1411 yn St Andrews (yn y cyfnod pan oedd Glyn Dŵr yn galw am ddatblygiad tebyg yng Nghymru), a sefydlwyd prifysgolion yn ddiweddarach yn Aberdeen yn 1454, a Chaeredin yn 1583. Felly, yr oedd gan yr Alban, yn wahanol i Gymru, draddodiad maith ac anrhydeddus o brifysgolion ac ysgolheictod cenedlaethol.

Yr oedd i'r traddodiad Albanaidd nodweddion a'i gwahaniaethai oddi wrth draddodiad Caer-grawnt a Rhydychen yn Lloegr. Rhoddasai'r prifysgolion Seisnig, ar eu gorau, bwyslais eithaf arbenigol ar astudio'r ieithoedd clasurol (Groeg a Lladin). Eithr pwysleisiai'r traddodiad Albanaidd ehangder amrediad y pynciau y disgwylid i fyfyrwyr eu hastudio, a'r pwnc uchaf ei fri oedd athroniaeth.

> It may be claimed – if gross over-simplification may be pardoned – that if Oxford gave the most thorough training in classics, and Cambridge in mathematics, the Scottish universities at the peak of their fame were pre-eminent in philosophy. It may even be argued, ... that in Scotland the approach to every subject was philosophical. That is to say, it was an attempt to stimulate youthful minds, not so much to precise scholarship as to the habit of thinking about what they were doing.[1]

Yn gymdeithasol, yr oedd prifysgolion yr Alban yn llai elitaidd o lawer na cholegau Oxbridge, ac nid oeddynt yn gwahardd neb ar sail enwadaeth. Yr oedd yn rhaid datgan ymlyniad wrth Eglwys Loegr cyn derbyn swydd don yn Oxbridge hyd at 1871. Rhyddhawyd myfyrwyr o'r cyfyngiad hwn yn 1854. Oherwydd y gwaharddiadau hyn yn Lloegr, yr oedd y Cymro, Dr Daniel Williams, wedi sefydlu ysgoloriaethau i alluogi ymneilltuwyr o Gymru a Lloegr i efrydu yn Glasgow (cafodd ef ei hunan radd D.D. o Gaeredin a Glasgow yn 1709). Yn wir, un yn unig mewn rhestr anrhydeddus o Gymry ymneilltuol a gafodd addysg uwch yn yr Alban yw Henry Jones.

---

[1] H.J. Paton, *The Claim of Scotland*, Llundain 1968, t. 238.

Yn Glasgow, yr oedd dwy gadair athroniaeth, y Gadair Resymeg a'r Gadair Athroniaeth Foesol, a bu Jones yn astudio dan y ddau athro, sef John Veitch ac Edward Caird. Bu'n rhaid iddo hefyd astudio Lladin dan George C. Ramsey, Groeg dan Syr Richard Jebb, Llenyddiaeth Saesneg dan John Nichol ac Athroniaeth Naturiol (sef ffiseg) dan yr Arglwydd Kelvin. Yr oedd ei faes llafur fel myfyriwr yn enghraifft deg o nodweddion yr addysg Albanaidd. Y pynciau a aeth â'i fryd, fodd bynnag, oedd Athroniaeth a Llenyddiaeth, a'r ddau athro trymaf eu dylanwad arno oedd Edward Caird a John Nichol. Yn ei sylwadau ar yr Athro Rhesymeg, John Veitch, rhaid dweud bod Jones yn grintachlyd braidd, er ei fod yntau, fel Caird, yn ymdrin â'i hoff bwnc. Rhan o'r rheswm dros hyn yn ddiau oedd gwrthwynebiad Veitch i'r safbwynt athronyddol a draddodid gan Caird a Nichol yn eu dosbarthiadau, ac a goleddwyd gyda brwdfrydedd gan Jones. Disgrifia Hetherington safbwynt Veitch fel "Hamiltonian philosophy".[2] Athronydd Albanaidd oedd William Hamilton a fu farw yn 1856 ac a geisiodd uniaethu athroniaeth Kant â'r Ymoleuo Albanaidd. Yr oedd Veitch yn feirniadol o Hegel a'i ddylanwad ar y to iau o athronwyr, ond hwy yn hytrach na Veitch a ysbrydolai Jones. Ei farn ar Veitch oedd:

> the food he deals to us is rich in bones and poor in meat. Scraggy and lean is his philosophy my friend, and I must have another mind before I can enjoy it.[3]

Yn *Old Memories* dywed nad oedd yn cofio fawr ddim am ddarlithoedd Veitch ar wahân i'r modd y byddai'n taranu yn erbyn athroniaeth Hegel a'i "meaningless jargon".[4]

Hegeliaid o ryw fath oedd Caird a Nichol, y ddau ohonynt wedi drachtio'n ddwfn o'r dyfroedd athronyddol Idealaidd yn Rhydychen, lle buont ill dau yn gydfyfyrwyr yng Ngholeg Balliol. Yr oedd gan y coleg hwnnw gysylltiadau arbennig â'r Alban, a deuai myfyrwyr disglair o'r wlad honno yno gyda nawdd ysgoloriaethau Snell. Yng nghyfnod Caird a Nichol fel myfyrwyr yn Balliol yr oedd Benjamin Jowett, un o gymrodyr (ac yn ddiweddarach meistr) y coleg, yn cynhyrfu'r dyfroedd syniadol. Bu Jowett yn gyfrifol am gyflwyno cenhedlaeth o fyfyrwyr Rhydychen i'r syniadaeth Idealaidd Almaenig. Yn ychwanegol at hyn, yr oedd ysbryd gwleidyddol radical yn cyniwair ymhlith rhai (lleiafrif dethol) o'r myfyrwyr, gan gynnwys Caird a Nichol. Sylfaenodd John Nichol gymdeithas i fyfyrwyr yn Rhydychen yn 1856 yn dwyn yr enw "The Old Mortality Society".

[2] LL, t. 19.
[3] TJ/U/2/1.
[4] OM, t. 139.

> The founder of the Old Mortality was John Nichol, a Snell scholar, from Glasgow, and although but a few years older than his English friends, much more worldly confident than they … Nichol already could count himself a friend of Kossuth and Mazzini, and an acquanitance of John Stuart Mill and Carlyle. He was already interested in German thought before his arrival at Balliol. More than anyone else he was responsible for the tone of the Old Mortality: philosophical, radical, even republican. There were no aristocrats among the members. In some circles they were known as a revolutionary set, and read Browning.[5]

Trosglwyddwyd y diddordeb hwn yn Browning gan Nichol i'r Henry Jones ifanc yn ddiweddarach. Llenyddiaeth ac athroniaeth oedd pynciau trafod yr Old Mortality. Cyfarfyddai'r gymdeithas yn wythnosol i wrando ar un o'r aelodau yn traddodi papur ar bwnc o'i ddewis ei hun neu ddarlleniad o waith awdur arbennig, cyn cynnal trafodaeth ar y pwnc. Yr oedd naws radicalaidd iawn i'r trafodaethau hyn. Un o'r hanner dwsin aelod gwreiddiol oedd y bardd A. C. Swinburne, a edmygai, fel Nichol, arweinwyr mudiadau cenedlaethol y cyfandir. Ymreolaeth genedlaethol oedd prif gonglfaen athroniaeth wleidyddol y ddau ohonynt yn y cyfnod hwn. Gosododd Swinburne, gyda chefnogaeth frwd Nichol, ddarlun o Mazzini yn ei ystafell, a hefyd ddarlun o Orsini, y Carbonaro a geisiodd yn aflwyddiannus lofruddio'r Ymerawdwr Louis Napoleon. "Swinburne danced around the table in his room, screamed abuse and advocated the murder of the Emperor."[6] Nid yw'n syndod mai'r pwnc y dewisodd ei gyflwyno i'r Old Mortality oedd cerdd Shelley, 'Ode to Liberty'. Bu'r arweinydd Hwngaraidd, Kossuth, yn aros yng nghartref tad Nichol, yr Athro John Pringle Nichol, a dywedir bod John, y mab, yn modelu ei hun ar Carlyle. (Fel y gwelsom eisoes, daethai Jones, yntau, dan gyfaredd Carlyle ymhell cyn iddo gyrraedd Glasgow.)

I blith radicaliaid tanllyd yr Old Mortality daeth Edward Caird yn 1860. Disgrifiodd ef drafodaethau'r gymdeithas fel hyn:

> The free discussion of everything in heaven or earth, the fresh enjoyment of intellectual sympathy, fearless intercommunions of spirits, the youthful faith that the key of truth lies very near to our hands, give a unique zest and charm to those meetings of students with students, before the inevitable parting of the ways of manhood has come.[7]

O ran personoliaeth yr oedd Caird mor wahanol ag y gellid bod i Nichol a Swinburne. Yr oedd yn gymeriad pwyllog, mwy cymedrol ei farn o lawer na hwy, a hyd yn oed yn nyddiau ei ieuenctid adwaenid ef fel 'Old Caird'. Serch, hynny, coleddiai yr un gwerthoedd a'r un achosion â'r lleill. Yn ei gofiant i'w hen athro, dywed Jones " … Caird also was a philosophic, religious, and political radical!"[8]

[5] Melvin Richter, *The Politics of Conscience: T. H. Green and His Age*, Llundain 1964, t. 80.

[6] ibid., t. 81.

[7] ibid., t. 82.

[8] Henry Jones & John Henry Muirhead, *The Life and Philosophy of Edward Caird*, Glasgow 1921, t. 34.

Cefnogai wrthryfel Garibaldi, ac yr oedd yn selog dros achos y Gogledd yn y Rhyfel Cartref Americanaidd.

Darganfu yn yr Old Mortality ŵr ifanc o'r un anian yn union ag ef, Sais o'r enw Thomas Hill Green. Cymaint oedd y gynghanedd ysbryd rhyngddynt fel y gallai Jones ddweud:

> 'Knights of the spirit' these two men were rightly called, and they went forth to battle, side by side, and fought for the same causes with the same weapons. Indeed, so fully did they share the same convictions, entertain the same purposes and seek to render the same services to their time, that we can learn more fully from Green's Memoir than from any other source what events mattered for Caird at this time and what meaning they carried for him.[9]

Gŵr ifanc dwys, ond nid amddifad o hiwmor, oedd T. H. Green a ddaeth i Balliol yn 1855 o ysgol enwog Rugby. Yr oedd yn fab i ficer o Swydd Efrog a berthynai i adain efengylaidd yr eglwys wladol. Lliniarwyd piwritaniaeth Green gan gydwybod gymdeithasol effro iawn. Meddai A. V. Dicey, cyd-aelod ag ef o'r Old Mortality (a chyd-fyfyriwr yn Balliol) amdano yn y dyddiau cynnar hynny:

> He was as enthusiastic as we all were about Italian freedom, but ... At a time when we were thinking of what one may call romantic politics, he kept constantly pointing out to us the evil of pauperism.[10]

Cefnogai Green y Blaid Ryddfrydol gyda brwdfrydedd, ond fel Caird, cadwai ei draed ar y ddaear yn sicrach o lawer na Nichol a Swinburne. Fe'i cyfareddwyd, serch hynny, gan yr Almaen, ei phobl, ei diwylliant, ac yn enwedig ei hathronwyr. Yng ngwaith yr athronwyr Hegelaidd yn arbennig, gwelai ddehongliad o Gristnogaeth a oedd yn gyffrous a pherthnasol i'r gwaith mawr o sefydlu'r 'Deyrnas' yma ar y ddaear. Pan wnaed ef yn ddarlithydd a chymrawd o Goleg Balliol yn 1860, ac yn enwedig ar ôl ei ddyrchafiad yn Athro Whyte mewn athroniaeth foesol yn 1878, cafodd gyfle i ledaenu ei syniadau ymhlith arweinwyr y dyfodol. Ond nid 'meddyliwr' yn unig mohono; ymroes yn egnïol iawn i weithgarwch cymdeithasol ymarferol, yn arbennig felly ym maes addysg a dirwest. Fe'i etholwyd ar gyngor tref a bwrdd ysgolion Rhydychen, a bu'n gwleidydda dan faner y Rhyddfrydwyr gydol ei oes fer. Bu farw yn 45 oed yn 1882 cyn gweld cyhoeddi ei lyfrau pwysicaf, *Prolegomena to Ethics* a *Lectures on the Principles of Political Obligation*. Bu llyfrau a bywyd Green yn ysbrydoliaeth i genhedlaeth Henry Jones. Edrychent arno fel rhyw fath o sant, a thrwy gyfrwng Caird, yr oedd Jones fel pe bai mewn olyniaeth apostolaidd uniongyrchol. Disgrifiodd J. L Strachan-Davidson y berthynas rhwng Green a Caird fel hyn:

---

[9] ibid., tt. 33-34.

[10] Melvin Richter, op. cit., tt. 81/82.

> Caird and Green were kindered souls, with strong resemblances in the essential points of character, with like aims in life and keenly in sympathy in that which we call Philosophy.[11]

Yr oedd Edward Caird wedi bod yn tiwtora yn Rhydychen fel cymrawd o Goleg Merton rhwng 1864 a 1866, ac felly yn cydweithio â Green. Ym mis Mai 1866 etholwyd Caird i Gadair Athroniaeth Foesol Prifysgol Glasgow, lle roedd Nichol wedi bod yn Athro Llenyddiaeth Saesneg er 1862. Chwenychai Nichol gadair athronyddol yn y Brifysgol a cheisiodd yn aflwyddiannus yn erbyn Veitch am y Gadair Resymeg yn 1864, ac roedd ar feddwl ceisio am y Gadair Athroniaeth Foesol yn 1866 ond tynnodd ei enw'n ôl o blaid Caird (a wrthodai sefyll yn erbyn Nichol!). Ailflodeuodd cyfeillgarwch y ddau 'Hen Feidrolyn' yn Glasgow, a gwelai'r ddau addewid mawr yn y myfyriwr o Langernyw.

Ni chawsant eu siomi. Enillodd Jones ei radd M.A. (gradd gyntaf yw hon yn yr Alban) ym mis Mawrth 1878 gan ennill clod a gwobrwyon mewn Groeg, Rhesymeg, Saesneg ac Athroniaeth Foesol. Yn ystod y tair blynedd y bu'n fyfyriwr cafwyd newidiadau mawr yn ei ffordd o feddwl, a hynny dan ddylanwad Caird a Nichol, ond Caird yn arbennig. Yn wir honnai iddo'n feddyliol gael ei eni drachefn yn narlithoedd Caird.[12] Yr oedd bod yn ei ddosbarth yn brofiad cwbl newydd iddo ef a'i gyfoedion. Disgrifiodd Caird fel un o athrawon athroniaeth mwyaf y cyfnod modern ar sail agwedd agored ei feddwl, dyfnder ei ysgolheictod, ehangder ei olygon, diffuantrwydd ei argyhoeddiad a grym ei bersonoliaeth. Dan ddylanwad ei athronyddu a'i ddysgu gweddnewidiai ddaliadau ei fyfyrwyr.

> Old things passed away, never to return. There was never any direct negative criticism of the traditional belief which we had, like others accepted without examination or criticism. We were led, rather, to assume a new attitude of mind, and articles of our creed simply became obsolete.[13]

Byddai Jones yn dod i weld maes o law nad oedd yr agwedd meddwl newydd yn cael derbyniad cynnes gan bawb, a bod sawl cwr o'r byd academaidd yn ddrwgdybus o'i lladmeryddion.

Er bod dull Nichol o draddodi, fel y gellid disgwyl, yn gwbl wahanol i ddull Caird, yr oedd ei ddylanwad ar Jones yr un mor ffurfiannol. Gallai Nichol draddodi darlith mewn dull 'ysgubol', a thybiai Jones na chlywsai unrhyw un erioed yn darllen barddoniaeth neu ryddiaith yn gyhoeddus gystal ag ef. I ddylanwad Nichol y priodolai ei gariad at lenyddiaeth, a diolchai fod chwaeth ei athro yn y materion hyn mor gatholig. Fel myfyriwr câi wahoddiad weithiau i fynd am bryd o fwyd i gartref Nichol a'i wraig, ac yno unwaith y cyfarfu Swinburne, mor wyllt yr olwg arno ag erioed.

---

11 Henry Jones & John Henry Muirhead, op. cit., t. 30.
12 LL, t. 20.
13 OM, t. 134.

Yr oedd barn ei athrawon amdano yn uchel iawn. Galwai Nichol ef, "The best essayist in my class". Talodd y deyrnged wych hon i'w alluoedd mewn tystlythyr unwaith:

> At Glasgow, without question, the foremost student of his time in the department of Mental Philosophy, his eminence in literature was almost equally conspicuous.[14]

Cytunai Caird â barn ei gyd-athro:

> He was one of the most distinguished students of his time in the University; in Philosophy and Literature undoubtedly the most distinguished.[15]

Eto, ar waethaf y cyffroadau syniadol a effeithiai gymaint ar ei feddwl, nid oedd wedi colli golwg ar y nod a'i harweiniodd i Glasgow. Yn ystod gwyliau'r haf 1876 ac 1877 dychwelodd i Gymru, lle y pregethai yng nghapeli ei enwad bob Sul. Treuliodd wyliau haf 1876 yn y Bala yn darllen *Gwladwriaeth* Platon gyda Lewis Edwards. Derbyniodd 'alwad' gan gynulleidfa'r Methodistiaid Calfinaidd yn Nolwyddelan, ac yno y byddai wedi mynd yn union ar ôl graddio oni bai i'r Athro Nichol ysgrifennu llythyr ato i ddweud y gellid 'gwneud rhywbeth ohono' pe na bai'n rhuthro i dderbyn swydd. Yr oedd yr awgrym yn ddigon. Penderfynodd sefyll arholiadau gradd anrhydedd yn yr hydref, a threulio'r haf gyda chyfaill mynwesol o'r enw Hugh Walker yn yr Almaen. Gwrthododd yr alwad i Ddolwyddelan.

Wrth droi tua'r Almaen, yr oedd yn dilyn ôl troed y nifer cynyddol o fyfyrwyr athroniaeth ym Mhrydain a chwenychai ddod i gysylltiad uniongyrchol â ffynhonnell yr Idealaeth newydd: gwlad Kant, Fichte a Hegel. Un o'r rhai cyntaf i fynd ar y bererindod hon oedd yr Albanwr, J. Hutchinson Stirling. Graddiodd Stirling mewn meddygaeth ym Mhrifysgol Caeredin yn 1842, a bu am gyfnod yn feddyg yng Nghymru. Yn ôl ei gofiannydd, yr oedd "to some extent, acquainted with the Welsh Language". Yn 1843 daeth i Bont-y-pŵl i wasanaeth rhyw Dr Lawrence, ond ni chredai ei fod yng Nghymru go iawn yn Sir Fynwy: meddai, "I longed to be able to set down my foot on soil that neither map nor mortal could deny to be Welsh." Dyna paham y symudodd i'r Hirwaun yn 1844 i wasaneth Frank Crawshay. Cododd o fod yn feddyg cynorthwyol i fod yn bartner meddygol ac yna yn unig lawfeddyg gweithfeydd haearn Crawshay. Symudodd i Lyn-nedd yn 1849, lle bu tan 1851. Ysgrifennodd hanes ei brofiadau yng Nghymru dan y teitl, "The Foreign Country at Home". Fe aeth Stirling i'r Almaen ar ôl clywed honiad rhywun mewn sgwrs fod Hegel wedi llwyddo i gysoni crefydd ag athroniaeth. Trwythodd ei

[14] *Application and Testimonials of Henry Jones, M.A. (Professor of Logic and Philosophy in the University College of North Wales. Candidate for The Chair of Logic and Metaphysics in the University of Edinburgh)*, Glasgow 1891, t. 11.

[15] ibid., t. 13.

hun yn llwyr yn athroniaeth Hegel a'i ddisgyblion, a chyhoeddodd glamp o lyfr yn 1865, *The Secret of Hegel.* Hwn oedd y llyfr cyntaf yn Saesneg ar Hegel, ond brawychwyd llawer gan natur ddyrys ei athroniaeth.

Yn 1865 hefyd penderfynodd Caird a rhai o'i gyfeillion dreulio'r haf yn Dresden a Weimar. Buasai T. H. Green yno eisoes, a gwirioni ar y wlad a'i phobl. Iddo ef, dyma ddiwylliant mwyaf gwareiddiedig Ewrop. Mae'n wir iddo gwyno bod merched yr Almaen yn dieithriad yn hyll, ond (o'r herwydd, efallai) fe wnaent well cydymaith i ddyn! Wyddom ni ddim beth oedd barn Jones am ferched yr Almaen yn gyffredinol, ond dywedodd fod gan ŵr y llety yn Bonn 'two fair daughters'. Roedd rhianedd ar feddwl Jones a Walker yr haf hwnnw. Ar y ffordd i'r Almaen galwasant heibio Mrs Roxburgh, a oedd bellach yn byw ym Metws-y-coed, ac yno syrthiodd Walker mewn cariad gydag un o'i merched. Ar ôl dychwelyd o'r Almaen, ymwelodd Jones â chartref Walker, a syrthio mewn cariad gydag un o'i chwiorydd.

Pan ddaeth yr arholiad am radd anrhydedd yn yr hydref y flwyddyn honno, llwyddodd Jones i ennill anrhydedd yn y dosbarth cyntaf, ac ar ben hynny ennill cymrodoriaeth fwyaf hael y brifysgol, Cymrodoriaeth Clark. Gallai ddilyn efrydiau uwch dan nawdd y brifysgol am gyfnod o bedair blynedd, a hynny ar incwm o £225 y flwyddyn – ffortiwn o'i gymharu â'r £40 y flwyddyn a gawsai dan Ysgoloriaeth Dr Williams. Ei fwriad oedd dilyn camre ei eilun a mynd yn 1879 i Goleg Balliol i ymgeisio am radd ym Mhrifysgol Rhydychen. Yn wir, fe aeth yno gyda Walker ar ôl taith arall i'r Almaen yn yr haf, i Dresden y tro hwn. Ond ar ôl tymor rhoes y gorau i'w fwriad, gan ei fod yn teimlo'n rhy hen, ac yn rhy ymroddedig i athroniaeth, i ddechrau ymboeni am ramadeg Groeg a Lladin unwaith eto, fel y gwnâi glasfyfyrwyr Rhydychen. Nid oedd ambell frecwast gyda Jowett i'w gymharu â chyfathrach feunyddiol gyda Caird, ac i Glasgow y dychwelodd i fod yn gynorthwy i'w hen feistr fel darlithydd ac arholwr, ac uwchben popeth i ddarllen a myfyrio a thrafod.

Esgorodd y trafodaethau athronyddol anffurfiol hyn ar gymdeithas arbennig ar ddechrau tymor y gaeaf 1879, y Witenagemot. Yr oedd Jones a'i gyfaill Mungo MacCallum wedi bod yn gwrando ar gyfaill arall o'r enw James Lambie yn pregethu rhyw fore Sul, ac wedi i'r tri ohonynt ddod i lety Jones yn Willowbank Street am sgwrs, dyma benderfynu sefydlu cymdeithas debyg i'r Old Mortality. MacCallum oedd yn gyfrifol am yr enw 'Witenagemot', sef Cyngor 'Gŵyr Doeth' y Sacsoniaid gynt! Cynhaliwyd y cyfarfod swyddogol cyntaf yng nghyffiniau'r Brifysgol mewn tafarn fechan yn Park Road (yn ôl *Old Memories* nid oedd adeilad Undeb y Myfyrwyr i'w gael bryd hynny) ac etholwyd Jones yn ysgrifennydd. Yr oedd y dadleuon yn anffurfiol ac yn danbaid a'r cyfarfodydd yn gyfle godidog i wynnyllu barn. Weithiau, fel eu tad hwy oll, deuai Caird i'w plith. Cyfeiriodd J. H. Muirhead at un achlysur o'r fath pan ddaeth yr Athro â chopi o lawysgrif ei ddiweddar gyfaill T. H. Green o'r gyfrol *Prolegomena to Ethics* gydag ef, a darllen tamaid ohono iddynt. "The text with the comments were perhaps an epoch in more lives than that of the writer," meddai.[16] Bu marw annhymig Green yn 1882 yn ergyd drom iawn i Caird. Ymddengys eu bod mor glòs â Dafydd a Jonathan: y ddau ar yr un donfedd ym mhob dim o bwys.

> Seldom have there been in the history of philosophy two men who so entirely understood each other, seldom, I think, two such friends as Caird and Green. The death of his old brother in-arms had come as a stunning blow to Caird. The friend who saw him off in Glasgow on his journey to Oxford to attend Green's funeral found him so 'bewildered with grief' that he thought it well to ask the guard to see he changed at Crewe.[17]

Marwolaeth Green oedd achlysur cyhoeddi papur athronyddol cyntaf Henry Jones. Yn 1883 cyhoeddwyd cyfrol o draethodau athronyddol gan naw o athronwyr, yn cynnwys Jones, fel teyrnged i Green, *Essays in Philosophical Criticism*. Yr oedd y gwaith hwn yn wir ar y gweill cyn i Green farw mor annisgwyl. Mor gynnar ag 1881 yr oedd grŵp o Hegeliaid ifanc yn awyddus i ddangos eu hanfodlonrwydd â'r cylchgrawn athronyddol safonol *Mind*, a oedd yn dal i lynu wrth y traddodiad empeiraidd Seisnig. Y bwriad gwreiddiol oedd sefydlu cylchgrawn annibynnol eu hunain, ac yn hyn cawsant sêl bendith Green a Caird, ond penderfynwyd mai gwell fyddai cyhoeddi cyfrol a fyddai yn fath o faniffesto dros yr athroniaeth newydd. Gobeithient fedru cyhoeddi mewn pryd i ddathlu canmlwyddiant ymddangosiad *Kritik der reinen Vernunft* (Saesneg: *Critique of Pure Reason*) Immanuel Kant yn 1781, ond rhoddodd marwolaeth Green achlysur dwysach iddynt ei nodi.

Golygyddion y gyfrol oedd Andrew Seth ac R. B. Haldane. Yr oedd Seth bedair blynedd yn iau na Jones, yn frodor o Gaeredin ac wedi graddio yn y dosbarth cyntaf yn y clasuron ac mewn athroniaeth ym Mhrifysgol Caeredin. Bu'n astudio am ddwy flynedd yn yr Almaen, gan gynnwys cyfnod dan R. H. Lotze. Fe'i penodwyd yn gynorthwywr i'r Athro Alexander Campbell Fraser yn ei hen brifysgol yn 1880, ac yn 1882 cyhoeddasai gyfrol ar *The Development from Kant to Hegel*. Yr oedd Richard Burdon Haldane yr un oed â Seth, yn gynnyrch Prifysgol Caeredin, a bu yntau'n astudio dan Lotze yn yr Almaen. Yn wahanol i Seth, nid oedd Haldane yn ŵr academaidd. Maes ei weithgarwch oedd y gyfraith a gwleidyddiaeth, lle cafodd lwyddiant nodedig iawn fel Ysgrifennydd Gwladol dros Ryfel (1905–12) ac fel Arglwydd Ganghellor (1912–15 a 1924). Dywedir amdano nad oedd yn unig yn fodlon cael ei alw'n Hegelydd, ond ei fod yn dymuno hynny!

Yr oedd yr *Essays in Philosophical Criticism* yn garreg filltir bwysig yn hanes athroniaeth ym Mhrydain, oherwydd yn yr ysgrifau mynegodd y genhedlaeth iau i ba gyfeiriad yr oedd athroniaeth am fynd. Yn ei Ragymadrodd dangosodd Caird yntau o ba gyfeiriad y daeth yr ysgogiad.

[16] Henry Jones & John Henry Muirhead, op. cit., t. 90.
[17] ibid., t. 131.

> The writers of this volume agree in believing that the line of investigation which philosophy must follow, or in which it may be expected to make most important contributions to the intellectual life of man, is that which was opened up by Kant, and for the successful prosecution of which no one has done so much as Hegel.[18]

Â Caird rhagddo i bwysleisio nad derbyn athrawiaeth 'a roddwyd unwaith' oedd y bwriad, eithr yn hytrach gyrru 'mlaen i'r cyfeiriad a ddangoswyd gan yr Almaenwyr. Dywed y dylid barnu safbwynt athronyddol yn ôl ei allu i ateb gofynion y presennol, nid yn ôl ei berthynas â'r gorffennol. Yr oedd gwaith Green yn ymgorfforiad o'r agwedd hon gan iddo fynnu dilysu ei athroniaeth drosto'i hun, ac nid gyda'r apêl at 'draddodiad'. Yn wir, datgelodd Caird fod Green yn credu mai beirniadaeth *debyg* i'r eiddo Hegel oedd ei hangen, ac nid beirniadaeth Hegel fel y cyfryw. Am waith Hegel dywedodd unwaith fod yn rhaid ail-wneud y cyfan! Eto i gyd Hegel oedd yr ysbrydoliaeth.

Teitl papur Jones oedd "The Social Organism" a chyfaddefodd wrth un o'r golygwyr ifanc, Andrew Seth, ei fod yn cael y gwaith yn orchwyl eithriadol o galed. Mewn llythyr arall cyfaddefai:

> I think if I had known all the worry and depression and despair that were to be my lot I would scarcely have undertaken the task, and even now the rejection of my paper seems to be not an impossible contingency … Caird has lavished upon me a goodness which I never deserved and which it is my sorrow that I cannot repay even by writing a paper in the least worthy of his kind help.[19]

Doedd ddim angen iddo bryderu. Yr oedd yr ysgrif yn deilwng iawn o'r gyfrol, a'r gyfrol yn sicrhau safle amlwg i bob un o'r cyfranwyr o hynny ymlaen yn y ffurfafen athronyddol.

Yr oedd ffurfafen bersonol Jones yn las iawn hefyd. Ar 11eg Ebrill 1882 priododd Annie Walker, gwraig a fu yn gynhaliaeth ddi-feth iddo drwy storm a hindda gydol ei fywyd. Cawsant fwrw-swildod yn Ardal y Llynnoedd a Llangernyw. Gan gyfeillion y Witenagemot cawsant ddesg dderw hardd yn anrheg priodas. Yr oedd Harri wedi derbyn galwad gan gapel yn Lerpwl, ond Caird a roes derfyn ar obeithion yr Hen Gorff y tro hwn drwy ddweud wrtho, "Why! I intend you to be a professor of philosophy." Doedd dim y dymunai'r darpar-weinidog ei glywed yn fwy na hynny, ac felly dyna siomi capel arall. Pan ddeuai'r Gymrodoriaeth Clark i ben yn haf 1882 bwriadai Caird ei gyflogi fel darlithydd cynorthwyol a thalu iddo o'i boced ei hun. Ond yn annisgwyl iawn, daeth cynnig swydd darlithydd mewn athroniaeth o'r coleg yn Aberystwyth. Dyma'r agoriad proffesiynol a geisiai, a dyna gyfle i wasanaethu ei wlad ei hun yn ei ffordd ei hun. Dyma ddechrau 1883 felly yn gweld Henry Jones yn dychwelyd i Gymru.

---

18 Andrew Seth & Richard B. Haldane (Gol.), *Essays in Philosophical Criticism*, Llundain 1883, t. 2.

19 TJFU/2/14.

Pennod 3

Dychwelyd i Gymru

Dechreuodd Henry Jones ar ei yrfa fel darlithydd yn Aberystwyth yn yr union gyfnod pan oedd cynnydd na welwyd mo'i debyg erioed o'r blaen mewn addysg uwch yng Nghymru a Lloegr. Yr oedd prifysgolion a cholegau prifathrofaol yn cael eu sefydlu, neu ar fin cael eu sefydlu, mewn sawl dinas fawr yn Lloegr rhwng dechrau wythdegau'r bedwaredd ganrif ar bymtheg a diwedd degawd cyntaf yr ugeinfed ganrif. Yng Nghymru, yr oedd Coleg Dewi Sant, Llanbedr Pont Steffan, a sefydlwyd gan yr Esgob Burgess yn 1827 (i gynhyrchu offeiriaid a fyddai'n addysgiadol gymwys i'w gwaith yn yr eglwys wladol yng Nghymru) wedi cael yr hawl i gynnig graddau er 1852, ac yr oedd Coleg Aberystwyth wedi bod ar agor er 1872 i baratoi myfyrwyr ar gyfer graddau Prifysgol Llundain. Yn 1881 yr oedd y Pwyllgor Adrannol a sefydlasai Gladstone dan gadeiryddiaeth Arglwydd Aberdâr wedi argymell bod y llywodraeth yn noddi dau goleg prifysgol yng Nghymru, y naill yn y gogledd a'r llall yn y de. I lenwi'r holl swyddi academaidd yn y sefydliadau newydd yr oedd galw mawr am raddedigion o hen brifysgolion yr Alban, ac roeddynt hwythau yn barod iawn i'w llenwi. Meddai'r Athro J. Gwynn Williams yn ei gyfrol swmpus ar hanes cynnar Coleg y Brifysgol, Bangor:

> The Scots were so firmly entrenched in the new colleges and universities south of the Tweed as to occasion gentle raillery for it was sometimes hinted that higher education in England and Wales had expanded in order to provide employment for Scotland's philosophy graduates.[1]

I Henry Jones a'i gyfoedion, disgyblion efengyl T. H. Green, yr oedd maes cenhadol yn agor o'u blaen a chyfle euraid i ledaenu'r Idealaeth newydd yn y colegau newydd. Pan gyrhaeddodd ef Aberystwyth yr oedd cydsefydlydd y Witenagemot, Mungo MacCallum, eisoes yno fel Athro Saesneg er 1879. Penodwyd ei gyfaill Hugh Walker, ei frawd yng nghyfraith bellach, yn Athro Saesneg yng Ngholeg Dewi Sant, a chyn diwedd y flwyddyn, dewiswyd Andrew Seth (un o olygyddion yr *Essays in Philosophical Criticism*) yn Athro Athroniaeth cyntaf y coleg newydd yng Nghaerdydd. Wrth longyfarch Seth ar ei benodiad dywedodd Jones mewn llythyr:

> It would be an immense advantage for the colleges, after the establishment of the Welsh University, if the professor of Philosophy in North Wales will be of the same faith as yourself.[2]

---

[1] J. Gwynn Williams, *The University College of North Wales: Foundations 1884–1927*, Caerdydd 1995, t. 66.

[2] TJ/U/2/21.

Yn wir, bu Jones a MacCallum yn gweithio'n ddiwyd o blaid Seth, gan geisio dylanwadu ar bawb a allai fod o gymorth. Yr oedd MacCallum am gael gair yng nghlust Jayne, Prifathro Coleg Llanbed, meddai Jones, ond er bod Jayne yn gynnyrch Rhydychen, "He is not of the Green, Wallace and Bradley lot"[3] (tri Hegelydd amlycaf Rhydychen) h.y. nid yn 'un ohonom ni'. Cafodd y cyn-Wittenagemotwr, J. H. Muirhead, ei benodi i ddarlithio yn Birmingham (lle bu mewn bri mawr fel Athro Athroniaeth) yr un flwyddyn, ac mae'n amlwg fod Jones yn awyddus iawn i gadw cywion Caird yn frawdoliaeth gyda'i gilydd wrth iddynt oll wasgaru i sefydlu adrannau neu weithio mewn adrannau a sefydlwyd yn ddiweddar. Mae lle i gredu ei fod wedi anfon at Caird a'i wahodd i lywyddu ar y fath frawdoliaeth. Nid oedd Caird yn awyddus i dderbyn rôl tad-yn-y-ffydd, fodd bynnag.

> The fraternity of young philosophers is not a bad thing in itself, but think it s'd postpone itself till the originator of it is at least a professor and the affairs of N S Wales settled. I think also the question of President should be postponed till the members have got together. They could not in any case expect help from me – who have never had much prowess of acting and social methods. But the generous enthusiasm that prompted the proposal is in itself an encouraging thing to a confined philosopher.[4]

Mae awgrym yn ateb Caird fod bwriad i'r frawdoliaeth wneud mwy na thrin athroniaeth, ac ymwneud â rhyw waith cymdeithasol yn ogystal. Os felly, byddai hynny'n gwbl gydnaws ag ysbryd T. H. Green, ond nid oes sôn fod dim wedi deillio o'r awgrym.

Un rheswm yn ddiau am hynny oedd y ffaith fod storm ofnadwy wedi torri yn Aberystwyth yn fuan ar ôl i Jones gyrraedd yno, a hynny yn bennaf oherwydd ei ymddygiad ef ei hun. Yr hyn a ddisgrifiai Caird fel "the affair of N S Wales" oedd wrth wraidd y mater. Pan argymhellodd Pwyllgor Aberdâr fod y llywodraeth yn noddi dau goleg, un yn y gogledd a'r llall yn y de, yr oedd Coleg Aberystwyth yn synhwyro bod perygl angheuol yn yr awgrym i sefydliad nad oedd yn amlwg wedi ei leoli yn y naill na'r llall. Wedi i safle gael ei nodi ar gyfer coleg y de (sef Caerdydd), yr oedd tynged Coleg Aberystwyth yn dibynnu ar agwedd cefnogwyr Coleg y Gogledd tuag ato. Ymunodd Henry Jones â staff Coleg Aberystwyth ar yr union adeg hon o ansicrwydd dwys.

Cyn trafod yr helynt a gododd rhwng Jones ac awdurdodau Coleg Aberystwyth, dylid egluro bod y Prifathro, Thomas Charles Edwards, yn edrych ymlaen at ei ddyfodiad a'i ddychweliad i Gymru. Mewn llythyr at ei dad, Lewis Edwards, Y Bala, yn Hydref 1882 dywedodd T. C. Edwards:

> Henry Jones of Glasgow will come here as Assistant Lecturer in January. I am anxious to give him a chance, and, if he proves satisfactory, to fix him in Wales.[5]

[3] TJ/U/2/22.
[4] TJ/U/2/23.
[5] TCEL/331.

Yn hyn yr oedd T. C. Edwards wedi llwyddo i achub y blaen ar ei dad, oherwydd mewn llythyr at Henry Jones yn Ebrill 1881 yr oedd Lewis Edwards wedi mynegi awydd i'w ddenu i Goleg y Bala. Ymateb i gais am gefnogaeth wrth geisio am swydd dysgu Saesneg yn Nottingham neu Northampton yw'r llythyr hwn (yn ôl Dr Thomas Jones). Agwedd Lewis Edwards oedd:

> Like yourself I should prefer your doing something in Wales, and I cannot but hope the door will open for you in some part of the Principality … The English Language and Literature is an interesting subject, though I cannot help thinking you would be be more at home with Philosophy. I wish some one would endow a Chair of Philosophy for this College, and in such a case I should certainly vote for you as first professor.[6]

Yn ddiau, yr oedd y Methodistiaid Calfinaidd yn ymfalchïo yn llwyddiant academaidd amlwg Jones a disgwylient bethau mawr ganddo maes o law. Yr oedd pob rheswm dros gredu y byddai Aberystwyth yn cynnig llwyfan godidog i'r athrylith ifanc. Yr oedd ei deimladau ef ei hun braidd yn gymysg, fodd bynnag. Mewn llythyr at Andrew Seth yn Hydref 1882 dywedodd:

> As to the Welsh lectureship I don't know what to say to you. I cannot allow you to congratulate me for the job is neither permanent nor well paid. I only trust that it will lead to a Chair in Philosophy in one of the new Welsh Colleges. The only chance I have is to make myself indispensable to the Aberystwyth staff: but then, that is a very hard matter for a mere Assistant or Lecturer. I could scarcely afford to accept the post; but still less could I afford to reject it. So I leave Scotland in January or December, and enter into the little, squabbling scandalmongering life of a country town. It is a trial to leave my Glasgow friends and Caird has been a father to me. Nor do I know that I have sufficient strength to live the higher life in my new surroundings, but I must try it, and hope that now and then I shall get a glimpse of the stronger race of philosophers and thinkers of the Scotch Universities.[7]

Nid oedd yr amheuon a lechai yng nghalon y Cymro alltud ynglŷn â'i ddychweliad adref yn argoeli'n dda.

Yn ystod degawd cyntaf oes y coleg gofelid am yr adran Athroniaeth gan y prifathro, y Parchedig T. C. Edwards ei hunan. Yr oedd cael rhywun arall i'w gynorthwyo yn mynd i ysgafnhau tipyn ar ei feichiau trymion. Nid oedd nifer y myfyrwyr yn fawr, ond roedd Jones yn cynnal darlithoedd cyhoeddus yn y dref, ac roedd ymateb da iddynt. Ymhlith myfyrwyr y Coleg yr oedd O. M. Edwards, a thyfodd perthynas gyfeillgar rhyngddynt.

> Henry Jones has come here to lecture us. As I was MacCallum's favourite last year, so I am his this year …"
>
> Now I have fallen into the hands of Henry Jones, who is rapidly widening and deepening the channel of my thoughts. He takes a great interest in us all …

[6] Trwy law Mr John Hughes.

[7] TJ/U/2/25.

> Last Friday, I spent the afternoon with Henry Jones, went together for a walk to Clarach, made me dream of Philosophy Honours … [8]

Yn ddiweddarach yn 1883 cafodd O. M. gyfle i fynd yn efrydydd i Glasgow gyda Puleston Jones (a oedd yn ddall, ac angen cydymaith cydnaws arno). Does dim amheuaeth fod Henry Jones a Mungo MacCallum wedi gwneud i Glasgow edrych yn ddeniadol iawn. Yn ôl W. J. Gruffydd, hwy oedd y ddau a gafodd y dylanwad trymaf ar Owen Edwards yn Aberystwyth.[9] Byddai MacCallum a Jones yn ei wahodd i'w cartrefi, ac yng nghartref y cyntaf, cyfarfu â John Nichol unwaith. Cafodd O. M. a Puleston dreulio blwyddyn wrth draed Caird a Nichol yn Glasgow cyn mynd i Rydychen yn 1884. Os bu yr O. M. Edwards ifanc yn dir ffrwythlon i'r Hegeliaeth a ddysgai Caird ("Bu ei athroniaeth yn fywyd meddyliol i mi")[10], nid oedd pawb yn Aberystwyth yn ymateb â'r un eiddgarwch i'r genadwri honno fel y'i lladmerid gan Jones. Sylweddolai yntau fod yn rhaid iddo fod yn ochelgar wrth ddatgelu ei ddaliadau crefyddol personol. Dywedodd wrth O. M. y byddai yn datgan wrtho ei gredo crefyddol wedi i'r berthynas rhyngddynt newid (rhag cael ei gyhuddo o gymryd mantais ar ei safle fel athro, mae'n siŵr.) Serch hynny, llwyddodd i gael O. M. i fynegi rhai o'i amheuon crefyddol wrtho, a hynny drwy ei 'dywys' i raddau gyda'i gwestiynau.

Nid ei ddaliadau athronyddol a aeth â Jones i drybini fodd bynnag, ond ei awydd mawr i wneud rhywbeth ymarferol dros addysg uwch yng ngogledd Cymru. Yr oedd y mudiad o blaid Coleg Prifysgol yn y gogledd wedi cynnal cynhadledd fawr yng Nghaer yn Ionawr 1883 lle gwrthodwyd cynnig Lewis Edwards, Y Bala, a David Davies, Llandinam, i gynnwys Sir Aberteifi ymhlith y siroedd i'w hystyried fel safle i'r coleg. Yn gynnar ym mis Mawrth ffurfiwyd Pwyllgor Safle i ddewis lleoliad derbyniol i'r sefydliad newydd ac i drefnu ymgyrch i godi arian drwy'r gogledd. Yr oedd y Pwyllgor yn awyddus i benodi dau drefnydd i hyrwyddo'r amcanion hyn, y naill yn Ymneilltuwr a'r llall yn Eglwyswr. Dewisodd Esgobion Llanelwy a Bangor reithor Llandyrnog, y Parch David Williams, fel y trefnydd Anglicanaidd. Dewis y Pwyllgor am y swydd arall, a'r person roeddynt yn awyddus dros ben i'w gael, oedd Henry Jones.

Cododd dau anhawster ar unwaith. Er ei fod yn awyddus iawn i weithio dros goleg i'r gogledd, nid oedd yn awyddus i gyflawni swydd trefnydd fel 'cynrychiolydd' yr Ymneilltuwyr gan ei fod gymaint o blaid addysg anenwadol. Nid oedd yn awyddus ychwaith i dorri cysylltiad gyda Choleg Aberystwyth. Yr oedd yn cael ei dynnu bob ffordd ac mewn argyfwng personol go arw. Daeth hyn yn amlwg i O. M. Edwards mor gynnar â Mawrth 8fed. Meddai yn ei ddyddiadur am y diwrnod hwnnw:

---

[8] W. J. Gruffydd, *Owen Morgan Edwards: Cofiant,* Aberystwyth 1937, t. 184.

[9] ibid., t. 182.

[10] Hazel Davies (Gol.), *Bro a Bywyd Syr O. M. Edwards,* Caerdydd 1988, t. 38.

> 'No philosophy lecture' this evening. There is something the matter with Henry Jones. He said after a half an hour's lecture to me this morning – 'This week has been a dreadful one for me, the "whole estate of man" is tottering with me. I can't tell you now, but you will soon know all.' His lips quivered convulsively as he showed me a copy of a Telegram beginning thus: "Difficulties have arisen. Meet me at once at the St. Pancras Hotel." He asked me to publish his non-attendance this evening and then vanished through the myriad minute snow-flakes which are drizzling round. What can be the matter with him?[11]

Mawrth 9fed gwnaed cais ar ran y Pwyllgor Safle gan y Capt. Edward H. Verney i T. C. Edwards am ei farn ar benodi Jones yn drefnydd. Bu Jones ei hun yn trafod y mater gyda'r Prifathro.[12] Yn ôl adroddiad Edwards o'r cyfarfod, fe geisiodd ei berswadio i beidio derbyn y swydd, gan ei annog i ganolbwyntio ar ei waith athronyddol.[13] O wneud hynny byddai yn siŵr o gael ei benodi i gadair yng Ngholeg y Gogledd, lle bynnag y'i lleolwyd. Byddai hynny'n rhagori ar gael cynnig cadair am ei fod wedi codi arian i'r coleg. Yn ôl Jones yn *Old Memories*, y dewis a gafodd oedd derbyn swydd trefnydd ac ildio'i le yn Aberystwyth, neu ei gwrthod a chael ei ddyrchafu ar unwaith i gadair yn Aberystwyth.[14] (Yn ôl cofnodion Cyngor y Coleg, yr oedd y Prifathro eisoes wedi paratoi'r ffordd ar gyfer y dyrchafiad hwn yng nghyfarfod 28ain Chwefror – "The Principal gave notice of his intention at the next Council meeting to propose the permanent appointment of Mr Henry Jones as Professor of Logic, Moral Philosophy and Political Economy".[15]) Methai Jones â gweld bod parodwydd i weithio dros Goleg y Gogledd yn arwydd o ddiffyg teyrngarwch tuag at Goleg Aberystwyth gan y credai ef yr adleolid Coleg Aberystwyth, ac y byddai'r coleg ar ei ennill o symud.

Mae'n amlwg mai gofyn i Jones ailystyried y mater a wnaeth y Prifathro a gofyn iddo ddod i'w weld drachefn. Ond yn ystod yr ail gyfarfod Edwards, ac nid Jones, a newidiodd ei feddwl. Lliniarodd y Prifathro gryn dipyn ar ei wrthwynebiad i'w 'fenthyg' i'r ymgyrch dros Goleg y Gogledd, gan ddweud na fyddai ef yn bersonol yn gwrthwynebu deisyfiad Jones pan ddeuai'r mater ger bron Cyngor Coleg Aberystwyth. Rhoddodd Edwards dri rheswm dros y newid agwedd mewn llythyr at Aberdâr, gan ddweud mai dan bwysau o du Jones y gwnaeth hynny. Yn gyntaf, dymunai iddo barhau gyda'r 'gwaith da' a wnâi yn y coleg; yn ail yr oedd am ymddangos yn gyfeillgar tuag at ymgyrch Coleg y Gogledd yn y gobaith y byddai hynny'n ennyn ystyriaeth ffafriol o achos Coleg Aberystwyth; yn drydydd oherwydd ei ewyllys da tuag ato, poenai beth a wnâi Jones am ei fywoliaeth ar ôl i'w dymor fel trefnydd ddod i ben pe na bai swydd Aberystwyth yn dal ganddo.

Yn ôl Edwards, dymunai Jones iddo awdurdodi ei ryddhad yn y fan a'r lle, ond dywedodd wrtho na allai wneud hynny heb gydsyniad y Cyngor. Dadleuai Jones fod

---

[11] W. J. Gruffydd, op. cit., t. 179.

[12] TCEL/336.

[13] TCEL/347.

[14] OM, tt. 167-8, paragraff rhif 4.

[15] *The Dragon,* Cyf XLV (1922/3), tt. 178-180.

y Cyngor wedi awdurdodi'r Prifathro i'w benodi, ac felly, drwy'r un awdurdod, dylai fedru ei ryddhau. Gwrthddadleuai Edwards mai awdurdod i ddewis y sawl a fynnai i'r swydd a gafodd gan y Cyngor, nid awdurdod i wneud penodiad fel y cyfryw. Yr argraff a gafodd Jones, fodd bynnag, yn ôl *Old Memories* oedd fod y Prifathro wedi rhoi 'caniatâd' iddo dderbyn y swydd trefnu, a hynny heb ildio ei swydd yn Aberystwyth. Gwadai Edwards iddo wneud y fath beth.

Awgrymodd Edwards fod Jones yn ysgrifennu'n uniongyrchol at Lywydd y Coleg, Arglwydd Aberdâr, i gyflwyno ei achos ger ei fron. Fe wnaeth yntau hynny mewn llythyr dyddiedig Mawrth 12fed, gan ddatgan na welai ef wrthdrawiad rhwng gweithio dros sefydlu Coleg y Gogledd a'i deyrngarwch i Goleg Aberystwyth.[15] Byddai'n trefnu i sicrhau darlithydd arall i gymryd ei le dros y cyfnod (yr oedd William Rathbone A.S. yn fodlon wynebu'r gost am hyn yn bersonol), ond os na fyddai hynny'n dderbyniol, gofynnai i Gyngor y Coleg, fel cymwynas bersonol, ei ryddhau o'i swydd yn Aberystwyth.

Achosodd cais Jones benbleth go arw i uchel swyddogion Coleg Aberystwyth, a bu yntau yn ceisio cyngor gan ei dad ysbrydol, Edward Caird. Mae'n amlwg ei fod yn anesmwyth iawn ynglŷn â pharodrwydd yr athronydd ifanc i ymroi i waith trefnu. Dywed yn ei ateb, dyddiedig Mawrth 12fed, fod ei "paternal fears somewhat awakened by your 'Do o'r die' language." Yr oedd ei gyngor yn ddiamwys:

> You must first of all be a philosopher and a teacher, and it would not be right – you would not eventually do so much good – if anything s'd lead you to subordinate that to anything else … I have every confidence that the work is a worthy one. But I think you s'd hold as to a sheet anchor to the conviction that you are to be teacher first, and an agitator even for university second. (Keep him to that my dear Mrs Jones!)[17]

Yr oedd yr Athro yn adnabod personoliaeth ei gyn-ddisgybl yn dda, a dyna a'i poenai: "It is hard for you to give anything less than the whole of yourself to anything". Wrth gwrs, ni allai Jones, fwy na neb arall, ymroi yn llwyr i fwy nag un peth. Anfonodd lythyr arall eto ar Mawrth 17eg yn mynegi'r farn ei fod yn ddoeth i beidio derbyn ieuad anghymarus gydag offeiriad yn y gwaith. Heb sicrwydd ar y mater hwn, " … you are well to keep out of it … "[18] (Mae'n ddiddorol fod Edwards yn gwybod am agwedd Caird.)

Yn y cyfamser, bu Aberdâr mewn cysylltiad ag Edwards. Mewn llythyr dyddiedig Mawrth 12fed, pwysleisia mor bwysig ydyw i'r Prifathro gael trafodaeth lawn gyda Jones ar y mater, ac egluro iddo fod ei gred ef ei hun nad oedd gwrthdrawiad rhwng ymgyrchu dros Goleg y Gogledd a gwasanaethu Coleg Aberystwyth yn safbwynt bregus iawn. Mae'n atgoffa Edwards o ddatganiad Stuart Rendel,

[16] TCEL/337 (Cymharer 347 a gweler hefyd OM, t. 168, paragraff rhif 5).

[17] TJU/2/16.

[18] TJU/2/17.

> 'That by the terms of the resolution passed at Chester, the money collected must be considered as received solely for the purpose of a college in – not for – N. Wales' – and that therefore the action of those who promote subscriptions in N. Wales must be considered as antagonistic to the College at Aberystwyth. Does Mr Jones propose to announce that his efforts to raise subscriptions include the possibility of their being applied to a N. Wales College at Aberystwyth? If so I fear that he will find that he has chilled the enthusiasm of his audiences.[19]

Ar ben hyn, yr oedd y Llywydd yn awyddus iawn i sicrhau gwasanaeth "so distinguished a Welshman" i Goleg Aberystwyth. Eisoes, fodd bynnag, yr oedd Jones wedi maentumio wrth y Pwyllgor Safle y byddai yn derbyn y swydd, a rhyddhawyd y wybodaeth hon i'r wasg.

Pan ymddangosodd ei enw yn y papurau ar Fawrth 16eg fel trefnydd tebygol i ymgyrch Coleg y Gogledd, ni adawyd Edwards mewn unrhyw amheuaeth ynglŷn â'u gwrthwynebiad gan nifer o aelodau Cyngor Coleg Aberystwyth.[20] Anfonodd Aberdâr at Edwards ar Fawrth 19eg yn amgáu ei ateb i Jones, sef gwrthod caniatâd i'w ryddhau ar gyfer y gwaith trefnu.[21] Syfrdanwyd Jones gan yr ateb ac fe aeth ar ei union i weld y Prifathro. Dyma adroddiad Edwards o'r hyn a fu rhyngddynt y dydd hwnnw, mewn llythyr at y Llywydd:

> The day on which your lordship sent me the telegram, stating that you would reply to Mr Jones through me, he came and asked to be allowed to see your reply before I went to lecture the following morning, because he was anxious to telegraph his acceptance to the North Wales Committee, which would be sitting that day. Next morning I handed him the reply. After reading it he said, with great emotion and in strong terms, that he would go and do the work in N. Wales in spite of everything: he would compress his instruction of our students to half the week and spend the other half of every week in N. Wales. I replied that that could not now be done, as the President had refused to permit his doing work which he (the President) considered to be inconsistent with his being on our staff at all. He said, in an ebullition of feeling, that he knew what he was about. I then said that I hoped he would do nothing that was not perfectly honourable. To this he answered that he also hoped all would act honourably, but that he knew where all this had come from. I asked what he meant, and said he could not surely suppose I had prejudiced his case. He replied that he did not name individuals, but that I knew as well as he. Those were his last words. He gave his concluding public lecture that evening. As I had previously promised, I took the chair. But he did not speak to me at the beginning of the meeting and did not come up to bid me good bye at the close. He left for North Wales next morning.[22]

Ysgrifennodd Jones at Aberdâr o ogledd Cymru, Mawrth 24ain, i egluro ei fod wedi derbyn y swydd trefnydd ar sail y 'caniatâd' a gafodd gan y Prifathro ar ôl pwyso'n drwm arno.

---

19 TCEL/338.

20 TCEL/340/341/343/344.

21 TCEL/342.

22 TCEL/347.

> The authority, then, which bound me to the Aberystwyth College at the first voluntarily permitted me to accept the organizing secretaryship of the N. Wales's committee; and I may assert that otherwise I should neither have been offered nor accepted the post.[23]

Os oedd y Llywydd yn awr yn gwrthod rhoi sêl ei fendith ar y cynllun i ganiatáu iddo rannu ei amser rhwng Aberystwyth a'r gogledd, byddai'n rhaid iddo ymddiswyddo o'i swydd fel darlithydd. Ysywaeth, ni chafodd hawl i wneud y naill na'r llall. Felly, ni chymerodd unrhyw ran yng ngwaith ymgyrch Coleg y Gogledd. Mewn llythyr at Edwards, dyddiedig Mawrth 31ain, cyhuddodd Aberdâr Jones o "want of candour" yn ei ymwneud â'r ddau ohonynt.[24]

Ar ôl cyfweliad gyda'r Prifathro ar Ebrill 5ed, bu'n ddigon grasol i anfon at Aberdâr i ymddiheuro'n llwyr am ddweud bod Edwards wedi rhoi 'caniatâd' iddo dderbyn swydd y trefnydd. Mae'n cydnabod mai ef yn ei eiddgarwch a ddehonglodd adwaith personol y Prifathro fel pe bai'n ddyfarniad swyddogol. Mae'n awyddus iawn i bwysleisio nad oedd unrhyw fai o gwbl ar Edwards. Dymuna roddi ei holl egni i'w swydd fel darlithydd mewn Athroniaeth yn y coleg a gofidia ei fod wedi rhoi'r argraff nad oedd yn ddigon ymwybodol o'i gyfrifoldeb tuag at Goleg Aberystwyth. Ychwanegodd fod y coleg wedi gweld yn dda i beidio talu ei gyflog iddo ar ddiwedd y tymor![25]

Yr oedd Arglwydd Aberdâr yr un mor rasol wrth dderbyn ymddiheuriad Jones, a gorchmynnodd fod y cyflog a ataliwyd (heb yn wybod iddo ef) yn cael ei dalu ar unwaith.[26] Ysgrifennodd Edwards at Aberdâr hefyd i ddweud bod Henry Jones wedi ymddiheuro wrtho. "I beg you, therefore, to consider him absolved so far as I am personally concerned in the matter."[27] Atebodd Aberdâr ei fod yn falch iawn o glywed am ddiwedd heddychlon y mater. Nid oedd eisiau dweud dim mwy am y peth. Eithr yr oedd perthynas Jones a'r coleg wedi suro. Sylwodd fod peth o'r cynhesrwydd tuag ato wedi cilio a bod amheuon ynglŷn â'i uniongrededd crefyddol ar gerdded.[28]

Credai Jones fod ei holl ofidiau yn tarddu o agwedd elyniaethus Thomas Charles Edwards tuag ato. Gyda threigl y blynyddoedd dyfnhaodd ei chwerwder tuag at Aberystwyth. Am y coleg hwnnw meddai, yn 1919, "That will never be a fine college, so long as it is in the power of the Cardis and the people who make religion do instead of rectitude!"[29] Dros amser hefyd, mae'n amlwg iddo symleiddio'r sefyllfa, gan borteadu T. C. Edwards fel dyn a geisiai ei orfodi i ddewis rhwng yr hyn a gredai oedd yn ddyletswydd i wasanaethu ei genedl (fel trefnydd ymgyrch

---

[23] TCEL/346.
[24] TCEL/348.
[25] TCEL/349.
[26] TCEL/350.
[27] TCEL/351.
[28] CM, t. 170.
[29] TJ/U/1/102.

Coleg y Gogledd) a'i fywoliaeth (fel darlithydd yn Aberystwyth). Ni werthfawrogodd erioed fod y Prifathro yn cael ei dynnu mewn mwy nag un cyfeiriad, a'i fod, beth bynnag, yn was i eraill. Wrth dystiolaethu i'w ffydd mewn Rhagluniaeth, disgrifiodd ddigwyddiadau Aberystwyth fel hyn mewn llythyr personol yn 1906:

> Somehow I feel confident we shall never want. There was a time when I had to choose between my livelihood and my conscience. I may tell you about it some day. A man called great and thought good, who was then my official chief, strove by bribes and threats to induce me to give up a public cause, which I thought it my duty at the time to serve. I begged him, as a man begs for what he holds dearest, not to force such an option (?) upon me, but I begged in vain; and I am thankful even yet for the reply I was led to make. 'It is my part to stand by my duty, and that of God's Providence to see that I shall not starve.' I never wanted. I was reduced to 10/- in the bank, apart from the little my wife owned, as a consequence of his act, but since then my means have grown ample for my needs. I never feared, and I have never had cause to fear.[30]

Ar y gorau, mae'n rhaid i ni ddweud mai fersiwn gywasgedig iawn yw hon o'r sefyllfa.

Serch hynny, y mae tystiolaeth fod agwedd T. C. Edwards tuag ato yn wir wedi troi'n elyniaethus. Daw tystiolaeth ddiddorol dros ben o ddyddiadur O. M. Edwards. Rhaid cloriannu'r dystiolaeth hon yn ofalus, fodd bynnag, oherwydd gwyddom gymaint yr edmygai O. M. Henry Jones (a sut na lwyddodd i glosio at T. C. Edwards). Y mae'n amlwg fod y Prifathro yn chwilio am dystiolaeth y gellid ei defnyddio i ddangos fod Jones yn aelod anfoddhaol o'r staff ac i'r diben hwn gwahoddodd O. M. i'w stydi ym mis Ebrill neu Mai.

> ... the Principal one day called me to his study, tried to get out, under the cloak of anxiety for the class, every thing I could say concerning Henry Jones, and did it all with such an apparent air of goodness that I was dumbfounded, expressing the greatest solicitude for the class he himself so grossly neglected, and an equally great concern for the man whom I instinctively knew he was trying to ruin, perhaps by means of what I might tell him. I looked demure and quiet, but my thoughts were angry and stormy when I thought I was perhaps used as means, and that without my knowing it, to ruin another. I was told to tell Mr Jones 'if he went from his course – and stay – you might perhaps tell me too'. I think the revered gentleman will not tell the Council anything I said concerning the Philosophy lectures, unless he is more friendly to Henry Jones than I take him to be.[31]

Yn ystod y sgwrs hon, neu ryw sgwrs arall, mynegodd y Prifathro'r farn, "It was not to teach a grand philosophy but to train men for London (h.y. graddau Prifysgol Llundain) that I asked him (Jones) here": arwydd pendant nad oedd Hegeliaeth Jones yn dderbyniol iawn i glustiau Methodistaidd Thomas Charles Edwards! Teimlai O. M. mai ei ddyletswydd oedd rhybuddio Henry Jones fod y Prifathro â'i

[30] TJ/U/3/195.

[31] W. J. Gruffydd, op. cit., t. 180.

gyllell ynddo. Aethant i ymgynghori gyda MacCallum, a daeth pethau eraill 'i'r golwg'. Er mawr syndod i O. M. darganfu nad oedd gan y Prifathro gyfaill o gwbl ar y staff. Gan fod MacCallum ar delerau da gydag Aberdâr, penderfynwyd y dylai ei rybuddio fod posibilrwydd y dywedid pethau camarweiniol wrtho parthed effeithiolrwydd Jones fel darlithydd.

Penodiad dros ddau dymor oedd y swydd a gymerasai Jones yn Aberystwyth. Nid oedd Edwards yn amcanu ailgydio yn y gwaith o ddarlithio mewn athroniaeth, felly byddai'n rhaid ei gosod ar sail barhaol. Disgwyliai Jones i'r Cyngor ei gadarnhau ynddi. Ond nid dyna ddigwyddodd. Heb ymgynghori ag ef yn gyntaf, aeth y Cyngor ati i hysbysebu am Athro Rhesymeg ac Athroniaeth. Byddai'n rhaid iddo gystadlu am ei swydd. Cymerodd hyn yn sarhad, ac nid oedd ei enw ymhlith yr un ymgeisydd ar ddeg am y gadair. Felly, mewn siom a chwerwder, a heb swydd i fynd iddi, daeth ei benodiad academaidd cyntaf i ben. Wrth ymadael, dywedodd y byddai'n gadael mater tysteb i ddoethineb y Prifathro a'i farn c'r hyn fyddai'n gyfiawn.[32] Atebodd Edwards y byddai'n falch o roddi llythyr o gymeradwyaeth iddo, "… I understood, when we last spoke, that we parted friends. I assure you I bear you no ill will …"[33] Ond ni chredodd Henry Jones hynny.

[32] TCEL/364.

[33] TCEL/365.

Pennod 4

Athro ym Mangor

Er ei fod heb swydd ganol 1883, nid oedd Henry Jones heb waith. Yr oedd yn awr yn rhydd i roddi cymaint o amser ag a fynnai i ymgyrch Coleg y Gogledd. Cafodd gais gan William Rathbone A.S. i wneud gwaith rhagbaratoadol ar gyfansoddiad y coleg arfaethedig. Gwaith yn y cefndir oedd hyn ond talodd Rathbone £50 am ei lafur.[1] Dewiswyd Bangor fel safle'r coleg newydd ar 24 Awst 1883.

Yr oedd gwaith ar ei gyfer yn yr Alban hefyd. Fe'i penodwyd yn arholwr mewn Athroniaeth a Saesneg ym Mhrifysgol Glasgow: swydd am dair blynedd a dalai £80 y flwyddyn. Golygai'r swydd gryn dipyn o deithio yn ôl a blaen i'r Brifysgol gan fod disgwyl i'r arholwr arolygu'r myfyrwyr wrth iddynt sefyll eu harholiadau. Un diwrnod, pan oedd Jones yn eistedd yn y neuadd yn arolygu gosododd Caird gopi o waith yn dwyn y teitl *Aids to Philosophy* o'i flaen gan ofyn iddo am ei farn. Yr oedd yn amlwg mai fersiwn garbwl ydoedd o ddarlithoedd Caird ei hun. Byddai caniatáu i'r fath waith gael ei gyhoeddi yn niweidiol i fyfyrwyr ac i Caird fel ei gilydd wrth gwrs. Penderfynwyd gwneud cais am waharddiad ar gyhoeddi'r llyfr yn y llysoedd. Nid oedd yn achos hawdd, ac ni chafodd Caird lwyddiant bob cam o'r ffordd. Ond yn y diwedd, ger bron Tŷ'r Arglwyddi, enillodd y dydd, a hynny i raddau helaeth oherwydd trylwyredd Jones, a gyflogwyd ganddo i fynd gyda chrib mân drwy'r *Aids* a theipysgrif o ddarlithoedd Caird i brofi'r cyhuddiad o lên-ladrad.

Y mae'n amlwg fod Jones yn ei elfen pan oedd ar drywydd llên-ladrad. Darganfu bod yr arfer afiach yn rhemp yn yr Eisteddfod Genedlaethol! Fe'i gwahoddwyd ef a'r Prifathro T. C. Edwards, ynghyd â'r Dr John Morris (Aberhonddu) i fod yn feirniaid cystadleuaeth y Traethawd Cymraeg yn Eisteddfod Genedlaethol Lerpwl, 1884. Cynigiai'r Eisteddfod £30 o wobr a Thlws Aur am draethawd ar y testun: "Athroniaeth Hegel, a'i dylanwad ar feddwl Ewrop". Ymgeisiodd chwe chystadleuydd. Dr John Morris yn unig a anfonodd feirniadaeth yn Gymraeg; dewisodd Jones ac Edwards Saesneg fel eu cyfrwng hwy. Anfonodd y Prifathro ei feirniadaeth ef drwy delegram, dair brawddeg o hyd! Yr oedd beirniadaeth Jones yn faith ac yn fanwl. Ef yn unig sydd yn tynnu sylw at y ffaith fod tri ymgeisydd wedi bod yn copïo gwaith awduron eraill.

Enillydd y wobr oedd y Parch David Adams, bryd hynny o Hawen, Sir Aberteifi. Cyhoeddwyd y traethawd yn y *Liverpool National Eisteddfod Transactions* [2] a hwn,

---

1 J. Gwynn Williams, *The University College of North Wales: Foundations 1884–1927,* Caerdydd 1985, tt. 51-52.

2 *Transactions of the Royal National Eisteddfod of Wales, Liverpool 1884*, Lerpwl 1885, tt. 111-173. Gweler y beirniadaethau tt. 109-111. Am astudiaeth o fywyd a gwaith Adams gweler E. Keri Evans & W. Pari Huws, *Cofiant y Parch. David Adams,* Lerpwl 1924.

mae'n debyg, oedd y gwaith cyntaf i'w argraffu yn Gymraeg ar Hegel. Yr oedd Adams wedi graddio yn Aberystwyth yn 1877, ac yn gyn-ddisgybl i T. C. Edwards (fel rhai o'r cystadleuwyr eraill, efallai). Blaenffrwyth gwaith ei fywyd oedd y traethawd, oherwydd cyhoeddodd lyfrau dylanwadol wedi hyn a lwyddodd i ogwyddo diwinyddiaeth yng Nghymru i gyfeiriad Hegelaidd. Mae'r ffaith fod yr Eisteddfod wedi gosod y testun hwn ar gyfer traethawd yn arwydd o amlygrwydd cyffyddol Hegeliaeth yn ymwybyddiaeth y deallusion. Wrth drafod dylanwad Hegel ar syniadaeth Ewrop mae Adams yn sôn am Ffrainc, Denmarc, Norwy, Sweden a'r Eidal yn ogystal â'r Almaen cyn troi ei sylw at Brydain. Ar ôl llafur arloesol Stirling, meddai, trosglwyddwyd lluman Hegeliaeth i Green a Wallace yn Rhydychen, a Caird yn Glasgow. A beth am Gymru? Mae Adams yn ei draethawd yn disgwyl y bydd dylanwad Seth (yng Nghaerdydd) a Jones yn foddion i ledaenu'r safbwynt Hegelaidd ymhlith y Cymry.

Coleg y Gogledd a roddodd i Jones ei gyfle mawr i wneud hynny. Aed ati i benodi Prifathro ac Athrawon i chwe chadair ym Mangor ym mis Mai 1884. Penderfynodd y byddai'n ymgeisio am swydd fel Prifathro neu Athro Athroniaeth yn y drefn honno. Yn y llythyr a anfonodd at Seth yn ei longyfarch ar gael cadair yng Nghaerdydd dywed am ei ymgeisyddiaeth ei hun ym Mangor:

> I shall of course go in with all my might, first for the Principalship and then for the Professorship, and if I succeed in either, we shall be able to work together.[3]

Bu'r misoedd cyn y cyfweliadau yn llawn pryderon iddo. Un ohonynt oedd y byddai Athrawon a Phrifathro Aberystwyth yn cael eu penodi i'r swyddi ym Mangor (yn unol â'i obaith cynharaf ef ei hun) er mwyn ennill coleg i'r gogledd heb golli'r un oedd yn bod eisoes, fel petai. Ysgrifennodd Caird ddau lythyr o leiaf ato yn poeni am y posibilrwydd hwnnw.[4] Wrth gwrs, gyda T. C. Edwards yn brifathro, byddai'n amhosibl i Jones hyd yn oed feddwl am ymgeisio am swydd o unrhyw fath yno. Ond hyd yn oed ar ôl iddi ddod yn amlwg na fyddai Edwards yn ymgeisio am brifathrawiaeth Bangor, gwelai Jones ôl ei ddylanwad yn gweithio yn ei erbyn yn y dirgel. Yr arf peryclaf yn arfogaeth ei elynion oedd amheuon ynglŷn â'i uniongrededd diwinyddol. Ni allai Jones yn hawdd ei amddiffyn ei hun yn erbyn cyhuddiad nas gwnaed yn gyhoeddus nac yn fanwl. Mae'n mynegi cri o rwystredigaeth mewn llythyr at y Parch Ellis Edwards, y Bala, gohebydd cyfeillgar:

> As for myself, I am freely resolved, that I shall not, come weal come woe, degrade myself and the post I seek by standing before the country to try to persuade it that I am no infidel.[5]

Ofnai na fyddai pob un o'i gefnogwyr yn ofalus o'i hunan-barch.

[3] TJ/C/2/21.
[4] TJ/C/2/18 & 19.
[5] Y/128.

> I had to write to prevent the Vale of Conway Presbytery from protesting vigorously against the injustice done me in these rumours.[6]

Mewn llythyr arall at Ellis Edwards, gofynnodd:

> Why am I asked always to preach if an infidel? Am I not still on the list of the preachers of the Calv. Meth? Why don t they deal with me? Let that unborn individual who has heard me deny God, the Atonement and the divinity of Christ be produced. It is a shame. But, to write more coolly: the thing is so absurd as to correct itself: and thank God, the whole tenor (?) of my life is against it. A thousand thanks for your kindness. I know you will not stand by to see me massacred in this way.[7]

Y mae'n anodd iawn dweud i ba raddau yr oedd T. C. Edwards yn bersonol y tu ôl i'r ensyniadau ynglŷn â daliadau diwinyddol Jones, ond fe gafodd gyfle i'w lledaenu. Cafodd gais am farn ar y cwestiwn gan aelod o Gyngor Coleg Bangor, John Bryn Roberts, Aelod Seneddol dros Dde Arfon a Methodist Calfinaidd pybyr, mewn llythyr dyddiedig 9 Mai 1884:

> You are probably aware that the Rev. (sic) Henry Jones is a candidate for the Principalship and Philosophy chair of the N.W. College. There is a general impression abroad that he is not orthodox in his theological views and he has in fact rationalist tendencies. He & his friends strongly deny this but I, and, I know, several other members of the Council, still feel considerable doubt about the matter. I feel that it would be a great calamity to the Country if a rationalist were appointed Principal or to the Philosophy Chair that I venture to write and ask you your opinion of him as he has been with you at Aberystwyth. One of our ministers informed me that he was told that Mr Henry Jones at a lecture in Aberystwyth gave expression to some doubtful theories and that you on that occasion cautioned the audience not to accept implicitly all the theories propounded by the Lecturer by which you incurred considerable hostility on his part. If you would kindly favour me, for my guidance, with your opinion on the matter and also on the merits or demerits of Mr Henry Jones as a Professor independent of his scholarship, I would be much obliged. If you do so and desire the communication to be treated as confidential you may implicitly rely on my doing so.[8]

Heb weld yr ateb a gafodd Roberts, mae'n amhosibl dweud beth oedd safbwynt Edwards ar yr agwedd hon ar bethau. Yr oedd llawer o gefnogwyr Coleg Aberystwyth, fodd bynnag, yn teimlo yn ddrwgdybus o Jones. Credent ei fod yn defnyddio sefydlu Coleg y Gogledd fel ffordd o wneud niwed i Aberystwyth drwy hudo'r staff i Fangor, lle, gyda grant y llywodraeth, yr oedd dyfodol sicrach. Er enghraifft dyma ddywedwyd mewn llythyr a gafodd Edwards gan J. B. Rogers fis Tachwedd 1883:

[6] ibid.

[7] Y/127.

[8] TCEL/383.

> Mr Stephen Evans had a conversation with Mr T. M. Williams concerning Mr Henry Jones. It quite confirms the opinion already formed as to his ingratitude. It appears that he has great confidence that he will be appointed Principal of the North Wales College. The question of the North Wales College was also spoken about and jestingly Mr Stephen Evans said in reply to a remark of Mr Williams that if our Professors chose to apply and be appointed there they were quite welcome to go – that there were none that could not be replaced. In this connection Mr Evans requested me to suggest from him that you should take a perfectly independent course with the Professors. He had in view the influence which Mr H. J. may be exercising amongst them.[9]

Roedd y sefyllfa yn wenwynig iawn. Credai Jones fod Edwards yn gweithio i'w rwystro rhag cael prifathrawiaeth na chadair ym Mangor, ac roedd rhai am i Edwards gredu bod Jones yn gweithio i sicrhau y byddai Bangor yn llyncu Aberystwyth. Heb os nac onibai fe gostiodd y ffrae gydag Edwards brifathrawiaeth Bangor i Jones. Y mae'n bosibl nad oedd y mwyafrif o Bwyllgor Penodiadau Bangor am ochri yn erbyn Jones cyn belled â bod sylwedd y ffrwgwd yn Aberystwyth yn y cwestiwn (er, i Arglwydd Aberdâr fynegi ei gred fod Jones 'in the wrong' wrth Arglwydd Powys),[10] ond sylweddolai nifer o'r aelodau fod yn rhaid i brifathrawon y colegau fedru cydweithio ac ymddiried yn ei gilydd os oedd addysg uwch yng Nghymru i sefyll ar seiliau cadarn. Hynny o bosib, lawn cymaint ag unrhyw ystyriaeth ynglŷn â'r dyn ei hun, a arweiniodd at y penderfyniad i benodi Harry Reichel, yr Eglwyswr a'r Tori o dras Ellmynig yn hytrach na Harri Jones, y Methodist a'r Rhyddfrydwr o Gymro, yn brifathro cyntaf Coleg y Gogledd. Yr oedd aflwyddiant Jones yn fêl ar fysedd yr hen Lewis Edwards yn y Bala. Meddai, mewn llythyr at ei fab dyddiedig 21 Mai 1884:

> And so Henry Jones is left out in the cold. Perhaps he may get a chair, though that is doubtful. There is a strong feeling against him in Carnarvonshire.[11]

Weddill ei oes, priodolodd Jones ei fethiant i sicrhau'r swydd i ddylanwad yr Edwardsiaid. Meddai, yn *Old Memories*,

> The Calvanistic Methodist influence, inspired and sanctified by Principal Edwards and his father, ran against me like a powerful stream.[12]

Yn wir, yr oedd Lewis Edwards yn aelod o'r Pwyllgor Dewis, ac yn bresennol pan wnaed y penodiad, ond fe geisiodd Trebor Lloyd Evans ddangos mai rhaniadau ymhlith y Rhyddfrydwyr Cymreig, y tu allan i reolaeth Lewis Edwards, oedd y cymorth pwysicaf i lwyddiant Reichel.[13]

---

9 TCEL/372.
10 J. Gwynn Williams, op. cit., t. 62.
11 TCEL/384.
12 OM, t. 173.
13 Trebor Lloyd Evans, *Lewis Edwards: Ei Fywyd a'i Waith,* Abertawe 1967, tt. 100-104, sef Atodiad, 'Cyhuddiad Syr Henry Jones'.

Cadwodd Jones ei urddas: daliodd i sefyll am y Gadair Athroniaeth, ac nid oedd ronyn o genfigen ynddo tuag at Reichel. Yn feddyliol, yr oedd yn ymbaratoi i fethu eto, a gwyddai fod ganddo swydd arall i fynd iddi yn yr Alban pe methai. Mewn llythyr at Ellis Edwards, dyddiedig 17 Mai 1884, mae'n dweud:

> Reichel is an admirable man, I believe, and if I am appointed Professor of Phils I shall do what I can to aid him in his work. But my election to that post too will be opposed by a certain number of men who 'were more anxious to keep me out than to get their "own man in".' I believe they will this time oppose me in vain. At least I am assured on all hands that the desire for me is strong and wide. Be it so. I shall be glad to get the Professorship: but I shall not stake much on it – not my hope of success not my comfort. Scotland has a post ready for me and I shall be able to take another defeat quite calmly. I believe that Wales will not willingly pass me over this time: and if I am opposed my opponents will do themselves more harm than me.[14]

Yr oedd Jones yn ymwybodol iawn o'i ddyletswydd i Gymru. Er iddo gael ei gythruddo mor arw gan y cyhuddiadau o heresi, teimlai y dylai gwasanaeth i'w wlad fod yn drech na'i ddicter personol.

> I am very indignant at this (h.y. yr ensyniadau): almost indignant enough, were it not my duty to myself and my country, to take a post here (h.y. yn yr Alban) which I can have and wh. is kept open for me.[15]

Ond, pe gwrthodai Gymru ef, ni thorrai ei galon:

> I can stand absolute exclusion from Wales with some calmness.[16]

Efallai'r mai'r hyn a'i cynhaliodd yn ystod y cyfnod anodd wedi'r siom ynglŷn â'r brifathrawiaeth oedd sylweddoli ei fod wrth reddf yn fwy o athro nag o weinyddwr. Disgrifiodd ei ymateb i aflwyddiant ei gais fel hyn wrth Ellis Edwards.

> I assure you that my rejection in this election was to me at the time and is now more than ever a matter of gratulation. I said truly, what none however but my best friends can believe, that if I counselled (?) my own happiness I wd not have sought the post of P.pal in N. Wales. I wd have devoted myself day and night to the Education of my countrymen: care for it wd have set behind me all my days. Now, however, I can calmly and peacefully pursue my proper studies and I am truly thankful that God did not call me to sacrifice my place & my prospects of writing and knowing more on this altar.[17]

Ac nid dweud hyn ar ôl methu yr oedd ychwaith. Cyn y cyfweliad, mewn llythyr at yr un gohebydd, dyddiedig 14 Mawrth 1884, dywedodd:

[14] Y/130.
[15] Y/127.
[16] ibid.
[17] Y/130.

> To be made Principal will be to be crowned – but with thorns, if one is earnest, so absurd are the prejudices and so great is the bigoted ignorance (?) of some people.[18]

Ond ni chafodd siom yr ail waith. Beth bynnag oedd amheuon y Pwyllgor Dewis am ei addasrwydd fel prifathro, ni fu amheuon ynglŷn â'i allu a'i ddoniau fel addysgwr. Yr oedd y priodoleddau hyn yn drech na'r amheuon ynglŷn â'i ddehongliad o'r Gyffes Ffydd. Ymatebodd i'w lwyddiant gyda brwdfrydedd, ac fel Boethius gynt, profodd gysuron athroniaeth,

> I shall plunge into philosophy if I get a class: and I shall endeavour, as far as God has given me the power, to fill my students; our preachers I hope, with a spirit of irrefragable loyalty to truth! 'That word,' says Hegel,'which makes our heart beat high'.[19]

Dyma ail gyfle felly i geisio lle iddo'i hun yn y gyfundrefn addysg uwch a oedd yn prysur ddatblygu yng Nghymru. O'r cychwyn, bu'n gwbl deyrngar i Reichel, ac roedd yntau yn ymddiried yn llwyr yn Jones. Datblygodd cyfeillgarwch dwfn rhyngddynt. Yr oedd eu hymgysegriad i lwyddiant y coleg ifanc yn sail ddiogel i'w cyfeillgarwch, a'r ffaith fod y coleg mor fychan yn eu clymu yn agos at weddill y staff. Yr oedd y Prifathro wedi ei ethol i'r Gadair Hanes, sef un o'r chwe chadair wreiddiol yn y coleg. Diddorol yw nodi bod tair o'r pum cadair arall wedi mynd i ymgeiswyr a chysylltiadau â Phrifysgol Glasgow: Henry Jones, yr Athro Athroniaeth; James Johnston Dobbie (Prifysgolion Glasgow, Caeredin a Leipzig), yr Athro Cemeg a Daeareg; Andrew Gray (Coleg Herriot Watt a Phrifysgol Glasgow), yr Athro Ffiseg. Bu ef yn gweithio dan yr Arglwydd Kelvin ym Mhrifysgol Glasgow, ac fe'i olynodd yn y Gadair yn Glasgow yn 1899. Pan adawodd Gray Fangor i ddilyn ei hen athro yn Glasgow, fe'i dilynwyd yntau ym Mangor gan hen ddisgybl iddo ef, Edward Taylor Jones. Brodor o Ddinbych oedd ef a enillasai ysgoloriaeth i astudio yn yr Almaen, ac un o hynodion ei yrfa wych yw iddo yn 1926 ddilyn Gray eto, fel ei olynydd yn y Gadair Ffiseg yn Glasgow! Byddai Jones yn dilyn yr un llwybr maes o law.

Pan symudodd y Jonesiaid o Aberystwyth i Fangor, yr oeddynt yn dri. Ganed mab i Henry ac Annie ym mis Medi 1883, Elias Henry Jones. Enw ei dad arno oedd 'Hal', a byddai ganddo ef gysylltiad ei hun â Choleg y Gogledd fel oedolyn. Rhwng 1933 a 1941 ef oedd Cofrestrydd Coleg Bangor. Cafodd Henry ac Annie Jones chwech o blant i gyd, sef Harry (Hal), Jim, Jeanie, Enid, Will ac Arthur. Bu'r teulu, sef y rhieni a phedwar o'r plant, yn byw mewn ffermdy o'r enw Ferfeddgoed, tua dwy filltir y tu allan i Fangor, ond i dŷ ym Mangor Uchaf y daethant i fyw ar y cychwyn.

[18] Y/ 27.

[19] Y/ 31.

Nid oedd Prifysgol Cymru wedi ei sefydlu pan esgynnodd Jones i Gadair Athroniaeth Bangor. Paratoi myfyrwyr ar gyfer arholiadau Prifysgol Llundain a wneid, ac ni chynhwysid athroniaeth ym maes llafur y radd B.A. tan y flwyddyn olaf, a hynny fel pwnc dewisol yn unig. Pan agorodd y Coleg ei ddorau am y tro cyntaf fis Hydref 1884 yr oedd yn gwbl bosibl na fyddai ganddo fyfyrwyr i'w dysgu! Er mawr ryddhad iddo yr oedd dau fyfyriwr wedi dewis astudio athroniaeth. Yr oedd y ddau eisoes wedi llwyddo yn adrannau dechreuol eu cwrs B.A. ac wedi cofrestru i gwblhau eu blwyddyn olaf yn y coleg. Yr oeddynt yn Fedyddwyr, yn ymgeiswyr am y weinidogaeth ac yn alluog. Llwyddodd un ohonynt, cyn-löwr o'r enw John Thomas, i gyrraedd brig rhestr y myfyrwyr llwyddiannus mewn athroniaeth ym Mhrifysgol Llundain y flwyddyn honno, a gwnaeth radd M.A. mewn athroniaeth wedyn. Arbenigodd y llall, Silas Morris, mewn Groeg, ond yr oedd yntau hefyd yn alluog iawn, a daeth maes o law yn ôl i Fangor fel Prifathro Coleg y Bedyddwyr. Bu'n golygu *Seren Gomer* am ddeng mlynedd.

Yn *Old Memories*, dywed Jones fod ganddo ddau fyfyriwr yn y flwyddyn ganlynol hefyd, ond nid oeddynt yn alluog. Yn wir, honnodd fod un ohonynt yn analluog i weld na ellir casglu fod pob anifail yn ddyn ar sail y gosodiad fod pob dyn yn anifail! Nid oedd myfyrwyr o'r fath yn ddeunydd addawol iawn i sefydlu Adran Athroniaeth ddylanwadol arnynt. Deallai Jones paham yr oedd cymaint o'r myfyrwyr galluocaf yn tueddu i ddewis y pynciau y disgleirient ynddynt eisoes, cyn dod i'r coleg, yn hytrach na mentro gyda phwnc cwbl newydd fel athroniaeth, ond gofidiai o'r herwydd, serch hynny. Megis yn Aberystwyth, yr oedd cyfle i sicrhau cynulleidfa y tu allan i furiau'r coleg, ond yma eto, ni châi fodlonrwydd. Dywed iddo gyrraedd rhyw dref yng ngogledd Cymru gyda'r bwriad o gynnal dosbarth allanol a darganfod ar ôl cyrraedd nad oedd neb wedi ymorol am logi ystafell na hysbysebu'r darlithoedd. Teimlodd y siom i'r byw (er bydd y sawl sy'n gyfarwydd â'r math hwn o waith yn gwybod o brofiad na ddylid ystyried un methiant yn drychineb!). Yn raddol aeth i deimlo nad oedd ganddo gyfraniad o bwys i'w wneud, neu o leiaf, fod eraill o'r farn honno. Arwydd o'r elfen groendenau ynddo oedd iddo ddechrau amau fod rhywrai am osod ei gannwyll fechan ef dan lestr er mwyn i'w goleuni hwythau lewyrchu yn ddisgleiriach, ond credai fod Reichel yn gwbl anrhydeddus yn hyn. Yr oedd ymddiswyddo yn ei feddwl y gaeaf hwnnw. Cyngor Caird iddo oedd gwyntyllu ei deimladau a pheidio â'u cadw iddo'i hun. Fe wnaeth hynny, a theimlo'n well wedyn. Fe aeth ati i geisio dangos i fyfyrwyr, nad oeddynt yn dewis astudio athroniaeth ar gyfer eu gradd, beth oedd y pwnc dieithr hwn. Gwahoddodd nifer o wŷr ifanc, y mwyafrif â'u bryd ar y weinidogaeth, i'w gyfarfod ar fore dydd Sadwrn i ddarllen *Introduction to the Philosophy of Religion* gan John Caird.

Brawd i Edward Caird oedd John Caird, a phan oedd Edward yn Athro Athroniaeth Foesol ym Mhrifysgol Glasgow, John oedd y prifathro. Yr oedd cartref swyddogol y Prifathro a chartref swyddogol yr Athro Athroniaeth Foesol

Y Cwm, cartref Henry Jones yn Llangernyw, fel y mae heddiw (1998). *(Llun Cambrian)*

Henry Jones a'i gyd-Athrawon a'r Darlithwyr ar Senedd gyntaf Coleg y Brifysgol, Bangor, 1884.
Rhes gefn: James J. Dobie (Cemeg), W. Rhys Roberts (Groeg), G. Ballard Matthews (Mathemateg), R. W. Phillips (Bywydeg).
Ail Res: G. McGowan (Cemeg), D. Morgan Lewis (Ffiseg), E. V. Arnold (Lladin).
Rhes flaen: E. Trechman (Ieithoedd Modern), Henry Jones (Athroniaeth), Harry R. Reichel (Prifathro), Andrew Gray (Ffiseg), W. Cadwaladr Davies (Cofrestrydd).

(Llun Archifdy Prifysgol Cymru, Bangor: copi Eryl Rothwell Hughes)

Yr Athro Edward Caird (portread mewn olew gan Syr George Reid.)

(Llun a hawlfraint yr Hunterian Art Gallery, Prifysgol Glasgow)

Yr Athro John Nichol (portread mewn olew gan Syr W. Q. Orchardson).

(Llun a hawlfraint yr Hunterian Art Gallery, Prifysgol Glasgow)

Henry Jones pan oedd yn fyfyriwr yn Glasgow.

(Llun J. Bowman, Glasgow, drwy garedigrwydd John Hughes)

Annie Jones (Walker gynt).

(Llun Ymddiriedolaeth y Cwm)

Plant Henry ac Annie Jones pan symudodd y teulu i Fangor: Harry, Jim, Will, Jean ac Enid. Nid oedd y chweched, Arthur, wedi ei eni.

(Llun Ymddiriedolaeth y Cwm)

Ystafelloedd Henry Jones ym Mhrifysgol St. Andrews (i'r chwith o'r drws yn yr ongl).

(Llun Gwyn Davies Williams)

'Noddfa', cartref Henry Jones a'i deulu yn Tighnabruaich o 1911 ymlaen. Yma bu Henry Jones farw yn 1922

(Llun Gwyn Davies Williams)

(No.1, The College) wedi eu lleoli ar y campws, gyferbyn â'i gilydd, yn Professors' Square. Dywedir y gellid gweld y ddau frawd yn mynd am dro ambell gyda'r nos yn sgwrsio a gosod trefn ar y byd a'r brifysgol mewn cytgord llwyr. Yr oedd y ddau yn Hegeliaid, ond fel diwinydd y cofir am John, yn fwy felly nag fel athronydd. Efallai mai'r prif reswm am hyn yw ei fod ef, yn wahanol i Edward, wedi ei ordeinio'n weinidog yn Eglwys yr Alban. Gellir mesur maint dylanwad Hegel ar lyfr John Caird o'r sylw a wnaed gan T. H. Green arno mewn adolygiad: "... we think that he has been too much overpowered by Hegel". [20] Noder mai Green sydd yn dweud!

Dyma'r llyfr yr oedd Jones am ei drafod gyda darpar weinidogion mewn grŵp gwirfoddol yn y coleg. O gael blas ar y pwnc dan yr amodau anffurfiol hyn, daeth nifer i ddewis astudio athroniaeth ar gyfer yr arholiadau terfynol. Bu'r arbrawf yn llwyddiant, ac mae Jones yn nodi yn ei hunangofiant fod rhai myfyrwyr disglair wedi dilyn y llwybr hwn megis John Owen Jones (Athro yn ddiweddarach yng Ngholeg y Bala) ac Edward Edwards (Athro yn ddiweddarach yng Ngholeg Aberystwyth, a brawd O. M. Edwards). Yn sicr, roedd â wnelo doniau eithriadol Henry Jones fel darlithydd lawer iawn â'r llwyddiant hwn.

Mewn oes pan oedd bri mawr ar bregethu ac areithio yr oedd ef yn cael ei osod yn y rheng flaenaf. Mae'n amlwg, fel y dywed yr Athro J. Gwynn Williams, fod Jones yn berson carismataidd. [21] Yn ei deyrnged iddo, cyfeiria Reichel at dystiolaeth un o'r myfyrwyr:

> A former Science student of the College remarked to me, the day after the news of his death, that it always seemed to him as if Henry Jones's face shot out rays of energy and light – a remarkable testimony from a man who had only seen him from a distance.[22]

Ac nid wrth iddo ddarlithio i fyfyrwyr y coleg yn unig y gwelwyd ei ddoniau areithiol ychwaith. Yr oedd yr un mor effeithiol yn annerch llond Pafiliwn Caernarfon o chwarelwyr ar Ŵyl Lafur. Dyma dystiolaeth llygad-dyst:

> Yr oedd rhai yn gwawdio'r syniad o gael gŵr o ddysg fel Henry Jones i annerch cynulleidfa anysgedig fel cynulliadau Gŵyl Llafur y Pafiliwn; ond bradychu eu hanwybodaeth oedd y gwawdwyr – eu hanwybyddiaeth o Henry Jones ac o'r chwarelwyr. Nid oedd Henry Jones wedi bod yn siarad am dros bum munud cyn iddo gael gafael ar lygad, a sylw, a chalon, a deall y dorf. Hwn, un o ddysgedigion pennaf ei oes, heb sôn am ei wlad, yn siarad â thorf yn cynnwys miloedd o weithwyr cyffredin, ar bynciau na fedrai'r gweithiwr Seisnig gadw ei feddwl arnynt am bum munud; ond yma yr oedd y pregethwr a'r gwrandawr yn deall eu gilydd i'r dim. Rhoddodd iddynt fwyd cryf, ond gofalai am ei dorri yn ddigon mân iddynt.[23]

[20] John Passmore, *A Hundred Years of Philosophy,* Llundain 1957 a 1966, t. 57 yn argraffiad Pelican Books, 1967.

[21] J. Gwynn Williams, op. cit., t. 233.

[22] *UCNW Magazine,* Mawrth 1922, t. 7.

[23] *Ysbryd yr Oes,* Cyf.1, Rhif 8, t. 142.

Bu i Goleg y Gogledd elwa mewn sawl ffordd ar enwogrwydd ac enw da Jones. Go brin y gellid dweud am unrhyw athronydd arall (ym Mhrydain beth bynnag) ei fod yn anwylyn ei bobl: ond teg dweud hynny amdano ef. Ychwanegu at ei faintioli a wnâi ei wreiddiau distadl, yn ôl yr ysgrif arno yn *Ysbryd yr Oes*:

> Un o'r bobl yw, ac a fydd efe. Gŵyr trwy brofiad beth yw bywyd, ac angen, a dyhead y werin. Mae eu bywyd hwy yn rhan o'i fywyd mewnol ef. Dichon fod hynny yn rhan o'r esboniad ar y ffaith nad oes ŵr o'i safle ef yn yr holl deyrnas yn gymaint ffafrddyn personol gan y werin.[24]

Cafodd awdur hyn o folawd afael ar hanesyn a osodai Jones ar dir i'w ganoneiddio.

> Yr oedd un o staff y coleg ar ei ffordd i gyfarfod yn Llanrug, pan ddigwyddodd gael chwarelwr yn gydymaith …
>
> 'Ydach chi am fynd i gyfarfod y Coleg?' gofynnai'r proffeswr.
>
> 'Ydwyf, yn tad! ac am roi'r gorau fedra i ato fo hefyd!' oedd yr ateb cynnes.
>
> 'Be?' ebe'r llall yn ymholgar; 'mae gynnoch chi olwg fawr ar y Coleg felly?'
>
> 'Na, nid cymaint,' ebe'r llall, 'nid er mwyn y Coleg bydda i'n rhoi, ond er mwyn Henry Jones!'
>
> Deffrodd hyn chwilfrydedd y proffeswr, a mynnodd gael y stori.[25]

Ymddengys bod Jones wedi cael cynnig lluniaeth yng nghartref y chwarelwr yn ystod streic fawr Llanberis (1885–86). Deallodd yn ystod y sgwrs nad oedd rhagor o fwyd yn y tŷ, a chyn ymadael arllwysodd hynny o arian oedd ganddo yn ei bocedi ar y bwrdd. Gadawodd heb ddatgelu ei enw. Flynyddoedd yn ddiweddarach mewn Gŵyl Lafur ym Mhafiliwn Caernarfon gwelsant eu hymwelydd hael ar y llwyfan, a synnu o ddarganfod mai'r Athro Henry Jones ydoedd! Dyma'r union fath o stori y carai pobl ei hailadrodd, ac fe wnâi hi, a straeon eraill tebyg iddi, les mawr i enw da Jones a'r coleg fel ei gilydd.

Tua diwedd yr wythdegau cyfarfyddai criw bychan o gyfeillion unwaith bob wythnos dros gyfnod o dair blynedd yn ei ystafell yn y coleg i drafod athroniaeth, crefydd a llenyddiaeth. Cyd-athrawon gydag ef yn y coleg oedd dau ohonynt, sef John Morris-Jones (Cymraeg) a William Lewis Jones (Saesneg), a gweinidogion gyda'r Hen Gorff oedd y ddau arall, sef John Puleston Jones (Capel Saesneg Princes Road) a William Matthews (Capel Cymraeg y Graig). Meddai Puleston Jones am gyfarfodydd y pum cyfaill:

> Ni welais i erioed gyfarfod a mwy o chwerthin ynddo na'r cyfarfod wythnosol hwn, ond ni welais un erioed chwaith a mwy (o) ddifrifwch ynddo. Pwnc o unplygrwydd amcan yw difrifwch, nid pwnc o dymer. Weithiau byddai testun wedi ei adael o'r cyfarfod o'r blaen, Moesoldeb Yr Efengyl, Peryglon Pregethu Cymru, y Gwyrthiau, Cariad Duw, Maddeuant, Tragwyddol Gosb, Ai rhywbeth nacaol yw pechod ynte gwrthwynebiad pendant i'r Brenin Mawr. Fe adawodd Henry Jones un argraff am byth ar bawb ohonom, yr argraff o bwysigrwydd tragwyddol ac anghymarol gwirionedd.[26]

---

[24] ibid.

[25] ibid., t. 143.

[26] R. W. Jones, *Y Parchedig John Puleston Jones,* Caernafon 1930, t. 85.

Yr oedd Puleston a Matthews yn gyfeillion agos iawn ac ystyrai Puleston fod ei gyfaill yn "un o'r meddylwyr miniocaf a fu mewn pulpud erioed."[27] Yr oedd hefyd yn ddadleuwr praff a phryfoclyd. Gwyddai sut i gorddi Jones. Edrydd Puleston atgof am y ddau:

> Cof gennyf i'r Athro agor rhyw ymddiddan trwy osod i lawr fod Duw yn bod. Ar hynny meddai Matthews wrtho: 'Rhoswch, Proffesor, profwch o!' Ffrwydiad ofnadwy fyddai wedyn.[28]

Bu Jones â rhan yn y gwaith o ddenu Puleston i Fangor. Wedi ei ordeinio yn 1880 gan y Sasiwn yn Ninbych, ni chafodd y gweinidog dall alwad gan gynulleidfa Gymraeg, ond yn yr hydref daeth un gan un o gapeli'r 'English Cause', sef Capel Saesneg Bangor. Ysgrifennodd Jones lythyr personol at Puleston yn canmol cynulleidfa Princes Road, yn arbennig felly'r gwŷr ieuanc.

> They are full of readiness to do that secular kind of good which is the unassuming manifestation of a true religious spirit … Further there is all the rising generations of students, many of whom will always attend the Church, and it is an unutterable pity if the Gospel Of Christ is to be presented to them in an unscholarly, and repulsive form.[29]

Yr oedd gan Jones le i gredu nad oedd perygl i hynny ddigwydd dan weinidogaeth Puleston, oherwydd, yn un peth, cyn mynd i Rydychen bu yntau hefyd (am flwyddyn) ym Mhrifysgol Glasgow, lle gwnaed argraff ddofn arno gan Caird a Nichol. Yn ôl ei gofiannydd, "Parhaodd y tân a gyneuodd Caird i losgi yn Puleston hyd ddiwedd y daith."[30] Mynegodd Caird a Nichol eu hedmygedd o bersonoliaeth a gallu Puleston fwy nag unwaith[31], a gwyddai Jones y câi ysbryd o'r un anian ag ef yn y gweinidog ifanc, pe deuai i Fangor. Serch hynny, mynegodd un pryder yn ei lythyr, sef "whether or not you will find your best sphere in the Welsh–English Church movement."

Derbyn a wnaeth Puleston, er mawr lawenydd i Jones. Ei ail blentyn, Jim, oedd un o'r plant cyntaf i Puleston ei fedyddio. Cais y tad oedd, "I want you to baptize my boy Jim. I want him to be received into the fellowship of this Good."[32] Nid ef oedd yr unig Athro o'r coleg i fynychu Princes Road. Yno y deuai W. Lewis Jones (Saesneg), J. Dobbie (Cemeg), P. J. White (Sŵoleg), A. Gray (Ffiseg) a Ballard Mathews (Mathemateg). Serch hynny, mae'n debyg mai iaith ei briod yn hytrach nag ansawdd deallusol carfan o'r gynulleidfa a barodd iddo gysylltu ei hun â chynulleidfa Bresbyteraidd Saesneg.

---

27 ibid.
28 ibid., t. 86.
29 ibid., t. 76.
30 ibid., t. 50.
31 e.e., ibid., t. 51.
32 ibid., t. 79.

Ni chyfyngwyd egnïon Jones yn y blynyddoedd hyn i hyrwyddo addysg golegol yn unig. Yr oedd Adroddiad Pwyllgor yr Arglwydd Aberdâr (1881) wedi gwneud argymhellion ar addysg ganolraddol yn ogystal ag ar addysg uwch. Gweithredwyd ar fyrder i sefydlu'r colegau prifathrofaol, ond disymud iawn oedd y llywodraeth i weithredu ym maes addysg ganolraddol. Yr oedd hyn yn fater o ofid mawr i Jones, a manteisiodd ar gyfle i fynegi ei anfodlonrwydd mewn sgwrs gyda William Rathbone A.S. Yr oedd hwnnw yn aros yng nghartref ei gyd-Aelod Seneddol, Richard Davies, yn Nhreborth, a Jones wedi ymuno â'r cwmni gyda'r nos. Y rheswm dros yr oedi ynglŷn â chyflwyno mesur seneddol ar addysg ganolraddol yng Nghymru, yn ôl Rathbone, oedd barn yr Aelodau Cymreig na fyddai eu hetholwyr yn fodlon derbyn dimai ar y dreth yn unol ag argymhelliad Pwyllgor Aberdâr i dalu am y ddarpariaeth. Yr oedd Jones yn argyhoeddedig fod y seneddwyr wedi camddehongli tymer y wlad ar y mater, ac addawodd Rathbone ystyried traddodi araith ar y pwnc yn Llangefni drannoeth.

Dyna'n wir a wnaeth, ac er mawr lawenydd iddo, canfu bod y gynulleidfa'n gefnogol iawn i symud ymlaen â chynllun Adroddiad Aberdâr, gan gynnwys y dreth ddimai. Galwodd i weld Jones yn y coleg, a'i annog i fynd ati ar unwaith i drefnu ymgyrch yn y wlad o blaid addysg ganolraddol. Gyda chymorth Cadwaladr Davies o'r coleg ac R. A. Jones, Lerpwl, fe drefnwyd llu o gyfarfodydd cyhoeddus led-led y gogledd, gyda Henry Jones yn annerch nifer ohonynt, i drefnu bod deisebau o blaid y datblygiad hwn yn cael eu hanfon at yr Aelodau Seneddol. Bu'r ymgyrch yn llwyddiant, a daeth yr Intermediate Education Act i rym yn 1889, gan roddi i Gymru gyfundrefn o ysgolion canolraddol (sef 'ysgolion uwchradd' yn ein terminoleg ni) dair blynedd ar ddeg cyn i'r fath ddarpariaeth gael ei hymestyn i Loegr.

Y cam nesaf oedd penderfynu ymhle i sefydlu'r ysgolion. Yr oedd dwy farn ar y cwestiwn. Credai rhai y dylid sefydlu cymaint ohonynt ag y gellid er mwyn sicrhau bod ysgol ganolraddol o fewn cyrraedd cymaint o blant ag oedd modd, ond credai eraill y dylid gofalu yn gyntaf am safon ac ansawdd yr ysgolion, hynny yw, sefydlu nifer gweddol fychan gan sicrhau eu bod o safon ragorol. Cefnogai Jones y farn gyntaf. Yn fuan ar ôl i'r mesur ddod i rym fe'i gwahoddwyd ef ac eraill gan yr Aelod Seneddol, Arthur Acland, i gyfarfod Tom Ellis yng Nghlynnog er mwyn cynllunio sut i weithredu darpariaethau'r ddeddf. Cynhwysai'r cwmni Cadwaladr Davies ac R. A. Jones, John Powell (Wrecsam) a'r Athro Ellis Edwards o'r Bala. Cyhoeddodd y ddau seneddwr lyfryn yn gosod allan eu safbwynt, a bu Henry Jones yn ddyfal iawn fel lladmerydd yn y wasg. Lluniodd gyfres o tua wyth o lythyrau, ac yn ôl *Old Memories*[33] ymddangosasant mewn saith papur Cymraeg ac wyth papur Saesneg.

[33] OM, t. 188.

Byrdwn y llythyrau hyn oedd mai dim ond drwy sicrhau i bob bro ei hysgol ganolraddol ei hun y gallai'r werin fod ar ei hennill.

> Y mae y darllenydd yn deall erbyn hyn fod dau amcan gwahanol i'r Ysgolion Canolradd. Un ydyw, agor llwybr rhydd i'r rhai fo a gallu ganddynt, boent hwy dlawd neu beidio, i fyned o'r Ysgolion Elfenol i'r Prifysgolion. Y llall ydyw, ychwanegu blwyddyn neu ddwy at addysg plant rhieni mewn amgylchiadau isel, modd y gallant tra yn dilyn eu galwedigaeth ddilyn hefyd ar ôl gwybodaeth. Y mae'r naill a'r llall o'r amcanion hyn yn dda, ac yn anhepgor i lwyddiant ein gwlad. Ond os oes un ohonynt yn fwy pwysig na'r llall, cynhyrchu parch at wybodaeth yn y dosbarth gweithiol yw hwnnw, a'u deffro i ymgais amdani, fel y dyrchafer eu cymeriad, ac eu gwneir yn well gweithwyr ac yn well dynion.[34]

Dyna fynegiant croyw o egwyddor addysg ryddfrydol barhaus, safbwynt a gynhwysai Jones flynyddoedd yn ddiweddarach i fod yn aelod o'r Comisiwn ar Addysg Oedolion. Clywir tinc bendant llais T. H. Green yn ei eiriau pan ddywed mai:

> ... amcan cyntaf a phenaf y Ddeddf Addysg Ganolradd yw galluogi dosbarth gweithiol Cymru i gymeryd meddiant lwyrach o etifeddiaeth deg byd y meddyliau.[35]

A thrachefn,

> A raid i'r werin byth ddisgyn i'r ffos, fel y rhodia eraill drosti yn droed-sych? Onid oes ganddynt hwythau hefyd hawl, ac hwyrach well hawl na neb arall, i leddfu eu llafur a mwynhad gwybodaeth? Ai ofer yw gobeithio y daw amser pan y gallo'r gweithiwr ar derfyn ei ddydd llafur fwrw baich ei ofalon oddiar ei war, ac ar ei aelwyd dawel ei hun, fwynhau cysuron byd y meddwl ...?[36]

Gwelai Jones fod y cwestiwn o faint o ysgolion y dylid eu codi ynghlwm wrth gwestiwn natur a swyddogaeth yr ysgolion.

> Y syniad a goleddir am brif amcan yr Ysgolion Canolradd a benderfyna eu rhif, dyweder a fyner. Os llanw'r colegau ydyw hwnw, fel y tybia llawer, a pharatoi bechgyn a genethod dosbarth canol y Cymry gogyfer â'r galwedigaethau bonheddig, bydd nifer bychan ... yn ddigon, ond os nad ofer ein hymbil am iawnderau gweithwyr Cymru, ac os mynwn roddi moddion bywyd uwch, mwy diwylliedig a mwy dedwydd, yn ngafael plant goreu gwŷr tlawd ein gwlad, rhaid i ni luosogi'r ysgolion hyd eithaf ein gallu.[37]

I'r diben o sicrhau'r nifer uchaf posibl o ysgolion, galwai Jones ar bwyllgorau lleol i beidio gosod eu golygon yn rhy uchel ar fater ansawdd yr adeiladau. Dygai i gof ei ddarllenwyr fel y bu i'r tadau Ymneilltuol ofalu yn gyntaf fod ganddynt eglwys fyw cyn mynd ati i godi teml iddi. Yn wir awgrymodd y gallai rhai o adeiladau'r

[34] *Y Goleuad,* 1 Ionawr 1891, t. 10.
[35] *Y Goleuad,* 18 Rhagfyr 1890, t. 11.
[36] *Y Goleuad,* 25 Rhagfyr 1890, t. 6.
[37] *Y Goleuad,* 22 Ionawr 1891, t. 11.

enwadau Ymneilltuol gael eu defnyddio gan yr ysgolion arfaethedig (syniad a oedd i'w wyntyllu eto yng nghyd-destun addysg oedolion). Apeliodd arnynt hefyd i beidio mynnu bod bechgyn a genethod yn cael eu dysgu ar wahân (mater y byddai Jones yn ei wynebu maes o law yn yr Alban eto). Nid yn y gwersi mae'r peryglon i foesoldeb, ond yn y teithio yn ôl a blaen i'r ysgol (yn enwedig os defnyddir y trên)! Dyna reswm ychwanegol dros beidio cael yr ysgolion yn rhy brin a gwasgaredig.

Yr oedd Henry Jones, y gwladwr, yn fyw iawn i'r anfanteision a wynebai blant y wlad pe gorfodid hwy i deithio i'r trefi am eu haddysg ganolradd. Ofnai y collent ormod o amser yn teithio, ac nid oedd yn hyderus y byddai aros mewn llety yn llesol iddynt ychwaith. Credai'n angerddol yn nylanwad da yr aelwyd ar ffurfiant cymeriad plant a phobl ifanc. Ofnai y byddai rhieni yn teimlo bod yn rhaid dilladu'r plant yn well os anfonid hwy o gefn gwlad i'r dref, ac y gosodai hyn faich ychwanegol, ond dianghenraid, ar rieni'r dosbarth gweithiol. Cydnabyddai y byddai codi llai o ysgolion yn sicrhau bod yr ychydig a fyddai'n cael eu sefydlu yn ysgolion o faint i allu cyflogi mwy o athrawon arbenigol. Serch hynny, yr oedd mantais mewn ysgolion llai lle gallai'r athrawon roddi mwy o sylw unigol i'r disgyblion. Unwaith eto, dadleuon Jones a'i gyfeillion a orfu.

Hawdd gweld ei fod yn yr ymgyrchoedd hyn yn edrych ar anghenion addysgol plant o gefndir tebyg iddo ef ei hun, ond mae'n syndod na fynegwyd gair ar le'r iaith Gymraeg yn y gyfundrefn newydd. Gellid tybied mai un o'r dadleuon cryfaf dros sicrhau bod plant gwledig yn cael eu haddysg ganolradd mewn ysgol wledig ei lleoliad a'i naws oedd y gellid darparu addysg iddynt yn eu hiaith eu hunain, yn haws felly nag mewn ysgol drefol. Nid yw Jones yn defnyddio'r ddadl hon, ac mae'n debyg na fyddai'n hapus â'r fath safbwynt beth bynnag.

Cawn olwg ar ei syniadau am le'r Gymraeg yn yr ysgolion cynradd yn y dystiolaeth a roddodd gerbron y Comisiwn Brenhinol ar Weithrediad y Deddfau Addysg Elfennol yn Lloegr a Chymru (1887). Fe'i gwysiwyd i roddi tystiolaeth ar ddau fater, sef dwyieithedd a chyfraniad y prifysgolion i hyfforddiant athrawon cynradd. Ar yr ail fater, gellir dweud ei fod o'r farn y gallai myfyrwyr y colegau normal fanteisio o ddilyn rhai cyrsiau academaidd mewn colegau prifysgol, a'i fod o blaid sefydlu adrannau addysg mewn prifysgolion. Yn y maes hwn tynnodd sylw at brofiad yr Alban lle'r oedd cyfartaledd sylweddol o athrawon cynradd yn raddedigion neu wedi dilyn cyrsiau mewn prifysgol.

Ar fater yr iaith, yr hyn a elwid gan y Comisiwn yn 'the bi-lingual difficulty', ei farn yn fras oedd y dylid sicrhau lle i'r iaith Gymraeg yng nghwricwlwm yr ysgolion cynradd (neu 'ysgolion elfennol' yn nherminoleg y cyfnod). Gwelai ei hun fel rhywun oedd yn galw am ymestyn y ddarpariaeth yn y Gymraeg yn yr ysgolion. Yr oedd am wrthod rhai ffyrdd o wneud hynny, fodd bynnag. Nid oedd o blaid cynnwys y Gymraeg fel pwnc ('class subject') ar draul y Saesneg fel pwnc, a chredai y byddai ychwanegu'r Gymraeg a chadw safle'r Saesneg (sef cynnwys dwy iaith fel 'class subjects') yn ysgolion Cymru 'braidd yn galed'.[38] Yr oedd ef o blaid cynllun a fyddai'n caniatáu i ysgolion ddarparu bod un o'r llyfrau dysgu darllen yn y dosbarthiadau isaf yn llyfr Cymraeg, a bod gwersi ysgrifennu'r dosbarthiadau uwch yn cynnwys hyfforddiant mewn ysgrifennu Cymraeg. Byddai gofynion y Bwrdd Addysg parthed dysgu darllen ac ysgrifennu Saesneg, felly, yn aros yr un fath yng Nghymru ag yn Lloegr. Credai hefyd fel mater o degwch y dylid sicrhau bod y plant a'r athrawon yn cael 'cydnabyddiaeth' o'u cymwysterau mewn iaith ychwanegol.

Yr oedd yn gwbl wrthwynebus i ddefnyddio'r Gymraeg fel cyfrwng addysg yn yr ysgolion cynradd.

> I would so far as possible maintain the teaching of English in its integrity … As the foundation of education, and as practically the only medium of communication between teachers and taught; because I think that English is taught not so much in connexion with English as a Subject in the schools, as on account of the fact that English is the medium of conversation between teachers and taught, wherever that is possible at all; and it is the medium through which other subjects are taught, such as arithmetic, geography, history, and so on; and I think that to make too ready a resort to the use of Welsh would do great harm; I mean in this connexion. Because it would weaken the child's effort to express himself in English; and I think that these two things taken together constitute the two chief means by which a language is learnt.[39]

Daliai at yr egwyddor hon, hyd yn oed pe byddai hynny yn amharu ar lwyddiant plentyn i ddeall ei athro ar y cychwyn.

> … very often the teacher is forced to explain the arithmetic processes in Welsh as well as in English; but the vocabulary used in teaching arithmetic is small, and the child's intuitive, or almost instinctive, power of learning a language is so great that I would be sorry, although the child should lose somewhat in the earlier part of his education, to use Welsh systematically as the medium of instruction.[40]

Mae hyn yn gwbl gyson â disgrifiad Reichel o'i safbwynt:

> When the movement for the utilisation of Welsh in the elementary schools was started, he held aloof, and told me he did so in consequence of his own experience. 'The master of the elementary school which I attended was an Englishman; he taught us English as French is often taught in English girls' schools, by making it a punishable offence to speak a word of the native tongue during school hours. The result was that we learnt English far more thoroughly than the children in most country schools, and even used to play in English.' To that power of thinking in English thus aquired he attributed in large measure the comparative ease with which he wrote the language, and no doubt it has something to do with the excellence of the style which is so marked a feature of his published writing.[41]

---

[38] *Third Report of the Royal Commission Appointed to Inquire into the Working of the Elementary Education Acts in England and Wales*, Llundain 1887, t. 321 (50,778).

[39] ibid. (50,774/5).

[40] ibid., t. 323 (50,823).

[41] TI/U/4/122.

Yr unig aelod o'r Comisiwn i holi Jones yn dreiddgar ar ei ddaliadau yn y cyswllt hwn oedd Dr Dale. Ceisiai gyffredinoli ei egwyddorion, a thrwy hynny ddangos yr elfen o annhegwch sydd ymhlyg ynddynt. Dyma enghraifft o'r holi ac ateb – Dale yn holi a Jones yn ateb.

> 50,824. Should you recommend that in an English school arithmetical lessons should be given in Latin or Greek? – Yes; if it were as important for an Englishman to learn Latin or Greek, as it is for a Welshman to learn English.
>
> 50,826. Do you not think that the first question that we should consider in educating a Welsh child is, how we can best do justice to its intellectual faculty and development, making the mastery of the English language the second consideration? – I am not willing to commit myself to such a collision as you make between the two.
>
> 50,827. I understand you to admit that the giving of instruction to an English child in a foreign language might, perhaps, mar and impair the efficiency of that instruction in its immediate object? – Yes.
>
> 50,828. And I imagine that that must be so in the case of a Welsh child? – Yes.
>
> ... (ateb Jones i gwestiwn 50,831) ... but you are more than repaid, I think, for the loss at first by the gain of entrance into the larger life and literature of the English people
>
> 50,832. But eight-tenths of the children in a Welsh school are never likely, as I understand from you, to enter fully into that larger life? – No, I think not fully.
>
> 50,844. Then do you not think that it is rather a serious thing, for the sake of the two-tenths, to be affecting rather injuriously the intellectual culture of the remaining eight-tenths? – I do not wish to endeavour to answer that question, because I do not know whether things ought to go by counting of heads or not, whether one man is not sometimes more valuable than ten, I cannot say.
>
> ... (ateb Jones i gwestiwn 50,846) ... I think that everything should be done to cultivate the knowledge of Welsh in Wales, consistent with the maintenance of English.
>
> 50,847. But which would you make the first thing? – The latter. [42]

Credai Jones fod Cymru yn symud yn raddol iawn o fod yn wlad uniaith Gymraeg i fod yn wlad uniaith Saesneg,[43] oni bai iddi fod yn bosibl i gymuned fod mewn cyflwr o ddwyieithedd sefydlog.[44] Ni ddymunai fynegi barn a oedd hynny'n bosibl ai peidio, ac mewn ymateb i osodiad y Cadeirydd fod cyfran helaeth o bobl Gwlad Belg yn ddwyieithog, dywedodd fod Lloegr, beth bynnag, wedi methu parhau yn

[42] *Third Report of the Royal Commission Appointed to Inquire into the Working of the Elementary Education Acts in England and Wales,* Llundain 1887, tt. 323-4.

[43] ibid., t. 321 (50,758).

[44] ibid. (50,765).

wlad ddwyieithog (Ffrangeg ac Anglo-Sacson).[45] Serch hynny, mae'n amlwg nad oedd yn fodlon ar effeithiau colli'r Gymraeg.

> ... Wales will never be made richer by neglecting its language; nor do I believe that English will be known better. For, on the border counties where they do lose their Welsh, or have done so and become English, there is degradation of intelligence because they do not really become English.[46]

Yn wir, wrth ateb Dr Dale yn ddiweddarach, mae'n dweud mai syniad hollol Seisnig yw'r dybiaeth fod unieithrwydd yn norm.

> ... It is surely almost exclusively an English idea that a man should speak only one language, or that one language should stand in the way of the other ...[47]

Mae'n gwneud y gosodiad hwn i gefnogi ei safbwynt fod modd cynyddu gwybodaeth plant o'r Saesneg heb amharu ar eu meistrolaeth o'r Gymraeg. Ar yr olwg gyntaf, o leiaf, nid yw'n ymddangos yn gyson iawn yn ei syniadau ieithyddol. Ac ar seiliau sigledig o'r fath y sefydlwyd polisïau iaith y gyfundrefn addysg yng Nghymru am ddwy genhedlaeth wedyn. Beth bynnag, cyn belled ag y gallai weld, ni fyddai tynged yr iaith yn gorwedd gyda'r addysgwyr:

> .. the fate of the Welsh language will not be determined in the schools; that is to say, even supposing that to make Wales wholly English at the shortest possible time (which is a view of the welfare of Wales that can quite be taken) it would be well to abolish Welsh, it cannot be done by the schools; because the real forces that keep Welsh alive are social and religious.[48]

[45] ibid. (50,776-7).
[46] ibid., t. 322 (50,781).
[47] ibid., t. 324 (50,850).
[48] ibid., t. 327 (50,926).

Pennod 5

Dychwelyd i'r Alban

Yr oedd Henry Jones, megis ei athro Nichol, yn adnabyddus am ei ddiddordeb mawr ym marddoniaeth Robert Browning, a phan fu'r bardd farw yn 1889 fe'i gwahoddwyd i draddodi darlith arno yng Nghaer-grawnt. Cafodd y ddarlith gystal derbyniad fel y llwyddwyd i'w berswadio i'w chyhoeddi, ond dan ei law yn ailweithio'r deunydd ar gyfer y wasg yn ystod 1890–1 tyfodd y ddarlith yn llyfr. Fe'i cyhoeddwyd ym Mehefin 1891 dan y teitl *Browning as a Philosophical and Religious Teacher*. Dyma ei lyfr cyntaf ac un o'i weithiau mwyaf llwyddiannus. Cafodd y llyfr dderbyniad cynnes ar unwaith. Gwerthwyd dros fil o gopïau o fewn deufis, a chafwyd sawl adargraffiad. Maclehose oedd y cyhoeddwyr cyntaf, sef cyhoeddwyr swyddogol Prifysgol Glasgow, ond cymerwyd y teitl drosodd gan Nelson a daeth y gwaith i sylw cylch eang iawn o ddarllenwyr. Y mae i'r llyfr le anrhydeddus ym maes beirniadaeth Browningaidd.[1]

Y mae ar gael o hyd lythyr at Jones oddi wrth ei rieni sy'n fynegiant hyfryd o'u balchder yn llyfr cyntaf eu mab. Meddai Elizabeth,

> May dy dad wedi gwirnoi (sic) yn lan hefo dy lyfr … dwi yn siwr ei fod yn ei ddallt hefud.[2]

Yr oedd nodyn trist yng nghenadwri Elias Jones, fodd bynnag, sef cyfleu ei gydymdeimlad ar achlysur marwolaeth Mrs Roxburgh. Ond yr oedd nodyn llawen hefyd:

> Mi welais ganmoliaeth i Ti a Du Lufr yn y faer (sic) Dudd Mercher Duwetha.[3]

Eithr, ni bu pob adran o'r wasg Gymraeg mor garedig â'r *Faner* fel y sylwasai O. M. Edwards yn *Cymru*.

> Anaml y cafodd llyfr Cymro gymaint o sylw y wasg Seisnig a llyfr y Proffeswr Henry Jones ar y bardd Browning fel dysgawdwr athroniaeth a chrefydd. Ca ganmoliaeth ac edmygedd digymysg gan y rhan fwyaf; ond y mae ambell i bapur fel y *Speaker*, – yr hwn sy'n ceisio siarad wrth fodd beirniaid sych-ddysgiedig a gwyw eu henaid sy'n mynychu clybiau Llundain, – yn tueddu i yrru arno. Y mae y *Goleuad*, hefyd, yn gofalu peidio colli'r cyfleusdra i roi sen i Mr Henry Jones, – yn ôl ei arfer. Y mae arddull y llyfr yn dlws a chlir; ac y mae rhyw onestrwydd a hyawdledd ynddo sydd yn gwneyd ei ddarllen yn waith mor iach ag anadlu awel y bore.[4]

---

[1] Gweler e.e., Boyd Litzinger, *Time's Revenges: Browning's Reputation as a Thinker 1889–1962*, Knoxville 1963.
Boyd Litzinger & K. L. Knickerbocker, *The Browning Critics*, Lexington 1965.

[2] TJ/U/2/63.

[3] ibid.

[4] *Cymru*, 1891, t. 33.

Yr oedd y *Goleuad* wedi bod yn cynhyrfu'r dyfroedd er mis Tachwedd 1890 pan roddwyd sylw i adroddiad yn y *News of the Week* am ddarlith a draddodwyd gan Jones yng Nghaerdydd lle gwnaeth sylwadau 'amharchus' am y diweddar Lewis Edwards yn ôl y gohebydd. Cyhoeddodd y *Goleuad* lythyr yn rhifyn 4 Rhagfyr oddi wrth Jones yn gwadu'r cyhuddiad, ond ni bu'r golygydd yn gwbl rasol yn ei sylw, "... y mae yn sicr nad oes neb a ofidia yn fwy na Mr Jones ei hunan oherwydd i'w eiriau gynhyrchu argraff wahanol ar feddwl y rhai oedd yn ei wrando."[5] Yr oedd awdur y 'Nodion Cymreig' yn yr un rhifyn yn llai grasol fyth. "Er yn derbyn yn llawn eglurhad y Proffeswr Henry Jones, drwg gennyf fod lle cryf i dybio nad oedd yr hyn a ddywedodd mor glir ag y dylusai fod."[6] Gwyddai nifer o ddarllenwyr y *Goleuad,* mae'n siŵr, nad oedd llawer o Gymraeg rhwng Jones a T. C. Edwards, ac yr oedd awgrymu ei fod wedi bod yn ysgafn o'r tad, sef 'pab' yr enwad, ac yntau bellach yn ei fedd (er 1887), yn fodd i gymylu ei enw da.

Ni rwystrodd y 'gamddealltwriaeth' hon ef rhag anfon wyth llythyr maith o blaid sefydlu cyfundrefn o addysg ganolraddol yng Nghymru i'w cyhoeddi yn y *Goleuad* rhwng 18 Rhagfyr 1890 a 12 Chwefror 1891. Ond pan esgorodd ar ei lyfr cyntaf, yr oedd y *Goleuad* yn barod amdano. Cyn cyhoeddi adolygiad o'r gyfrol fe'i collfarnwyd yn y termau mwyaf ysgubol yn y golofn olygyddol yn rhifyn 16 Gorffennaf 1891.

> Mae ieuenctyd yn llyncu syniadau penrydd am lawer o'r pethau a gredid yn ddiameu gan y tadau. Un o arwyddion yr amserau ydyw ymddangosiad llyfr galluog Proffeswr Henry Jones – sypyn o baganiaeth diledrith dan ffurf Hegeliaeth – yn yr hwn y cymysgir nefoedd a daear, ac nad oes modd gwahaniaethu cydrhwng pechod a rhinwedd, drwg a da, o ran ei hanfod. Yr unig gysur yw, fel y dywed y *Speaker*, mai ychydig sydd yn debyg o ddarllen y traethawd, ac mae nifer fechan o'r ychydig yma sydd yn debyg o allu deall meddwl yr awdur drwy dywyllwch ei arddull. Ond fe gyfyd dynion cyn hir a fyddant yn medru egluro eu syniadau gwyrdraws, ac fe'u credir gan Gymru, a rhaid cael dysgawdwyr crefyddol a allant ddadrys cylymau athroniaeth, neu eu tori a chleddyf yr Ysbryd. 'Hawyr bach! a ydych chwi am godi cenhedlaeth o bregethwyr i wrthwynebu Hegeliaeth a phob damcaniaeth arall; rhodder yr hen efengyl syml i mi, ac ymaith ag athroniaeth!' Ni raid i mi sicrhau neb na thueddir myfyrwyr a ddeuant o'r Bala i bregethu dim ond Crist a hwnw wedi ei groeshoelio. Bydd esiampl a dysgeidiaeth Dr Edwards yn ddigon i argraffu ar feddwl pob un ohonynt, mai dyma yw sylwedd pregethu i fod;[7]

Yr oedd T. C. Edwards wedi hysbysu Cymdeithasfa Llanidloes ym mis Mehefin 1891 ei fod yn derbyn y gwahoddiad i fod yn Brifathro Coleg y Bala. Dyma gyfle felly i ddyrchafu'r gynnen rhwng Jones ac Edwards i lefel dadl ddiwinyddol a gwrthdaro rhwng dau fath o goleg.

---

[5] *Y Goleuad,* 4 Rhagfyr 1890, t. 11.

[6] ibid., t. 4.

[7] ibid., 16 Gorffennaf 1891, t. 9.

Nid oedd Jones yn amddifad o amddiffynwyr, fodd bynnag. Y cyntaf i'r adwy oedd Puleston gyda llythyr meistrolgar, Jesuitaidd ei resymeg, yn rhifyn 30 Gorffennaf. Mae'n amau sut y gallai llyfr ar Robert Browning, o bawb, fod yn baganaidd.

> Ond os ydyw dweyd fod llyfr ar Frowning yn llyfr paganaidd yn ddweyd afresymol, y mae un gair mwy afresymol fyth ynglyn a'r dywediad hwn. Dywedir ei fod yn sypyn o baganiaeth dan ffurf Hegeliaeth. Beth, tybed, ydyw ystyr y gair 'ffurf' yn y fan yma? Ai ffurf yn golygu sylwedd, ynte ffurf mewn gwrthgyferbyniad i sylwedd a feddylir? Os y diweddaf, yr ystyr yw fod y Proffeswr yn cuddio ei baganiaeth ddi-ledrith dan gochl Hegeliaeth, a bod Hegel felly yn rhywbeth gwahanol i bagan, ac mewn gair yn dipyn o Gristion. Ond os dyna yr ystyr, mewn difri', pa gysondeb sydd yn y geiriau? Y maent cystal a dweyd fod Hegel ei hun yn rhyw fath o Gristion, a'r gwr a ystyrir yn ddisgybl selog iddo yn bagan. Eithr tebycach mai yr ystyr oedd mewn golwg, ffurf yn cynnwys sylwedd. Os felly, yr ydym i olygu mai ffurf ar baganiaeth ydyw Hegeliaeth, mai paganiaeth yn y ffurf Hegelaidd ydyw athrawiaeth y Proffeswr Jones, a'i fod ef, a Hegel, a Browning, debyg, yn baganiaid gyda'u gilydd. Ofn sydd arnaf na wna y sylw fawr o les i'r Proffeswr tuag at ei argyhoeddi, oherwydd fod ganddo ef, fel pawb arall call, feddwl go lew o'i gyd-baganiaid.[8]

Yn yr un rhifyn ceir llythyr gan D. D. Jones, Bangor, yn ymosod ar y sylw a wnaed o'r llyfr yn y Golofn Olygyddol am ei fod yn "anfoneddigaidd, annheg ac anghrefyddol."[9]

Ymddangosodd adolygiad o *Browning as a Philosophical and Religious Teacher* yn rhifynnau 27 Awst a 3 Medi o'r *Goleuad*. Mae'r adolygwr yn agor drwy ddweud, "Mae enw Proffeswr Henry Jones, Bangor, yn adnabyddus trwy Gymru oll." Mae ei enwogrwydd yn seiliedig, meddir, ar ei ymdrech wych i ddringo i'r entrychion academaidd. Fe'i gelwir yn "un o athrawon mwyaf poblogaidd Cymru." Yn ychwanegol "mae ei frwdfrydedd a'i gymwynasgarwch yn swyno yr myfyrwyr." Ond nid yw ei ragoriaethau personol yn ddigon i'w ddiogelu rhag cael ei gollfarnu am y safbwynt athronyddol a chrefyddol a goleddir ganddo yn ei lyfr. Crynhoir y feirniadaeth i dri phwynt sef, "darnio Browning i geisio egluro ei gredo" – h.y. credo Hegelaidd Jones (er nad oedd Browning ei hun yn Hegelydd); "diffyg eglurder yr arddull yn codi o ddiffyg eglurder meddwl yr awdur"; a "gochelgarwch gwyliadwrus yr awdur wrth esbonio egwyddorion ei gredo, a'r dull amwys ymha un y defnyddia frawddegau ac ymadroddion cyffredin rhai y mae eu golygiadau cyn belled a'r dwyrain oddiwrth y gorllewin oddiwrth syniadau Hegel."[10]

Mae'r trydydd pwynt yn un diddorol dros ben oherwydd mae'n dangos nad oedd y *Goleuad* am ymosod ar Hegeliaeth fel y cyfryw, ond yn unig ar Hegeliaeth 'honedig' Jones. Eithr y mae'n gwbl amlwg oddi wrth yr adolygiad ei fod yn tramgwyddo fwyaf pan fo buraf ei Hegeliaeth. Prysurodd Puleston Jones a

[8] ibid., 30 Gorffennaf 1891, t. 10.

[9] ibid., t. 11.

[10] ibid., 27 Awst 1891, t. 10

D. D. Jones i'w amddiffyn yn erbyn y cyhuddiad o baganiaeth unwaith yn rhagor. Newidiodd cyweirnod yr amddiffyn yn rhifyn 24 Medi gydag ymyrraeth John Morris-Jones.

Yn gyntaf, mae'n galw'r adolygwr yn anonest. Fe'i cyhudda o roddi camargraff lwyr o ddyfarniad y *Speaker* ar y gyfrol: fel y sylwodd y *Genedl Gymreig* "pentyru canmoliaeth ar y llyfr" a wnaeth y papur Saesneg hwnnw, nid ei gollfarnu fel yr awgrymodd y *Goleuad*. "A raid wrth gelwydd i amddiffyn y wir ffydd?" gofynnodd John Morris-Jones. Hefyd, cyhudda'r adolygwr o ystumio ystyr rhai o'i frawddegau drwy wyro eu gramadeg gan droi yr hyn oedd eglur a'i wneud yn dywyll. Wrth ddamnio ei arddull yr oedd yr adolygwr wedi gofyn yn un man, "Beth atolwg yw ystyr yr *although*?" Mae John Morris-Jones yn egluro, ac yn cynnig ei frawddeg enghreifftiol, ddeifiol, ei hun, "he is orthodox, though dishonest"!

Yn ail, nid yw am ei amddiffyn ar sail ei gysondeb â'r hyn a "gredid yn ddiameu gan y tadau." I'r gwrthwyneb, y mae'n dewis amddiffyn ei gyd-athro ar sail gwreiddioldeb ei safbwynt. Wrth gymeradwyo radicaliaeth ddiwinyddol Henry Jones yr oedd Morris-Jones yn ei amddiffyn ar sail a oedd, mewn gwirionedd, yn anghyson â haeriad Puleston Jones, y gellid dehongli ei ddaliadau mewn modd a ddiogelai ei uniongrededd.

> Pwnc mawr yr adolygydd yw dangos fod dysgeidiaeth y Proff. Jones yn Anghristionogol. Ac yma yr wyf am brotestio yn bendant yn erbyn arfer, fel y gwna efe, y gair 'Cristnogaeth' am ei gyfundrefn ddiwinyddol fach ef, nac am un Dr Lewis Edwards, er cymaint fy mharch iddo; nac am yr un cyffes ffydd arall. Oblegid yr wyf yn credu o'm calon y bydd Cristnogaeth fyw byth; yr wyf yn credu'n drwyadl hefyd y bydd credoau presenol Cymru farw, fel y bu'r hen rai farw o'r blaen. Mawr yr heretic a fuasai'ch adolygydd i ancr y Canol Oesoedd![11]

Ennynnodd amddiffyniad mor ysgubol nifer o atebion chwyrn, gan gynnwys llythyr gan yr adolygwr ei hunan yn synnu fod J. Morris-Jones "wedi anghofio ei hunan i'r fath raddau nes ymostwng i arddull ddichwaeth." Yn wir, yr oedd ambell ohebydd yn wawdlyd o gymhwyster John Morris-Jones i fynegi barn ar fater diwinyddol o gwbl, megis Edward Jones, Lerpwl:

> Pwy ydyw y gŵr da, a pha beth a ŵyr pan mae'n fforddio gwawdio Lewis Edwards o'r Bala? Mi adwaen J. M. Jones care of Dafydd ap Gwilym, ac a adwaen J. M. Jones care of William Owen Pughe; ond pwy atolwg yw J. M. Jones y difeinydd? Ym mha le yr astudiodd efe dduwinyddiaeth, a phwy a'i cenhadodd i udganu i fod y Gyffes Ffydd newydd? Ymha le y bu y cyngor a ddeorodd y syniad? Ai yng ngwely brwd Cymdeithas Dafydd ap Gwilym?... Ai dyma syniadau y dynion ieuanc sydd yn meddwl arwain y genedl? Gobeithio nad yw J. M. Jones yn cynrychioli dim ond dau, – y ddau Jones, John a Henry.[12]

[11] ibid., 24 Medi 1891, t. 7.
[12] ibid., 8 Hydref 1891, t. 5.

Yr oedd W. E. Griffith, Pentre, Rhondda yn fwy amharchus fyth o Athro Cymraeg Coleg y Gogledd:

> Bum yn sylwi yn ddistaw er's llawer o fisoedd ar y cwrs oedd pethau yn ei gymeryd gyda rhai dynion ieuainc sydd yn hawlio i ni eu galw yn arweinwyr Cymru Fydd, a'm cred yw fod yr amser yn nesu pan y rhaid dweyd wrth rai o'r dynion ieuanc hyn pa le y mae eu safle. Meddylier am laslanc – maddeuer y gair os yw'n gableddus am broffeswr, – nad ydyw ond yn dechrau agor ei lygaid ar y byd, yn rhuthro i wawdio rhai o'r meddyliau aeddfetaf a welodd Cymru erioed!... Mae'r syniad am weled y Proff. J. Morris Jones yn dyfod allan fel apostol y grefydd newydd – "y Gristnogaeth a fydd byw byth!" – i mi yn wrthun ... [13]

Ni lwyddodd John Morris-Jones i ymatal rhag taro'n ôl. Mêl ar ei fysedd oedd y newyddion a gawsai 8 Hydref 1891 fod argraffiad cyntaf *Browning as a Philosophical and Religious Teacher* wedi ei lwyr werthu a bod ailargraffiad yn y wasg.

> Go dda, onide, 'i baganiaeth ddiledrith' sy'n rhy 'dywyll' i neb ei ddeall. Nid wyf yn meddwl ychwaith y newidir y *not* na'r *although* yn yr argraffiad hwn.[14]

Yr oedd Morris-Jones wedi gweld yn ymosodiad yr adolygwr arno gadarnhad o'i farn mai'r un person oedd wedi adolygu'r llyfr ag a'i condemniodd wythnosau ynghynt yn y golofn olygyddol. Byddai'n dwyn ymosodiad mwy difrifol na hyn yn erbyn yr adolygwr maes o law. Datgelodd mewn llith yn rhifyn 29 Hydref mai ar ôl cyhoeddi'r farn fod y llyfr yn "sypyn o baganiaeth diledrith dan ffurf Hegeliaeth" y gofynnodd golygydd y *Goleuad* i'r awdur am gopi i'w adolygu!! Pan basiodd yntau'r cais ymlaen i'r cyhoeddwyr atebasant nad oedd copïau ar ôl, ond serch hynny fe gafwyd adolygiad yn y *Goleuad*.

Yr oedd ffyrnigrwydd yr ymosodiadau ar John Morris-Jones ("This overgrown schoolboy", fel y galwodd 'P.T.J.' ef yn y rhifyn uchod) yn gasach o lawer na'r anghytuno a gaed gydag amddiffyniad Puleston o'r llyfr oherwydd iddo herio'r sefydliad diwinyddol Methodistaidd. Gwelai ef geidwadaeth yn ceisio mygu, ac yn wir yn ceisio erlid, unrhyw ddatblygiad newydd ym myd syniadau am grefydd.

> Yr ysbryd hwn sydd i raddau helaeth, wedi peri ein bod yn ein hunman yn Nghymru er's cymaint o amser; ac nad oes ond un neu ddau Gymro yn adnabyddus fel duwinyddion allan o Gymru, er mai duwinyddiaeth yw'r hoff efrydiaeth. Gwelir yr un peth yn y ffaith na ymosodwyd ar lyfr y Proff. Jones ond yng Nghymru neu gan Gymry.[15]

O'u rhan hwy, credai 'amddiffynwyr y ffydd' fod Jones o'r diwedd wedi datgelu gwir natur ei ddaliadau diwinyddol, ac wedi ei gondemnio â'i eiriau ei hun.

[13] ibid., 15 Hydref 1891, t. 6.
[14] ibid., t. 7.
[15] ibid., 12 Tachwedd 1891, t. 7.

Mynegodd y gohebydd 'P.T.J.' yn ei lythyr craff ond beirniadol agwedd y sefydliad tuag ato gyda gofid yn hytrach na dicter, "… we are forced to relinquish those hopes in which he figured as a religious pioneer of his country and a guide of his denomination …" [16]

Pan oedd y ffrae yn ei llawn wres torrodd y newyddion fod Jones am ymddiswyddo o'i gadair ym Mangor a gadael Cymru am gadair yn yr Alban, ym mhrifysgol hynafol St Andrews. Yr oedd yn naturiol i'r symudiad gael ei ddehongli fel adwaith i'r condemniad a gafodd ei lyfr yng Nghymru, a parhaodd traddodiad hyd heddiw ei fod wedi ei alltudio o Gymru gan y sefydliad diwinyddol. Teimlai ei gefnogwyr ei fod wedi cael cam gan ei enwad a'i genedl. Meddai John Morris-Jones yn un o'i lythyrau at y *Goleuad*:

> Ni chafodd Henry Jones erioed mo'i le priodol yn Nghymru. Gwrthodwyd ef gan ei bobl ei hun.[17]

Ond nid oedd ei feirniaid yn mynegi unrhyw ofid am hynny. Yn wir, yr oedd tinc fuddugoliaethus yn ateb 'Adolygydd' yn y rhifyn canlynol:

> 'Ni chafodd Henry Jones erioed mo'i le priodol yn Nghymru', medd ei amddiffynydd. Nis gallaf baso barn am hynny, ond os felly, ar bwy mae y bai? Pan ddaeth i Gymru udgenid ei glod gan bob newyddiadur. Gwnaethpwyd lle iddo yn Aberystwyth, ond ymadawodd oddiyno mewn mwg. Daeth i Fangor, derbyniwyd ef yn llawen, mawrhawyd ef ymhob cylch, cafodd bob mantais i wneyd ei fare. Os na chafodd 'ei le priodol' pwy sydd i'w feio? Beth ydyw ei le priodol, wys? Ai lle yr Apostol Paul? A Mr J. M. Jones yw Dimotheus? Beth yw lle priodol Henry Jones yn Nghymru? A fwriadwyd ef gan Ragluniaeth fawr i fod yn Fahomet Cymru, yn broffwyd newydd i gymeryd lle yr hen broffwydi gynt? Drwg gennyf gael ar ddeall fod Proff. H. Jones yn ŵr siomedig yn Nghymru. Gobeithiaf yn fawr y gwna dau lythyr maith ei gyfaill Mr J. Morris Jones, 'i achub ei gam', weinyddu llawer o gysur iddo. Diau y gwnant. Tosturiaf bob amser wrth weld dyn a gafodd bob mantais i gyrraedd ei nod yn cwyno trwy ei gyfeillion na chafodd ei le priodol! Mewn dynion cyffredin, mae peth felly yn *small* ys dywed y Saeson, ond yn yr amgylchiad presenol nid yw yn llai na bod yn wir *tragical*, … Peidied Proff Jones a'i gyfeillion a gwneyd camgymeriad a chwerwi. Mae Cymru yn dechrau dyfod i adnabod gwahaniaeth cydrhwng ysgolheictod a gwir allu. Rhaid i'r ysgolheigion wneyd rhywbeth i brofi eu gallu defnyddiol, a'u hawl i arwain y genedl, heblaw enill graddau. Mae gwŷr yn llenwi lleoedd uchel yn ein hathrofeydd, – nid wyf yn cyfeirio at Proff. H. Jones na'i gludydd arfau – sydd wedi enill graddau da yn y prif ysgolion, ond sydd yn druenus amddifad o gymwysderau i lenwi eu swyddau, ac fe fydd chwalfa eto cyn hir, pryd y bwrir mwy nag un Jonah difudd i'r mor.[18]

Faint bynnag o ddiffuantrwydd oedd y tu ôl i eithrio'r ddau Jones o'r cystwyo ysgolheigion yn y paragraff olaf, y mae sawyr maleiusus iawn i weddill yr epistol. Yr oedd y frawddeg agoriadol yn wawdlyd dros ben – "Mae yn hwyr i'r Proff. Henry Jones ymadael i'r Alban neu rywle arall, fel y gallo ddianc rhag y cyfeillion

---

[16] ibid., 29 Hydref 1891, t. 12.

[17] ibid., 15 Hydref 1891, t. 7.

[18] ibid., 22 Hydref 1891, t. 7.

eiddil sydd yn ymladd drosto." Hynny yw, mewn geiriau unsillafog, 'a gwynt teg ar 'i ôl o.' Ond, heretic neu beidio, byddai digon o ddarllenwyr y *Goleuad* yn gwybod os oedd rhywun erioed wedi gwneud "rhywbeth i brofi eu gallu defnyddiol, a'u hawl i arwain y genedl, heblaw enill graddau", Henry Jones, gyda'i ymgyrch fawr dros addysg ganolraddol ac addysg uwch i feibion a merched gwerin Cymru oedd hwnnw.

A glwyfwyd Jones gan y difrïo cyhoeddus a fu arno yn y *Goleuad*? Nid dyna'r argraff a roddai i'w gyfeillion ar y pryd. Dyma dystiolaeth John Morris-Jones, eto yn y *Goleuad*:

> Yn hytrach na bod yn chwerw at Gymru, yr oedd Henry Jones yn drist iawn wrth feddwl am ei gadael. Cafwyd cinio ymadawol er parch iddo echnos. Dywedodd wrthyf tua'r diwedd na bu hi erioed yn galetach arno, a phrudded oedd. Yn hytrach na bod erthyglau'r adolygydd wedi effeithio arno, gwybydded y dienw na ddarllenodd Henry Jones mohonynt.[19]

Eithr mae'n amlwg ei fod yn gwerthfawrogi ymdrechion ei gyfaill drosto, fel y dengys y sylw isod ar un o epistolau John Morris-Jones.

> Miniog fel cledd yw'r llythyr. Ni faidd y Dienw ddod i'r golau – y mae ei lygaid wedi eu duo a'i wyneb wedi ei bydru yn ormod gan eich dyrnodiau diarbed.[20]

Y mae digon o sail dros gredu nad ffieidd-dra'r ymosodiadau o fewn ei enwad a barodd iddo adael Bangor yn 1891. Yr oedd, ys dywedir am weinidogion, eisoes yn 'symudol'. Ym mis Mai 1891, deufis cyn i'r *Goleuad* 'ddarganfod' Browning, yr oedd Jones wedi gwneud cais am Gadair Rhesymeg a Metaffiseg Prifysgol Caeredin a ddaethai yn wag ar ymddeoliad yr Athro Campbell Frazer. Yr oedd nifer o'r ysgolheigion a gefnogai ei gais wedi darllen ei lyfr ar Browning (cyn ei ddyddiad cyhoeddi), ac y mae eu sylwadau arno yn wrthgyferbyniol iawn i'r hyn a gafwyd yn y *Goleuad*. Er enghraifft, dyma dystiolaeth y Parchedig Athro Dr A. B. Bruce, un o brif ddiwinyddion Eglwys Rydd yr Alban:

> His forthcoming work on Browning will I am certain make its mark. I have never read anything as instructive and inspiring on the views of God, man, and the world, which underlie the writings of that noble poet. It serves little purpose to say to what sect or school of philosophy a man belongs. The great question is, does he teach what tends to exalt our idea of human nature and to throw the light of hope on human life. That Browning did this is well known. That Professor Jones does so also is certain. His influence as a Professor of Philosophy will be altogether for good; morally wholesome, thoroughly Christian in spirit.[21]

[19] ibid., 29 Hydref 1891, t. 11.

[20] JMJ/77. Anfonwyd o 13 North Bell St., St Andrews.

[21] *Application and Testimonials of Henry Jones, M.A., Professor of Logic and Philosophy in the University College of North Wales. Candidate for the Chair of Logic and Metaphysics in the University of Edinburgh.* Glasgow 1891, t. 27.

Cartŵn o Henry Jones (gweler 'The Jone' t. 68).

(Llun Archifdy Prifysgol Glasgow)

Prifysgol Glasgow ar droad y ganrif.

(Llun Archifdy Prifysgol Glasgow)

Henry Jones tua diwedd ei oes (portread mewn olew gan Christopher Williams a wnaed ar gyfer Prifysgol Glasgow yn 1923 ar sail portread a wnaeth i Goleg y Brifysgol, Bangor, yn 1920).

(Llun a hawlfraint yr Hunterian Art Gallery, Prifysgol Glasgow.)

Henry Jones ychydig cyn triniaeth lawfeddygol 1913.

(Llun Annan & Son, Glasgow gan Archifdy Prifysgol Glasgow)

Cartref Henry Jones a'i deulu ym Mhrifysgol Glasgow 1894-1911,
No. 1 Professors' Square.

(Llun Gwyn Davies Jones)

William George, H. Cernyw Williams a Henry Jones.

(Llun Lettsome and Sons, Llangollen: trwy law y diweddar Margaret Williams).

Y Gofeb yn y Cwm.

(Llun Ymddiriedolaeth y Cwm)

Bedd Henry Jones yn Kilbride (yma hefyd claddwyd Annie yn 1932 ac Enid yn 1953.

(Llun Ymddiriedolaeth y Cwm)

Gwnaeth John Morris-Jones ddefnydd o'r dyfyniad hwn ac eraill yn ei frwydr gyda'r adolygwr Cymraeg yn ddiweddarach, ond y pwynt yw fod Henry Jones â'i lygad ar gadair Albanaidd cyn i'r helynt yn y *Goleuad* dorri. Ymddengys mai Edward Caird a'i hanogodd i ymgeisio am Gaeredin, er iddo gytuno ag ef na fyddai ganddo obaith cipio'r swydd yn erbyn ymgeisyddiaeth Andrew Seth. Cynnyrch Prifysgol Caeredin oedd Seth, a symudasai o Gaerdydd i St Andrews yn 1887. Yr oedd ef eisoes wedi gwneud cryn enw iddo'i hun gyda dau lyfr, *Scottish Philosophy* (1885) a *Hegelianism and Personality* (1887). Yn wir, fe gynhyrfodd y dyfroedd Hegelaidd yn arw gyda'r ail lyfr, oherwydd ei safbwynt beirniadol, ond wrth gwrs, daeth hynny ag amlygrwydd yn ei sgil. Credai Caird, fodd bynnag, y byddai'r profiad o ymgeisio am gadair Albanaidd yn fantais fawr i Jones pe dymunai ddilyn Seth yn St Andrews. Yn hyn yr oedd yn hollol gywir. Cafodd Seth gadair Caeredin, a gwnaed argraff ffafriol iawn gan Jones. Mewn llythyr at Stuart Rendel ym mis Gorffennaf dywed iddo ddeall mai ef oedd yn sefyll ail yn yr ymgeisyddiaeth honno. Yr oedd yn fwy hyderus ynglŷn â chipio cadair St Andrews, ac yn y llythyr hwn mae'n mynegi pam yr oedd y gadair honno yn apelio ato:

> I should much like a larger sphere for working at phy & teaching it, …[22]

Ac wedi iddo gael y swydd, dywedodd wrth Macelhose,

> I'll try hard to lecture well. I shall now for the first time get a field.[23]

Y mae'n amlwg, felly, nad mewn pwd y gadawodd Fangor. Uchelgais yn hytrach na dicter a'i dygodd yn ei ôl i'r Alban. Efallai, yn wir, iddo deimlo bod culni diwinyddol yn llesteirio datblygiad athroniaeth yng Nghymru. Wrth gyfeirio at y posibilrwydd o gynnwys darpariaeth ar gyfer diwinyddiaeth yn siarter Prifysgol Cymru, mynegodd mewn llythyr at Cadwaladr Davies yn 1892 ei ddirmyg tuag at y sefydliad enwadol:

> My view is that the black beetles have too much power in Wales and they had better keep out of the University till they are better educated. The creeping things will be out place there and do much harm …[24]

Yn yr Alban, lle cafodd athroniaeth safle breiniol yn y prifysgolion ers y canol oesoedd, yr oedd Jones yn medru anadlu'r awyr iach hwnnw a gynhaliodd athronwyr gwir fawr fel David Hume, Adam Smith, Thomas Reid, William Hamilton, Edward Caird a chwmwl tystion anrhydeddus. Ym Mangor llwyddodd i

---

22 LlGC, llsgr. 1945D (324).

23 TJ/U/3/192.

24 TJ/U/2/64.

wneud cyfraniad sylweddol, ac unigryw yn wir, i ddatblygiad addysg yng Nghymru. I wneud cyfraniad at athroniaeth, i'w ymestyn ei hun fel athro a meddyliwr, teimlai fod yn rhaid iddo ymfudo i'r lle a alwodd O. M. Edwards yn "wlad athroniaeth".

> Y mae Henry Jones, Athraw Athroniaeth Coleg y Gogledd, wedi ei roddi yng nghader Athroniaeth Prif Ysgol St. Andrews. Y mae cadeiriau'r Alban yn rhai yr hiraethir amdanynt gan athrawon Lloegr a'r Iwerddon a Chymru, heblaw athrawon yr Alban ei hun. Nid yn aml y rhoddir cadeiriau athroniaeth yr Alban i estron, – y mae'r Albanwyr eu hunain yn athronyddion goreu'r ynysoedd. Yn ddiau, defnydd llawenydd ydyw gweled Cymro yn un o brif gadeiriau athronyddol gwlad athroniaeth.
>
> Bydd llawer, y mae arnaf ofn, yn llawenhau wrth weled Henry Jones yn troi ei gefn ar Gymru. Yr oedd rhai yn ofni ei athrylith, gan feddwl mai athrylith ddinistriol ydyw; yr oedd llawer yn meddwl drwg ohono oherwydd na fyddai bob amser yn gwisgo ac yn siarad ac yn cerdded fel y dymunai pob Sir Fopling Flutter a Mr Courtly Nice iddo wneyd.
>
> Bydd dau fath o Gymry o leiaf, yn galaru fod Henry Jones yn gadael ei wlad. Y dosbarth cyntaf ydyw'r efrydwyr Cymreig a fu ym Mhrif Ysgol Glasgow ar ei ôl. Yn y Brif Ysgol honno rhoddodd Henry Jones safle i'r Cymro, ac edrychir hyd heddyw ar ei gydwladwyr gyda pharch. Bu llawer un sy'n canu'n uchel am Gymru heddyw yn ddigon anfoddlon i gyfaddef yn ei Brif Ysgol mai Cymro oedd; ond ni chlywais Albanwr erioed yn sôn am Henry Jones heb ddweyd yn gyntaf peth mai Cymro oedd.
>
> Dosbarth arall alara wrth weld yr athraw hwn yn gadael Cymru ydyw ei hen fyfyrwyr. Nis gallaf gredu fod yr un gelyn i Henry Jones – os oes ganddo un, – wedi bod yn ei gwmni yn hir nac yn ei adnabod yn dda. Anaml y gwelais un a'i gymeriad mor gyson â'i gredo, – gwelais ef yn aberthu pob peth er mwyn ei ddisgyblion ac er mwyn y gwir, nis gwelais ef erioed yn meddwl am dano ei hun nac yn arbed ei hun.[25]

Wedi gadael Bangor, ni ddychwelodd i Gymru i fyw. Ond ni throdd ei gefn ar Gymru. Ni phallodd ei ddiddordeb mewn materion Cymreig, a pharhaodd i roddi gwasanaeth cyhoeddus i'w wlad enedigol. Eto, mewn ffordd, yr oedd mynd i'r Alban megis 'troi am adre' yn ysbrydol iddo.

Prin y gellid gorliwio'r gwahaniaeth rhwng bywyd academaidd ym Mangor ac yn St Andrews. "The contrast between this and my life in Wales is very strong," meddai Jones wrth ohebydd ym Mangor.[26] Sefydliad bychan, saith mlwydd oed, yn paratoi myfyrwyr ar gyfer graddau Prifysgol Llundain ac wedi ei leoli mewn hen westy oedd Coleg Bangor. Ymestynnai hanes Prifysgol St Andrews yn ôl hyd at 1410, ac yr oedd yn sefydliad â mwy nag un coleg yn perthyn iddo. Ar un adeg yr oedd tri choleg yn y brifysgol, sef colegau St Salvator (1450), St Leonard (1512) a St Mary (1537), ond unwyd y ddau goleg cyntaf yn 1747. Pan etholwyd Jones yn Athro Rhesymeg a Rhethreg yn 1891, yr oedd Prifysgol St Andrews yn ehangu drwy ymgorffori Coleg Prifathrofaol Dundee fel un o'i sefydliadau cyfansoddol. Yn anffodus, nid oedd y briodas rhwng St Andrews a Dundee yn mynd rhagddi'n

[25] *Cymru,* 1891, t. 133.

[26] TJ/U/2/64 (at Cadwaladr Davies?).

esmwyth, ac yr oedd cryn dipyn o ddrwgdeimlad ar y ddwy ochr. Bu ymron i hyn arwain at ymadawiad Jones o fewn awr iddo gael ei sefydlu yn ei Gadair!

Yr oedd wedi cael ei ethol drwy fwyafrif o un bleidlais yn llys unedig St Andrews a Dundee. Dim ond un o etholwyr St Andrews a bleidleisiodd drosto, ond pleidleisiodd holl etholwyr Dundee o'i blaid. Canlyniad hynny oedd gwneud y bleidlais yn gyfartal, ond yn ffodus i Jones, bu'n rhaid i un o etholwyr St Andrews fynd i angladd yng Nghymru ar ddiwrnod y pencdiad gan roddi iddo ei fwyafrif o un. Mawr oedd ei ddyled i'w gydwladwr ymadawedig ac anhysbys! Heb yr un bleidlais hon o'i blaid byddai'r Prifathro Donaldson o St Andrews wedi bwrw ei bleidlais fel Is-ganghellor a chadeirydd y llys, ac nid ef fyddai wedi ei chael.

Dechreuodd ar ei yrfa academaidd yn yr Alban felly dan gwmwl y rhaniad pendant rhwng y colegau ynglŷn â'i benodiad, ond ar ddechrau ei gyfarfod cyntaf o senedd y brifysgol gwnaed datganiad ysgytwol. Cyhoeddodd y Prifathro Donaldson fod uniad Coleg Dundee a Phrifysgol St Andrews yn gyfreithiol wallus ac felly'n ddirym! Canlyniad hynny, meddai Prifathro Coleg St Mary (y Prifathro Cunningham), oedd fod penodiad Jones yn annilys. Gwawriodd enbydrwydd ei sefyllfa arno ar unwaith. Yr oedd am yr eildro yn ei yrfa yn ddiwaith, gyda'r gwahaniaeth y tro hwn ei fod wedi gollwng ei swydd flaenorol o'i wirfodd! Meddyliodd ei fod wedi cymryd cam gwag gwaethaf ei fywyd.[27] Ymatebodd ar unwaith drwy gynnig ymneilltuo o'r ystafell er mwyn i'r senedd fedru trafod ei sefyllfa yn rhwyddach. Ond cododd hynafgwr y senedd (yr Athro Lewis Campbell) ar ei draed gan ddatgan yn chwyrn yr elai yntau allan hefyd pe gadawai'r Athro Jones yr ystafell. Gyda hynny trodd y fantol o'i blaid. Cafodd gefnogaeth lwyr ei gyd-athrawon, a'r tri phrifathro, y dydd hwnnw a thra bu yn St Andrews.

Cadair mewn Rhesymeg a Rhethreg, yn y dull hynafol, oedd un Jones yn St Andrews. Golygai hynny ei fod yn darlithio ar athroniaeth a llenyddiaeth Saesneg. Fel rhywun oedd newydd wneud enw iddo'i hun gyda llyfr ar Robert Browning, yr oedd y cyfuniad wrth ei fodd, a darlithiai ar Burns, Scott, Coleridge, Shelley a Wordsworth fel Athro Saesneg. Yn ystod ei ail a'i drydedd flwyddyn aeth i Goleg y Brifysgol, Dundee, i ddarlithio ar resymeg a seicoleg a chymerodd yr Athro M'Cormick o'r Coleg hwnnw gyfrifoldeb am ddosbarthiadau llenyddol Jones yn St Andrews. Dyma'r unig fater y llwyddodd Dundee a St Andrews i gytuno arno yn ystod ei gyfnod ef yno, meddai Jones. Yr oedd yr ymrafael yn y senedd yn ddi-baid ac yn ddi-ildio. Maes o law, cytunwyd ar uniad dilys a barhaodd tan 1967 pan gafodd Prifysgol Dundee ei siarter fel prifysgol annibynnol.

O'r cychwyn cyntaf bu Prifathro Coleg Dundee (y Prifathro Peterson) yn garedig a chefnogol tuag at Jones. Mwynheai gymdeithas glòs y frawdolaeth athronyddol. Yr oedd ysgol athroniaeth gref yn St Andrews gyda dau Athro, sef Jones a'r Athro Knight yn y Gadair Athroniaeth Foesol. Yr oedd ganddynt ddau ddarlithydd disglair

[27] OM, t. 211.

yn eu cynorthwyo: H. H. Joachim (a fu rhwng 1919 a 1935 yn Athro Wykeham mewn Rhesymeg yn Rhydychen, lle'r oedd yn fawr ei ddylanwad) a Robert Latta (Athro Rhesymeg a Rhethreg yn Glasgow yn ddiweddarach). Yr oedd gan y myfyrwyr glwb athronyddol, gyda myfyriwr galluog dros ben yn ysgrifennydd, sef Norman Kemp-Smith (Athro Rhesymeg a Metaffiseg yng Nghaeredin yn ddiweddarach ac athronydd 'ysgolheigaidd' o fri). Yr oedd olynydd Lewis Campbell yn y Gadair Roeg, yr Athro John Burnet, yn awdurdod ar athroniaeth y Groegiaid, ac erys ei lyfr ar athronwyr cynnar Groeg yn waith safonol hyd heddiw. Gallai Jones gyfrif y rhain oll ymhlith ei gyfeillion. Yr oedd hen gyfeillion Glasgow, gan gynnwys Caird, o fewn cyrraedd hefyd. Darganfu Caird ar ei ymweliadau â St Andrews ei fod yn ennill parch ac edmygedd:

> I have given two lectures at St. Andrews – and have had the pleasure of finding Jones gaining golden opinions there both from his colleagues as far as they know him and still more from his students whose ears his persuasive Celtic tongue has caught. He is working for them with all his might ... Me he treats like the most devoted of sons.[28]

Y boddhad pennaf oedd cael awdurdod llwyr dros gynnwys ei gyrsiau fel Athro mewn prifysgol annibynnol.[29] Mewn llythyr o St Andrews at Cadwaladr Davies ym Mangor dywedodd:

> To a man who loves his subject and his students, freedom of teaching is what he would prize above almost all other things.[30]

Yr oedd yn cael ei flino gan yr ymrafael rhwng Dundee a St Andrews, fodd bynnag, a bu'n rhoi tystiolaeth o blaid diwygio'r drefn gerbron Comisiwn Brenhinol ar ad-drefnu prifysgolion yr Alban. Mynegodd ei bryderon wrth Cadwaladr Davies, a chanmol yr argymhellion ar gyfer cyfansoddiad Prifysgol Cymru, a oedd ar fin cael ei sefydlu:

> We are under the reign of King Muddle here, and I don't know what will come of the present struggle to undo the knots he has tied. Your combination of academic and democratic power in the University would be ideal.[31]

Er na fu ef ei hun erioed yn Athro ynddi, bu Jones â barn bendant ar gyfansoddiad Prifysgol Cymru drwy gydol ei fywyd.

Ni thorrodd ei gysylltiad â Choleg Bangor ychwaith, a sicrhaodd ei gyfeillgarwch gyda Reichel ei fod yn gwybod am holl droeon yr yrfa yno. Yn fuan wedi iddo ddod

[28] Henry Jones & John Henry Muirhead, op. cit., t. 175.
[29] OM, t. 213.
[30] TJ/U/2/64.
[31] op. cit.

i St Andrews, bu helynt dychrynllyd ym Mangor rhwng Pennaeth Neuadd y Merched (sef Bron Castell heddiw) a'r Coleg.[32] Ducpwyd llu o bobl amlwg gogledd Cymru i'r ffrae a bu gohebu yn y *Times*, yr *Educational Review* a'r *Weekly Dispatch*, heb sôn am y wasg leol. Cyfeiriwyd at y sefyllfa yn Nhŷ'r Cyffredin a Thŷ'r Arglwyddi gan beryglu'r mesur seneddol i sefydlu Prifysgol Cymru. Methodd Jones â chadw draw:

> I had been all last week at Bangor amongst my old colleagues, where there is the bonniest fight between the snobs and the Tories on the one side and my old colleagues on the other. I have been helping to put the fat in the fire. There will be a libel against *The Times* and others and the Tory Party in Wales, if things are as they are represented, will have one of the nicest lickings they ever had. If the case breaks down, a professor will have to go, but the College will gain in any case. This has taken my whole mind and time for the last week.[33]

Ei olynydd ef ei hun yn y Gadair Athroniaeth, yr Athro Keri Evans, a ymddiswyddodd. Fel Jones, cafodd Evans Ysgoloriaeth Dr Williams i Glasgow (yn 1884, wedi i Jones ddychwelyd i Gymru), eisteddodd wrth draed Edward Caird, enillodd Gymrodoriaeth Clark, a bu'n ddarlithydd cynorthwyol ac arholwr allanol i Caird. Er i Evans dderbyn ymddiheuriad am athrod ynghyd â hanner canpunt gan y *North Wales Chronicle*, dyfarnodd senedd y coleg ei fod heb ymddwyn yn ddigon gochelgar yn ei berthynas â myfyrwyr benywaidd. Cwbl bitw oedd y gŵyn yn ei erbyn, ond ymhen deunaw mis yr oedd wedi ymddiswyddo a thorrodd ei iechyd. Fe'i ordeiniwyd yn weinidog gyda'r Annibynwyr yn 1897. Llanwodd Gadair Athroniaeth Gristnogol Coleg Presbyteraidd Caerfyrddin rhwng 1901 a 1907. Mae'n adnabyddus fel awdur *Fy Mhererindod Ysbrydol*.

Gyda'r holl ymgecru yn St Andrews a Jones yn cadw'i fys mewn sawl potes yng Nghymru, nid oedd unrhyw wir berygl iddo foddi mewn esmwythdra yn ei amgylchedd newydd. Meddai wrth Cadwaladr Davies,

> I trust my Welsh life has been long and stirring enough to prevent me from becoming a stuffed beast, with glass eyes and a skin gradually losing its fur and returning into dry dust.[34]

Eto, yr oedd uwchben ei ddigon a'i deulu yn medru byw yn gyffyrddus:

> Y mae yma awyr ysgafn a hen dre fonheddig dawel. Credaf mai da i mi yw dod yma. Yr wyf wrthi ddydd a nos yn paratoi at fy nosbarthiadau … Ni welais le hoffusach erioed o ran yr awyr, a'r dref, a'r môr, a'r creigiau.[35]

Yn St Andrews ganwyd chweched plentyn Jones, Arthur, y plentyn olaf. Yr oedd Annie yn ôl ymhlith ei chydwladwyr wrth gwrs, ac mae'n amlwg fod ei gŵr mewn

[32] J.Gwynn Williams, op. cit., tt. 106-111.
[33] TJAJ/2/65.
[34] TJAJ/2/64.
[35] JMI/77.

cariad â'r wlad. Mynegodd ef hynny ei hun wrth un o'i gyfeillion newydd yn St Andrews.

Ronald Munro-Ferguson oedd y cyfaill hwn, ac ar yr olwg gyntaf mae'n ymddangos yn gyfaill annhebygol. Gŵr uchelwrol ei wedd ydoedd, ond yr oedd yn Rhyddfrydwr brwd. Cyflwynodd ei hun i Jones drwy gyfaddef iddo bleidleisio yn ei erbyn pan benodwyd ef i'w gadair, ond ei fod ers hynny wedi ei oleuo gan Tom Ellis ynglŷn â'i ragoriaethau. Daeth Jones yn ymwelydd cyson â chartref Munro-Ferguson yn Raith a pharhaodd eu cyfeillgarwch yn glòs a chynnes drwy'r blynyddoedd. Yr oedd St Andrews yn etholaeth Asquith, a Jones yn awyddus i weithio drosto. Meddai wrth Munro-Ferguson:

> I have promised to go out campaining for Asquith ... I like the statesman in him and believe in his cause; but the one I should like to stump with is yourself. It would give me a rare time if I could put the powder in. My difficulty is the want of a good Scotch grievance, like the Welsh Church. A good grievance would get us Home Rule for Scotland, which I am more in love with than ever; e.g. if we had a Scotch House we would be able to thrash out our University matters ...[36]

Yng nghanol yr holl ddarlithio a'r gwleidydda (academaidd a gwladol) cafodd Jones amser i ysgrifennu hefyd. Cyhoeddwyd y ddarlith gyhoeddus a draddodwyd ganddo gerbron Prifysgol St Andrews ar gael ei sefydlu yn ei Gadair yn y cylchgrawn *Mind*. 'Natur ac Amcanion Athroniaeth' oedd teitl y ddarlith honno. Ychydig yn ddiweddarach yn 1893 ymddangosodd papur arall ganddo yn *Mind* ar 'Idealaeth a Gwybodeg'. Mae'r papur hwn yn ddiddorol oherwydd ceir ynddo feirniadaeth o safbwyntiau ei ragflaenydd, Andrew Seth. Yr oedd Seth wedi bod yn torri cwys annibynnol hyd yn oed cyn gadael Caerdydd, a gwelir ef fel prif ysgogydd y mudiad athronyddol a adwaenir fel 'idealaeth bersonol'. Yn ei feirniadaeth o Hegel yr oedd Seth yn dilyn yr un trywydd â'r athronydd Almaenig, Rudolf Hermann Lotze (1817–81). Nid yw hyn yn syndod pan gofiwn fod Seth wedi astudio am gyfnod byr dan Lotze ym Mhrifysgol Gottingen, ond yr oedd miniogrwydd ei feirniadaeth o Hegel yn annisgwyl gan un o gywion Caird. Yr oedd y nyth yn dechrau chwalu. Ceisiodd Jones feirniadu'r anuniongrededd newydd, a gwnaeth hynny gyda mwy o arddeliad nag y dymunai Caird iddo ei ddangos.[37] Y cam naturiol nesaf iddo oedd ysgrifennu llyfr ar athroniaeth Lotze.

Ymddangosodd *A Critical Account of the Philosophy of Lotze: the Doctrine of Thought* yn 1895. Y mae wedi ei gyflwyno i goffadwriaeth John Nichol. Ni chafodd y llyfr yn un hawdd o bell ffordd i'w ysgrifennu. Ysgrifenasai'r rhan fwyaf o'r gyfrol dair neu bedair gwaith drosodd cyn bod yn fodlon.[38] Yr oedd ail gyfrol i fod i ddilyn, gyda'r is-deitl 'The Doctrine of Reality', ond ni welodd honno olau dydd

[36] TJ/U/2/64.
[37] LL, t. 57.
[38] LL, t. 70.

ysywaeth. Mae'n resyn, oherwydd dywedodd wrth F. H. Bradley mai dyna'r agwedd yr ymddiddorai fwyaf ynddi.[39]

Ar sawl cyfrif dyma lyfr gorau Jones. Fe'i hanelwyd, yn fwy felly nag unrhyw un o'i lyfrau eraill, at ei gyd-athronwyr. Dyma'r unig astudiaeth estynedig o waith athronydd arall iddo ei chyhoeddi. Mae ei arddull yn fwy cynnil a'i fynegiant yn fwy uniongyrchol na'r hyn a gafwyd ganddo o hynny ymlaen. Un rheswm dros hyn efallai yw fod cymaint o'i weithiau cyhoeddedig yn seiliedig ar ddarlithoedd a draddodwyd ganddo yn wreiddiol ar lafar. Mae'n bosibl hefyd i'r ffaith ei fod yn ysgrifennu dan bwysau amser gael effaith lesol ar ei arddull. Dywed iddo gwblhau'r fersiwn terfynol mewn ychydig wythnosau.[40]

Daeth amser yn elfen bwysig yn yr ysgrifennu oherwydd bod Edward Caird wedi derbyn swydd Meistr Coleg Balliol, Rhydychen. Byddai Prifysgol Glasgow yn penodi olynydd iddo ar gyfer dechrau blwyddyn academaidd 1894. Ef oedd y cyntaf i gael gwybod gan Caird ei fod yn ymadael â'i Gadair, a mynegodd ei awydd i'w weld yn ymgeisio amdani. I gryfhau ei safle yn y gystadleuaeth, ymroes Jones â'i holl egni i ysgrifennu ei lyfr ar Lotze, y gwaith mwyaf academaidd iddo ei gyhoeddi. Hoffai wybod pa argraff a gawsai ei ysgrifennu ar athronwyr o ddylanwad gwleidyddol, a cheisiodd gael Tom Ellis i ddarganfod agwedd Haldane a Balfour.[41] Teimlai yn sicr o ewyllys da Caird, ond ni allai hwnnw ddangos cefnogaeth amlwg i neb. Yn wir, yr oedd Caird yn bleidiol hefyd i gyn-fyfyriwr arall, yr Athro Watson o Brifysgol Kingston, Canada. Serch hynny, roedd yn gwbl anfodlon gweld Jones yn tynnu allan o'r ornest. Yr oedd ei frawd, y Prifathro John Caird, yn ôl *Old Memories*, yn ffafrio'r ymgeisydd arall, gan awgrymu y byddai'n well ganddo weld Jones yn ymgeisio am yr ail Gadair athronyddol yn Glasgow, sef Cadair Rhesymeg, a ddeuai'n rhydd yn fuan ar ymddeoliad yr Athro Veitch.[42]

I Jones, fodd bynnag, cael esgyn i Gadair Edward Caird oedd y posibilrwydd a'i swynai. Fel y dywedodd wrth Tom Ellis, yr oedd dan anfantais oherwydd mai Albanwyr oedd yr ymgeiswyr eraill. Am hynny, teimlai'n hy i bwyso ar Gymry dylanwadol i weithio drosto:

> I am, I need hardly say, exceedingly sorry to trouble you and George. But by your help it is just possible that I may be able to show to some Welshman the way up; and I sh'd dearly like to see a Welsh flag flying in my old University, for the first time in History, amongst the rest.
>
> I am happy here, and able really to do some philosophical work. But what a sphere there is in Caird's chair – the most important in Scotland in my line, with its 218 students, this year.[43]

[39] LL, t. 188.
[40] OM, t. 224.
[41] LLGC, Papurau Tom Ellis, 1069.
[42] OM, t. 224 a 226.
[43] LLGC, Papurau Tom Ellis, 1069.

Yn y diwedd, rhwng Jones a Watson oedd hi, a Jones a gipiodd y wobr. Fe'i etholwyd yn Athro Athroniaeth Foesol ym Mhrifysgol Glasgow ym mis Mehefin 1894. Ni chaniataodd i fantell Edward Caird ei fygu ychwaith, ond llanwodd y Gadair yn ei ddull dihafal ei hun gan ennill parch mawr fel un o athrawon mwyaf nodedig ei ddydd. Yma y cyflawnodd waith mawr ei fywyd.

Pennod 6

Athro yn Glasgow

I Henry Jones yn bersonol, mae'n sicr nad oedd braint uwch na chael esgyn i Gadair Edward Caird, ac yn wir yn ôl y safon fwyaf gwrthrychol, roedd wedi cyflawni camp fawr iawn. Safai yn awr mewn olyniaeth oedd yn cynnwys enwau meddylwyr o fri fel Francis Hutcheson, Adam Smith a Thomas Reid. Bu Cadair Athroniaeth Foesol Prifysgol Glasgow yn eiddo iddynt oll yn eu tro, a hawdd y gallai ymwybyddiaeth o'r ffaith hon droi'n fwrn ar y diweddaraf o'u holynwyr. Nid felly y bu. Penderfynodd Jones o'r cychwyn nad cysgod o unrhyw un arall y disgwylid iddo fod, ond Henry Jones ar ei orau.

Cafodd ei benodi'n ffurfiol gan Lys y Brifysgol ar 5 Gorffennaf 1894. Er mawr ryddhad iddo, mae'n siŵr, penderfynodd Senedd y Brifysgol na fyddai disgwyl iddo draddodi darlith mewn Lladin ar gael ei sefydlu yn y swydd.[1] Fe'i derbyniwyd yn aelod o'r Senedd ar 9 Hydref, ac aeth ati ar unwaith i ddechrau diwygio'r drefn! Gwnaeth gais am ganiatâd i ddysgu dosbarth cymysg o feibion a merched. Yn ystod ei holl hanes maith, nid oedd Prifysgol Glasgow wedi gweld myfyrwyr o'r ddau ryw yn gwrando ar ddarlith yn yr un ystafell. Yn wir, nid oedd merched wedi derbyn unrhyw fath o addysg yn Glasgow cyn 1845, pan gafwyd cyfres o ddarlithoedd arbennig iddynt gan yr Athro Hutton Balfour. Sylw Henry Jones ar y fenter honno oedd, "the subject being Botany, no harm to the women was expected to ensue"![2]

Ni chafwyd unrhyw ddarpariaeth ffurfiol ar gyfer addysg i ferched tan 1868 pan drefnodd Mrs Campbell o Tullichewan gwrs o 'Lectures for Ladies'. Traddodwyd y darlithoedd hyn gan bedwar o Athrawon ifanc y Brifysgol, sef Young, Veitch, Nichol a Caird. Cawsant gefnogaeth frwd y Prifathro, John Caird, a than ei gadeiryddiaeth ef sefydlwyd y Glasgow Association for the Higher Education of Women yn 1877. Nid oedd mwyafrif senedd y brifysgol o'r un farn â'r prifathro. Yn wir, yn 1874 John ac Edward Caird oedd unig aelodau'r senedd a gefnogai addysg uwch i ferched.[3] Yr oedd yr holl aelodau eraill am wrthwynebu mesur gerbron Tŷ'r Cyffredin i alluogi merched i dderbyn graddau meddygol. Erbyn 1877, fodd bynnag, cafodd Athrawon yr hawl i ddefnyddio ystafelloedd yn y Coleg ar gyfer darlithio i ferched, ond byddai'n rhaid iddynt ymgynnull a gwasgaru ar adegau pan oedd y meibion o'r golwg wrth eu gwaith mewn darlithfa neu labordy. Yn 1883 trawsnewidiwyd yr 'Association' yn goleg merched, Queen Margaret College, gydag Edward Caird yn cynrychioli senedd y brifysgol ar y bwrdd llywodraethol. Gwelodd Caird ei lafur maith dros addysg uwch i ferched yn

---

[1] Cofnodion Senedd Prifysgol Glasgow, Cyf. 101, t. 29.

[2] Henry Jones & John Henry Muirhead, op. cit., t. 96.

[3] Ibid., t. 97.

cyrraedd y nod gydag ymgorfforiad Coleg y Frenhines Margaret ym Mhrifysgol Glasgow yn 1892. Serch hynny, ar wahân y cawsai'r meibion a'r merched eu dysgu.

Ymgais i newid y drefn hon oedd cynnig Jones. Gofynnodd y senedd am adroddiad gan y gyfadran, ac yn yr adroddiad hwnnw a gyflwynwyd ar 1 Tachwedd argymhellwyd cefnogi'r cais am un sesiwn yn unig. Pleidleisiodd y senedd, 11 o blaid a 9 yn erbyn. Cafwyd sêl bendith llys y brifysgol ar 29ain o'r mis,[4] a llwyddodd Jones yn ei ymgyrch gyntaf. Ond er iddo ennill buddugoliaeth dros hawliau merched ym myd addysg, lled oleuedig yn unig oedd ei syniadau ar ennill hawliau gwleidyddol iddynt. Nid oedd yn erbyn estyn y bleidlais i ferched, ond cydnebydd yn 1897 nad oedd yn frwdfrydig o blaid ychwaith:

> I am no enthusiast for this matter of women's political rights but I cannot see that we have the least ground for denying them a share of the priviledges, seeing they wish them. We have defended their rights too badly in the past, to deny them in the future. And it is possible that this is the only way to educate women into capacity for union amongst themselves. The one thing that prevents me from being warm in the matter is, that I am loath, loath to see women enter into an arena that is so trampled into deep mud: they are much too good for the work in some respects.[5]

Go brin y byddai unrhyw ferch heddiw yn gwerthfawrogi ei gonsŷrn, ac yn wir mae ei sylwadau yn diraddio'r bywyd gwleidyddol mewn ffordd anghydnaws â'r pwysigrwydd moesol a roddai Jones ar ddinasyddiaeth.

Dyma'r math o ymgyrch lle roedd ar ei orau: ymgyrch fer heb ormodedd o fanylion a chymhlethdodau. Yr oedd yn gymeriad rhy eirias i feistroli doniau diplomatyddol a Maciafelaidd y pwyllgorwr greddfol. Serch hynny, yr oedd yn berswadiwr heb ei ail. Er enghraifft, pan oedd yn ciniawa gyda rhai o'i gyfeillion o fyd masnach (yr oedd ganddo nifer o'r rhain, megis: Dr William Lorrimer, pennaeth cwmni peirianyddol mawr; Syr James Murray Smith, perchennog y *Glasgow Evening News*; Syr John Mann, pennaeth cwmni o gyfrifwyr; Dr Paul Rothenburg, a fu'n gadeirydd y Siambr Fasnach; Syr D. M. Stevenson, a fu'n dal swydd Lord Provost y ddinas 1911–14; ac wrth gwrs, y teulu a gyhoeddai ei lyfrau, y Maclehoseiaid), datblygodd sylw o'i eiddo nad oedd modd i fyfyrwyr fedru rhannu copi'r llyfrgell o'r llyfrau y cyfeirid hwy atynt i ddibenion paratoi eu traethodau yn apêl yn y fan a'r lle am arian i sefydlu llyfrgell i'r adran. Cyn pen dim yr oedd wedi casglu £200!

---

[4] Integreiddiwyd Coleg y Frenhines Margaret a'r Brifysgol yn llwyr yn 1935 a daeth i ben fel sefydliad, ond goroesodd yr enw yn yr ymadrodd 'Queen Margaret Students' am fyfyrwyr benywaidd y Brifysgol. Gweler *The University of Glasgow through Five Centuries,* Glasgow 1951 a 1985, t. 80.

[5] TJ/U/2/88. Cellwair, mae'n siŵr, oedd ei sylw at Carpenter yn Rhydychen yn 1913, "I am surprised to hear that Rhys & Murray shd think of not clinging to the party & fighting for it through thick and thin. I would vote for the Liberals even though they did give the vote to women!" Coleg Harris Manceinion, Rhydychen, llsgr. Casgliad Carpenter, 57.

Gwerthfawrogai Jones ei gysylltiadau â'r byd dinesig a masnachol bron gymaint â'r frawdoliaeth academaidd, ac yr oedd hynny yn gwbl gydnaws â'r olwg a gymerai ar alwedigaeth yr athronydd. Ymhlith ei gyfeillion agosaf ar staff y Brifysgol yr oedd A. C. Bradley, Athro Iaith a Llên Saesneg a brawd yr athronydd F. H. Bradley. Saif F. H. Bradley gyda T. H. Green fel cynnyrch athronyddol disgleiriaf Rhydychen ail hanner y bedwaredd ganrif ar bymtheg. Fe'i gelwir yn fynych yn Hegelydd, ond er cymaint ei ddyled iddo, nid yw'r label yn gwbl briodol. Yr oedd ei frawd iau, A. C. Bradley, a gyfrifir yn ysgolhaig Shakespearaidd o'r radd flaenaf, yn hyddysg iawn mewn athroniaeth ac yn amlwg ar yr un donfedd â Jones; yr oeddynt yn eneidiau cytûn. Yr oedd deiliaid y Gadair Resymeg a Rhethreg, cadair arall ysgol athronyddol Prifysgol Glasgow, yn gyfeillion iddo, er nad oeddynt o'r un anian ag ef. Tan 1902, pan fu farw'n annhymig, yr Athro Adamson oedd yr Athro Rhesymeg; ysgolhaig gwych iawn, wedi ei drwytho yn hanes athroniaeth. Ei olynydd oedd yr Athro Latta, sef cynorthwy-ydd Jones yn St Andrews.

Dros y blynyddoedd deuai cyfeillion hen a newydd i Glasgow, megis Andrew Gray, hen gyd-weithiwr o Fangor a ddychwelodd yn ei ôl i Glasgow i ddilyn ei hen athro yntau yn y Gadair Ffiseg; olynwyr Bradley, Sir Walter Raleigh a W. MacNeile Dixon; a'r Athro Groeg, Gilbert Murray. Yr oedd Jones, yn sicr, yn uchel ei barch ymhlith ei gyd-athrawon, nid efallai fel ysgolhaig mawr, ond fel darlithydd ac athro eneiniedig.

Roedd y Jonesiaid yn byw yn y tŷ hwnnw ar y campws (yn 'Professors' Square') lle trigai Edward Caird gynt, sef No. 1, The College. Mae'n adlewyrchiad o statws yr Athro Athroniaeth Foesol mai ef a breswyliai yn Rhif Un. Buont yn byw yn y Sgwâr tan 1911 pan aeth awyr fyglyd Glasgow yn drech nag iechyd Annie. Prynodd Jones dŷ yn Tighnabruaich, gyda dyfroedd y Kyles of Bute yn ymestyn o'i flaen wrth iddynt gofleidio Ynys Bute. Nid nepell o'r tŷ yr oedd y cei lle cyfarfyddai'r cwch a'i dygai ar hyd y Kyles i Greenock at y trên a'i cludai'n ddiffwdan i Glasgow. Ni fyddai neb yn mynd o Tighnabruaich i'w waith yn Glasgow mewn dull mor waraidd ac mewn cyn lleied o amser heddiw! Yr oedd y tŷ yn y Coleg yn dal at ei wasanaeth ar ôl 1911, ac yn y tŷ hwnnw y bu byw hwyaf ar wahân i'r Cwm.

Rhoddodd Hetherington gipolwg diddorol i ni o *routine* feunyddiol Jones yn Glasgow. Yr oedd yn foregodwr, bob amser cyn 6 y bore, ac mor gynnar â 4.30 yn ystod y gaeafau cyntaf. Gwnâi baned o de a chynnau'r tân cyn dechrau ar ei baratoadau ar gyfer y ddarlith wyth o'r gloch. Y Jones a ddarlithiai am wyth oedd yr Athro a welai'r mwyafrif o'i fyfyrwyr, oherwydd hwn oedd y dosbarth 'cyffredin'. Byddai'r dosbarth hwn yn cyfarfod am wyth o'r gloch bum bore'r wythnos yn ystod y sesiwn (h.y. yn ystod y ddau dymor rhwng Hydref a Mawrth; nid oedd trydydd tymor, sef Ebrill i Fehefin, ym Mhrifysgol Glasgow cyn 1907), a darlithiai Jones ar bedwar bore iddynt.

Byddai oddeutu 160 neu 190 o fyfyrwyr yn y dosbarth hwn, rhai ohonynt wedi dechrau ar eu taith mor gynnar â chwech o'r gloch y bore. Teithient i'r coleg, meddai Hetherington, drwy'r gwyll oerllyd a nodweddai foreau gaeafol Glasgow, ac wedi cyrraedd y ddarlithfa dechreuent ganu a churo eu traed i godi tipyn o wres. Yna, yn union wedi i gloch y coleg orffen taro wyth, caeid y drws, ac o'r ystafell arwisgo ymddangosai Jones. Un ystum â'i law, ac yr oedd y gynulleidfa yn sefyll mewn tawelwch ar gyfer y weddi agoriadol, arferiad a etifeddwyd o gyfnod Caird.

> Almighty and everlasting God, in whom we live and move and have our being, who hast created us for Thyself, so that we can find rest only in Thee: Grant unto us purity of heart and strength of purpose, so that no selfish passion may hinder us from knowing Thy will, no weakness from doing it; but in Thy Light may we see light clearly and in Thy service find perfect freedom.

Wedi galw'r gofrestr a gwneud un neu ddau o gyhoeddiadau, dechreuai â'r agorawd, "Yesterday, we were considering ..." Er fod ganddo nodiadau newydd ar gyfer pob darlith, ni chadwai atynt yn hir. Byddai rhyw bwynt neu'i gilydd wedi hawlio sylw a'i harweiniai i ymhelaethu neu chwilio am enghreifftiau neu ddyfyniadau o weithiau'r beirdd neu'r Beibl (cyfieithiai adnodau Cymraeg yn ei feddwl weithiau, gan roddi mynegiant gwreiddiol iawn i'r Ysgrythur!) Ar adegau fel hyn, dechreuai gerdded yn ôl a blaen ar ei lwyfan, ac yn aml deuai i lawr i ganol y ddarlithfa, ei lygaid yn pefrio a'i holl gorff yn mynegi ei frwdfrydedd. Meddai Hetherington:

> He would state the case against his own theory as fairly and fully as he could. He knew very well how prone he was to enforce his own doctrine, and in his statements of contrary views he was anxious to redress the balance; for above all he wanted his students to think. But the mischievous impulse was never far away, and every now and then it would find expression. The whole lecture seemed to go just where it liked. It wore all the air of 'unpremeditated art', though it was very far from that; and one found, when one looked back on the lectures and on the course, that somehow they had been woven together to expose and to illumine a systematic body of doctrine.[6]

Bu Hetherington yn eistedd ar y meinciau yn gwrando'n blygeiniol ar 'berfformiad' a oedd yn hysbys i genedlaethau o fyfyrwyr Glasgow. Byddai llu mawr ohonynt yn trysori'r atgof o'r 'Ddarlith Wyth' weddill eu dyddiau. Yr oedd y weddi agoriadol yn draddodiad o ddyddiau Caird, ond dyna'r unig debygrwydd rhwng arddull ddarlithio'r ddau.

Am naw o'r gloch, byddai'n dychwelyd i'r tŷ i gael ei frecwast, a gwahoddai fyfyrwyr i ddod gydag ef o bryd i'w gilydd. Erbyn deg o'r gloch byddai'n ei ôl yn y stydi yn gweithio tan ganol dydd. Am un o'r gloch ar ddyddiau Llun, Mawrth a Iau cyfarfyddai'r dosbarth anrhydedd. Byddai'n paratoi yn fanwl iawn ar ei gyfer: criw bychan o ddeg neu lai o fyfyrwyr arbenigol. Dewisai destun diweddar, o waith

[6] LL, tt. 77-78.

F. H. Bradley neu Bosanquet, neu waith mawr modern o eiddo Kant neu Hegel, neu hyd yn oed glasur o athroniaeth Groeg gyda'r bwriad o dywys y dosbarth drwy'r testun hwnnw gyda manylder beirniadol. Gyda'r math hwn o ddosbarth nid oedd gofyn am huodledd ac arabedd, ac nis cafwyd. Y nod, gyda'r arbenigwyr, oedd galluogi'r myfyrwyr i ymarfer eu doniau dadansoddol ac ymresymol. Byddai disgwyl iddynt fod yn gyfarwydd â'r testun dewisedig yn ei gyflawnder fel canlyniad i'w hymdrechion eu hunain. Gwelai mai ei swyddogaeth ef oedd eu gosod ar ben ffordd; ond byddai disgwyl iddynt ddarllen a meddwl drostynt eu hunain

Yn oedd paratoi ar gyfer ei ddarlithoedd a darllen traethodau'r myfyrwyr yn waith diddiwedd a digon trwm, ond gyda'r agweddau hyn ar ei swydd, yr oedd Jones yn ei elfen. Ambell brynhawn, fodd bynnag, byddai disgwyl iddo wasanaethu, fel unrhyw athro arall, ar un o'r amryfal bwyllgorau sydd ynghlwm wrth waith prifysgol. Pan oedd y prynhawn yn rhydd ganddo, hoffai fynd allan i'r wlad gyda'i ddaeargwn Cymreig i saethu a physgota neu i chwarae golff neu hwylio. Roedd diddordebau'r gwladwr yn agos i'r wyneb o hyd, fel y dengys y dyfyniad o'r llythyr hwn a anfonwyd o Tighnabruaich at gyfaill yn Llangernyw:

> You say 'mae yma llawer iawn o wnhingod bach iw gweld.' I cant understand where they come from! I think it cant be from the farms Evan and I ferretted! I believe they must have come from Ned Wynne's preserves and probably Jack Lewis left a good lot too. But I am very glad to hear that the Gwytherin snipe is getting better as Llwynsaint will be able to have some more practice at it – tell him he needs to practice all he can if he hopes to take Hendre Ddu and shoot the Hendre ddu rabbits! I have been fishing in Islay an island off the west coast of Scotland but though we had good sport it was not the same thing as Llangernyw. There was no good company at the inn, no joking & laughing over the beer mugs, no challenging and story telling and fun after the day's sport. Indeed it was more of a business than of a bit of sport. Give me Llangernyw every time, – I want nothing better in this world, and if I can have a few rabbits & fish and Evan bach to help me catch them, & a nice inn like the Bridge to meet my friends of an evening in the next world, then I shall be fairly satisfied with it. I would rather be busy doing that than sitting in a cold cloud twanging at a harp I dont know to play. Dont you think so, William? There is something wrong with those pictures of Heaven they used to show us when we were children …
>
> Yours ever,
> Harry Ferreter.[7]

Rhwng amser te a chinio hwyrol fe ymneilltuai i'r stydi eto, ond gyda'r nos hoffai ddiddanwch ei aelwyd a chwmni cyfeillion. Yn y stydi, ac ar yr aelwyd, mwynheai gysur ei getyn.

Cydnabuwyd Jones fel un o athrawon mwyaf ei gyfnod yn ystod ei oes ei hun ac am flynyddoedd wedi ei farw, hyd yn oed gan rai na chytunent yn llwyr â'r hyn a

[7] Trwy law John Hughes.

ddysgai. Mae teyrnged ei hen gyfaill coleg, James Denney, pan oedd hwnnw'n Brifathro ar yr United Free Church College yn Glasgow, yn enghraifft dda o hyn:

> He is far the most influential university teacher in Scotland. All our students are strongly impressed by him, and a good many who ought to be our students are diverted from the Church – and, as I am convinced, from the Gospel – by his influence.[8]

Nid gormodiaith fyddai dweud bod rhai o fyfyrwyr Jones yn hanner ei addoli. Dywedodd Syr John Mann mai eistedd wrth ei draed yn Gilmorhill oedd un o freintiau mwyaf ei fywyd. Nid oedd wedi cyfarfod unrhyw un mor ysbrydoledig, mor anhunanol ac mor ysbrydol ei feddwl â Henry Jones, ac yr oedd yn hyderus na wnâi fyth eto ychwaith. Yr oedd yn ymdebygu, meddai, i'w ddarlun dychmygol o Iesu Grist![9] Dyma deyrnged fwy cymedrol gan Agnes Saville, M.A., M.D:

> Many can say of him, as he said of Caird, that they were reborn in his classroom, that for their whole lifetime they bore his mark on their every intellectual endeavour, on their every moral problem. Was any Professor more loved? Did any other classroom ring with cheer after cheer, as so often occurred after these famous lectures, when every young and generous spirit felt as if inspired with his contagious enthusiasm for the good?[10]

Yr oedd rhai o'i fyfyrwyr yn medru dangos eu gwerthfawrogiad ohono mewn ffyrdd tipyn llai 'parchus'. Yn 1899, er enghraifft, cyhoeddodd myfyrwyr Prifysgol Glasgow lyfryn doniol yn dwyn yr enw *The College Picture Book*. Ynddo ceir cartwnau a nodiadau gogleisiol ar yr athrawon. Mae'r cartŵn o Jones yn ei bortreadu fel crwban ac yn dwyn y teitl, 'The Jone'. Dyma'r nodyn amdano:

> This dear little creature is loved by everybody. It crawls along and tries to do good. When it is aroused, it can speak quite beautiful, and never repeats itself. Sometimes it pretends to be in a rage, and then, when you are horribly frightened, it smiles sweetly, and you cannot but love it more than ever. It lives on Hegel and Kant, and other things, but always has Browning for dessert. It is a very funny beast at times. If you make a noise with your feet, it tells you to use the other end.[11]

I raddau helaeth, yr hyn a'i gwnaeth yn athro mor enwog oedd ei huodledd. Y mae'n amlwg fod ganddo ddoniau areithio arbennig, a'i fod yn gwneud defnydd llawn ohonynt wrth ddarlithio. Yr oedd ei ddull yn fwy trawiadol o bosib oherwydd

[8] LL, t. 82.

[9] TJ/U/4/6. Yr oedd Jones ei hun yn credu y gallai bod ym mhresenoldeb ambell bersonoliaeth fod yn brofiad dyrchafol i fyfyrwyr: "I am quite sure that the students & Oxford generally wd gain from Prof Royce (lladmerydd syniadau ysgol arbennig o Hegeliaid yn yr Unol Daleithiau). The question of agreeing with such men is really quite secondary to the young men: it is the contact with personalities that signify which has value". Coleg Harris Manceinion, Rhydychen, llsgr. Casgliad Carpenter, 53.

[10] TJ/U/4/132.

[11] Archifau Prifysgol Glasgow, llsgr. 34933.

fod dysgu athroniaeth fel arfer yn gofyn am ddoniau tawelach ac arafach. Fel y nododd Reichel,

> Intellectual speculation usually conveys a suggestion of coldness. In him it always glows and often rises to a white heat …[12]

Eithr nid oedd y dull hwn o draddodi at ddant pawb. Ni feirniadwyd Jones yn gyhoeddus am ei 'dân Cymreig', ond mewn hunangofiant preifat i'w deulu, cyfaddefodd un hen fyfyriwr, William Boyd (a ddaeth maes o law yn gynorthwy-ydd iddo) fod dull Jones yn medru bod yn faen tramgwydd weithiau.

> In some ways, Jones's Welshness rather spoiled him for the Glasgow students. The best of them found him stimulating and some of them became imitators, not only of his thinking but of speech and gestures (among them the present Principal of the University, Sir Hector Hetherington, not among them ME). But most ordinary students did not get a great deal out of them and some of them became antagonistic to what they considered his verbalism.[13]

Ymhlith y myfyrwyr na fu gymaint â hynny ar eu helw o fod yn ei ddosbarth, mae Boyd yn cynnwys ei wraig a'i frawd ("he got more and more dissatisfied with the Jonesian talk"), ond mae'n datgan ei fod ef ei hun yn ddyledus iawn iddo.[14]

Er fod y myfyrwyr a'r coleg yn ganolog i'w fywyd, yr oedd llawer iawn o alwadau academaidd a chyhoeddus eraill ar ei amser a'i egni. Yr oedd galw cyson am erthyglau ac adolygiadau ganddo o gyfeiriad y cylchgronau dysgedig a chrefyddol, yn enwedig yr *Hibbert Journal*, y cylchgrawn crefyddol rhyddfrydol amlycaf. Mewn llythyr, dyddiedig 4 Mawrth 1905,[15] y mae'n rhestru'r canlynol fel pethau i'w gwneud cyn 2 Mai: (1) Ysgrif feirniadol ar Balfour i'r *Hibbert Journal* (bron yn barod); (2) erthygl ar etifeddeg fel cyflwyniad i gyfrol o draethodau erbyn wythnos gyntaf Ebrill; (3) adolygiad o lyfr gan Bradley ar gyfer yr *International Journal of Ethics* erbyn 20 Ebrill; (4) paratoi arolwg ac adroddiad ar lyfrau Sorley (W. R. Sorley oedd olynydd Seth Pringle-Pattison fel Athro Athroniaeth Coleg y Brifysgol, Caerdydd [1887-94]. Yr oedd yn gyfrannwr, gyda Jones, i'r *Essays in Philosophical Criticism.*) o fewn pythefnos ar gais Prifysgol Caer-grawnt, a fwriadai ei gydnabod â D. Litt.; (5) anerchiad i'w draddodi yn Kilmarnock; (6) anerchiad i'w draddodi i Lyfrgell Stirling ar 11 Ebrill gyda'r bwriad o'i gyhoeddi; (7) cynnal arolwg ar ysgol a pharatoi adroddiad erbyn 12 Ebrill; (8) paratoi anerchiad i ddathlu canmlwyddiant Martineau yn Rhydychen 1af neu 2il Mai; (9) adolygu llyfr i Maclehose, y cyhoeddwyr. Mae'n amlwg na ddeuai ysgrifennu yn

---

12 TJ/U/3/135.

13 Archifau Prifysgol Glasgow, teipysgrif *Memorabilia Guilielmi Boyd, Civis Universitatis Glasguensis*, t. 123.

14 ibid., tt. 123-4.

15 TJ/U/2/125.

rhwydd iddo. Gwaith llafurus a gymerai lawer o'i amser oedd paratoi erthyglau, darlithoedd a llyfrau. Meddai amdano'i hun:

> You never knew a more toilsome worker than I am, nor probably one who tears up and re-writes so much – & always up to the last moment.[16]

Yr oedd hyn i gyd ar ben cynnal yr arholiadau gradd a'r holl ddyletswyddau a ddeilliai o gyfarfodydd y senedd a'r llys yn ystod y cyfnod hwnnw.

Mae'r cyfeiriadau uchod at yr *Hibbert Journal* a'r ddarlith yn Rhydychen ar Martineau yn arwydd o'r cysylltiad diddorol oedd gan Henry Jones â'r Undodiaid. Er iddo feirniadu Undodiaeth fel credo, yr oedd yn edmygu'r enwad fel arloeswr crefydd ryddfrydol. Edmygai'r Undodiaid yntau, fel y dengys ei benodiad yn 1906 yn Ddarlithydd Hibbert mewn Metaffiseg yng Ngholeg Manceinion, Rhydychen. Swydd oedd hon a olygai deithio i lawr o Glasgow i draddodi darlith yn y coleg unwaith bob pythefnos yn ystod dau dymor y gaeaf. Daliodd y swydd hyd 1912.

Coleg diddorol iawn yw Coleg Manceinion. Er ei fod er 1990 yn rhan o Brifysgol Rhydychen (ac wedi mabwysiadu'r enw 'Harris Manchester College'), nid oedd felly yn y cyfnod hwnnw. Sefydlwyd y coleg ym Manceinion yn 1786 ar ôl cau Academi Ymneilltuol Warrington (agorwyd 1757) fel sefydliad a oedd yn cynnig addysg uwch i Ymneilltuwyr, a waherddid bryd hynny rhag ymaelodi ym Mhrifysgolion Rhydychen a Chaer-grawnt. Symudodd y coleg ei leoliad nifer o weithiau, gan ddod am gyfnod yn rhan o Brifysgol Llundain, cyn ymsefydlu yn Rhydychen yn 1889. Coleg diwinyddol rhyddfrydol ydoedd, ac athrofa i ddarpar-weinidogion gyda'r Undodiaid. Yr oedd Jones eisoes yn amlwg yn y cylchoedd hyn, fel y dengys ei aelodaeth o fwrdd golygyddol yr *Hibbert Journal*, prif gylchgrawn crefydd ryddfrydol ers ei sefydlu yn 1902.

Yr oedd ganddo le cynnes iawn i'r coleg oherwydd y rhyddid a warentid i bawb yno i draethu ei farn yn rhydd – heb ofn cythruddo unrhyw esgob na Chyfarfod Misol. Meddai unwaith am Goleg Manceinion:

> When I survey the theological world, with its creeds and sects and shibboleths, this little College seems to me to stands out as a happy exception, like a green oasis in a vast waste, or, better, like a clear place amidst the entangling undergrowths of a thick forest.[17]

Mae'n amlwg fod croeso cynnes iddo yn y coleg. Deuai myfyrwyr, yn feibion a merched, darlithwyr, clerigwyr, ambell Athro hyd yn oed, o'r coleg a'r tu hwnt i wrando ar y cyfresi darlithoedd a draddodai o flwyddyn i flwyddyn. Yn ei anterth, yr oedd yn denu cynulleidfa o tua chant a hanner – mwy nag y gallai'r ddarlithfa eu cynnwys. Meddai Prifathro'r coleg am y darlithoedd hyn:

---

[16] Coleg Harris Manceinion, Rhydychen, llsgr. Casgliad Davis, 185.

[17] *Divine Transcendence*, Manceinion 1907, tt. 3-4.

> They were eloquent, apt in literary illustration, and distinction of style was never lacking. To the critical, however, he seemed to be preacher rather than philosopher. 'Idealism' writes an old Oxford Greats man, 'was not so much a theorem to be argued and expounded, as a gospel and religion to which converts must be made.' Such students found him of little use for examination purposes, and their interest and attendance declined. But the charm of his personality was felt by all.[18]

Yr oedd un hyfrydwch arbennig iawn iddo ynglŷn â'r teithiau i Rydychen. Yr oedd yn rhoi cyfle iddo weld Caird yn ei flynyddoedd olaf. Hyd at ei farw yn 1908, gydag ef y lletyai.

Ni chyfyngwyd ei gynulleidfaoedd i wledydd Prydain yn unig. Yn 1908 cafodd wahoddiad i fynd ar daith ddarlithio i Awstralia. Yr oedd ei hen gyfaill Mungo MacCallum (cyd-sefydlydd y Witenagemot a chyd-ddarlithydd yn Aberystwyth) eisoes yn Awstralia er 1879. Fe'i penodwyd yn Athro Saesneg ym Mhrifysgol Sydney yn 1886, ac ef a awgrymodd wrth Fwrdd Estyn y Brifysgol eu bod yn gwahodd Jones i draddodi cyfres o ddarlithoedd cyhoeddus yn Sydney yn ystod ei wyliau haf. Cychwynnodd o Glasgow ym mis Ebrill, a chymerodd seibiant gyda'i fab Harry, a oedd bellach yn was sifil yn Burma, cyn cwblhau'r siwrnai ddechrau Gorffennaf.

Yr oedd y daith yn llwyddiant mawr. Rhoddodd Jones 'berfformiadau' ysbrydoledig i neuaddau gorlawn yn Sydney, Melbourne, Adelaide, Hobart a Brisbane. Yr oedd yn darlithio i gynulleidfa o dros 700 yn Brisbane, a'r cyfarfod dan lywyddiaeth Llywodraethwr Queensland. Ar y cyfan, themâu athronyddol oedd i'r darlithoedd hyn, ond roedd y mynegiant ohonynt ar ffurf eithaf poblogaidd. Cyhoeddwyd y brif gyfres a draddodwyd yn Sydney yn ddiweddarach dan y teitl, *Idealism as a Practical Creed*. Drwy gyfrwng barddoniaeth Wordsworth a Browning, yn ogystal ag athroniaeth Hegel, mae'n trafod esblygiad rhyddid a'r mynegiant diriaethol ohono yn y byd cyfoes. Dyma ei lyfr mwyaf 'poblogaidd', ac y mae'n llwyddo o fewn ei gyfyngiadau i gyfleu gwerthoedd y mudiad Idealaidd. Cafodd gyfle hefyd i annerch ar faterion cyhoeddus, yn arbennig felly, addysg.

Dychwelodd drwy Fiji a Gogledd America, gan fanteisio ar y cyfle i ymweld ag Efrog Newydd, lle'r oedd cyn-fyfyriwr o ddyddiau St Andrews, Norman Kemp Smith, yn Athro Athroniaeth ym Mhrifysgol Princeton. Yno hefyd, cyfarfu â Woodrow Wilson, Llywydd Princeton ar y pryd. Cafodd gyfle i ddychwelyd i'r Unol Daleithiau yn 1912 fel aelod o ddirprwyaeth o academyddion Ewropeaidd ar achlysur sefydlu Prifysgol Texas yn Houston. Yno, cafodd gyfle i ddarlithio ar 'Gerrig Milltir Athronyddol', darlithoedd a gyhoeddwyd yn ddiweddarach gan y Rice Institute. A thrachefn, bu yn yr Unol Daleithiau yn 1918 fel rhan o ddirprwyaeth Brydeinig i geisio sefydlu perthynas agosach rhwng y prifysgolion o boptu Môr Iwerydd. Cyfarfu â Wilson eto, yr Arlywydd Wilson erbyn hynny.

[18] LL, t. 111.

Am y deuddeg mlynedd cyntaf fel Athro, un cynorthwy-ydd yn unig oedd gan Jones i'w helpu i ofalu am adran mor fawr; ond cynyddodd y nifer i ddau ac yna, maes o law, i dri. Rhyddhaodd hyn ef o lafur enfawr asesu gwaith myfyrwyr lluosog y dosbarthiadau cyffredin. Ymhlith y cynorthwywyr yr oedd dau a ddeuai'n athrawon i Gadair Athroniaeth Caerdydd, sef H. J. W. Hetherington (Caerdydd, 1915–20) a'i olynydd J. W. Scott (Caerdydd 1920–44). Gallai Jones yn awr roddi mwy o sylw i faterion dinesig a chyhoeddus. Nid oedd yr Hegeliaid yn fodlon cyfyngu eu gweithgareddau i ddadansoddi cymdeithas yn y ddarlithfa: credent fod ganddynt genhadaeth gymdeithasol ehangach, ac mae'r agwedd hon ar ei yrfa lawn cyn bwysiced â'i waith fel athro. Credai fod angen goleuo dynion busnes, arweinwyr llafur a gwleidyddion lleol a chenedlaethol ynglŷn â natur foesol dinasyddiaeth a'u cyfrifoldebau dinesig. I'r diben hwn aeth ati i sefydlu'r Glasgow Civic Society yn 1897. Yn y gwaith hwn cafodd gefnogaeth yr Athro George Adam Smith a Syr James Bell, Lord Provost y ddinas. Bell oedd y llywydd cyntaf ac ymhlith y swyddogion ac aelodau'r pwyllgor yr oedd cynghorwyr amlwg fel Robert Crawford a Bailie Chisholm, a chyfeillion o'r Brifysgol megis Ker a Bradley. Yr oedd nifer yr aelodau i'w gyfyngu i gant ac o fewn mis yr oedd mwy o geisiadau am aelodaeth nag oedd o leoedd.[19] Yr oedd y rhain yn cynnwys cyfeillion personol Jones o fyd busnes y ddinas ac arweinwyr llafur, ac ef oedd cyd-ysgrifennydd a phrif ysgogydd y gymdeithas o'r cychwyn.

Yn ôl y cyfansoddiad, diben y gymdeithas oedd hyrwyddo gwell dealltwriaeth o faterion cymdeithasol drwy drafodaeth, darlithoedd ac unrhyw ddulliau eraill y cytunai'r Pwyllgor arnynt o bryd i'w gilydd. Mae'n diddorol sylwi bod y cyfansoddiad yn gwahardd cymryd pleidlais ar ddim ond materion gweinyddol. Dyma danlinellu'r ffaith mai fforwm oedd y cyfarfodydd ac nid dadl. Meddai Jones mewn llythyr, wrth sôn am y gymdeithas, "it is a great idea to reflect the unity of our clashing interests". Gallai ymfalchïo, "… if I were to name its members, I could show that to a unique extent they are the leaders of our civic life, and the representatives of its manysided interests."[20]

Cyfarfyddai'r Glasgow Civic Society yn Undeb y Myfyrwyr tua hanner dwsin o weithiau yn ystod dau dymor y sesiwn academaidd. Yn gyffredinol, byddai aelod yn agor y drafodaeth gyda phapur ar ryw bwnc neu'i gilydd, ond weithiau, yn enwedig wrth agor neu gloi gweithgareddau'r flwyddyn gwahoddid darlithydd arbennig. Yn eu plith hwy yr oedd nifer o athronwyr, megis yr Athro Adamson ar 'Athroniaeth a'r Broblem Gymdeithasol' (1898), Bernard Bosanquet ar 'Unigoliaeth, Amgylchiadau a'r Wladwriaeth' (1899), ac Edward Caird, a ddaeth o Balliol i draddodi'r ddarlith yn y cyfarfod a sefydlodd y gymdeithas, ar 'Unigoliaeth a Sosialaeth' (1897). Dengys amrediad y pynciau a ddewiswyd i'w trafod gan yr

[19] TJ/U/2/87.
[20] TJ/U/2/86.

aelodau ehangder eu consýrn cymdeithasol, e.e. 'Cyfrifoldeb Awdurdodau Dinesig wrth Atal Diciâu' (1899), 'Agweddau Cymdeithasol Gwallgofrwydd' (1900), 'Dyfarniadau Gorfodol mewn Anghydfod Diwydiannol' (1898), 'Deddf Iawndal Gweithwyr' (1897), 'Cwestiwn y Tir' (1901), 'Agweddau Cymdeithasol Llafur Merched' (1901), 'Deddfwriaeth i Amddiffyn Plant' (1906), 'Gamblo' (1902), 'Adfer Bywydau Egwan' (1902). Dengys y detholiad hwn hefyd (yn enwedig felly'r pwnc olaf) ddiddordeb mawr yng ngallu a hawl cymdeithas i ymyrryd ym mywyd unigolion er eu lles eu hunain a'r gymuned. Dyma bwnc canolog gwleidyddiaeth ac athroniaeth gymdeithasol yr oes.

Un o'r problemau cymdeithasol y teimlai Jones yn gryf yn ei chylch oedd problem meddwdod. Cafwyd trafodaeth yn y Civic Society ar 'Problem Meddwdod: Ei Hagweddau Cymdeithasol a Deddfwriaethol' (1900). Cafodd Jones flas ar y drafodaeth, mae'n amlwg:

> We had a discussion of the Liquor Question in the Civic Society here, the other day, and a capital discussion it was. The trend of opinion was strongly in the lines you [h.y. Ronald Munro-Ferguson] indicate. And it is evident that the teetotallers are getting gradually persuaded to adopt saner methods and accept less than the whole, which, of course, is utterly impracticable if not also equally undesireable. The Liberal Party is an idiot if it does not take up the question and press hard for legislation.[21]

Yr oedd alcoholiaeth yn broblem gymdeithasol ddifrifol yn Glasgow yn y bedwaredd ganrif ar bymtheg, ond erbyn i Jones ddod yno i fyw yn 1894 yr oedd y sefyllfa wedi gwella. Yn nhridegau'r ganrif honno yr oedd Albanwyr dros bymtheg oed yn yfed ar gyfartaledd tua pheint o wisgi (cyfreithlon) yr wythnos yn ogystal â pheint o gwrw'r wythnos. Ar ben hynny yr oedd peth wmbredd o wirod anghyfreithlon yn cael ei yfed. (Darganfuwyd dros 700 o ddistyllwyr anghyfreithlon rhwng 1833 ac 1835 yn unig.) Yn Glasgow yr oedd tafarn o ryw fath ar gyfer pob 130 o'r trigolion. Pan gofiwn fod llawer o'r gwragedd yn yfed y nesaf peth i ddim, fe sylweddolir faint yr oedd rhai o'r dynion yn llwyddo i'w yfed mewn wythnos. Erbyn blynyddoedd olaf y ganrif, gostyngodd graddfa yfed wisgi i ychydig dros hanner peint y pen ar gyfartaledd mewn wythnos. Yr oedd yfed cwrw yn cynyddu yn ystod yr un cyfnod, ond roedd hwnnw'n rhatach ac yn llai alcoholaidd na wisgi.

Mae peth o'r clod am y gostyngiad mewn yfed yn Glasgow, a'r Alban yn gyffredinol, yn ddyledus i weithgarwch y mudiad dirwest. Yn 1829 sefydlwyd cymdeithas yn Glasgow gan gyhoeddwr efengylaidd o'r enw William Collins i hyrwyddo ymwrthod â gwirodydd (yn yr ystyr gyfyng o 'Spirits' yn hytrach na diod gadarn o bob math), a sefydlwyd cymdeithas debyg yn Greenock gan yr ynad, John

[21] TJ/U/2/93. Gweler ymhellach, T. C. Smout, *A Century of the Scottish People 1830-1950*, Llundain 1986, tt. 132-158.

Dunlop. Erbyn canol y ganrif tyfodd dau fath o raniad yn rhengoedd y dirwestwyr. Yn gyntaf, datblygodd gwahaniaeth barn parthed llwyredd yr ymwrthod â diod gadarn. Bu dirwestwyr Lloegr yn ymgyrchu dros lwyrymwrthod *(teetotalism)* yn hytrach na chymedroldeb (neu ymwrthod rhannol, fel yr argymhellai Collins a Dunlop), a'r farn hon yn y diwedd oedd gryfaf ei dylanwad yn yr Alban hefyd. Yn ail, datblygodd gwahaniaeth barn ynglŷn â chyfrifoldeb y wladwriaeth dros reoli'r fasnach ddiod. Safbwynt y Scottish Temperance League oedd mai'r unig ffordd i ddiwygio cymdeithas yn y cyfeiriad hwn oedd drwy gael trwch y boblogaeth i droi cefn ar ddiod feddwol yn wirfoddol, h.y. fel gweithred foesol. Gwrthwynebwyd y safbwynt hwn gan yr United Kingdom Alliance, a ymgyrchai dros waharddiad cyfreithiol ar y fasnach drwy ddeddf.

Cymedrolwr oedd Jones. Meddai amdano'i hun mewn llythyr at Ferguson unwaith, "I ... who knew and enjoyed your fine wines, my friend, and who have neither a drunken nor a teetotal fibre in my body."[22] Credai hefyd fod dyletswydd ar y wladwriaeth i ddeddfu er mwyn rheoli'r fasnach ddiod, ac yr oedd yn ddiamynedd iawn gyda phetruster y Rhyddfrydwyr i gofleidio safbwynt digymrodedd. Yr oedd T. H. Green (a fu'n Is-lywydd yr United Kingdom Alliance) wedi gosod seiliau athronyddol y Ryddfrydiaeth Newydd a gysonai ymyrraeth gan gymdeithas a'r cysyniad o ryddid yr unigolyn. Mae Jones yn annog Ferguson i ddarllen Green:

> ... By the bye, you might read T. H. Green's minor works. He is first rate; heavy but very strong.[23]

Yn yr un llythyr, mae'n mynegi ei frwdfrydedd dros ddod â'r tafarndai dan reolaeth a pherchenogaeth llywodraeth leol.

> Why can't the public houses be handed over to the local authorities to close, multiply, confine or expand as they darned please? Why shouldn't Edinburgh try one scheme and Glasgow another?

Yr ymgyrchwr amlycaf dros gynllun fel hwn oedd gŵr o'r enw Arthur Sherwell, dirwestwr o Loegr, a gefnogai'r hyn a elwid yn Gothenburg System. Tarddodd y drefn hon yn Sweden, lle meddiannai'r awdurdodau lleol y tai yfed gan ddefnyddio'r holl elw tuag at ddibenion cymdeithasol. Gwnaent ymdrech hefyd i wneud y tafarndai mor blaen a digysur ag y medrent! Bu arbrofi ar y llinellau hyn ym maes glo Fife. Felly, yn Kelty, caed 'Goth No. 1' a 'Goth No. 2', a 'Red Goth' yn Lochore.

Dim ond un ochr i'r geiniog, fel petai, oedd ceisio pylu rhywfaint ar allu'r tafarndai i fod yn ddeniadol. Yr ochr arall oedd ceisio lleddfu anghysur llym cartrefi

[22] TJ/U/3/5.

[23] TJ/U/2/85.

haenau isaf cymdeithas yn Glasgow. Dyma gyfnod gosod seiliau gwasanaeth cymdeithasol, a bu rhai o'r prifysgolion, gan gynnwys Glasgow, yn amlwg yn y gwaith. Yr oedd T. H. Green, yn Rhydychen, wedi llwyddo i ddwysbigo cydwybod rhai o fyfyrwyr y Brifysgol drwy eu gwneud yn ymwybodol o'u breintiau o'u cymharu â thrwch y boblogaeth yn y dinasoedd diwydiannol. Drwy ei esiampl a'i ddysgeidiaeth creodd awydd eirias ym mynwes nifer o wŷr ifanc i weithredu mewn modd ymarferol i rannu peth o'u breintiau hwy gyda'r difreintiedig. Pan awgrymodd y Canon Barnett yn 1883 wrth gynulleidfa yng ngholeg St Ioan, Rhydychen, y dylai myfyrwyr ystyried trigo a gweithio mewn ardaloedd tlawd, disgynnodd yr awgrym ar dir oedd eisoes wedi ei fraenaru. Aed ati ar fyrder i sicrhau eiddo yn Whitechapel, ardal dlotaf yr East End yn Llundain, a threuliodd y myfyrwyr eu noson gyntaf yn yr adeilad nos Nadolig 1884. Rhoddwyd yr enw Toynbee Hall ar y sefydliad, er cof am Arnold Toynbee, hanesydd ifanc a symudasai i Whitechapel i weithio gyda'r Charity Organization Society, ond a fu farw yn 1883. Fel hanesydd dadlennodd gost ddynol llwyddiant a chynnydd y Chwyldro Diwydiannol. Cafodd ei waith a'i esiampl, fel yr eiddo Green, ddylanwad dwfn ar wŷr ifanc Rhydychen. Esgorodd Toynbee Hall ar nifer o sefydliadau cyffelyb a adwaenid fel 'University Settlements'. Erbyn 1911 yr oedd tua 45 'university settlement' wedi eu sefydlu,[24] ac roedd un ohonynt yn Glasgow.

Byrdwn cenadwri Barnett oedd fod angen mwy na bwyd ar y tlodion. Yr oedd arnynt angen gwybodaeth a'r moddion i ddatblygu eu hunain, moddion a syrthiasai i feddiant y goludog. Dylai pethau dyrchafol bywyd fod o fewn cyrraedd pawb yn ddi-wahân, a dyletswydd y lleiafrif breintiedig a gawsai fanteision addysg uwch oedd bod yn lladmeryddion dysg a chelfyddyd mewn cymdeithas yn gyffredinol, i fod yn lefain yn y blawd. Effaith waethaf tlodi oedd gwneud i'r tlodion eu dibrisio eu hunain. Tasg aelodau'r 'settlements' oedd tywys y difreintiedig i ailwerthuso eu hunain, a thrwy ddefnyddio eu hadnoddau ysbrydol eu hunain, i sylweddoli eu posibiliadau. Eithr nid trwy weithredu fel cenhadon y gallai'r dysgedigion lwyddo eu hamcanion. Pwysleisiai Barnett mai drwy gymdeithasu o fewn y gymuned, a thrwy gyfeillgarwch a bontiai agendor dosbarth y cyflenwid dibenion y mudiad. Daeth Toynbee Hall yn ganolfan i waith gwirfoddol amlochrog iawn, gan ddylanwadu ar ddatblygiad gwaith allanol y prifysgolion a'r symudiad i sefydlu Cymdeithas Addysg y Gweithwyr (yn 1903). Ond nid proses unffordd oedd yr addysgu, wrth gwrs. Yr oedd y profiad o fyw ymysg y dosbarth gweithiol yn addysg uniongyrchol iawn i'r academyddion; a bwriadai Barnett iddi fod felly. Yr oedd y 'settlements' i gyfoethogi pawb oedd yn gysylltiedig â hwy, ac yn ddiau llwyddasant i wneud hynny.

[24] Am hanes y mudiad gweler Andrew Vincent & Raymond Plant, *Philosophy Politics and Citizenship,* Rhydychen 1984, t. 132-149.

Mae'n amlwg fod Glasgow yn ddinas â phroblemau cymdeithasol cyn waethed pob gronyn â rhai'r East End yn Llundain. Yr oedd gan Caird gyfle ar garreg ei ddrws i weithredu'r argyhoeddiadau a rannai mor llwyr gyda Green.[25] Felly yn 1886 sefydlwyd The University Settlement Association yn Glasgow. Sicrhawyd tŷ yn Parson Street, ond nid oedd yn addas i fyfyrwyr fyw ynddo. Serch hynny yr oedd yn ganolfan i'w galluogi i wneud gwaith cymdeithasol ymarferol. Erbyn 1892 llwyddwyd i sicrhau safle gwell yn Cathedral Street, a galwyd y sefydliad newydd yn Toynbee Hall. O'r diwedd, dyma gyfle i weithredu'r cynllun yn llawn, ac Edward Caird oedd prif ysgogydd y datblygiad, ef a'i briod gweithgar. Yn ei araith agoriadol ailfynegodd Caird ddibenion y mudiad.[26] Pwysleisiodd resyndod sefyllfa lle'r oedd 'Treftadaeth y ddynoliaeth' yn eiddo i leiafrif bychan, a mynegodd ei farn y dylai'r da eu byd deimlo 'a generous shame' o'r herwydd. Eu dyletswydd hwy oedd pontio'r agendor rhyngddynt a'r tlodion, a hynny drwy gyfathrach gymdeithasol, fel y gallai'r genedl fod yn un corff. Cysylltodd Caird ddelfrydau tri arloeswr gyda'r fenter, sef John Ruskin, Thomas Hill Green ac Arnold Toynbee. Nid Toynbee Hall oedd yr unig 'settlement' yn Glasgow. Yr oedd un arall wedi cael ei sefydlu gan fyfyrwyr a welai'r fath waith fel ymestyniad o'u hargyhoeddiadau Cristnogol. Prif symbylydd y mudiad oedd Henry Drummond, y diwinydd. Ychydig cyn i'r settlement hwnnw agor ei ddrysau, yn 10 Possil Road, dywedodd Drummond amdano, "It will be on earnest evangelical lines, and ought to be a great blessing to the university."[27] Fe'i hagorwyd gan Drummond ar 28 Tachwedd 1889,[28] ac o'r deg ar hugain myfyriwr a weithiai o'r ganolfan, byddai pymtheg yn byw yno. Ymddengys bod ei naws wedi newid rhywfaint erbyn 1894, fodd bynnag, gyda llai o bwyslais ar yr elfen genhadol.[29] Gellid dweud hefyd fod aelodau 'settlement' Possil Road yn iau nag aelodau 'settlement' Parson Street, ac ar y cyfan yn perthyn i haenau is mewn cymdeithas, sef y dosbarth gweithiol a'r dosbarth canol is.[30]

Diau y gwyddai Jones am yr holl ddatblygiadau hyn, ond ni fu ef â rhan yn y gwaith, gan ei fod yn ei ôl yng Nghymru er 1883. Pan ddychwelodd i Glasgow yn 1894 yr oedd y mudiad wedi cael ei gefn ato. Ond ar y dechrau, ymddengys mai digon llugoer oedd ei agwedd at weithgareddau'r 'settlements'. Meddai un o'i fyfyrwyr, gyda golwg ar ei agwedd tuag at sefydliad Possil Road,

> I remember Henry Jones when he came to Glasgow being very critical of what seemed to him a diversion of the students' interests from what he called their proper work of study. He was not long in discovering that the men from the Settlement who took his class were much better students for it and in due course he sent his own son, Arthur, to live there, though his home was in Glasgow.[31]

[25] Henry Jones & John Henry Muirhead, op. cit., t. 114.
[26] ibid., t. 116.
[27] George Adam Smith, *The Life of Henry Drummond,* Llundain 1899, t. 286.
[28] ibid., t. 291.
[29] William Boyd, op. cit., t. 130.
[30] ibid., t. 125.
[31] ibid., t. 130.

Yr argraff a roddai i genedlaethau diweddarach o fyfyrwyr oedd ei fod yn gefnogol iawn i'r 'settlement'. Meddai Hector Hetherington, a ddaeth i Glasgow fel myfyriwr yn 1905,

> Jones was deeply interested in the students' settlement, an institution which, springing from the inspiration of Professor Henry Drummond of the Free Church College, was carried on by a dozen students, residing together in one of the slum areas of Glasgow. Partly *through his influence*, many of his best students lived and worked there, and his youngest son spent in it the greater part of his short university life.[32]
> (Fy italeiddio i)

Deuai Hetherington o gefndir nid annhebyg i Jones. Fferyllydd a phostfeistr pentref Tillicoultry oedd ei dad (a gof ym mhentref Lockerbie oedd ei daid), ac mae'n siŵr fod dod wyneb yn wyneb â bywyd y slymiau yn Glasgow wedi bod yn brofiad ysgytwol iddo. Daeth i'r Brifysgol gyda'r bwriad o'i gyflwyno ei hun i'r weinidogaeth, ond meddai ei gofiannydd:

> It seems probable that it was his experience of Glasgow slum conditions which turned his thoughts away from the church and towards more practical aspects of social and economic planning. Hetherington's experience of slum life came as a result of his participation in the affairs of the University Settlement at Possil Road ... It was an essay in practical social rehabilitation, and though the small scale of enterprise and the poverty of its resources limited its effectivness – there were scoffers who compared it to throwing snowballs into a volcano – nevertheless there can be no doubt that it and its likes provided the seeds from which our modern social welfare state has grown.[33]

Un arall o hoff fyfyrwyr Jones a drigai yn Possil Road ac a fwriadai yn wreiddiol fod yn weinidog oedd Thomas Jones, Cymro o Rhymni, yng Ngwent. Yr oedd ef wedi dod o Goleg Aberystwyth i Glasgow yn fyfyriwr cryn bum mlynedd o flaen Hetherington.

> Round about the time I joined the group there was a turning from the ordinary orthodox outlook to a socialistic view of life combined with the Christian. Philosophy was always a predominant interest, especially in its theological applications, but gradually Economics came to take its place ... The neighbourhood was poor and overcrowded and one would need the hide of a rhinoceros to be indifferent to the misery around us, or to be satisfied with prescribing Moody and Sankey's evangelical salvation as the one and only remedy. I was allotted a 'close' which had forty-four families on six floors on one staircase in forty-four rooms – the famous ticketed houses. We went about, it was said, unpacking our hopes of a blissful future, with a New Testament in one pocket and a Fabian tract in the other, seeking to reconcile the other worldliness of the one and the this – worldliness of the other.[34]

---

[32] LL, t. 88.
[33] Charles Illingworth, *University Statesman,* Glasgow 1971, t. 10.
[34] Thomas Jones, *Welsh Broth,* Llundain 1950, t. 12.

Credai Thomas Jones fod y cyfuniad a gaed yn Possil Road o'r crefyddol a'r 'seciwlar' yn llesol i'r ddwy elfen fel ei gilydd.

> Not the least advantage of residence at the Settlement was the mingling of divinity students with the rest of us and they helped to keep us abreast of the freshest theological thought. It was, for example, well to compare what Henry Jones was preaching at Gilmorehill with what James Denney was teaching at the Free Church College.[35]

Yn ddiau, yr oedd dylanwadau dynol ac ymarferol y 'settlement' lawn cyn bwysiced â dim a ddaeth o'r ddarlithfa i roddi cyfeiriad i yrfa ddisglair Thomas Jones fel Ysgrifennydd Comisiynwyr Yswiriant Cenedlaethol, Dirprwy Ysgrifennydd y Cabinet, ac yn ddiweddarach, prif ysgogydd sefydlu Coleg Harlech.

Elfen ganolog yng ngweithgareddau'r 'settlements' oedd addysg oedolion, a bu Henry Jones yn egnïol iawn yn hyrwyddo'r achos hwnnw. Bu'n cynnal darlithoedd a dosbarthiadau i'r cyhoedd yn Aberystwyth ac mewn sawl lle yng ngogledd Cymru pan oedd ym Mangor. Yn ystod ei gyfnod yn Glasgow, tyfodd y mudiad addysg oedolion yn aruthrol drwy wledydd Prydain yn gyffredinol. Cafodd y mudiad hwn ei gefnogaeth frwdfrydig gydol ei oes. Iddo ef, nid dysgu techneg a medrau newydd yn unig oedd addysg, ond math o 'foddion gras' i oleuo a chyfoethogi pobl fel personau dynol. Ychydig cyn iddo farw, pwysleisiodd mewn llythyr at A. C. Bradley parthed addysg, "I want the human conditions of wellbeing to be in the foreground instead of the economic."[36] At Tom Jones, ysgrifennodd fel hyn yn dilyn cyfarfod o'r Comisiwn ar Addysg Prifysgol yng Nghymru:

> We had the coal-owners yesterday, not on Education, but on the manufacture of raw humanity into money-making machinery. The Philistianism of it all made me sick, and I felt with terrible force the need of educating, not merely the working man, but those who employ and manage him. ... Tom! the unconscious attitude of the mind of these coalowners was appalling. When are we going to teach ethics to the people and slacken the speed of our going towards materialism like unto Germany's. I almost despair.[37]

Dwysaodd y Rhyfel Mawr ei ymwybyddiaeth o'r angen am addysg oedolion. Credai fod goruchafiaeth ideoleg lygredig yn yr Almaen wrth wraidd y rhyfel, a phryderai y gallai pobl Prydain fynd yn ysglyfaeth i'r un perygl. Felly pan ddaeth gwahoddiad gan yr Y.M.C.A. i baratoi llyfr ar egwyddorion dinasyddiaeth yn 1918, yr oedd yn eiddgar i dderbyn. Cwblhaodd *The Principles of Citizenship* mewn wythnosau, a hynny ar amser prysur iawn yn ei fywyd.

Yr oedd eisoes yn aelod o Bwyllgor Addysg Oedolion y 'Ministry of Reconstruction' a sefydlasai Lloyd George yn 1917. Cadeirydd y Pwyllgor oedd

---

[35] ibid., t. 46.

[36] TJ/U/3/173.

[37] TJ/U/1/18. Gweler ymhellach LL, t. 131.

A. L. Smith (Meistr Coleg Balliol), ac yr oedd cewri'r mudiad Addysg Oedolion, pobl fel R. H. Tawney ac Albert Mansbridge (sylfaenydd y W.E.A.), yn aelodau ohono. Yr oedd gan y Pwyllgor 18 o aelodau yn ychwanegol at y Cadeirydd a 2 ysgrifennydd. Cynhwysai adroddiad y pwyllgor atodiad ar Addysg Oedolion yng Nghymru a ysgrifennwyd gan Mrs A. H. Davies, Cymraes ac aelod amlwg o'r Women's Labour League. Cwynodd hi gymaint bod cyn lleied o sylw wedi ei roddi i amgylchiadau unigryw Cymru yn y prif adroddiad, fel y bu'n rhaid i R. H. Tawney blannu cyfeiriadau at Gymru yma ac acw drwy'r adroddiad terfynol a gyflwynwyd i'r senedd yn 1919![38]

Hyd heddiw, fe ystyrir 'Adroddiad 1919' fel prif destament y mudiad addysg oedolion ym Mhrydain. Meddai'r Athro R. D. Waller wrth gyflwyno adargraffiad o ddetholion ohono yn 1956, "This great Report has no parallel ... It is certainly the most notable and useful monument in our adult education literature."[39] Ailgyhoeddwyd yr adroddiad yn ei grynswth mor ddiweddar â 1980.[40] Awgrymir na fu gan Jones ran amlwg yn y gwaith o ddrafftio'r adroddiad terfynol,[41] ond serch hynny mae'n ymgorffori ei brif syniadau. Mae'n gweld addysg oedolion fel proses sydd yn parhau drwy gydol oes yr unigolyn gyda'r bwriad o ehangu ei orwelion a'i gymhwyso i gymryd rhan ym mywyd ei gymuned. Dyna paham y dylai fod o fewn cyrraedd pawb. Anogir y Llywodraeth i ddiwallu'r galw mawr am gyrsiau yn y pynciau 'dyneiddiol' gan y cyhoedd oherwydd fod poblogaeth ddeallus yn fwy tebygol o lwyddo yn y gwaith mawr o ailadeiladu'r economi a gweithredu'r ddelfryd ddemocrataidd. Cydnabyddir yr un pryd fod galw mawr am hyfforddiant 'technegol' i gyrraedd y nod economaidd, ond pwysleisir bod modd cyflwyno hyfforddiant mewn ffordd 'ryddfrydol' a fydd yn cyfoethogi dychymyg a miniogi deall.

Cafodd Jones gyfle i leisio rhai o'r egwyddorion hyn yn ei anerchiad fel Llywydd y Dydd yn Eisteddfod Genedlaethol Corwen, 1919, pan alwodd am ymgyrch genedlaethol yng Nghymru i hyrwyddo addysg oedolion. Gwelai le blaenllaw i'r eglwysi yn yr ymgyrch. Mewn gwlad ddigon prin ei manteision, credai fod gan yr eglwysi adnoddau arbennig at y gwaith, megis adeiladau, trefniadaeth ac adnoddau dynol ardderchog y weinidogaeth. Cafodd ei alwad ymateb brwd, ond heb ei bresenoldeb ef yng Nghymru, ac efallai gydag ofn ambell elfen yn y sefydliad capelyddol o'r seciwlareiddio oedd eisoes ar gerdded, ni chafwyd rhwydwaith ffurfiol o ddosbarthiadau yn seiliedig ar y capeli. Serch hynny, buont yn gefn mawr i fudiadau megis y W.E.A. gan adael i'r dosbarthiadau ddefnyddio festrïoedd ar hyd

[38] John Taylor, 'The Making of the Report', *Studies in Adult Education,* Cyf. 8, Rhif 2, tt. 134-148, ac yn 40 isod.

[39] Cyflwyniad i Max Parrish, *A Design for Democracy,* Llundain 1956.

[40] Harold Wiltshire, John Taylor, Bernard Jennings (Goln), *The 1919 Report,* Nottingham 1980.

[41] ibid., t. 32, a LL, tt. 132-3.

a lled Cymru ar delerau ffafriol iawn, ac ni ellir mesur gwerth gwasanaeth clodwiw llu o weinidogion ac offeiriaid fel tiwtoriaid. Bu araith Henry Jones o leiaf yn fodd i greu amgylchedd ffafriol i addysg oedolion yng Nghymru.

Pennod 7

Y Cymro Alltud

Yn ystod blynyddoedd Glasgow daeth sawl galwad ar Henry Jones i roddi gwasanaeth i Gymru. Weithiau byddai hyn yn wasanaeth y gellid ei gyflawni oddi yno, ond dro arall cawsai wahoddiad i ddychwelyd i Gymru. Yn 1901 bu farw Viriamu Jones, prifathro cyntaf Coleg y Brifysgol, Caerdydd, yn bump a deugain mlwydd oed, a bu sôn am Jones fel olynydd iddo.[1] Nid oedd y swydd yn apelio ato, ac efallai nad oedd Caerdydd wrth ei fodd ychwaith. Mewn llythyr at Syr Henry Hadow parthed prifathrawiaeth y coleg yn 1918 dywedodd, "... Cardiff is not Wales. It is the least lovable, I almost said the one abominably vulgar place in Wales ..."[2]

Derbyniodd wahoddiad i Gaerdydd yn 1905, fodd bynnag, i annerch cymdeithasau'r ddinas ar gwestiwn llosg dyfodol Prifysgol Cymru. Sefydlwyd hi yn 1893, yn fuan wedi i Jones adael Coleg Bangor am St Andrews, felly nid oedd ganddo brofiad uniongyrchol o weithio fel Athro dan y gyfundrefn ffederal. Serch hynny, pan amlygwyd awydd gan rai am ddiwygio'r drefn ar ddiwedd degawd gyntaf ei hanes, mentrodd i'r maes gyda mynegiant cyhoeddus o'i farn ar rai o'r materion hyn.

Mae'n bwysig sylweddoli bod y colegau cyfansoddol cyntaf yn bodoli cyn ffurfio'r brifysgol, ac er diogelu eu dyfodol hwy y sefydlwyd Prifysgol Cymru. Medd ai Syr Emrys Evans yn ei lyfr ar hanes yr hanner canrif cyntaf,

> Certainly the champions of the University idea were less influenced by the desire to create a national institution to satisfy a national sentiment than by their solicitude for the colleges, which they wished to strengthen by breaking down their isolation and giving their teachers the greater scope and opportunity they would obtain when set free from dependence on the University of London.[3]

Efallai y dylai Syr Emrys fod wedi dweud 'most champions', oherwydd yr oedd carfan a welai sefydlu prifysgol yng Nghymru fel cam ar ffordd tuag at ennill i Gymru fywyd cenedlaethol llawnach. Dywedodd y Prifathro T. C. Edwards unwaith, "O gael Prifysgol Genedlaethol, fe dyfwn yn genedl."[4] I'r garfan hon (heb gynnwys Edwards, a fu farw yn 1900), yr oedd methiant cyfansoddiad y brifysgol i sicrhau un arweinydd cenedlaethol wrth y llyw yn ddiffyg. Heb arweinydd pendant ei hun, go brin y gellid disgwyl i'r brifysgol arwain y genedl.

---

[1] LL, t. 99.

[2] TJJ U/3/64.

[3] D. Emrys Evans, *The University of Wales: a Historical Sketch,* Caerdydd 1953, t. 44.

[4] Geraint H. Jenkins, *Prifysgol Cymru: Hanes Darluniadol,* Caerdydd 1993, t. 3.

Er bod ganddi ganghellor parhaol, un brenhinol a seremonïol oedd hwnnw. Yr oedd swydd yr is-ganghellor, sef y gwir bennaeth yn y mwyafrif o brifysgolion, yn swydd a lenwid gan bob un o brifathrawon y colegau cyfansoddol am ddwy flynedd yn eu tro. Gwelai rhai hyn yn wendid sylfaenol yn y drefn ffederal. I raddau cuddiwyd natur wasgarog y swydd gan bresenoldeb dirprwy-ganghellor hŷn. Llanwyd y swydd hon ar y dechrau gan Dr (Syr yn ddiweddarach) Isambard Owen, meddyg o Lundain a ddaeth, drwy'r Cymmrodorion, yn brif awdur cyfansoddiad Prifysgol Cymru. Meddai ar ddoniau trefnu unigryw a gwych, ac er nad oedd yn academydd nac yn derbyn tâl am wneud y swydd, pwysai holl swyddogion eraill y brifysgol yn drwm arno am ei arweiniad. Cymaint oedd galwadau Prifysgol Cymru arno fel y dechreuodd ei waith meddygol yn Llundain ddioddef. Felly, pan gafodd gynnig swydd Prifathro'r Armstrong College of Science yn Newcastle-upon-Tyne, fe'i derbyniodd ar unwaith, ond fe syfrdanwyd rhai o'i gyd-weithwyr ym myd addysg uwch yng Nghymru gan ei benderfyniad. Ychwanegwyd at eu pryder gan ei fwriad i barhau fel dirprwy-ganghellor hŷn Prifysgol Cymru.

Gwelodd y rhai oedd am weld cryfhau peirianwaith canolog a chenedlaethol y brifysgol gyfle, gyda newid amgylchiadau Owen, i gychwyn ymgyrch o blaid creu swydd pennaeth gweithredol i Brifysgol Cymru. Yn naturiol, nid oedd prifathrawon y tri choleg yn awyddus i weld datblygiad fel hyn, ond ni fyddai'n briodol iawn iddynt ymosod yn rhy ffyrnig ar gefnogwyr y syniad, oherwydd hawdd y gellid dehongli hynny fel ymgais i ddal gafael yn eu statws eu hunain o fewn y Brifysgol. Yr oedd Reichel wedi sicrhau bod Jones yn gwybod am yr holl ddatblygiadau, ac yr oedd yn awyddus i'w ddwyn i mewn i'r frwydr. Yr oedd sôn am ei enwebu ar Lys y Brifysgol, ond gwrthododd yntau dderbyn.[5] Poenai'n ddirfawr fod yr Anghydffurfwyr a'r Rhyddfrydwyr i'w gweld yn cefnogi'r syniad o bennaeth gweithredol.[6]

Yn 1905 fe ddaeth i lawr o Glasgow i annerch cyfarfodydd yn Niwbwrch, Bangor, Aberystwyth a Chaerdydd. 'The University of Wales: The Line of its Growth' oedd teitl yr araith a draddodwyd yng Nghaerdydd, ac fe'i hargraffwyd. Y mae'r prif bwyntiau yn syml iawn. Yn gyntaf, y mae Prifysgol Cymru yn sefydliad sydd yn gyfrifol am ddysgu ac ymchwil yn ogystal ag arholi ymgeiswyr am ei graddau. Yn y colegau cyfansoddol y bydd y dysgu a'r ymchwil yn cael ei wneud, ac mae'n gwbl angenrheidiol felly fod athrawon y colegau yn gwbl rydd i ddilyn eu trywydd academaidd eu hunain heb ymyrraeth o'r tu allan i'w coleg. Yn ail, ni ellid rhoi digon o gyfrifoldebau i 'bennaeth gweithredol' y brifysgol i gyfiawnhau ei swydd heb ddwyn peth o gyfrifoldebau swyddogion eraill oddi arnynt, yn enwedig athrawon a phrifathrawon y colegau. Yn drydydd, fel y bydd y colegau yn cynyddu a chryfhau, bydd tuedd anochel iddynt geisio statws prifysgolion annibynnol. Ni ddylid llesteirio'r datblygiad hwn.

[5] TJ/U/2/138.
[6] TJ/U/2/133.

Mae Jones yn cydnabod y ddadl genedlaethol hefyd, neu'r "cry for 'Cymru'n Un" fel y geilw ef hi. Ei ateb yw gofyn a fyddai unrhyw un yn honni y byddai undod yr Alban yn ddyfnach pe unid ei phrifysgolion hi dan un pennaeth? Go brin! Ni welai fod sefyllfa Cymru'n wahanol.

Ni chyfyngodd ei sylwadau i sylwedd y ddadl, ond ymosododd gyda dirmyg ar gefnogwyr y syniad yn ogystal:

> But the truth is that the conception of a 'working head' will not bear close analysis or practical investigation; and it seems to me that something like German barm has been 'working' in the 'heads' of those who projected it. The proposal is ill-considered, it is unnecessary and wasteful, and it is mischievous.[7]

Drwy ei ymosodiad *ad hominem* fe roddodd Jones gyfle i wrthwynebydd a fedrai ddefnyddio'r dull hwn o ddadlau gydag effeithiolrwydd ysol ymosod arno yntau. Y gwrthwynebydd miniog hwn oedd Syr T. Marchant Williams, Warden Urdd y Graddedigion, a phrif ysgogydd yr alwad am ddiwygio'r cyfansoddiad. Dywed Geraint Jenkins amdano ei fod "ymhlith aelodau mwyaf lliwgar, cecrus ac eofn Llys y Brifysgol ... ac roedd ganddo ddawn ddigymar i wneud gelynion."[8] Ef oedd sylfaenydd a golygydd cylchgrawn *The Nationalist*, ac yr oedd yn Ynad Cyflogedig Merthyr Tudful. Fis ar ôl i Jones annerch gwyrda Caerdydd, daeth cyfle Williams i annerch Cymmrodorion y ddinas ar 'The University of Wales: Its Past, its Present, and its Future'. Argraffodd yntau ei anerchiad hefyd, ac ynddi mae'n sychu'r llawr gyda Jones![9]

Ymosodiadau *ad hominem* diflewyn-ar-dafod yw deuparth pamffled Williams – a dyna sy'n ei wneud yn un difyr iawn i'w ddarllen! Wrth gyfeirio at "my impulsive and rhetorical friend Professor Henry Jones", dywed nad oes neb academaidd wedi mentro i'r maes eto gyda chyn lleied o gymwysterau i amddiffyn y *status quo* ag ef. Nid oedd ganddo unrhyw brofiad o weithio dan y drefn ffederal, ac (fel y gallodd Williams ddangos) nid oedd ei afael ar y ffeithiau yn sicr bob amser. Wrth gwrs, beio'r sawl a baratôdd y *brief* a wna'r ynad – "his four friends (or shall I call them his employers?)" – sef Isambard Owen a'r tri phrifathro. I Marchant Williams, deiliaid swyddi breision y colegau oedd y tu ôl i'r gwrthwynebiad i sefydlu pennaeth gweithredol i'r brifysgol, ac amddiffyn eu breintiau hwy oedd swyddogaeth "the moral philosopher from the banks of the Clyde". Dyfynna Williams o'i anerchiad:

> I once more give you his words:
>
> The gown of the professor is as pure as the ermine of the judge. His dignity and authority and good name is (sic) a public asset, which vulgarity, whatsoever its source, must not be allowed to touch or tarnish.'

[7] Henry Jones, *The University of Wales: The Lines of its Growth,* Bangor 1905, t. 21.

[8] Geraint H. Jenkins, op. cit., t. 2[illegible].

[9] T. Marchant Williams, *The University of Wales: Its Past, its Present and its Future,* Caerdydd 1905.

> Here we have sounded the keynote to the tune invariably chanted by some of the professors and the academic officers of our University whenever they are brought in contact with the lay members of its Court and Committees. A more perfect example of academic snobbishness has rarely, if ever, come under my notice. And coming too from Henry Jones of Llangernyw of all persons in the world![10]

Clwyfa Jones ychydig ymhellach pan ddywed, "Whatever one may say of Professor Henry Jones, nobody can deny that he is loyal and true to his class", h.y. yr 'hierarchy' academaidd.

Dim ond ar ddiwedd ei araith ysgubol y mae Williams yn trafod natur y swydd newydd yr hoffai ei sefydlu. Byddai wedi gwneud mwy o les i'w achos drwy fod yn llai deifiol yn ei sylwadau personol, megis datgelu diddordeb Reichel mewn ymgeisio am swydd pennaeth gweithredol Prifysgol (ffederal) Llundain, ond ar yr un pryd yn gwrthwynebu sefydlu swydd o'r fath ym Mhrifysgol Cymru, a chanolbwyntio ar y manteision a welai'n deillio o greu'r swydd. Does dim ffordd sicrach o golli'r dydd na bychanu gwrthwynebwyr pwysigfawr.

Barn Jones am Marchant Williams oedd "... a man whose spite is very enduring and who is not held in by any code of honour known to me ..."[11] "... a resolute and vindictive creature ..."[12] Mae'n anffodus iawn fod safon y ddadl wedi gostwng mor isel, oherwydd gyda phleidwyr mwy cymedrol fe ellid bod wedi cyfuno egwyddorion hanfodol y ddwy ochr mewn un cynllun. Yr oedd y ddwy blaid yn awyddus i ddylanwadu ar bwyllgor Syr Thomas Raleigh a oedd yn cynnal ymchwiliad i anghenion addysg uwch yng Nghymru ar gyfer y llywodraeth. Darganfu Jones gyda braw fod Lloyd George wedi cael ei ddylanwadu gan syniadau Marchant, a gwnaeth yn siŵr ei fod yn ei ddarbwyllo.[13] Yn y diwedd, ar ôl ystyried troi'r colegau yn brifysgolion llawn ar y naill law a chanoli mwy ar y drefn ffederal ar y llall, penderfynodd pwyllgor Raleigh argymell cadw'r drefn fel ag yr oedd. Mae'n ddiddorol nodi mai un o bleidwyr cadw'r brifysgol yn un ffederal, a hynny i raddau ar dir y ddadl genedlaethol, oedd hen athro Groeg Jones ym Mhrifysgol Glasgow, Syr Richard Jebb.

Ailwyntyllwyd llawer o'r dadleuon drachefn yn 1916 pan sefydlwyd Comisiwn Brenhinol ar Addysg Uwch yng Nghymru dan gadeiryddiaeth Arglwydd Haldane, Hegelydd brwd a ddiarddelwyd o'r cabinet yn 1915 oherwydd cydymdeimlad honedig â'r Almaen! Yr oedd Jones yn aelod o'r comisiwn, a bu'r un mor wrthwynebus ag erioed i unrhyw symudiad tuag at ganoli awdurdod yn y brifysgol neu unrhyw ymgais i roddi cyfeiriad mwy cenedlaethol i'w gweithgareddau. Ysgrifennodd at Reichel yn 1917 i dawelu ei ofnau ynglŷn â'r posibilrwydd y ceid argymhelliad bod y Gymraeg o hyn allan yn ofynnol mewn rhyw fodd.

[10] ibid., t. 15.
[11] TJ/U/2/144.
[12] TJ/U/2/145.
[13] TJ/U/2/142.

> I should say (in your ear) that there is not the remotest chance that Welsh will be made compulsory in the way you mention. A bow and arrow is more than enough to keep the battlements secure at that point. I would not have the matter disturb your thoughts for a single moment. Let them blether! There is a curious tendency to distrust and run down the 'academical element' in some of the witnesses. I gave some of them something to think over on Thursday and Friday simply by pressing them for the grounds on which they based their opinions as to the standard of teaching in the Welsh colleges, the absence of the 'national spirit' (bless the mark) amongst the College staffs and all that rot.[14]

Fel mae'n digwydd, Reichel oedd un o'r ddau a bwysodd am sefydlu Bwrdd Gwybodau Celtaidd ym Mhrifysgol Cymru. Deillia'r Bwrdd a Gwasg y Brifysgol o argymhellion niferus y comisiwn doeth hwn.

Yr oedd ei gyfeillgarwch gyda Lloyd George yn sicrhau bod Jones yn cael ei ddewis i eistedd ar bwyllgorau cyhoeddus pwysig – yn enwedig rhai Cymreig. Felly yn 1906, cafodd ei ddewis yn aelod o'r Comisiwn Brenhinol ar Waddoliadau'r Eglwys ac Adnoddau'r Enwadau yng Nghymru. Mewn gwirionedd, darganfod mwy am gyflwr yr holl enwadau cyn mentro ar lwybr Dadgysylltiad Eglwys Loegr yng Nghymru oedd pwrpas y Comisiwn a eisteddai dan gadeiryddiaeth y Barnwr Vaughan Williams. Ymddiswyddodd Jones cyn i waith y Comisiwn gael ei gwblhau, fodd bynnag, gan honni bod atgasedd cynrychiolwyr y gwahanol enwadau tuag at ei gilydd yn drech nag ef. "Such an atmosphere of distrust, suspicion, and pious malice I never breathed before or since," meddai tua phymtheng mlynedd yn ddiweddarach.[15] Mae'n anodd credu bod Henry Jones, o bawb, yn methu dygymod ag awyrgylch cecrus! Yr oedd pawb yn cytuno mai profiad blin iawn oedd eistedd ar y Comisiwn hwn, a bod y rhan fwyaf o'r bai am hynny i'w briodoli i'r Cadeirydd.[16] Eithr nid oedd Jones yn ddifai yn y mater, yn ôl un dystiolaeth o leiaf.

> I may here relate a little incident that may show that Henry Jones (as he then was) was not altogether free from responsibility for the extra-ordinary feeling that disgraced that Commission. I was on my way to the Commission room on my first and only visit there when I encountered Mr D. A. Thomas (afterwards Lord Rhondda), who was returning from his first visit there. He had seen Henry Jones for the first time, and had witnessed one of those frequent 'scenes' that characterised the Commission, the actors in that particular 'scene' being the chairman and Henry Jones. 'What a peppery chap he is!' he said to me of the latter when describing with some gusto the 'scene'. Nonconformist though he was, Mr Thomas's sympathies were manifestly with Lord Justice Vaughan Williams …[17]

---

[14] TJ/U/3/50. Cymh. rhybudd Jones i Hadow (aelod arall), "You will find a strong attempt to bring the University under National control and therefore Philistinised." TJ/U/3/64 Am waith y comisiwn gweler Geraint H. Jenkins, op. cit., tt. 83-90; D. Emrys Evans, op. cit., tt. 68-82. LL, tt. 127-132.

[15] LL t. 95.

[16] Archbishop of Wales (sef A. G. Edwards), *Memories,* Llundain 1927, tt. 233-4.

[17] The Vicar of Aberpergwm (sef Joseph Llewelin Thomas), *Western Mail,* 6.11.1924.

Dywedodd Jones o'r cychwyn nad oedd y gwaith hwn at ei ddant; "… om llwyr anfodd y gosodwyd fi ar y Commission …"[18] Serch hynny, nid mewn ysbryd diduedd a chymodlon yr aeth o gwmpas ei waith. Mae'n amlwg oddi wrth ei lythyrau at John Morris-Jones fod ei agwedd at Eglwys Loegr yn anghyfeillgar.

> A phwy ddwed ac a brawf mai estrones ydyw'r Eglwys heddiw? A phwy ddengys pa elfen yn y wlad sy'n caru ac yn cadw i fyny lenyddiaeth Gymraeg heddyw? Pwy gar ddysg? Plant pwy sydd yn mynychu'r Colegau Cymreig? Pwy aberthodd fwyaf i'w sefydlu a'u cynnal?[19]

Mae'n awyddus hefyd i ddefnyddio tactegau a fydd yn ffafrio tystion Ymneilltuol. Yr oedd yn awyddus i alw John Morris-Jones, a gwneud hynny mewn modd na fyddai'n adlewyrchu'n rhy bleidiol ar Goleg Bangor.

> … mi fynna i gael lle i chwi ateb y gelyn … Ond dweud y gwir ofn *farce* sydd gen i, … Cadwch ein gohebiaeth yn gyfrin John.[20]

> Nid oes neb yng Nghymru all roddi y dystiolaeth a allwch chwi. Ond mi ragwelais i'r anhawsder. Dywedwch wrth W. L. Jones am fod yn barod. Ni raid iddo ef na chwithau ddod os na chewch chwi *orchymyn* i ddyfod. A bydd *gorchymyn* yn fwy na digon o fantell. Wnawn ni ddim gadael i neb o'r gelyn fygu ein tystion goreu; ac nid oes berygl am y Coleg. Pe buasai mi gawsoch lonydd gin i.
>
> Fy mwriad ydyw gofyn i'r Commissiwn *wysio* amryw: Anwyl, er enghraifft, ac O.M.E., a'i frawd Ed. Edwards, & Registrar Aberystwyth – Mi dendia i, John, am fod yn ochelgar, a'r gochelgarwch goreu ydyw *gwysio* o *amryw golegau*. Ond peidiwch dweyd dim am hyn wrth neb ond W. L. Jones, rhag ofn i'r gelyn chwythu yng nghlust yr hen Gadeirydd. A rhoddwch W.L.J. ar ei lw i dewi.[21]

> Er mwyn gochel drwg, bwriedaf fi gael Llanbedr i fewn yn *gyntaf* … Sicrhewch y brodyr fy mod i am gael eu help, ac, yn ail, nad wyf fi mor ddall ag i dynnu tân ar y Coleg a garaf oreu yng Nghymru …[22]

Eithr ni pharhaodd Jones hyd rownd derfynol y sgarmes hon!

Yn 1906 cafodd gyfle i gynnig gwasanaeth addysgol i Gymru. Yr oedd ym mwriad y llywodraeth Ryddfrydol i sefydlu Cyngor Addysg i Gymru, a thrwy ddylanwad Lloyd George (Llywydd y Bwrdd Masnach), cafwyd darpariaeth i'r perwyl hwnnw ym Mesur Addysg Birrell. Ond trechwyd y Mesur yn Nhŷ'r Arglwyddi. Felly, fe aeth Lloyd George a Birrell ati i greu Adran Addysg Gymreig a fyddai'n gweithredu o fewn y weinyddiaeth Seisnig, ond gyda chyfrifoldeb ac awdurdod arbennig dros addysg yng Nghymru.

[18] JMJ.84.
[19] ibid.
[20] JMJ.85.
[21] JMJ.86.
[22] JMJ.87.

Tra oedd y cynllun yn dal yn gyfrinachol iawn, yr oedd George a Birrell wedi dechrau ymgynghori â Jones gyda golwg ar ei benodi ef yn Ysgrifennydd Parhaol i'r Adran arfaethedig. Gwelai yntau fod y swydd yn un a allai fod yn ddylanwadol iawn. Mewn gwirionedd dyma'r mesur cyntaf o wrthganoli i Gymru, a sylweddolai gymaint y gellid ei gyflawni mewn swydd mor allweddol. Yr oedd yn llawn edmygedd o George am yr hyn a geisiai ei wneud. "Y *mae* Lloyd George yn un garw – yn cipio mesur o annibyniaeth addysgol i Gymru o ganol *wreck* Bill Burrell," meddai mewn llythyr at John Morris-Jones i geisio cyngor ganddo (yn gyfrinachol).[23] Derbyniai ddilysrwydd dadl Birrell y byddai cael Cymro i weithredu Deddf Addysg amhoblogaidd Balfour, ac yn enwedig felly, Cymro Cymraeg yn esmwytháu doluriau Cymreig. Ei brif ddiddordeb, fodd bynnag, oedd cael y cyfle i 'gwblhau' perthynas yr ysgolion canolraddol â'r colegau, a'r cyfle i sefydlu perthynas rhwng y colegau a fyddai'n diogelu eu rhyddid (sef eu diogelu rhag unrhyw ddatblygiad ar linellau cynllun Marchant).

Amheuai ai ef oedd y person gorau i gyflawni'r swydd, fodd bynnag. Nid oedd erioed wedi bod yng ngofal swyddfa, yr oedd y gwaith yn gwbl ddiethr iddo, ac yn yr Alban yr oedd yn hapus iawn ac yn llwyddo yn ei waith. Yn y diwedd fe roes gynnig ger bron George, Morant a Birrell: fel arbrawf, byddai'n cymryd y swydd yn ystod ei wyliau, sef o ddiwedd Mawrth tan ddechrau Hydref. Ar ben y cyfnod hwnnw, gallai'r ddwy ochr ddod i benderfyniad mwy parhaol. Er ei syndod, ni wrthodwyd yr awgrym yn syth. Mae'n amlwg fod Jones yn cael ei dynnu ddwy ffordd; meddai wrth ei gyfaill,

> A pe bawn i'n anfon telegram y cymerwn' i job, cawn delegram yn ôl ei bod hi i mi. Y mae fy ysbryd 'n ddigon tawel wedi dod yn ôl fel hyn: ond fedra i yn fy myw beidio â troi a throsi pethau. Be feddylech chwi, John bach? Fuasem ni yn medru gwneyd rhywbeth o honni hi, deydwch?[24]

Beth bynnag oedd cyngor John Morris-Jones, yr oedd arwyddion digon cadarnhaol yn cyrraedd Glasgow. Mor ddiweddar â 10fed Ionawr 1907 yr oedd Jones yn anfon drachefn at Morris-Jones i ddweud ei fod wedi derbyn gan Birrell "Llythyr caredig dros ben ag sydd yn cymryd yn ganiataol debygaf i, eu bod yn derbyn fy nhelerau."[25] Eithr, rhyw fath o lythyr ymadawol oedd hwnnw, gan fod Birrell yn cael ei symud i swydd Prif Ysgrifennydd Iwerddon. Yn y cyfamser derbyniasai air gan Reichel (a wyddai, mae'n amlwg, am y datblygiadau gweinyddol arfaethedig) yn cydnabod y byddai'n debyg o fod dan ystyriaeth, ond yn syrthio'n fyr o'i annog i dderbyn y cynnig pe deuai.

[23] JMJ.88.
[24] ibid.
[25] JMJ.89.

> Mi gefais lythyr oddiwrth Reichel yn dweyd 'fe allai fy mod wedi cael cynnyg y swydd, ac y gallwn ei gwneyd *'ar y cyfan'* (in many *respects*) fel ag i fod o wasanaeth mawr i Gymru: (gŵr gofalus ydyw ef) ac yna yn gwasgu adref rinweddau Bruce.[26]

Dwysaodd penbleth Jones gan ddatblygiad arall yn Glasgow. Bu farw'r Prifathro Storey, ac roedd ei statws gyfryw fel bod sôn amdano fel pennaeth posibl Prifysgol Glasgow. Felly, ymhen naw niwrnod mae'n anfon llythyr pellach at Morris-Jones i egluro ei amgylchiadau newydd.

> Credaf y cymer pethau wythnos neu bythefnos eto cyn *setlo*. Yna setler hwy yn *derfynol* y naill ffordd neu'r llall. Y mae'r Ysgotiaid yma yn ymladd fel *teigrod* i'm gwneyd yn Ben y Coleg yma: a dyna'r gwaith y credaf y gallwn ei wneyd oreu. Cymeraf ef, os caf ef. Os na chaf ef, ac os bydd telerau y *Secretaryship* yn foddhaol deuaf oddi yma i Gymru ...[27]

Anodd yw osgoi dod i'r casgliad fod y posibilrwydd o Brifathrawiaeth Glasgow wedi gwthio'r swydd Gymreig yn llwyr o'i feddwl. Yn wir, dau ddiwrnod ar ôl ysgrifennu'r uchod, yr oedd yn ysgrifennu at ei gyn-ddisgybl, Tom Jones, i'w hysbysu ei fod am osod ei enw ef gerbron ar gyfer swydd Ysgrifennydd Parhaol yr Adran Addysg Gymreig.[28] Ni ddatgelodd hynny wrth Morris-Jones, ond cyfaddefodd rhyw wythnos yn ddiweddarach,

> ... yr wyf fi wedi rhyw ddiflasu ar y swydd Gymreig. 'Chawn i mo'm dwylo'n rhydd, John. Mi fyddai rhyw bolitician neu gilydd uwch fy mhen yn penderfynnu prif linellau'r policy. Daeth hyn i'r golwg pan roeddwn yn Llundain yr wythnos diwethaf; ac mae gin i ofn y tresi, a minnau wedi bod yn byw cyhyd ar awelon yr anialdir fel asyn gwyllt! Addewais edrych i mewn i'r Swydd Gymreig os na enwir fi i swydd arall, a *gwnaf* hynny. Ond y mae *set of my disposition* yn mynd (?) yn erbyn symud.[29]

Yn y diwedd, cyfreithiwr o Sir Fflint, A. T. Davies, a gafodd y swydd pan sefydlwyd yr Adran yn Chwefror 1907, ac O. M. Edwards, a benodwyd yn Brif Arolygydd.

Yr oedd yr hawl i benodi Prifathro Glasgow ym meddiant y Goron, ond yn ymarferol gwneid y penodiad gan Ysgrifennydd Gwladol yr Alban. Credai Jones fod ganddo siawns dda am y swydd.

> Y students ar y naill law, a'r businessmen a phobl y dref ar y llaw arall ydyw fy ffrindiau goreu: a'm gwrthwynebwyr ydyw (1) y *Snobs*, wrth gwrs, sydd yn credu na fedr Mrs Jones a minnau ... (?) cadw y 'Social position' i fyny ac (2) pleidwyr gweinidog *U.F.* sectoraidd sydd eisieu rhoi slap i'r Eglwys Wladol yma.[30]

---

26 ibid.
27 JMJ.90.
28 TJ/U/1/1.
29 JMJ.91.
30 JMJ.90.

Erbyn 30 Ionawr 1907 yr oedd yn ffyddiog mai ef a benodid, serch ei fod yn gofidio mai ar air un dyn y gwneid y penodiad.

> Yn ôl yr arwyddion presennol anhawdd peidio rhyw ddisgwyl y bydd Ysgrifenydd y Sgotiaid yn anfon fy enw i i'r brenin rai o'r dyddiau nesaf yma. Ond, wrth gwrs, nis gellir bod yn sicr o gwbl. Dibynna y peth ar ewyllys benrydd un dyn. Pe buasai pwyllgor yn apwyntio, pwyllgor cyffredin, byddai fy etholiad yn bur sicr. Ond y mae y swydd ar drugaredd mympwy.[31]

Ond er bod ganddo gyfeillion yn y Cabinet, gormod oedd disgwyl i Gymro gael blaenoriaeth dros Albanwyr i swydd mor amlwg ym mywyd cenedlaethol y wlad.[32] Syr Donald Macalister a enwyd yn olynydd i Storey, ac fel yn achos methiant ei gais am Brifathrawiaeth Bangor, ni chwerwodd Jones. Ei farn yn 1920 oedd, "I am glad I have been always a teacher, and on the two occasions when I would have accepted a Principalship I was not chosen."[33]

O ystyried ei fod wedi bod mor amlwg fel lladmerydd egwyddorion dinasyddiaeth ar hyd ei yrfa, nid yw'n syndod iddo ystyried gwneud cyfraniad i fywyd gwleidyddol Cymru fel Aelod Seneddol. Gwelai rhai yng Nghymru ddeurydd ymgeisydd seneddol cryf iawn ynddo ar gyfer sedd newydd Prifysgol Cymru. Enillodd Prifysgol Cymru'r hawl i anfon ei Haelod Seneddol ei hun i Dŷ'r Cyffredin yn 1917 megis y gwnâi prifysgolion eraill, a dechreuodd Thomas Jones wneud ymholiadau i weld faint o gefnogaeth fyddai i'w hen athro fel ymgeisydd. Yr oedd Henry Jones yn ffigwr mawr ei barch yng Nghymru, yn ysgolhaig enwog ac yn Rhyddfrydwr a oedd wedi ymgyrchu gymaint â neb i hyrwyddo addysg o bob math. Ar lawer cyfrif, byddai'n gwneud ymgeisydd delfrydol i sedd brifysgol.

Cysylltodd Tom Jones ag un o weinyddwyr addysg amlycaf gogledd Cymru, J. C. Davies (Cyfarwyddwr Addysg Sir Ddinbych) yn Chwefror 1918 i weld beth fyddai ei adwaith.[34] Rhyddfrydwr oedd Davies,[35] a byrdwn neges Tom Jones wrtho oedd fod Henry Jones yn Rhyddfrydwr y byddai darpar ymgeisydd (sosialaidd) fel Silyn Roberts yn fodlon sefyll o'r neilltu i sicrhau etholiad diwrthwynebiad iddo. Atebodd Davies ar fyrder yn llawn brwdfrydedd dros ei ymgeisyddiaeth.

Nid oedd Jones am dderbyn awgrym ei hen ddisgybl fodd bynnag, ac awgrymodd y byddai Herbert Lewis yn gwneud ymgeisydd rhagorol. Yn anffodus, cafodd y wasg yng Nghymru afael ar enw Jones fel ymgeisydd posibl. Efallai fod ei gefnogwyr yn credu y byddai'n anos iddo wrthod cymryd ei enwebu pe bai'r galw arno i sefyll yn dod yn hysbys, ond ei ymateb cyntaf oedd anfon at Tom Jones

---

31 JML.91.

32 Fe lwyddodd un Cymro lle methodd Henry Jones, Syr Alwyn Williams (Prifathro Prifysgol Glasgow 1976-88).

33 TJ/J/2/125.

34 TJ/J/1/34. Gweler hefyd David Thomas, *Silyn,* Lerpwl 1956, tt. 125-6.

35 Gwasanaethodd fel A.S. Dinbych, 1922-3. Gweler Geraint Morgan yn *Trafodion Cymdeithas Hanes Sir Ddinbych*, Cyf. 20, tt. 230 a 234-5. Bu'n ymgeisydd Rhyddfrydol aflwyddiannus yn erbyn Syr Henry Morris-Jones yn Ninbych yn 1935. Gweler Henry Morris-Jones, *Doctor in the Whips' Room,* Llundain 1955, t. 100.

ddiwedd Mawrth 1918 i ofyn iddo wneud datganiad yn gwadu ei fod am ganiatáu i'w enw fynd ymlaen.[36] Ond, bedwar diwrnod yn ddiweddarach, anfonodd at Tom Jones drachefn i ddweud y byddai'n sefyll pe bai Llys y Brifysgol yn dymuno iddo wneud.[37]

Yr un diwrnod, anfonodd lythyr diddorol a phwysig at Sidney Webb mewn ymateb i wahoddiad a estynnodd iddo i ymuno â'r Blaid Lafur. Mae'r llythyr yn ddogfen ideolegol ddiddorol, ond mae'n dangos hefyd ei gyflwr meddwl parthed yr ymgeisyddiaeth yng ngwanwyn 1918.

> And now, as to my canditature. I am *not* a candidate as yet. It is very doubtful if I shall be a candidate. Were it not for the urgency of friends in Wales, and especially amongst them, one whom both of us know, namely Mr Thomas Jones, I should have written to the press to correct its erroneous statements. They want me to wait, and I for my part want them to look round to find some other instrument of their purposes, for I have no least (?) personal desire to go into Parliament.[38]

A beth oedd y 'purposes' y gobeithid y byddai Jones yn gyfrwng i'w sylweddoli fel Aelod Seneddol?

> Their main purposes, which they think I ought to try to help, is precisely that of breaking down the isolation of the Universities and making them feel their responsibility and take it upon their shoulders, of throwing themselves open to the working classes. Adult education, especially in the humanities, should be as universal and continuous as that of the care of bodily health. Not two years ago I was *alone* with Mr Thomas Jones, in advocating measures in Wales that would help to this end: I refer to a penny rate for the maintenance of its university; which would bring it sufficient means both to abolish fees and to establish in *every* centre of population, *always*, classes such as those of the WEA ... But the whole thing may end on paper. And it is because that I could help to prevent this catastrophe that they desire, (and I am tempted to yield to their desire if circumstances permit) that I should accept nomination as candidate for representing the Welsh University in Parliament.[39]

Pe safai dan yr amgylchiadau hyn, meddai, ni allai ddweud a fyddai'r Blaid Lafur yn dymuno ei wrthwynebu. Ar un wedd (a dim ond un), byddai'n croesawu gwrthwynebydd Llafur er mwyn cael cyfle i danlinellu ei farn ar y cyfeiriad y dylai Llafur ei ddilyn.

Yr oedd J. C. Davies yn siomedig iawn fod Jones yn anfodlon sefyll[40] ac yn awyddus i gychwyn deiseb i apelio arno i newid ei feddwl.[41] Cafodd gais ym mis Mai gan undeb athrawon yr AMA i sefyll,[42] ac ymhen pythefnos anfonodd Rhys

[36] TJ/U/1/43.
[37] TJ/U/1/44.
[38] TJ/U/1/45.
[39] ibid.
[40] TJ/U/1/47.
[41] TJ/U/1/65.
[42] TJ/U/1/62.

Morgan o Bontypridd ato i ddweud bod athrawon Morgannwg yn awyddus i gefnogi ei ymgeisyddiaeth.[43] Ond, aflwyddiannus oedd yr ymdrechion hyn, a Herbert Lewis a etholwyd i'r Senedd fel yr Aelod cyntaf dros Brifysgol Cymru. Mae'n amlwg fod y syniad o roddi gwasanaeth cyhoeddus i Gymru yn apelio at elfen ym mhersonoliaeth Jones, ond deuai'n ôl o hyd at yr argyhoeddiad mai fel athro yn Glasgow y gallai roddi o'i orau mewn gwasanaeth.

Dechreuodd Jones ar ei yrfa fel myfyriwr yn Glasgow gyda'r bwriad o wasanaethu'r Methodistiaid Calfinaidd yng Nghymru. Pan adawodd Gymru am St Andrews yn 1891, yr oedd ef a'i syniadau yn cael eu fflangellu ar dudalennau papur wythnosol yr enwad. Ond, dros y ddau ddegawd y bu allan o Gymru bu cryn newid yn ei hinsawdd ddiwinyddol.[44] Gellir priodoli hyn i raddau i'r ffaith fod athroniaeth wedi dod yn elfen amlycach yn y drafodaeth ddeallus ar grefydd, a'r safbwynt athronyddol mwyaf dylanwadol yn y cyfnod hwnnw oedd Hegeliaeth. Lladmerydd mwyaf effeithiol yr agwedd hon ar ddiwinyddiaeth oedd David Adams, ac er bod digon yn gwrthwynebu'r tueddiadau newydd, o'u gwyntyllu collasant eu hamharchusrwydd. Hefyd, yr oedd cyfartaledd uchel o weinidogion Ymneilltuol Cymru yn ddynion llengar, a daethant yn gyfarwydd â syniadau a ddeilliai yn uniongyrchol neu'n anuniongyrchol o Idealaeth yr Almaen, syniadau y gallai Methodistiaid (ac eraill) eu traethu a'u clywed yn haws yn eu cerddi nag yn eu pregethau.

Erbyn diwedd ei yrfa yr oedd yn ŵr y gallai'r enwad ymfalchïo'n agored ynddo, nid yn gymaint oherwydd ei fod yn un o arloeswyr rhyddfrydiaeth grefyddol, ond oherwydd ei amlygrwydd yn fel un o ddoethion yr Ymerodraeth Brydeinig a gynigiai arweiniad moesol iddi ar awr ei hargyfwng mawr. O blith yr holl anrhydeddau a ddaeth i'w ran, mae'n sicr mai un o'r rhai a werthfawrogodd fwyaf oedd y gwahoddiad i fod yn siaradwr gwadd yn un o gyfarfodydd Cymanfa Gyffredinol y Methodistiaid Calfinaidd yn Llundain ym Mehefin 1915. Wrth estyn gwahoddiad iddo ddod i Gymanfa Gyffredinol Llundain dywedodd yr ysgrifennydd lleol, Y Parch J. Thickens:

> Nid ydym yn cofio i chwi gymeryd rhan bwysig yng nghyfarfodydd y Corph ynglŷn ag unrhyw Gymdeithasfa neu Gymanfa, a chredwn fod gennych genadwri a gwelediad sydd yn apelio at amryw ohonom yn Llundain …[45]

Wedi'r holl ffraeo a'r siomedigaethau o'r ddwy ochr, yr oedd lle cynnes eto i Henry Jones yng nghesail y Gymru Gymraeg Fethodistaidd.

[43] TJ/U/1/66.

[44] Gweler R. Tudur Jones, *Ffydd ac Argyfwng Cenedl,* Cyf. 2, tt. 7-44.

[45] TJ/U/3/181.

Pennod 8

Cysgodion

Enillodd Henry Jones gydnabyddiaeth y byd academaidd yn yr Alban, yng Nghymru a Phrydain oll, fel y dengys yr anrhydeddau a ddaeth i'w ran. Derbyniodd Ll.D. Prifysgol St Andrews yn 1895 a D.Litt. Prifysgol Cymru yn 1905. Yn 1904 fe'i hetholwyd i Gymrodoriaeth yr Academi Brydeinig, braint fawr iawn yn wir. Cafodd gydnabyddiaeth wladol hefyd. Yn 1912 fe'i hurddwyd yn farchog.

Nid oedd yn gwbl esmwyth wrth dderbyn yr anrhydedd. Cyfaddefodd wrth Reichel, "I was very, very loath … I felt so keenly that my people are the common people."[1] Wrth yr Athro Gilbert Murray dywedodd ei fod wedi troi a throsi llawer cyn derbyn, gan feddwl am adwaith pobl fel yntau a Ker a Bradley ("plead for me with Bradley"). Yn y diwedd fe'i derbyniodd er mwyn ei feibion, ei bwnc a Chymru.

> And then, as Ll. George insisted, there is 'Wales', a very wee country, which 'likes this sort of thing', as he said; and 'You know, Jones,' he added, 'you and I must buck up for it.'[2]

Ddeng mlynedd yn ddiweddarach dyfarnwyd Medal Aur Anrhydeddus Gymdeithas y Cymmrodorion iddo.

Yn Glasgow profodd uchafbwynt ei lwyddiant academaidd a chyhoeddus, ond yno hefyd y cafodd ef ac Annie brofi oriau duaf eu bywyd. Taflodd afiechyd a rhyfel gysgodion dros ddyddiau haf yr yrfa ddisglair yn Glasgow. Yr oedd y Jonesiaid yn deulu o wyth pan symudasant i mewn i No. 1, The College, yn Professors' Square. Yng Nghymru, fel eu tad, y ganed pump o'r chwe phlentyn, sef Harry, Jim, Jeanie, Enid a Will, ac yn yr Alban, fel ei fam, y ganwyd Arthur (yn St Andrews).

Y brofedigaeth fawr gyntaf i daro'r teulu oedd colli Will yn 1906 yn fachgen un ar bymtheg mlwydd oed. Clafychodd y bachgen yn frawychus o sydyn gydag *appendicitis*, a methodd ei rieni â chyrraedd ei wely angau cyn ei golli. Yr oedd ei dad yn Rhydychen, a'i fam yn Lesmahagow yn gofalu am Jeanie, a oedd wedi cael *pleurisy* ar ôl triniaeth lawfeddygol. Jim yn unig oedd gydag ef yn y cartref yn Glasgow ar y pryd, ond methodd ef â chyrraedd yr ysbyty cyn i Will fynd yn anymwybodol. Yr oedd hon yn ergyd gwbl annisgwyl, ond yr hyn sy'n drawiadol iawn yw cryfder ffydd grefyddol y rhieni. Cawn ymdeimlad o hyn yn y gair a anfonodd Jones i gydnabod llythyr o gydymdeimlad a dderbyniwyd gan John Morris-Jones:

---

[1] LL, t. 223.

[2] ibid.

> Diolch i chwi. Yr oedd yn dda gennyf deimlo eich llaw yn eich llythyr. Marw heb ei fam na'i dad, ddarfu'r bachgen, a dieithriaid i gyd o amgylch ei wely: a phan ddaeth ei frawd nis gwyddai Wili ... Fe gafodd y gwynt ddod y tu fewn i'r babell, John, ac y mae wedi bod yn gwneud sport o'r trodrefn. Ond mi wn i am feistr y gwynt. Ac nid ydym yn ofni dim, dim.[3]

Ysgrifennodd gofiant tyner i'w fab, ac yn hwnnw mae mynegiant bendant o ffydd mewn Rhagluniaeth ac anfarwoldeb.[4]

Bedair blynedd yn ddiweddarach, sef 1910, bu farw Jeanie, y ferch hynaf. Yr oedd yn ferch ifanc osgeiddig a'i bryd ar yrfa mewn meddygaeth. Unwaith eto bu'n rhaid rhoi i orwedd 'lloer ifanc mewn lle rhyfedd'. Wrth gydnabod gair o gydymdeimlad gan yr Athro Macneile Dixon, dywed Jones ei fod wedi gwirioni ar ei ferch erioed, ond o'i cholli, ni chwerwodd.

> These are the things that Mrs Jones and I feel at present. Desolation may come, and I am afraid of later times. But as yet I can't say that 'God has been unkind.' You see, we had Jean for twenty-five years, and that was no mean privilege but something that makes us lift our heads.[5]

Hal, y mab hynaf, oedd achos y pryderon nesaf. Yr oedd ef dramor yn y Gwasanaeth Gwladol yn Burma, ond torrodd ei iechyd, a bu'n rhaid iddo ddod adref i atgyfnerthu. Bu iechyd ei fam yn fregus iawn hefyd, a phenderfynwyd bod yn rhaid symud o amgylchedd afiach y ddinas er lles iechyd y teulu. Cawsant gartref newydd yn Tighnabruaich, swydd Ayr. Erys yr enw a osodwyd ar y tŷ ganddynt hwy hyd heddiw, sef 'Noddfa'. Felly, rhwng 1910 a 1912 bu iechyd aelodau ei deulu yn bryder mawr i Jones, ond yn 1913 darganfuwyd ei fod ef ei hun yn dioddef o gancr yn y genau.

O fewn wythnos i ddiwedd tymor yr haf, aeth i Lundain am driniaeth lawfeddygol gan wybod y gallai ei fywyd fod mewn perygl. Daeth drwyddi'n llwyddiannus, ond o'r cyfnod hwn ymlaen tyfai farf i guddio ôl y graith ar ei wyneb. Yr oedd amheuaeth a fedrai fyth ddarlithio wedyn, neu hyd yn oed lefaru o gwbl yn wir. Ond yn raddol, a chyda chryn ddewrder, ailgydiodd yn ei ddyletswyddau. Erbyn dechrau 1914 yr oedd yn ei ôl yn y tresi drachefn.

Daeth cyhoeddi rhyfel yn Awst 1914 â chwmwl du dros y cartref a thros holl gartrefi'r wlad. Eto, o ran ei ddaliadau gwleidyddol, yr oedd Jones yn barod am y rhyfel. Yr oedd ei genhadaeth fawr dros ddinasyddiaeth yn gorwedd yn esmwyth â'i gred mai yn yr Ymerodraeth Brydeinig yr ymgorfforid orau y ddelfryd o ryddid dinesig. Hefyd, yr oedd ei ddadansoddiad Hegelaidd o natur yr hunan yn peri iddo ystyried bod tynged unigolion yn anwahanadwy oddi wrth dynged eu gwlad. Mae'n bwysig iawn deall hyn wrth geisio deall ei ymateb i'r rhyfel. Hynny yw, beth bynnag a ddywedir am adwaith rhai Cymry amlwg i'r argyfwng yn 1914, ni ellir

[3] JMJ.83.

[4] LL, tt. 285-302.

[5] LL, t. 220.

cyhuddo Jones o ymateb mewn modd anghyson â'i Ymneilltuaeth Gymreig.[6] Ni chofleidiodd ef erioed safbwynt moesol na chaniatâi iddo gyfiawnhau ymladd mewn rhyfel cyfiawn; ac iddo ef, yr oedd achos yr Ymerodraeth Brydeinig yn 1914 yn gyfiawn.[7]

Yr oedd sesiwn cyntaf cyfnod y Rhyfel yn amser diflas yn y coleg. Ni allai lawenhau o weld bechgyn addawol yn ymadael â'u gyrfa golegol i ymuno â'r lluoedd arfog, ond ni allai lawenhau o'u gweld yn dal at eu hefrydiau chwaith!

> I have just brought to a close without a break, the most difficult of College sessions. There was no satisfaction in seeing any of the lads not enlisting and not much in parting with them. They have done well. The whole country has done well so far as enlisting is concerned.[8]

Yr oedd yn fater o foddhad dwfn i Jones fod ei fab Arthur wedi ymrestru i wneud ei ddyletswydd ar unwaith, fel yn wir y gwnaeth Hal a Jim. Yr oedd gwerth moesol mawr ym mharodrwydd unigolion i wirfoddoli, er bod gan y wladwriaeth yr hawl foesol i wneud gwasanaeth milwrol yn orfodol.

> I know no argument against compulsion during the war; even tho' it is second best. But "*Second*" is too favourable a term to use, when one thinks of the *moral* compulsion, the categorical imperative of the Best, which took your boys and mine into the fight, and, Thank God! hundreds of thousands of others.[9]

Yn Arthur, rhamanteiddiodd alwedigaeth y milwr gyda delweddau'r chwedlau:

> Arthur is 2nd Lieut Durham Light Infantry drilling at Barnard Castle, getting to be a strong broad backed laddie, not wanting to be in the army but could not hesitate a moment and looks like doing his part as long as he is to the fore, like a real knight, a fine clean chivalrous, calm and fearless laddie.[10]

Ni fu galw arno ef ei hun i wneud gwasanaeth milwrol, ond gwelodd yr awdurdodau fod modd defnyddio ei ddoniau areithyddol i berswadio eraill i ymuno â'r rhengoedd. Credent y gallai fod yn ddylanwadol iawn yng Nghymru, a threfnwyd teithiau areithio ar ei gyfer. Yr oedd ef yn bendant iawn pa fath o naws y dymunai i'r cyfarfodydd recriwtio ei gyfleu.

---

6 Faint bynnag o wirionedd sydd i'r haeriad am Lloyd George, sef "drwy rym ei garisma gallai wyrdroi ac ail ddiffinio traddodiadau Ymneilltuaeth yn 1914" (Gerwyn Williams, *Y Rhwyg*, Llandysul 1993, t. 3), yr oedd Jones wedi ei baratoi yn feddyliol ar gyfer gofynion 1914 ymhell cyn hynny.

7 'Why we are Fighting', *Hibbert Journal*, Cyf. 13, tt. 50-67.

8 TJ/U/3/5.

9 TJ/U/3/30.

10 TJ/U/3/5.

> I would like, were it possible, for meetings to have the high seriousness which religious meetings have, and the influence of religious leaders let loose. Surely! this war is a *Jahad* if ever there is one.[11]

> You know what I want to do, it is to strengthen those who are in mourning or in fear and anxiety. And I know no such strength as that which comes from regarding the War in a *wide* context, the moral context.[12]

Yn unol â'r agwedd hon, awgrymodd Reichel y patrwm hwn ar gyfer cyfarfod recriwtio i'w annerch gan Jones yng Nghaergybi:

> Would the "Spiritual aspect of the War" do for the title of your address? I propose opening the meeting with a hymn – "O God our help in ages past", and closing with a Welsh hymn "O Arglwydd Dduw Rhagluniaeth".[13]

Awgrymodd yntau wrth Thomas Jones y dylid sicrhau cyfarfodydd dyrchafol, â'u bryd ar 'big ends'. Uwchben popeth dylid osgoi dadleuon ar faterion fel heddychiaeth a'r croestynnu rhwng Cyfalaf a Llafur. Da o beth fyddai cael y Maer i'w gadeirio os oedd yn bosibl, a sicrhau bod cynrychiolwyr o bob plaid wleidyddol a gweinidogion yr Efengyl yn eistedd ar y llwyfan. Dylid trefnu bod cynnig yn cael ei gyflwyno i'r cyfarfod, fel y gallai pawb ei gefnogi, a mynd â'r genadwri i'r pentrefi cyfagos. Annerch ei gyfarfodydd mawrion fel athro athroniaeth foesol a fynnai Jones, wrth gwrs, nid fel propagandydd bocs sebon ('I should be appalled at the prospect of wrangling meetings at pit mouths'[14]).

Ar y cyfan, fe aeth y cyfarfodydd rhagddynt yn esmwyth a llwyddiannus. Ni thorrodd neb unwaith ar eu traws, prin oedd yr holi ar derfyn ei areithiau, ac yn ddi-ffael cefnogwyd y cynnig ar y diwedd. Yng nghyfarfodydd gogledd Cymru dim ond dau a wrthododd gefnogi'r cynnig, a gweinidogion Ymneilltuol oeddynt hwy! Yn y De cafwyd cyfarfodydd gwych yn Nowlais a Merthyr, er enghraifft, er bod elfennau 'peace-at-any-price' ar waith yno, yn cymylu uchel-amcanion y rhyfel, a bod 'malcontents, socialistic & other' yn chwyddo pob anhawster diwydiannol neu brinder bwyd i'w dibenion eu hunain.[15]

Adlewyrchu profiadau 1917–18 a wna'r sylwadau hyn. Erbyn hynny yr oedd y Llywodraeth wedi 'benthyg' Jones o Brifysgol Glasgow ar gyfer y gwaith propagandyddol yma. Bu wrthi drwy gydol y rhyfel yn annog ei gynulleidfaoedd i gefnogi'r rhyfel fel crwsâd ysbrydol. Mynegodd ddiffyg cydymdeimlad llwyr â'r gwrthwynebwyr cydwybodol:

---

[11] TJ/U/9.
[12] TJ/U/3/17.
[13] TJ/U/3/20.
[14] TJ/U/1/27.
[15] TJ/U/1/41.

> *Pacifists*. Because an ignorant will is a bad will I have not felt able to petition for their being let off. To me they were criminals, though I admit our way of dealing with them has been silly.[16]

Yn wir, collodd ei barch at hynny o fyfyrwyr oedd yn weddill ganddo yn ei ddosbarthiadau:

> ... it is harder to lecture *well* to a mere remnant of fellows either bodily or spiritually (or both) incapable of giving to their country the help it most needs.[17]

Ysywaeth, synhwyrodd ambell un o'r myfyrwyr eu bod yn cael eu hesgeuluso. Yn ei hunangofiant preifat i'w blant, dywedodd William Boyd am eu mam:

> Mum is another of Jones's critics. She had him during the War years, when he was going about the country orating. He did that very well, but in Mum's case at the expense of his students.[18]

Os yw'r cyhuddiad hwn yn wir, gallwn fod yn sicr ei fod yn gweithredu'n unol â'r hyn a welai ef fel ei ddyletswydd pennaf ar y pryd. Perthyn i'r cyfnod hwn y mae'r llun ohono yn sefyll ar garreg y drws yn Downing Street gyda Lloyd George a'r arch-recriwtiwr Methodistaidd, Y Parchedig Ddr John Williams, Brynsiencyn. Diddorol dros ben, yn wyneb taerineb yr olaf wrth annog meibion cefn gwlad Cymru i ymrestru yn y rhengoedd, yw llythyr a anfonodd at Jones yn gofyn a allai ddefnyddio ei ddylanwad i sicrhau bod un o'i gydnabod yn cael ei esgusodi rhag mynd i'r gad, ond yn hytrach yn cael ei osod mewn swydd weinyddol![19] Yn anffodus iawn nid yw ateb Jones ar gael.

Nid annerch cyfarfodydd oedd ei unig weithgarwch dros yr achos. Fe geisiodd, drwy nifer o erthyglau, drafod cynsail moesol y rhyfel. Hefyd, cafodd wahoddiad gan Syr Henry Hadow i ysgrifennu llyfr ar ddinasyddiaeth y gellid ei ddefnyddio gan yr Y.M.C.A. yn y dosbarthiadau a drefnai'r mudiad hwnnw ar gyfer y milwyr yn Ffrainc. Roedd gweithio ar y llyfr hwn yn gynhaliaeth ysbrydol iddo ar gyfnod o bryder a gofid personol dwys iawn. Er nad oedd y llyfr yn addas i'w ddiben gwreiddiol, y mae *Principles of Citizenship* yn fynegiant clir o'i safbwynt. O ran arddull, mae'r gyfrol fach hon yn rhagori ar rai o'i weithiau mwy enwog.

Ceisiodd weithredu mewn dulliau ymarferol hefyd. Bu'n weithgar yn sefydlu lloches i ffoaduriaid o Wlad Belg yn Tighnabruaich. Gwelodd gyfle yn yr argyfwng i hybu achos dirwest. Ceisiodd berswadio'r Llywodraeth y byddai gweithwyr ffatrïoedd arfau Dyffryn Clyde yn fwy effeithiol a chynhyrchiol pe cyfyngid ar y fasnach ddiod yno! Ond er iddo lwyddo i argyhoeddi arweinwyr yr undebau a pherchenogion y cwmnïau peirianyddol, ni lwyddodd gyda'r bragwyr, ac er mawr

[16] TJ/U/3/94.
[17] TJ/U/3/33.
[18] William Boyd, op. cit., t. 124.
[19] TJ/U/3/62.

ofid iddo, hwy a lwyddodd i ddylanwadu ar y Llywodraeth. Rhoddodd y bai am ei fethiant ar elfennau yn y wasg Doriaidd.

Fe gducpwyd Jim a Hal i mewn i'r rhyfel yn ogystal ag Arthur. Gwasanaethodd y ddau ohonynt ym Mesopotamia, ond nid gyda'i gilydd. Yr oedd Hal yn swyddog yn y fagnelaeth a Jim ar ddyletswydd feddygol. Clafychodd Jim gyda phara-typhoid a dychwelodd yn wael iawn i India, ond nid cyn ennill y D.S.O. Cymerwyd Hal yn garcharor a'i gludo i Yozgad yn Anatolia. Clwyfwyd Arthur yn Ffrainc, ac am ei ymdrygiad yn y frwydr, cafodd M.C. Ym mis Mawrth 1918, enillodd far ar ei M.C. am wrhydri, ond yn Ebrill derbyniodd ei rieni newyddion ei fod wedi ei glwyfo ac ar goll. Gwnaeth Jones ymholiadau taer am ragor o wybodaeth, ac roedd ef mewn safle da i gael mynediad i'r ffynonellau uchaf, ond yn ofer. Tristwch o'r mwyaf yw dilyn ei ohebiaethau yn y cyfnod hwn, a gweld ei obeithion ef ac Annie yn graddol ddiffodd. Bachgen annwyl iawn oedd Arthur, y tyneraf o feibion dynion. Yn ôl Boyd, dywedwyd amdano ei fod yn gofalu mynd ar hyd ffosydd maes y gad cyn eu gadael i agor drysau'r trapiau, rhag ofn i'r llygod mawr lwgu i farwolaeth!

Yr oedd pryder pellach yn pwyso'n drwm ar deulu Noddfa. Derbyniwyd newyddion, a ddaeth drwy law llysgenhadaeth yr Iseldiroedd yng Nghaergystennin fod Hal wedi cyrraedd ysbyty yn y ddinas mewn cyflwr o wallgofrwydd. Cyn bo hir, fodd bynnag, derbyniwyd neges gan y Jonesiaid gyda rhai llythrennau Saesneg wedi eu nodi yn y fath fodd ag i ddatguddio geiriau Cymraeg a awgrymai mai ffugio gwallgofrwydd oedd Hal mewn gwirionedd. Wedi'r rhyfel daeth yr holl fyd i wybod am yr antur hon pan gyhoeddodd Hal ei hanes mewn llyfr poblogaidd iawn, *The Road to En-dor*. Erbyn canol Rhagfyr 1918 yr oedd Hal adref gyda'i rieni a'i wraig a'i blant bach ifanc, a daeth Jim adref o India hefyd. Felly, y Nadolig hwnnw yr oedd Hal, Jim ac Enid yn Noddfa, y tri o'r chwe phlentyn oedd ar ôl.

Er cilio o gwmwl du'r rhyfel, daeth pryder arall i flino'r teulu. Daeth yn amlwg fod cancr Jones yn dechrau ailffyrnigo. Cafodd lawdriniaeth ysgafn yn 1919, ond erbyn 1920 yr oedd yn amlwg nad oedd gwella i fod. Eto, cafodd ysbrydoliaeth newydd i wynebu'r diwedd pan etholwyd ef i draddodi'r Darlithoedd Gifford fel olynydd Iarll Balfour. Anrhydedd a gyfyngir i brif athronwyr eu dydd yw hon, felly dyma goroni gwaith ei yrfa gyfan. Gwelodd y Darlithoedd Gifford fel cyfle i grynhoi ac i fynegi ei genadwri athronyddol a chrefyddol. Yn wir, dylid ystyried y darlithoedd hyn, a gyhoeddwyd dan y teitl *A Faith that Enquires* fel ei destament athronyddol a'i bregeth olaf. Wrth droi eu tudalennau, daw'r darllenydd yn ymwybodol o'r pregethwr sy'n llefaru drwy'r athroniaeth.

Gweithiodd yn ddygn drwy fisoedd yr haf yn eu paratoi a disgwyliai eu traddodi yn ystod sesiwn 1921–22. Daeth yn amlwg i'r rhai oedd yn agos ato, fodd bynnag, fod gwir berygl na fyddai ei nerth yn dal cyhyd â hynny. Bu Balfour mor rasol â gohirio traddodi ei ail gyfres ef er mwyn ei alluogi i ddechrau blwyddyn ynghynt. Bu o gwmpas ei waith yn y brifysgol drwy gydol 1920, ac erbyn dechrau tymor y gaeaf yr oedd wedi cyfansoddi dros hanner y darlithoedd. I esmwytháu pethau iddo, fe'i gwnaed yn bosibl iddo ddychwelyd i fflat yn ei hen gartref, No. 1 The College, a oedd bellach wedi ei droi yn swyddfeydd (ac sy'n parhau felly). Felly, tua diwedd mis Hydref 1920 dechreuodd draddodi'r Darlithoedd Gifford mewn ystafell weddol fechan, rhag bod gormod o dreth ar ei lais a'i egni. Dim ond cyfran fechan o'r nifer luosog a ddymunai ei glywed a lwyddodd i gael mynediad. Serch hynny, gordrethodd ei hun, a methodd â chwblhau'r bedwaredd ddarlith.

Dychwelodd i Tighnabruaich yn ddyn gwael iawn. Wedi cyfnod o orffwys dechreuodd gryfhau, ac yn gynnar yn 1921 daeth am seibiant i Bwllheli i aros gyda mab ei frawd, John. Parhaodd i weithio ar ei Ddarlithoedd Gifford, ac erbyn Ebrill yr oedd yn ei ôl yn y brifysgol yn darlithio ddwywaith yr wythnos. Dychwelodd i Gymru eto ym mis Mehefin. Y tro hwn arhosodd yn ffermdy'r Cefn, Llanengan, ar benrhyn Llŷn. Ni chawsai driniaeth ers dechrau'r flwyddyn ac yr oedd y boen yn cynyddu. Gallai ymgolli i raddau yn y gwaith o gyfansoddi'r Darlithoedd Gifford, ond weithiau byddai'r boen yn rhy enbyd i hynny. Ar adegau felly, byddai'n ysgrifennu atgofion am y dyddiau cynnar yn Llangernyw a'r ymdrech arwrol am addysg. Tyfodd yr atgofion hyn i fod yn hunangofiant nodedig. Fe'i cyhoeddwyd wedi marwolaeth Henry Jones dan y teitl, *Old Memories*, a hwn mae'n debyg yw'r hunangofiant Saesneg mwyaf poblogaidd ei apêl i'w gyhoeddi gan unrhyw Gymro Cymraeg erioed.

Cysur mawr iddo tra bu'n aros yn Llanengan oedd cwmni ei fab Jim, a oedd wedi cael dychwelyd adref o India am seibiant er adfer ei iechyd yntau. Yn ystod y dyddiau hyn cafodd olwg newydd ar ddigwyddiad mwyaf enbyd ei yrfa, sef yr ymadawiad o Aberystwyth, drwy lygaid ei fyfyriwr hoff, O. M. Edwards. Bu Syr O. M. farw ym mis Mai 1920, ac fe gafodd gyfle annisgwyl i weld dyddiadur ei hen fyfyriwr dros gyfnod yr helynt. Disgrifir yr amgylchiadau yn y llythyr hwn a anfonwyd at Thomas Jones gan G. P. Williams, Llanelli yn 1922:

> Dichon y cofiwch fod papurau cyfrinachol Owen Edwards gennyf i. Yn y papurau hynny cofnodir ffeithiau – (a chasgliadau oddi wrthynt) gan Owen Edwards am y tro gwarthus hwnnw, na wyddai Syr Henry ei hun mohonynt – i gyd, beth bynnag, hyd nes y gelwais i'w weld, a'r papurau gyda mi, yn Llanengan ym mis Medi diwethaf.
>
> Aethum yno yn un swydd. Ofnwn mai hwnnw a fyddai y cyfle olaf i mi i'w weld ac nid oeddwn yn rhyw sicr iawn beth a garai i mi ei wneud a phethau cyfrinachol felly pan ddeuwn i drafod y rhan honno o fywyd Owen Edwards.
>
> Pan anturiais guro wrth ddrws y Cefn, y prydnawn tesog hwnnw, gorphwysai, druan, yn lluddiedig iawn a'i wedd wedi curio'n enbyd ers pan y gwelswn ef cynt. Dywedais fy neges, darllennodd yntau'r papurau'n awchus, a chyn pen dim bron, cynhyrfodd ei enaid tanbaid nes dod ag ynni rhyfedd i'w gorff llesg. Rhoes i mi yn hyawdl yr holl hanes i gyd a thorodd y ddadl a'm penbleth ar unwaith. Heb un ias o betrusder meddai – 'Cyhoeddwch y cwbl' – 'mae pob gair yn wir'. 'Cyhoeddwch y cwbl pe na bai ond fel tystiolaeth i graffter a barn Owen Edwards y myfyriwr.' Yn awr ac eilwaith, wrth ddarllen dywedai 'Bravo! Edwards!' 'Well done Edwards'.[20]

[20] TJ/U/4/19.

Ym mis Medi cwblhaodd ddrafft cyntaf y Darlithoedd Gifford, a dychwelodd i Glasgow ar gyfer dechrau'r sesiwn newydd. Er ei fod yn dal ati gyda gwaith yr adran, yr oedd mewn poen cyson. Cyfaddefodd wrth Thomas Jones:

> It is an awful fight, Tom dear – the pain is *always* present and at times overwhelming. But, so far, I have not given in.[21]

Serch hynny, penderfynwyd ei fod yn traddodi pump o'r Darlithoedd Gifford y tymor hwnnw yn yr ystafell Athroniaeth Foesol. Yr oedd yr ystafell yn orlawn, a phawb yn synhwyro eu bod yn gyfrannog o fraint fawr, cael clywed tystiolaeth dyn a lefarai, nid bellach yng nghwrs ei yrfa, ond ar gost enbyd iddo'i hun oherwydd ei argyhoeddiad mai dyma fyddai ei gymynrodd i'r oesau. Traddododd ei ddarlith olaf ar 11 Rhagfyr 1921. Meddai un a oedd yno:

> The memory of his last lecture is ineffaceable. From out of the dark and rain we came in to the Moral Philosophy Room, where there was not a soul but felt the supreme sadness of the occasion. Sir Henry was very ill, and had lost his old buoyancy. But still he held on. He contrived to finish on a cheery note, far removed from the tones which a man might well have used, quitting as he was for ever a rostrum from which he had led and inspired thousands of students.[22]

Ysgrifennodd at Thomas Jones dridiau yn ddiweddarach,

> I am not getting better Tom, the pain is somewhat less but the disease is slowly, very slowly, eating its way.[23]

Gadawodd Glasgow a Professors' Square am y tro olaf a dychwelyd i Noddfa dros y Nadolig. Drwy ymdrech lew ar ran Cwmni Macmillan cafodd weld cyfrol o'r Darlithoedd Gifford, *A Faith that Enquires*, wedi ei rhwymo cyn dyddiad eu cyhoeddi. Yna, ar ddydd Calan 1922 cyhoeddodd Lloyd George fod y brenin wedi enwi Henry Jones fel Companion of Honour. Erbyn hyn, fe'i cyfyngwyd i'w wely, a'r diwedd yn amlwg yn agos. Cafodd y boddhad o dderbyn insignia ei anrhydedd gan Ysgrifennydd y Cabinet, sef ei hoff fyfyriwr, Thomas Jones. Mewn llythyr ato yn diweddarach dywedodd Mary Jones (nith Henry Jones):

> I know you will always be glad you were able to see him, so laterly, it was an untold pleasure to him. I shall remember how his eyes lighted with joy when I told him you were downstairs. 'God *is* good to me' he said.[24]

Ni phallodd ei hiwmor drwy'r holl ddioddef. Parhaodd y direidi hyd y diwedd, fel y dengys yr hanesyn bach yma.

---

21 TJ/U/1/128.
22 J. R. Peddie yn LL, t. 151
23 TJ/U/1/130.
24 TJ/U/1/137.

> On the night of 3rd February, a few hours before he died, his niece Mary and the nurse who was helping her came into his room. He asked, 'Which of you is going to sit up with me to-night?' Mary, understanding his mood, answered, 'Which of us would you like?' At once a gleam of the old mischief shone in his eye. 'The prettier. Now fight for it.'[25]

Ond gwyddai o'r gorau ei fod bellach wedi cyrraedd y trothwy. Yr oedd eisoes wedi gofyn y prynhawn hwnnw i Annie am neges i'w rhoi i'r plant 'yr ochr draw'. Bu farw'n dawel fore Sadwrn 4 Chwefror am hanner awr wedi saith o'r gloch y bore. Ei gyffes olaf oedd, "The Lord reigneth. Let the earth rejoice."

Claddwyd ei weddillion yn Kilbride ger Tighnabruaich ym mhen ucha'r fynwent. Yn ei deyrnged iddo, dywedodd yr Athro Macneile Dixon ei fod yn argyhoeddedig y byddai cael ei gofio fel dinesydd da yn bodloni Henry Jones yn fwy na chael ei gofio fel athronydd mawr. Yr oedd ei fywyd yn gyfuniad o fyfyrdod y meddyliwr a llafur y gweithredwr, ond rhoddwyd cyfeiriad i'w holl weithgareddau gan ei ddadansoddiadau athronyddol.

[25] LL, t. 154.

Rhan 2

Athroniaeth Syr Henry Jones

The influence of metaphysics, for good and evil, upon a nation's mind and therefore on its history is far greater than the practical man dreams.

Henry Jones
(*Hibbert Journal*, XIII, 1914, t. 62)

Pennod 9

Rhyddfrydiaeth Newydd mewn Crefydd

Fe gawn yn *Old Memories* ddisgrifiad cryno o'r modd y trawsnewidiwyd daliadau crefyddol cynnar Henry Jones dan ddylanwad darlithiau cyfareddol Edward Caird.[1] Cawn yr argraff ei fod yn hollol gartrefol yn feddyliol ac emosiynol gyda *Chyffes Ffydd* y Methodistiaid Calfinaidd pan ymadawodd â Chymru am Glasgow y tro cyntaf. Edwino yn hytrach na chael eu gwrthbrofi a wnaeth ei ddaliadau uniongred, ond parhaodd i fod yn ddyn crefyddol iawn gydol ei oes. Profodd yr Harri ifanc rymuster Diwygiad '59 yng Nghapel y Cwm; nid ffurfioldeb marw oedd y grefydd y magesid ef ynddi.[2] Eto, wrth edrych yn ôl, galwodd grefydd ei febyd yn "legal and vindictive"[3] a gofidiai fod ei hadeiladwaith yn gynnyrch dwylo eraill.[4]

Nid ymosododd Edward Caird yn uniongyrchol o gwbl ar erthyglau'r *Gyffes Ffydd*, ond wrth iddo osod crefydd yng nghyd-destun eang bywyd yr ysbryd yr oedd yn anochel y byddai'r hen athrawiaethau yn graddol wywo. Credai'r Idealwyr fod unoliaeth sylfaenol i holl fyd y meddwl (neu'r ysbryd), sef rheswm. Drwy reswm y ceir gwybodaeth o'r gwirionedd a'r dirweddol ym mhob un o feysydd ein profiad. Meddai Jones yn ei Ragymadrodd i *A Faith that Enquires*,

> Let man seek God by the way of pure reason, and he will find him.[5]

Ym mhob cylch arall o fywyd, drwy ymarfer ein rheswm, drwy rydd ymofyn, y deuwn i ehangu gwybodaeth ac yn yr ysbryd hwnnw y traddododd ei Ddarlithiau Gifford:

> Believing with all my heart that in the last resort there is only one way of knowing, ...[6]

Ni chafodd unrhyw anhawster i dderbyn amod Arglwydd Gifford wrth sefydlu'r darlithoedd:

> I wish the lecturers to treat their subject as a strictly natural science ... without reference to or reliance upon any supposed special exceptional or so-called miraculous revelation. I wish it considered just as astronomy or chemistry is.[7]

---

1 OM, t. 134.
2 ibid., tt. 51-2.
3 ibid., t. 135.
4 ibid., t. 53.
5 FTE, t. vii.
6 ibid., t. 15.
7 ibid., t. 2.

Ond, mae rheswm yn cwmpasu llawer mwy na rhesymeg, a phan fydd Jones yn mynnu mai drwy reswm yn unig y mae ennill gwybodaeth, y mae'n cynnwys y cyfan o brofiad yr ymwybyddiaeth ddynol. Mae'n siŵr fod elfen hunangofiannol yn y brawddegau hyn yn *The Idealism of Jesus*:

> ... subtle changes may take place in the tone or temper of experience, which may alter the perspective of all the facts it contains. Without conscious controversy, even with oneself, a new attitude towards life may react upon and change the meaning of facts and doctrines which have never been definitely refuted. When men rise to a new spiritual level – it may be from suffering, or bereavement, or defeat in the struggle for finite and perishable ends; when for any reason, they gain insight and acquire a deeper faith in the divine love which sustains the world, they will find the whole body of their religious and moral belief suffer change. Every term in their theology will have a new significance: the life of Jesus, the love of God, the meaning of the world, the destiny of man, pass through a strange and subtle alchemy which is priceless, and which the methods of controversy most rarely produce.[8]

Mae alcemi yn ddelwedd ddiddorol iawn, oherwydd un o'r beirniadaethau ar Jones a'i debyg yw eu bod yn defnyddio'r un eirfa â'r uniongred, ond gydag ystyr newydd a gwahanol.[9] Fe'u cyhuddir o draws-sylweddu iaith crefydd.

Yr oedd Jones yn gwbl agored ynglŷn â'r newidiadau yn arwyddocâd ac ystyr ei ddaliadau crefyddol. Yn wir, dywedai eu bod yn anochel oherwydd natur bywiol rheswm. Nid cyflwr statig yw ymwybyddiaeth. O holl gylchoedd astudiaeth dim ond diwinyddiaeth erbyn hyn sy'n ofni neu'n gwrthod newid daliadau yn wyneb gwybodaeth newydd. Ond ni ellir cyfyngu'r gwirionedd a'i gadw gyda hualau'r gorffennol. Mae'r byd seciwlar eisoes wedi darganfod hyn, meddai.

> Truth, which in its very nature is one and eternal, is also, so far as concerns the growing consciousness of man, always *in the making*.[10]

Os mai rheswm, yn yr ystyr eang, yw cyfrwng ein gwybodaeth mewn crefydd, y mae'r adnabyddiaeth o Dduw o fewn cyrraedd pawb. Fel y dywedodd Caird,

> Every creature, who is capable of the consciousness of an objective world and of consciousness of a self, is capable also of the consciousness of God.[11]

Os felly, ni raid wrth ddatguddiadau gwyrthiol a neilltuol mewn gwir grefydd. Pa awdurdod pellach a berthyn i ysgrythurau, neu i eglwysi, os yw pob bod rhesymol, yn rhinwedd ei reswm, yn medru amgyffred y gwirionedd? Mewn sgwrs ochelgar

[8] IOJ, tt. 13-14.

[9] Un o'r rhai a gollfarnai'r Idealwyr am y modd y defnyddient eu geirfa oedd L. T. Hobhouse. Gweler ymateb Jones yn WFSR, tt. 199-200.

[10] Henry Jones, *Divine Transcendence*, Manceinion 1907, t. 4.

[11] Edward Caird, *The Evolution of Religion*, Glasgow 1899, Cyf. 1, t. 68.

gydag O. M. Edwards, yn nyddiau Aberystwyth, gwelodd Jones ei fod ef a'i fyfyriwr ar yr un donfedd ar y pwynt yma. Dyma'r sgwrs fel y'i croniclir yn nyddiadur O. M.: mae Jones newydd ofyn iddo, "What are you now?", ac mae Edwards yn cyfaddef, " … anything you like."

> He looked down –
> 'Found difficulties, I suppose.'
> 'Yes.'
> 'With inspiration perhaps?'
> 'Yes often'
> 'Don't you believe that the Bible is inspired?'
> 'Oh yes, and so was Shakespere, and so am I.'
> He looked at me from the corners of his eyes, and quoted – 'which lighteneth every man that cometh into the world.' The conversation dropped.[12]

Yr oedd y gred fod Duw wedi ymwneud ag un genedl, Israel, mewn ffordd arbennig yn enghraifft o gred wedi goroesi ym marn Jones, ac yn dangos y modd y mae ciffyg dynion i garu eu hil yn gyffredinol yn cael ei adlewyrchu yn y Duw a addolant.[13] Mae hanes pob cenedl yn fynegiant rhannol o Dduwdod i Hegelydd, ond nid yw hanes unrhyw un genedl yn fynegiant cyflawn ohono.

> There is no spot of earth anywhere that is not holy ground, and no bush that does not burn, where a leader of men may not meet the Best he knows and receive the message of his God.[14]

Dyma agwedd a apeliai at y Bardd Newydd yng Nghymru, a gwelir yr union syniad, a'r un ddelwedd yn wir, ag a ddefnyddiodd Jones uchod yng ngherdd Gwili 'Tu hwnt i'r llen':

> Pa le y mae Horeb? Ai dim ond un berth
> A welodd Jehofa erioed yn werth
> Dyfod i'w brig yn fflamiau byw?
> Mae pob un o'r perthi yn llosgi gan Dduw!
> …
> Ai yn y Nefoedd mae Duw uwchben?
> Mae yn yr holl berthi, tu hwnt i'r llen!

Syniad a gafodd ei gyfleu yn llinellau cyfarwydd cerdd fawr Islwyn, tad-bedydd y Bardd Newydd, 'Y Storm':

[12] W. J. Gruffydd, *Owen Morgan Edwards: Cofiant,* Aberystwyth 1937, t. 230.
[13] IPC, t. 245.
[14] FTE, t. 42.

> Mae'r oll yn gysegredig,
> ...
> Pa beth yw ffynnon Jacob? Y mae delw
> Un mwy na Jacob ym mhob ffrwd trwy'r byd.

O ddilyn trywydd fel hwn, fe ddeuwn at gwestiwn mwy canolog fyth, sef arbenigrwydd y datguddiad o Dduw gan Grist, ac yn wir, arbenigrwydd Iesu Grist yn ei Berson. Nid oedd Jones yn ddiwinydd, ond mae'n amlwg ei fod yn ymwybodol o ymgais diwinyddion ar hyd yr oesau i ddarganfod ffordd briodol i'w cyfnod o fynegi'r hyn a gredent ac a deimlent am Berson Crist. Yn y diwedd, fodd bynnag, meddai Jones, ni chredai unrhyw ddiwinydd fod deall (heb sôn am dderbyn) cysyniadau astrus fel cydsylweddiad y Tad a'r Mab yn angenrheidiol i fod yn Gristion. Eto, fe erys *arwyddocâd* yr athrawiaeth hon i bob crediniwr, hyd yn oed y symlaf.

> And whatever more 'consubstantiality' meant when the term was in vogue, it implied, and it still implies, even for simple men, that Jesus of Nazareth was in some way one with God; and the acceptance or rejection of this view was regarded as vital.[15]

Hyd yma, byddai mwyafrif y diwinyddion uniongred yn cytuno. Mae Jones yn dyfynnu o waith un o brif ddiwinyddion yr Alban, James Denney, ysgolhaig mawr iawn (a chyfaill personol, fel y gwelsom), i ddangos cefnogaeth geidwadol i'r fath safbwynt.

Y cwestiwn sy'n peri gwahaniaeth barn rhyngddynt yw – pa mor arbennig oedd undod Iesu a Duw? I Denney yr oedd mabolaeth Iesu yn gwbl unigryw. Er ei fod yn cydnabod bod llacrwydd ymhlith Iddewon a'r cenhedloedd ynglŷn â thadogi'r teitl 'Mab i Dduw', yn y cyswllt Cristnogol mae'n gwbl bendant ac unigol. Meddai am yr Iesu:

> ... in that filial consciousness He stands alone in the world. He is not, as He conceives Himself and as Christian faith recognizes Him, a Son of God, but the Son.[16]

Cred Jones fod angen gwahaniaethu rhwng dau gwestiwn sydd ymhlyg yn y gosodiadau a wneir am Berson Crist. A oedd Iesu o Nasareth yn ddwyfol? Ai'r Iesu *yn unig* o blith dynion sydd yn ddwyfol? Bydd llawer yn cymryd yn ganiataol, meddai, fod ateb negyddol i'r ail gwestiwn yn diddymu gwerth ac ystyr ateb cadarnhaol i'r cyntaf. Ond dyna sut y dewisiai ef ateb. Un o'r hanesion enwog amdano yw'r modd yr ymatebodd pan eglurodd John Morris-Jones wrtho unwaith

[15] IOJ, t. 20.
[16] ibid., t. 21.

paham yr oedd blaenoriaid Methodistaidd Llannerch-y-medd yn hwyrfrydig i'w wahodd yn ôl atynt, ac yntau wedi cael cystal hwyl ar bregethu yno. Ceisiodd ei gyfaill egluro, "Maent wedi clywed si eich bod yn gwadu dwyfoldeb Crist." "Y fi," atebodd, "yn gwadu dwyfoldeb Crist! Ni wedais i ddwyfoldeb unrhyw ddyn erioed!"

Yn y gorffennol, meddai Jones, diben athrawiaeth dwyfoldeb yr Iesu oedd tanlinellu'r *gwahaniaeth* rhyngddo ef a gweddill y ddynolryw. Bellach, fodd bynnag, mae diben newydd iddi, sef tanlinellu'r hyn sy'n *gyffredin* rhwng yr Iesu a'r ddynolryw. Dyma arwyddocâd gweledigaeth yr Idealwyr. Wrth gwrs, mae'r dehongliad hwn yn groes i draddodiad yr Eglwys ar hyd y canrifoedd, ond nid yw'n gwbl ddigyswllt ag ef ychwaith. Bu'n rhaid i'r Eglwys Fore ymgodymu â safbwyntiau a wadai wir ddyndod yr Iesu, ac fe'u condemniwyd fel heresïau. Er enghraifft, gwadai canlynwyr Apolinarius fod gan yr Iesu enaid dynol: credent mai gwisg neu gostrel oedd ei gorff i gynnal ei natur ddwyfol. Credai canlynwyr Eutyches fod y natur ddynol a'r natur ddwyfol wedi cydgymysgu yn yr Iesu i ffurfio trydydd natur nad oedd yn ddynol na dwyfol. Yr oedd nifer o safbwyntiau eraill tebyg i'w cael, ond fe'u condemniwyd gan yr Eglwys am iddynt wadu gwir ddyndod yr Iesu.

Dadleuai Jones fod datgan bod dwyfoldeb Iesu o Nasareth yn unigryw yn peryglu dilysrwydd ei ddyndod. Credai ei bod yn hanfodol bwysig medru dweud am Grist, gyda'r Epistol at yr Hebreaid, "wedi ei demtio ym mhob peth yr un ffunud â ninnau, eto heb bechod."[17] Ond tanseilir yr honiad yma yn llwyr os oedd dimensiwn unigryw i'w Berson ef. Sut y gallai gael ei demtio yr un ffunud â ninnau os oedd ganddo adnoddau dwyfol *unigryw* o'i du?

> The disparity is too stupendous. Jesus is man, but he is also more than man: more by the momentous addition of the divine. Does his manhood remain unaffected by this addition? Is the manhood that has, the same as the manhood that has not, the divine on its side?[18]

Dywed ei fod yn deall yn iawn paham yr oedd credinwyr wedi bod mor awyddus i wahaniaethu rhwng yr Iesu a dynolryw yn gyffredinol. Cawsant fod Iesu yn anghymharol, a dyna yn wir oedd profiad Jones hefyd. Yn anffodus, fodd bynnag, mynegwyd yr anghymaroldeb hwnnw mewn modd sy'n ysgaru Crist o fyd dynion a'r byd real. O wneud hynny, dibrisiwyd yr hyn y ceisir ei honni amdano. Trosglwyddwyd ffydd i lefel ofergoel.[19]

Er ei fod yn selog dros arddel dyndod cyflawn a chyffredin yr Iesu, yr oedd Jones yr un mor selog dros arddel ei ddwyfoldeb cyflawn.

---

[17] Hebreaid, IV, 15.

[18] IOJ, t. 46.

[19] Ibid., tt. 24-5.

> I believe Jesus was divine. But when it is said that the splendour with which he was clothed, and which was divine, was his only, that it made him stand absolutely alone in the world, I must demur.[20]

> The error, I would fain make clear, does not spring from maintaining the divinity of Jesus, but from denying the divinity of man.[21]

Yr oedd Jones mor wrthwynebus â *Chyffes Ffydd* y Methodistiaid i unrhyw ymgais i ddad-ddwyfoli Crist. Diraddio dyndod fyddai hynny yn ei dyb ef. Dyma paham na ellir ei gyfrif gyda'r hen ryddfrydiaeth ddiwinyddol. Nid oes ganddo fawr o ddiddordeb yn yr ymchwil am 'Iesu hanes'. Datgysylltai ei hun, er enghraifft, â safbwynt yr ysgolhaig Llydewig, Ernest Renan, a geisiodd yn ei lyfr dylanwadol *La Vie de Jésus* (1863) ddehongli honiadau'r Iesu amdano ei hun fel gosodiadau a wnaed dan ddylanwad gorfoledd a chyflyrau dyrchafedig. Nid oes dim i'w ennill o geisio gosod cyfyngiadau lle ac amser ar Iesu hanesyddol.

> I confess that I cannot foresee that any great advantage can accrue to religious faith from the attempts which are being made to demonstrate the limitations of Jesus, or to prove, through such limitations, that he was 'merely a pious Jew of more than usual purity and depth of character'.[22]

Datgysylltai ei hun hefyd â'r hen Undodiaeth a roddasai'r holl bwyslais ar ddadlau mai 'dim ond' dyn oedd Iesu, yn hytrach na chyhoeddi dwyfoldeb Iesu a phob person arall. Ni ddylid gwahaniaethu rhwng y dwyfol a'r dynol fel hyn.

> It is the error of the Unitarianism of the past and of the theology to which it was opposed.[23]

Y mae awgrym cynnil yma nad oedd yr Undodiaeth gyfoes yn syrthio i'r un bai. Digwyddasai newid mawr iawn yng nghyfeiriad diwinyddiaeth Undodaidd yn ystod ail hanner y bedwaredd ganrif ar bymtheg, yn bennaf dan arweiniad James Martineau. "Ni welir safbwynt Undodiaid heddiw ond yn nrych meddwl Martineau," meddai T. Oswald Williams yn *Undodiaeth a Rhyddid Meddwl* (1962).[24] Ef oedd prif ladmerydd y rhyddfrydiaeth grefyddol newydd. Sylfaenwyd yr hen ryddfrydiaeth ar ysgolheictod hanesyddol a thestunol manwl. Meddai Williams am yr hen ryddfrydwyr:

> Yr oeddent hwy yn barod i gredu athrawiaeth y Drindod neu'r Iawn neu Gosbedigaeth Dragwyddol o cheid hwynt yn yr ysgrythur. Fe'u gwrthodent nid am eu bod yn afresymol ond am eu bod yn anysgrythurol. 'For my own part', meddai Martineau, 'I must confess myself unable to adopt this language'.[25]

---

[20] ibid., t. 52.
[21] ibid., t. 51.
[22] ibid., tt. 16-17.
[23] ibid., t. 52.
[24] T. Oswald Williams, *Undodiaeth a Rhyddid Meddwl,* Llandysul 1962, t. 272.
[25] ibid., tt. 273-4.

Anallu oedd hynny a ddeilliai o anawsterau moesol ac athronyddol. I'r rhyddfrydwyr newydd, rheswm a phrofiad oedd ffynhonnell awdurdod mewn crefydd bellach. Megis yn yr Oesoedd Canol, daeth perthynas athroniaeth a diwinyddiaeth yn un agos iawn. Ni chyfrifir Martineau ymhlith yr Hegeliaid, ond mae'n amlwg o ddarllen ymdriniaeth Jones o'i waith yn *The Philosophy of Martineau in Relation to the Idealism of the Present Day*[26] fod y ddau ar donfedd debyg i'w gilydd. Gallai Jones yn hawdd fod wedi ysgrifennu'r geiriau hyn o eiddo Martineau:

> The Incarnation is true, not of Christ exclusively but of man universally and of God everlastingly. He bends into the human to dwell there and humanity is the susceptible organ of the Divine ...[27]

Yr oedd yr hen ryddfrydwyr crefyddol yn barod iawn i wrthod athrawiaethau traddodiadol y ffydd Gristnogol, hyd yn oed y rhai mwyaf canolog fel athrawiaeth y Drindod ac athrawiaeth yr Iawn, fel rhan o'u cenhadaeth i adfer purdeb dysgeidiaeth yr Iesu a'r apostolion. Eithr adeiladu yn hytrach nag adfer a wnâi'r rhyddfrydwyr newydd, symud crefydd ymlaen, darganfod 'rhyw newydd wyrth'. Iddynt hwy daeth y fenter grefyddol yn debyg iawn i wyddoniaeth: mesurir ei llwyddiant yn ôl y gallu i ddarganfod gwirioneddau newydd, nid yn ôl y gallu i amddiffyn gwirioneddau'r gorffennol. Wrth gwrs, y mae'r gwirioneddau eu hunain yn dragwyddol, ac ymhlyg (os hefyd yn ddirgel) yn y ffydd Gristnogol drwy'r oesoedd. Yr oedd hyn yn cyd-daro'n hynod o hapus gyda'r syniad Hegelaidd o ysbryd yn cynyddu mewn hunan-wybodaeth.

Eto i gyd, yr oedd angen angori'r weledigaeth helaethach wrth yr efengyl gyntefig, wrth eiriau'r Iesu ei hun. Felly, fel sail i'r syniad o ymgnawdoliad cyffredinol, yr oedd Jones yn awyddus i ddangos fod yr Iesu yn dysgu nad peth unigryw iddo ef oedd bod yn Fab Duw. Oni ddysgodd ef *bawb* i gyfarch Duw fel "Ein Tad"? Onid dangos bod perthynas Iesu a Duw yn berthynas agored i'r ddynoliaeth oll yw gwir arwyddocâd y geiriau a lefarodd yn ei weddi o ymgysegriad, "Rwy'n gweddïo ar iddynt oll fod yn un, ie, fel yr wyt ti, O Dad, ynof fi a minnau ynot ti, iddynt hwy hefyd fod ynom ni ..."?[28] Dehonglwyd y geiriau gan Edward Caird fel hyn:

> Christ is thus proclaimed to be the unique revelation of God, but only as the first born of many brethren ... In fact, it *was* through Jesus Christ that that capacity of men to become sons of God, which was in humanity from the first, was actualised or clearly revealed ...[29]

---

[26] Henry Jones, *The Philosophy of Martineau in Relation to the Idealism of the Present Day*, Llundain 1905.

[27] T. Oswald Williams, op. cit., t. 275.

[28] Ioan, XVII, 21. Trafodaeth yn IOJ, tt. 29 a 35.

[29] Edward Caird, op. cit., Cyf. 2, tt. 231.

Diwinyddiaeth yn ymateb i ofynion athroniaeth yw hyn. Y mae mor bellgyrhaeddol ei effaith ag unrhyw weddnewidiad athrawiaethol a ddigwyddodd yn ystod y Diwygiad Protestannaidd. Ond oherwydd y parodrwydd i roddi dehongliad newydd i hen athrawiaethau yn hytrach na'u gwrthwynebu a'u gwrthod, nid esgorodd y rhyddfrydiaeth newydd ar enwadau newydd. Ni welodd Caird na Jones yr angen i droi cefn ar Bresbyteriaeth ac ymuno â'r Undodiaid. Radicaleiddiasant Undodiaeth a Phresbyteriaeth a phob 'iaeth' arall o'r tu mewn drwy ddehongli athrawiaethau diwinyddol traddodiadol fel gwisg dros dro i sylwedd y gellid ei adnabod yn ei noethni pur drwy gyfrwng athroniaeth.

Felly, gyda'r athrawiaeth am fodolaeth Duw: y mae Duw yn athronyddol angenrheidiol, sut bynnag y bu i draddodiadau crefyddol yr oesau geisio portreadu ei ddatguddiad ohono'i hun yn eu hiaith symbolaidd liwgar. Cawn enghraifft o'r math o ymresymiad sy'n gwneud bodolaeth Duw yn angenrheidiol gan T. H. Green yn *Prolegomena to Ethics*. Y mae'n ceisio pontio'r agendor rhwng gwybodaeth oddrychol a gwybodaeth wrthrychol.

> ... we cannot suppose that those relations of facts or objects in consciousness, which constitute any piece of knowledge of which a man becomes master, first come into being when he attains that knowledge; ... They must exist as part of an eternal universe or universe of consciousness ...[30]

Oherwydd bod cysylltiad a pherthynas pethau â'i gilydd wedi eu dal mewn un ymwybyddiaeth dragwyddol mae gwybodaeth wrthrychol yn bosibl i ni. Dyma paham y teimlwn oll ein bod yn byw yn yr un byd â'n gilydd yn hytrach na bod pawb yn byw yn ei fyd preifat ei hun. Y mae'r ffeithiau sydd yn fy meddwl i yn gyson ar y cyfan â'r ffeithiau sydd ym meddyliau pobl eraill. Mae gwybodaeth yn beth cyhoeddus ac yn feddiant cymdeithasol oherwydd bod unoliaeth iddo, ond mae'r unoliaeth honno wedi ei hangori yn yr ymwybyddiaeth dragwyddol.

Ai'r ymwybyddiaeth dragwyddol oedd 'Duw Abraham a Jacob', y Duw y dysgodd yr Iesu ei ddilynwyr i'w alw'n 'Abba', 'dad'? Nid oedd unfrydedd ymhlith yr Idealwyr ar yr ateb i'r cwestiwn hwn. Yr oedd Henry Jones yn bendant yn ei ateb cadarnhaol iddo. Yr oedd yr un mor barod â Green a Caird i weld yn y cysyniad o Dduw amod y posibilrwydd o ganfod gan unrhyw feddwl. Heb y fath gysyniad ni fyddai unrhyw gysondeb (*coherence*) i'n profiad.[31] Y mae Duw yn fetaffisegol angenrheidiol i Jones fel y mae i Green a Caird. Yr oeddynt hwy yn medru uniaethu Absoliwt metaffiseg â Duw ffydd, ond wrth i'r mudiad Idealaidd ddatblygu ym Mhrydain daeth y safbwynt hwn dan feirniadaeth o fwy nag un cyfeiriad.

Dadleuai F. H. Bradley mai diben metaffiseg yw bodloni rheswm. Bodlonir rheswm gan yr hyn sy'n gyfanrwydd ac yn rhydd o anghysondeb, sef y real. Nis bodlonir gan yr hyn sy'n rhannol ac anghyson, sef yr hyn sy'n ymddangosiadol. Y

[30] T. H. Green, *Prolegomena to Ethics,* Rhydychen 1883, t. 83

[31] Edward Caird, op. cit., Cyf. 2, t. 68.

mae'r Absoliwt yn gyfanrwydd, yn gyson ac yn real, ond nid felly Duw, meddai Bradley. Yn ôl dysgeidiaeth crefydd y mae Duw yn bodoli mewn perthynas â'i greadigaeth, ac nid yw unrhyw beth sy'n bodoli mewn perthynas ag arall yn gyfanrwydd ynddo'i hun. Mewn gwirionedd mae'r Absoliwt yn cynnwys y greadigaeth a Duw fel ymddangosiadau rhannol o fewn ei gyfanrwydd real.

Canlyniad ymresymiad fel hyn, meddai Jones, yw fod Bradley yn gorfod derbyn *dau* Fod Mawr ("two supreme beings")[32], y naill yn ateb gofynion crefydd, a'r llall yn ateb gofynion athroniaeth. Nid yw Bradley yn gweld anghysondeb yn hyn. Gwelai ef le i fwy nag un math o wirionedd, gwirioneddau crefydd (serch eu bod yn wirioneddau anghyflawn) a gwirioneddau metaffiseg (a fydd, oherwydd eu cyflawnder, yn wahanol i wirioneddau crefydd). Mae'n datgan bod ymddangosiadau crefydd yn ddigonol *i grefydd*: metaffiseg sydd yn gorfod cyrchu heibio'r ymddangosiadol tuag at y real.

Enghraifft glir o gysyniad sydd yn ganolog i grefydd ond sydd yn amhosibl i fetaffiseg yw personoliaeth Duw. Meddai Bradley:

> A God that can say to himself 'I' as against you and me, is not in my judgement defensible as the last and complete truth for Metaphysics.[33]

Rhaid i'r Absoliwt fod yn ddi-bersonoliaeth neu oruwch personoliaeth. Mae'n cwmpasu pob personoliaeth, eto heb bersonoliaeth, oherwydd o reidrwydd y mae personoliaeth yn cyfyngu, a thrwy ddiffiniad nid oes cyfyngiad ar yr Absoliwt.

Gwêl Bradley anawsterau hyd yn oed o fewn syniadaeth grefyddol ei hun â'r cysyniad o bersonoliaeth Duw. Yr oedd ef mor awyddus â Jones i gyhoeddi dwyfoldeb dynolryw. Mae'n frwd yn ei groeso i'r 'bantheistiaeth' sy'n nodweddu barddoniaeth, celfyddyd a chrefydd yr oes,[34] ond sut mae cysoni'r syniadaeth bantheistaidd gyda chred mewn un bersonoliaeth ddwyfol sy'n bodoli mewn arwahanrwydd trosgynnol – sef Duw sy'n medru dweud 'Myfi'? Ni fedr gwir bantheist briodoli'r fath unigoliaeth ynysig ("external individuality") i Dduw, meddai Bradley.

Ateb Jones i hyn yw gwrthod dadansoddiad Bradley o hanfod personoliaeth. Nid yw unrhyw bersonoliaeth yn gwbl ynysig a digyswllt â'r arall. Mae'r arall yn gyfrwng ffurfiant hunan. Mae ymwybyddiaeth o'r hunan ac o'r arall yn cydsefyll neu'n cyd-ddarfod. Rhan o wead yw pob hunan, ac mae hyn mor wir am bersonoliaeth Duw ag unrhyw bersonoliaeth arall. Ymhell o fod yn anghyson â phantheistiaeth, mae personoliaeth Duw yn sail iddi. Mae'n mynd ymlaen i ddadlau bod gwadu personoliaeth i'r Absoliwt yn amddifadu'r cyfanfyd o'i unoliaeth.

---

32 FTE, t. 314.

33 F. H. Bradley, *Essays on Truth and Reality,* Rhydychen 1914, t. 428.

34 ibid., t. 437. Am drafodaeth bellach gweler David Boucher ac Andrew Vincent, *A Radical Hegelian*, Caerdydd 1993, tt. 56-60.

> ... there is nothing save self-consciousness which does overcome external relations. It alone achieves unity in difference. Self-consciousness is one with itself only through its relation to objects; for a subject that has no object, that does not say 'I' as over against something else is not possible. In denying personality, or self-consciousness to the Absolute, Mr Bradley is thus permitting external relations to be final; and his Universe is in no sense a unity.[35]

Yr oedd perthynas yr hunan â'r arall yn elfen ganolog yng ngwaith Hegel ei hun, wrth gwrs, ac yn thema bwysig mewn meysydd eraill heblaw metaffiseg ac athroniaeth crefydd. Yr oedd yn un o themâu canolog y rhyddfrydiaeth newydd mewn gwleidyddiaeth hefyd.

[35] FTE, t. 321.

Pennod 10

Yr Athronwyr a'r Beirdd

Bardd, yn hytrach nag athronydd, oedd gwrthrych llyfr cyntaf Henry Jones, *Browning as a Philosophical and Religious Teacher*. Ni ddylai hynny beri syndod: yr oedd wedi bod yn astudio llenyddiaeth ymhell cyn iddo ymddiddori mewn athroniaeth, ac yn wir trwy gyfrwng llenyddiaeth y daeth gyntaf i gysylltiad â'r syniadau hynny a fyddai'n llywodraethol yn ei athroniaeth maes o law. Treuliodd ran o'i ddwy flynedd fel myfyriwr yn y Coleg Normal yn astudio llenyddiaeth Saesneg, ac yn llyfrgell y coleg hwnnw darganfu waith un o'r awduron a ddylanwadodd drymaf arno, Thomas Carlyle.[1]

Yr oedd llenyddiaeth Saesneg yn faes astudiaeth iddo ym Mhrifysgol Glasgow hefyd, a bu John Nichol, ei athro Saesneg, yn ddylanwad llawn cyn drymed arno â Caird. Dwysawyd y dylanwad hwn oherwydd bod Nichol a Caird ar yr un donfedd yn syniadol: y ddau ohonynt yn gynnyrch yr 'Old Mortality'. Gallai Nichol yn hawdd fod wedi esgyn i gadair athroniaeth, a dyna'n wir oedd ei ddymuniad ar un adeg.[2] Yr oedd Caird yntau'n ysgrifennu ar bynciau llenyddol o bryd i'w gilydd.[3] Ystyriodd Jones geisio am swydd fel darlithydd Saesneg unwaith[4] a phan symudodd i St Andrews yn 1891, fe esgynnodd i Gadair Rhesymeg a Rhethreg, sef swydd lle darlithiai ar lenyddiaeth Saesneg yn ogystal ag ar athroniaeth.

Nid oedd felly yn ystyried ei fod yn 'tresmasu' y tu allan i ffiniau diffiniedig ei arbenigedd fel athronydd wrth ddarlithio ac ysgrifennu ar farddoniaeth. Gwelai ef a'i gyfoedion gysylltiad rhwng barddoniaeth yr oes a chyfeiriad athroniaeth y dyfodol. Yn wir, credent eu bod yn fwy dyledus i feirdd Saesneg nag i athronwyr Saesneg. Am ryw reswm, meddai A. C. Bradley (cyfaill a chyd-weithiwr i Jones yn Glasgow, ac Athro Barddoniaeth Prifysgol Rhydychen yn ddiweddarach), nid yw athronwyr y Saeson ar yr un donfedd â'u beirdd.

---

1 Nid yw'n ymddangos bod llenyddiaeth Gymraeg wedi cael fawr ddim dylanwad ar Jones. Pan anfonodd Elfed ato i ofyn am restr o lyfrau Cymraeg a fwynhaodd (ar gyfer cyfres yn *Y Cyfaill*) atebodd Jones, "Y mae fy ngwybodaeth o lenyddiaeth Cymru yn rhy brin i fod o unrhyw les i undyn." (LlGC, Papurau Elvet Lewis, 10572B.) Dywedodd wrth John Morris-Jones unwaith, "Feiddia i ddim honni fy mod yn Gymro ysgolheigaidd: ond y mae Gymraeg di-lediaith mam a nhad gin i – iaith y gegin a'r siop grydd." (JMJ.92.). Yn Gymraeg yr ysgrifennai at ei hen gyfaill bob amser, ond heb lawer o hyder, er fod ei iaith yn ddilychwin. "Jones! mae n well gin i ysgrifennu Cymraeg atoch chwi na Saesneg – gan mil o weithiau. Ond os ydyw fy Nghymraeg i mor ddrwg nes merwino eich clustiau mi beidiaf. Ches i'r un lesson iawn gan neb … "(JMJ.86.)

2 Gweler Pennod 2, t. 17.

3 Cyhoeddodd Edward Caird *Essays on Literature* yn 1892.

4 Gweler Pennod 3, t. 24.

> ... if we read first Pindar and the Greek dramatists, and then Plato and Aristotle, we feel no incongruity or want of kinship in the poetry and the philosophy, and no inadequacy of either to the other. Neither do we feel this after reading German poetry from Goethe to Heine, and German philosophy from Kant to Hegel ... But this is just what we do feel when we pass from the poetry of Shakespeare's or Wordsworth's Age to Locke or Hume or any our most purely native philosophers. We find ourselves in the presence, not merely of an inferior degree of genius, but of a view of the world incongruous with the substance of the poetry.[5]

Wrth sôn am waith Thomas Carlyle, awdur nad oedd neb, gan gynnwys ef ei hun, yn ei ystyried yn athronydd, dywed un arall o gyfeillion Jones, John Henry Muirhead,

> Philosophy, like experience, is a house of many mansions. There is a place in it for everyone who by word or act gives typical expression to the deeper mind of the race in any one of the departments of its operation. A man may thus be of service to philosophy by the deepening of consciousness that comes from speaking to his time from a level of experience more truly representative of that of his nation than any others.[6]

Dyma wnaeth Coleridge, Carlyle, Wordsworth a Browning. Wrth gwrs, y mae gwahaniaeth rhwng athroniaeth a barddoniaeth, ond yn ôl Jones cyfyd y ddau o'r un ysgogiad. Buddiol i'r athronwyr fyddai sylweddoli hynny, meddai, oherwydd y perygl mwyaf i ddyfodol athroniaeth yw cael ei hynysu. Yr ysgogiad hwnnw yw'r ymwybyddiaeth o undod sylfaenol popeth mewn un cyfanfyd. Heb ragdybied yr undod hwn nid oes sail i wybodaeth wyddonol ac athroniaeth, na sail ychwaith i'r ymdeimlad hwnnw o gynghanedd yn y cread sydd wrth wraidd barddoniaeth a chelfyddyd.

> ... if the conception of the world as a whole is held to be impossible, if philosophy is a futility, then poetry will be a vain sentiment and religion a delusion.[7]

Fel mater o hanes, y mae rhai cyfnodau pan fydd yr ymwybyddiaeth hon yn wan neu'n absennol. Geilw Jones y fath gyfnod yn 'age of prose and scepticism'.

Yn y bôn, agwedd meddwl yn hytrach na rhyw athrawiaeth arbennig yw athroniaeth. Ni cheir felly ddamcaniaeth derfynol mewn athroniaeth na safbwynt disyfl;[8] yr hyn a geir yw cysondeb dull. Y dull sy'n briodol i athroniaeth yw'r dull dadansoddol, a dyma sy'n gwahanu athroniaeth oddi wrth y celfyddydau yn gyffredinol, a barddoniaeth yn arbennig. Lle bydd y bardd yn ceisio priodas

---

[5] A. C. Bradley, *English Poetry and German Philosophy in the Age of Wordsworth,* Manceinion 1909, t. 10.

[6] John Henry Muirhead, *The Platonic Tradition in Anglo-Saxon Philosophy,* Llundain 1931, t. 126.

[7] BPRT, t. 26 (37).

[8] IPC, t. 7.

berffaith rhwng syniad a'i fynegiant, a hynny mewn cyfanwaith gorffenedig, bydd yr athronydd yn gorfod chwalu'r undod hwnnw wrth geisio cael gafael ar y 'cynnwys' cysyniadol.

Eithr ni ddylid cymryd annibyniaeth celfyddyd ac athroniaeth i olygu na fedr athronwyr a beirdd elwa o ymgydnabod â gwaith ei gilydd. Rhaid i'r athronwyr dderbyn mai yn eu barddoniaeth y costrelodd rhai cenhedloedd eu syniadau mwyaf treiddgar am natur moesoldeb. Ni chynhyrchodd yr Iddewon neu'r Saeson athronwyr i ragori ar Job neu Shakespeare. Nid llai ychwaith yw dyled yr athronwyr i feirdd y cenhedloedd 'athronyddol' megis Sophocles a Goethe. Ac "yn ein dyddiau ni" (h.y. 1891), pan yw awdurdod crefydd ar drai, a diffyg unfrydedd yn nodweddu'r athronwyr, llwyddodd y beirdd i ennill gwrandawiad. Mae eu gwaith hwy yn fwy diriaethol na gwaith yr athronwyr ac yn haws 'cael gafael ynddo'. Ac er i ni dderbyn mai priod waith yr athronwyr yw dadansoddi a dadelfennu, y mae serch hynny wir angen hefyd iddynt feddu'r gallu i weld pethau yn eu cyfanrwydd fel y gwna'r artist. Mae hyn yn arbennig o wir yn achos y gwyddorau moesol lle mae angen cydbwysedd rhwng yr angen i ddadansoddi a'r angen i weld dynion a'u gweithredoedd yn gyfain ac yn eu crynswth.

Ond, am yr union reswm nad dadansoddi yw priod waith y bardd, gall ei waith bylu miniogrwydd beirniadaeth a suo'r ysbryd ymofynnol. Nid da fod y bardd ei hunan a heb gymdeithas yr athronydd. Yn wir, i lawn werthfawrogi gogoniant undod gwaith o gelfyddyd bydd angen ymarfer y ddawn (a berthyn o briodoldeb i athronwyr) i ddadelfennu'r hyn a unir yn y cyfanwaith. Ac ni raid i'r bardd bryderu os teflir golwg athronyddol dros ei waith ambell dro gyda'r bwriad o ddarganfod ac ystyried ei syniadau, oblegid nid apêl at y synhwyrau yn unig yw celfyddyd. Nid rheswm moel yw dyn, ond nid talp o deimlad diddeall mohono ychwaith. Wrth gwrs, ni ddylid ystyried darn o farddoniaeth fel petai'n athroniaeth fydryddol, ond gwnawn fwy fyth o gam â barddoniaeth drwy ei darllen er budd y synhwyrau'n unig.[9]

Yng Nghymru, fe gododd to o feirdd yn negawd olaf y ganrif a gymerodd y genadwri hon yn sylfaen i'w gwaith, sef yr ysgol a adwaenir fel 'Y Bardd Newydd'. Eu diffyg mawr oedd tybied mai dim ond iddynt gael gafael sicr ar y syniadau, fe edrychai'r farddoniaeth ar ei hôl ei hun. Dyma'r safbwynt sy'n egluro dull cywaith Rhys J. Huws ac R. Gwylfa Roberts o gynhyrchu pryddestau. Yn ôl Alun Llywelyn-Williams,

> Byddai'r naill yn darllen o gwmpas y testun, yn penderfynu ar gynllun ac yn ysgrifennu'r defnyddiau mewn rhyddiaith, a'r llall wedyn yn nyddu'r cwbl yn daclus ar fydr. Ffrwyth y bartneriaeth ryfedd hon oedd pryddestau arobryn Blaenau Ffestiniog ym 1898, ar *Charles o'r Bala*, a Chaerdydd y flwyddyn ddilynol, ar *Y Diddanydd Arall*.[10]

[9] BPRT, t. 8 (20).

[10] Yn Dyfnallt Morgan, *Gwŷr Llên y Bedwaredd Ganrif ar Bymtheg,* Llandybïe 1968, t. 269.

Afraid dweud nad oes sail o gwbl i'r dull hwn o 'farddoni' yn namcaniaethau esthetig Jones. Mae'n wir i J. T. Job, wrth feirniadu cystadleuaeth yr awdl yn Eisteddfod Merthyr Tudful (1901), gyhuddo Ben Bowen o fod dan ddylanwad llyfr Jones:

> Dyma awdl braidd yn eithriadol o ran ei meddylwaith, wedi ei chanu ar hyd llinell nad yw bellach yn newydd ym marddoniaeth Cymru. Y sawl sydd wedi darllen llyfr y Proffeswr Henry Jones ar 'Browning' (a pha fardd yn Nghymru nad yw yn hen gynefin â'r llyfr rhagorol hwnw, bellach?) – a ŵyr am y llinell o feddwl y cyfeiriwn ati. Yr ydym wedi sylwi ar rai cyfansoddiadau barddonol diweddar – a ystyrir yn 'wreiddiol' a 'newydd' – er nad ydynt yn ddim amgen o ran eu prif syniadau nag arall-eiriad o brif syniadau y llyfr uchod.[11]

Eto, nid yw Jones yn unman yn cymeradwyo mydryddu llyfrau athronyddol (hyd yn oed rhai a ysgrifennwyd ganddo ef!). Yn achos y 'Bardd Newydd' yr hyn a dry diffyg yn drychineb yw'r ffaith nad oedd y syniadau y ceisient eu mydryddu yn deillio o unrhyw weledigaeth eglur. Ni ellid dwyn y cyhuddiad hwnnw yn erbyn gwrthrych llyfr Jones, wrth gwrs.

O blith y beirdd, Browning, meddai ef, allai oddef archwiliad 'syniadol' orau, oherwydd fe saif ef ar y ffin sy'n gwahanu barddoniaeth ac athroniaeth. Eto i gyd, cydnebydd Jones ei fod yn amcanu gwneud rhywbeth sydd mewn gwirionedd yn amhriodol wrth chwilio barddoniaeth Browning am athrawiaeth foesol a chrefyddol. Daw'r cyfiawnhad dros wneud hynny gyda'r gosodiad fod pawb sydd yn meddwl yn aelodau o un frawdolaeth gyffredinol.[12] Beth bynnag yw maes ein hymdrechion, cemeg, celfyddyd neu foeseg, yr un yw'r nod,[13] sef adnabod y byd yr ydym yn trigo ynddo. Trwy gyfrwng y meddwl y deuwn i adnabyddiaeth ohono ac y sefydlwn berthynas ag ef.

Wrth i ni ddod i'w adnabod, byddwn i raddau yn ei greu hefyd.[14] Yn yr ymwybyddiaeth ddynol cysylltir elfennau a wahanwyd gan amser, amgylchiadau a gofod. Meddwl dyn a ddyry i bopeth ei arwyddocâd, fel y canodd Browning:

> The winds
> Are henceforth voices, wailing or a shout
> A querulous mutter, or a quick gay laugh,
> Never a senseless gust now man is born.
> (Paracelsus)

Trwy'r meddwl dynol bydd natur yn medru bod yn brydferth, oherwydd yn absenoldeb meddwl ni ellir ac ni fydd prydferthwch, trefn, diben nac arwyddocâd i

[11] Gweler David Bowen (Gol.), *Cofiant a Barddoniaeth Ben Bowen,* Treorci 1904, td. cxlii. Gweler hefyd bennod Dyfnallt yn yr un gyfrol, yn enwedig td. cliv-clv.

[12] BPRT, t. 35 (45).

[13] ibid, t. 46 (56).

[14] IPC, t. 147.

ddim.[15] I Wordsworth, rhyw fath o ddrych oedd natur lle gallai dyn adnabod adlewyrchiad ohono'i hun, a dyna paham yr oedd ef yn:

> well pleased to recognize
> In nature and the language of the sense
> The anchor of my purest thoughts, the nurse,
> The guide, the guardian of my heart, and soul
> Of all my moral being.
>
> (Tintern Abbey)

Ond, meddai Jones, nid oedd Browning yn uniaethu dyn a natur mewn ffordd mor uniongyrchol â Wordsworth. Nid ystyriai Browning natur yn ysbrydol ynddi ei hun, yn absenoldeb dyn fel petai. Dim ond trwy gyfrwng meddwl dyn y cyflawna natur yr addewid ysbrydol a fu ynddi o'r cychwyn.

> Hints and previsions . .
> Are strewn confusedly everywhere about
> The inferior natures, and all lead up higher,
> All shape out divinely the superior race,
> The heir of hopes too fair to turn out false,
> And man appears at last.
>
> (Paracelsus)

Gwelai Jones yng ngwaith y beirdd Saesneg hyn flaenffrwyth y chwyldro syniadol a gafwyd eisoes yn yr Almaen yng ngwaith athronwyr a beirdd fel Kant a Lessing, Fichte a Schiller, Goethe a Hegel. Llwyddasant hwy i bontio'r agendor rhwng y materol a'r ysbrydol. Synhwyrodd Shelley a Wordsworth bresenoldeb yr ysbrydol mewn natur, ond Browning a'i gwelodd yn cyrraedd uchafbwynt mewn dyn.

Nodweddir meddwl dyn gan y gallu i wahaniaethu rhwng y byd fel y mae ac fel y gallai fod. Unwaith y sylweddolwn nad da lle gellir gwell, ni allwn fodloni ar dderbyn y byd fel y cawn ef. Unwaith y bwytasom o bren gwybodaeth da a drwg agorodd agendor rhyngom a'r byd a'i gwnaeth yn amhosibl i ni ei dderbyn yn ddigwestiwn. Fe'n gwahanwyd i raddau o drefn natur, ac mae angen ein cymodi â hi. Oherwydd bod Browning wedi sylweddoli hyn ni fedr fod yn 'fardd natur' yn yr un ystyr â Wordsworth, meddai Jones.[16]

Y berthynas rhwng natur a moesoldeb oedd thema ei Ddarlith Agoriadol fel Athro Athroniaeth Foesol ym Mhrifysgol Glasgow yn 1894, *Is the Order of Nature Opposed to the Moral Life*?[17] Yr oedd y ddarlith hon yn ymateb i ddarlith a draddodwyd yn ystod y flwyddyn flaenorol gan T. H. Huxley ar *Evolution and Ethics* (Y Ddarlith Romanes). Sŵolegydd oedd Thomas Henry Huxley

[15] Ibid, t. 148.
[16] Ibid., t. 177.
[17] Henry Jones, *Is the Order of Nature Opposed to the Moral Life*?, Glasgow 1894.

(1825–1895) a Darwinydd brwd gyda diddordebau yn ymestyn ymhell y tu hwnt i ffiniau gwyddoniaeth bur. Ysgrifenasai lyfr bychan ar athroniaeth David Hume yn 1879, ac yn 1863 cyhoeddodd y llyfr, *Zoological Evidences as to Man's Place in Nature*.

Yr ysgytwad pennaf a ddaeth yn sgil damcaniaeth esblygiad a detholiad naturiol oedd y sylweddoliad na weithredai'r byd naturiol ar sail cyfiawnder. Yn ôl y ddamcaniaeth hon," … swyddogaeth detholiad naturiol oedd gweithredu fel gogor gan nithio'r rhai 'gwerthfawr', yn nhermau goroesiad, oddi wrth y rhai llai gwerthfawr."[18] Yn nhermau goroesiad ac nid yn nhermau moesoldeb y clorianna trefn natur yr hyn sydd yn 'werthfawr'. Y mae dau ymateb yn bosibl i'r sylweddoliad yma. Un ymateb yw dweud bod yn rhaid i ni wrth foesoldeb newydd, wedi ei sylfaenu ar y patrwm biolegol, a'r ymateb arall yw dweud bod yn rhaid i ddyn ei hun (ac yn unig) gynnal y gwerthoedd moesol mewn bydysawd di-foesoldeb.

Enghraifft o'r safbwynt cyntaf yw'r eiddo Friedrich Nietzsche (1844–1900). Tua'r adeg hon cyhoeddodd ei lyfr *Der Antichrist* lle mae'n dweud:

> Gelwir Cristnogaeth yn grefydd *tosturi*. Saif tosturi mewn gwrthgyferbyniad â'r teimladau cryfhaol hynny sy'n atgyfnerthu'r angerdd bywiol: ei effaith yw gwanhau. Fe gyll dyn nerth pan dosturia. Mae'r colli nerth, a ddigwyddodd i fywyd eisioes yn y dioddef gwreiddiol, yn cael ei gynyddu a'i amlhau ymhellach drwy dosturi. Daw dioddefaint yn haint drwy dosturi; weithiau gall arwain at erydu bywyd ac angerdd bywiol ar raddfa dorfol afresymol o'i gymharu â maint ei achos gwreiddiol (– marwolaeth y Nasaread, er enghraifft). Un wedd yw hon, ond mae un arall sy'n bwysicach. Pe baem yn gwerthuso tosturi yn ôl gwerth yr adwaith arferol iddo, gwelem pa mor beryglus yw mewn gwirionedd. Yn gyffredinol bydd tosturi yn tanseilio deddf esblygiad, sydd yn ddeddf *detholiad*. Mae'n diogelu'r hyn sy'n aeddfed i'w ddinistrio; mae'n amddiffyn y sawl a gondemniwyd ac a ddietifeddwyd gan fywyd ei hun; drwy gynnydd yr erthylod o bob math sy'n cael cynhaliaeth drwyddo mae'n troi bywyd ei hunan yn dywyll a gwyriedig.[19]

Enghraifft o'r ail safbwynt yw un Huxley. Y mae'n cytuno nad yw esblygiad yn gweithredu ar sail foesol a chyfiawn, ond yn hytrach nag argymell dynolryw i ddynwared natur, mae'n datgan mai dyletswydd y ddynoliaeth yw gweithredu'n groes i drefn natur. Byddai wedi ategu profiad Cristnogol Ann Griffiths pan ganodd hithau:

> Er mai cwbl groes i natur
>   Yw fy llwybyr yn y byd.

Yn wir gwêl Huxley ddyn fel unig wrthwynebydd y drefn naturiol yn y bydysawd wrth iddo geisio sefydlu ffordd o fyw ar werthoedd cwbl groes iddi. Rhaid i ddyn, meddai Huxley, "combat and check the cosmic process, and bend the Titan to his will." Felly, ateb cadarnhaol sydd ganddo i gwestiwn Jones: '*Ydyw*, y mae trefn natur yn groes i'r bywyd moesol'.

---

[18] Diffiniad R. Elwyn Hughes yn *Darwin* (Cyfres y Meddwl Modern), Dinbych 1981, t. 93. Gweler hefyd, Harri Williams, *Duw, Daeareg a Darwin*, Llandysul 1979.

[19] Friedrich Nietzsche, *Der Antichrist* (1888), Adran 7.

Gellid disgwyl efallai, yng ngoleuni'r hyn a ddywed am arwyddocâd meddwl dyn yn y bydysawd, y byddai Jones yn cytuno â Huxley, ond nid dyna wnaeth. Mae'n gwrthod y safbwynt hwnnw am nad oedd Huxley wedi sylweddoli bod trefn natur a'r bywyd moesol yn agweddau ar yr un cyfanfyd. Wrth iddo wrthgyferbynnu trefn natur ar y naill law a moesoldeb ar y llall, mae Huxley wedi hollti cyfanfyd yn ddau ac yna wedi trafod yr hanerau fel pe baent yn ddau gyfan. Eithr, meddai Jones, yn union fel na fedr planhigyn ddwyn ffrwyth ond drwy gyfrwng y drefn naturiol a'i cynhyrchodd, ni fedr dyn fyw bywyd moesol ond drwy gyfrwng y byd a'i cynhyrchodd yntau. Ynddynt eu hunain nid yw'r materol na'r meddyliol yn hunanddigonol. Y ffaith yw, trefn natur sydd wedi cynhyrchu'r meddwl dynol sy'n gyfrwng moesoldeb a gwybodaeth yn y bydysawd. Ymhell o fod yn groes i natur, mae moesoldeb yn gynnyrch natur, meddai Jones.

Yr oedd gwrthwynebiad Jones i safbwynt hiwmanistaidd Huxley yn sathru ar gyrn diwinyddol fodd bynnag, a gwyddai hynny o'r gorau. Anghytunai â'r crefyddwyr hynny oedd o'r farn fod olrhain tarddiad gwerthoedd ysbrydol yn ôl i drefn natur yn gwadu arbenigrwydd yr ysbrydol.

> The derivation of spiritual from natural laws thus appears to be fatal to the former; and religious teachers naturally think that it is necessary for their cause to snap the links of the chain of evolution, and, like Professor Drummond, to establish absolute gaps, not only between the inorganic and the organic worlds, but also between the self-conscious life of man and the mysterious, spiritual life of Christ, or God … On the contrary, this idea (h.y. esblygiad) is, in all the history of thought, the first constructive hypothesis which is adeqate to the uses of ethics and religion.[20]

Paragraffau fel yr uchod a osododd sail i gyhuddiad y *Goleuad* fod Jones yn 'cymysgu nefoedd a daear'.[21] Ond, meddai ef, unwaith y tybir bod mater a meddwl yn gyflawn ynddynt eu hunain fe gyfyd problemau gwaelodol iawn, nid yn unig ynglŷn â statws moesoldeb, ond ynglŷn â'r posibilrwydd o unrhyw fath o wybodaeth o gwbl. Os ynysir y meddwl, fel sylwedd cyflawn ynddo'i hun, fe gyfyd cwestiwn dyrys profi bod realiti 'yn y byd allanol' yn cyfateb i'r hyn sydd 'yn y meddwl'. Mae athronwyr y Gorllewin wedi cynnig sawl ateb i'r problemau hyn. Gwadodd rhai fod gennym unrhyw wybodaeth am fodolaeth byd 'allanol'; mynnodd eraill fod rhywbeth yn bodoli y tu allan i feddyliau, ond na feddwn wybodaeth amdanynt 'fel y maent', dim ond amdanynt fel yr 'ymddangosant' i'r meddwl. Rhoddodd eraill y flaenoriaeth i'r byd materol, gan weld byd y meddwl fel agwedd yn unig ar y materol. Ond problemau athronyddol a greodd athronwyr iddynt eu hunain yw'r rhain, yn ôl Jones, oherwydd iddynt ddechrau gyda'r dybiaeth fod meddwl a mater yn gyflawn ynddynt eu hunain. Dyma paham y mae ef yn pwysleisio gyda'r fath arddeliad mai gwisg ddiwnïad yw'r cyfanfyd.

---

[20] BPRT, tt. 200-1 (207).

[21] Gweler Pennod 5.

> There are not two worlds – the one of thoughts, the other of things – which are absolutely exclusive of each other, but one universe in which thought and reality meet … The inference is not from thoughts to things, nor from things to thoughts, but from a partially known world to a systematic theory of that world. Philosophy is not engaged in the foolish enterprise of trying to discover whether the world exists; its problem is how to account for our knowledge. It asks what must the nature of things be, seeing that they are known; and what is the nature of thought, seeing that it knows facts?[22]

Gwelodd Jones yn namcaniaeth Darwin adlewyrchiad a chadarnhad gwyddonol o'r idealaeth Hegelaidd. Trwy gyfrwng gwybodeg, rhesymeg, seicoleg a hanes yr oedd Hegel wedi ceisio adrodd stori fawr meddwl yn y byd yn ei lyfr cyntaf, *Ffenomenoleg Ysbryd* (1807), ac yn ei *Descent of Man* (1871) yr oedd Darwin wedi dadlau na ellid eithrio dyn o'r broses esblygol. Credai Jones mai yn y meddwl dynol y costrelir cynnyrch uchaf esblygiad, ond bu'r posibilrwydd yno drwy gydol oesau materol bore'r byd.

> Natural science corroborates the truth which the poets and philosophers divine. Man, it tells, is not an exception to the scheme of things … he was present in promise at the dawn of being, waiting to be evolved. The potencies of his spirit slumbered amongst the molten masses and the fiery vapours. For all is one scheme. Evolution tolerates no break, brings forth nothing altogether new, permits nothing to become altogether old. It builds the living present from the dying past, forgetting nothing, abandoning nothing in its course, least of all the dormant promise of the emerging ideal. That is immortal, present from first to last and maintaining itself in every change. Every step in the cosmic process is its self-emancipation, until at length it stands declared in a form worthy of itself; and it shows itself as spirit.[23]

Gair digon anodd ei ddehongli yw 'spirit'. Ceisiodd Jones ei egluro fel hyn:

> 'Spirit' is the best word I know for thought and feeling and will and all the powers of man in interpenetration and indivisible unity.[24]

Priodoleddau a berthyn i fodau ymwybodol yw'r rhain, ac yn wir, efallai y dylid eu cyfyngu i fodau hunanymwybodol. Er bod y term 'ysbryd' i'w ddeall fel gair sydd yn cyfleu undod a chydymdreiglad y priodoleddau hyn, bu athronwyr o gyfnod y Groegiaid ymlaen yn pwysleisio'r gwahaniaethau rhyngddynt a'r duedd sydd ynddynt i wrthdaro. Rhyw ymbarél o air yw 'ysbryd', felly, ond nid yw Jones am osod yr un bri ar bob un o'r priodoleddau sy'n llechu dano.

Er maint ei edmygedd o Browning, credai fod un gwendid cwbl sylfaenol yn nysgeidiaeth y bardd. Cytunai â Browning mai'r gwerth moesol uchaf yw cariad.

> There is no good of life but love – but love!
> What else looks good, is some shade flung from love,
> Love gilds it, gives it worth.
>
> (In a Balcony)

[22] BPRT, tt. 205-6 (211-2).

[23] IPC, t. 146.

[24] IPC, t. 36, troednodyn.

Ond fe aeth Browning ymlaen i ddatgan bod cariad yn y pen draw yn gorfod diystyru gwybodaeth oherwydd bod y deall dynol yn analluog i amgyffred sut y gallai trefn natur fod yn sylfaenol foesol a da yn wyneb yr holl ddrygioni sydd yn y byd.

> Wholly distrust thy knowledge then, and trust
> As wholly love allied to ignorance!
> There lies thy truth and safety.
>
> (A Pillar at Sebevar)

Dyma gam gwag Browning ym marn Jones: disodli deall gyda 'ffydd y galon'. Dibrisir popeth unwaith y'i cyplysir ag anwybodaeth. 'Allied to ignorance' fe gyll hyd yn oed cariad ei werth. Dadleuai Browning, fodd bynnag, fod elfen o anwybodaeth yn hanfodol mewn moesoldeb. Pe bai ein gwybodaeth ni yn gyflawn, ni fyddai gan foesoldeb le i weithredu, oherwydd gellid disgrifio pob gweithred yn nhermau deddf achos ac effaith. Pe baem yn hollwybodol ni fyddai angen delfrydau arnom. Byddai 'dylai' y ddeddf foesol wedi ei ddisodli gan 'mae' deddf natur, a ninnau yn gweithredu'n beiriannol. Ofer ffydd lle bo gwybodaeth. Ond, er bod ein gwybodaeth yn ddiffygiol, cred Browning fod ein teimladau yn llefaru wrthym yn sicrach o lawer.

Mae Browning yn unigryw yn y modd y gwnaeth anwybodaeth yn elfen ganolog mewn moeseg. Ym mhob damcaniaeth foesegol arall mae anwybodaeth yn ein hesgusodi rhag gorfod derbyn cyfrifoldeb moesol, ond gwnaeth Browning anwybodaeth yn *amod* cyfrifoldeb moesol. Ei gamgymeriad, yn ôl Jones, oedd methu â gweld bod perthynas hanfodol rhwng ein teimladau a'n gwybodaeth.

> In the life of man at least, the separation of the emotional and intellectual elements extinguishes both. We cannot know that in which we have no interest. The very effort to comprehend an object rests on interest, or the feeling of ourselves in it; so that knowledge, as well as morality, may be said to begin in love. We cannot know except we love; but, on the other hand, we cannot love that which we do not in some degree know. Wherever the frontiers of knowledge may be it is certain that there is nothing beyond them which can either arouse feeling, or be a steadying centre for it. Emotion is like a climbing plant. It clings to the tree of knowledge, adding beauty to its strength. But, without knowledge, it is impossible for man. There is no feeling which is not also incipient knowledge – that face of the known fact which is turned inwards.[25]

Cynnyrch gwybodaeth yw gwrthrych cariad, a chynnyrch y deall yw gwybodaeth. Er mor eang yw ystod yr hyn a gwmpasir gan ysbryd, angorir y cyfan wrth y deall. Mae ein holl brofiad yn deillio o ymwneud ein deall â'n hamgylchedd. Felly wrth i ni ymresymu a dadansoddi'r profiad hwnnw, boed hynny'n agwedd ar foesoldeb neu grefydd neu gelfyddyd, yr hyn a wnawn mewn gwirionedd yw symud o reswm tuag at reswm.[26]

[25] BPRT, t. 321 (324-5).
[26] ibid., t. 332 (336).

Wrth gwrs, nid y pwyslais ar reswm sydd yn newydd yma, ond yn hytrach y gydnabyddiaeth fod ysbryd mor amlochrog. Mae Jones, er enghraifft, yn derbyn pwysigrwydd cyfraniad yr isymwybod. Cyfeiria at ddamcaniaethau seicolegol William James[27] parthed ehangder a dyfnder y rhan honno o'r meddwl sydd allan o gyrraedd ymwybyddiaeth. Nid yw am wadu pwysigrwydd yr elfennau hyn, ond bydd yn awyddus i'n hatgoffa fod y cyfan sy'n llifo trwy brofiad i selerau tywyll y meddwl yn brofiadau a ffurfiwyd yn y lle cyntaf gan ymateb y deall i'w amgylchedd. Drwy ridyll y deall y cafodd yr isymwybod y delweddau a'r teimladau sydd yn anodd eu dehongli pan gyffyrddant haen ymwybodol a 'rhesymegol' y meddwl.

Yr un modd, cydnabu Jones bwysigrwydd y dylanwadau cymdeithasol sydd yn cyflyru deall yr unigolyn. Mae'n derbyn dilysrwydd pwyslais Balfour ar arwyddocâd traddodiad ac awdurdod yn ffurfiant ein syniadau.[28] Hyn, yn hytrach na rheswm pur, yw ffynhonnell ein syniadau crefyddol, gwleidyddol a moesol, meddai Balfour. Yn y diwedd, swyddogaeth ddigon distadl sydd gan reswm yn ffurfiant y rhain, sef rôl catalogydd. Mae'n derbyn, trefnu, cofnodi a throsglwyddo'r traddodiadau sy'n ffurfio gwir sylwedd profiadau pobl. Ond, meddai Jones, er bod hyn i gyd yn wir, nid yw traddodiad heb darddle. Epil rheswm ydyw yn y pen draw.

> There is no customary opinion which was not once a bold conception, and no habit which was not at one time a venturous enterprise. Reason built tradition, and reason alone receives and transmits it ... To bind reason in chains at the feet of tradition is to enslave it to its own past.[29]

Nid rhywbeth a 'roddwyd unwaith' i ni gan reswm yw traddodiad ychwaith. Fe'i dygir yn gyson gerbron brawdlys rheswm i'w adnewyddu a'i addasu os yw'r gymdeithas yn fyw ac iach. Dywedodd Balfour mai'r hyn sy'n gwahaniaethu dyn oddi wrth y bwystfilod yw ei ymwybyddiaeth o draddodiad, nid ei allu i ymresymu. Ond, gofynnodd Jones, a oedd Balfour wedi sylweddoli paham y mae'r bwystfilod yn amddifad o draddodiad?

> Brutes have instincts, but not traditions: for though they may be conscious, they are not self-conscious. They can not by reflexion make their own lives an object of their thought, and so enlarge them.[30]

[27] IPC, t. 47.
[28] ibid., t. 45.
[29] ibid., t. 50-1.
[30] ibid., t. 50.

Pennod 11

Cymdeithas, Cenedl a Gwladwriaeth

Gydag esblygiad dyn esgorodd ymwybyddiaeth ar hunanymwybyddiaeth. Yn ôl Hegel, ni fydd hunanymwybyddiaeth yn deffro mewn dyn nes y daw ei ymwybyddiaeth unigol i gysylltiad a gwrthdrawiad â'i amgylchedd ac â dynion eraill. Mynega Jones y syniad hwn gyda'r gymhareb hon:

> As the chemist brings out the qualities of a gas or liquid, by observing 'its give and take' with other substances, … so are man's powers made evident – and indeed, made real also – through his interaction with the world and with his fellows.[1]

Wrth bwysleisio natur ffurfiannol dylanwad ei gyd-ddyn ar yr unigolyn gwrthodai'r Hegeliaid y ddamcaniaeth ryddfrydol glasurol am berthynas yr unigolyn a chymdeithas, sef mai creadigaeth unigolion yw cymdeithas. I'r gwrthwyneb, gwelai'r Hegeliaid unigolion fel creadigaeth cymdeithas.

> … rhaid i ni dewi sôn am bersonau unigol fel pe gallent byth hanfodi ar wahan oddiwrth gymdeithas, neu gyrhaedd eu hamcanion oddieithr trwy ddyfod yn organau iddi a chario allan ei hamcanion hi.[2]

> … *the nature of the individual is essentially social*. That is to say, a man's relations to his fellows are not addenda to his personality, but the inmost content and reality of it.[3]

Mae pob un o briodoleddau'r unigolyn wedi eu derbyn yn etifeddiaeth gan gymdeithas a thrwyddi, gan gynnwys y rhai mwyaf creiddiol megis iaith, cysyniadau, moesau, amcanion bywyd.

> Fel y sugna plentyn bach ei faeth o fronnau ei fam, felly y sugnwn ninnau holl gynhaliaeth ein meddwl a'n hysbryd o fronnau Cymdeithas … Iaith pwy sydd ar dy wefus di, onid iaith dy wlad? Arferion pwy a welaist, ac a ddynwaredaist ac a gofleidiaist ti, onid arferion dy wlad? Ai ti a ddyfeisiodd y gwahaniaeth a weli di rhwng y drwg a'r da? A ddyfeisiaist ti unrhyw un o elfennau bywyd gwâr? Ai ti a sefydlodd ddeddfau dy foes, ac a osododd sylfaeni dy gred grefyddol? Na! benthyg ydynt bob un.[4]

Dyna paham na allai cymdeithas fod wedi ei ffurfio drwy benderfyniad bwriadol unigolion. Cyn cymdeithas ni fyddai unrhyw unigolion yn bod. Erthyl o beth fyddai bod dynol heb iaith na syniadau nac amcanion. Mae'r holl etifeddiaeth

---

[1] IPC, t. 34.

[2] 'Y Corff Cymdeithasol', *Y Traethodydd,* 1884, t. 266.

[3] WFSR, t. 233. Cymh., "As a man becomes more of a man, a greater individual, he becomes less particular. As he knows more truth, he possesses more of that which is universal, true to everybody, a common possession." Llawysgrif McLeish, Prifysgol Glasgow, Darlith 18.

[4] DB, t. 30.

gymdeithasol wedi cronni ym mhob aelod, eithr yn anwastad, a dyma sy'n sicrhau mai unigolyn ac nid clôn yw pob person aeddfed.

> The difference between individuals in significance and worth comes from the different degrees in which they have been able thus to incorporate in themselves these social relations, and to constitute themselves into *foci* of the general life.[5]

Heb yr etifeddiaeth gymdeithasol bydd dyn yn anghyflawn. Mewn gwirionedd y mae unigolion yn aelodau o gorff (cymdeithas), ac o'u gwahanu oddi wrth y corff ni allant fyw. Maent yn dibynnu ar y corff am eu maeth megis aelodau organebau, ac eto fe berthyn i bob aelod o gymdeithas hunaniaeth gwbl annhebyg i achos aelodau o gorff biolegol. Y paradocs hwn oedd testun y papur cyntaf i Jones ei gyhoeddi sef, 'The Social Organism'.[6] Yn sicr, nid rheidrwydd biolegol yw sail cymdeithas. Mae'r rheidrwydd yn fwy grymus na'r biolegol oherwydd ei fod yn medru goresgyn arwahanrwydd yr aelodau, a'u cloi mewn un cyfanrwydd.[7] Cyfyd y rheidrwydd o fod mewn sefyllfaoedd lle bydd unigolyn yn dod yn ymwybodol o ofynion eraill arno. Bydd amcanion a gweithredoedd unigolion yn deillio o'r cyd-destun rhyngbersonol yma. Dyma darddiad y rhwymau sydd yn clymu unigolion fel aelodau o gymdeithas, a dyma gnewyllyn moesoldeb. Profir y berthynas gyntaf oll yng nghyd-destun y teulu. Meddai Jones am y teulu:

> Y mae ganddo un bywyd; y mae y bywyd hwnw *yn* y fam a'r tad, a'r plant, ac o hono y tardd eu dyletswyddau, eu breintiau, eu dedwyddwch, a'u gofidiau. Eu cysylltiad a'u gilydd ydyw achos gweithredol eu hymddygiadau: *dros* eu plant, ac yn wir *yn* eu plant, y bydd y rhiaint fyw ... Dyma rwymyn ysbrydol annatodol; ac er nas gwêl llygad ef, eto y mae yn bod, ac yn gryfach a dyfnach hyd yn nod na'r cysylltiad naturiol.[8]

Yr hyn sydd mor ddyrchafol am y berthynas deuluol yw ei bod yn ymestyn ymwybyddiaeth yr hunan i gynnwys unigolion eraill. Yr wyf yn rhan o'm teulu: mae fy nheulu yn rhan ohonof fi. Mae'r berthynas hefyd yn sail i'r ymwybyddiaeth o ddyletswydd tuag at eraill. Dyma eginyn moesoldeb.

---

5 WFSR, t. 233.

6 Andrew Seth & Richard B. Haldane, *Essays in Philosophical Criticism,* Llundain 1883, tt. 187-213. (Cafwyd cyfieithiad Cymraeg, 'Y Corff Cymdeithasol' yn *Y Traethodydd,* 1884, tt. 261-282.)

7 ibid., t. 194 (t. 267).

8 'Anghenion Cymru I', *Y Geninen,* 1889, t. 211. (Cyfieithiad o 'Some of the Social Wants of Wales' yn *Transactions of the Liverpool Welsh National Society,* 1888, tt. 23-34.)

> Yn y teulu y gwelir deddf uchaf bywyd dyn, sef cariad, yn llywodraethu am y tro cyntaf. Trwy ddefnyddio y cysylltiadau anianol sydd yn rhwymo anifail y maes (yn gystal â dyn) wrth ei epil i daro i lawr raib naturiol yr anwarddyn, y mae yr ysbryd sydd yn arwain dyn yn ei lwybr esgynol yn rhoddi iddo ei wers gyntaf yn yr hyn sydd *dda* – yn dysgu iddo elfennau cyntaf bywyd uchaf dyn, sef bywyd o geisio lles arall fel yr eiddo ei hun. Y teulu ydyw yr *experiment* gyntaf yn moesoliad dyn; prawf, presenol ar bob tu, y gall dyn ddiangc allan o hono ei hun i fywyd eangach, a bod yn dda.[9]

Serch hynny, rhaid sylweddoli mai man cychwyn yn unig yw'r teulu.

> ... arbrawf ar y raddfa leiaf ydyw ... O anian y teulu y deillia y gallu sydd i oresgyn y byd. Nid ydyw y teulu, fodd bynnag, yn ddim ond tarddiad: rhaid i'r afonig lwybro ei ffordd yn mlaen drwy hanes dynoliaeth, gan enill dyfnder a lled a grym wrth fyned yn mlaen, nes o'r diwedd y bydd cariad y tad at ei blentyn yn dyfod yn gariad gwlad-garwr at ei bobl, a chariad dyn – Crist at y ddynoliaeth.[10]

Tarddiad cnawdol sydd i'r teulu a'r genedl fel ei gilydd, a gwahaniaeth o raddfa yn unig sydd rhyngddynt. Y mae ymhlyg yn y ddau hefyd addewid o gyflenwad i anghenion ysbrydol dwfn.

> Y mae cysylltiad anianol, neu waed-gysylltiad teulu, yn rhagdueddu at ac yn sail y cysylltiad uwch a phrydferthach a ffurfir gan gariad, ac felly hefyd, y mae fod pobl o'r un haniad, iaith, crefydd, a hanes, yn eu tueddu at unoliaeth cenedl; ond nis gall y pethau hyn ynddynt eu hunain ffurfio na chenedl na theulu. Gall yr holl elfenau hyn gydfod lle nad oes cenedl; ac y mae gennym hanes cenhedloedd yn ngwir ystyr y gair nas meddent un, neu ychwaneg, o'r nodweddion hyn ... Ysbrydol o ran eu natur ydyw y teulu a'r genedl. Sefydliadau ydynt yn mha rai y mae y da sydd yn gweithio yn y byd wedi cymeryd iddo ei hun ffurf allanol a pharhaol, ac nis gellir eu hesbonio ond fel cynnyrch y gallu moesol hwn. Y teulu ydyw'r amlygiad prydferthaf o hono; ond y genedl ydyw'r mwyaf, a'r mwyaf aruchel.[11]

Byddai coleddu'r safbwynt hwn fel y'i gosodir yma yn gwneud Jones yn genedlaetholwr, ond nid dyna oedd ei safbwynt terfynol. Credai ef fod mynegiant uwch eto o ysbryd ac o foesoldeb i'w gael, sef y wladwriaeth. Yn gyffredinol ni ddewisodd wahaniaethu yn ei ysgrifennu rhwng 'cenedl', 'gwlad' a 'gwladwriaeth': gwendid anesgusodol mewn athronydd. Serch hynny, yr oedd o'r farn fod gwahaniaeth pendant iawn rhwng y genedl a'r wladwriaeth.

Mae'r genedl yn rhagori ar y teulu oherwydd, er bod i'r ddau wreiddyn biolegol, a gallu yn y ddau i ddeffro ynom ymwybyddiaeth o anghenion cyd-ddyn, ehanga'r ysbryd cenedlaethol ein consýrn am eraill y tu hwnt i'r cylchoedd mwyaf hunanol.

---

9 ibid.

10 ibid.

11 ibid.

> A common descent and a common language are organic filaments which, so far, make us sensitive to the needs of others and aware of the identity of their welfare with our own. From this point of view one cannot but regard the revival of the idea of the national spirit as a moral good for any country. It is a standing protest against personal, and family, and class selfishness; ... But such a community, while it is probably the basis and condition of all others has to pass into something higher. The blood-relationship from which it grows is purely natural, and the social reason which it exercises is unconscious. But man progresses from nature to spirit ... The natural bond of the flesh loses such of its rights as are not consistent with, or capable of being transformed into, the higher form of the common spiritual purpose of a people or of a race.[12]

Megis yr esblygodd y genedl o ffurf fwy cyntefig y teulu, felly hefyd y bydd y genedl yn ei thro yn esgor ar ffurf llai cyntefig eto, sef y wladwriaeth.

> The same truth holds with reference to the 'nation'. The natural elements which primarily constitute it fall into the background; that is to say, the tie of blood-relationship, together with its natural concomitants lose their importance. The community comes to consist of all persons who are able more or less, to identify some element of its welfare with their own. The definitive characteristic of the true state appears. For a state is based upon some conception, generally a most inadequate one, of a common good that is desired by each of its members as a condition of their own welfare.[3]

Iddo ef, felly, mae'r wladwriaeth yn ffurf uwch ar ysbryd na'r genedl, ac yn rhagori fel uned foesol.

> ... the State as a moral organism whose ends come into existence in being freely willed as a common good for a number of individuals, stands far higher than the Nation as we have described it.[14]

Awgryma fod y drafodaeth wleidyddol yng Nghymru yn rhy dueddol i fod yn gyfyngedig i lefel y genedl.

> ... the idea of the State seems to me to be a more adequate practical [h.y., moesol] ideal than the idea of the Nation which, in Wales at least, is more frequently spoken of.[15]

Wrth gwrs, nid yw'n anodd deall paham y mae mwy o drafod ar y genedl na'r wladwriaeth yng Nghymru. Cenedl ac nid gwladwriaeth oedd Cymru. Fe gyfyd hyn broblem. Er nad yw Cymru yn wladwriaeth, fe berthyn i wladwriaeth, ond i wladwriaeth sydd yn cynnwys cenhedloedd eraill yn ogystal. Mae hyn i raddau yn cymylu'r drafodaeth athronyddol a gawn gan Jones ar berthynas cenedl a gwladwriaeth. Iddo ef y mae'r ffaith fod y Wladwriaeth Brydeinig yn cynnwys nifer o genhedloedd yn un rheswm dros ragoriaeth y wladwriaeth dros y genedl fel mynegiant o ysbryd (yn union fel mae'r genedl, sydd yn cynnwys nifer fawr o

[12] 'The Idea of the State', *Transactions of the Liverpool Welsh National Society,* 1895-6, tt.18-19.

[13] ibid., tt. 19-20.

[14] ibid., t. 20.

[15] ibid., tt. 20-21.

deuluoedd gwahanol, yn rhagori ar un teulu fel mynegiant o ysbryd). Ond beth am y wladwriaeth un genedl? Byddai'n dda cael trafodaeth ar ragoriaeth y wladwriaeth dros y genedl mewn achos fel Denmarc, er enghraifft. Nid yw Jones yn trafod y cwestiwn mewn cyd-destun mor syml â hynny, felly mae'r drafodaeth bob amser yn rhagdybied bod y wladwriaeth yn aml-genedlaethol. Mae diffyg arall ar y drafodaeth hefyd. Nid yw'n gwahaniaethu fel arfer rhwng y Wladwriaeth Brydeinig a'r Ymerodraeth Brydeinig. Nid yw pob gwladwriaeth yn ymerodraeth, ac nid yw'n amlwg a yw ymerodraeth yn ffurf fwy esblygedig ar ysbryd na gwladwriaeth. Yn bendant credai mai'r Ymerodraeth Brydeinig, yn benodol, oedd uchafbwynt esblygiad cymdeithas yn ei oes ef.

> Cyfuniad pobloedd gwahanol oddifewn i'r Ymerodraeth Brydeinig ydyw y ffurf uchaf ar fodolaeth politicaidd y galwyd ar y byd hyd yn hyn i'w sefydlu …[16]

Yn anffodus tuedda i siarad am y Wladwriaeth a'r Ymerodraeth Brydeinig ar yr un gwynt. Mae'r llacrwydd ieithyddol hwn, sy'n peri bod termau fel 'gwlad', 'cenedl', 'gwladwriaeth' neu 'ymerodraeth' yn gyfnewidiadwy yn achosi stomp weithiau. Meddylier amdano, er enghraifft, yn annerch torf o chwarelwyr Cymraeg eu hiaith, ac (yn achos y mwyafrif ohonynt) ymneilltuol eu crefydd, fel hyn:

> A ystyriasoch chwi erioed yr hyn a ddygir i ni gan y cysylltiadau cymdeithasol yn y Wladwriaeth, ac mor dlawd y byddem hebddynt? Ddeallasoch chwi na byddai gennym ddim; y buasem heb na iaith, na moes na chrefydd, a'n henaid yn noethlwm?[17]

Hawdd y gallent hwythau ateb fod ganddynt iaith a moes a chrefydd *ar waethaf* ac nid *oherwydd* eu 'cysylltiadau cymdeithasol yn y Wladwriaeth'! Eithr ni all neb wadu iddynt eu derbyn oherwydd eu cysylltiadau cymdeithasol yn y genedl.

Ar rai achlysuron prin bydd yn gwahaniaethu'n glir rhwng y wladwriaeth a'r cenhedloedd ym Mhrydain.

> … the Welsh 'nation', like the English, Irish and Scotch, is part of a 'state' which is more comprehensive than any one of these, and which means something different from a compound or agglomeration of them all.[18]

Er bod y wladwriaeth yn ffurf uwch ar ysbryd na'r genedl, nid yw Jones am weld hunaniaeth y cenhedloedd cyfansoddol yn ymdoddi i'w gilydd, neu a bod yn fwy manwl, nid yw am weld Cymru yn esblygu i fod yn rhan o Loegr. Mae'n amlwg yn gwahaniaethu rhwng ymdoddi mewn gwladwriaeth fwy ac ymdoddi mewn cenedl fwy. Hynny yw, ni all unrhyw genedl gadw ei hunaniaeth mewn cenedl fwy, er y

[16] 'Anghenion Cymru II', *Y Geninen*, 1890, t. 12.
[17] DB, t. 30.
[18] 'The Idea of The State', *Transactions of the Liverpool Welsh National Society*, 1895-6, t. 21.

gall ei gadw mewn gwladwriaeth fwy. Mae'n bosibl i Gymru brofi'r ddau fath o ymdoddi: mae'n gefnogol i'r ail fath, ond nid i'r cyntaf.

> Rhaid i ni un ai glynnu ynghŷd er mwyn enill ein hamcanion cenedlaethol, neu ynte fod yn rhanbarth ddienw o Loegr. Y mae yn rhesymmol gofyn, ac yn wir y mae yn hen ofyniad, pa un o'r ddau beth hyn sydd fwyaf i'w ddymuno. Onid oes rhai gwŷr, awyddus am ddaioni ein cenedl, a dybiant mai ymgolli yn Lloegr fyddai tynged oreu Cymru; ac a gredant fod pob ymgais i ddyfnhau y gwahaniaeth rhwng y ddwy wlad yn tueddu i gynhyrfu dig Lloegr ac i ddistrywio Cymru? Y mae yn ddiammeu fod rhai yn synied felly; ac mor werthfawr yn fy ngolwg i ydyw undeb a Lloegr, fel pe tybiwn ei fod yn anghyson a delweddau [delfrydau ?] ac amcanion Cymreig, y byddai yn well gennyf i aberthu y pethau olaf hyn na'r blaenaf. Y mae Cymru Annibynol yn yr ystyr hwn o'r gair, mor ddiwerth yn fy ngolwg, fel yr adsefydlwn Dderwyddaeth yn Sir Fon mor gynted a Senedd Gymreig yn Sir Gaernarfon. Y mae undeb a Lloegr yn angenrheidiol i'n bodolaeth; ac y mae amodau bodolaeth yn rhagflaenu amodau llwyddiant. Ond nid oes raid i undeb, a hwnw o'r fath agosaf, beri fod Cymru yn cael ei Seisnigeiddio.[19]

Nid yw'n eglur a yw'r undeb â Lloegr yn 'angenrheidiol i'n bodolaeth' fel cenedl neu fel gwladwriaeth. Ni ddywedir ychwaith beth yw natur yr angenrheidrwydd – economaidd, gwleidyddol, moesol? Y tebyg yw fod 'Annibynol' yn y dyfyniad presennol yn golygu 'sofran', oherwydd yr oedd yn gefnogol i senedd Gymreig fel rhan o gynllun datganoli ym Mhrydain.

> My opinion about Wales is quite distinct. I would gladly have Home Rule (or Devolution, which really must mean the same thing in practice) ... Personally I am strong for Devolution and like you, think Scotland would be very foolish not to insist upon it, for its own sake and everyone's.[20]

Beth bynnag am hynny, mae'n tynnu sylw at elfen bwysig ym mharhad cenedligrwydd, sef 'ysbryd cenedlaethol'.

> Dywedai Fichte, yn ei ddull eofn ei hun, fod y fath bobl a hyn yn anorchfygol; ac na ddistriwyd cenedl erioed cyn diffodd ei hysbryd cenedlaethol, a chyn aberthu o'i thrigolion les y cyffredin er mwyn esmwythyd, a gloddest, ac amcanion hunanol. Pa un bynnag a yw hyn yn wir llythrenol ai pheidio, cydnebydd pob gwr cyfarwydd a hanesiaeth mai gwladgarwch yw arfogaeth oreu pobl bob amser i'w hamddiffyn rhag traha estroniaid, ac mai hi hefyd ydyw y gallu cryfaf i ddadblygu ei hadnoddau mewnol. Ac os yw Cymru i fod yn rhywbeth gwell nag adran ddirywiedig o Loegr, rhaid i'w thrigolion deimlo mai sylweddoliad amcanion y genedl ydyw ei dyletswydd uchaf, a chael eu llanw gan gariad at wlad eu tadau i'r fath raddau fel ag i fod yn barod i'w hamddiffyn fel y peth gwerthfawrocaf yn eu meddiant.[21]

Mae Jones yma'n cyplysu dau gysyniad, sef 'ysbryd cenedlaethol' a 'sylweddoliad amcanion y genedl'. Teimlad yw'r cyntaf, amgyffrediad o ddyletswydd, neu ymwybyddiaeth foesol yw'r ail. Beth felly yw'r amcanion

[19] 'Anghenion Cymru II', *Y Geninen*, 1890, tt. 11-12.
[20] Llythyr at Syr Ronald Ferguson, TJ/U/2/191.
[21] 'Anghenion Cymru II', *Y Geninen*, 1890, t. 13.

cenedlaethol a berthyn i'r Cymry? Gellir eu rhestru yn fyr ac yn syml – Ymneilltuaeth a Rhyddfrydiaeth. Mae'r ddau'n costrelu gwerthoedd y Cymry, ac maent yn fynegiant o'u cenedligrwydd. Nid yw am ddyrchafu'r gwerthoedd Cymreig uwchlaw'r gwerthoedd Seisnig gwrthgyferbyniol, ond mae'n pwysleisio mai moesol yw mewnbwn y Cymry i fywyd dinesig y deyrnas, a phe diddymid Cymru, byddai'n golled foesol i'r Ymerodraeth gyfan.

> Y mae yn lled debyg fod nodweddion cymeriad cenedlaethol y Saeson, a'u cymryd gyda'u gilydd, yn rhagorach nag eiddo cenhedloedd eraill yr Ymerodraeth Brydeinig: os na addefir hyn, y mae yn anhawdd, os nad yn amhosibl, cyfrif am oruchafiaeth boliticaidd Lloegr arnynt. Ond er hynny, nid oes un bobl na fyddai yn gan-mil gwell aelod i ymerodraeth wrth fod yr hyn ydyw wrth natur nag wrth ddynwared pobl arall. Fe allai fod Esgobyddiaeth yn well nag Ymneilltuaeth Gymreig; Toriaeth y Sais yn well na Rhyddfrydiaeth y Cymro; y cymeriad Seisnig, ynghyd a'i uniondeb penllew yn well na theimladaeth barod ac uchelgais anymarferol y cymeriad Cymreig: ond os proselytir Cymru gan orfodaeth deddfwriaeth na chydymdeimla a'n gwlad i fabwysiadu yr elfennau Seisnig hyn, diffodda ei bywyd goreu. Byddai Cymru heb ei thueddiadau cenedlaethol, hyd yn nod pe na byddai y tueddiadau hynny y rhai uchaf a goraf, yn wlad farw i bob daioni, – fel cragen anghyfanedd. Ond mewn undeb a Lloegr, byddai dan y fath delerau a'r rhai hyn yn ffynonell gwendid i'r ymerodraeth, ac nid nerth; byddai fel aelod marw, trwy yr hwn na cherdda y bywyd cenedlaethol.[22]

Cred mai cyfraniad moesol yw'r cyfraniad gwerthfawrocaf y gall cenedl ei wneud i fywyd y ddynoliaeth. Dengys hanes na fu maint cenhedloedd bychain yn rhwystr iddynt rhag gwneud y fath gyfraniad.

> Tra nas gall bychander Cymru yn yr ystyr naturiol, na'i dibynaeth boliticaidd, sefyll rhyngddi hi a'i llwyddiant, gosodant derfyn ar ei dylanwad ac amodant ef, os na luddir hwynt gan rywbeth arall. Oer ei huchelgais cenedlaethol, os na orbwysir ei hanfanteision materol gan ddoniau meddyliol a moesol. Ni ddeilliodd mantais i Judea a Groeg o'u bychander. Oni bae am allu gwrthbwys, ni fuasent fyw mewn hanes; ond gwthasid hwy o'r golwg gan eu cymdogion galluoccach. Ond yr oeddynt hwy yn fwy yn yr ystyr foesol na'u cymdogion. Yr oeddynt hwy yn bobl oleu yng nghanol tywyllwch, a thywynnai eu gweithredoedd da mewn byd drwg. Felly, hefyd, rhaid i Gymru – am ei bod ym mhob ystyr faterol mor ddistadl, o'i chymharu a rhannau eraill yr ymherodraeth – ragori arnynt hwy yn noniau uwch y meddwl, os ydyw i ddal meddiant o'r eiddo ei hun. Rhaid i'w thrigolion ymroddi yn fwy llwyr i ddiwylliant, credu yn fwy dwfn mewn gwybodaeth, cadw eu bywyd yn fwy pur, ac ymgeisio at bethau uwch na'u cymdogion; oblegid yn y pethau hyn y mae cuddiad cryfder gwlad.[23]

---

[22] 'Anghenion Cymru II', *Y Geninen*, 1890, t. 12.

[23] Henry Jones, *Fy Ngwlad a'i Rhagolygon*, Dinbych 1890, t. 16.

Pennod 12

Rhyddfrydiaeth Newydd mewn Gwleidyddiaeth

Y wladwriaeth yw uchafbwynt datblygiad dyn yn y byd a phrif gyfrwng ei ddatblygiad pellach. Y mae gan Jones felly barch aruthrol ati, ac y mae am i holl ddinasyddion y wladwriaeth (neu'r 'wladwrfa' fel y geilw ef hi weithiau) ymagweddu ati gyda'r un parch.

> Cysegredig ydyw'r Wladwrfa, fy nghyfeillion; cynnyrch araf yr oesoedd ydyw ei moesau, a'i harferion, ei sefydliadau a'i chyfreithiau. 'Perth yn llosgi heb ei difa' ydyw; ac nid wyf fi yn petruso dweyd wrth y neb ddyneso ati hi: 'Diosg dy esgidiau oddi am dy draed.'[1]

Er mai 'cynnyrch araf yr oesoedd' yw'r wladwriaeth ymron ymhob achos, nid ar gyfrif ei hynafiaeth yr haedda barch yn bennaf, ond fel uchafbwynt datblygiad ysbryd. Megis ei gyd-Hegeliaid, gwelai Jones y wladwriaeth fel cyfrwng i wneud dyn yn dda ac yn rhydd. Mae cysylltiad agos iawn rhwng y ddeubeth. Rhaid bod yn rhydd cyn medru bod yn foesol dda, a pho fwyaf yw ein rhyddid, cymaint â hynny'n fwy yw ein cyfle i fod yn dda. Hynny yw, dim ond am yr hyn y mae gennym reolaeth drosto y gellir ein hystyried yn gyfrifol. Felly, y mae rhyddid a chyfrifoldeb yn anwahanadwy.

Yn sylfaenol, rhyddid yw'r cyflwr croes i gaethiwed. Mae caethiwed bob amser yn fath o gyfyngiad, boed gorfforol neu feddyliol, yn gyflwr o fod dan reolaeth neu orfodaeth neu ddylanwad oddi allan i'n hewyllys ein hunain. O'i ddiffinio fel hyn, peth negyddol yw rhyddid – sef absenoldeb rheolaeth oddi allan. Y diffiniad negyddol hwn,

> A'r maglau wedi eu torri,
> A'm traed yn gwbl rydd;

sydd wrth wraidd y syniad rhyddfrydol traddodiadol o ryddid. Rhoddir yr holl bwyslais ar dorri'r hualau. Yng nghyd-destun bywyd cymdeithasol, mae hyn yn golygu pwysleisio rhyddid rhag ymyrraeth allanol ym mywyd yr unigolyn. Mewn gwleidyddiaeth ymarferol golyga hynny wrthwynebu unrhyw ymgais ar ran y wladwriaeth i ymestyn elfen orfodol y ddeddf i mewn i agweddau personol ar fywyd yr unigolyn.

Cyfoethogir y cysyniad o ryddid, fodd bynnag, drwy ei ddiffinio mewn termau cadarnhaol. Yn hytrach na phwysleisio'r hyn mae rhywun yn rhydd ohono, gellir pwysleisio'r hyn mae rhywun yn rhydd i'w wneud. I Jones, mesur ein rhyddid yw

---

[1] DB, t. 11.

ffiniau'r hyn y gallwn ei gyflawni. Po fwyaf y gallwn ei wneud, mwyaf yw ein rhyddid. Os galluogir ni i gyflawni pethau na fedrem eu cyflawni yn ein nerth ein hunain, cynyddir ein rhyddid. Yn y byd modern mae'r wladwriaeth yn medru ein galluogi i ymestyn ein hunain gyda chymorth ei hadnoddau. Yr enghreifftiau amlycaf o hyn yw ehangu gorwelion a chynyddu medrau'r dinasyddion drwy addysg, diogelu hawliau'r gwan yn erbyn gormes y cryf drwy rym y gyfraith, ymgeleddu'r afiach a'r llesg drwy nawdd cymdeithasol, ac yn y blaen. Bydd sicrhau'r amodau sy'n gwneud y 'bywyd helaethach' hwn yn bosibl yn golygu elfen o reolaeth ac o orfodaeth, ond yr effaith yw cynyddu ein posibiliadau fel unigolion ac fel cymdeithas.

> Mae yr ewyllys gorfforedig ac ewyllysiau personau unigol yn fwy rhydd, yn yr ystyr o fod yn fwy effeithiol: … Yr ydym yn gwneyd y wladwriaeth yn fwy effeithiol o flwyddyn i flwyddyn, oblegid gyda'n holl gyrff deddfwriaethol mae yr ychwanegiadau a wneir at ein deddf-lyfrau bob blwyddyn yn anferth. Yn ddiameu y mae pob deddf ychwanegol yn golygu mwy o rwymau – ar rywun neu gilydd, … Ond a ydym wedi dweyd yr holl wirionedd am y deddfau pan alwasom hwynt yn gyfyngiadau? Ai nid ydyw yn wir, yn hytrach, fod y cyfyngiadau newyddion a ar-osodir gan y cyfreithiau a wneir yn barhaus, hefyd yn foddion effeithiol i gario allan ewyllysiau pob un o'r dinaswyr?[2]

Serch hynny, yr oedd Jones yn glir na ellid 'gorfodi dyn i fod yn rhydd' (a defnyddio ymadrodd Rousseau). Y mae i ryddid ei agwedd oddrychol a mewnol, oherwydd hanfod rhyddid yw dewis, a'r elfen hon sy'n gosod gwerth moesol i'r hyn a wneir, boed dda neu ddrwg. Mae'n bwysig felly fod agwedd y dinesydd yn gefnogol tuag at ddeddfwriaeth a fwriedir i'w gyfoethogi fel person ac i gynyddu ei effeithiolrwydd fel unigolyn. Y delfryd yw sicrhau cynghanedd rhwng ewyllys yr unigolyn a deddfau'r wladwriaeth. Dyna ryddid sydd yn gadarnhaol heb fygu cyfrifoldeb moesol.

> The law within and the law without may coincide. Man may be obedient and yet free, and the more obedient because he is free. The social authority may be still steadfast, and the more steadfast and imperative because it is rooted in the heart of its subjects.[3]

Dyna yw'r delfryd, ond mae hanes yn frith o enghreifftiau o ryddid yr unigolyn yn cael ei aberthu er hyrwyddo 'lles' y wladwriaeth. Dyma darddiad y gormes a ddaeth yn sgil sawl chwyldro oedd i fod i ehangu rhyddid. Er bod Jones wedi rhoi cymaint o bwyslais ar ei argyhoeddiad na ellir cael unigolion heb gymdeithas, yr oedd yr un mor bendant fod y cyfosodiad yn wir, sef:

> … fel y mae natur y person unigol yn hanfodol gymdeithasol, felly fod natur cymdeithas yn hanfodol unigol; ac mewn canlyniad, fod beth bynnag sydd yn gwanhau neu yn niweidio y person unigol ac yn atal ei ddatblygiad, i'r un radd a thrwy yr un weithred yn gwanhau ac yn niweidio cymdeithas ac yn atal ei chynnydd.[4]

---

[2] 'Cymdeithas a'r Person Unigol', *Y Traethodydd*, 1898, tt. 5-6.

[3] IPC, td.108.

[4] 'Cymdeithas a'r Person Unigol', *Y Traethodydd*, 1898, t. 2.

Mae'n bwysig nodi ei fod yn pwysleisio fod modd i gymdeithas, yn ogystal â'r unigolyn, fod yn anghyflawn. Ni ellir cael unigolion heb gymdeithas, ond ni ellir cael cymdeithas heb unigolion chwaith.

> If the nature of the individual is essentially social, *the nature of society is essentially individual* – or 'personal' ...[5]

Yr allwedd i ddeall Jones yma yw ei ddehongliad o gymdeithas fel organeb. Yn wahanol i organeb fiolegol nid oes gan gymdeithas un *sensorium* canolog, neu un canolbwynt i'w hunanymwybyddiaeth, ond yn hytrach mae'n bodoli yn ymwybyddiaeth pob aelod unigol. Nid yw cymdeithas wedi llwyr ddatblygu nes y bydd ganddi gymaint o ganolbwyntiau gweithgaredd ymwybodol ag sydd ganddi o aelodau. Am y rheswm yma dywed Jones y byddai'n fwy priodol i alw cymdeithas yn *hyper-organism.*

> The truth of individuality is thus to be found in a fully organised society; and of society in a fully developed individual.[6]

Ni ellir gorbwysleisio'r agwedd hon ar ei safbwynt. Camddehongliad yw ei bortreadu fel tyndra rhwng hawliau'r unigolyn a hawliau cymdeithas. Dim ond i ni iawn ddeall y berthynas rhwng yr unigolyn a chymdeithas, meddai Jones, gwelwn mai'r un yw buddiannau'r naill a'r llall (mae 'essential coincidence' rhyngddynt).[7] Dylai'r egwyddor hon fod mor sylfaenol mewn moeseg ag egwyddor unffurfiaeth natur mewn gwyddoniaeth. Nid yw moesoldeb yn fater o wrthwynebiad yr hunanol a'r allgarol, nac yn fater o gyfaddawd rhwng gofynion lles yr unigolyn a lles cymdeithas. Camsyniad llwyr ar ran damcaniaethwyr gwleidyddol oedd meddwl mai'r gamp bwysig i gymdeithas yw sicrhau cydbwysedd rhwng gofynion gwrthwynebus unigolion a chymdeithas. Y pwynt yw, meddai, na fu unrhyw gynnydd ym muddiannau'r unigolyn nad oedd ar yr un pryd yn llesol i gymdeithas, na chynnydd ym muddiannau cymdeithas nad oedd hefyd o les i aelodau'r gymdeithas. Mae'r unigolyn a chymdeithas wedi cyd-ddatblygu, y naill yn elwa ar gynnydd y llall. Ysywaeth, mae'r traddodiad rhyddfrydol wedi dehongli'r esblygiad hwn fel datbygiad y naill ar draul y llall.

Drwy gyfrwng cymdeithas y datblyga'r unigolyn a thrwy gyfrwng yr unigolyn y datblyga cymdeithas, y naill yn cyfoethogi'r llall. Fel Hegel, yr oedd Jones yn gweld cadarnhad o hyn yn hanes gwareiddiad.

---

5 WFSR, t. 233.

6 ibid., t. 234.

7 "The functions of the state and the individual are supposed to increase in inverse ratio. It looks awfully obvious. But if you compare modern society with ancient, you will find both individual and state functions have increased together. The individual is capable of wider and greater enterprises than at any other time." Llawysgrif McLeish, Prifysgol Glasgow, Darlith 25.

> Impossible as it may at first seem to be, that both society and its members may at the same time enlarge their sphere of activity, history shows us that this has actually been taking place. Indeed, I am not sure that anything else of the highest moment has been taking place. For this more intense integration and fuller articulation of the moral cosmos, this synthesis and analysis at one stroke, this growth of society as an active unit and of its members as free and effective personalities within it, is the very essence of civilisation.[8]

Eto esblygodd y berthynas rhwng yr unigolyn a chymdeithas drwy gyfnodau lle bu gogwydd eithafol tuag at awdurdod cymdeithas yn y naill begwn ac annibyniaeth yr unigolyn yn y llall. Dyma thema *Athroniaeth Hanes* Hegel, a neilltuodd Jones Bennod 3 o *Idealism as a Practical Creed* i roddi amlinelliad o'r patrwm.

Yn y Dwyrain y caed y gwladwriaethau cynharaf, hen ymerodraethau lle nad oedd ond un ewyllys, sef ewyllys yr unben, ac felly un oedd yn rhydd. Gyda'r Groegiaid y gwelir gwawrio'r syniad o ryddid torfol, yn yr ystyr fod holl ddinasyddion y ddinas yn rhydd. Yr oedd bywyd y ddinas yn fynegiant o fywyd ei dinasyddion. Yr oeddynt wedi uniaethu â hi i'r fath raddau fel mai mater o awydd yn hytrach na mater o ddyletswydd oedd y bywyd dinesig iddynt hwy. (Ni phrofasant rym cydwybod, meddai Hegel.) Torrwyd ar yr undod hwn gan yr athronwyr. Yr oedd y Soffyddion wedi dysgu mai 'dyn ydyw mesur popeth', ac yn y cyswllt hwn ystyr 'dyn' yw yr unigolyn. Dyma osod bri felly ar unigoliaeth. Yn ôl yr athrawiaeth hon gallai'r unigolyn benderfynu drosto'i hun pa beth sydd gywir a pha beth sydd iawn. Pwy all wrthbrofi chwaeth? Ond tanseiliwyd safbwynt y Soffyddion gan Socrates a ddysgodd fod modd gwybod beth sydd rinweddol oherwydd fod Da gwrthrychol a chyffredinol yn bod. Dyma ddeffro'r ymwybyddiaeth o gydwybod, sef awdurod uwchlaw deddfau unrhyw wladwriaeth. O reidrwydd, condemniodd tadau dinesig Athen ef i'w ddienyddio. Ni allai'r wladwriaeth ddinesig Roegaidd ddygymod â'r awdurdod uwch yng nghydwybod unigol ei dinasyddion.

Dyrchafwyd cydwybod i safle breiniol mewn Cristnogaeth, ond 'mewnol' oedd ei rhyddid. Gallai Cristnogaeth 'orchfygu'r byd', ond gwnâi hynny heb newid y ffurfiau gwleidyddol ar y ddaear. Gyda'r Ymoleuo a'r Chwyldro Ffrengig y gwelwn yr ymgais ymwybodol fwyaf mewn hanes hyd hynny i orfodi'r byd fel y mae i gydymffurfio â'r weledigaeth o'r byd fel y dylai fod. Ond ysywaeth, fe ddeilliodd y Brawychaeth o'r mynegiant hwn o rym cydwybod. Serch hynny yr oedd Kant, prif athronydd yr Ymoleuo, wedi gosod delfryd gwaraidd iawn ger bron, sef cymdeithas o bobl sydd yn byw yn unol â gofynion ewyllys daionus. Ewyllys yw hon sydd yn cydymffurfio â rheswm, ac sydd, o'r herwydd yn gyffredinol ac unigol, gan y gwêl pawb drosto'i hun beth sydd yn ofynnol. Bydd aelodau'r fath gymdeithas yn ddeiliaid yn gymaint â'u bod yn ufudd, ac yn frenhinoedd yn gymaint â'u bod drwy eu rheswm eu hunain yn gorchymyn. Ond ni fydd eu rheswm yn gweithredu mewn

8 WFSR, t. 243.

rhyw wagle haniaethol. Fel y gwelsom eisoes, cred Jones gyda Hegel y bydd ein dyletswyddau yn amlygu eu hunain i ni mewn ffyrdd diriaethol yng ngwead ein bywyd cymdeithasol.

> Society exists only in the individual, and the individual exists only in society. Apart from society the individual cannot realise his freedom; neither his own particular self nor the Universal will could afford him a single motive. The individual is free only because he finds his duties in society, and his duties are his ethical life. And, on the other hand, it is the freedom of the component of a society that gives the society real and permanent existence. It is because the State is a higher realisation of freedom that it has greater permanence than the family.[9]

Nid y teulu yw'r unig elfen yn y gwead cymdeithasol sydd yn sail i'r wladwriaeth. Un arall ohonynt yw dosbarth. Rhoddai gryn bwysigrwydd i rôl dosbarth yn ffyniant yr unigolyn.

> He is now one of a *class*, and it is in union with it that he fails or prospers: his fate is united with that of others in similar circumstances to his own. ... The sphere of responsibility for the individual is widened, and even fidelity confined to one's own class is far better than loyalty to one's own self alone.[10]

Parodrwydd Jones i gydnabod arwyddocâd aelodaeth o ddosbarth a'i barodrwydd i annog y dosbarth gweithiol i gyd-sefyll a'i gwnaeth yn areithiwr mor dderbyniol yng Ngwyliau Llafur Undeb y Chwarelwyr. Amddiffynnodd yn rymus werth undebaeth lafur i'r gweithwyr yn ei araith 'Amodau Llwyddiant y Chwarelwyr'[11], ac yn yr enwocaf o'r areithiau hyn, 'Dinasyddiaeth Bur', mae'n amlygu dealltwriaeth o natur perthynas llafur a chyfalaf na allai unrhyw sosialydd ar yr olwg gyntaf anghytuno â hi.

> Ni fwriedir byd gwych i'r gŵr gwasaidd, ac ni wêl yr hwn sydd foddlawn i fod dan draed brinder pobl barod i sarnu arno. Cyhyd ag yr oedd y dosbarth gweithiol yn edrych ar eu gwaith fel yr edrycha cardotyn ar elusen, hur wael elusengarwch a gaent; a fflangell oedd eu dioddefiadau i'w gyrru i hawlio iawnderau dynion. Safwch ochr yn ochr, weithwyr, pan yn bargeinio am gyflog: oblegid nid oes yr un llwybr arall ond trwy greu ewyllys gyd-bwys ag ewyllys gref Cyfalaf i sicrhau yr hyn sydd ddyledus i chwi.[12]

Ond cydbwysedd grym rhwng Cyfalaf a Llafur yn hytrach na buddugoliaeth Llafur dros Gyfalaf yw'r nod, yn ôl Jones. Y rheswm dros hyn yw'r ffaith mai dim ond elfennau mewn undod uwch yw'r dosbarthiadau, sef y wladwriaeth.

---

[9] 'The Social Organism', Andrew Seth & Richard B. Haldane, *Essays in Philosophical Criticism,* Llundain 1883, t. 207.

[10] IPC, tt. 213-14.

[11] DB, tt. 33-46.

[12] ibid., t. 28.

> Dyma gyfundrefn a myrdd o elfennau ynddi, a'r rhai hynny mor gydbwys ac yn ymddibynu y naill ar y llall i'r fath raddau nes bod y genedl yn un, er gwaethaf pob gwahaniaeth safle, ac ymryson ei dosbarthiadau. Y mae i'r Wladwriaeth, fel i bopeth byw, ei hegwyddorion na faidd eu hangofio, a deddfau bod nas gall sarnu arnynt heb ei dinistrio ei hun.[13]

Mae rhywbeth mwy gwaelodol na'i ddosbarth cymdeithasol yn perthyn i'r gweithiwr.

> Y mae'r gweithiwr nid yn unig yn weithiwr ond yn ddyn, ac yn ddinesydd; ac nid oes gwahaniaeth dinesig rhwng gwreng a bonedd.[14]

Byddai i un dosbarth, pa ddosbarth bynnag y bo, sicrhau rheolaeth dros yr holl wladwriaeth er mwyn hyrwyddo ei fuddiannau ei hun yn gyfystyr â dinistr y wladwriaeth honno. Un o brif nodweddion y wladwriaeth lwyddiannus yw ei gallu i gynnal yr holl elfennau gwrthgyferbyniol a gwrthwynebus mewn undod drwy sicrhau cydbwysedd rhyngddynt.

Cafwyd adwaith beirniadol i syniadau 'Dinasyddiaeth Bur' (a'r fersiwn Saesneg, 'The Corruption of the Citizenship of the Working Man'[15]) gan awduron Sosialaidd. Cyhoeddodd David Thomas ateb dan y teitl *Y Blaid Lafur a Dinasyddiaeth y Gweithiwr.*[16] Byrdwn ei feirniadaeth oedd fod Henry Jones wedi anwybyddu'r agweddau ymarferol ar wleidyddiaeth. Cefnogai undebaeth lafur fel y ffordd effeithiolaf i hyrwyddo buddiannau gweithwyr, ond edrychai ar Dŷ'r Cyffredin "fel rhyw Gysegr Sancteiddiolaf lle ni ddylai dim hunanoldeb na phleidgarwch wthio'i ben i mewn."[17] Ond yr oeddynt eisoes wedi gwneud hynny, meddai Thomas.

> Ceir digon o enghreifftiau i ddangos mai brwydr rhwng gwahanol fuddiannau ydyw'r prif frwydrau gwleidyddol heddyw. Gwelir hyn ... pan fo perchenogion glofeydd yn gwrthwynebu Mesur Wyth Awr, a gwelwyd hyn yn arbennig yn y brwydrau caled a fu y llynedd uwchben Mesur a basiwyd gan y Blaid y perthyna Syr Henry Jones iddi, sef y Mesur Yswirio.[18]

Fel y dangosodd Ramsey Macdonald yn ei ateb yntau i'r fersiwn Saesneg, mae Jones yn camddehongli natur llywodraeth gynrychioliadol os yw am ddadlau mai halogi dinasyddiaeth bur yw gweithio i sicrhau cynrychiolaeth sy'n gefnogol, ac yn agored gefnogol, i fuddiannau un dosbarth yn y wladwriaeth.

---

13 ibid., t. 17.
14 ibid., t. 26.
15 *Hibbert Journal,* Hydref 1911, tt. 155-178.
16 David Thomas, *Y Blaid Lafur a Dinasyddiaeth y Gweithiwr,* Caernarfon 1912.
17 ibid., t. 11.
18 ibid.

> We think that there is an authority which is custodian of the common interest – the State; and if we, the victims of the conflict [rhwng gwahanol fuddiannau], ask the State to settle it, what evil do we do? True we take one side. But the Legislature is a Court of Conciliation in which both *sides* sit, as sides, and agree as best they can upon the conclusions satisfactory to the community composed of the conflicting interests. After a careful reading of the opening pages of the paper, I think that Professor Jones has a notion that Parliament should be an impartial tribunal every member of which is a just man made perfect. That is an utterly impossible view. Parliament is not a committee of judges … Professor Jones … entertains mistaken views of Parliament, politics and representative government.[19]

Beth bynnag, nid buddugoliaeth un dosbarth ar draul pob dosbarth arall yw nod terfynol Sosialaeth yn ôl David Thomas.

> Oherwydd y mae gan arweinwyr y Blaid Lafur nod uwch na buddiannau dosbarth; y delfryd uchel y gweithiant ac yr ymestynant hwy ato yw'r Wladwriaeth Sosialaidd, 'Gwladwriaeth fydd yn bodoli er mwyn pawb, ac yn cael ei gwasanaethu gan bawb,' Gwladwriaeth lle y bydd pawb yn ddinesydd rhydd, ac yn cyfranogi o holl freintiau a dyletswyddau dinesydd. Ni cheir Gwladwriaeth felly tra bo'r gallu gan rai dynion i arglwyddiaethu ar eu cyd-greaduriaid, a'u twyllo a'u hysbeilio a'u newynnu; ni cheir hi tra bo bywyd cymdeithas yn nwylo gwahanol ddosbarthiadau, a buddiannau rheiny yn groes i'w gilydd, a phob un ohonynt yn ymladd i gael y llaw uchaf ar y llall. Cyn y bydd Gwladwriaeth a Dinas yn bosibl, mae'n rhaid i ni chwalu sylfeini pob rhagorfraint a gormes dosbarth … Dyna'r pryd y bydd Dinasyddiaeth Bur yn bosibl; cyn cael Dinasyddiaeth, mae'n rhaid cael Dinas.[20]

Ni fyddai ymresymiad fel hyn yn tycio gyda Jones, oherwydd yn ôl y ddadl hon, amod dinasyddiaeth bur yw goruchafiaeth un dosbarth yn gyntaf. O reidrwydd, bydd y dosbarth hwnnw yntau wedi llwyddo i ennill ymddiriedaeth y dosbarthiadau eraill, neu mi fydd wedi eu dileu (beth bynnag y mae hynny yn ei olygu).

Eto, yn *Principles of Citizenship* mae Jones yn llai llawdrwm ar y Blaid Lafur. Deil i gredu y gallai gwrthdaro rhwng y dosbarthiadau beryglu bodolaeth y wladwriaeth, ond o'r peryglon newydd fe gyfyd cyfleoedd newydd hefyd.[21] Fel canlyniad i ddatblygiadau economaidd yr ugeinfed ganrif fe ddygir y wladwriaeth (os yw'n dymuno hynny ai peidio) fwyfwy i'r dasg o sicrhau cyfiawnder cymdeithasol, ac yn sgil hynny bydd ei dylanwad yn treiddio i fwy o agweddau ar fywyd y dinesydd, gan ei alluogi yntau i gyflawni cymaint mwy o bethau nag a fedrai fyth eu gwneud ar ei ben ei hun.

---

[19] J. Ramsey Macdonald, 'A Reply', *Hibbert Journal,* Tachwedd 1911, t. 358.

[20] David Thomas, op. cit., t. 15.

[21] PC, tt. 169-177.

Pennod 13

Dinasyddiaeth Dda

Yr oedd syniadau Hegelaidd Henry Jones am natur ac awdurdod y wladwriaeth yn wahanol iawn i'r damcaniaethau rhyddfrydol a fu mor amlwg yn nhraddodiad athroniaeth wleidyddol Lloegr ers yr ail ganrif ar bymtheg. Yn ôl John Locke (1632–1704) cyfyd y wladwriaeth allan o gyfamod a wnaed gan unigolion o'u rhydd ewyllys eu hunain. O'i flaen ef, yr oedd Sais arall, Thomas Hobbes (1588–1679), wedi ceisio egluro tarddiad cymdeithas fel cyfamod rhwng unigolion. Ysgrifennodd yr athronydd o'r Swistir, Jean Jacques Rousseau (1712–1778), lyfr dylanwadol iawn yn 1762 ar y cyfamod cymdeithasol. Nid yw'r athronwyr hyn yn cytuno, fodd bynnag, paham y gwnaeth unigolion gyfamod. Yn ôl Hobbes, fe ildiodd unigolion rhydd eu hannibyniaeth cynhenid mewn cyfamod cymdeithasol er mwyn creu grym canolog a fyddai yn eu hamddiffyn yn well nag y gallent ar eu pen eu hunain, ac a sicrhâi felly well amodau iddynt ddilyn eu buddiannau unigol yn fwy llwyddiannus. Unigolwyr hunanol yw pawb wrth reddf, meddai Hobbes. Ni chredai Locke ein bod yn gynhenid hunanol. Iddo ef, prif gymhelliad yr unigolion a ymrwymodd mewn cyfamod cymdeithasol oedd sicrhau awdurdod diduedd i weinyddu cyfiawnder pan fyddai gwrthdaro rhwng unigolion. Ond er i'r athronwyr hyn anghytuno ynglŷn â chymhellion y cyfamodwyr a natur y cyfamod, yr oeddynt yn gytûn mai unigolion a'i gwnaeth, ac mai unigolion a greodd gymdeithas drwy'r cyfamod.

Credai Locke fod gan bob unigolyn hawliau cynhenid, a'u bod yn rhai naturiol na ellid byth eu diddymu. Nid eu derbyn gan gymdeithas a wna'r unigolyn oherwydd mae iawnderau'r unigolyn yn rhagflaenu cymdeithas ac yn sefyll yn annibynnol arni. Y mae gan bob unigolyn, yn ôl Locke, yr hawl sylfaenol i fywyd, rhyddid ac eiddo. Yn y ddeunawfed ganrif ymgorfforwyd y syniad o hawliau sylfaenol a naturiol yr unigolyn mewn datganiadau cyfansoddiadol gan weriniaethau America a Ffrainc. Nid oes modd i unrhyw wladwriaeth neu gymdeithas ddileu'r hawliau hyn, yn ôl Locke. O reidrwydd felly, awdurdod cyfyngedig sydd gan y wladwriaeth.

Credai Locke hefyd fod rhai agweddau ar fywyd yr unigolyn yn fater i gydwybod yr unigolyn yn unig, e.e., addoli. Yn y bedwaredd ganrif ar bymtheg cafodd y traddodiad rhyddfrydol clasurol hwn ladmerydd dylanwadol iawn yn John Stuart Mill (1806–1873). Daliai ef nad oes a wnelo'r wladwriaeth ddim â moesoldeb unigolion, ac eithrio pan fo ymddygiad un unigolyn yn amharu ar unigolyn arall. Fe berthyn i bawb gylch preifat o fywyd sydd wedi ei ynysu rhag ymyrraeth y wladwriaeth a'r cyhoedd.

Nid oedd Jones yn derbyn man cychwyn Locke a'r traddodiad rhyddfrydol clasurol. Camsyniad dybryd iawn oedd damcaniaeth y cyfamod cymdeithasol yn ei olwg ef; camsyniad yn deillio o ddiffyg dadansoddi'r cysyniad o unigolyn. Unwaith y derbynnir mai creadigaeth gymdeithasol yw'r unigolyn, fe gyll damcaniaeth y cyfamod cymdeithasol ei hystyr, ac fe gyll y ddadl fod hawl unigolion yn blaenori ar hawl cymdeithas ei sail. Felly athroniaeth wleidyddol wahanol iawn i safbwynt Locke a Mill a gawn ganddo. Yn gwbl groes iddynt hwy gwadodd fod hawliau 'naturiol' gan unigolion. Ni welai arwyddocâd moesol i unigolion ynddynt-eu-hunain. Mewn gwrthgyferbyniad llwyr â rhyddfrydiaeth glasurol, mae Jones yn gwadu ar y naill law fod terfynau i hawl y wladwriaeth (pan yw'n hyrwyddo'r hyn sy'n foesol dda) i ymyrryd ym mywyd y dinesydd, ac ar y llaw arall fod terfynau i ddyletswyddau'r wladwriaeth tuag at y dinesydd. Mae'n gwadu hefyd fod terfynau i'r hyn y gall y wladwriaeth foesol ei hawlio gan y dinesydd.

Gallwn ystyried y pum gwadiad yn eu tro, gan ddechrau gyda'r gwadiad fod gan unigolion hawliau naturiol. Yn *Principles of Citizenship* (1920) dywed am hawliau naturiol:

> It has been maintained that man is born free, that he has ... indefeasible and inalienable rights against the State. The State has not granted them and it cannot take them away ... The State has not instituted these rights, and yet it must respect them. As natural they were held to be superior to the State and independent of it. They are individual and not social. They define a territory into which the State must not intrude. ... the rights which are represented as natural are supposed to belong to man independently of society: he has them before and apart from his becoming a member of society. But who is he and what can he be or do apart from society? We have seen already that he is a being without a self and without the power of becoming a self. There is a long history, the strains of a very long and varied parentage, a vast social inheritance in the child when he is born into the world; and he grows with his world. 'When he can separate himself from it' – as a self to be given or denied rights – 'and knows himself apart from it, then by that time his self ... is penetrated by the existence of others.' In a word, the self to which such natural rights are assigned is a pure fiction of the imagination and an impossible being.[1]

Yn wyneb y ffaith fod yn rhaid wrth fewnbwn cymdeithasol i ffurfio unigolyn, ni wêl Jones fod synnwyr mewn sôn am hawliau a berthyn i unigolyn cyn iddo ddod yn aelod o gymdeithas. Nid yw hyn yn golygu, fodd bynnag, nad oes gan unigolyn hawliau sylfaenol. Mae'n bendant iawn fod ganddynt y fath hawliau, ond o gymdeithas y tarddant.

> Nevertheless, that the human being, as human, has rights cannot be denied. They are innate, and they are inalienable, and their ground is in the man himself. They are intrinsic. But they are in him as a social being.[2]

[1] PC, t. 145.

[2] ibid., t. 148.

Mae'r gwadu bod arwyddocâd moesol i unigolion-ynddynt-eu-hunain yn deillio o syniadau Hegelaidd am gyd-ddibyniaeth yr unigolyn a chymdeithas. Nid oes modd gwneud synnwyr o'r naill heb y llall, ac fe'n harweinir i gors syniadol os ceisiwn osod gwerth moesol arnynt yn annibynnol ar ei gilydd.

> The State 'in itself', we say (quite truly), is nothing. But we do not realize that the individual 'in himself' may also be nothing, and that to think to any purpose of either, we must dismiss these abstractions, and endeavour to understand the State and the individual as we find them, not as they might be when severed and held asunder.[3]

Wrth ffurfio unigolion o'i haelodau, bydd cymdeithas yn gwneud rhywbeth arall sy'n perthyn i hanfod dyndod, sef creu'r amodau angenrheidiol i foesoldeb.

> Not less than two persons can be moral; for not fewer than two can come under a 'common law', which both must respect … Passion meets passion and desire desire, and both have a new nobility; mind looks mind in the eye and sees its own reflection; will confronts will and out of their very strain is born mutual restraint and consideration, and the faint promise of regard and reverance. A common law emerges, and with its control the first beginning of the moral life. Man in order to become man, must find himself amongst rivals.[4]

> Alone with nature (could we conceive him),'monarch', like Crusoe on his island. 'of all he surveys', he could not become a moral being. At best he would be a powerful and dangerous brute. There would, in such a case, be no limit to his claims, except the limit of his power to enforce them; and he would have no means of making them good except force. But none of his claims could be *rights*, and he would have no duties.[5]

Gyda dyfodiad moesoldeb i'r byd (drwy gyfrwng cymdeithas) fe ddaw hawliau ac iawnderau hefyd.

Fel y gwelsom eisoes, prif ddiben gwladwriaeth yw sicrhau i'w dinasyddion y bywyd helaethach drwy ddatblygu i'r eithaf y potensial sydd ynddynt. O fewn terfynau'r amcan hwn, nid oes sail foesol dros geisio gosod cyfyngiadau ar hawl y wladwriaeth i ymyrryd ym mywyd personol ei dinasyddion.

> Within the limits of this, the ultimate end of the State, I am not able to see that there is anything which the State may not do, or any department of man's life, however private, into which its entrance would be an invasion and interference.[6]

> … the State must have the bearing of its actions upon character … continually in view, and having that in view as the end it may do *anything*. In contravention of that end it can do *nothing*.[7]

---

[3] ibid., t. 55.
[4] ibid., tt. 104-5
[5] ibid., t. 103.
[6] ibid., t. 137.
[7] ibid., t. 150.

Nid yw Jones hyd yn oed yn eithrio moesoldeb a chrefydd o gylch priodol gweithgaredd y wladwriaeth.

> Can it teach morality, it may be asked, and religion? I should answer that it can and ought to do so, always provided that it does so with a view to fostering the moral and religious spirit. This implies that it can teach definite moral and religious doctrines, affirming some and refuting others.[8]

Meithrin 'ysbryd y gwirionedd' mewn unigolion yw dyletswydd y wladwriaeth, meddai, nid gwthio dogma ar bobl. Yr oedd gan Rousseau safbwynt tebyg i hyn, ond rhaid cyfaddef fod hon yn athrawiaeth annisgwyl, a dweud y lleiaf, gan un a gefnogai ddatgysylltu'r eglwys wladol yng Nghymru, ac a eisteddodd fel Ymneilltuwr ar y Comisiwn Brenhinol ar yr Eglwys yng Nghymru yn 1906!

Dyletswydd yn ogystal â hawl yw dysgu'r dinasyddion yn ôl Jones. Er iddo osod hawliau'r wladwriaeth yn uchel iawn, mae'n gosod dyletswyddau'r wladwriaeth yr un mor uchel. Mae'n gwadu bod terfynau i ddyletswyddau'r wladwriaeth tuag at y dinesydd. Unwaith eto mae'n groes i ryddfrydiaeth glasurol yn ei safbwynt.

> Ychydig flynyddau'n ôl tybiai y gwleidyddion doethaf mai dyletswydd bennaf y ddeddfwriaeth oedd sicrhau i bob dinesydd gylch clir i fyw, heb ymyrryd o neb ag ef nac ymyrryd ohono yntau a neb. Ei nod oedd ei adael yn llonydd i ddilyn ei amcanion ei hun, heb wneuthur dim erddo na throsto ond yn unig ei rwystro i wneuthur na derbyn cam ... Ond erbyn heddyw y mae'r ddeddf yn gallu dywedyd nid yn unig 'Paid!' ond 'Gwna !' Ymae iddi swydd gadarnhaol, ac y mae yn ymyrryd â'n bywyd a'n hamgylchiadau ni ymhob cylch o'r bron, a'i llaw arnom o'r cryd i'r bedd.[9]

Mae'n cymeradwyo'r newidiadau deddfwriaethol a alluoga'r wladwriaeth i 'ymyrryd â'n bywyd ... ni ymhob cylch o'r bron'. (Cofier, iddo ef, creadigaethau'r wladwriaeth yw'r dinasyddion beth bynnag, felly go brin fod sail ganddynt i wrthwynebu ymyrraeth eu 'crëwr' â hwy!) Canlyniad yr ymyrraeth yw galluogi'r dinesydd i gyflawni pethau na allai fod wedi eu cyflawni yn ei nerth ei hun. Cynyddir ac estynnir ei hunaniaeth fel unigolyn gan ddeddfwriaeth ar iechyd, addysg, diogelwch diwydiannol, yswiriant cenedlaethol, etc. Dyma ni yn ein holau yn nhiriogaeth y syniad cadarnhaol o ryddid. Drwy wneud y gofal hwn dros fuddiannau gorau'r unigolyn yn fater o ddyletswydd, mae'n tanlinellu ei farn fod y wladwriaeth yn sefydliad moesol. Bydd yn mynegi hyn weithiau drwy wadu mai corff 'seciwlar' yw'r wladwriaeth.

Ei bumed gwadiad oedd gwadu fod terfynau i'r hyn y gall y wladwriaeth foesol ei hawlio gan ei dinasyddion. Gan mai'r wladwriaeth a'n lluniodd fel unigolion, ac mai trwyddi hi y sylweddolir ein potensial llawnaf, ni fedr yr unigolyn wrthsefyll ei galwadau arno – hyd yn oed yr alwad i roddi i'r eithaf drosti. Hawdd dadlau,

---

[8] ibid.

[9] DB, t. 18.

meddai Jones, mai gwadu cyfle i'r unigolyn i sylweddoli ei dda pennaf yw disgwyl iddo farw (a lladd eraill) dros y wladwriaeth. Ond dadl yw honno sy'n seiliedig ar ddealltwriaeth wallus o natur moesoldeb.

> There are two assumptions implicit in the argument which are inconsistent with the nature of morality. These are, first, that the good of the citizen and that of the State are distinct, separable, indpendent, respectively the private possesion of each: secondly, that the good of each is its own as it stands, and consists in the right merely to exist.[10]

Unwaith y gwahenir yr unigolyn a'r wladwriaeth oddi wrth ei gilydd fe gyll y ddau y cysylltiad sy'n rhoi iddynt eu gwir briodoleddau. Dyma wendid rhai dadleuon sydd yn ceisio sail foesol dros wrthwynebiad cydwybodol i ryfel. Maent yn cychwyn drwy ragdybied bod rhyw werth cynhenid mewn bod dynol unigol fel y cyfryw, ond, meddai Jones, heb yr holl gysylltiadau sy'n ei wneud yn berson ac yn unigolyn arbennig, nid oes arwyddocâd moesol iddo. Y mae'n amau, yn wir, a oes unrhyw werth moesol mewn bodoli, fel ffaith foel, i unrhyw beth.

Rhaid pwysleisio ei fod yn credu y gall gwladwriaeth golli ei gwerth. Ar wahân i les moesol a ffyniant ei dinasyddion nid oes unrhyw werth iddi fel y cyfryw. Nid oes gan unrhyw wladwriaeth hawl i fodoli yn unig. Ei feirniadaeth o'r Almaen dan y Kaiser oedd ei bod wedi colli golwg ar wir natur y wladwriaeth gan osod gwerth arni 'ynddi ei hun'. Eilunaddoliaeth ohoni oedd hynny, yn ei farn ef.

> No particular fact, be it a man or a State, or any other object we can name, has absolute value in itself. The 'sovereignty' of natural life is as little absolute as that of the State – pacifist and German theorist commit the same blunder. Value comes from relation to the whole, ... Except as a servant of the good neither man nor State has a right to live.[11]

Y mae'n barod iawn i gydnabod y gall gwladwriaeth fod yn llygredig. Beth wedyn yw dyletswydd y dinesydd os daw'r alwad i ymladd drosti? Ei ddyletswydd yw ei gwrthwynebu, ond (ac y mae hwn yn 'ond' pwysig iawn) dim ond er lles y wladwriaeth y dylai wneud hynny.

> Not only may the individual citizen judge whether the war in which he is required by his country to serve is or is not just, it is his duty to do so, and to act in accordance with his judgement. If he is convinced that the war is wrong, it is his duty to refuse to fight. It may even be his duty to fight against his country.[12]

> .. the individual can resist the will of the community or the extension of the functions of his city or State only when he has identified his own will with a will that is more universal, more concrete, and the source of higher imperatives than either. And this means that he can resist the State only for the good of the State, and never *merely* for his own profit.[13]

---

[10] PC, t. 156.
[11] ibid., t. 73.
[12] ibid., t. 158.
[13] WFSR, tt. 113-14.

Un hawl y mae Jones yn ymddangos yn amharod i'w ganiatáu yw hawl yr heddychwr i sefyll o'r neilltu gan gondemnio rhyfel pan fo ei wladwriaeth eisoes yn rhyfela. Yn anffodus nid yw'n mynegi ei safbwynt yn glir. Ni chawn oleuni ganddo ar beth yn union y dylai heddychwr ei wneud mewn rhyfel. Dyma ddywed Jones am yr heddychwr:

> What cannot be his duty is that of taking no side when the question of the right and wrong is being decided by means of war. The pacifist's protest against war, when his country is fighting, is the affirmation of a moral principle when it cannot be applied; and it has no more value than the affirmation of a hypothesis which is not applicable to facts.[14]

> Let the pacifist stand by his conscience, seeking to know the good ever more fully and to be ever more humbly loyal to its deliverances: and meanwhile, let him take his chance, and endure the consequences with as little fuss and sense of martyrdom as do they who suffer, and die and take the life of others whom they do not hate, *also* in obedience to *their* conscience.[15]

Anodd iawn dehongli'r paragraffau hyn. Ar un wedd, mae Jones fel pe bai'n dweud mai dim ond mewn adegau o heddwch y dylai'r heddychwr wneud ei brotest! Efallai mai'r hyn y ceisiai ei ddweud oedd y dylai'r heddychwr gydnabod, unwaith y dechreuodd rhyfel, fod yn rhaid i'r ddadl foesol symud ymlaen i ganolbwyntio ar agweddau eraill o'r argyfwng. Pa ddiben dadlau na ddylid rhyfela unwaith y mae rhyfel yn ffaith? Pan fydd y wladwriaeth y mae'n aelod ohoni yn mynd i ryfel, dyletswydd yr heddychwr yw ymladd a derbyn y clwyfau i'w gydwybod, megis y bydd disgwyl iddo dderbyn a rhoi clwyfau corfforol, fel rhan o ddioddefiadau rhyfel. Nid yw'n amlwg beth yn ymarferol a olyga Jones gyda'r ymadrodd 'stand by his conscience'.

Er iddo gredu bod dyletswydd ar y dinesydd mewn rhai amgylchiadau i ymladd dros ei wlad, nid oedd yn credu bod rhyfel fel y cyfryw fyth yn foesol dda. Meddai yn 1914:

> I think that the present war, like every war that was ever waged, is wrong, and that nothing can make it right … No context of circumstance, no compulsion of conscience, no sense of the imperative nature of duty can turn the waging of war into either a natural or a moral good.[16]

Serch hynny, mae'n cyfiawnhau ymladd yn y Rhyfel Byd Cyntaf drwy ddweud bod dyletswydd arnom weithiau i ddewis rhwng dau ddrwg. Yr unig ddau ddewis i Brydain, fel y gwelai ef bethau, oedd derbyn trais arfog yr Almaen neu ei wrthsefyll. Mae'r naill ddewis fel y llall yn ddrwg, ond mae un ohnonynt yn llai drwg. Dyma sut y mae'n disgrifio dilema Prydain Fawr:

---

[14] PC, 158.

[15] ibid., 159.

[16] 'Why we are Fighting', *Hibbert Journal,* Hydref 1914, tt. 50 a 52.

> There is no right thing left in the world for it to do. Its very best, its duty, is the tragical choice between two great evils.[17]

Er nad oes dewis moesol dda i'w gael, nid ymwacawyd y sefyllfa o arwyddocâd moesol: mae dyletswydd yn dal i alw.

> It is precisely this contradiction between 'duty' and 'rightness' that we must try not to obscure.[18]

Mae'n cydnabod pa mor baradocsaidd yw ei safbwynt. A ddichon bod dyletswydd i wneud yr hyn nid yw dda? Nid yw'n cynnig ateb eglur, ond mae'n ein cyfeirio tuag at ateb drwy ddweud (fel y gwelsom) na ddylid ceisio datrys y broblem ar sail cyfundrefn o werthoedd sydd yn gosod y gwerth uchaf ar unrhyw un elfen yn y sefyllfa yn unig. Hefyd mae'n rhaid ehangu terfynau cwmpas moesoldeb i gynnwys meysydd y buwyd hyd yma yn fodlon i'w hystyried y tu hwnt i'w gafael, sef yn benodol perthynas gwladwriaethau a'i gilydd.

> The truth is that the problems of international relationship, like those of individual men, are moral, and that everything depends upon the recognition of this fact. It is the failure of the moral powers which has made the present appeal to force necessary. 'So long as mere force is in any way influential in human life, so long we are not civilisied or moral ... a state of war is equivalent to 'the suspension of morality.' The situation is infra-human. It cannot be justified except on the ground that it is inevitable. But that is not *moral* justification. It means that the very principle of morality, namely, the free choice of an end conceived as good, is not operative ... As it is the failure of morality which has brought war, so it is the restoration of the authority of the moral powers, and that alone, which can bring peace.[19]

O ystyried y wladwriaeth fel y ffurf uchaf ar ysbryd y cyfyd y broblem. Ar wahân i'r ffaith fod rhai gwladwriaethau'n fwy 'datblygedig' nag eraill, fe gyfyd cwestiwn ynglŷn â'r posibilrwydd o gydnabod awdurdod uwchlaw'r gwladwriaethau. Yr oedd Hegel wedi gosod y wladwriaeth sofran fel pinacl esblygiad cymdeithas, ac ni welai sut y gallai'r dinesydd fod â theyrngarwch at unrhyw elfen 'uwch'. Fel canlyniad, gwelai ef berthynas gwladwriaethau â'i gilydd fel un gystadleuol yn ei hanfod. Mae ei ddisgrifiad o natur y berthynas yn ein hatgoffa o ddisgrifiad Hobbes o berthynas unigolion â'i gilydd yn eu cyflwr naturiol cyn ffurfio cymdeithas. Mae'n wahanol iawn i safbwynt Kant. Yr oedd ef, fel un o wŷr yr Ymoleuo, yn credu ym mhosibilrwydd brawdoliaeth gyffredinol dyn, ac yn ceisio gosod seiliau athronyddol i drefn newydd o gyfraith ryngwladol.

Mae Jones yn ymwybodol iawn o safbwynt Hegel, ac mae'n rhoi mynegiant croyw ohono (ond heb enwi Hegel). Dyma ychydig frawddegau sy'n cyfleu'r safbwynt hwn yn eithaf clir:

[17] ibid., t. 54.
[18] ibid., t. 53.
[19] ibid., tt. 57-8.

> Now, as all States have ideally the same obligations to their citizens, and therefore the same unlimited rights, they are natural rivals; and the normal relation between them is that of mechanical strain. ... And just as the obligations of a State to its own inhabitants are primary, so the duties of the citizen to his country must override all others. His sentiments may be cosmopolitan, but his practice must be patriotic.[20]

Ond mynegi'r safbwynt er mwyn ei feirniadu a wna Jones. Megis T. H. Green, mae ef yn gwrthod y syniad nad yw llwyddiant un wladwriaeth yn bosibl ac eithrio ar draul gwladwriaethau eraill, ac am gydnabod bodolaeth dyletswyddau tuag at ddynolryw yn gyffredinol. Mae'n cydnabod, fodd bynnag, fod gwahaniaeth ansawdd rhwng dyletswydd dinasyddion tuag at eu gwladwriaeth a dyletswydd gwladwriaethau tuag at ei gilydd.

> It is easy to show that the individuality of a State is intrinsically much more rich, concrete, and strong than that of any private person; and, at the same time, that the larger society of mankind is a far more empty and impotent universal than any single State is in relation to its members.[21]

Colyn yr holl gyfundrefn o ddyletswyddau a hawliau yw'r wladwriaeth. Ar y naill law, mae'n galluogi ei dinasyddion i sylweddoli eu posibiliadau fel unigolion, ac ar y llaw arall, mae'n gyfrwng i alluogi ei haelodau i gysylltu â byd ehangach. Ond byd teneuach yw'r byd ehangach yn yr ystyr fod llai o gysylltiadau ynddo yn dal ei elfennau gyda'i gilydd. I Hegel, yr oedd mor denau nes bod yn lledrithiol, ond credai Jones, fel Green, fod gwladwriaethau yn gyd-ddibynnol ar ei gilydd.

> As between individuals the egoistic ethical doctrine of the middle of the last century has been refuted; and as regards its own citizens the State's negative legislative practice has been discredited. We know, we have been forced to recognise even by Acts of Parliament, that whether we will or no we are one another's keepers. But the relations between one political State and another are still normally frankly egoistic. Each stands for its own good – which is right; but each is apt to interpret that good in a highly exclusive way, which is very wrong; for it is the characteristic not of moral but of natural or material good to be exclusive.[22]

Yr oedd Jones, felly, yn credu bod gwladwriaethau, lawn cymaint â'u dinasyddion, y tu mewn i gwmpas moesoldeb.

> ... there cannot be one morality for men, and another, or none at all, for States.[23]

Nid yw'n egluro beth neu pwy sydd yn ymgorffori'r foesoldeb uwchwladwriaethol. Efallai iddo newid ei feddwl ar y mater yn ystod y Rhyfel. Yr

[20] WFSR, t. 140.
[21] ibid., t. 145.
[22] 'Morality and its Relation to the War', J. E. Carpenter, *Ethical and Religious Problems of the War,* Llundain 1916, t. 37.
[23] ibid., t. 22.

argraff a gawn ganddo yn 1915/16 yw mai'r gwladwriaethau eu hunain sy'n ymgorffori ac yn gweithredu'r foesoldeb ryngwladol.

> 'No nation,' we are told by Mr Fisher, 'has yet consented, or in the present state of public ethics, is likely to consent to refer matters affecting its vital interests, independence, or honour, to an international tribunal.' I agree, and I go further. No nation ought to do so. A nation like an individual may consult its neighbours as to its duty, borrow light from its neighbours to see what it should do, but it cannot delegate the responsibility of choosing. There is a certain isolation and sacredness of soul in this matter of morality. We can send no proxies to meet duty or death.[24]

Diddorol iawn felly yw thema ei gyhoeddiad Cymraeg olaf a ymddangosodd yn 1918, *Ffurfiwch Gyngrair Heddwch yn Awr!* (Faint o'r Gymraeg sy'n llifo o law Syr Henry Jones a faint o law Syr John Morris-Jones, sydd yn fater i'r uwchfeirniaid: yn Saesneg y cyhoeddwyd y pamffledyn hwn gyntaf.) Cyhoeddwyd y gwaith gan The League of Nations Union, ac mae'n trafod amodau 'heddwch parhaol' wedi diwedd y Rhyfel.

> Coleddir y syniad mewn cylchoedd eang mai trwy 'Gyngrair y Cenhedloedd' yn unig y gellir sicrhau byd – heddwch ...[25]

Ond annelwig iawn yw'r cysyniad o gynghrair. Yn fwyaf arbennig, nid yw'n trafod y posibilrwydd o ddwyn grym awdurdod rhyngwladol i ddylanwadu ar ymddygiad y gwladwriaethau, er iddo ddyfynnu o sylwadau'r Arlywydd Wilson yn *Enforced Peace*, sef *Proceedings of the First Annual National Assemblage of the League to Enforce Peace, Washington,* Mai 26–27, 1916. Sylwer ar y gair 'enforced'.

> Y mae'n anghenraid moesol am i genhedloedd rhydd y byd ymuno mewn Cyngrair Hedd yn gyfryw na wiw i ni oedi. Rhoes y gwladweinydd doeth uchod (Wilson) fawr bris ar y syniad syml am dano fel amcan i'w sylweddoli. 'Pe na chyflawnodd y rhyfel hwn ddim arall ... symudodd feddwl gwladweinwyr y byd oes gyfan ymlaen. Gwnaethpwyd yn eglur gan sylwadau prif wladweinwyr y teyrnasoedd mawr sydd ar hyn o bryd yn rhyfela ... fod yn rhaid i egwyddor hawl gyhoeddus o hyn allan gymryd y blaen ar fuddiannau unigol cenhedloedd arbennig, a bod yn rhaid i genhedloedd y byd ymuno rhywsut neu'i gilydd, i ofalu fod yr hawl honno i dycio yn erbyn unrhyw fath o ymosodiad hunangar ... ond fod yn rhaid wrth gytundeb cyffredin ar amcanion cyffredin ...'[26]

A ddychmygai fod hyn yn ddichonadwy heb gyfyngu ar ryddid neu sofraniaeth lwyr 'y ffurf uchaf ar ysbryd' – y wladwriaeth? Ni ddywedodd ddigon i ni fedru deall ei agwedd at y posibilrwydd o sefydliadau cyfreithiol uwchwladwriaethol. Mae'r ffaith ei fod yn credu bod un sefydliad rhyngwladol a oedd, er yn amddifad o rym cyfreithiol, â digon o rym moesol i fedru trawsnewid agweddau'r gwledydd at ei

[24] ibid., t. 41.

[25] Henry Jones, *Ffurfiwch Gyngrair Heddwch yn Awr!,* Llundain 1918, t. 11

[26] ibid., t. 13.

gilydd, sef yr Eglwys, yn awgrymu mai drwy newid 'mewnol' yn hytrach na thrwy orfodaeth grym 'allanol' y sicrheid heddwch byd. Yn y pen draw, mater i ddinasyddion y gwladwriaethau yw dylanwadu ar eu gwleidyddion, meddai Jones, ac fe ddylai'r Eglwys weld hyn fel her a chyfle.

> Pe dechreuai ar hyn o orchwyl mewn modd ymarferol a didroi'n ol, fe'i gwelai ei hun yn fuan yn arweinydd mewn anturiaeth foesol ardderchog, y fwyaf eang a mawrfrydig a ymrithiodd erioed o flaen llygaid ein gwylwyr gwleidyddol ar y mur, gweledigaeth ysblennydd yn ymgodi uwch gorwelion diorffwys bywyd dyn.[27]

[27] ibid. Gweler sylwadau ar wahanol bwyslais Hegel a'r Idealwyr Prydeinig ar fater moesoldeb gwladwriaethau yn David Boucher ac Andrew Vincent, *A Radical Hegelian*, Caerdydd 1993, tt. 173-7.

Pennod 14

Y Gymynrodd

Gellid cyfleu amrediad diddordebau athronyddol Henry Jones gyda'r geiriau 'ysbryd' ac 'ymerodraeth'. Gyda'i gilydd maent yn cyfleu'r agwedd lled-grefyddol oedd ganddo tuag at y wladwriaeth, agwedd na fyddai heddiw yn cael ei hystyried yn un iach o gwbl.

> … the nation as organised into a political State is the highest moral being in the world, harmonising, however imperfectly, wider and more various forms of good than any other. It is the worst sinner and the most heroic saint; and for the individual, it stands most frequently of all and most fully for the moral Absolute.[1]

Mae'r agwedd uchel hon at y wladwriaeth yn deillio o Hegel, ac yn peri bod Jones ar adegau yn gweld y wladwriaeth fel sefydliad mwy moesol ac ysbrydol na'r Eglwys.

> … there is a sense in which the Church at its best, witnessing as it does sometimes to the highest truths, is only a preliminary and preparatory institution to the State. It is the arsenal where the weapons are stored, the commissariat and the training school; but it is not the battle field. … In the social life which has assumed in civilized nations the form of the State, the moral powers of which we hear in the Church, are to be seen in actual play.[2]

Y wladwriaeth yw'r ymgorfforiad llawnaf o Ysbryd a hi yw prif gyfrwng datblygiad ysbrydol dynion oherwydd ei bod yn rhydd o'r arallfydolrwydd hwnnw sydd yn nodweddu'r Eglwys mor aml. Yr olwg hon ar bosibiliadau'r wladwriaeth yw prif gymynrodd Jones. Credai fod y wladwriaeth wedi dod fel y caem fywyd ac fel y caffom ef yn ei lawnder eithaf. Ond ar waethaf ei agwedd addolgar tuag ati nid yw'n ddall i'w methiannau. 'It is the worst sinner', meddai am y wladwriaeth ar ei gwaethaf. A theg yw dweud nad oedd yn gwbl naïf yn ei agwedd at y wladwriaeth odidocaf a welodd daear erioed, yr Ymerodraeth Brydeinig. Nid oedd yn gwbl unllygeidiog wrth holi a oedd dwylo Prydain yn gwbl lân yn 1914.

---

1 'Why we are Fighting', *Hibbert Journal,* Hydref 1914, t. 63.

2 'The Idea of the State', *Transactions of the Liverpool Welsh National Society,* 1895/6, t. 27. Cymh., " … the civic state … comprises all the other forms of society – such as the family and industrial societies and the church." Llawysgrif McLeish, Prifysgol Glasgow, darlith 25.

> Isolated excellence, exclusive salvation, is a fiction both for nations and for individuals. The moral world is One. Nations like men, share one another's guilt, as well as bear one another's punishment. If, therefore, in attempting to find the cause of the present war we are driven to turn the light of inquiry mainly upon another people, it is not because our own hands are spotless. It was not by converting the heathen that we acquired their lands, nor for the sake of "the end of civilisation" that we drove the savages out of their hunting grounds. We may say, with much truth, that our conquests have followed our trade, and that what we now possess has come "in the way of business". But at what time in our history were our business ways with crude peoples honourable; or how often has the right of the savage to his wigwam been respected? We have been as ruthless, and we have been as ready to plead "the rights of a higher civilisation over a lower", as the German people are to-day.[3]

Trafodwyd rhai o agweddau gwrthgyferbyniol Jones tuag at y wladwriaeth gan yr Athro Huw Morris Jones yng nghyfrol XVI o'r *Efrydiau Athronyddol*.[4] Yr oedd eisoes wedi cyhoeddi crynodeb byr campus o waith Jones yn Saesneg, sef anerchiad yng Ngholeg y Brifysgol Bangor ar achlysur dathlu canmlwyddiant ei eni. Fe'i cyhoeddwyd gydag anerchiad Cymraeg yr Athro Hywel D. Lewis.[5]

Mae'r ymdriniaeth yn yr *Efrydiau Athronyddol* yn hynod o feirniadol, mor feirniadol yn wir fel bod y term 'athroniaeth' yn cael ei atal wrth ddisgrfio gwaith Jones ar natur cymdeithas a'r wladwriaeth.

> Gelwais yr ysgrif hon yn "syniadau gwleidyddol" ac nid yn "athroniaeth wleidyddol" Syr Henry Jones, oblegid yr argraff a adewir arnaf yw mai nifer o syniadau gwleidyddol a geir yn ei weithiau, nad ydynt yn tarddu i gyd o'r un ffynhonnell, ac nad ydynt yn gwbl gyson a'i gilydd.[6]

Prin iawn fyddai'r gweithiau y gellid eu disgifio fel 'athroniaeth' yn unrhyw iaith pe defnyddid y safon hon yn gyffredinol! Nid yw amrywiaeth yn nharddiad syniadau, nac anghysonderau rhwng nifer ohonynt, yn ddigon o sail dros wrthod ystyried cyfundrefn syniadol arbennig fel athroniaeth. Dull yr ymdriniaeth sydd yn penderfynu hynny. Y mae dehongliad Huw Morris Jones o waith Jones yn nodweddu barn lled gyffredin am yr Idealwyr Prydeinig, sef bod tyndra rhwng eu Hegeliaeth a'u Rhyddfrydiaeth.

Yn yr ysgrif fe wneir ymgais i ddosbarthu syniadau Jones yn ôl eu tarddiad. Y ddwy brif ffynhonnell yw'r 'cefndir crefyddol Cymreig' a'r athroniaeth a ddysgid yn Glasgow. O'r cyntaf deilliodd y diddordeb mewn addysg, dirwest a datgysylltiad Eglwys Loegr yng Nghymru. Gallai Jones, meddir, fod wedi gweithio dros y pethau hyn 'petasai heb fynd o gwbl i Glasgow'. Ond o fynd i Glasgow, maentumir ei fod wedi ei 'drwytho' mewn Hegeliaeth i'r fath raddau ag i'w orfodi i ysgwyddo ieuad anghymarus Rhyddfrydiaeth ac Idealaeth. Darlunnir y gwrthgyferbyniad ar ei eithaf fel hyn,

[3] 'Why we are Fighting', *Hibbert Journal*, Hydref 1914. t. 56.

[4] Huw Morris Jones, 'Syniadau Gwleidyddol Syr Henry Jones', *Efrydiau Athronyddol,* Cyf. XVI (1953), tt. 1-9.

[5] Huw Morris-Jones & Hywel D. Lewis, *Henry Jones* 1852-1922, Caerdydd 1953.

[6] Huw Morris Jones, 'Syniadau Gwleidyddol Syr Henry Jones', *Efrydiau Athronyddol,* Cyf. XVI (1953). t. 1.

> Yn yr Almaen felly Hegel yw awdur y dogmâu athronyddol a gynhyrchodd genedlaetholdeb dotalitaraidd y wlad honno. Ond ym Mhrydain daeth syniadau hanfodol Hegel i'w coleddu gan wŷr fel Caird a Henry Jones a oedd yn gwbl wahanol eu hagwedd wleidyddol, yn Rhyddfrydwyr argyhoeddiadol, ac a wnaeth eu rhan mewn bywyd cymdeithasol i ehangu a diogelu rhyddid dyn a'i hawl i feithrin a mynegi barn yn annibynnol ar orchmynion offeiriadaeth eglwysig neu swyddogaeth wleidyddol.[7]

Mae'n anodd iawn dweud beth yn union yw ystyr 'awdur' yn y cyswllt hwn, ond mae'r portread o Hegel wedi ei lurgunio gymaint fel prin y gellir ei adnabod fel yr athronydd a roddodd gymaint o bwys ar hunanymwybyddiaeth a chydnabyddiaeth o'r unigolyn. Beth bynnag fyddai daliadau Jones ar 'ryddid dyn' pe na bai wedi mynd i Glasgow, gellir yn hawdd ddangos bod y syniadau a arddeliai yn tarddu'n uniongyrchol o Hegeliaeth. Nid yw hynny, wrth gwrs, yn profi eu bod yn gwbl gyson â'i gilydd nac ychwaith eu bod yn ddilys.

Mae man cychwyn Jones yn gwbl ddilys, sef na ellir cael unigolyn yn absenoldeb eraill. Fel y dywed Huw Morris Jones,

> Dyma'r thema sy'n allwedd i Henry Jones i ddatrys y gwrthdrawiad ymddangosiadol rhwng budd yr unigolyn a budd y wladwriaeth. O gymdeithas y cafodd yr unigolyn bob dim a fedd – hyd yn oed ei ymwybyddiaeth ohono'i hun fel personoliaeth. Oherwydd nid yw'n bosibl dod yn ymwybodol o'r hunan heb fod yn ymwybodol o rywun arall fel personoliaeth. Trwy adnabod ein gilydd y down i'n hadnabod ein hunain. A pho lwyraf yr adnabyddwn eraill, llwyraf ein hadnabyddiaeth o'n hunain. Yn llythrennol ni ellir cael unigolyn unig.[8]

Eithr, wrth geisio amlinellu rhai o oblygiadau ei ddehongliad o natur yr hunan mae Jones yn cyfeiliorni. Mae'n gweld egin moesoldeb yn yr ymdeimlad sy'n cynyddu yn yr unigolyn fod gan eraill ofynion arno, oherwydd o'r ymdeimlad hwn y tardd y cysyniad o ddyletswydd sydd wrth wraidd moesoldeb. Hwn yw'r cwlwm anweledig sy'n dal teulu wrth ei gilydd, ac o'i ehangu sy'n dal cymdeithas a gwladwriaeth wrth ei gilydd hefyd. Y cysylltiad honedig hwn sy'n peri ei fod yn ystyried y teulu a'r wladwriaeth fel cyfryngau moesoldeb. Ond mae wedi gorsymleiddio'r berthynas. Beth bynnag yw tarddiad yr ymwybyddiaeth foesol mewn unigolion, byddai'n cytuno gyda Kant mai wrth eu hansawdd ac nid eu tarddiad y mae adnabod gweithredoedd moesol. Byddai'n barod i gyfaddef y gall y teulu neu'r wladwriaeth alw ar unigolyn i weithredu'n anfoesol, a phan ddigwydd hynny, dyletswydd y gweithredydd yw gwneud yr hyn a wêl yn foesol gywir. Mae'n amlwg felly nad oes unrhyw gyfiawnhad dros ystyried ufudd-dod i alwadau'r wladwriaeth ar y dinesydd fel dyletswydd hanfodol foesol. Nid yw hyn yn anghyson â safbwynt arall a goleddir ganddo, sef bod gallu gan y wladwriaeth i sicrhau'r amodau hynny

[7] ibid., t. 2.

[8] ibid., t. 5.

sy'n debygol o wneud dynion yn foesol dda. Mae hyn yn wir, ond nid yw'n gyfystyr â chydnabod y wladwriaeth fel sefydliad sydd, drwy ddiffiniad, yn foesol ynddi ei hun.

Y mae dyletswydd yr unigolyn tuag at gymdeithas yn deillio o'i ddyled iddi am ei wneud yr hyn ydyw, meddai Jones. Mae hyn yn rhagdybio bod yr unigolyn yn fodlon ar yr hyn ydyw, ond ni ellir cymryd hynny yn ganiataol. Fe all yr unigolyn fod yn feirniadol iawn o'r etifeddiaeth gymdeithasol a gafodd, a gofidio fod ei gymdeithas wedi ei ffurfio fel y gwnaeth. Ateb Jones i hyn, mae'n debyg, fyddai dweud, oni bai am ei gymdeithas, ni fyddai gan yr unigolyn yr adnoddau meddyliol i'w beirniadu. Mae hyn yn hollol wir, ond nid oes ganddo le yn ei ddamcaniaeth i gydnabod cymhlethdod perthynas unigolion â'u cymdeithas. Mae graddfeydd o berthyn. Mewn ymdriniaeth nodweddiadol dreiddgar trafodir mathau gwahanol iawn o berthyn i gymdeithas gan Raymond Williams yn ei lyfr *The Long Revolution,* gan gynnwys y 'rebel' a'r 'alltud' yn ogystal â'r 'aelod'.[9] Gogwydda damcaniaeth Jones tuag at ystyried ymwrthod â gwerthoedd y gymdeithas a roes fodolaeth iddo gan unigolyn fel gweithred anfoesol neu afresymol, ond unwaith yr aeddfedodd yr unigolyn rhaid ei ryddhau i dderbyn, gwrthod neu ddiwygio'r gymdeithas a esgorodd arno.

Canlyniad derbyn cymhlethdod y ffyrdd o berthyn i gymdeithas yw sylweddoli na all cymdeithas hyrwyddo buddiannau ei holl aelodau i'r un graddau. Yn wir ei hanallu, neu ei hamharodrwydd i wneud hynny sy'n peri bod rhai o'i haelodau yn ymddieithrio ac yn cefnu arni neu yn ymosod arni. Ar brydiau bydd Jones yn swnio fel pe bai'n derbyn dilysrwydd syniad Rousseau am yr 'ewyllys gyffredinol', sef yr ymwybyddiaeth honno o les y gymdeithas gyfan sydd yn galluogi aelodau unigol i roddi blaenoriaeth iddo dros eu buddiannau fel unigolion. Efallai'n wir fod y fath 'ewyllys' yn amlwg ar adegau hanesyddol arbennig, megis cyfnod o ryfel, ond mae cymdeithasau modern mor gymhleth fel bo sôn am un 'ewyllys' yn hynod artiffisial. Â llawer o feirniaid yr Idealwyr cyn belled â dweud mai dim ond unigolion sy'n feddiannol ar ewyllys. Efallai fod y mwyafrif ohonom wedi teimlo'n rhan o rywbeth mwy na ni'n hunain, ond cynghanedd rhwng ewyllysiau unigol yn hytrach na ffurfiant un ewyllys gyffredinol sy'n gyfrifol am hynny.

Craidd y feirniadaeth Farcsaidd ar gymdeithas yw fod ei threfniadaeth ar y cyfan yn hyrwyddo buddiannau un dosbarth ar draul y lleill. Cyn medru chwyldroi'r sefyllfa, credai Marx fod yn rhaid dyfnhau ymwybyddiaeth dorfol y dosbarth gweithiol, a gwrthweithio ymgais y dosbarth llywodraethol i greu ymwybyddiaeth gyfun a fyddai'n cofleidio holl aelodau'r gymdeithas fel pe bai ganddynt oll yr un buddiannau. Yr elfen hon mewn sosialaeth oedd yn cythruddo Jones yn fwy na dim. Nid oes raid i ni yma ddewis pa ymwybyddiaeth ddylai gael y flaenoriaeth, digon yw nodi bod lle i ddadl ar ba ymwybyddiaeth ddylai gael y flaenoriaeth. Nid yw'n

[9] Raymond Williams, *The Long Revolution,* Llundain 1961, tt. 89-102.

amlwg o gwbl mai'r ymwybyddiaeth o berthyn i wladwriaeth arbennig sydd â'r hawl foesol gryfaf arnom, fel y credai Jones.

Man gwan amlwg iawn yn ei ddamcaniaeth gymdeithasol yw ei ddadansoddiad o berthynas y genedl a'r wladwriaeth. Weithiau yn wir mae ei barodrwydd i gyfnewid termau fel 'gwlad', 'cenedl', 'pobl' a 'gwladwriaeth' yn awgrymu eu bod yn gyfystyr, ac nad oes berthynas i'w dadansoddi o gwbl. Weithiau bydd yn sôn am y wladwriaeth fel y genedl ar ei ffurf wleidyddol neu gyfreithiol. Mae tuedd yn Jones i ddamcaniaethu heb dalu unrhyw sylw i dystiolaeth hanes. Nid yw fel pe bai'n ymwybodol o natur fyrhoedlog llawer o wladwriaethau. Mae map gwladwriaethau'r byd yn newid o genhedlaeth i genhedlaeth, ond nid felly map y cenhedloedd. Gall gwladwriaeth ddod i fodolaeth neu gael ei diddymu drwy gyfamod neu gytundeb dros nos, ond fel y tystia Jones ei hun, cynnyrch datblygiadau'r canrifoedd yw'r genedl. O ddarllen dadansoddiad Simone Weil, er enghraifft, o'r rhesymau dros gwymp disymwth Gweriniaeth Ffrainc yn 1940, gwelwn mai haen fregus dros lu o ymwybyddiaethau cenedlaethol a dosbarthol oedd y wladwriaeth honno. Nid oedd wedi tyfu fel cenedl, a dyna paham y rhoddodd Weil y teitl *Yr Angen am Wreiddiau* i'w chyfrol.[10]

Heddiw, unigoliaeth (onid unigoliaeth hunanol yn wir) sydd mewn bri, a'r wladwriaeth ar drai. Mae buddugoliaethau y credai Jones a'i gyfoeswyr eu bod wedi eu hennill am byth wedi eu gwyrdroi, ac nid yw'n amlwg y bydd unrhyw un yn barod i arfogi i'w hadennill. Ond o edrych ar hanes Prydain dros y can mlynedd diwethaf gellir dweud mai'r dehongliad Idealaidd o ryddid a roes i ni'r Wladwriaeth Les. Cafodd y syniad y gellid defnyddio'r wladwriaeth i sicrhau bod potensial pob unigolyn yn cael ei ddatblygu i'w eithaf afael yn nychymyg llunwyr polisi cyhoeddus bob plaid wleidyddol tan 1979. Dyna brif gymynrodd Henry Jones a'i gyd-Idealwyr i'r ganrif hon, ac y mae'n un y mae miliynau ohonom yn ddyledus iddynt amdani.

[10] Simone Weil, *The Need for Roots,* Llundain 1952.

Llyfryddiaeth Fer

(Ychwanegwyd ychydig at y llyfryddiaethau o weithiau Henry Jones a gafwyd gan Hetherington [isod 70] a Peter Nicholson yn Boucher a Vincent [isod 71].)

I Gweithiau Henry Jones

A. Gweithiau Cymraeg Henry Jones

1. 'Y Corff Cymdeithasol', *Y Traethodydd*, 1884, tt. 261-282 (cyfieithiad o 11 isod).
2. 'Moesoldeb fel Rhyddid', *Y Traethodydd*, 1888, tt. 357-369 (cyfieithiad o 14 isod).
3. 'Anghenion Cymru', *Y Geninen*, 1889, tt. 209-212 (cyfieithiad o rhan o 13 isod).
4. 'Anghenion Cymru II', *Y Geninen*, 1890, tt. 9-14 (parhad o 3 uchod).
5. *Fy Ngwlad a'i Rhagolygon*, Dinbych 1890 (gweler 38 isod am y fersiwn Saesneg).
6. 'Addysg Ganolradd', *Y Goleuad*, cyfres o ysgrifau ar ffurf llythyrau i'r golygydd:
   - 18 Rhagfyr 1890, t. 11.
   - 25 Rhagfyr 1890, tt. 6-7.
   - 1 Ionawr 1891, tt. 10-11.
   - 15 Ionawr 1891, t. 7.
   - 22 Ionawr 1891, tt. 11-12.
   - 12 Chwefror 1891, tt. 6-7.
7. 'Cymdeithas a'r Person Unigol', *Y Traethodydd*, 1898, tt. 1-13.
8. *Y Diwygiad: a'r hyn eill ddod ohono*, Caernarfon, 1905 (hefyd yn 9 isod).
9. *Dinasyddiaeth Bur ac Areithiau Ereill*, Caernarfon, 1911.
10. *Ffurfiwch Gyngrair Heddwch yn Awr!*, Llundain, [1919?] (cyfieithiad o 60 isod).

B. Gweithiau Saesneg Henry Jones

[1] Cyfraniadau i gylchgronau neu lyfrau a olygwyd gan eraill (Ni chynhwysir erthyglau a ymddengys yn *The Working Faith of a Social Reformer and Other Essays*, Llundain 1910 ac *Essays on Literature and Education*, Llundain 1924)

11. 'The Social Organism', A. Seth ac R. B. Haldane (Goln.), *Essays in Philosophical Criticism*, Llundain 1883 a Bryste 1990.

12. 'Adjudication of Prof. HENRY JONES, University College of North Wales, Bangor', *Transactions of the Royal National Eisteddfod of Wales, Liverpool, 1884*, Lerpwl 1885.
13. 'Some of the Social Wants of Wales', *Transactions of the Liverpool Welsh National Society*, Lerpwl 1888.
14. 'Morality and Freedom', *Time*, CN 7, 1888.
15. 'Home Rule for Wales', *Westminster Review*, CXXXIII, 1890.
16. 'The Nature and Aims of Philosophy', *Mind*, CN II, 1893.
17. 'Idealism and Philosophy', *Mind*, CN II, 1893.
18. 'The Idea of the State', *Transactions of the Liverpool Welsh National Society*, Lerpwl 1895/6.
19. 'Browning as a Dramatic Poet', *Boston Browning Society Papers 1886-97*.
20. 'How to Attain Liberal Unity', *New Liberal Review*, 21, 1902.
21. 'The Late Professor Adamson', *Mind* CN XI, 1902.
22. 'The Present Attitude of Reflective thought Towards Religion', *Hibbert Journal*, I a II, 1902/3 a 1903/4.
23. 'Mr Balfour as a Sophist', *Hibbert Journal*, III, 1904/5.
24. 'The Child and Heredity', Thomas Stephens (Gol.), *The Child and Religion*, Llundain 1905.
25. 'Divine Immanence', *Hibbert Journal*, V, 1906/7.
26. 'The Ethical Demand of the Present Political Situation', *Hibbert Journal*, VIII, 1909/10.
27. 'Ethics and Politics', *Quarterly Examiner*, XLIV, 1910.
28. 'Modern Science and Philosophical Thought Regarding Human Society', J. B. Paton, P. W. Bunting ac A. E. Garvie (Goln.) *Christ and Civilization*, Llundain 1910.
29. 'The Corruption of the Citizenship of the Working Man', *Hibbert Journal*, X, 1911/12.
30. 'Why We Are Fighting', *Hibbert Journal*, XIII, 1914/15.
31. 'Philosophical Landmarks: Being a Survey of the Recent Gains and the Present Problems of Reflective Thought', *Rice Institute Studies*, I, 1915.
32. 'Morality and Its Relation to the War', J. E. Carpenter (Gol.), *Ethical and Religious Problems of the War*, Llundain 1916.
33. 'The Huge Machinery of Sin and Sorrow', *The Free Catholic*, I, 1916.
34. 'The Education or the Citizen', *The Round Table*, VII, 1916/17.
35. 'A League of Learning', *Rice Institute Studies*, VI, 1919.
36. 'The Obligation and Privileges of Citizenship – A Plea for the Study of Social Science', *Rice Institute Studies*, VI, 1919.
37. Detholiad o sylwadau yng nghwrs ymweliad y Genhadaeth Addysg Brydeinig, *Rice Institute Studies*, VI, 1919.

[2] Llyfrau a phamffledi

38. *On Some of the Social and Economic Aspects of the Land Question in Wales*, Glasgow 1888.
39. *Wales and its Prospects*, Wrecsam 1889.
40. *Browning as a Philosophical and Religious Teacher*, Glasgow 1891 (a Llundain yn ddiweddarach).
41. *Browning as a Dramatic Poet*, Boston 1894.
42. *Is the Order of Nature Opposed to the Moral Life?* Glasgow 1894.
43. *The Higher Learning in its Bearing Upon the National Life of Wales*, Bangor 1895.
44. *A Critical Account of the Philosophy of Lotz: The Doctrine of Thought*, Glasgow 1895.
45. *Corporate and Individual Charity*, Glasgow 1897.
46. *Principal Caird*, Glasgow 1898.
47. Ar y cyd gyda C. M. Douglas, *Scottish Education Reform: A Scheme of District School Boards and a National Council*, Glasgow 1903.
48. *The Philosophy of Martineau in Relation to the Idealism of the Present Day*, Llundain 1905.
49. *The Immortality of the Soul in the Poems of Tennyson and Browning*, Llundain 1905.
50. *The Function of the University in the State*, Aberystwyth 1905.
51. *The University of Wales: The Line of Its Growth*, Bangor 1905.
52. *Social Responsibilities*, Glasgow 1905.
53. *Francis Hutcheson*, Glasgow 1906.
54. *Divine Transcendence*, Manceinion 1907.
55. *The Idealism of Jesus*, Llundain 1909.
56. *Idealism as a Practical Creed*, Glasgow 1909.
57. *The Working Faith of the Social Reformer and Other Essays*, Llundain 1910.
58. *Social Powers*, Glasgow 1913.
59. *North Wales Heroes Memorial*, Bangor 1917.
60. *Form a League of Peace Now*, Llundain [1919?]
61. *The Principles of Citizenship*, Llundain 1919.
62. Ar y cyd gyda J. H. Muirhead, *The Life and Philosophy of Edward Caird*, Glasgow 1921.
63. *A Faith that Enquires*, Llundain 1922.
64. *Old Memories*, (Gol. Thomas Jones) Llundain 1922.
65. *Essays on Literature and Education*, (Gol. H. J. W. Hetherington) Llundain 1924.

[3] Llythyrau

66. Cyhoeddwyd tua 90 o lythyrau a chofiant i Will ei fab yn H. J. W. Hetherington, *The Life and Letters of Sir Henry Jones*, Llundain 1924.

[4] Llawysgrifau nodiadau myfyrwyr o ddarlithoedd Henry Jones

67. Nodiadau Thomas Jones am y cyfnod 1897–1900 – yn Llyfrgell Genedlaethol Cymru, Aberystwyth.
68. Nodiadau Donald A. S. McLeish am y cyfnod 1911–12 – ym Mhrifysgol Glasgow.
69. Nodiadau Thomas R. Morton am y cyfnod 1919–20 – ym Mhrifysgol Glasgow.

II Gweithiau am Henry Jones

70. H. J. W. Hetherington, *The Life and Letters of Sir Henry Jones*, Llundain 1924. (Gwaith bywgraffiadol gyda phennod ar athroniaeth Jones, llyfryddiaeth o weithiau Jones a detholiad o'i lythyrau wedi eu golygu.)
71. David Boucher ac Andrew Vincent, *A Radical Hegelian: The Political and Social Philosophy of Henry Jones*, Caerdydd 1993.
(Trafodir athroniaeth wleidyddol a chymdeithasol Jones yn ei chyd-destun gyda chyfeiriadaeth helaeth at waith meddylwyr eraill gan ddau ysgolhaig amlwg cyfoes; llyfryddiaeth gyfoethog.)

III Cefndir cyffredinol

Llyfrau addas i'r darllenydd cyffredinol

72. E. Gwynn Matthews, *Hegel – Y Meddwl Modern*, Dinbych 1984.
73. Charles Taylor, *Hegel and Modern Society*, Caer-grawnt 1979.
74. H. S. Harris, *Hegel: Phenomenology and System*, Indianapolis/Caer-grawnt, 1995.
75. Peter Robbins, *The British Hegelians 1875–1925*, Efrog Newydd/Llundain 1982.
76. Andrew Vincent a Raymond Plant, *Philosophy, Politics & Citizenship*, Rhydychen 1984.
77. Alan P. F. Sell, *Philosophical Idealism and Christian Belief*, Caerdydd 1995.

Mynegai

Aberdâr, Arglwydd 22, 26–29, 31, 35
  Pwyllgor 22, 23, 42
Aberystwyth 21, **22–31**, 34–35, 38, 39, 53, 77, 82, 86, 105
Absoliwt, Yr 110, 111
Acland, Arthur 42
Adams, David 32, 91
Adamson 65
Adelaide 71
addysg (*gweler hefyd*: Aberdâr, Pwyllgor)
  Addysg, Adran Gymreig 86, 88
  addysg brifysgol (Comisiwn ar Addysg Brifysgol yng Nghymru) 78
  Addysg, Cyngor i Gymru 86
  Addysg, Deddf Balfour 87
  addysg elfennol (Comisiwn Brenhinol 1887) 44
  addysg ganolraddol, Deddf Addysg Ganolraddol Cymru (1889) 42, 54
  addysg Gymraeg (cynradd) 44–47 (uwch) 85
  addysg oedolion 43, 44, 78, (Adroddiad 1919) 78–80
  addysg ryw 11
  addysg uwch (Comisiwn ar Addysg Uwch yng Nghymru 1917 – Haldane) 84
Alban, Yr
  undod 83
  ymreolaeth 60
Almaen, Yr 9, 18–20, 33, 37, 78, 84, 91, 141, 142, 149
America, Unol Daleithiau 71
Anwyl, Syr Edward 86
Asquith 60
Awstralia 71

Balfour 61, 69, 97, 122
Baner ac Amserau Cymru 48
Bangor 82
  Capel Princes Road 41
  Coleg y Brifysgol (Coleg y Gogledd) 22, 26–30, **32–47**, 53, 55, 56, 58, 65, 78, 86, 148
  Esgob 25
Bardd Newydd, Y 105, 115
Barnett, Canon 75
Bell, Syr James 72
Birmingham 23
Birrell 86, 87
Bonn 19
Bosanquet, Bernard 67, 72
Boyd, William 10, 11, 69, 96
Bradley, A. C. 65, 72, 78, 92, 113, 114n
Bradley, F. H. 23, 61, 65, 67, 69, 110
  Essays on Truth and Reality 111
Brisbane 71
Browning, Robert 15, 48, 50, 54, 57, 68, **113–122**
Bruce, A. B. 54
Brynaman 10
  Capel Moriah 11
Burnet, John 58

Caerdydd 22, 23, 33, 49, 55, 60, 69, 72, 81, 82
Caeredin 13, 18, 20, 37, 54, 55, 58
Caerfyrddin
  Y Coleg Presbyteraidd 59
Caer-grawnt 13, 48, 69, 70
Caergybi 95
Caernarfon
  Y Coleg Hyfforddi 9
Caird, Edward 14, 15–17, 19–21, 23–25, 27, 32, 33, 39, 55, 58, 59, 60, 61, 62, 63, 66, 71, 72, 76, 103, 104, 109, 110, 113, 149
  The Evolution of Religion 104n, 109n
  Essays on Literature 113n
Caird, John 38, 39, 61, 63
  Introduction to the Philosophy of Religion 38
Campbell, Lewis 57, 58
Carlyle, Thomas 7, 15, 113, 114
  Sartor Resartus 9
cenedl, cenhedloedd **123–129,** 151
Charity Organisation Society 75
Coleg Balliol (Rhydychen) 14, 16, 19, 61
Coleg Dewi Sant (Llanbedr Pont Steffan) 22, 23, 86
Coleg Harlech 78
Coleg Manceinion (Rhydychen) 70
Coleg Merton (Rhydychen) 17
Coleg Normal, Y (Bangor) 8–10, 12, 13, 113
Coleg y Bala 18, 24, 39, 49
Coleg y Gogledd *gweler* Bangor, Coleg y Brifysgol
cosb gorfforol 11
Crawshay, Frank 18

Cunningham, Y Prifathro 57
cyfamod cymdeithasol 137, 138
cymdeithas **123–129,** 131–133, 137, 138, 139, 140, 143, 150
Cymdeithas Addysg y Gweithwyr (W.E.A.) 75, 79, 90
Cymraeg
  llenyddiaeth 86, 113
Cymru 48
Cymru Fydd 52

Chwyldro Ffrengig, Y 133

Dafydd ap Gwilym 51
  Cymdeithas Dafydd ap Gwilym 51
Darwin, Charles 120
Davies, Cadwaladr 8, 42, 55, 58, 59
Davies, David (Llandinam) 25
Davies, J. C. 89, 90
Davies, Richard 42
Denney, James 68, 78, 106
Dicey, A. V. 16
dinasyddiaeth (*gweler hefyd* Jones, Syr Henry) 78
Dinbych 7n, 37, 41
dirwest (alcohol/meddwdod) 16, 73–75
Diwygiad '59 5
Dixon, W. MacNeil 65, 93, 100
Dobbie, James Johnston 37, 41
Dolwyddelan 18
Donaldson 57
dosbarth (cymdeithasol) 134, 135, 150
Dowlais 95
Dresden 19
Drummond, Henry 76, 77, 119
Dundee 57, 58
Duwdod 105
dwyfoldeb 106, 107

Edwards, Edward 39, 86
Edwards, Parch Ellis (Y Bala) 33, 36, 42
Edwards, Lewis 18, 23, 24, 35, 49, 51
Edwards, O. M. 24, 25, 30, 31, 39, 48, 56, 86, 98, 105
Edwards, Thomas Charles **23–31**, 32–35, 49, 81
Eglwys Loegr (yng Nghymru) 60
  Comisiwn Brenhinol ar Waddoliadau'r Eglwys ac Adnoddau'r Enwadau yng Nghymru 85, 86, 140

Eisteddfod Genedlaethol, Yr
  Corwen 1919 79
  Lerpwl 1884 32
Ellis, Thomas 42, 61
esblygiad 118, 123, 126, 127
Essays in Philosophical Criticism gweler Pringle-Pattison, Andrew Seth
Evans, Syr Emrys 81
Evans, Keri 59

Faner, Y *gweler Baner ac Amserau Cymru*
Ferguson 74
Fichte 18, 117
Fraser, A. C. 20, 54

Genedl Gymreig, Y 51
George, Lloyd 78, 84, 85, 86, 87, 94n, 96
Gifford
  Darlithoedd 97–99, 103
Glasgow 10–15, 17–19, 24–25, 32–33, 37, 59, 61, 62, **63–80,** 81, 82, 84, 87, 88, 91, 92, 95, 99, 113, 117, 149
  Glasgow Association for the Higher Education of Women/Queen Margaret College 63
  Glasgow Civic Society 72–73
  United Free Church College 68, 77, 78
Glyn-nedd 18
Goleuad, Y 43n, 48–55, 119
Gothenberg System 74
Gray, Andrew 37, 41, 65
Green, Thomas Hill 16–17, 19–23, 33, 43, 74, 76, 110, 144
  Prolegomena to Ethics 16, 19, 110
  Lectures on the Principles of Political Obligation 16
Griffiths, Ann 118
Gruffydd, W. J. 25
gweddi cyn darlithio, Caird a Jones 66
gwladwriaeth 94, **123–129,** 130–136, 137–144, 147, 149, 151
  gwladwriaeth les 77, 151
gwrthwynebwyr cydwybodol 95

Hadow, Syr Henry 81, 96
Haldane, R. B. 20, 61, 84
Hamilton, William 14, 55
heddychwr 142
Hegel 14, 18, 19, 21, 33, 37, 39, 50, 60, 67, 68, 71, 112, 114, 117, 120, 123, 132, 133, 134, 143, 144, 146n, 149

Hegelydd, Hegeliaid 23, 39, 50, 72, 84, 105, 123, 130, 139
Hegeliaeth, Hegelaidd 25, 30, 33, 50, 52, 91, 93, 137, 148, 149
Hetherington, Hector 14, 65, 66, 69, 72, 77
Hibbert Journal 69, 70
Hobbes, Thomas 137, 143
Hobhouse, L. T. 104n
Hume, David 55, 118
Hutcheson, Francis 63
Huxley, T. H. 117, 118, 119

Idealaeth, Idealwyr 14, 22, 103, 104n, 110, 146n, 148, 150, 151
Iesu Grist 106–109
International Journal of Ethics 69
Islwyn 105
Israel 105

James, Y Parchedig Thomas (Llanelli) 11
James, William 122
Jayne, Prifathro 23
Jebb, Syr Richard 14, 84
Joachim, H. H. 58
Jones, Annie gynt Walker 22, 37, 59, 92
Jones, Arthur 37, 59, 76, 92, 94, 97
Jones, D. D. 50, 51
Jones, Edward Taylor 37
Jones, Elias 3, 4, 6, 48
Jones, Elias Henry (Hal) 5, 37, 92, 93, 94, 97
Jones, Elizabeth (Williams gynt) 3, 4, 7, 48
Jones, Enid 37, 92, 97
Jones, Syr Henry 68 ('The Jone')
'Anghenion Cymru' 124n, 127n, 128n, 129n
Browning as a Philosophical and Religious Teacher 48, 50, 52, 54, **113–122**
Critical Account of the Philosophy of Lotze, A 60
Dinasyddiaeth Bur 134, 135, 140n
Divine Transcendence 104n
Faith that Enquires, A 97, 99
Fy Ngwlad a'i Rhagolygon 129n
Ffurfiwch Gyngrair Heddwch yn Awr! 145
'Idea of the State, The' 127n, 147
'Idealaeth a Gwybodeg' 60
Idealism as a Practical Creed 71, 123n, 133
Idealism of Jesus, The 104
Is the Order of Nature Opposed to the Moral Life? 117
'Morality and its Relation to the War' 144
'Natur ac Amcanion Athroniaeth' 60
Old Memories 3, 4, 6, 7, 9, 11, 14, 19, 26, 35, 38, 42, 61, 98, 103
Philosophy of Martineau in Relation to the Idealism of the Present Day, The 109
Principles of Citizenship, The 78, 96, 136, 138, 141n, 142n
'Social Organism, The' 21, 124, 134n
'Why we are Fighting' 142, 147, 148n
Working Faith of the Social Reformer, The 104n, 123n, 124n, 132n, 141n, 144n
Jones, Huw Morris 148
Jones, Jeanie 37, 92, 93
Jones, Jim 37, 41, 92, 94, 97
Jones, John 4, 6, 8, 10, 98
Jones, Puleston 25, 41, 50, 51, 52
Jones, R. A. (Lerpwl) 42
Jones, Dr Thomas 24, 77–78, 88, 89, 90, 95, 99
Jones, Viramu 81
Jones, Will 37, 92, 93
Jones, William 4, 6, 10
Jones, William Lewis 40, 41
Jowett, Benjamin 14, 19

Kant 14, 18, 20, 21, 67, 68, 114, 117, 133, 143, 149
Kritik der reinen Vernunft 20
Kelvin, Arglwydd 14, 37
Kemp-Smith, Norman 58, 71
Ker, W. P. 72, 92
Kilbride 100
Knight 57
Kossuth 15

Lambie, James 19
Latta, Robert 58, 65
Leipzig 37
Lerpwl 21
Lewis, Syr Herbert 89, 91
Lewis, Hywel D. 148
Lloyd, Y Parchedig Thomas 12
Locke, John 137, 138
Lotze, R. H. 20, 60

Llafur 95, 134
Plaid 90, 136
Llanbedr Pont Steffan
Coleg Dewi Sant *gweler* Coleg Dewi Sant (Llanbedr Pont Steffan)
Llanberis
y streic fawr 40

Llanengan 98
Llangernyw 3, 5, 7, 9, 11, 21, 67, 98
Capel y Cwm 3, 5, 6, 103
Y Cwm 3, 4, 7
eglwys 6
ysgol 4, 6, 10
Llannerch-y-medd 107
Llanrwst 4, 7

MacCallum, Mungo 19, 22, 23, 25, 31, 71
Macdonald, Ramsey 135, 136n
Maclehose 64, 69
Mansbridge, Albert 79
Martineau, James 69, 70, 108, 109
Marx, Karl 150
Mathews, Ballard 41
Matthews, William 40, 41
Melbourne 71
Merthyr Tudful 83, 95, 116
Methodistiaeth Galfinaidd 5, 24, 30, 34, 35, 52, 91, 96, 107, 108
Y Gyffes Ffydd 37, 103
Mill, John Stuart 15, 137
Mind 60
Morris, Dr John (Aberhonddu) 32
Morris, Silas 38
Morris-Jones, John 40, 51, 52, 53, 54, 86, 87, 92, 106, 113n, 145
Muirhead, J. H. 19, 23, 114
Munro-Ferguson, Ronald 60, 73
Murray, Gilbert 65, 92

Nationalist, The 83
Nichol, John 14, 15, 16, 17, 18, 25, 41, 48, 60, 63, 113
Nietzsche, Friedrich 118
Niwbwrch 82

Old Mortality Society 14, 15, 16, 19, 113
Owen, Syr Isambard 82, 83

Pandy Tudur 7, 8
Penny Readings 6
Platon 18, 114
Powell, John 42
Powys, Arglwydd 35
Presbyteriaeth 110
Price, John 7, 8
Prifysgol Cymru 38, 55, 58, 81–85, 89, 90, 91
Prifysgol Glasgow *gweler* Glasgow
Prifysgol Llundain 22, 30, 38, 56, 70, 81, 84
Prifysgol Princeton 71
Prifysgol Sydney 71
Prifysgol Texas 71
Pringle-Pattison, Andrew Seth 20, 21, 22, 24, 33, 55, 60, 69
The Development from Kant to Hegel 20
Essays in Philosophical Criticism (cydolygydd) 20, 22, 69
[am 'The Social Organism' *gweler* Jones, Syr Henry]
Hegelianism and Personality 55
Scottish Philosophy 55
Pwllheli 98

Raleigh, Syr Thomas 84
Raleigh, Syr Walter 65
Ramsey, George C. 14
Rathbone, William 27, 32, 42
Redfern, Tom 7, 8
Reichel, Syr H. 35, 39, 45, 69, 82, 84, 87, 88, 95
Reid, Thomas 55, 63
Rendel, Stuart 27, 55
Roberts, John Bryn (A.S.) 34
Roberts, Sam 7
Rogers, J. B. 34
Rousseau 131, 137, 140, 150
Roxburgh, Mrs 6, 7, 9, 11, 19, 48

Rhondda, Arglwydd 85
Rhydychen 12, 13, 17, 19, 23, 25, 33, 58, 70–71, 75, 92, 113
Rhyddfrydiaeth, Rhyddfrydwr/wyr (gwleidyddol) 35, 74, 89, 129, 137, 140, 148
rhyddid 71, 74, 130, 131
rhyfel 142
Rhyfel Byd Cyntaf 78, 94, 142, 144, 145

St Andrews 13, 53, 55, 56, **56–62**, 65, 81, 91, 113
Sandbach, Mr 6
Sandbach, Mrs 9
Sartor Resartus *gweler* Carlyle, Thomas
Scott, J. W. 72
Seren Gomer 38
Seth, Andrew *gweler* Pringle-Pattison, Andrew Seth
'settlements' 75–78
Shelley 15, 57
Smith, Adam 55, 63
Smith, George Adam 72
Socrates 133

Sorley, W. R. 69
sosialaeth 136
Stirling, J. Hutchinson 18, 33
    The Secret of Hegel 19
Strachan-Davidson, J. L. 16
Swinburne 15, 16, 17

Tawney, R. H. 79
teulu 124, 126, 127, 149
Thomas, D. A. *gweler* Rhondda, Arglwydd
Thomas, David 135, 136
Thomas, Parch John 38
Thomas, Mr (Y Coleg Normal) 10, 12
Thomas, Y Parchedig Joseph Llewelin 12, 85
Tighnabruaich 65, 93, 98, 100
    yr ysgol 10
Times, The 59
Toynbee, Arnold 75, 76
    Toynbee Hall (Llundain) 75–76
    Toynbee Hall (Glasgow) 76

Undodiaeth 70, 108, 110
unigolyn, unigolion 123, 124, 132, 137, 138, 140, 141, 150
United Kingdom Alliance 74
University Settlements (Association) *gweler* 'settlements'

Veitch, John 14, 61, 63
Verney, Capt. E. H. 26

Walker, Hugh 18, 19, 22
Wallace 23, 33
Watson 61, 62
Webb, Sidney 90
Weil, Simone 151
Weimar 19
White, P. J. 41
Wilson, Woodrow 71
Williams, Dr Daniel 13
Williams, Parch David (Llandyrnog) 25
Williams, Dr John (Brynsiencyn) 96
Williams, J. Gwynn 39
Williams, Raymond 150
Williams, Syr T. M. 35, 83, 84
Williams, Y Barnwr Vaughan 85
Witenagemot 19, 21, 22, 23, 71
Wordsworth, William 57, 71, 114, 117

Y.M.C.A. 78, 96
Ymerodraeth Brydeinig 93, 126, 127, 129, 147
Ymneilltuaeth 94, 129
Ymoleuo, Yr 133, 143
ymwybyddiaeth 123, 124
    hunanymwybyddiaeth 123
ysbryd 120, 125, 127, 145, 147

The Flying Boat Days

The Early Aviation History of Lord Howe Island 1931 to 1974

This book was researched and written on Lord Howe Island over an eight year period. It is proudly produced and printed in Australia.

Thank you for supporting this wonderful country.

Peter A.R. Phillipps

Requests and inquiries concerning reproduction and rights should be addressed to Mr Peter Phillipps, Neds Beach Road, Lord Howe Island, NSW, Australia, 2898.
The Flying Boat Days can be purchased via email from,
peterphillipps@bigpond.com

First Published 2002; reprinted 2003, 2004, 2005, 2006, 2007, 2008, 2009, 2010, 2011, 2012, 2013, 2014, 2015, 2016, 2017, 2018, 2019, 2022, 2023

Typesetting:
Seaview Press

Printed by:
Fuji Xerox DMS, 123 Hayward Avenue, Torrensville, South Australia, 5031

Cover picture of the Trans Oceanic Sunderland *Australis* on the lagoon late 1940s by courtesy of John Wilson.

National Library of Australia Cataloguing-in-Publication entry.

Phillipps, Peter A. R.
The flying boat days : the early aviation history of Lord Howe Island.

ISBN 1 74008 179 X.

1. Aeronautics - Lord Howe Island - History. 2. Seaplanes - Lord Howe Island - History. I. Title.

387.73347099481

An early liveried Ansett Sandringham coming in to alight.

courtesy Don Kerr

Flying off the water and sailing into the sky

About the author

Peter Phillipps was born in New Zealand in 1962 and grew up in Christchurch on the South Island.

Peter's initial interest in aviation was sparked by the roar of Pratt and Whitney radial engines mounted on Harvard trainers from the nearby air force base. His father entertained him with stories of World War Two fighter pilots and he became a totally dedicated aviation enthusiast after seeing the 1969 film "Battle of Britain".

Peter's family moved to Australia in 1979 and in 1991 he married a Lord Howe Islander, Janine Thompson, who was working in Sydney as a teacher. They moved to Lord Howe a year later and have two daughters Bronte and Abbey.

Whilst Peter's interests include surfing, skiing, photography and model making his main passion continues to be aviation. After ten years as the island's postmaster Peter and his wife Janine these days conduct guided tours sharing their knowledge of their wonderful home's natural and social story both current and historic.

Peter continues to photograph and document the visits of all interesting aircraft to Lord Howe Island and has published two magazine articles, the "World's Last Flying Boat Service" (Australian Aviation November 1999) and "A Ship At Sea" (Pacific Flyer December 1999).

Some twenty of his photos have been published in various journals and he was a key organiser in the commemorative restoration of a Catalina propeller undertaken by the R.A.A.F. as a memorial to the seven air force men who died in the tragic Catalina crash on Lord Howe in September 1948.

He also played his part in the Sandringham float restoration by Ten Squadron of the R.A.A.F. This item is now in the island's museum and is believed to be the largest piece of this type of aircraft in existence in Australia.

For Nina

Bronte, Janine, Peter and Abbey Phillipps with Catalina ZK-PBY in New Zealand September 2005.

David Russell

Contents

About the author iv
Foreword by Chris Murray vii
Introduction xi
Chapter 1: Francis Chichester and *Madame Elijah* 1
Chapter 2: The War Years 5
Chapter 3: The R.A.A.F.; Serving the Island; Catalina Visits 9
Chapter 4: Tragedy in paradise: The loss of Catalina A24-381 17
Chapter 5: Airstrip Proving Flight 21
Chapter 6: Radio Communications 22
Chapter 7: The Planes, the Place and the People 35
Chapter 8: Marinair 43
Chapter 9: Trans Oceanic Airways 46
Chapter 10: The First Airstrip 50
Chapter 11: A Second Airline 52
Chapter 12: The Catalina Incident 56
Chapter 13: The Last Big Boat Service in the World 67
Chapter 14: Crop Duster on the Cricket Pitch 75
Chapter 15: Flying Boat Culture 76
Chapter 16: The End of an Era 78
Epilogue 98
Appendices 107
Technical details for the Catalina, Sunderland and Sandringham . . .108
Extracts from the Court of Enquiry regarding
the Catalina A24-381 crash 110
Flying Boats Elsewhere 119
Acknowledgements 122
Bibliography 126
Flying boat DVD 127
Gallery of additional pictures 128

Foreword by Chris Murray

Islands are few and far between in the Tasman Sea, but Lord Howe Island is exceptional, being the remnant of a mighty shield volcano that erupted from the sea floor some seven million years ago.

At latitude 31 S and located some 500 km from the east coast of Australia and 600 km from the nearest island neighbour Norfolk Island, it was so isolated from the lanes of human commerce that no human footprint touched the Island until 1788. No one was to settle on the island for a further 46 years.

Oceanic islands are often isolated, and their history, economy, and society is inevitably linked to their degree of contact with the outside world and the manner in which that contact takes place. For isolated communities, transport is a key link with commerce, and civilisation, and Lord Howe Island is a classic case of an island society shaped by changing modes of transport and communication. Unique historical époques are defined by the way in which island men and women transacted their business with the world at large.

So, when Lord Howe Island was first settled in 1834, its inhabitants were sustained by the whaling ships that scoured the Pacific in the hunt for whale oil. Located in the whaling area known as the "middle grounds", up to 40 whaling vessels per year called for water and fresh produce. In return they bartered for the necessities that the islanders could not provide for themselves.

As the commerce developed one or two small trading ketches began to voyage intermittently from Sydney to the Island, transporting produce and residents to the mainland and returning with supplies, mail and home bound islanders.

However, the fragility of this supply line was underscored when whaling collapsed in the 1870's and a locally owned vessel *Sylph* disappeared at sea in April 1873 with a cargo of onions and eight passengers and sailors. Had it not been for the robust subsistence economy and the self sufficiency of the islanders in basic foodstuffs, the early settlers might well have given up and left for good!

Fortunately their hand to mouth, day by day existence improved from the 1880's with the discovery that the seed from the indigenous Howea (or Kentia) palm was a marketable commodity owing to a rising passion in Europe for exotic indoor plants and palms.

The commerce based upon the palm seed trade elevated Lord Howe from the barter into a money-based economy. The timely expansion of Burns Philp into the

Pacific started a new era on Lord Howe in 1893 with the establishment of a regular steamer service between Sydney, Lord Howe Island and continuing onto Norfolk Island and the Hebrides.

It was not long before Burns Philp began to systematically promote tourism in the Pacific and visitors from the outside world began to call regularly at Lord Howe. At first they would come ashore whilst the vessel anchored, to off load and back-load cargo. But soon they were staying between ship arrivals and Island families saw the business opportunity and began to provide accommodation for them.

The Island remained strongly sufficient in vegetables, meat, fish and dairy produce, proving to be very fortunate when the Second World War arrived and both tourism and the palm trade collapsed over night and the regular steamer service diminished from a near fortnightly to an erratic trickle of a service, that sometimes did not arrive for several months!

Ironically, with transport services at the lowest ebb for over 50 years, seeds of a new era were being sown when the Royal Australian Air Force (R.A.A.F.) opened up a lifeline from their flying boat base at Rathmines. Approximately once a month they sent out Catalina flying boats to bring vital supplies, transport passengers and carry out medical evacuations.

The magnificent lagoon on the western side of the Island, which was sheltered by the most southerly coral reef in the world became the landing strip for these versatile wartime flying boats.

The lagoon at Lord Howe Island was also surveyed as an emergency alighting site for the trans-Tasman Empire Class flying boat service that operated between Sydney and New Zealand throughout the war.

Lord Howe Island's role in this link was significant as it was the site of a trans Tasman radio navigation beacon, and provision of 24 hour radio communication with passing aircraft.

All this wartime flying activity had not been lost on the Lord Howe islanders who saw the potential of reviving their pre war tourist industry by using a flying boat service from Sydney. Enthusiastic residents, like George Kirby at *The Pines* actively lobbied the Federal and State governments to support the proposal. However, it did not become a reality until August 1947 when Trans Oceanic Airways (T.O.A.) operated the first regular commercial flights in a converted wartime Sunderland flying boat. Qantas Empire Airways (Q.E.A.) then followed, using Catalinas, in December of the same year.

The flying boat era which commenced in 1942 and lasted 32 years until 1974 (when the airstrip was built) was a golden era in Island history. For the first time in over a century of settlement, the island had a regular and reliable form of transport that brought mail, freight and passengers up to five times a week (except over the blustery winter months when the schedule was reduced to a fortnightly service).

Whilst this brought many of the benefits of civilisation — including a stable economy, it also filtered out the liabilities. Under most conditions, the service could only operate once daily, when the tide was high at Lord Howe and was never attempted on weekends owing to congestion at Sydney Harbour.

This, coupled with the gradual phasing out of flying boats on other routes, left Lord Howe Island with a truly unique airline service that brought genuine prosperity to the island without inundating the island with thousands of visitors!

As town planning concepts did not develop to any great degree in Australia until the 1960's and 70's, Lord Howe was spared the high rise development that engulfed many of Australia's beautiful holiday places, by the simple fact that its transport system simply couldn't deliver more than 250 visitors per week to its shores. By the time the service finished in 1974, and an airstrip enabled more passengers to travel, a planning scheme had been formulated for the Island to carefully control future growth.

And so today we owe the Island's relatively unspoilt beauty and low key development to its unique flying boat service of the 40's, 50's, 60's and early 70's, that enabled visitors to enjoy the Island and residents to prosper without ruining the environment through a catastrophic avalanche of numbers.

However, these comments say little about the wonderful quality of life that imbued the Island throughout the years of the flying boats — an era I was privileged to live through. My own father, David Murray, arrived on Lord Howe Island in 1957 as the port manager for Ansett Flying Boat Services and I arrived a year later to attend primary school on the Island. Along with all other passengers, my memories of the flying boats include spectacular take-offs and landings on Sydney Harbour and leisurely, comfortable hours in the air with wonderful cabin service which included bar and hot meals!

Above all, there was the excitement of landings on the lagoon at Lord Howe, with the water hissing under the hull and spraying over the windows, as 42 passengers all strained to see the lovely clear waters of the lagoon and spectacular scenery of the Island beyond. Even when the aircraft moored at Lord Howe, the final transfer by small boat to the jetty was charged like a tonic with a fresh breeze and salty tang in the air, to blow away the cobwebs of city dross! The flying boats inevitably extended a Lord Howe holiday, beyond the Island itself. Excitement mounted at the Rose Bay base in Sydney well before departure and ended on the journey home only as the majestic aircraft swept past the Harbour Bridge and touched down on the harbour.

As it was too congested on Sydney Harbour to operate flying boats on Saturdays and Sundays, the weekends on the Island were also free, leaving the Island community to enjoy a wide array of sporting and social activities including cricket, sailing, golf, bowls, dances, concerts, and picnics in which visitors were invited to participate.

Community life flourished and even those holidaying for a week or two felt a welcome part of it.

When the airstrip opened in 1974 the pattern changed completely with most holiday packages running from weekend to weekend and most flights arriving on Saturday or Sunday. The weekends became busy for lodges, shops and tour operators and so community recreation in the wider sense died.

Today a community concert, picnics, dances, golf or bowls have to be squeezed into weekday afternoons and can now involve only some of the Island's residents. Understandably, Island residents have developed a love and passion for the "flying boat era" on Lord Howe because, in retrospect, it had so many exceptional qualities which have since faded.

Peter Phillipps has done us a remarkable service by researching and writing a wonderful book about this *Golden Age.* By combing through the archives, writing to countless people and recording dozens of interviews with pilots, flight attendants, engineers, traffic officers, civil aviation employees and many others, Peter has brought back to life one of the happiest epochs of the Island's history. This was an era when the Island and its people still had their rustic charm and strong community ethic and spirit which made them wonderful hosts.

Visitors came to share the stunning beauty of the Island with a generous people who made them feel welcome. Their holiday started not from the point from which they arrived but from the very moment they set foot in the Rose Bay base for their flight.

Who amongst us would not wish to voyage to a magic isle in the Pacific in a great *seabird*, avoiding the congestion of big passenger terminals, busy runaways and the like, and setting down in the turquoise waters of a sub-tropical lagoon.

Peter has recaptured this era for us — defined entirely by a special mode of transport. Peter's efforts are all the more remarkable considering he only settled on the Island in 1992 and did not personally experience the flying boat era on the Island.

Peter occasionally gets a flight to remember (like his scenic tour of the Island skies in a visiting Grumman Albatross — including three touch and goes on the lagoon), but his greatest pleasure of all will be the publication of this book 'The Flying Boat Days'.

Introduction

Lord Howe Island is situated off the east coast of Australia approximately 482 nautical miles north east of Sydney.

A volcanic remnant, the Island is flanked by a ridge known as the Northern Hills which climbs gradually from the west to a peak in the north eastern corner of the Island known as "The Malabar".

Ten kilometres to the South lie the impressive Mount Gower (2850 feet) and Mount Lidgbird (2550 feet).

Joining the mountains and northern hills is the settled lowlands area. To the west is the lagoon which is enclosed by the world's most southern coral reef.

The Island was discovered in 1788 by Henry Lidgbird Ball, the Captain of His Majesty's ship *Supply*. The Island is probably most famous for a small flightless bird, the Lord Howe Island Woodhen. By the late 1970's the native Woodhen was close to extinction and it was believed only thirty birds remained — all of which were living on the summits of the two mountains.

Aviation played a part in saving the Woodhen when, in May 1980, a Jet Ranger helicopter using long range tanks, was flown to the Island to bring down some surviving pairs from the mountain tops. These were bred in captivity and the Woodhen was successfully re-established on the Island. Lord Howe is also known for its endemic Kentia Palm which for over one hundred years has been exported all over the world.

The early aviation history of this small island in the Tasman Sea is both interesting and unique and from its beginning in 1931 to this day, flying to and landing at Lord Howe has been difficult.*

Sir Francis Chichester, the first aviator to visit the Island wrote of his 1931 flight across the Tasman Sea. He renamed Norfolk and Lord Howe Island, *Scylla* and *Charybdis* respectively. From Greek mythology passing seafarers would have to navigate the narrow passage between each monster. Too close to the six-headed *Scylla* each head would take a living man. *Charybidis* was more threatening: three times a day she would engulf the surrounding waters often taking whole ships!

* Author's note: I learnt very early in my research that flying boats do not land they "alight". I have used this term through-out the text. I have also used feet and miles as this was used at the time and still is by aircraft today.

After researching some of the incidents of the Island's early aviation history it is easy to see why Chichester drew these comparisons.

Between 1931 and 1974 seven marine aircraft were washed ashore or damaged due to weather. Of these only two could not be repaired and were lost. Two out of the seven were refloated without damage. Four land based aircraft also arrived on the Island before the airstrip was completed — one being a helicopter.

'The Flying Boat Days' not only refers to the obvious but describes an era in the Island's history which saw a major change — that being the beginning of an efficient lifeline with mainland Australia.

This is the story of a small community living on an isolated and naturally spectacular island. The story of a group of people who saw a better future for themselves.

Some of the events described in this book took place a long time ago but despite this, I believe that which follows, is as close to the truth as it could be.

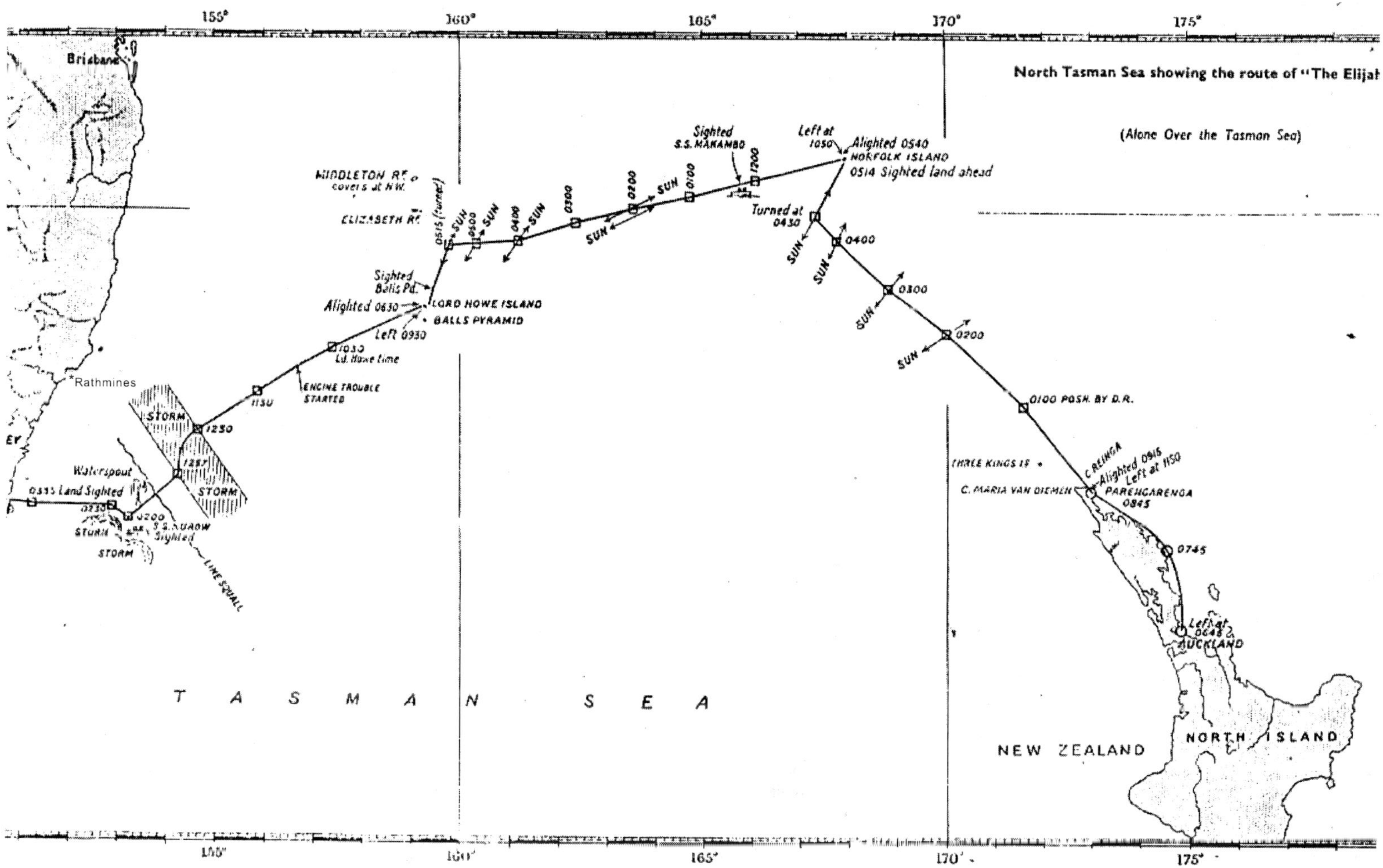

Map of ZK-AKK's route across the Tasman Sea.
*Note: Rathmines has been added to show where the R.A.A.F. Catalinas flew from.

Lord Howe Island

Locations of main incidents.

A. 1931 Gipsy Moth *Madame Elijah* overturned in a storm.
B. 1943 R.A.A.F. Catalina A24-33 washed from mooring.
C. 1947 trans Tasman Ercôupe landed on lagoon beach.
D. 1948 R.A.A.F. Catalina A24-381 crashed below the *Malabar.*
E. 1949 Q.E.A. Catalina washed from mooring.

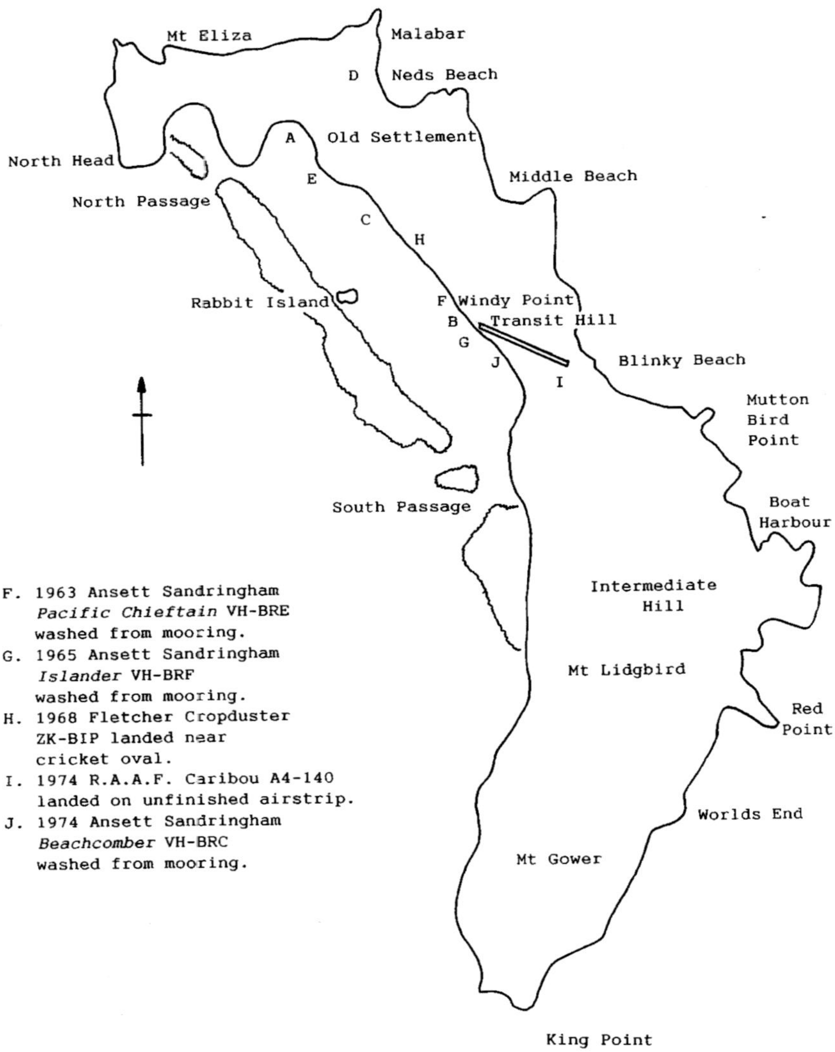

F. 1963 Ansett Sandringham *Pacific Chieftain* VH-BRE washed from mooring.
G. 1965 Ansett Sandringham *Islander* VH-BRF washed from mooring.
H. 1968 Fletcher Cropduster ZK-BIP landed near cricket oval.
I. 1974 R.A.A.F. Caribou A4-140 landed on unfinished airstrip.
J. 1974 Ansett Sandringham *Beachcomber* VH-BRC washed from mooring.

Chapter 1: Francis Chichester and *Madame Elijah*

Lord Howe Island aviation history began on 1 April 1931 when Englishman Francis Chichester alighted on the lagoon in a single engine floatplane.*

In 1967 Chichester was knighted for his many solo long-distance journeys. At the age of sixty-five he had sailed solo around the world in his yacht, Gipsy Moth. This yacht and the vessels he used before, were all given this name after a craft of his first love.

Long before that, in 1929, Chichester purchased a DH60 Gipsy Moth. The 25-ft. long biplane was constructed with a timber frame covered in a fabric skin; the 85-hp engine enabled a comfortable cruising speed of approximately 90-mph in favourable conditions. This aircraft preceded the ever-popular Tiger Moth which these days is much sought after by collectors.

After only five months flying training, Chichester set out from his native England bound for Australia, on what was to be the beginning of a life of many such journeys!

Both aircraft (now named *Madame Elijah*) and pilot performed with few hitches over the 14, 308 mile flight. The aircraft was then shipped across the Tasman Sea to New Zealand, where a business he had begun on a previous trip was in need of his attention. Francis Chichester, it seems, could not resist a challenge. Not long after his arrival in New Zealand he began planning a flight across the Tasman.

He calculated that with accurate navigation he could fly from the North Island of New Zealand to Norfolk Island, that being 481 miles and after refueling continue to Lord Howe, that being 561 miles and the longest leg of the journey. Then he would refuel again and complete the crossing to Australia, another 480 miles.

Both these small islands had no suitable area to land so a water alighting would be the only solution. After a search, floats suitable for a Gipsy Moth were finally located in the possession of the Royal New Zealand Navy but they were reluctant to sell.

At first the Navy thought Chichester's plans were too risky, and secondly the floats had been badly damaged when they were accidentally dropped along with the

* A floatplane alights on floats usually attached via struts whereas a flying boat alights on its hull-shaped fuselage.

aircraft to which they were attached, some twenty feet onto the deck of a battleship. Finally though, with skilful negotiation and added charm, Chichester won through.

On 31 March 1931, *Elijah* and her pilot set off from Parengarenga Harbour at the tip of the North Island of New Zealand and made his way to Norfolk Island. After nearly missing the island, a safe open sea alighting was accomplished. The frail Gipsy Moth was lifted ashore by crane, for maintenance on the cylinder head, which had suffered two leaking valves. After a brief stay for repairs the floatplane was refueled and hoisted once again onto the ocean. The extra weight of fuel combined with the swell of the open sea caused another problem and after a number of attempts it became obvious that a successful take-off would be unlikely. A decision was made to remove all but the minimum of fuel and fly to Emily Bay, a narrow reef protected lagoon where a laden take-off would be easier. This was accomplished with a fair amount of good fortune and finally Chichester continued his journey.

However, not long after leaving Norfolk Island, Chichester noticed that *Elijah* had a developed a bad vibration. He correctly guessed that this was related to the pounding *Elijah* had taken whilst trying to take-off from the open sea. Knowing that was where he would end up if he returned, *Elijah* and her pilot pressed on for Lord Howe Island. He also discovered the aircraft could not be trimmed for level flight and a severe pull to starboard meant the joystick had to be held between Chichester's knees while he took sun shots with his sextant.

Some time later, a small split was found in the starboard float, which was probably a result of the earlier accident, when the Royal New Zealand Navy owned the floats. While on the water the starboard float slowly filled and very slowly emptied whilst in the air, consequently, the extra weight caused a pull to the starboard.

He arrived in the area of Lord Howe Island. The Island was not where Chichester had calculated. Suddenly, to the south he noticed what looked like land, not the Island but the monolith of rock that is Balls Pyramid.

On arrival over Lord Howe, Chichester was greeted by a violent storm with gusting winds tearing at the fragile craft. Despite this, a hasty, yet safe alighting was made.

Being the first aircraft ever to visit the Island, the locals approached with some hesitation and after some raised voice requests, *Elijah* and her master were towed to Sylph's Hole, a sheltered boat mooring near Old Settlement Beach. Over the short distance Chichester realised the people of the Island were very capable when it came to handling their vessels on the water. Although the storm had begun to subside, the locals suggested that they secure the plane on the bank near the beach. Chichester made it quite clear this would not be necessary, as he would be leaving the next morning. With a heavy mooring line attached the weary aviator retired to the Dignam house for a much-needed meal and a good night's sleep. That night the wind returned with one gust waking Chichester "bolt upright in the bed".

Young Phil Dignam woke Chichester at dawn and they made their way down the sandy track along the lagoon. After turning the corner at the headland known as the Flagstaff they could see down to where ZK-AKK lay. Young Phil commented "She looks queer to me". Poor *Elijah* had been lifted and flipped at her mooring, she lay upside down with her engine completely submerged, with just the lower wing visible.

In Chichester's words "she was done for" and the completion of the crossing now seemed out of the question. The aircraft was towed to the shallows on the high tide and left until the tide receded.

Chichester decided to salvage what he could. Luckily the regular steamer, *Makambo,* was due so he could at least get some money from the parts he was able to save. All the Island people came out to help with the dismantling. The wings were removed and placed on the bank and then the floats and fuselage were carried up and placed near the jetty shed. All of this took less than an hour and for the second time during his stay Chichester was impressed with the local people's efficiency. None of them had ever dealt with a fragile airplane before but yet with little fuss they had placed everything in orderly piles. In fact the only parts lost were two wing bolts which fell through the holed pockets of Chichester's borrowed shorts.

While waiting for the arrival of the *Makambo* and his departure, Chichester spent his time dismantling and cleaning the parts he could sell. The thought of completing his journey to Sydney by steamer was both miserable and humiliating.

The challenge of it all finally got to him especially after one of the local people commented "Why not rebuild her, man?" To rebuild her seemed impossible with her wings bent and broken and instruments and engine full of salt water not to mention the fuselage was soaked through. Whilst it seemed impossible perhaps it could be done thought Chichester. He took another look at the plane and decided that in a new light and a lot of hard work, as well as the right help (and a lot of luck!) just maybe the Palm Island Plane Factory could rebuild *Madame Elijah*!

Palm Island Plane Factory

The people of Lord Howe, due to their isolation, have always been resourceful. This tradition proved to be of great assistance with the rebuilding of the delicate floatplane. Whenever a seemingly insurmountable problem arose, someone would show up and after a day or so return with the problem solved.

Roly Wilson, a skilled carpenter, became Chichester's right hand man. William Thompson, the Island's administrator, owned and operated a forge and was able to make some steel items for the rebuild. Gerald Kirby was a skilled mechanic and did a lot of the engine repairs.

The women of the Island also played a vital role. Among others, Minnie Dignam and Eileen Wilson, sewed a lot of the intricate lockstitching on the fabric skin before the dope was applied for tension. For the third time during his visit Chichester was impressed and no sooner had he showed the ladies the type of stitch needed and they were off as if they had done it for years!

Chichester enjoyed the hospitality of the Dignam family for the length of his stay. Young Phil or *Tid,* as he was known, was a keen gardener and his mother Emmaline made fantastic meals using local fish and vegetables, which the grateful guest would praise for years to come. It would be fair to say the entire community helped with the rebuild in one way or another!

Luck was also on their side as the necessary replacement parts were ordered and just made it to the *Makambo* before she left Sydney on her regular run to the Island. Finally, the day arrived when *Elijah* could be returned to the air.

Gower Wilson directed the ever-present volunteers who lifted the aircraft down over the rocks near the jetty and lowered her onto to the clear waters of the lagoon.*

To thank the locals for their help and hospitality, Chichester took many of the locals for a short flight. Island resident, Frank Payten, went on one of these short flights and once airborne he asked Chichester if he could fly down low over his house so he could wave to his wife. The sight which greeted them did not please Frank — his startled horse, two cows and a mixed gaggle of ducks and hens were so frightened that they tore through the fence into his vegetable garden trampling everything to a pulp! Needless to say that Frank did not enjoy the rest of the flight! The aircraft performed well beyond expectations and Chichester commented that she was as good as the day he had bought her.

On June 10 1931, just over two months after *Elijah* had been wrecked, she left Lord Howe Island for mainland Australia. The first aviator to visit the Island arrived at Jervis Bay, south of Sydney, and successfully completed his Tasman Sea crossing. The total actual flying time from New Zealand to Australia was just under twenty hours.

Kingsford Smith and Ulm in the famous *Southern Cross* had already successfully crossed the Tasman Sea in Sept 1928; the second crossing being their return flight to Australia in October of the same year.

The third crossing was flown in secret by twenty-one year old Guy Menzies, also in 1928. His single engine Avro Avian, named *Southern Cross Junior,* had been previously owned by Kingsford Smith. The fourth crossing was Chichester's and the fifth, Kingsford Smith and P.G. Taylor again, in *Southern Cross,* with this flight carrying the first paying passenger across the Tasman Sea.

Francis Chichester and *Madame Elijah* became both the first to cross the Tasman Sea in a westerly direction solo and to use Lord Howe Island and Norfolk Island as stopovers. He was second to Menzies to fly the distance in a single engine aircraft.

Many years later, Chichester sailed close by Lord Howe on his 1965 solo around the world voyage. A radio message was passed on to the people of the Island expressing his gratitude for the help and hospitality he had received 34 years earlier.

* Sadly in November 1936 Gower Wilson along with his son Jack and four other men, Messrs W. Hammill, L. Hart, H. Higgs and F. Murray, were lost at sea with no trace.

Chapter 2: The War Years

The next visit to the Island by an aeroplane was not to be for another eleven years during the troubled times of World War Two.

During the war the R.A.A.F. made frequent visits performing both exercises and medical evacuations.

Flying Catalinas from their Lake Macquarie Base, Rathmines, these men and their machines were welcomed by the Island's people. During the war shipping to the Island was greatly reduced not only due to the demands of the war effort but also the very real and deadly threat of enemy submarines operating along the East Coast of Australia. On more than one occasion unidentified ships were seen off the Island.

The visiting Cats would not only bring welcome supplies but also the reassurance that the Island and its inhabitants were not alone and mainland Australia had not forgotten the small Island community.

The first Catalina to visit the Island arrived in May 1942 under the command of Wing Commander Scotty Allen. This visit was for the medical evacuation of the Island resident Maude Payten and proved to be the beginning of an association with R.A.A.F. Catalinas and their crews which would last for the best part of a decade. Before their story can be told, a little needs to be explained of Lord Howe Island's situation at the beginning of the war in the Pacific.

Up until the arrival of the Catalinas, the only transport to and from the Island was by steam ship belonging to Burns Philp & Co which began a freight and passenger service to Lord Howe and Norfolk Islands around 1893.

A number of ships were used: *Havilah, Katoomba, Ysabel, Tambo, Ovalau, Makambo* and *Morinda.*

The *Makambo* was used for a number of years until the *Morinda*, which made her first voyage to the Island on 14 January 1932, replaced her. She continued bringing passengers and freight throughout the war until the early 1950's.

Journeys made during the war years were quite different to those made earlier in less troubled times. Firstly, the regular visits went from three monthly to an irregular six monthly service and the tourist trade all but ended with only a limited number of berths available to the Island people wanting to return or to leave their home.

It should also be noted that out of one hundred and sixty people on the Island, twenty-four would leave for war. Sadly, three of these young men were not to return home.

A number of vessels were sunk along Australia's eastern seaboard and the *Morinda* had her own defences on board with sand bags for protection and a twin Bofors cannon which was mounted on the rear deck. In addition to this she had a machine gun mounted on either side of the bridge.

Island resident, Thelma Wilson, along with her sister Lois Whistler, made a number of voyages to and from her Island home. On one such trip from Sydney to Lord Howe she remembers very well. "She only left the safety of the harbour heads after the approaches had been patrolled and permission to leave had been granted. On this voyage we left at night and all shipping travelled unlit for obvious reasons."

She had not long left Sydney when the captain called all the passengers from their cabins to the rear deck. After quite some time we were allowed to return to our cabins. We had only just settled down to our beds when we were called to the deck again. I remember how black the water looked and we were all very scared. After what seemed like an eternity, we were once again allowed to return to our cabins and we weren't disturbed again." It was later found that that an unknown vessel had shadowed the *Morinda* on the surface!

In September 1941, Arthur Le Navez with his wife Joan, came to the Island on the *Morinda* to take up the position of officer in charge of radio communications and held this position until 1953. Not long after his arrival he received a report from the captain of the *Morinda*. She had come across two ships close together with their lights on. No allied ship would have dared such a risk in hostile waters, so these vessels were presumed to be the enemy. Luckily the *Morinda* slipped by undetected and made it safely to the Island.

Throughout the war years, the radio station was surrounded by a protective wall of sandbags and an emergency radio set was also hidden in the bush on top of Transit Hill. There was a small shack on the top of *Malabar* — the peak hill at the north end of the Island. This was manned around the clock with anything suspicious being reported. The radio station on the Island also provided a point of contact for the R.A.A.F. Catalinas all of which were ferried across the Pacific, at first by Q.E.A. crews, then R.A.A.F. crews and occasionally American crews.

Strict radio silence was maintained during these flights. However, Arthur Le Navez can remember communicating with at least two crews with minor problems. It is interesting to note that the first R.A.A.F. Catalina ferried from the United States to Australia in February 1941, was in fact only the third aircraft ever to cross the Pacific Ocean.*

During the war years ships were sunk near the Island with the nearest being approximately 90 miles to the south west.

Debris from these wrecks was often washed up on the Island's beaches. The misfortune of some bringing fortune to others and the Island people put to good use

* Surprising as it may seem most of the new Cats were flown to Central Victoria to the then secret flying boat repair and maintenance base at Lake Boga.

what ever they could with the most welcome being drums of fuel, which was in very short supply.

On one occasion some high-octane aviation fuel was used in the Island's one and only plough, a small Howard rotary cultivator.

Island resident, the late Cobby Robins, had the controls and had slipped her into high gear and she was off with Cobby struggling to keep up! Due to the higher rated fuel the performance of the plough was somewhat improved. Unable to get the plough out of gear he elected to remove the spark plug leads. This proved to be a shocking experience, the renegade escaped, finally falling over and digging a circular hole till it ran out of fuel!

Island resident Norman Simpson also remembers "A lifeboat was washed over the reef near the North passage. The inverted vessel was towed in alongside the jetty and a line attached to one side and she was soon righted. We were all relieved to find nothing underneath! On the next visit by the *Morinda* it was loaded aboard and taken back to Sydney."

On another occasion a not so welcome mine was washed ashore on a reef just north of Middle Beach. The authorities on the mainland were contacted for advice and their suggestion being to detonate the mine from a safe distance with a rifle. After half the Island locals had had a pot shot or two and without success, the mine was eventually exploded with a very long fuse and a stick of gelignite.

As mentioned earlier, unidentified shipping was often seen close to the Island. On one occasion Thelma Wilson again with her sister Lois, were sitting on a rock above the shelter at Neds Beach when they saw what they thought was a strange looking ship in the Sugar Loaf passage between the main island and the nearby Admiralty Islands.

They hastily made their way to Arthur Le Navez, not entirely sure what they were trying to describe. Arthur drew a quick sketch confirming it was in fact a submarine that the girls had spotted. A report was sent to Sydney and a message was sent back reporting no Allied activity in the area.

By far the most dramatic sighting of the enemy happened when on 22 February, 1942 a small seaplane was sighted approaching from the north At approximately half a mile from the Island it turned east and headed back out to sea.

Yokosuka Floatplanes (allied Code Name Glen) made a total of four flights over Sydney during the Second World War. These small submarine-launched monoplanes, had a crew of two and were stored in a small water tight hangar forward of the conning tower.

These purpose built subs of the Imperial Japanese Navy had a launching ramp in front of the hangar from which the small floatplane was catapulted. On return from a flight the aircraft would have to alight alongside the sub and then be hoisted aboard, this being an especially difficult task in the open ocean.

The first reconnaissance flight over Sydney Harbour was made on 18 February

1942 and then a second on 23 May, and a third flight just seven days later on 30 May of that year. A second Japanese floatplane made the third unchallenged flight to locate targets for the famous midget sub raid, which followed on the night of the 31 May 1942. That same night, an Island resident, the late Eileen Douglas along with a number of Island people were on board the *Morinda* having just returned to Sydney after a trip from the Island. As she prepared to enter the harbour the attack began.*

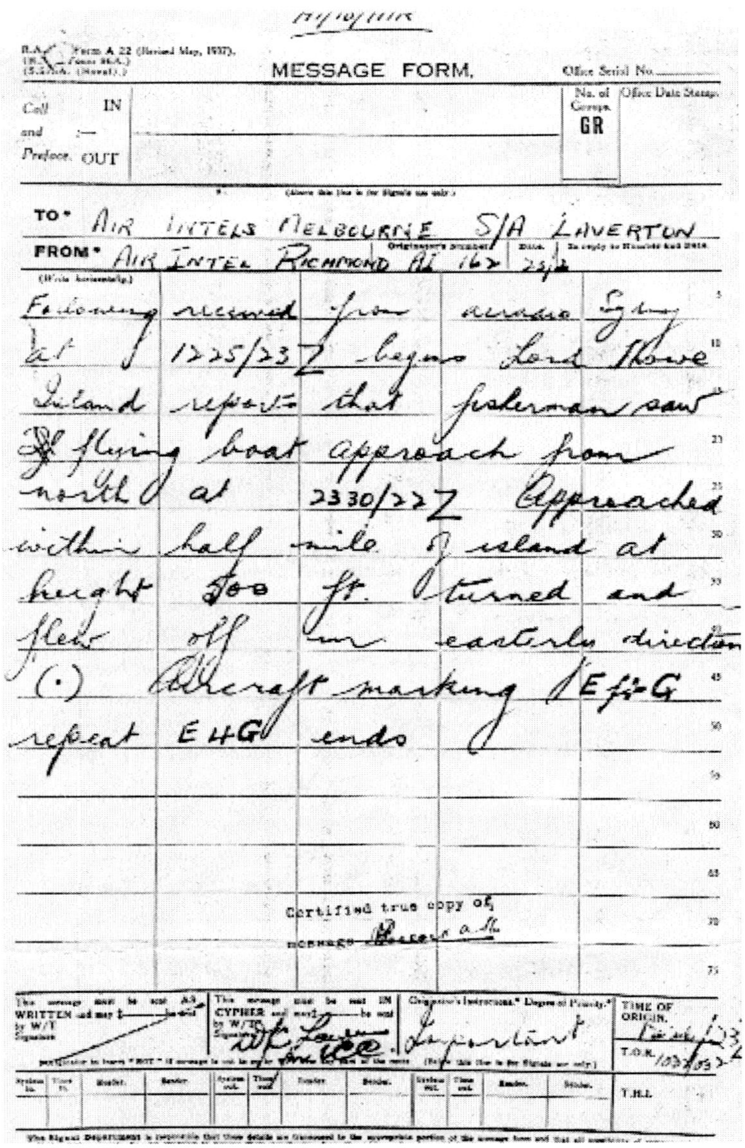
MESSAGE FORM.

Office Serial No.

Call and Preface IN — OUT

No. of Groups GR

Office Date Stamp

TO: AIR INTELS MELBOURNE S/A LAVERTON

FROM: AIR INTEL RICHMOND AI 162 23/5

Following received from ... Sydney at 1225/23Z begins Lord Howe Island reports that fisherman saw flying boat approach from north at 2330/22Z Approached within half mile of island at height 500 ft. turned and flew off in easterly direction (.) Aircraft marking 1E4G repeat E4G ends

Certified true copy of message

Important

TIME OF ORIGIN.

T.O.R.

T.H.I.

Document relating to Japanese plane's visit

courtesy Chris Murray

* It wasn't until the fourth and final flight at around midnight on the 25 January 1943 that one of these aircraft was actually challenged. However, the searchlights and anti-aircraft guns used failed to find the intruder.

Chapter 3: The R.A.A.F.; Serving the Island; Catalina Visits

The arrival of the first Catalina in May 1942 marked the beginning of an association with the Island and the R.A.A.F., which still exists to this day. The R.A.A.F. Catalinas were to fly to the Island for the best part of a decade. To this day the R.A.A.F. still fly to the Island only these days flying the impressive and very capable C 130 Hercules.

As mentioned previously a Scotsman Scotty Allan was the first captain of a R.A.A.F. Catalina to alight on the Island lagoon. George Urquhart Allan had flown under age during the First World War over France. In 1929 he was recruited in London by Charles Ulm to fly with Australian National Airways headed in partnership by Ulm and Kingsford Smith. With commercial aviation still in its infancy Smith and Allan flew the first airmail from Australia to England and back. In 1933, Allan, Ulm and P.G. Taylor flew a record-breaking flight from England to Australia in less than seven days.

In 1934 Scotty Allan joined Q.E.A. and in 1938 flew the first Q.E.A. C Class Empire Boat *Coolangatta* from England to Australia. At the outbreak of World War Two Allan had over 10,000 hours in his logbook. He was reluctantly released by Q.E.A. and joined the R.A.A.F. with the rank of Wing Commander.

As stated earlier the R.A.A.F. Cats flew from their Rathmines base usually via Sydney then out to Lord Howe. The Cats began to visit the Island on an almost monthly basis. Mostly they performed medical evacuations, flew in doctors, dentists, teachers, freight and even local residents returning to or leaving their Island home.

The Island also became the unofficial rest and recreation spot for the weary Catalina crews. Lord Howe was also used as a navigational training point where aircraft overflew and would not alight. Often Catalinas were heard at night or seen during the day. After leaving the Island they frequently flew to Middleton and Elizabeth Reefs, some hundred miles to the north of Lord Howe and then home to Rathmines.

The Cat crews considered themselves lucky to be allotted a trip to the Island. They would usually stay around for two or three days; that gave them the opportunity to explore the Island's natural beauty, perhaps do a little fishing and generally enjoy the local hospitality.

Squadron Leader Vic Hodgkinson made two visits to the Island during the war. His following contribution sums up many a Cat crew's visit, "The allocation of crew members to billets always caused some problems among the local people, as there was never enough to go around, almost to the point of aggression! The hospitality was out of this world and every time one opened one's mouth they put food in it!

Questions were continuous to the point that on return trips, one was asked to explain things discussed on the previous visit a month or so before. Daytime was taken up by an Island picnic where the entire population gathered complete with hampers which were placed on an old truck. One and all followed this to the chosen beach where swimming and racing competitions (including climbing the local palm trees) filled the day.

At night the Island Community Hall filled and the food and dancing continued into the early hours. On the morning of departure we would gather on the beach for our fond farewells to these wonderful people whose hospitality seemed to have no bounds. We would depart with baskets made from palm leaves full of goodies. Some oranges were at least a pound in weight!"

Vic Hodgkinson had flown Sunderlands with 10 Squadron earlier in the war. He was credited with sinking a U-boat in the Bay of Biscay and awarded the Distinguished Flying Cross. It was during this time with 10 Squadron that he met and flew with Ron Gillies who in later years flew to Lord Howe Island on the Ansett Sandringhams.

While the R.A.A.F. Catalinas performed quite a number of medical evacuations there was also one occasion in April 1943 when they came to the rescue of a stranded civil flying boat.

An Injured Albatross

Late in 1937 a New Zealander named John Burgess captained a Shorts Empire flying boat named *Centaurus* across the Tasman. The purpose of this flight was to determine the viability of the route for a commercial operation.

Centaurus arrived in the north Island city of Auckland then proceeded south to the nation's capital Wellington.

The author's father, the late Brian Phillipps, witnessed the arrival of the flying boat as it alighted in Wellington Harbour.

In April 1940, nearly three years later, Tasman Empire Airways Limited (T.E.A.L., now Air New Zealand) began a regular service across the Tasman Sea. Lord Howe Island's lagoon became an emergency alighting location for obvious reasons. A permanent buoy was put in place to the south of Rabbit Island. Air radio was installed and maintained from the commencement of the service. Official time was also altered on the Island due to this service, as the following extract from a letter to all residents describes:

Circular No.42 Lord Howe Island Board Of Control
Sydney, 19 March 1940

Circular Memorandum to all shareholders
Kentia Palm Industry*

Alteration of standard time at Lord Howe Island: following representations from the Commonwealth Authorities, The Board of Control decided that the local standard time at Lord Howe Island shall, in future, be recognised as 10 hours 30 minutes ahead of Greenwich Mean Time instead of 10 hours 36 minutes as at present. As Sydney is 10 hours ahead of Greenwich Mean Time the variation made in respect of Lord Howe Island was designed to avoid confusion which otherwise might arise and also to facilitate the transmission of reports from the Island in connection with the trans-Tasman flying boat service.

S.L Anderson.
H.H Hicks.
R.H Hicks.
Members. Lord Howe Island Board Of Control

Throughout the war T.E.A.L. operated two Shorts S30 'Empire Boats' the *Aotearoa* (ZK-AMA) and *Awarua* (ZK-AMC). These machines were predecessors to the Sunderlands and Sandringhams, which were later flown to the Island.

The Auckland-Sydney service began with a weekly service carrying up to 16 passengers over the 1200-mile flight, which took around 9 hours in favourable conditions. The Bristol Perseus engines that powered the S.30 Empire boats proved very reliable. Laurie Martin flew with T.E.A.L. as a radio operator from the 7 October 1942 to the 8 July 1946 and during the many crossings he made there were only two occasions when the aircraft had engine problems.

On April 14 1943 on Lord Howe Island the local people were greeted with the unexpected arrival of the T.E.A.L. boat *Awarua*. On the 13 April the flying boat had left Sydney for Auckland with K.A. Brownjohn as Captain. A few hours into the flight the crew experienced heavy showers and shortly aftwards the port inner was shut down due to faulty operation.

Jack Felton, the flight engineer, takes up the story "I was not satisfied with the pilot's decision so it was decided to start the port engine again. The engine operated satisfactorily from that time onwards."

Soon after the starboard inner engine began to vibrate and backfire considerably and both magnetos were tried with no change to the situation. It was decided to shut the engine down and feather the airscrew.

* All eligible residents had a share in the Kentia Palm Industry.

Jack Felton: "The symptoms pointed to ignition trouble and since we had been flying through heavy showers for one and half hours with one engine suspect and another shut down, the Captain made a decision to divert to the nearest landfall and turned north west to Lord Howe Island."

Laurie Martin remembers well the magnificent sight of Balls Pyramid. Not only was the 1850-ft monolith of rock an impressive sight it also told them they had made it. Luck was with the crew and passengers of *Awarua* as the tide had almost reached its height and the large flying boat came in over Blinky Beach and alighted without further incident.

9 hours 19 minutes after leaving Sydney, ZK-AMC arrived in the morning of 14 April — this probably still stands today as the longest flight time from Sydney to Lord Howe Island!

The flying boat had actually passed well south of Lord Howe but from the point the decision to divert was made the Island was the closest landfall.

The importance of this aircraft, or more so the service it provided between Australia and New Zealand, is enforced by the fact that a Royal Australian Navy (R.A.N.) vessel was ordered to steam at full speed from its position 150 miles south of Lord Howe and patrol the area.

The arrival of such an aircraft was quite an event for the local people. Gerald Kirby, with his wife Beth, owned and operated the guesthouse *The Pines*. "Kirb", as he was known to one and all decided to treat the local school children with a closer look at the 'ship of the sky'.

His launch, the *Albatross*, had been on the slip for sometime. Built on the Island of Oregon timber in 1936 the planks had dried and opened up. Halfway across the lagoon it became obvious the vessel was slowly filling with water. Luckily, a homemade wooden bilge pump was on board. Eager hands manned the pump for the entire visit. The *Albatross* managed to stay afloat and all made it back to shore, safe and sound.

This event may well have been that which kept the *Albatross* on the Island. Two American officers, passengers on the aircraft, made Kirb a more than handsome offer for the vessel. They intended shipping her north to be used in the war effort. After seeing the water she was taking on, their interest waned and they quickly withdrew their offer.

Meanwhile the crew of *Awarua* had a dilemma. Firstly, the reliability of the engines was dubious and, more importantly, there wasn't enough fuel in the tanks to make it back to the mainland. There was actually some aviation fuel on the Island that had floated ashore in drums with other cargo from a ship which had been sunk nearby. It was decided unanimously that it couldn't be used due to the risk of salt water contamination.

On 15 April, a radio signal was sent by Island resident Stan Fenton to the mainland. The following is an extract from that message: "Only 410 gallons of petrol left sufficient oil. Stop. No petrol supply here. Stop. Will send you further signal in morning immediately after taxiing tests. Brownjohn."

On the morning of the following day the R.A.A.F. dispatched two Catalinas from Rathmines with spare fuel. A24-37 captained by Flight Lieutenant Keith Bolitho and A24-1 under the command of Squadron Leader Gilbert Thurston. Although the rough trip indicated that conditions would not be ideal on arrival at the Island both flying boats alighted without trouble. Fuel was drained from the Catalina's tanks into drums then ferried by boat to the T.E.A.L. machine — a tricky operation with all three machines bucking about in the wind and swell.

After refueling, both inner engines were run at 1200rpm and found to be satisfactory. It was decided to do a test flight to see if all was well. *Awarua* took off but the starboard inner still vibrated on both magnetos at cruising boost and over, so the aircraft alighted after a 50 minute flight. It was agreed she should be able to make her way back to Sydney, however, it would not be safe to do so with passengers aboard.

The following morning permission was granted to Bolitho to proceed to New Zealand with the passengers. Thurston would escort *Awarua* back to Sydney. The Empire boat took off first, struggling into the air, obviously still with engine problems.

A24-37 took off and headed south east for New Zealand. A24-1 went with the T.E.A.L. boat. All three flying boats experienced very rough turbulence. Most of the passengers on board A24-37 became ill with the cramped hull not adding much to their comfort.

Not long into the flight A24-37's radio operator, Pilot Officer Rob Hutchinson, received a call from Thurston's A24-1 saying they were experiencing very strong headwinds and were getting worried that they may not have enough fuel to make it back.

Bolitho had no choice, he turned around and set a course south of the Island to intercept the others. A24-37 was now heading into the wind, which greatly reduced their speed. On Hutchinson's suggestion Bolitho climbed to see if they could find lighter winds. Luckily they did and quickly caught the Sydney bound flying boats. Hutchinson called the other two aircraft and suggested they also climb — which they did and, although a lot colder, the conditions improved a great deal.

All three flying boats alighted at Rose Bay without further incident however Thurston's A24-1 ran out of fuel while taxiing and had to be towed to her mooring. If this had happened only minutes earlier the end result would have been quite different.

Both the T.E.A.L. Empire boats continued to fly the Tasman until 1947 when they were firstly offered for sale then scrapped.

T.E.A.L. then purchased four specially modified "Tasman Class" Sandringhams from Shorts. These machines took over the Tasman route until 1950 when Q.E.A. purchased two which became VH-EBW and VH-EBX.

The other two were purchased by Barrier Reef Airways, the first in 1950 becoming VH-BRC and the second in 1951 became VH-BRD. Three of these four machines were destined to visit Lord Howe Island.

T.E.A.L. continued to fly the Tasman with five of the last Short Brothers line of big boats, the mighty Solent. Their last Tasman Sea crossing was in June 1954. They too were replaced by land planes. T.E.A.L. flew their final flying boat service to Fiji in September 1960. It must be said that the T.E.A.L. ground staff and aircrew did a magnificent job. On only one occasion was an aircraft forced to use Lord Howe Island in an emergency.

Whispering Death and the Wooden Wonder

The visit by the T.E.A.L. boat wasn't the only aircraft other than a Catalina to fly to the Island during the war. RAAF Beaufighters often flew navigational training missions out to the Island.

The author's father in law, Barry Thompson, remembers the Beaufighter visits quite vividly. "How could I forget them — as kids we'd fish off the jetty when all of a sudden, all hell would break loose! You'd swear they'd miss the jetty by only a few feet."

It soon became common practice for locals out in their boats to get close in under the cliffs whenever Beaufighters were about the Island. These twin-engined aircraft were used by the R.A.A.F. mainly for ground attack and shipping strikes throughout the South West Pacific Area. They were very heavily armed with four 20mm cannons and six 0.303 machineguns. There was also a single rear facing 0.303 operated manually by an observer, mounted on the top of the fuselage. In addition to guns, the Beaufighter could also carry eight rockets, two bombs or a single torpedo. They were powered by the unique sleeve-valved Bristol Hercules engines, which were a lot quieter than other aircraft of the time.

The Beaufighter was given the nickname "Whispering Death" due to its ability to seemingly appear from nowhere and reap havoc with its devastating firepower. The other aircraft to visit on similiar training missions was perhaps the most successful twin engine aircraft of the war. The de Havilland Mosquito was built almost entirely of balsa and plywood. The 'Wooden Wonder' was produced in bomber and fighter versions and served with extraordinary success throughout World War Two.

Catalina on the beach

By 1943 Catalinas made visits on an almost monthly basis. They continued to visit the Island throughout and after the war. The difficulties of flying to then mooring on the lagoon was a constant concern for the visiting Cat crews. The problem of mooring was brought home on 17 September 1943 when Catalina A24-33 made a trip to the Island. Squadron Leader Vic Hodgkinson was the captain with his crew including Pilot Officer Rob Hutchinson as Radio Operator. Hutchinson had also been on board A24-37 when she came to the aid of the T.E.A.L. boat earlier that year.

Pilot Officer Rob Hutchinson: "We went to Rose Bay first picking up a doctor and dentist as well as nine other passengers. Our crew consisted of Squadron Leader Hodgkinson with two trainee pilots up front; Bob Calwell in the middle with two trainee engineers while I had Pilot Officer Ashcroft and Sergeant Lane as trainee radio operators. The trip out to this Island was quite rough taking over 4 hours".

Squadron Leader Vic Hodgkinson takes up the story: "When we arrived there was a very strong wind, around 60 knots, blowing from the east. I could see by the surface conditions on the Lagoon that the wind was gusting and alighting would take particular caution."

Between the mountains to the South and the ridge to the North is a low plateau causing severe down draughts in the lee and the lagoon where the Catalina had to alight.

Vic Hodgkinson continues: "I flew a circuit to estimate the hazards of the turbulence and it was quite rough! I set the Cat up for a full stall alighting with floats up and power around 15 inches of manifold pressure, 2300 rpm and airspeed at 65knots. I intended to alight as far from the shore as possible. On approaching the intended spot at around 100 feet the Cat literally fell out of the sky and with full power applied we hit the water with a thump, the power was pulled back and the control column forward, the flying boat stuck and we were there. The floats were lowered and we taxied up to the mooring."

Rob Hutchinson: "It was a truly magnificent piece of airmanship which went completely unnoticed by the civilians on board whose main concern was either for their queasy stomachs or the best way to keep their baggage away from the swishing bilge water."

A24-33 was moored at the flying boat buoy at Comet's Hole on the south side of Rabbit Island. The crew made their way ashore to be billeted in various Island homes. After a hearty meal of the local vegetables and fresh fish the now traditional dance was put on for the Air Force men.

That night the wind swung round to the west and increased to an estimated 90 mph. The Cat was now on her own to face the full fury of the wind and swell. The following morning the locals were met with the sorry sight of a "Catalina on the beach" those being the very first words that woke Squadron Leader Hodgkinson.

Vic Hodgkinson: "I was awakened at dawn by one of the fisherman to be told that the Cat was on the beach. She had come ashore just over the sand dune near the Superintendent's house where I was staying. There was no damage, it appeared the fitting of the suction plate to which the buoy was attached was broken. The rest of the buoy was still attached to the flying boat. As the tide was out it was simple matter of running a line out to the Cat to a large anchor. All we did then was wait for the tide to rise and with the help of the engines she was pulled off and returned to the sea. Not long after this, good-byes and thanks were passed on to all for their hospitality and help. The crew boarded and made their way safely back to Rathmines."

Squadron Leader Hodgkinson was to return to the Island on 7–9 January 1944. As a token of his thanks for their help and hospitality he took a group of Island people for a flight to Middleton Reef some 100 miles north of Lord Howe.

Vic Hodgkinson: "We also had on board an R.A.A.F. photographer who took some shots of the *Annosona*, an old square rigger which had been wrecked there in January 1907. From then on the wreck became part of the Catalina's training course. When the crews were formed their final exercise was to find the wreck at night, photograph it, and then bomb it with a practice bomb. No one hit it in my time as Chief Flying Instructor."

George Woods also visited the Island as part of Flying Officer Hill's crew aboard A24-28 on 25 November 1944.

"My job as Fitter/Airgunner was to man the front turret. After we had alighted I made ready the mooring lines. I was also responsible for sounding and calling depths to the captain. I was very surprised to find we were actually in 40 feet of water with the sandy bottom and clarity, it looked a lot shallower.

The crew were put up by a number of the local people in their homes, I was kindly accommodated by the Dignam family. That night a dance was put on for us, with all the local people in attendance. I was very keen to see one of these Mutton-Birds everyone was talking about. One of the locals satisfied my curiosity by taking me outside to a burrow, reaching down and then plucking one out. I was ribbed about this for some time and earned the name "Mutton-Bird George" for the rest of my stay."

The R.A.A.F. Catalinas continued to visit the Island for some time until the late 1940's when firstly T.O.A. and later Q.E.A. began their commercial operations to the Island. The R.A.A.F. Cats did not visit the Island as frequently after this but they used the Island as a navigational point and overflew both day and night.

Chapter 4: Tragedy in paradise: The loss of Catalina A24-381

On the 28th September 1948, R.A.A.F. Catalina A24-381 from 11 Squadron hit the ridge near the North peak known as the *Malabar*. Seven of a crew of nine died:

F/Lt. M.D. Smith (Captain)
F/Lt. J.B. McCoy
F/Lt. W.D. Keller
F/Lt. A. McKenzie
Pilot 111 S. Piercy
W/O S.H. Bacon
W/O D.E. Salis
The survivors were:
F/Lt. B.R. Bradley
W/O J.D. Lea

The crew were briefed to take-off from Rathmines on a training mission which was to search for, locate and shadow the 'enemy' that being H.M.A.S. *Australia* off the east coast of Sydney. This was to be done until Beaufighter aircraft from 30 Squadron attacked the ship. The second part of the mission was a navigation exercise flying from daylight into darkness to Lord Howe and then on to Middleton Reef and home to Rathmines.

After leaving the East Coast the captain decided the navigation exercise would be to Lord Howe and then return to Rathmines instead of the extra leg to Middleton Reef.

On arrival the Cat circled the Island at 3,000 feet then headed west towards Rathmines. After approximately twenty minutes on the homeward leg a serious fuel leak developed. Having a high mounted wing, the fuel tanks are housed in the wing behind the engines. The wing is mounted to the fuselage on a streamlined pedestal, which is where the engineer sits. It is believed that the leak started above the engineer's compartment.

A decision was made to return to Lord Howe Island and attempt an after dark alighting on the lagoon. Unfortunately when crossing the Island east to west the Cat struck the ridge below the north peak.

Roy Wilson and his good friend Bill Davis were dining at a house very close to where the remains of the Catalina came to rest. With flames everywhere both Roy and Bill threw caution to the wind and ran into the inferno. They managed to pull two of the crew clear until a huge explosion lit the sky.

Roy's brother Allen and a guest staying at *Oceanview* guesthouse, Clyde Parrish, arrived on the scene not long after Roy and Bill and helped to get the two survivors back to *Oceanview* for medical attention.

When the aircraft crashed, Clyde had run in the direction of the blazing wreck. He nearly didn't get to the crash site at all as a well which Clyde hadn't seen in the darkness had been recently dug at the back of the guesthouse. Sure enough, in he went and whilst there wasn't any water in the well the sides were too steep to climb out. Luckily, Allen Wilson wasn't far behind and had heard his calls. Allen pulled him free and the pair continued to the crash site albeit with valuable minutes wasted.

The day after the incident the late Gerald Kirby wrote to Wing Commander Wearne the then Base Commander at Rathmines:

Dear Wing Commander Wearne:

> The loss of your crew and aircraft has deeply affected the Island people and I want to express our sincerest sympathy to the relatives and friends of the chaps who lost their lives. The aircraft was circling high over the Island at about 7.30pm last night.
>
> I wasn't taking much notice as we had heard that a Catalina was over on exercise. She circled several times and then came in over the ridge which connects North Peak to a place called "Pooles Lookout" (at the back of *Oceanview*).
>
> The next thing we knew was a terrific flash that lit up the whole north end of the Island and all hands cleared off to see if they could be of assistance. As I went I called at the Doctor's residence and got him organised. The aircraft was burning fiercely when I got there. The two survivors had been laid out on stretchers and were being carried away. This was about 8 p.m. or perhaps a bit later.
>
> I waited till some chaps came down off the hill behind the wreck where they said they had discovered nothing. It subsequently transpired that these chaps had not been to the top of the ridge but only where the aircraft entered the trees. I felt pretty rotten over the whole business and another chap and myself went back about 10.30 p.m. and climbed the ridge. On the extreme crest we discovered that the aircraft had grazed the top about 600 feet up (not North Peak but the ridge below it). A portion of the keel and hull were strewn around and also bits of Perspex.
>
> The story I heard was that the aircraft was full of petrol vapor and the crew were not risking ignition from a spark from the transmitting set. There are unconfirmed reports of white flashes coming from the aircraft believed to be signals. No one I have heard of said same. There is no doubt in my mind that if the aircraft was full of petrol vapor the sparks associated with the bottom scrubbing across the rock would ignite the mixture and there is no doubt that she was on fire after the first contact with the ridge.

We followed her course slowly through the bush zig-zagging to make sure that we missed nothing. We found the navigator's tables partly charred about a hundred yards down the hill along with portions of burnt out radio equipment, spoons in a small enamel bowl and sundry pieces of metal. Her speed after hitting the ridge kept her clear of trees for a couple of hundred yards. There she entered again and for about another 100 yards tore down everything in her way. It was amazing to see the trees cleaned up by her last dive. The float and portion of one wing was about a hundred yards from the final position of the wreck. After clearing a swathe during which she started to disintegrate she came onto a clearing where she finally broke up and burnt.

The tail sections broke off at the blister and two chaps were thrown out, both on fire, but the flames were put out by Roy Wilson and Bill Davis. Another chap was thrown through the fuselage on fire and probably unconscious before being thrown out and quite impossible to save.

It was quite impossible to get within yards of the blaze which looked like a movie picture of an oil well fire.

I felt sure that with the terrific buffeting the aircraft received that it would be most unlikely that anyone was conscious when the flaming tanks finally wiped the others out. We gave the area between the first bit and the final area a thorough do over and did not leave the area till 12.45 by which time I felt certain that no one had been thrown out. I think that death must have been instantaneous.

It has been the greatest disaster on the Island. With the exception of sailing boat wrecks with undisclosed losses there has been nothing comparable. It has left a gloom over the whole community.

Yours sincerely

G.M Kirby

The tragic loss of the 11 Squadron Catalina was the highest loss of R.A.A.F. personnel in a peacetime accident.

By the early fifties the R.A.A.F. had sold off or scrapped its Catalinas. Either T.O.A. using ex-R.A.A.F. Sunderlands or Q.E.A. who also used ex-R.A.A.F. Catalinas then carried out medical evacuations.

Paper Runs

The R.A.A.F. replaced the Catalinas with the Lockheed Neptune known locally as the *Nepies*. The role of this aircraft was long range over water patrols. Following on from the Catalinas these aircraft also used Lord Howe as a navigation training point. Although they couldn't land they often brought bundles of newspapers which were dropped and greatly appreciated by the local people.

Island resident John Wilson remembers the *Nepies* visits well. "They used to approach from the west over the lagoon and head towards a paddock just below our home. They were so low all you could see from where we stood was their tail just above the grass bank. They'd roar in, drop a bundle of papers then head away to the east; absolutely fantastic they were!"

The R.A.A.F. operated the Neptune for twenty-six years. During this period only one aircraft was lost. This tragedy occurred on 4 February 1959 when 11 Squadron's A89-308 crashed near its Richmond base. The loss of the entire crew of eight took Catalina A24-381's place in R.A.A.F. history as the highest loss of personnel in a peacetime accident.

The R.A.N. also made visits to the Island and it was in fact a naval helicopter which became the second land based aircraft to visit the Island. In 1957 a Bristol Sycamore landed on the Island and took two of the residents, Stan Fenton along with Jim Whistler, out to its ship, the H.M.A.S. *Melbourne* for morning tea. During the Sycamores' service life they were to visit the Island on a number of occasions. The R.A.N. operated thirteen Sycamores from 1951 to 1965.

It was to be almost a quarter of a century before a R.A.A.F. fixed wing aircraft was to land on the Island. Once again, it was an emergency medical evacuation which brought about this event.

Chapter 5: Airstrip Proving Flight

The first aircraft to use the Island airstrip was far from planned. The aircraft, a R.A.A.F. Caribou, came to the aid of Island resident Wally Wilson who had suffered a compound fracture of the right leg and nearly severed his foot when a tree that he was cutting for firewood rolled on top of him.

There was grave concern for the patient and it became essential he went to a major hospital urgently or he would lose his leg. A bad storm had whipped up the sea thus ruling out the flying boats. R.A.A.F. base Richmond in Sydney was contacted and on 12 August 1974 a 38 Squadron Caribou was despatched.

When A4-140 arrived overhead, the weather had really set in. It was raining and the wind was gusting up to 70 knots from the south west, direct crosswind to the partially sealed airstrip.

On the first attempt at landing this plane, a gust hit the aircraft and slewed it sideways — up went the revs and the undercarriage. The Caribou tried a northerly approach from the opposite direction only to get the same result! Finally, after four attempts, the aircraft touched down in the mud and reverse pitch was selected. Much to the relief of the sizeable audience she was down safely.*

The pilot, Wing Commander Dave Middleton, later said his fifth attempt would have been his last. If he didn't land he would have had just enough fuel to get back to the mainland. The wind was so strong on the ground an Army multi roller was used to anchor the plane before refuelling. Soon after this was completed the Caribou and her grateful patient took off and made their way to Brisbane. Wally's leg was successfully operated on and he later returned to the Island to make a full recovery.

Caribou A4-140 was the second of twenty nine Caribous to serve with the R.A.A.F. She served in Vietnam receiving some damage from ground fire. The aircraft was still in service with the R.A.A.F. in 2000.

* The Army had just started to seal the airstrip only having completed the first third of the southern end when the Caribou arrived. The Army asked if the pilot could avoid the fresh seal if possible. A credit to Wing Commander Middleton's flying skill, as the tyre marks in the mud where the aircraft touched down were a mere two feet from where the seal finished.

Chapter 6: Radio Communications

Radio, of course, is vital to the operation of aircraft and was first installed on the Island by A.W.A in 1929.

Island resident, the late Stan Fenton, had been at sea as a radio operator and returned to the Island to take up a position as Radio Operator and Postmaster. Stan Fenton eventually became an employee of the Department of Civil Aviation (D.C.A.). He retired as Officer in Charge of Communications.

Power for the early transmitter was provided by a small engine which was started on petrol then, once it was running, it was changed over to kerosene. In the early days communications were by Morse code with messages being sent three to four times a day. During the war the building, which still stands alongside the power station was blacked out and sand bagged.

From the 1950's voice communications via High Frequency were introduced and while this was an improvement it was not 100% reliable. The D.C.A. made the radio available to the locals for a one hour period in the morning and afternoons. It wasn't until the 1980's that a designated H.F. radio was installed for phones.

A. W. A. radio installation 1929.

courtesy Norman Simpson

S.S Morinda.

author's collection

With local assistance Chichester begins the salvage of his Gipsy Moth after she was flipped.

courtesy Kerry McFadyen

Roly Wilson and Frank Payten with the best wing which had every rib broken.

author's collection

Chichester and Minnie Dignam working on the repairs.

author's collection

The rebuilt float plane is carried down to the lagoon.

author's collection

ZK-AKK *Madame Elijah*.

courtesy Kerry McFadyen

The repaired Gipsy Moth taxis past The Flagstaff before departing for mainland Australia.

courtesy Kerry McFadyen

Mine on the reef at Middle Beach.

courtesy Thelma Wilson

R.A.A.F. Catalina overflies during the war.

author's collection

Cat crew moored on the lagoon.

courtesy Vic Hodgkinson

A24-33 on the beach in 1943.

courtesy Vic Hodgkinson

War weary Black Cat with Rabbit Island behind.

courtesy John Wilson

Late model PB2B-2 Catalina on the lagoon.

courtesy John Wilson

ABOVE: R.A.A.F. crew enjoying the Island.
courtesy Vic Hodgkinson

AT LEFT: R.A.A.F. crew and locals gather around the old Thornycroft lorry.
courtesy Vic Hodgkinson

BELOW: Locals waving off a departing Cat.
courtesy Vic Hodgkinson

R.A.A.F. Rathmines during the war.

courtesy Hazel Payten

R.A.A.F. Catalina A24-381 mid 1948

courtesy Denis Saunders

Tail section and port wing tip of A24-381 the morning after the crash.

courtesy Hazel Payten

Tail section of A24-381.

courtesy Hazel Payten

Another view of the tail.

courtesy Hazel Payten

R.A.A.F. Caribou A4-140 on one of her five attempts to land on the new airstrip.

courtesy Hazel Payten

Attempts to land were also made from the north.

Mick Bloomfield

The wind was so strong that the Caribou was tied to a multi roller.

courtesy Hazel Payten

Chapter 7: The Planes, the Place and the People

To get a true appreciation of flying boat operations to Lord Howe Island a short general explanation is required on the aircraft used, the situation on the Island, and finally the people who lived, worked and came to depend on the "Ships that Flew".

The flying boat as an airliner evolved from the golden age of aviation which was a time when flying was reaching both 'up and out' across the world. Both men and women aviators were breaking long distance, height and speed records almost as soon as they were set. Aircraft manufacturers were also continuously looking for ways to improve performance, reliability, safety and so sell aeroplanes. The outbreak of World War Two saw an acceleration of aircraft development through necessity.

The flying boat had proved before the war to be ideal as a passenger liner to the many waterways of the world. As a military machine this type of aircraft also proved ideal for the many and varied tasks it was asked to perform. The very war which saw the development of the flying boat also brought about its downfall. Throughout World War Two, airstrips were built all over the world, thus eliminating the extra expense of flying operations off water. Also the improvement of land based aircrafts' reliability and range meant they could reach these strips safely.

Maintenance time and costs for aircraft operating off water are a lot higher than that of land planes. The harsh nature of the elements — saltwater, wind, swell and currents all offer their own challenge.

Although major maintenance such as engine swaps were performed on the water most major repairs and servicing were much easier when performed on land. This meant a flying boat would first have to be beached and then large wheels were attached to the fuselage on either side with a smaller wheeled arrangement being attached to the rear of the hull.

Land aircraft can of course have all their servicing performed within the protection of a hangar, often alongside the runway where they take-off and land.

Of the many thrills associated with flying, lifting off and alighting on water in a large flying boat would be difficult to equal. To fly to Lord Howe Island on one of these magnificent machines and arrive to the tranquillity and natural beauty of the Island could only enhance such an occasion. Flying boat skippers genuinely appreciated the Lord Howe route as once they left the controlled airspace of the east coast to the point where they tied their aircraft to the buoy on the Island's lagoon, the aircraft was totally under their command. They were totally free to do as they saw fit to ensure a safe and comfortable journey for their passengers. Land plane operations on the mainland were very controlled with courses all set and altitudes fixed, totally under the command of a controller.

The Planes

The Consolidated PBY Catalina

The PBY Catalina was built to a 1933 United States Navy requirement for a Long Range Patrol flying boat. The prototype flew on 28 March 1935 and proved to be an excellent aircraft. The hull featured a single deck with very shallow draft and even when fully laden a Catalina would only draw two and a half feet. As well as its incredible range and endurance the flying boat was capable of alighting in very rough water conditions. These two factors combined well for the many open sea rescue missions they were to perform.

The first flying boats to visit Lord Howe were Catalinas of the R.A.A.F. during World War Two. In total the R.A.A.F. received 168 Catalinas of varying models from 1941 to 1945. Two PBY-4s were acquired from the Dutch Air Force. These machines had slightly lower capacity engines than the later models and they also lacked the distinguishing blisters.

The most common version was the PBY-5 and a total of sixty six were purchased. The R.A.A.F. also purchased forty-six of the PBY5A, a tricycle undercarriage amphibian version. PB2B-1s were similar to the PBY-5, only they were manufactured by Boeing as opposed to Consolidated; seven were delivered. The final version, the PB2B-2, was again similar to the PBY-5, only this version featured a much taller and less broad tail fin. Only sixty-seven of this model were manufactured in total, forty-seven of which entered service with the R.A.A.F.

The Catalina never flew defensive missions in R.A.A.F. service. In fact, in the early days of the war in the Pacific it was the only aircraft of the R.A.A.F. to fly offensively. The R.A.A.F. Catalina's continued this role throughout their entire period of service during World War Two. Perhaps the least known and most daring missions were the laying of mines in Japanese harbours. The R.A.A.F. painted their Catalinas black for these missions with this camouflage proving ideal at concealing the slow and vulnerable flying boats from Japanese night fighters.

As well as mines and bombs, depth charges and even torpedoes were slung under the wing. Not only were these ordnance heavy, they were also very blunt and not at all streamlined. With a full load of fuel and mines, take-offs were often achieved after as much as a three mile run! Some Black Cat crews returned from such missions after having spent over 20 hours in the air!

The Catalina is probably best known for its role in air-sea rescue. In the South West Pacific area Cats were used to cover strikes by attacking bombers and fighters. Many downed aircrew owe their lives to the Catalina and the crews that flew them.

The PBY Catalina had a 104 foot wingspan with no flaps. Positioned close together above the cockpit were two Pratt and Whitney fourteen cylinder, dual row radial engines. A unique feature were the wing tip floats. As the aircraft approached to alight, an electric motor would be activated and the neatly fitting wing tips would fold down to become stabilising floats. The floats were also designed to act as air-brakes; the extra drag helping the flying boat alight at lower speeds. The most recognisable feature along the 63 foot long fuselage were two observation blisters just aft and below the wing trailing edge.

Most R.A.A.F. Cats had a 0.50 calibre machine gun mounted in each blister and the lower half of the blister could be lifted similar to one's eyelid. From this position the gunners had a 180 degree field of fire. Forward of the cockpit was a manually operated nose turret with a smaller 0.303 calibre machine gun.

Both these positions also proved useful once the flying boat was on the water. From the blister, under the orders of the captain, crew men would deploy drogues which would assist by slowing, and with the engines, help turn the boat. By alternating the power to either of the R-1830-92 Twin Wasp engines, the flying boat could, in favourable conditions, be turned. From the blister, passengers, freight and crew could easily be transferred to boats and taken ashore.

In the nose turret a crewman would prepare the mooring lines, or if a buoy was not available, the collapsible anchor would be made ready. Often this crewman would also have to sound, using a weighted line to determine the depth ahead of the boat. If the bowman made a mistake and missed the mooring buoy or if the Captain went too fast or not close enough the flying boat would simply have to go around and try again as there were no brakes or reverse!

The Short Sunderland

Short Brothers Motto: *We don't build planes that float, We build ships that fly** The Sunderland evolved from the earlier and much travelled "C Class Empire Boats". Shorts made a variety of aeroplanes for both land and sea but it was their great four-engine flying boats built to serve the far-off corners of the British Empire that they are perhaps best remembered for.

This version only visited the Island on one occasion when one of the two operated by T.E.A.L. had to use the lagoon in an emergency.

With the outbreak of World War Two a new design rolled off the Short Brothers production line, the "Sunderland". Designed as a long range maritime patrol boat, the Sunderland proved ideal for seeking out and destroying German U-Boats which threatened the supply convoys to Britain during the war.

* This was true: the construction was to lay the keel then build up from there.

The Sunderlands gained a fearsome reputation with both the enemy, U-Boat crews of the Kriegs Marine, as well as the long range fighters of the Luftwaffe who were sent out to shoot them down. Often a sole Sunderland would be attacked by a number of enemy aircraft. The Sunderland had three power operated turrets with a single machine gun in the nose, two in the middle upper and four machine guns in the tail turret. Many crews also fitted extra guns in the galley windows.

When attacked the slow flying Sunderland would get down low to the water from where they could fight off the enemy with every gun they had. The pilots of the Luftwaffe nicknamed the Sunderland *The Flying Porcupine* due to the many guns fired at them during attacks.

R.A.A.F. 10 Squadron flew the Sunderland from England and accounted for thirty of the two hundred U-Boats sunk by aircraft during the war. Twenty-five "Distinguished Flying Crosses" were awarded to crews from this Squadron.

10 Squadron also played their part in developing the Sunderland with the ground crews replacing the ageing and under-powered Bristol Pegasus engines "on the sly" with the proven and more powerful Pratt and Whitney, the same engine as the Catalina.

This adaptation resulted in a lot more power although it took some time to solve the over-heating problem especially when they were used in the warmer climates of the South Pacific.

Back in Australia, due to an immediate need for reconnaissance aircraft, two Empire Boats were initially impressed from Q.E.A. to the R.A.A.F. In total five Q.E.A. Empire Boats saw service with 40 Squadron — three were lost during the transport missions they performed.

40 Squadron later operated six Pegasus-powered Sunderlands (A26-1 to A26-6) successfully in a transport role up and down the east coast of Australia and north into the South West Pacific Area. One of these aircraft, A26-6 was damaged and converted to components in November 1944.

After the war there was a large demand for aircraft capable of carrying passengers long distances in the comfort of the times. Short Brothers could see a role for their Sunderlands as a passenger airliner. Many Sunderlands had their military equipment removed, the galley upgraded, and they were fitted with seating with some for as many as forty or more passengers.

The first of these conversions, officially known as 'Hythes', kept the front turret, as it had been designed to retract and allow crew to get forward to the mooring gear.

On the water the Sunderland was quite different to the Catalina. Firstly it was a larger aircraft with a wingspan of 112 feet, 9.5 inches and the fuselage from bow to stern measured 85 feet, 4.1 inches. Unlike the Catalina the floats hung permanently under the wing with struts and bracing wires for support. The tip of the fin stood some 30 feet above the water's surface.

The hull had a very steep vee with a lot more wetted area than the Catalina. A

Sunderland drew over 4 feet fully laden, well over 6 feet when they settled during the end of their alighting run. Taxiing was also a little easier as the Catalina had its engines close together almost directly above the fuselage while the Sunderland on the other hand had four engines. After alighting the Captain would shut down the inner engines and steer the boat by alternating the throttles of the outer engines.

The Sandringham

The ultimate conversion had the nose turret removed altogether and a much more streamlined and appealing bow section with a flush fitting hatch. The Sandringham also had the thick flat panels of the windscreen replaced with more streamlined curved perspex. Upper and lower decks of seating were fitted with sound proofing, a fully appointed galley and some even had a bar and smoking lounge!

This model also benefited from 10 Squadron's modifications as all the Australian Sandringhams had the extra power of the Pratt and Whitney engines.

Sunderland or Sandringham?

One hybrid was converted by Ansett at their Rose Bay Flying Boat Base in 1963 for use on the Lord Howe route. Named *Islander*, this boat was unique in that she was a Sunderland converted for civil use to Sandringham standards. She lost her nose turret yet kept her bulbous Sunderland nose shape, mainly in order to accommodate the many odd shaped items of freight taken to the Island. She also held on to her military past by keeping the flat panelled windscreen glass. She could not really be called a Sandringham nor was she any longer a Sunderland!

The Place

The Tasman Sea has a world wide reputation for being both unpredictable and hazardous. The Island lies in an area of disturbed westerlies for most of the year. During the summer months, subtropical highs can provide changeable conditions.

Tropical cyclones often form near the east coast of northern Australia, then move south, bringing strong winds and heavy rain. In winter the freezing level can be as low as 3,000 feet. In general the weather is unpredictable throughout the year for more than a few days in advance. In strong winds, violent turbulence can be experienced with the Island's peculiar topography often causing both horizontal and vertical rotors which still cause problems for modern aircraft.

Due to the varying tides, flying boats could only alight roughly an hour and a half either side of high. Many small reefs in the lagoon are exposed at low tide. Pilots also had to deal with a sand bar which stretched from Rabbit Island across the lagoon to the beach. The flying boats were taxied at speed over this area, known as 'flying the bar' to keep the hull clear of the bank.

On a few very rare occasions, when the wind was a light easterly, flying boats actually taxied out the north passage and down the reef, to take-off in the larger southern end of the lagoon.

This situation only occurred when the captain considered it a risk to taxi over the bar due to the tide being too low. Safe mooring could be made at quite a large area just to the south of Rabbit Island, known as Comet's Hole where a flying boat could moor through the tide.

Before a flying boat could alight, the lagoon would have to be swept of any debris as a floating log could easily puncture a thin aluminium hull. Shallow reefs and sandbanks were also marked with small temporary buoys. Of course, a flying boat's runway was mobile and the direction of the wind determined its location. The large mooring buoy had to be dressed, which involved a light line with a loop sitting on the top of the buoy, then a heavier line was attached as soon as all was secure.

The memory most people recall when alighting on the Island's lagoon was the aqua blue water splashing up over the port-holes and occasionally, passengers on the lower decks believed they went under water.

The author's wife, Janine, recalls, "After the flying boat came off the plane and the spray cleared, the hull would settle quite noticeably. This instant, while looking out over the water of the lagoon, is still with me, a feeling only a flying boat passenger arriving at Lord Howe would know. This was also a feeling that told me I was home."

Once on the water, the pilots had to be careful. Unlike a land plane, a flying boat had no brakes and the engines were the only means to manoeuvre the ship up to her mooring buoy.

By this time a crew member, usually the steward, had made his way to the forward hatch with a boat hook; his job being to guide the pilots up to the mooring. As soon as he had the line he would indicate to the pilots who would cut the engines. The co-pilot also had the important job of "parking the props" whereby the three bladed propellers were moved by a small motor into such a position that the passenger boats would not hit them.

The Department of Civil Aviation (D.C.A.) provided its employees with a small launch known as the crash boat, and apart from the obvious, this vessel was used to sweep the lagoon of any debris, to flag sand banks and reef areas, and to relay weather conditions by radio.

Over the years a number of vessels were used for this task and the *Venture* and the *Dawn* were the first. Both were 24 feet long and modelled on surf boats. The oldest of the two, the *Venture,* was on the Island when Chichester visited in 1931. They were initially used as crash boats and later to transport passengers between the jetty and the flying boats. The *Venture* and the *Dawn* were both ceremoniously burnt on the beach on the last day of the Ansett Service in 1974.

Other crash boats included the *La Maude*, *Butterbox* and finally the *Moorei*. The vessels used to transport passengers included the *Venture* and *Dawn* along with the

Albatross, Lulawai, Pacific Chieftain and the *Viking*. Of the above the *Albatross, Lulawai, Moorei* and *Viking* are still in use.

The D.C.A. employees also had the unusual task of scraping the lagoon! This involved two of the Island launches dragging a chain joined to each vessel's stern, knocking down any coral heads which threatened a flying boat's fragile hull.

On a number of occasions a flying boat's engine would have to be changed on the lagoon. In the later years a spare engine was kept on the Island and such tasks as engine swaps involved a specially made gantry which attached to the wing.

First the propeller would be lowered into a boat followed by the engine.

Working on a narrow plank, fifteen feet above the lagoon in adverse weather, was not fun and every now and then a spanner or two would slip. I have been told there is probably the equivalent of a box of tools buried in the sands of the lagoon.

The water is only deep enough to take-off and alight during a 2 to 3 hour period through the high tide*. This did not leave a lot of time to alight passengers and unload their luggage, then reload with departing passengers and take-off. The flying boats always carried enough fuel to return to the mainland, however, on the odd occasion, the tanks would have to be topped up. All these tasks would be easily performed as long as the weather co-operated.

Inevitably a flying boat would have to stay the night as after dark take-offs were not permitted. The most common reason for an overnight stay would be a deterioration in the weather. Not only did this create a delay for the passengers but it often created a problem for the crew.

The reef would keep the ocean swells at bay at low tide, but as the tide rose, the lagoon could become quite rough. An incoming swell would pull tight at the mooring lines, then raise the flying boat into a nose high position. The 112 foot wing of a Sandringham was designed for lift. The twenty ton ship of the sky would again pull tight on the mooring lines as she tried to fly!

As the swell passed, her nose would drop into the trough and she would gather speed, only to slam into the next oncoming swell. On really rough nights it was not uncommon for a crew to stay on board running the engines to keep their charge on the mooring.

From the first aeroplane in 1931 to the end of the flying boats in 1974, a total of seven marine aircraft had come ashore due to weather and/or sea conditions while visiting the Island. Of these only two machines suffered little or no damage and were refloated. It is also interesting to note that on three separate occasions fixed wing aircraft put down and took off from the Island during the flying boat era. Only one of these aircraft used the then incomplete airstrip.

---

* Often, depending on the time of year, the turn around period could either be lengthened for a high tide or shortened for a low high tide.

The People

The people of Lord Howe Island that feature in the flying boat era are many. The Island's residents lived on a small and very isolated paradise removed from the rest of Australia. Perhaps the credit for the success of the commercial operation should go to those that first flew regularly to the Island.

The R.A.A.F. flew the first flying boats to the Island during the war. They brought with them, among other things proof that flying boats could operate safely between the mainland and the Island. Many of these wartime crews formed fond and long-standing friendships with the people of Lord Howe.

A number of these battle-hardened aircrew went on to fly with the many commercial operations which started up after the war. The commercial operators brought tourism, and with this, employment for the Island people. In 1947, when the first commercial operator commenced a service to the Island there were only two major guest houses, *The Pines* and *Oceanview*. When the flying boats sadly came to their end twenty seven years later, the Island had almost a dozen places of accommodation. To the people visiting the Island the flying boats provided a unique mode by which they travelled to a beautiful island. For Lord Howe's residents, they were more than this as they not only carried freight, they also brought contact with the outside world that being an all-important lifeline with the mainland of Australia.

To this day the flying boats are held dearly in the hearts and minds of those that travelled on them. The planes, the place and the people were all unique in their own way; creating a special time in the Island's history, commonly referred to, even today, as the 'flying boat days'.

Chapter 8: Marinair

In 1946 P.G. Taylor made a number of inquiries about obtaining an airline licence to operate Catalinas to Lord Howe Island. Taylor, along with Mr A.C.M. Jackaman and Mr R. Mueller, formed a syndicate under the name of Marinair and purchased the following R.A.A.F. Catalinas: A24-350, -351, -358, -366 and -384, all later model PB2B-2's. These aircraft were flown from Rathmines to Rose Bay in Sydney, then onto the Cooks River near Kingsford Smith Airport.

They were hauled up a provisional slipway and completely modified to meet Civil Aviation regulations for transporting passengers.

The airline was plagued with difficulties. After a lot of paper shuffling and bureaucracy the venture eventually failed. Not long after all the Catalinas were refitted and sold. Marinair only ever made one commercial flight which was in July 1946. P.G. Taylor with H. Birch as First Officer, flew to Lord Howe Island and back carrying the first fare paying passengers to the Island.

Hugh Birch retired from the R.A.A.F. with the rank of Group Captain; he had amassed over 12,000 flying hours. He made a few flights with T.O.A., who were the next operator to the Island and finally worked for Q.E.A. in an administrative role.

Sir Gordon Taylor

'Bill' Taylor was a great pioneering airman with a fantastic vision for the future. He made a number of long distance flights, perhaps his most ambitious being the crossing of the Southern Pacific Ocean from Australia to South America in 1951. This epic journey involved pinpoint navigation to a number of small islands for refuelling, one of which, Easter Island, involved an open sea alighting.

Taylor also flew the Tasman Sea with Kingsford Smith in the triple engined Avro Ten which were built under licence, direct copies of Smithy's famous Fokker *Southern Cross*. These aircraft had a high wing with a single engine mounted in the nose the other engines were mounted under the wing and fixed undercarriage mounted via struts to the bottom of the outer engines and across to the fuselage.

It was during one memorable flight across the Tasman that Taylor really showed his stuff! On the 15 May 1935, with the crew of C. Kingsford Smith, P.G. Taylor and J. Stannage, *Southern Cross* set out from Sydney on a mail flight for New Zealand. All went well for the first 6 hours when suddenly there was a loud bang and the starboard engine began to vibrate violently. 'Smithy' quickly shut the engine down and turned back for Australia where it was discovered about 1 foot of the wooden propeller blade had broken off.

With all the power now being provided by the centre and port engine, the aircraft became very difficult to control. To make matters worse the port engine started to lose oil pressure and *Southern Cross* would not fly for long on one engine. In an extreme act of bravery Taylor climbed out into the slipstream and drained oil from the shut down starboard engine into a small thermos. The oil was collected into a small leather suit case within the cabin.

Taylor then climbed out onto the strut of the ailing port engine and topped up the oil. He made a total of twelve trips out into the slipstream transferring oil. *Southern Cross* made it back to Sydney and the oil splattered crew of Taylor, Kingsford Smith and John Stannage had to be assisted from the aircraft, exhausted but alive!

In June 1939 Taylor arranged the charter of a civil Catalina named *Guba*, and made the first crossing of the Indian Ocean. This journey opened up an alternate route from Australia to England and included stop-overs at Port Hedland in Western Australia, Batavia, Cocos Island, Diego Garcia and the Seychelles.

The total distance of the trip from Sydney to Mombasa in Kenya was in excess of 9,000 miles and no problem was encountered with the aircraft over the entire journey. Q.E.A. later flew Catalinas on this epic route which became the longest regular passenger service in history. Known as the 'Double Sunrise Route' due to the fact that some passengers experienced two sunrises and on some occasions occupants often disembarked after more than 28 hours in the air.

The following piece was written by P.G. Taylor. It could be about Lord Howe, or one of the many islands he visited.

Bird of the Islands

She passed the entrance islands and opened out into the great lagoon,
the wind was steady from the east
offering itself for the take-off.
The moon was drawing the ocean
to the time of high water and the swell was coming in over the reef.
I sat and watched the swell
as we ran through the pre-flight checks
then I let her come round and up to the wind
she faced the lagoon for a moment of contemplation
then I gave her full power.
The swell was there but harmless
she protested a little bit
but it was only to let me know her mood
slight backward pressure on the control column
restored her equilibrium and suggested a way of escape to the air.
She responded with confidence and soon was running light
and true upon the surface.
A touch of tail trim and I broke her away when she was ready.

Chapter 9: Trans Oceanic Airways

Trans Oceanic Airways (T.O.A.) was the first airline to make regular commercial flights to Lord Howe Island.

Bryan Monkton, the founding Director, was born in Melbourne and grew up in Adelaide. At the outbreak of World War Two he joined the R.A.A.F. and learned to fly on Tiger Moths at R.A.A.F. Base Richmond on the outskirts of Sydney. Not long after gaining his wings he was posted to England, where early in the war, he flew Hawker Hurricanes over France.

Just before Japan entered the war, Monkton was posted back to Australia, where he was made a Flying Instructor. It didn't take long for him to realise this wasn't for him and he asked what alternatives were available. He was given one option, Catalina flying boats, which he readily accepted and flew throughout the South West Pacific Area until the end of the war.

Bryan Monkton had never intended to go into aviation after the war. His good friend Stewart Middlemiss, who eventually started Barrier Reef Airways (B.R.A.), asked Monkton to come with him to Rathmines to look over some Catalinas being sold off by the R.A.A.F.

Monkton and Middlemiss had flown Catalinas together during the war. In future years as their respective airlines grew they maintained close contact, occasionally lending each other both aircraft and crew as the need arose.

While at Rathmines looking over the Catalinas, Monkton noticed five Sunderlands moored out in the bay. During his Air Force career he had flown the single engine Kingfisher, the twin engined Catalina and the German triple-engined Dornier*, never however getting a chance at the mighty four-engined Sunderland. He made a comment "I've never flown a Sunderland." The chap who was with him said, "Well, why don't you buy one?"

He made his way to the Commonwealth Disposals Commission in Sydney and said, "I'm interested in buying a Sunderland." They said, "We're sorry you can't tender for one, they are going as a job lot, five Sunderlands, twenty-two spare engines and a whole hangar full of spare parts."

Monkton went away thinking how much to put on the disposals form. He knew the Cats went for a thousand pounds so he decided the same amount per Sunderland, and another thousand pounds for the engines and spares.

---

* The Dornier D024K was the only axis aircraft officially operated by an allied Air Force during the war. The R.A.A.F. used six Dorniers attached to 41 Squadron, mainly in a transport role.

Much to his surprise the tender was accepted!

He was so caught out he had to borrow from a friend to help pay the six thousand pounds and on 4 October 1946 Bryan Monkton became the proud owner of five ex-40 Squadron Sunderlands (A26-1 to 5) along with engines and spare parts.

In Monkton's words, "Not the best way to start an airline!"

On 19 November 1946 Monkton was familiarised by Hugh Birch on A26-4. The aircraft was delivered, still in its camouflage paint from Rathmines to the Rose Bay flying boat base on 21 November 1946.

The remaining Sunderlands were prepared and delivered as follows: A26-5, 16 December 1946; A26-3, 27 January 1947; A26-2, 5 March 1947; and A26-1, April 1947.

The new residents to the Sydney Harbour Flying Boat Base were not welcomed with open arms. The then Labour Government had decreed Q.E.A. would be the only international airline for Australia. Monkton had plans to operate internationally, especially to the nearby Pacific islands.

T.O.A. was incorporated in Sydney on 24 February 1947. On 7 March 1947 an application for an airline licence was lodged but was unsuccessful. This meant the airline had to operate on a charter basis and permission for flights could only be obtained the day before departure. This made it very difficult for the airline to advertise its service.

A26-4 was the first Sunderland to be converted to a civil airliner. This involved removal of wartime camouflage and all military equipment not of use then fitting seats for up to forty passengers. On 5 May 1947 she was registered VH-AKO and given the name *Australis.*

The official name for a Sunderland converted to a civil airliner was "Hythe", but this name was never widely accepted on the Island, generally the T.O.A. boats kept the name Sunderland.

On 20 May 1947, T.O.A. began operations when *Australis* departed for New Guinea with a load of freight under charter of Mr J. Stubbs. The crew for the airline's first flight were B.A.W. Monkton, L.G. Taylor, G. Walker, D. Froggatt and H. Wright.

Due to the lack of shipping at the time there was a high demand for Monkton and his Sunderland. Routes were opened up to Vila, the New Hebrides, Honiara, Lingetau, Tulagi, Noumea and Fiji.

It was around this time that Gerald Kirby from Lord Howe approached Monkton about flying to the Island. The only way for visitors to visit the Island at the time was by the regular steam ship, the *Morinda.*

A regular air service would prove ideal for the fledgling tourist trade.

Monkton had not considered flying to Lord Howe but 'Kirb' must have been pretty convincing and Monkton made inquiries with the D.C.A. only to be told they would allow Catalinas which only drew two and a half feet; the Sunderland which needed over six feet was not allowed.

It can be done

As things turned out the first visit to Lord Howe by a T.O.A. Sunderland was never planned. On 30 June 1947, *Australis* had been chartered to deliver a large ship's propeller shaft to Fiji. The return trip to Sydney involved a stopover in Noumea for fuel. On 4 July 1947 *Australis* left Noumea for Sydney. This course took her close to Lord Howe Island. After circling the Island, then gaining permission via local radio, VH-AKO alighted on the lagoon.

The local people were ecstatic and a hasty meeting was held at *Oceanview* Guesthouse near the jetty. It was unanimously decided Monkton should get back to Sydney and tell them, "It can be done, a Sunderland can use the Island's lagoon."

The flying boat had alighted just after high tide, but by the time the crew were ready to depart the tide was well on its way out. Monkton's First Officer Gordon Taylor (not to be confused with P.G.Taylor, although he often was!) takes up the story: "As we taxied out for take-off, we touched the bottom making the need to get airborne a priority.

We radioed ahead requesting an immediate beaching on arrival at Rose Bay. As it turned out, the damage was only minimal and was repaired with ease."

On arrival back in Australia, Monkton found himself in trouble. Firstly, he had arrived in an Australian territory without a customs clearance; secondly, the Sunderland had been deemed to have too great a draught for the Island's lagoon. Captain Monkton had to face the Regional Director of Civil Aviation, who had been a high ranking officer in the Air Force during the war. After reading the riot act he eventually calmed down and asked, "Do you really think you could operate a service to Lord Howe?" Monkton replied, "We could as long as we kept our arrivals and departures to one hour either side of the high tide." He told Monkton to resubmit his application for the Lord Howe route and he would do his best to get it approved.

T.O.A.'s first air service to the Island commenced on 1 August 1947, departing Rose Bay with twenty two passengers on a flight arranged by David Jones Travel Services.

The crew for this first service were: Captain B. A. W. Monkton, First Officer L.G. Taylor, Radio Operator J. Deuchars, Flight Engineer R. Froggart and Flight Steward J. Dutton.

These early trips were more or less of an exploratory nature, advertised as "Weekends in the South Seas". The flying boat, her crew and passengers would all stay on the Island for three or four days before returning to Sydney. After a couple of these trips, the demand made it quite clear that a regular service would prove viable.

Up until this time T.O.A. had operated with Monkton as pilot and L.G. Taylor as First Officer. It became very obvious that not only more crew would be needed, but another Sunderland would have to be put into service. The commencement of the

T.O.A. service also created the need for a local agent. This position was filled initially by Phil Dignam then later by Hazel and Popie Payten.

Monkton called on another old war-time friend Phil Mathieson, who had returned to his home in Townsville, Queensland. Mathieson had flown flying boats during the war, with most of his hours on Martin Mariner transports. After a chat with his wife, the thought of flying again got the better of him and they made their way to Sydney.

Mathieson made his first trip to the Island with Bryan Monkton on 27 Aug 1947. During this stay their Sunderland *Australis* somehow came loose from her mooring!

Island residents Jim Whistler and the late Mickey Nichols played their part in saving the Sunderland. Jim takes up the story: "I used to get up before first light and walk the beach looking for squid, by far the best bait for fishing. I met the late Mickey Nichols at around 4 a.m., on his way home after his shift as a weather observer. He told me he'd found a flying boat on the beach near Windy Point! We quickly woke the pilots who were staying at the nearby *Pines*. They managed to get aboard start the engines and taxi back to the safety of the mooring."

It was later discovered that a shackle had come loose and the Sunderland had simply drifted in the light westerly wind on to the beach. Luckily the wind was in the west; if it had been from an easterly direction, *Australis* would have almost certainly ended up on the lagoon's coral reef!

Due to their hull shape a Sunderland would always weather cock and point into the wind. This meant if they did break free from their mooring they would usually drift backwards; therefore the stern would be grounded first, and the bow would point towards any oncoming swell. Like the R.A.A.F. Catalina in September 1943, she came ashore near Windy Point; no damage occurred. If the wind and swell had been up, things could have been quite different.

After surviving what could easily have been the end of the service within the first month, T.O.A. began to operate regularly to the Island, firstly with weekly trips, then, in the summer months and school holidays, two to three trips a week.

Phil Mathieson remembers, "It became fairly obvious with our early morning departures we would have to serve some form of breakfast, something simple and not too messy, as the galley was quite limited. We decided on boiled eggs and coffee. From that day until I left, we used the same water from the boiled eggs in the coffee, with no-one the wiser."

On 24 October 1947 the second Sunderland, A26-5, had her conversion completed and entered service. She was registered VH-AKP and given the name *Antillies*. It didn't take long for this boat to get the nickname "The Leaky Seal", due to its drab grey colouring and also due to the amount of water which entered her bilge when she was moored.

The people of the Island were to be surprised and perhaps a little bewildered by the next aircraft to visit, a single engined monoplane which became the first aircraft to land on the Island.

Chapter 10: The First Airstrip

The first airstrip on the Island was in fact the beach which runs almost the entire length of the Lagoon.

On 9 October 1947, the Island's air radio station received an unusual request; the pilot of a small aircraft wanted a report on the condition of the beach and whether or not the sand would be firm enough to permit a landing!

The aircraft was an American-made single-engine Ercoupe piloted by New Zealander Harry Newton. During World War Two, Newton had won a Distinguished Flying Cross, logging some 1,700 hours with the Royal Air Force. Two years after he returned to New Zealand, Newton decided he would return to Europe to visit friends he had made during the war.

Eventually he decided to make his way home. It seemed everyone at the time had similar plans, as all berths south to New Zealand were booked. Newton promptly decided to fly himself home, his only problem being what aeroplane would be suitable for the journey.

In 1940 the Engineering and Research Corporation of Maryland U.S.A. began production of a new and quite advanced aircraft. The Ercoupe featured an all-metal construction with fabric covered control surfaces, tricycle undercarriage, and a unique control system which had no rudder pedals, thus eliminating the pilot's need to coordinate pedals and stick. The rudder and aileron were linked and operated by the control column.

The aeroplane was almost impossible to stall and spin. Due to this, the then minimum qualification time of 35 hours was reduced to 25 hours for those trained on Ercoupes.

Only one hundred and twelve Ercoupes were assembled before wartime restraints halted production. However, after the war the aeroplane was reintroduced. In 1946 over four thousand Ercoupes were made, most being purchased within America.

While staying in Brussels, Newton met a representative of the Ercoupe Company, who was selling and assembling the 75 hp machines in Europe. Newton suggested buying an Ercoupe, then flying the 14,000 odd miles back to New Zealand. After a few raised eyebrows, Newton became the proud owner of a brand new Ercoupe registered 00-EXC. He made a few modifications, fitting extra fuel tanks, a constant speed propeller, artificial horizon and direction finding loop; two instruments which aid flight in bad visibility and over long distances.

Newton set out from Antwerp, to include stop overs at Marseilles, Corsica, Malta, El Adem, Lydda, Shaibah, Sharjah, Karachi, Gwalior, Calcutta, Akyab, Rangoon, Butterworth, Singapore, Palembang, Batavia, Bali, Koepang, Darwin, Katherine, Daly Waters, Camooweal, Rockhampton, then Brisbane, and finally Coffs Harbour!

Newton was nearly home, yet he now faced perhaps the most daunting task, the 1,200 mile leg across the Tasman Sea. He put in a flight plan direct from Coffs Harbour to his home, Urenui Taranaki, on the North Island of New Zealand.

Despite his previous achievements the authorities did not take too kindly to Newton's direct route, and insisted he track north to Norfolk Island, stop for fuel and rest, then complete his journey. Newton resubmitted a flight plan; however he had no intention of going home via Norfolk Island, being a firm believer in the old adage, the shortest route between two places is a straight line.

For the first 200 miles all went well, then an engine cowl latch popped open. With some distance to go, Newton called up Lord Howe Island, asking if the sand was firm enough to permit a landing! Luck was on his side. If the tide had been high, only the steep section of beach, with a lot softer sand, would have been available. A landing on the soft sand would almost definitely prove disastrous.

The little Ercoupe was only on the ground for 15 or so minutes. The offending latch was repaired, and with some help from the ever eager locals, the aeroplane was turned around and took off for New Zealand.

This last leg proved to be the worst of the entire trip. Nearing the east coast of New Zealand, heavy rain and strong winds were encountered; visibility was down to zero. Newton and his faithful Ercoupe were so close, yet he couldn't see a thing. With darkness descending, and fuel getting low, Newton turned back out to sea and retraced his track. After 40 miles he turned north towards Auckland; shortly afterwards he spotted the search lights of Whenuapai airport piercing the gloom.

You can imagine his feelings as he touched down. His epic journey set a record for the lowest powered aeroplane to fly from Europe to New Zealand, which still stands today!

On Lord Howe the local people's lives really began to change. The end of 1947 saw a second airline begin commercial flights to the Island.

Chapter 11: A Second Airline

Q.E.A. joins T.O.A. on the Lord Howe route

Q.E.A. had also begun to branch out it's operations into the Pacific. The airline acquired a number of Catalinas from the R.A.A.F., A24-372 was purchased February 1947, followed by A24-378 in October the same year. Both these machines were the later model PB2B-2, and were registered VH-EAX and VH-EAW respectively.

The Catalinas were flown to Rose Bay, where they were converted to civil airliners. This involved the removal of the front gun turret, and this area was then, faired over with a flush hatch: extra passenger windows and a spartan galley were also fitted.

On 20 November 1947 a non-passenger carrying survey flight to Lord Howe was made under the command of Captain Len Grey. Grey coincidentally had been Phil Mathieson's flight commander at one stage during the war. Catalina VH-EAW returned the following day, the total flying time to the Island and back being 7 hours 38 minutes.

On 3 December 1947 VH-EAW departed on its first passenger carrying flight to the Island. Unfortunately the weather then played its part. The Catalina arrived over the Island, only to find the surface conditions too rough to attempt alighting. Captain Grey had no choice but to return to Sydney, VH-EAW finally arriving at Rose Bay 8 hours and 53 minutes after it had departed.

Things were looking up for the small Island community. In the space of six months they had gone from an infrequent shipping service to, not one, but two major airlines. Mail and freight now arrived on a regular basis; the tourist trade picked up dramatically, as did the construction of buildings for accommodation.

The agents appointed to handle the affairs of Q.E.A. on the Island were Babe and Tom Payten.

1948 looked like being the beginning of a new era of tourism for the community of Lord Howe Island. Sadly this year of prosperity also brought about one of the Island's worst tragedies when on 24 September 1948 R.A.A.F. Catalina A24-381 crashed with the loss of seven of the crew of nine. This tragedy deeply affected the locals, as it was the Cat crews of the R.A.A.F. that proved it possible to operate a safe reliable service. It is perhaps to these men that the commercial operators, who followed, owed their success.

T.O.A. also opened other routes within Australia. On 2 October 1948 the first flight was made to Grafton and Maclean alighting on the Clarence River, which runs between the two towns.

Then on 8 October 1948, T.O.A. announced that P.G.Taylor would join the airline as an active pilot and director. Taylor had written to Monkton commenting, "I liked your spirit and if a place could be found I would like to join the airline". Bryan Monkton grabbed this opportunity with both hands. Not only did he gain a very experienced pilot; the appointment also brought a man with a number of contacts, and, of course, great publicity for the airline.

The airline actively pursued charters to other parts of the world as well. On 25 October 1948, VH-AKO captained by Phil Mathieson, departed for Europe on the first of many immigrant flights. He returned on 5 December 1948 from Augusta, Sicily with 40 new Australians.

On Lord Howe, the increase in tourism did provide a few problems with accommodation. On 5 January 1949 the State Transport Department refused permission for T.O.A. to carry passengers to the Island, stating all available accommodation was booked out. There was however no restriction on freight, this being an area where Q.E.A., with the smaller Catalina, could not compete. On 6 January 1949 VH-AKO, once again skippered by Phil Mathieson, flew to Lord Howe with one thousand eight hundred and forty pounds of freight, and four local people, therefore outside the Transport Department's restriction. This flight set a record of 2 hours 40 minutes! T.O.A. with their much larger Sunderlands, had the edge on Q.E.A., especially when it came to freight.

The Sunderland had been designed for 'Long Range Maritime Patrol', and during the war proved especially successful dropping depth charges in attacks on enemy submarines. A flying boat needed its water tight hull. For obvious reasons, a bomb bay was out of the question. The designers at Short Brothers came up with an ingenious winch system for the delivery of ordnance. An electric powered winch was mounted inside the fuselage directly under the wing. When the Captain gave the order, large hinged doors under each wing would open, the ordnance would then slide out into the slip stream on rails, from which they were dropped, hopefully straddling their target.

This winch system also proved ideal for the loading and unloading of freight. One of the more frequently carried items to Lord Howe in the early days were pianos, which were very popular at the time. These and other heavy items were simply lifted by the winch from inside, then slid out on the rails and lowered to a waiting boat under the wing.

The Island also exported large quantities of produce: fish, as well as Kentia Palm seed and potatoes, were transported to the Sydney markets.

Both T.O.A. and Q.E.A. operated regularly and without mishap until the events of June 1949. Both services had been delayed leaving Sydney due to bad weather. As is often the case in winter, winds from the sou-westerly quarter had meant flying to the Island was out of the question.

Finally on 22 June 1949, with a slight improvement in the weather, Q.E.A. Catalina VH-EAX departed Rose Bay, followed shortly after by T.O.A. Sunderland VH-AKO.

On arrival at the Island the weather was still bad. The Q.E.A. Cat took up the north mooring just off the jetty. The passengers and crew quickly disembarked for warmth and shelter after the rough flight. The T.O.A. Sunderland, under Phil Mathieson's command, arrived shortly afterwards taking up the south mooring in Comet's Hole just south of Rabbit Island.

After seeing his passengers safely ashore, Mathieson elected to keep his crew on-board as he did not like the look of the weather.

This turned out to be a very wise decision. During the night *Australis* broke from her mooring seven times!

For some periods during the night all four engines were run to aid the mooring. The actual mooring chain and buoy stayed firm, the problem was with the lines from the buoy to where they were attached to the flying boat. After all the internal bollards had been damaged, the anchor was used, only to have its winch torn from its mounting bracket.

The final solution was to pay out 100 yards of manilla rope, but with no attachments left, Mathieson lifted the floorboards and tied off to the fuselage stringers.

Without the efforts of Mathieson and his crew *Australis* almost certainly wouldn't have survived the night.

The next morning, with the wind still howling, the passengers for the return flight were quickly ferried aboard, and without waiting for a full tide the flying boat took off for Sydney.

Local newly-weds Jim and Lois Whistler left on this flight for their honeymoon. Lois recalls, "The flight back to Sydney still stands as the worst flight I have ever made from my Island home!"

The Q.E.A. Catalina meanwhile had survived the night with no problems, and with the weather still bad, the crew elected to stay another night and wait for fairer conditions.

VH-EAX did not survive the night! She broke from her mooring and came ashore on the rocky beach just south of the jetty.

She was too badly damaged and unfortunately could not be saved. Q.E.A. engineers came to the Island and salvaged what was of use. The ever industrious locals used what parts they could; a large part of the wing was taken across to the eastern side of the Island, where it was used as a retaining wall near the shelter at Neds Beach.

Chapter 12: The Catalina Incident

As if the loss of an aircraft on the Island wasn't enough, Q.E.A. suffered another blow when the other Catalina used on the route blew up at 2.22 a.m. on 27 August 1949.

VH-EAW had been fueled on the afternoon of the 26 August for an early morning departure for Lord Howe Island. It was discovered when the remains were recovered that a crude battery-powered sparking device had ignited fuel fumes from the smashed glass fuel flow meters in the engineer's compartment. It was quite obvious the explosion had been deliberate.

Before long Bryan Monkton was accused of the sabotage. He fought to get an immediate trial, but was frustrated by many delays. Eventually he stood his trial and, in his own words, "justice prevailed and I was acquitted." The sabotage remains a mystery to this day.

With the loss of not one, but two of their Catalinas in the space of two months, at this time Q.E.A. made its only flights to the Island using their Sandringhams.* One of these, VH-EBX *Pacific Chieftain*, was later to return to the Island in Ansett colours, with the same name, but a different registration: VH-BRE.

The bad publicity following the Catalina incident and T.O.A.'s association with it did irreparable damage to the airline.

Despite the problems, T.O.A. continued to move forward. Late in 1949 VH-AKO and VH-AKP had their names changed to *Samoa Star* and *Tahiti Star* respectively. A third Sunderland, A26-2, was also brought on line, registered VH-BKQ and named *Pacific Star*.** All three flying boats were repainted, the now patchy matt silver being replaced with a more appealing gloss white on the topsides. It was also around this time that the perspex of the turrets was replaced with aluminium plating.

On 2 December 1949 Q.E.A. and T.O.A. agreed to cease competition on the Lord Howe route. A deal was struck where Q.E.A. would operate the New Hebrides on its own, and leave the Lord Howe route to the T.O.A. Sunderlands. New routes also

---

* Author's note. I have not been able to prove whether or not Q.E.A. used their Sandringhams on the Lord Howe route. I am however very confident they did as a number of people on the Island have told me they can remember them.

** The final two ex R.A.A.F. Sunderlands, A26-1 and A26-3, were allotted the civil registrations VH-BKO and VH-BFX respectively. However these two boats where only ever used for spares for the other three Sunderlands.

commenced within Australia. On 24 December 1949, regular services to Port Macquarie and Taree began. On 16 August 1950, a service from Sydney to Hobart was added. On 19 December 1950, the first and faithful VH-AKO *Samoa Star* was retired from service.

On 10 December 1950 British Overseas Airways Corporation (B.O.A.C.) ceased flying boat operations, advertising their remaining boats for sale. The upgrading of the many wartime airstrips on their routes meant flying boats were now superseded by more economical land-based aircraft.

B.O.A.C. operated the last of the long line of the famous Short Brothers flying boats, the Solent. These magnificent machines maintained the appearance of the earlier Sandringham, but differed slightly, having a much deeper hull and the more powerful Bristol Hercules engines. The final version, the Solent Mark 4, had seating in style and comfort for forty-four passengers.

With the expansion of their routes and the future looking prosperous, the opportunity to obtain these machines was seized by T.O.A. With the injection of funds by an English shipping company, The Clan Line, T.O.A. eventually purchased a total of four Solents.

Bryan Monkton made his way to England to ferry the first Solent back to Sydney. This first of the B.O.A.C machines, with the British registration G-AKNO, was obtained on 28 January 1951, given the Australian registration VH-TOA and named *Star of Australia.*

Due to its deeper hull, the Solent never operated to Lord Howe Island; however the last of the Short boats did play a big part in the expansion and eventual demise of T.O.A.

"Lady Luck" deserted Captain Monkton on the ferry flight of VH-TOA back to Australia. On departure from Malta, with thirty nine French building site workers, the newly acquired flying boat struck a large wave which knocked off a float. The Solent rolled over and was lost. Sadly one of the passengers drowned.

The problems continued for T.O.A. on 16 April 1951, when one of the earlier converted Sunderlands bound for Grafton lost a propeller from the port outer engine! Captain H. Broadbent, with twenty five passengers on-board, returned to Rose Bay with no further problem.

On 2 April 1951 the second Solent, G-AKNP, arrived safely from England. She entered service with a flight to Hobart on 2 May 1951. This Solent was given registration VH-TOB, and named *Star of Papua*. She had not long been in service when on 18 June 1951 she struck a fruit boat while taxiing out for take-off from the Brisbane River. The damage put her out of action for several months.

The third ex-B.O.A.C. Solent, G-AHIV, arrived at Rose Bay on 14 July 1951. Registered VH-TOC, she entered service named *Star of Hobart*. She too was also badly damaged on the same stretch of water as her sister before her.

Before first light on the morning of 28 October 1951 she struck a dredge just after lifting off; 15 feet of the starboard wing was completely severed. Captain Mathieson managed to get the aircraft back on the water and with a great amount of skill run her up on the bank. No injury was sustained by either the eight crew or the ten passengers on-board.

The fourth and final ex B.O.A.C Solents G-AHIO was registered VH-TOD on 10 December 1951; she was honoured with the name *Star of Samoa* after the first Sunderland used by the airline. VH-TOD entered service the following day with a flight to Hobart.

1951 was a hard year for T.O.A. when the airline industry was becoming more and more competitive, and land planes becoming more economical. The day of the flying boat was perhaps coming to an end.

Just when the airline didn't need it they received what proved to be the beginning of the end. On 11 February 1952 *Star of Papua* which had been repaired after the damage caused by the fruit boat in Brisbane, lost a propeller from the starboard outer over Bass Strait. Captain A. Frame was en route to Hobart with forty passengers. The Solent alighted without further incident.

Finally an unforeseen world-wide fuel shortage severely curtailed operations. T.O.A. operated until 11 July 1952 when a meeting of shareholders decided to voluntarily liquidate the company.

All through this time, 'AKP' and 'AKO's' replacement, 'BKQ', had maintained the Lord Howe route with very few problems. As things turned out, T.O.A. made a fair profit on the Lord Howe run and lost money on all the others! It was looking as if, through no fault of their own, the people of the Island would lose the air service they had, in such a short time, become very attached to!

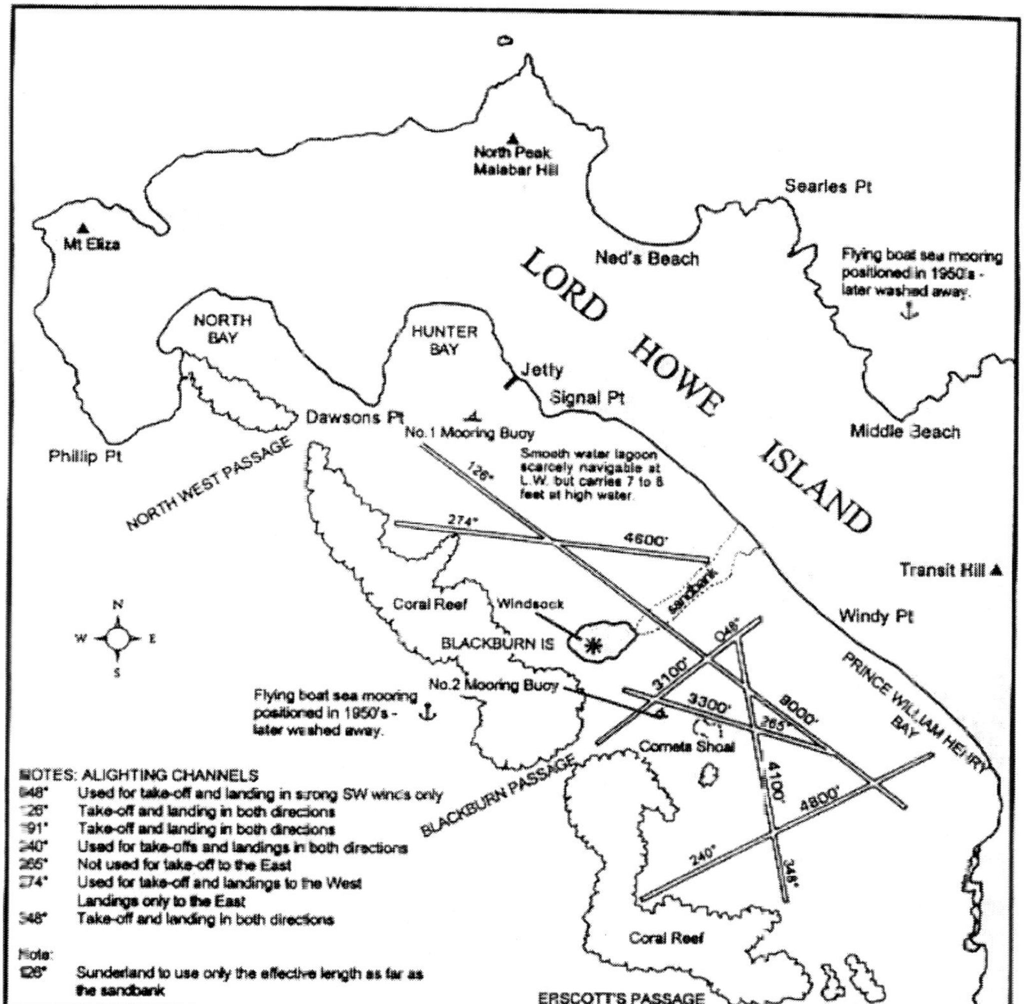

Lord Howe Island alighting areas surveyed for the Trans Oceanic operation of Sunderlands on the lagoon. By the 1950's these runways had been changed. See map on page 81.

Courtesy John Wilson

AT LEFT: Early photo of a Bristol Pegasus powered Sunderland.
author's collection

BELOW: T.O.A. Sunderland *Australis* on the lagoon.
courtesy Hazel Payten

T.O.A. Sunderland on the north mooring.

courtesy Hazel Payten

Harry Newton's Ercoupe on the beach in 1947.

author's collection

T.O.A. Sunderland takes on departing passengers, note the people leaning out the bomb bay door.

courtesy Hazel Payten

Tahiti Star formerly *Antilles* coming in to alight.

Arthur Le Navez

Q.E.A. Catalina VH-EAX on the beach near the jetty.

Arthur Le Navez

"Well we'll have to stay longer." Stranded visitors in front of VH-EAX.

courtesy John Wilson

Q.E.A. PB2B-2 Catalina ex R.A.A.F. A24-372.

courtesy Arthur Le Navez

Barrier Reef Airways Sandringham VH-BRD on a Trans Oceanic Charter.

courtesy John Wilson

VH-BRD *Capricorn* departs the island.

courtesy Arthur Le Navez

Capricorn was later to sink at her mooring on the Brisbane River.

courtesy John Wilson

Qantas Sandringham VH-EBV *Pacific Warrior* about to alight on the Brisbane River.

courtesy John Wilson

T.O.A. Solent on the Brisbane River.

courtesy John Wilson

Chapter 13: The Last Big Boat Service in the World

With the demise of T.O.A. the people of Lord Howe were not, as perhaps might be expected, "left in the lurch".

Stewart Middlemiss, Bryan Monkton's wartime friend, had been operating his airline, Barrier Reef Airways (B.R.A.), using two ex-R.A.A.F. Catalinas to Heron, Lindeman and Daydream Islands, off the Queensland coast. In addition to his Cats, Middlemiss also acquired two Short Sandringhams from T.E.A.L. ZK-AMH *Auckland* he renamed *Beachcomber* VH-BRC and ZK-AME *New Zealand* he renamed *Capricorn* VH-BRD. As stated earlier, this boat was lost when she sank at her mooring on the Brisbane River in October 1952. A replacement was acquired from Qantas* *Pacific Chieftain* VH-EBX. This machine had also formerly been with T.E.A.L. as ZK-AMD *Australia* Middlemiss kept the name *Pacific Chieftain*, however she was re-registered as VH-BRE.

To finance the purchase of these Sandringhams, Middlemiss was forced to sell shares in his B.R.A. to Reginald Ansett who at the time owned a small land plane airline which was showing potential. In 1953, Ansett purchased the liquidated T.O.A., along with the Rose Bay Flying Boat Base licence. Not long after this, he became the major shareholder in B.R.A. In 1957 Australian National Airways came under his control.

Two of the pilots at this time were Ron Gillies, who had flown with 10 Squadron alongside Vic Hodgkinson during the war, and Lloyd Maundrell, who was to stay on the Lord Howe route until the end of the service in 1974. For the entire period of the Ansett service the co-pilots came and went; the captains did not change very much at all.

The pilots were not the only crew to fall under the flying boat's spell. After three personal interviews Margaret Holle presented herself at the Rose Bay Flying Boat Base to take up her position as an Air Hostess. The following text is an extract written by Margaret who has kindly allowed the author to use it.

---

* By the 1950's Qantas Empire Airways was generally referred to as Qantas. In 1952 the airline made this their official name.

"Flying Boat Memories" By Margaret (Bellingham) Holle

Arriving at the Flying Boat Base I was overwhelmed with new sounds and smells. The Stewards were loading the aircraft with food for the outward and return flights. In the terminal there was a Hostess serving complimentary tea and biscuits to the passengers and their families. The passengers had often come a long way in the early hours of the morning.

I was immediately seconded to help and I was soon getting in everyone's way so I was directed to take tea to the Captain who I was told was upstairs. I was pointed in the direction of the door and told the stairs were outside. I wandered around feeling rather foolish, the tea began to get cold and eventually I found myself facing the water and a ladder! It seemed to lead to the roof. Surely I was not meant to climb up there with a cup and saucer?

I stood there trying to make up my mind what to do and was rescued by Norman Lynch from the Department of Civil Aviation (D.C.A.). He saw my dilemma and showed me the narrowest little stairway I have ever seen. It did lead upstairs. I still maintain I was set up by the Stewards! Captain Les Butterworth was in the tower getting the weather reports and doing the flight plan for our intended flight.

The views were marvellous; it was a beautiful morning and Sydney Harbour was glistening in all its splendour. Next we were off to board the aircraft. What a sight it was resting there in the dock gently rocking in the morning breeze.

From the floating dock it was a big step on board and then one more and I was in the entryway. In front of me were the two powder rooms (that's what they were called), to my left in the nose was the bow where the anchor and drogues were stored. Beside this was the freight locker also in the nose. The aircraft was literally a flying boat with all the structure of a boat, i.e. bilges, bulkheads and a galley etc. It had two decks and both aircraft I worked had galleys upstairs. These were VH-BRC and VH-BRE *Beachcomber* and *Pacific Chieftain*. The configuration were the same, however, there were subtle differences; I always preferred BRE and I don't know why.

The flightdeck was also upstairs. The entrance to the flight deck was from a ladder in the entry adjacent to one of the toilets. It was quite large with accommodation for the two pilots, flight engineer and on international flights a navigator. The engineer's panel was rear facing.

The flightdeck was also the host to many a visitor. The crews who flew these giant boats were always very generous with their time and allowed many visitors access. It was only ever in bad weather or during check or training flights that passengers were not made welcome. Many a flight to Lord Howe Island was livened up by visits to the cockpit of the young women on board. Full skirts were the dress of the day and the girls queued up to visit the crew. Halfway up the ladder the pilots would open a window (these aircraft were not pressurised) and Whoosh! up the skirts would go over their heads catching them completely by surprise. They would then have to climb the rest of the way holding their skirts down and blushing madly. Of course by the time they arrived the window had been shut and they were none the wiser!

On my first flight, as I was only in training and not needed in the cabin, Les Butterworth and Ron Gillies invited me upstairs for the take-off. I can assure you that it was something I will never forget.

We taxied out into Sydney Harbour; the runway had already been laid down by the D.C.A. crew who manned the two boats that were always there for our departures and arrivals. For our early morning flights to Lord Howe Island and evening arrivals at Rose Bay, the runway was a flare path. On subsequent early morning departures, Sydney Harbour was like fairyland. Daylight departures were also fantastic, cruising around the harbour.

The Captain, First Officer and Engineer went through all their pre-flight checks, the Steward was in the bow looking up at us through the hatch, waiting for the signal to release the bow line and store it. The tail line was released; this was a little hook on the rear underbelly of the fuselage that was called the "Cockie's Beak".

Once in a while it would fail to release and either the Engineer or Steward would have to run through to the back of E cabin, down the steps, into the rear freight locker, over the baggage and up into the tail to unhook it manually. This was always disconcerting for the pilots as the poor old aircraft would be trying to go forward and of course as it was still hitched up it couldn't. Also a little startling for the passengers was the Steward or Engineer thundering through and disappearing into the rear hold. Passengers were always fascinated to hear what was happening and liked to be well informed. It was often a first flight for many and so I guess it was just as exciting for them as it was for me.

Back to take-off … We taxied around and then started our run-up gathering speed and roaring along through the water and waiting for the inevitable lift-off. I was supposed to be strapped in like everyone else but of course I wasn't. I would not have had the thrill that was to come if I had been. I stood between the two pilots, hanging on to the backs of their chairs, and finally we were airborne. WOWEE! I was on my way. I could not believe that here I was having the most thrilling time and they were going to pay me for it!

Landings, I was to discover, were just as exciting. Once, approaching Lord Howe Island from the back and coming in skimming over the palms, I was sitting on the jump seat in B cabin and a lady opposite looked up and said: "If we don't hurry up and land, we'll be in the water." I could only reply, "I certainly hope so."

I was only on trial for this job as it did not suit everyone. The work was constant, meals were all prepared on board. Carrying food and drinks up and down the stairs in high heels was not always easy. The days could be very long in unpressurised conditions.

The aircraft consisted of five cabins which were known as A, B, C, D and E. The first cabin at the front was A and seated eight people. Next was B with three forward facing seats and one sideways-facing seat. (I called it the Barber's Chair). Across the aisle was a single rear facing seat and a pulldown cabin attendant's seat.

C cabin had eight seats, four forward facing seats and four rear facing (one on the aisle) on the port side. D cabin was great, it was at the rear and seated seven people comfortably. E cabin was upstairs and always seemed to be a favourite cabin, it seated fourteen. The back step into the tail also had a seat belt for cabin staff. Forty two seats in all.

Seats were not allocated until the passengers were on board. We knew which cabins were best suited to the people's needs. C cabin was quite cramped and it was not a good idea to have anyone in there with long legs. Also anyone who was on the large side because it was sometimes awkward to get out. The rest of the cabins were quite roomy.

Cabin A could be quite cool as it was closer to the front and seemed to be draughty, especially on early winter mornings. Cabin D was always thought to be best suited to anyone travelling with young children because of the space it afforded."

In 1963 Margaret married Noel Holle, an Engineer and Chief Maintenance Inspector at Rose Bay. Noel worked there from 1947 to 1974 with Qantas, T.O.A. and Ansett. It was due to the efforts of people like Noel Holle that these aircraft were able to be preserved as they are today.

As land planes became more efficient, all flying boat operations throughout Australia, and the rest of the world, gradually reduced until only the Lord Howe route remained. The advertising power of Ansett promoted not only the Island and its natural attractions, but also the unique form of transport by which passengers were taken to the Island. *Beachcomber* and *Pacific Chieftain* continued the service with few hitches and surprising reliability until the weather once again took its toll in the winter of 1963.

On 3 July 1963 *Pacific Chieftain* had stayed overnight, only to be torn from her mooring by a violent storm. Once again it was the winter westerlies that did the damage. The following morning the crew, passengers and local people were greeted by a sad sight. The port float had been smashed off; she lay on the badly damaged wingtip with the wind and rising tide threatening further damage. A hasty decision was made to return her to the water as soon as possible. Sand bags were placed above the intact starboard float; with the tide rising, a concerted effort was made by all to prepare her for a return to the ocean; then with the tide at its height, all four engines were used to pull her back into the lagoon.

She was taxied around to the more sheltered water of Sylph's Hole, off Old Settlement Beach. Little else could be done until her sister ship *Beachcomber* could fly in a new float and rigging. The next morning the same feelings felt by Chichester and the local people thirty two years earlier were again experienced.

The wind and waves had torn at the good starboard float and with the extra weight of the sand bags on the wing above, this float had given way. The starboard wing had submerged past the outer engine and the end of the wing was badly damaged by the rock and coral. The Ansett engineers arrived on the Island only to declare what most already knew: *Pacific Chieftain* was a write off!

The service could not continue with only the one boat. As salvage of all useable items from the now beached *Pacific Chieftain* began, so to did a world wide search for a replacement. The problem was that in 1963 there weren't many 1940s vintage flying boats left! The few that did had long since ceased flying and were now treasured museum pieces.

It turned out help was not far away. The Royal New Zealand Air Force (R.N.Z.A.F.) had in 1953 purchased sixteen refurbished military Sunderlands. The 'Kiwis' had used the boats with great success as transports. The R.N.Z.A.F. provided emergency services to many communities of the South Pacific which come under their protection. Being able to alight on the many sheltered lagoons of the area, they proved ideal for the variety of tasks they were asked to perform. The R.N.Z.A.F. Sunderlands were all retired by the mid 1960s and put into storage.

The New Zealand Government agreed to sell one Sunderland; NZ 4108 was selected. Captain Stewart Middlemiss and his crew made their way across the Tasman and delivered her to Ansett's Rose Bay workshop.

NZ 4108 was a military Sunderland, and while she did not have the middle upper turret, she was still fitted with the nose and rear turrets; her interior was that of a spartan yet functional Warbird. By this time all useable items from the stricken *Pacific Chieftain* had been ferried back to Rose Bay on board *Beachcomber*.

On the Island, approaches were made to Ansett to keep the hull of *Pacific Chieftain* with the idea of converting her to a museum, which at that time the Island did not have. Sadly these requests fell on deaf ears. The now-butchered old girl was to be towed to sea and scuttled.

Island resident Brian Simpson, known to all as *Carter* remembers what he believes has been one of the saddest jobs he has ever been asked to do:

"We were given these fine axes by the D.C.A. to chop holes in the old girl's skin; I climbed aboard knowing full well that the axe was going to a more caring home after this unpleasant deed. I was one of the last to step off into the waiting launch, I gave one last swing for good luck, the axe slipped from my hand, and beat everything to the bottom!"

All previous conversions of the military Sunderland to their close relative, the civil Sandringham, had been performed by the flying boat's manufacturer, Short Brothers. Rochester in the United Kingdom was considered too far away, and Ansett needed the boat urgently.

In September 1964 VH-BRF, appropriately named *Islander*, emerged from the Rose Bay hangar. The Ansett engineers had kept her bulbous Sunderland nose, to allow for the many items of bulky freight she would be required to carry to the Island. For fourteen months *Beachcomber* had continued the service alone, a credit to her design, and the people who maintained her. It is interesting to note the only difference between the handling of the two boats, both in the air and on the water, was that *Islander* was a little bit more susceptible to crosswinds when taxiing, due to her larger profiled nose area. Once airborne the two machines were identical to fly.

The service could now again return to normality, with *Islander* following on where *Pacific Chieftain* left off. Little did the people of the Island know *Islander* was to follow in *Pacific Chieftain's* webbed footsteps in more ways than one.

In May 1965, *Islander* stayed overnight after returning from a charter flight from Fiji back to Australia. Sure enough, that night a severe blow broke her from her mooring and she was driven up on the beach at Windy Point! Only eight months on the route and she was washed ashore at almost the exact same place as her predecessor.

Ansett, and the local people, now knew from previous experience, to first repair the damage then return her to the water. *Islander* was pulled above the high tide mark. The damage was not as bad as had first appeared. This time the starboard float had been knocked off, however, the wing only suffered minor damage at its tip. For the second time *Beachcomber* was asked to provide the service on her own. With an extensive effort by all, *Islander* was only on the beach for ten days before being flown back to Sydney for more extensive repairs and back into service.

Reliable *Beachcomber* also suffered some damage—whilst unloading one of the passengers noticed water coming up through the floor.

Jack O'Brien was the Flight Engineer on this trip. He takes up the story: "As we came to take up the mooring, the shackle from the mooring chain had flicked up, and without our knowledge, punched a hole in the skin directly under the boarding door. The first we knew of the problem was as the passengers walked forward the last few noticed their feet were getting wet! As soon as all the passengers were clear we started all the engines and hurriedly motored over to Old Settlement and ran her up on the beach."

Island resident and the Marine Section Coxswain, Harry Woolnough came up with the idea of a plywood patch on either side of the hole, with seat foam as packing in between. With a number of people's assistance the temporary repairs proved successful. The bilge was pumped out, and she was refloated. The following day *Beachcomber* flew back to Sydney with a full complement of passengers for more permanent repairs.

By now the people of Lord Howe had become very attached to *Islander* and *Beachcomber*. They had begun to believe they had a form of ownership over the old girls. Not only did they bring the all-important visitors and mail, they also provided a regular freight service. The demand for freight also contributed to the efficiency of the airline, as there was always a backlog of freight at Rose Bay waiting to go to the Island. If there wasn't a full load of passengers extra freight would be taken, in the later years livestock, building material and motor bikes were among some of the items carried.

Over the years the Island people formed many long-standing friendships with the crews, occasionally being invited up to the flight deck for a take-off or alighting. Gower Wilson took such an opportunity on one of his many flights to and from his Island home.

Gower takes up the story: "The flight back to Lord Howe was full, the skipper Keith Mansfield invited me to take a seat in the bridge for the flight home.* We hadn t long left Rose Bay and started our climb to cruise altitude; the Captain ordered the flaps to be retracted."

Sunderlands and Sandringhams have huge Fowler flaps which slide out and angle down at the trailing edge of the wing, helping by creating lift on take-off and slowing the aircraft on approach when alighting.

Gower continues: "The electric motor which operates the flaps is mounted in the roof behind the pilots. The flaps clunked into the retracted position, however the motor did not turn off! Smoke started to billow about the bridge until finally the power supply was cut and we all settled down. Who knows what they were thinking down in the passenger compartment! Of course we couldn't continue the journey so we made our way back to the harbour. Without flaps, and full fuel, the crew had a few concerns, however after an extended alighting run we safely returned to the mooring for repairs."

The arrival on the Island was a big event, almost all the visitors and residents would go to the jetty or The Flagstaff, a small headland south of the jetty which overlooks the lagoon. The thundering four engines of the ships of the sky gave ample warning of their imminent arrival.

David Murray was employed by Ansett for over twenty years as their agent on the Island. He arranged for a sign to be erected on the small terminal building near the jetty, which read, "Welcome to Lord Howe Island". This became a common greeting, still used to this day. While obvious it perhaps meant more than it implied, when greeted by the more than welcoming people of the Island.

The agent often had to warn all the guesthouse owners of delays. This involved riding his push bike from one end of the Island to the other at very early hours, calling through bedroom windows, "twenty four hour delay" in the event of a flight not leaving the mainland for what-ever reason. David Murray later graduated to a small motor scooter and on many occasions was assisted in this task by the late Frank Charters, a long-time visitor to the Island.

Departing visitors were regularly given leis of locally grown hibiscus and frangipani flowers. It became an Island tradition that these leis be cast to sea as you were ferried out to the flying boat. If the leis washed ashore the people who had been

*The cockpit of a flying boat was often referred to as the bridge as flying boats are ships.

wearing it would also one day return to the Island shores. Many of these people have returned and to this day the flying boats hold a special place in the hearts and minds of those who were lucky enough to travel on them.

If you have visited Lord Howe Island it is easy to imagine why this is so. With its stunning natural beauty, clean white sandy beaches, palm lined roads and tranquil south sea Island pace, Lord Howe has it all! Travelling to such a destination and alighting on the lagoon on board the graceful and majestic flying boats could only have enhanced such a holiday.

Ansett newspaper advertisment

source unknown

Chapter 14: Crop Duster on the Cricket Pitch

On 7 March 1968 the local people were to be surprised by what became the second fixed wing aircraft to land on the Island before an airstrip had been constructed.

The pilot, Derek Stubbs, was in the process of ferrying a Fletcher crop duster ZK-BIP from his homeland, New Zealand, via Norfolk Island to Australia. The Pacific-Aerospace Fletcher FU-24 was purpose built for crop dusting. Directly behind the cockpit is a huge hopper. This is loaded on the ground from above then the contents is sprayed from the underside when airborne. This hopper can also easily be used as a fuel tank for long range ferry flights.

A number of people witnessed the Fletcher overfly the Island. Gower Wilson was helping unload the regular freight ship the *Jacques Del Mar* and remembers the events of the day well.

"Firstly he overflew the Island in a westerly direction at quite a low altitude. An hour or so later someone came down to the jetty saying the aircraft was returning and had asked where he might be able to land! Apparently he had come across a wall of weather and after a few attempts had been unable to penetrate it. Without fuel to return to Norfolk, he had no choice but to attempt a landing on Lord Howe."

It was decided the best place was a small clear area between the lagoon beach and the road near the cricket oval, coincidentally not far from where the only other fixed wing aircraft (also piloted by a 'Kiwi') had landed more than twenty years earlier. White markers were placed at either end of the area and after a couple of passes to have a close look the Fletcher landed with ease.

After a two day wait for the weather to clear Stubbs made ready for his departure.

Gower continues, "It was decided he'd get a longer take-off run if he took off across the oval; the fence was dismantled and the Fletcher was moved down to the south eastern corner. With the brakes on, full power was applied. The aircraft took off with ease and completed its journey to the mainland safely."

Chapter 15: Flying Boat Culture

The difficult nature of the operation also added adventure for some visitors. The take-off time from the mainland was determined by the tide on the Island. This meant take-offs were very often as early as 2 am should the high tide be at dawn on the Island. On a number of occasions a flying boat would leave Sydney at an early hour, fly out to the Island, only to find the weather had deteriorated and the lagoon had become too rough for a safe alighting to be made!

The author's wife Janine went to boarding school in Sydney and recalls quite clearly such an incident.

"The taxi dropped me off at the Rose Bay terminal around 8 a.m., soon after we were winging our way home. After three and a half bumpy hours we passed close by the Island. After another pass an announcement was made and we set our course back to Sydney. After seven weary hours I stepped off at Rose Bay only to be told, "See you tomorrow and we'll try again."

Keith Mansfield captained the Ansett boats on the route for over ten years. He got even closer and still had to return to Sydney!

"We arrived over the Island to be greeted by a strong southerly wind with a large swell. The wind wasn't a problem: the swell sweeping across the lagoon was our main concern. The trick in these conditions was to put the hull down just in front of the crest and stay there until you lost enough speed to allow her to settle. If the hull moved off the crest of the swell, a float could easily catch which would be disastrous. We ended up touching down on three separate occasions; each time I was not happy so I "poured on the coal" and went around for another go. After the third attempt I decided it was too risky and reluctantly made the announcement to the passengers that we were returning to Sydney."

When new guests did eventually arrive, they would be taken to their recently vacated rooms at the various guesthouses. Occasionally a crew would elect not to leave. They could have an engine problem, the weather may have deteriorated, or due to a hold up, the tide may have gone out too far to allow a safe take-off. I have been told on more than one occasion a boat overnighted because a pilot fancied an Island girl! (Officially a technical problem)

This, of course, created a problem with the out-going guests, their old rooms now occupied by the new visitors. If it was the busy season it was not uncommon for guests to be billeted at the local people's private homes. If these became full guests slept in the bars and games rooms of their guesthouse. Not one person ever complained; after all it meant another day on the Island. The people it did upset were at Ansett, who picked up the tab.

The harbour waters of Sydney were too congested to allow operations on the weekends, so this left the Island people free to arrange all sorts of sporting and social events. In the evenings the whole Island, from babies to the elderly, attended dances which went to the early hours. During the day picnics, sailing regattas and cricket matches were arranged. It is no wonder the people of Lord Howe treated the old girls as their own; they played such an important part in their lives.

Chapter 16: The End of an Era

By the 1970's the government had begun to subsidise Ansett Flying Boat Services, as maintaining 1940's vintage flying boats as well as their Rose Bay Base cost a lot of money. Many of Sydney's residents, as well as the Harbour Authorities, were keen to see the flying boats go. The flying boats needed large areas of water when taking off and alighting, thus restricting water bound traffic. As for the residents the early morning noise of four 1,200 hp Pratt and Whitneys was not to their liking. On the other hand many residents saw the flying boats as much a part of Sydney Harbour as the Opera House and the Bridge! Despite their popularity, the "powers that be" began to look long and hard at building an airstrip on the Island, thus doing away with the harbour problems and eliminating the costly subsidy.

Phil Dengate worked as Passenger Services Officer at the Rose Bay Base from 1972 to the end of the service. Phil remembers an amusing phone call just after an early morning departure.

"It was a warm summer night, the flying boat had taken off from down near the bridge heading in an easterly direction, scraping over the roof tops of Dover Heights. With the humidity and heavy load it often took some time for the old girls to climb away. I was finalising a few things when the phone rang; on the other end a gentleman asked, 'Would you mind telling me the name of the captain who just took off in that flying boat?' I replied, 'Why do you ask?' He answered with, 'Because the next time that fellow flies through my front door, down the hall and out the back door I'd like to know his name so I can offer him a cup of coffee!'"

Finally the unfortunate but inevitable. In March 1974 a detachment of the Army's First Field Engineer Regiment arrived on the Island and began clearing a three thousand foot area from the middle of Blinky Beach in the east, diagonally across the Island to the Windy Point area in the west.

Many of the Island people looked upon the airstrip with apprehension. The first concern was whether the small aircraft could keep up with the demand. Secondly, due to the hilly surrounds and weather, the pilots who were to use it would have to be very competent.

So the days of *Beachcomber* and *Islander* were numbered. Ansett regrettably put the much travelled and loved old girls up for sale. An entrepreneurial American named Charles Blair made an offer which was accepted. His company, Antillies Airboats, had plans to fly luxury charters in the Caribbean.

Islander was pulled up on to the slip at Rose Bay for the last time; preparations for her long flight across the Pacific were begun. It would be left to *Beachcomber*, the longest serving on the route, to close down the last big boat service in the world.

It then seemed as if the Island itself made its claim on the beloved flying boats. In May 1974 *Beachcomber* was washed ashore in a severe storm. All three of the Ansett boats had now spent time on the beach. *Beachcomber* came up just north of 'Cobby's Corner', not far from the nearly completed airstrip. She suffered somewhat more than her sisters before her; the starboard float was knocked off and the leading edge, along with the wing tip were badly damaged.

Islander was rapidly returned to service but it took three months to repair *Beachcomber*. Finally, in August, VH-BRC was repaired; the heavy beaching wheels were fitted under the wings and the smaller trolley under her stern. With two launches attached to her bow and the afternoon sun glistening off her hull, her four Pratt and Whitneys roaring, she proudly entered the waters of the lagoon.

On 10 September 1974 *Beachcomber* left the Island with a full complement of passengers for the last time. Her last departure is best described by Island resident Jim Whistler, who then and still does at the time of writing, produce the Island's paper 'The Signal'.

Flying boat *Beachcomber,* which less than three months ago almost ended her days on the Lagoon beach, arrived shortly after noon and many residents were on the foreshore to see the historic last landing. The plane's crew, tourists and residents gathered at the jetty area for a light snack and cuppa. Speaking on behalf of the Island Committee, Mr J. Whistler said:

> "Flying boats have been coming here for 27 years ... that is at least one third of the lifetime of us all ... in fact it is the complete lifetime of many gathered here today ... the flying boat is very much part of our life and I feel quite inadequate as I attempt to express our thoughts at this time.
>
> The boats have made more than 5,000 flights to the Island and have brought close on 200,000 tourists to our shores ... our whole way of life has been linked to the flying boat service. We will carry on without the flying boats ...we must look to the future with confidence. But I doubt if any of us realise just how much we are going to miss the boats. I venture to say that we will indeed be lucky if the future brings us the enjoyment, comradeship, safety and economic security that the flying boat era has given us. We have already during past weeks said thank you and farewell to those who have been responsible for the operation of the flying boat service. We are grateful to Committee members Phil Dignam and Bill Retmock who have, with the help of others, arranged this gathering today. But how do you say farewell to a flying boat? In less than an hour's time Captain Lloyd Maundrell and Captain Bill Wilcher will fly

Beachcomber out of our lives. It will be a historic moment. I suppose that it is a privilege to witness and be part of this historic moment.

We wish it didn't have to happen!

Mr Phil Dignam speaking on behalf of the residents of the Island, then paid tribute to the service rendered to the community by Mr David Murray In his capacity as Island Manager for Airlines of New South Wales, Mr Dignam said that the service rendered had always greatly exceeded duty. He told David that the community wished to thank him for a job well done.

The only bright spot on this sad day is that you are going to spend your retirement living among us.

Mr Dignam then called on Mr H. Ward, Island Superintendent, to present Mr Murray with a token of the community's appreciation. Mr Ward supported Mr Dignam's remarks and noted that David organised the unloading and loading of the flying boats so smoothly that it was only during his absence on leave that residents realised what a good job he did!

Mr Ward told David that many innovations introduced by him were appreciated ... especially the "Welcome to Lord Howe Island" which was the greeting each arrival received on the jetty steps.

Replying, Mr Murray said that he too will miss the flying boats. He said that he greatly appreciated the gift and gesture from Island residents.

The Flagstaff Hill was crowded as *Beachcomber* took off towards the south-west, turned, banked over Dawsons Point and headed for the Flagstaff and then flew right along the lagoon that had been the site for so many graceful landings. There was no cheer from those on Flagstaff Hill, but there were heavy hearts and many a tear."

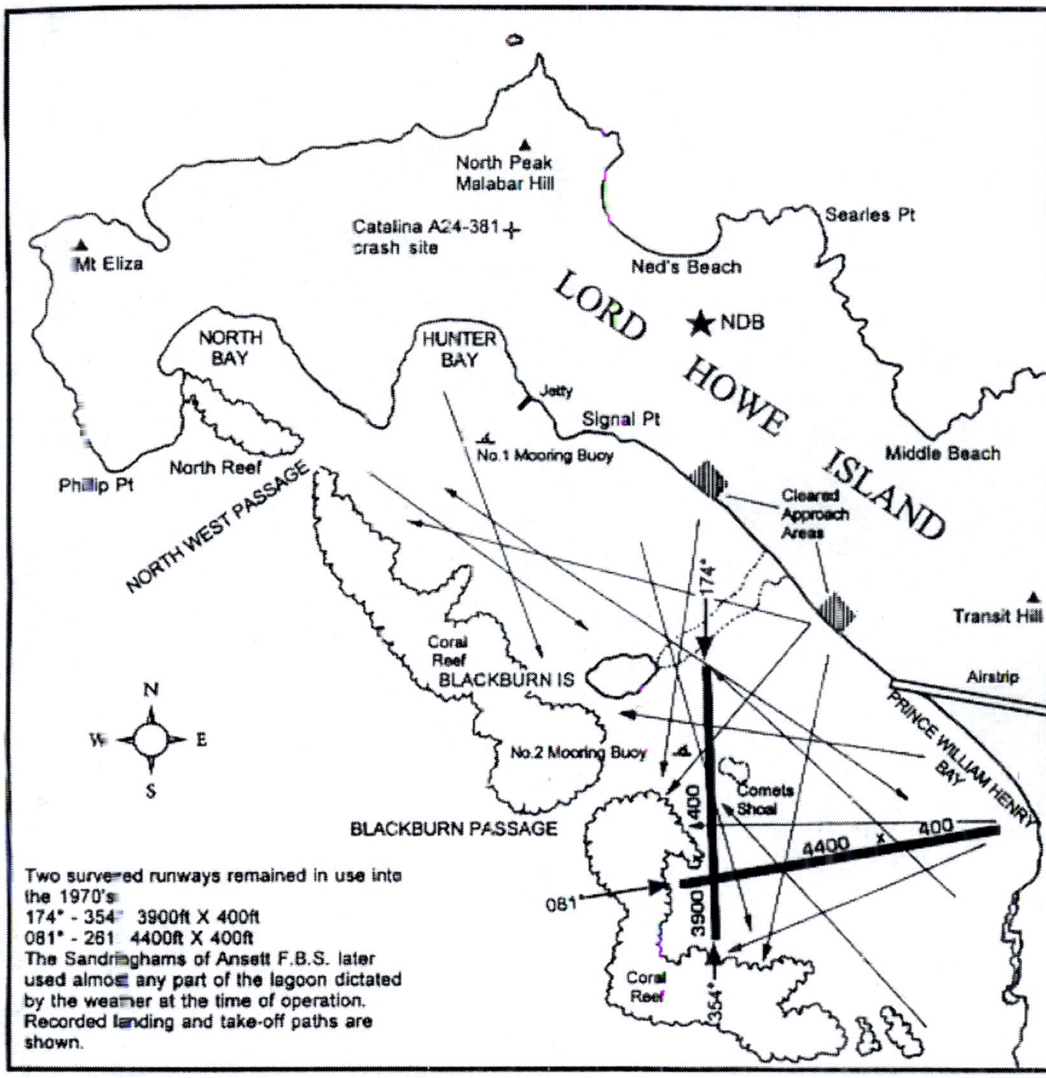

By the late 1950's the runway pattern at Lord Howe Island had changed considerably with aircraft using almost all parts of the lagoon.

Courtesy John Wilson

VH-BRC *Beachcomber* this Sandringham was to fly to the island for the best part of twenty one years.

courtesy Arthur Le Navez

Ansett Sandringham, at the start of her take-off run off the jetty

author's collection

VH-BRE *Pacific Chieftain* on the hard stand at Rose Bay.

courtesy John Wilson

Passengers' view from a Sandringham

courtesy Mary Biddle

Beachcomber on the north mooring.

author's collection

Pacific Chieftain washed ashore in 1963.

courtesy Hazel Payten

Locals working under the port wing.

author's collection

Pacific Chieftain was refloated without her port float.

author's collection

VH-BRE: in Sylphs hole after the starboard float had given way.

courtesy Hazel Payten

The Sandringham is pulled ashore to be salvaged.

courtesy John Wilson

All usable items were removed as a world wide search began for a replacement.

author's collection

Pacific Chieftain is scuttled west of the Island — see also pictures next page

courtesy Janine Phillipps

ABOVE and BELOW: The sad end to a once proud queen of the skies. *Pacific Chieftain* is scuttled west of the island — see also picture previous page

courtesy Janine Phillipps

courtesy Janine Phillipps

A replacement was not far away ex R.N.Z.A.F. Sunderland N.Z.4108 after she arrived at Rose Bay.

Keith Brent

The military Sunderland was soon to lose its nose and rear turret.

Keith Brent

After only a year and a half of ownership *Islander* was washed ashore

courtesy John Wilson

Islander on the beach at Windy Point

courtesy Kerry McFadyen

Group of locals act as counter balance on the port wingtip.
courtesy Kerry McFadyen

Starboard float repaired *Islander* is ready to return to the sea
courtesy Lord Howe Island Museum

Fletcher cropduster flies down the lagoon, *Jacques Del Ma*r outside the reef.

courtesy Hazel Payten

Fletcher about to land.

courtesy Hazel Payten

The author s wife looks the other way in excitement.

courtesy Janine Phillipps

ZK-BIP crossing the road on its take-off run to the west.

courtesy Janine Phillipps

Beachcomber with a D.C.A. launch on Sydney Harbour.

courtesy John Wilson

VH-BRF *Islander* on the lagoon.

Ron Cuskelly

Beachcomber on the beach north of Cobby's Corner.

Mick Bloomfield

An army bulldozer along with her engines return VH-BRC to the ocean.

courtesy John Wilson

Beachcomber on the step with the *Lulawai* in the foreground.

Mick Bloomfield

Islander and *Beachcomber* on the lagoon.

author's collection

Islander makes her last pass over the newly finished airstrip.

courtesy Hazel Payten

Beachcomber's last departure from the island September 1974.

courtesy Hazel Payten

Epilogue

It would be silly to suggest that this is the Island's early aviation history in its entirety. It is more the collection of a few people's memories of an era which eventually became an important part of their lives. It also should be considered that as we are all individuals, a person may see and describe the same event in quite a different manner to another, even so you can't do any better than an eyewitness

By far the most pleasurable part of researching and writing this book has been talking and corresponding with many of the people who played their part in this unique piece of history. The least enjoyable task was finding a date for an event from one source then finding the same event with a different date elsewhere; hopefully there are not many errors.

Elsewhere in the world flying boat operations had long gone due mainly to the better economics of land-based aircraft. The operation continued until September 1974, which means many of the people who made trips on the aircraft are present on the Island today. I believe Lord Howe would contain the largest number of ex-big boat passengers than any other community anywhere else in the world.

Of course this history would not have been possible if it weren't for the Island, and more importantly, its lagoon, initially no suitable area was available for a runway, flying boats were the only solution. There is also the importance of the fact that the Island is so naturally unique in many areas and rightly had to be protected.

It must be remembered that the Sandringham evolved from the Sunderland which first flew before the outbreak of World War Two. They were still flying to the Island in the 1970's. Everywhere else in Australia (in fact the world) these magnificent old aircraft had long since been replaced by more modern land-based aircraft.

If you ever visit Lord Howe Island you will immediately be impressed by the diverse natural beauty. To visit via a four engine flying boat and alight on the aqua coloured lagoon must have enhanced such a visit.

Due to the efforts of a number of people from both the Island and mainland the events of the pioneers of the Island's aviation history have been celebrated and remembered.

There are also a number of remnants of this bygone era held either by the Island's Museum or in forward thinking people's private collections.

Francis Chichester

You would think it unlikely seventy years after the event that anything would be left of Francis Chichester's "Gipsy Moth". However after a chat on the subject with my good mate Ian Fitzgerald, I was shown a piece of fabric, which Ian's grandfather, Alec Innes, had kept as a souvenir in 1931. Ian's father Jim had spotted it in an old shed which was being knocked down during the airstrip's construction in 1974, he put it aside, and it is now safely preserved in his possession.

In 1988 as part of Australia's bicentennial celebrations Boyd Munro flew a "Tiger Moth", which he had won in an air race, across the Tasman Sea via Norfolk and Lord Howe Island re-enacting Chichester's flight. Munro named his little biplane *Lady Sheila* after Chichester's widow. He safely completed the journey and still owned and flew aircraft in the 1990's.

Catalina A24-381

The remains of R.A.A.F. Catalina A24-381 are still able to be viewed in the paddock where they fell in 1948. Although there is very little recognisable of the smashed remains, the nose turret somehow survived not only the crash but also 48 years of salt air, wind and sun.

Early in 1996 the R.A.A.F. began a static restoration of a civil Catalina to military standards. When the work is completed the amphibian will be displayed at the R.A.A.F. Museum at Point Cook in Victoria, where it will stand as a monument to those who fought, flew and died in Catalinas during their service with the R.A.A.F. The task of restoring the Catalina was given to 23 Squadron based at R.A.A.F. Base Amberley in Queensland, the Restoration Project Manager being Group-Captain L. Armstrong* along with Warrant Officer Dennis Doggert, the Restoration Project Co-ordinator. 23 Squadron had not long completed the recovery and restoration of two Boston Attack Bombers to static standards, one for the R.A.A.F. Museum at Point Cook in Victoria, the other for the New Guinea Air Force Museum.

During its civil life in Australia the Catalina had been used for mineral survey work and had long since lost its distinctive blisters. The nose turret had been removed and replaced with a more streamlined fairing and much of the interior had been either modified or removed. The R.A.A.F. acquired the Catalina in the late 1980's and a world-wide search was started to find the necessary parts to restore her to a static representation of a war time R.A.A.F. Catalina.

In November 1996 Group Captain L. Armstrong was notified of the presence of the somewhat dented turret on Lord Howe Island. After making trips to as far off and remote places as the United States and the Northern Territory, chasing parts, a trip to Lord Howe was simple. The R.A.A.F. visit the Island for navigational training and

* Les Armstrong retired from the Air Force mid 1998.

medical evacuations as they did in the 1940's, only the aircraft in the late 90's is the C-130 Hercules of 36 and 37 Squadrons.

Group Captain Armstrong arranged to be on-board the next scheduled training flight to the Island. Coming to view the turret via a Hercules also gave Group Captain Armstrong an easy method by which to transport it back to the restoration project at Amberly. Components from A24-381's turret, as well as another turret donated by the Bell family of Albany, West Australia have now been repaired and incorporated in the restoration.

It came as quite a surprise when Group Captain Armstrong contacted the Island and announced he had restored a propeller from his spares and was arranging for it, along with a suitable mounting pole, to be transported to Lord Howe.

A plaque was designed with the help of Mr Ken Pilley, the Secretary of the Catalina Association of N.S.W. Funding was gained for the plaque via the Federal Government program called "Their Service Our Heritage".

The following is an extract from a piece written by Ken Pilley in application for the plaque's funding;

> The people of the Island were greatly saddened by the tragedy and are uniting in their wish to commemorate the sacrifice of Catalina A24-381 on the fiftieth anniversary of the crash. This commemoration will enable them to express their thanks to the R.A.A.F. and the next-of-kin of the crewmen. It will also serve as a focus for the Island's remembrance of the difficult years of the Second World War and the special relationship between the Island and the R.A.A.F., also to educate the younger members of the population both on the Island and through media interest on the mainland about this tradition of service.

With the donation of materials and labour by the Lord Howe Island Board, the Catalina Monument was erected and now stands at Old Settlement Beach near the site where A24-381 fell.

The plaque reads; DEDICATED TO THE MEN AND WOMEN OF AUSTRALIA'S DEFENCE FORCES WHO HAVE SERVED THIS ISLAND AND THEIR COUNTRY; ESPECIALLY THE CREW OF R.A.A.F. CATALINA FLYING BOAT A24-381 WHICH CRASHED AT LORD HOWE ISLAND ON SEPTEMBER 28TH, 1948.

The above inscription is followed by the names of the crew who died and the two survivors; the plaque also includes a detailed and accurate profile of a PB2B-2 Catalina.

Trans Oceanic Airways

On 1 August 1997, a plaque was unveiled at the old freight shed near the Island's jetty. The building these days houses the local radio station, as well as showers and washing facilities for visiting yachtees. The plaque commemorates the date of the first commercial flight by T.O.A. to the Island. Present for the unveiling was Captain of that flight, Bryan Monkton.

Qantas Empire Airways

The Museum holds one of the control wheels of Catalina VH-EAX also the centre section of the wing of this machine is buried near the shelter at Neds Beach.

Harry Newton's Ercoupe

The little Ercoupe which became the first aircraft to land on the Island in 1947, surprisingly, still exists in New Zealand. The current owner has plans to one day restore it to flying condition. I wrote to and then received a reply from Matthew Newton, the pilot's son. He informed me that Harry was fit and well, still working on the family farm. Matthew recently imported an Ercoupe from North America, it is now registered ZK-EXC. Harry's aircraft wore the European registration 00-EXC.

The Ansett Boats

It is undoubtably due to the service going on for so long that the two boats that Ansett used on the route still exist today. When the service ended both *Islander* and *Beachcomber* were bought by American Charles Blair.

He used *Beachcomber* (renamed *Southern Cross*) for charter flights throughout the Islands of the Caribbean. He had a lot of problems getting a Certificate of Airworthiness for *Islander* (renamed *Excalibur VIII*) as the authorities were not happy with the non-Short Brothers conversion, despite the fact that she had carried passengers safely to and from Lord Howe Island for over ten years previously. Tragically, Charles Blair was killed in a flying accident, both boats were put into storage and left to rot.

It wasn't long before the realisation that these were the last of a magnificent breed got the better of some ex-flying boat people. Both *Beachcomber* and *Islander* were eventually made airworthy and flown back to their place of birth, the United Kingdom.

Beachcomber finally found a home in the "Southampton Hall of Aviation" Museum. Interestingly Vic Hodgkinson who flew to the Island on two occasions as skipper of R.A.A.F. Cats, now plays a major part in the ongoing upkeep of the old girl. He is assisted by his good friend Dick Froggart, who flew as flight engineer, with Bryan Monkton of T.O.A. Froggart also made a number of trips to the Island while working for the company.

Islander spent a number of years under the ownership of Mr Edward Hulton; after many setbacks he sold her to a well known American collector of vintage and classic aeroplanes, Kermit Weeks. This well travelled old girl is now at his Museum, 'Fantasy of Flight' in Florida. He plans to keep her in flying condition, perhaps even one day returning her to original Sunderland configuration.

It is thanks to the efforts of the local museum's curator, Jim Dorman, and his team, that the Lord Howe Island Museum has an extensive collection of photographs and memorabilia from the era. Perhaps the most notable items being the starboard float and aileron which were replaced when *Beachcomber* was washed ashore in 1974.

By far one of the Museum's most impressive items is a donation made to the Island community of a 1/10 scale model Sandringham. Geoff Reichelt of the Gold Coast built and kindly donated the model which will eventually be displayed for all to see in the planned new Museum. The model is painted as Ansett's *Beachcomber* on one side and Qantas's *Pacific Chieftain* on the other. Geoff and his family visited the Island in July 1997. As well as the donation of the non-flying model, Geoff also bought his remote controlled model Sunderland. He successfully flew off the Island's lagoon, fifty years to the month after the first Sunderland captained by Bryan Monkton of T.O.A. visited Lord Howe Island.

Geoff Reichelt's model with locals and visitors who flew on the boats.

Peter Phillipps

Lord Howe Island was one of the first places in Australia to greet the new millennium who knows what is in store for us? Sadly it is highly unlikely the flying boats will ever return. Despite this there are still aircraft which go very close to capturing this magnificent era of the past.

One such machine is the Grumman Albatross. The people who happened to be on the Island during November 1996 were fortunate to experience a visit by a meticulously restored example. The Grumman Corporation manufactured a line of amphibians, beginning with the Widgeon, followed by the Goose, then the Mallard, ending with the 85 foot wingspan Albatross. This aircraft perhaps had its greatest hour rescuing downed pilots from the sea, often under fire, during the Korean and Vietnam Wars.

The owner of N3HU which visited Lord Howe, Dr Rich Sudgen, has a number of ex-military types in his collection, perhaps the most impressive being his HU-16A Albatross. He and a group of friends were on the last leg of a journey around the Pacific Rim.

Due to the interest in his machine, and on learning about the Island's flying boat past, Dr Sudgen decided to put on a display flight for the people present. This included three touch and goes on the Island's lagoon. I was very fortunate in being invited along for the flight, which for someone with my interest, now stands as a highlight of my life!

This flight in itself was quite historic, as it had been twenty two years since a flying boat had used the waters of the lagoon. I was later told many of the watching residents were close to tears, as the Albatross from a distance looked very similar to the Sandringhams from the flying boat days.

The Fiftieth Anniversary of the Catalina Crash

On the 27 September 1998 the Lord Howe Island Historic Society put on a welcome night for the one hundred-odd visitors who came to the Island for the anniversary. On display were many photos and memorabilia from the Catalina years, including a 1/10th scale model of Catalina A24-381, the second model made and donated by Geoff Reichelt. The highlight of the night was listening to the relatives of the crew talk of their loved one from the crew. Sad yet rewarding and perhaps healing.

The following night the official ceremony dedicating the propeller monument and Geoff Reichelt's replica of 381. This was followed by a service with an emotional laying of wreaths then a fantastic meal put on for one and all by the local people. The flying boat captains of old smiled on all, not only on that evening but in fact for the whole week leading up to the anniversary with summer weather, quite out of character for late September on Lord Howe Island.

Twenty five years since the last flying boat

It was around this time the Lord Howe Island Historic Society was approached by Number 10 Squadron of the R.A.A.F. to see if they could borrow the Museum's float and aileron for their Sixtieth Anniversary since the squadron's formation. To cut a long story short, Number 10 have now borrowed these items for a three year period. During this time the squadron's maintenance section has kindly offered to restore the items. As a result of the restoration work the fabric which covered the aileron was no longer required.

The Lord Howe Island Historic Society produced a limited number of certificates for the twenty fifth anniversary of the last passenger service from the Island on 10-September 1974. The certificate included: a photo of *Beachcomber* overflying the waving crowd on that last day, a full service history of the aircraft; and a photo of Geoff Reichelt's model of *Beachcomber* with a group of residents and guests who travelled on the boats. This photo was taken on 10 September 1999 — twenty five years to the day since that last flight.

I am sure there are other events which have been left out. If the research and writing of this book surfaces such stories, I can only see this as a good thing. This project has been a labour of love, I am not a pilot nor have I experienced any of the events between 1931 to 1974. I hope you have found it enjoyable.

Peter A.R. Phillipps

Bronte and Abbey Phillipps with the restored float in the Island's museum.

Peter Phillipps

Rich Sudgen's Albatross

Peter Phillipps

A24-381 ceremony with Geoff Reichelt's model in foreground.

Peter Phillipps

Kermit Weeks Sunderland, *Fantasy of Flight* formerly *Islander*.

Donna Bushman

The Catalina Club's Cat on Lake Wakatipu in the south island of New Zealand.

courtesy Marlene Gray

Appendices

1. Technical details for the Catalina, Sunderland and Sandringham

ii. Extracts from the Court of Enquiry regarding the Catalina A24-381

iii. Flying boats elsewhere

iv. Acknowledgements

v. Bibliography

Technical details for the Catalina, Sunderland and Sandringham

Consolidated PBY Catalina

Powerplants

Two Pratt and Whitney R-1830-92 Twin Wasp fourteen cylinder, dual row, geared and supercharged air cooled radial, piston engines each rated at 1,200 hp for take-off and 1,050 hp at 7,500 ft; three bladed Hamilton Standard constant speed propellers; fuel capacity 1,452 imp gal in two centre section integral tanks, capacity reduced to 1,246 imp gal if one tank is self sealing.

Dimensions

Wing span 104 ft; length 63 ft 10 in; wing area 1,400 sq ft; height 18ft 10 in.

Performance

Max speed 196 mph at 7,500 ft;. typical range cruise 117 mph; initial climb 660 ft per min at max weight; service sealing 18,100 ft; time to 5,000 ft at normal weight 4.5 min to 15,000 ft 16.00; max range 3,100 mls.

Short Sunderland/Sandringham.

Powerplants

Sunderland: Four Bristol Pegasus XXII nine cylinder single row air cooled radial, piston engines with single speed superchargers each rated at 1,010 hp for take-off and 865 hp at 6,500 ft; De Havilland three bladed two-pitch propellers. Fuel capacity 2,025 imp gal in six wing tanks.

Sandringham: Four Pratt and Whitney R-1830-90 Twin Wasp fourteen cylinder dual row, air cooled radial, piston engines with two speed superchargers each rated at 1,200 hp for take-off and 1,050 hp at 13,000 ft; De Havilland three bladed constant-speed and feathering propellers; fuel capacity 2,552 imp gals in ten tanks.

Dimensions

Sunderland/Sandringham: Wing span 112 ft 9.5 in; length 85 ft 4.1 in; height (on beaching gear) 32 ft 2in; wing area 1,487 sq ft.

Performance

Sunderland: Max.speed 209 mph at 5,000 ft; cruising speed 170 mph at 5,000 ft; time to 5,000 ft 7.2 min at normal weight; service ceiling 15,000 ft; range with max load 1,790 miles; range with max fuel 2,110 miles at 170 mph, 2,500 miles at 136 mph. Sandringham: Max speed 207 mph at sea level, 213 mph at 5,000 ft, long range cruise 133 mph at 2,000 ft; initial climb 814 ft per min; service ceiling 17,900 ft; max range 2,690 miles at 133 mph.

Catalina monument erected near the crash site in 1998.

Peter Phillipps

Extracts from the Court of Enquiry regarding the Catalina A24-381 crash

Tragedy in Paradise — The Catalina Crash

Island resident witness reports

Here follows witness reports taken from the Court of Inquiry following the Catalina A24-381 air crash.

Witness 1. Mr. Roy Wilson, Co-proprietor of the 'Oceanview' Guest House at Lord Howe Island having duly been sworn in states:

> I am Roy Lance Wilson, Co-proprietor of the Oceanview guest house at Lord Howe Island. On the evening of 28th September, 1948 I was having my evening meal at Mrs. Cunningham's residence. At approximately 0830Z I heard an aircraft moving from East to West showing a red navigation light.
>
> The engines sounded to be functioning quite normally. I then went back inside. Some 5 or ten minutes later I heard an aircraft again which sounded to be using a lot of engine power and I remarked "That fellow is either in a dive or in a steep climb."
>
> At that stage the sound appeared to be coming from the West.
>
> The sound of the engines then died away although I heard them intermittently in different positions which gave me the impression that the aircraft was circling the Island.
>
> Then I heard nothing for three or four minutes and then I heard a terrific roar of an aero motor at which stage I raced to the door heard a crashing sound and saw a sheet of flame coming down the side of Malabar Ridge.
>
> Then I saw and heard an explosion as the flaming mass hit the ground. I raced towards it and stopped momentarily at a fence about fifty yards from the crash and remarked to Mr. Bill Davis who had joined me "I don't think there is much we can do" he said "I thought I saw something move to the left of the plane" I replied "OK come on and see what it is."
>
> I raced up to the crash which was burning fiercely at the time and saw a body about 20 feet from the tail of the plane. This man spoke to me and said "Don't worry about me get my mate Snowy he's in there."

I approached the tail of the plane and heard a moan but could not see a human form.

I went further under the tail and saw a burning object, touched it and it proved to be a man. I immediately endeavoured to smother the flames and dragged the man clear of the wreckage. About a minute later an explosion occurred and the fire spread further.

After I dragged the second man clear I found Mr. Bill Davis and my brother Allen Wilson with the first crew member I had spoken to.

I was then also joined by a Mr. Parish, a visitor to the Island who assisted me to carry the second man further away from the flames.

Bill Davis and my brother Alan carried the first man away from the wreck.

Questions by the Court

Q: Have you been associated with aircraft very much?
A: Yes. I was a fitter Motor Boat Crew in the R.A.A.F for three years. I had a lot to do with the flying boats of the R.A.A.F. at Rathmines,Townsville and Madang.
Q: You said in your previous evidence that you heard the roar of an aero engine just prior to the crash. Could you say whether it was one engine or two making the noise?
A: No. I can only describe the noise as a definite roar.
Q: From your experience would you say the noise you heard was consistent with the noise normally made by a Catalina at full throttle.
A: Yes — definitely.
Q: Did that full-throated roar continue as you saw the flaming mass coming down the Hillside?
A: Virtually — no, but it was quite obvious to me that it was an aircraft

Witness 2. Mr. William Ernest Davis — resident of Lord Howe Island having been sworn states:-

I am William Ernest Davies, resident of Lord Howe Island. On the evening of Tuesday 28th September 1948 I was having my evening meal at Mrs. Cunninghams home. At about 08.40Z I heard an aircraft overhead and I went outside and saw it fairly high up coming from a westerly direction showing a red light. It appeared from the engine noise I heard to be circling the Island.

The engines sounded quite normal to me. I went back inside and took no further notice until Roy Wilson mentioned that he thought the aircraft was climbing or diving at which stage I heard the engines again.

I then went outside but I could see the house I heard an explosion. I turned and saw a plane coming down the hillside on fire.

I ran to the back of the house where I met Roy Wilson and we ran towards the plane.

We stopped about 50 yards from the plane and I saw something moving under the tail. I said: There is somebody under there" and then Roy started off and I followed right behind him.

I caught up with Roy as he was dragging a man from near the tail and I helped him beat out the mans burning clothing. I then noticed another chap with a broken foot so I ran to him and started to undo his Mae West.

I was then joined by Mr. Allen Wilson and Norm Simpson and between us we shifted the two men away from the wreckage.

We searched as we were able but could see only one other body in the flames.

Questions by the Court

Q: Did you hear any sounds consistent with the roar of aero engines immediately prior to the first explosion you heard?

A: No.

Q: Could you see the outline of the aircraft as it slid down the hill?

A: Yes. It looked almost as if it was still flying and appeared to be intact until it hit the bottom. It appeared to be burning around the engines until it hit the bottom when it burst completely into flames.

Note: Map does not have a witness 3.

Witness 4. Mr. Ronald Hugh Payten — resident of Lord Howe Island having been duly sworn states:

I am Ronald Hugh Payten resident of Lord Howe Island. On the evening of Tuesday 28th September 1948 I was at my house when about 0830Z I heard an aircraft in the vicinity of the Island but took no further notice.

I left my home at about 0835Z and went out on to the road. I saw an aircraft which I recognised as a Catalina and which was gliding without engine power in a N.E direction. Also noticed lamp signals being made from the starboard side. It passed out of my sight in that N.E direction and then about two minutes later I saw it glide in towards the Island from a N direction and very shortly after I saw a flash and simultaneously I heard a roar and I realised the aircraft had struck the hills . Right up to the moment of impact I could see the red port navigation light quite clearly. A few seconds later I heard a larger explosion.

Questions by the Court

Q: How far would you have been from the point that the aircraft struck when you saw the first flash?

A: About one mile.

Q: You say that you saw the aircraft gliding out in N.E direction. Why did you say it was gliding?

A: I knew it was gliding because there was no engine noise and I could hear it swishing through the air.
Q: You mentioned that as you saw the flash as the aircraft hit you heard a roar. Was it the roar of aero engines?
A: No. In my opinion it was the roar of the crash.
Q: Do you know that a Catalina has two powerful head lamps set in their wings which throw a powerful white light ahead and downwards and which are used for landing at night?
A: Yes
Q: As the aircraft was approaching the Island just before it crashed did you see any light that would indicate that its landing lights were switched on?
A: None at all.

Witness 5. Mr. Harry Ovalau Payten, a resident of Lord Howe Island having been duly sworn states:-

I am Harry Ovalau Payten, resident of Lord Howe Island. On the evening of 28th September 1948 I was at my home on the north side of the Island. At about 0830Z I heard an aircraft and then saw it manoeuvring above the Island high up.

I took no further notice then. At about 0845Z I saw an aircraft flying in a NW direction approximately parallel with the coast.

As it went along I heard no engine noise except an occasional popping sound.

It seemed to me very low and I thought it was going into the sea.

I could see his red navigation light as he went along. I thought it was going around behind the hills at the N of the Island but just as it was going from my vision I heard the sudden roar of its engines. A few seconds later I heard an explosion and I realised that the plane had hit the hills.

Questions by the Court

Q: Are you certain in your own mind that the sudden roar you heard was the roar of the engines?
A: Certainly, there was no mistaking it.
Q: Do you know that a Catalina has two powerful head lamps set in their wings which throw a powerful white light ahead and downwards and which are used for landing at night?
A: Yes.
Q: As the aircraft was approaching the Island just before it crashed did you see any light that would indicate that it's landing lights were switched on?
A: None at all.

Note: Mr Herbert John Edwards does not have a witness number.

Mr. Herbert John Edwards Aeradio operator of Department Civil Aviation at Lord Howe Island having been duly sworn in states:

I am Herbert John Edwards, Aeradio Operator of Dept. Civil Aviation at Lord Howe Island. I went on duty at the Radio Station at 0230Z on 28th September 1948. I carried out my normal duties and during which time I heard an aircraft giving the call sign ESP working Sydney.

At 0704Z ESP called me, I gave him the go ahead but received no reply. I produce to the court my Log for the period 0626Z 28th September 1948 to 1400Z 28th September 1948 which covers all the signals I heard from or sent to ESP.

At approximately 0848Z I heard an aircraft in the vicinity and I went outside and saw an aircraft showing a light which appeared to be turning pretty well overhead. I saw him head out in an easterly direction at which stage I went back into my station building and closed the door.

A little while later I heard what sounded to me like an aircraft again and I said to Mr. Bedger who was with me "That fellow must be coming back."

We took no further notice at this stage and did not open the door. Some few minutes later Mr. Ron Payten came to the station and told me that an aircraft had crashed.

Further actions I took regarding the accident are recorded in my log.

Questions by the Court

Q: When you heard an aircraft the second time could you say if the engines were running smoothly or otherwise?

A: When I heard it at first on this second occasion the noise from it sounded normal but then I heard what sounded to be a sudden increase in the volume of noise.

Q: Was there much noise in your own building from your radio gear?

A: The usual moderate noise was going on.

Q: After the sudden increase in noise you mention above did you still hear the aircraft?

A: I can't recollect having heard it after that.

Note: Mr Allen Wilson does not have a witness number.

Mr. Allen Wilson, co-proprietor of the Oceanview guest house at Lord Howe Island having duly been sworn states:

At about 0800Z on the evening of 28th September 1948 as we sat down to our meal I heard an aircraft so I went outside and saw it flying eastward at a considerable height burning navigation lights.

The engines seemed to me to be running quite normally. I then went back inside. After the meal I went out the back of the building and at about 0835Z I heard a distinct thud followed by the roar of aero engines. I rushed on to the lawn to see a heavy explosion.

I ran straight towards the explosion and on reaching the vicinity I saw it was an aircraft and I saw my brother Roy and Bill Davis at the tail of the plane attending to the two men.

I helped them from then on and after the flames died a little we searched as well as we could for other survivors.

Catalina crew witness report

No. 442553 Warrant Officer Lea John Deans W.O.A.G of No. 11 G.R Squadron, having been duly sworn in states:

> I was a member of the crew of A24-381 engaged in a naval co-op Exercise on 28 September 1948. The flight was quite normal until some little time after we turned for Rathmines at Lord Howe Island.
>
> I was n/t watch at this time and at the Captain's request I obtained permission for the aircraft to climb to 7,000 feet.
>
> We had settled down at this height — I was still at the radio — when a few minutes later petrol began to enter the rear compartment in a real shower. It was absolutely pouring in.
>
> I immediately turned off all radio power and went forward to tell the captain about the leak. He sent the second pilot out to have a look at the leak and told me to do up his safety straps.
>
> I went through to the aircraft telling all crew members to take up ditching positions as the Captain intended to ditch.
>
> The Captain had turned back by this time and I went through into the blister, compartment, unlocked the blisters, put my Mae West on and checked that both dinghies were ready for immediate use.
>
> By this time I thought that the Captain was probably on his down wind or approach leg, so I took my ditching position and braced myself.
>
> When the machine hit, my first thought was that we had hit the water very hard but soon after that I must have become unconscious.

Questions by the Court

Q: Would you be able to say whether the Captain was able to apply power to his engines at will?

A: After we had turned back for Lord Howe Island the engines were spluttering and I got the impression that the Captain was having trouble keeping them going. The final approach seemed normal to me and there was power on the engines immediately prior to the first impact. However, I cannot say whether or not the captain was able to use power at will.

Flight Lieutenant Bert Raymond Bradley (414301) W.O.A.G G.R Squadron having been duly sworn in states:

I was detailed as a member of the crew of Aircraft A24-381 in an instructional capacity for the Naval Co-ops and Naval exercise on the 28th September 1948.

We carried out the first part of our exercise and the flight was quite normal until we reached the vicinity of Lord Howe Island at approximately 0830 hours GMT

For the first half hour of our flight everything appeared to function normally. My first indication of trouble was the inter-communication system ceasing to function.

On tracing the cause I found that a bad petrol leak had developed in the navigation department. All radio equipment and electrical equipment had been switched off to minimise risk of explosion.

At this time Warrant Officer Salis took over engineers duties from Warrant Officer Bacon. The Captain ordered ditching position for all crew members and being an excess member of the aircrew, I took up ditching position in the port blister.

At this time the port engine began to splutter and Warrant Officer Salis kept trying repeatedly to re-start this engine. I could hear him working the priming pump.

At this time, we turned for Lord Howe Island, with all aircrew in ditching positions. The Captain's idea at this time was to make the sheltered waters to the south of the Island as a very strong wind and sea was running in open water.

An Aldis lamp was installed in the port blister. By this time, the petrol fumes inside the aircraft were almost stifling. Permission was obtained from the captain to open both blisters and the air vents in the bunk compartment. This action cleared the aircraft temporarily of fumes. The Aldis lamp was then used in an endeavour to locate the source of the petrol leak with negative results but at this time petrol in the port slip-stream showed indication of source in the port superstructure.

In view of fire hazard the Aldis lamp circuit was disconnected. At approx. five minutes to seven Lord Howe came into view on the port bow. During the period covered by this statement on one occasion both engines cut and we appeared to glide toward the Island. We approached from a southerly direction past the radio towers, then the aircraft struck the mountainside.

Just prior to hitting the mountainside the starboard engine appeared to gain power. So far as I know crew positions prior to the crash were Flight Lieutenant Smith at the controls Wireless Officer Piercy in second pilot's position. Flight Lieutenant Keller in the navigation compartment Wireless Officer McKenzie in the starboard bunk. W/O Salis in engineer's position, W/O Bacon on seat in Starboard blister and myself and W/O Lea in the port blister.

It may be noted that both blisters were left open for proposed alighting. The reason for this being the amount of petrol fumes within the aircraft. The captain of the aircraft and W/O Salis tried consistently until the time of the crash to get either motor in operation.

The hill that we struck was in a direct line with the sheltered lagoon on our landing approach.

Questions by the Court

Q: Do you think the captain would have been able to use power from his engines at all?

A: No.

Q: Have you had any experience of petrol leaks in Catalina aircraft before?

A: Yes, on two other occasions. On a flight to Melbourne with Flt/Lt Mutch as captain, when a bad petrol leak developed from the superstructure into the Nav compartment. It was necessary to cut all radio and electrical switches to minimise fire hazard. The second occasion being with F/lt Delahunty on a night flight between Rathmines and Port Moresby in A24-385. On this occasion it was necessary to return to Bowen. On inspection the following morning the hose clips on the strainer drain had worked loose, thus allowing petrol to flow into the Nav. Compartment. On all three of these occasions when I have experienced these leaks we were flying in PB.2.B.2 aircraft.

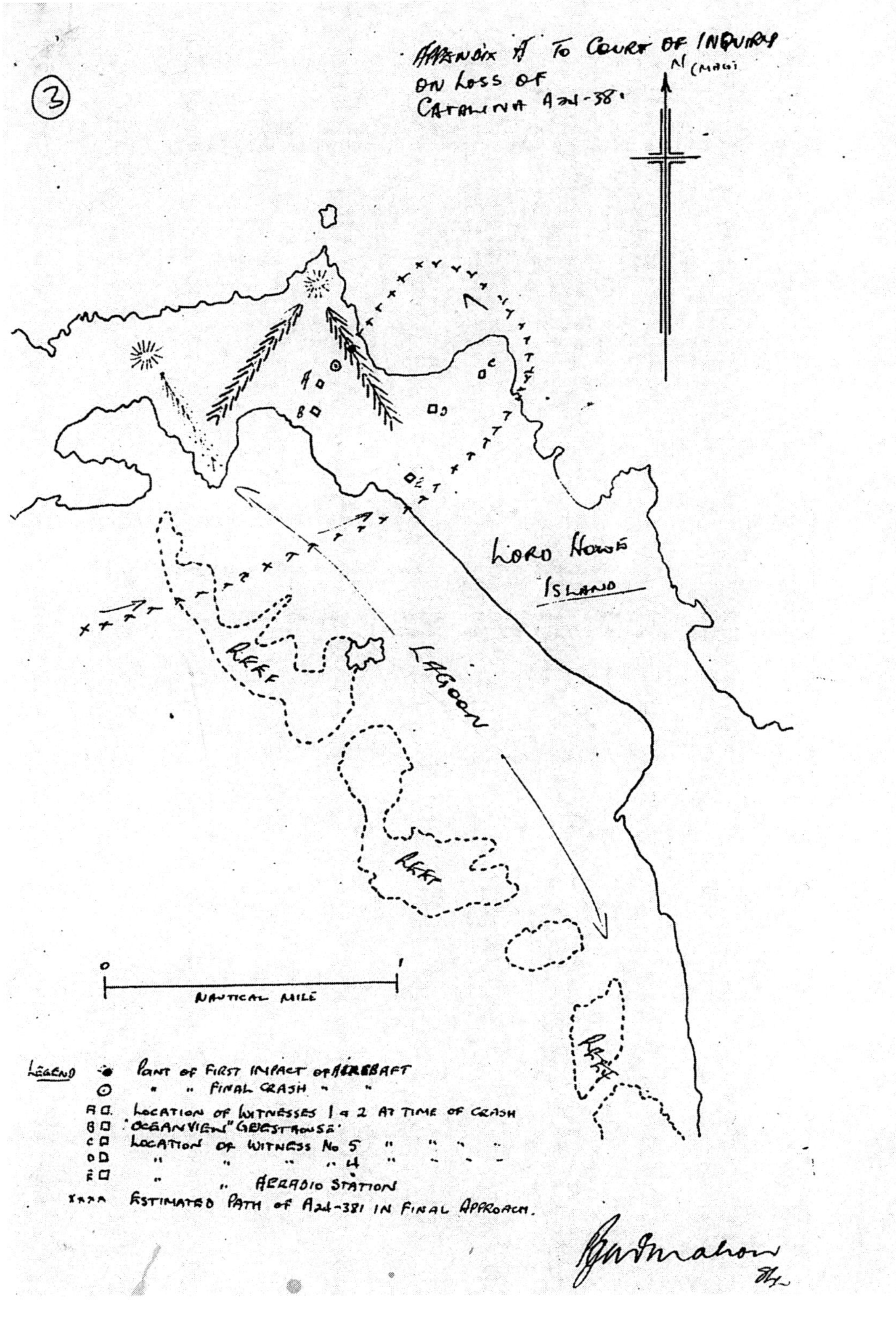
3
APPENDIX A TO COURT OF INQUIRY
ON LOSS OF
CATALINA A24-381
N (MAG)
LORD HOWE
ISLAND
LAGOON
REEF
REEF
REEF
0
1
NAUTICAL MILE
LEGEND
POINT OF FIRST IMPACT OF AIRCRAFT
" " FINAL CRASH " "
A LOCATION OF WITNESSES 1 & 2 AT TIME OF CRASH
B 'OCEANVIEW' GUESTHOUSE
C LOCATION OF WITNESS No 5 " " " "
D " " " " 4 " " " "
E " " AERADIO STATION
xxxx ESTIMATED PATH OF A24-381 IN FINAL APPROACH.

Flying Boats Elsewhere

It is across the Tasman where flying boat enthusiasts look with envy to the Catalina Club's airworthy Catalina ZK-PBY. After losing their first Cat on her ferry flight to New Zealand, in January 1994, a second example was obtained which regularly attends airshows through out the country reminding young and old of the flying boat era.

It is also in New Zealand where both an ex R.N.Z.A.F. Sunderland, a sister ship to *Islander* and an ex T.E.A.L. Solent can be viewed at Auckland's Museum of Transport and Technology.

While Australia does not boast an airworthy big boat, a static Catalina can be seen at the Whale World Musuem in Albany, Western Australia. I was fortunate to visit this composite airframe and talk at length with its owner restorer John Bell in 1995. Sadly John was killed on the 13 March 1996 when the aircraft he was piloting crashed. John Bell was very dedicated to restoring his Catalina; he told me in the early days of collecting bits and pieces from the eastern states, he made many trips across the Nullabor Plain, asserting he knew every rock on that long and desolate stretch of road! John's son, Peter, now carries on the work started by his father and in recent times loaned and donated a number of items to the 23 Squadron Catalina restoration; the R.A.A.F. in turn have helped out Peter Bell where they can.

There is also a Catalina displayed at *Catalina Park* on the shores of Lake Boga in Victoria; it was on these shores that many wartime flying boats were repaired. There is now also a Museum in one of the old underground wartime bunkers housing memorabilia from the Base's active days. The late Dr Browne, O.A.M, M.B. B.S. was the medical Officer at Lake Boga from 1942 to 1947. After the war he travelled with his wife in Europe then on return to Australia, Dr Browne took a position on Lord Howe Island where he practised from 1952 to 1973.

The Powerhouse Museum in Sydney displays what is perhaps Australia's most famous Catalina Sir Gordon Taylor's *Frigate Bird* VH-ASA (Australia South America)-the very machine he used to cross the Southern Pacific to South America and back!

Finally the soon to be completed R.A.A.F. restoration of what will become A24-104. This Catalina was one of the amphibious versions acquired by the R.A.A.F. during the war. It was used to trial Jato rockets which were attached to the sides of the fuselage and fired to reduce the take off run in rough conditions. A24-104 performed a famous post-war mission when on the 6 August 1948 it flew to Macquarie Island with a replacement engineer for a Mr C. Noble who sadly drowned when the thin ice he was skiing across broke. The amphibian then took off with the assistance of the Jato rockets and due to strong winds made its way to the R.N.Z.A.F. Base Wigram at Christchurch, New Zealand. The total distance travelled from Australia via Macquarie Island then on to New Zealand being 2,960 nautical miles! The well travelled Cat then returned safely to Australia.

As a result of my research I discovered a number of links between Catalinas A24-104, A24-381 and the aircrew that flew them.

These interesting links begin at the Flying Boat Repair Depot on Lake Boga August 6 1947. Catalina A24-381 under the command of Flight Lieutenant B. Delahunty was the last Cat to alight at Lake Boga before the base officially closed. On board was the then Pilot Officer M.D. Smith and his crew; nine days later Pilot Officer Smith departed as Captain of Supermarine Walrus HD874. A Walrus had in fact been the first aircraft to alight at Lake Boga, HD874 and her crew had been allotted to the newly formed R.A.A.F. Antarctic Flight. On the 28 November 1947 LST 3501 departed Australia from Perth; securely lashed and covered on deck was Walrus HD874.

LST 3501 set a course for Heard Island, 2,400 miles to the south-souwest eventually arriving on December 11. The biplane amphibian only made one flight under Smith's command before it was destroyed on the beach in a severe gale.

Smith was later promoted to Flight Lieutenant; sadly he died along with six of his crew of nine, on 28 September 1948 as Captain of Catalina A24-381 when it crashed at Lord Howe Island.

In the early 80's the R.A.A.F. recovered the remains of HD874 and in the year 2000 are not too far from completing its restoration. Eventually the Walrus will be put on static display at the R.A.A.F. Musuem at Point Cook in Victoria. The Catalina being restored at R.A.A.F. Base Amberly, using some components from A24-381, will eventually make its way to Point Cook to also be displayed as a static example of A24-104.

One of the two survivors from the crash of A24-381, Flight Lieutenant B.R. Bradley, had also been part of the crew on board A24-104 when she performed the Macquarie Island mission not two months earlier. It doesn't end there; Flight Lieutenant B. Delahunty, who delivered Smith and his crew to Lake Boga aboard A24-381 to pick up the ill-fated Walrus, was the Captain of A24-104 on the flight to Macquarie Island.

The end result being the restored Catalina displayed as A24-104 will, fifty years on perhaps be more than just a representation of the flying machine these men had flown, fought and died aboard.

Author's note: As we were about to go to print I discovered that Australia was in fact to gain not one but two additional Catalinas. The first, a static restoration, will be displayed at the site of a former U.S. Navy Catalina base on the bank of the Swan River in Perth. The N.S.W. based Historic Aircraft Restoration Society also hopes to acquire an airworthy example of a Catalina which will mean Australian skies will once again be graced with the sight and sound of one of these magnificent flying boats.

Historic Aircraft Restoration Society's Black Cat.

source unknown

Catalina on the shores of Lake Boga, Victoria.

Judith Phillipps

Acknowledgements

This document is the result of around eight years research, during this time many people have been of assistance. Flying boat people are a special breed, interest and passion, like the boats themselves crosses vast oceans. The flying boat spirit gets into your blood, It would be fair to say I have immersed myself and my family in this subject, whether they liked it or not.

To all the flying boat people, both near and far, I say thanks!

My wife Janine and our children Bronte and Abbey. It was Janine who first inspired me with her stories of journeys to and from her magnificent Island home.

Helen and Jeremy Palmer with out whose skill, patience and financial commitment this project would never have reached completion.

The people of the community of Lord Howe Island, both past and present. This is part of their history which helped shape the present, it has been put together for current and the future generations so as they can learn how the modern services and the tourist industry on the Island came to be.

*Indicates author has taped interview with person

I would also like to thank the following individuals for their assistance.

Mick Bloomfield, Ian Fitzgerald, Pam Goyne, the late Gerald Kirby, Hazel Payten,* Bill and Matthew Retmock, Bing, Brian and Norman Simpson, Barry Thompson, Andrew, Clive,* Gower,* John and Thelma* Wilson, Harry and Wally Woolnough.

Jim Whistler the editor of the local paper *The Signal.*

Photographs

The late Dick Morris took many photos during the early days of the flying boat era, and he was unknowingly responsible for capturing a lot of the history of the Island during his lifetime.

John Wilson, a Brisbane based flying boat enthusiast, who has kindly allowed me the use of his photos and maps.

Hazel Payten who has a magnificent collection of photographs and kindly allowed me free access to them.

The following people who allowed me access to their collections of photos used in this book.

Mary Biddle, Donna Bushman, Marlene Gray, Vic Hodgkinson, Don Kerr, Arthur Le-Navez, Janine Phillipps, Norman Simpson, Gower and Thelma Wilson and Dennis Saunders.

The Lord Howe Island Historic Society. Special thanks to all the volunteers who have willingly given their time and effort both at the Museum and with other Historic Society projects.

My eternal thanks must go to Chris Murray for his foreword and for the loan of his personal collection of photos, documents and audio recordings which greatly assisted this project.

The Lord Howe Island Board.
Lord Howe Island Seafreight. *The Island Trader.*
Lord Howe Island Shipping. *The Sitka.*

Arthur and Joan Le Navez.*

Ex R. A. A. F.
Vic Hodgkinson, Norm Smith,* George and Betty Woods.*

The Catalina Association of New South Wales. Rob Hutchinson,* Joe Leach, Neville Mason, Ken Pilley and Keith Stevens.

The Families and relatives of the crew of Catalina A24-381.

Airline Personnel

Trans Oceanic Airways

Captain Phil Mathieson.
Captain Bryan Monkton.*
First Officer Gordon Taylor.*
First Officer Hugh Hamilton.

Qantas Empire Airways

Captain Len Gray.
Bruce Costello.* (Flight Engineer)

Ansett

Phil Dengate.* (Customer Services Officer)
Margaret Holle.* (Flight Attendant)
First Officer Jim Hughs.
Jack Kennedy.* (Flight Attendant)
Jack O'Brien.* (Flight Engineer)
Captain Keith Mansfield.*
David Murray. (Ansett Agent Lord Howe Island)

R.A.A.F.

23 Squadron, Group Captain Les Armstrong (retired)
Warrant Officer Dennis Doggert. 10, 11, 36 and 37 Squadrons.
Janet Beck and David Wilson (R.A.A.F. Historical Records.)

The Lord Howe Island Branch of the Returned Serviceman's League. Esven Fenton, Stan Fenton and Les King.

Merle and Clyde Parrish, Geoff Bayliss.

Geoff, Trish, Mellisa and Tory Reichelt.

Alan Bond, Nigel Arnott, John Botton Riley, Mark and Ray Hanna, Barry Hempel, David Lowy, Tom Middelton, Colin Pay, The Roberts family, Rich Sudgen, Tim Wallis, Guido Zucoli.

Frank Charters, Mike Clayton, Don Dennis, Rohan Garnett, Jon Johanson, Boyd Munro and Paul Teft.

Harry Newton and his son Matthew.

John Bell and his son Peter of the Albany Whale Museum.

Marlene Gray and the Catalina Club of New Zealand.

The Southampton Hall of Aviation, United Kingdom. Dick Freggert and Vic Hodgkinson.

The Museum of Transport and Technology, New Zealand. Brian Crooks, Geoff Freer, Geoff Rodliffe. Crew members of *Awarua*. Jack C. Felton, Laurie Martin,* Fred L. Willans.
The following Aviation Magazines Australian Aviation, Classic Wings, Fightpath, Pacific Flyer.

Those who assisted with production.
Jodi Bills, Russell Geoffries, David Gudex, Lisa Makiiti, Lex McAulay, Chris Murray, Barney Nichols, James Phillipps, Doug Speedy and Jenny Thompson.

Bill Phippard and Susan Rintoul. Seaview Press.

My late father Brian, my mother Judith, sister Debbie and brother James.

Two historians who inspired me, the late William J. Phillipps and Max Nicholls.

I have spoken to a number of visitors to the Island who have passed on their stories, my thanks to you all.

Thanks also to the partners and families of all the people listed.

Finally, thank you to the men and women of the defence forces of Australia to whom this Island will always be in debt especially the crew of Catalina A24-381.

Died in accident
Warrant Officer Sydney H. Bacon.
Flight Lieutenant William D. Keller.
Flight Lieutenant Alex Mackenzie.
Flight Lieutenant James McCoy.
Pilot 111 Sydney L. Piercy.
Warrant Officer Donald E. Salis.
Flight Lieutenant Malcolm D. Smith. (Captain)

The survivors
Flight Lieutenant Bert R. Bradley. Warrant Officer John D. Lea.

Bibliography

Chichester, Francis, *Alone over the Tasman Sea*, Allen & Unwin Ltd, 1945.

Freeman, Brett, *Lake Boga at War*, Catalina Publications, 1995.

Fysh, Hudson, *Wings of the World: The story of Qantas 1945-1966*, Angus and Robertson, 1966.

Gunn, John, *Challenging Horizons*: Qantas 1939-1954. U.Q.P. 1987.

Hutchinson, Rob, *Out of my mind*, Floreat Press, 1989.

Parnell, Neville, Boughton and Trevor. *A Record of Aviation in Australia*. A Civil Aviation Authority Bicentennial Project. 1988.

Rendel, David, *Civil Aviation in New Zealand*, A.H. and A.W. Reed. 1975.

Wilson, Stewart, *Beaufort, Beaufighter and Mosquito in Australian Service*, Aerospace Publications, 1990.

Wilson, Stewart, *Catalina, Neptune and Orion in Australia Service*, Aerospace Publications. 1991.

Wilson, Stewart, *Anson, Hudson and Sunderland in Australian Service*, Aerospace Publications 1992.

Vincent, David, *Catalina Chronicle*, L.H.P. 1976.

DVD documentary of the Flying Boat Days out now!

This movie came about as a result of my research into a book that I produced after an eight or so year period researching this wonderful era of Australia's aviation history. During the course of this research I managed to collect many pictures and footage of the Flying Boats.

For many years it had been a dream of mine to produce a movie that tells the story of the "Flying Boat days." In 2008 the dream became a reality.

Francis Chichester and his Gypsy Moth "Madame Elijah"
The Royal Australian Air Force, the loss of Catalina A24-381
The civil services of Trans Oceanic Airways, Qantas Empire Airlines and Ansett Flying Boat Services
Caribou A4-140, the first aircraft to land on the runway
(Documentary features rare 8mm and 16mm colour footage.)

Bonus footage (Hi8 and slide film)
The Island's restored Sandringham float, 2008
1/10th scale R/C Sunderland off the lagoon, 1997
* Grumman Albatross touch and goes off the lagoon, 1996*
Flying boat era photo collage, 1931 to 1974

For copies of book or DVD go to peterphillipps@bigpond.com or write to Double P Publishing at PO Box 103, Lord Howe Island, NSW 2898, Australia.

Qantas Empire Airlines Catalina on the Blackburn Island mooring.

Le Navez family

Trans Oceanic Airways Sunderland coming in to alight.

Le Navez family

VH-AKP “Tahiti Star” alighting, Intermediate Hill behind.

Le Navez family

Trans Oceanic Airways Sunderland “flying the bar,” see page 39.

Le Navez family

On the jetty mooring unloading passengers.

Le Navez family

Notice the bomb bay doors open to unload freight, see page 53.

Le Navez family

"Tahiti Star" taxing for departure.

Le Navez family

Le Navez family